Pro Visual Studio.NET

BILL SEMPF, DONALD XIE, JAMES GREENWOOD,
ROB HARROP, COLT KWONG, JAN MACHACEK,
BRIAN BISCHOF, JON REID, AND KUNAL CHEDA

Pro Visual Studio.NET

Copyright © 2004 by Bill Sempf, Donald Xie, James Greenwood, Rob Harrop, Colt Kwong, Jan Machacek, Brian Bischof, Jon Reid, and Kunal Cheda

ISBN (pbk): 1-59059-368-5

Printed and bound in the United States of America 9 8 7 6 5 4 3 2 1

Trademarked names may appear in this book. Rather than use a trademark symbol with every occurrence of a trademarked name, we use the names only in an editorial fashion and to the benefit of the trademark owner, with no intention of infringement of the trademark.

Lead Editor: Dominic Shakeshaft
Technical Reviewer: Christophe Nasarre
Editorial Board: Steve Anglin, Dan Appleman, Ewan Buckingham, Gary Cornell, Tony Davis, Jason Gilmore, Chris Mills, Steve Rycroft, Dominic Shakeshaft, Jim Sumser, Gavin Wray
Project Manager: Sofia Marchant
Copy Edit Manager: Nicole LeClerc
Copy Editor: David Kramer
Production Manager: Kari Brooks
Production Editor: Janet Vail
Compositor and Artist: Kinetic Publishing Services, LLC
Proofreader: Patrick Vincent
Indexer: John Collin
Cover Designer: Kurt Krames
Manufacturing Manager: Tom Debolski

Distributed to the book trade in the United States by Springer-Verlag New York, LLC, 233 Spring Street, 6th Floor, New York, NY 10013 and outside the United States by Springer-Verlag GmbH & Co. KG, Tiergartenstr. 17, 69112 Heidelberg, Germany.

In the United States: phone 1-800-SPRINGER, e-mail orders@springer-ny.com, or visit http://www.springer-ny.com. Outside the United States: fax +49 6221 345229, e-mail orders@springer.de, or visit http://www.springer.de.

For information on translations, please contact Apress directly at 2560 Ninth Street, Suite 219, Berkeley, CA 94710. Phone 510-549-5930, fax 510-549-5939, e-mail info@apress.com, or visit http://www.apress.com.

The information in this book is distributed on an "as is" basis, without warranty. Although every precaution has been taken in the preparation of this work, neither the author(s) nor Apress shall have any liability to any person or entity with respect to any loss or damage caused or alleged to be caused directly or indirectly by the information contained in this work.

The source code for this book is available to readers at http://www.apress.com in the Downloads section.

Contents at a Glance

Contents

About the Authors

BILL SEMPF has spent an inordinate amount of time in the last several years writing about XML Web Services. He is a coauthor of *Effective Visual Studio.NET*, *Professional ASP.NET Web Services*, and *Professional VB.NET*, and a frequent contributor to *Builder.com*, *Hardcore Web Services*, *Inside Web Development Journal*, and *Intranet Journal*, and has recently been an invited speaker for the International XML Web Services Expo and the Association of Information Technology Professionals. A graduate of Ohio State University with a bachelor's of science in business administration, Microsoft Certified Professional, Certified Internet Business Strategist, and Certified Internet Webmaster, Bill has developed over one hundred web applications for startups and Fortune 50 companies alike.

Bill began his career in 1985 helping his father (also Bill) to manage Apple IIe systems for the local library. Since then, he has built applications for the likes of Lucent Technologies, Bank One, Nationwide Insurance, and Sears, Roebuck and Co. He specialized in data-driven web applications of all types, both public and private. Currently, Bill is a Senior Technology Consultant at Products Of Innovative New Technology in Grove City, Ohio. He can be reached at bill@sempf.net.

DONALD XIE is a software architect who specializes in enterprise application development in both the private and public sectors. He has coauthored several other programming books, mostly on Microsoft .NET. He also teaches programming classes at Element K and BNU.

Away from work, Donald enjoys every minute with his wife, Iris, and two beautiful girls, Belinda and Clare.

JAMES GREENWOOD is a technical architect and author based in the north of England. He spends his days (and most of his nights) designing and implementing .NET solutions from mobile integration platforms to financial systems, all the while waxing lyrical on the latest technologies and agile development techniques. His professional interests include research into distributed interfaces, the automation of application development, and alternative software-engineering processes.

While not at the keyboard, James can be found out and about, indulging in his other great loves: British sports cars and Egyptology. James can be reached at js_greenwood@hotmail.com or via his weblog at http://weblogs.asp.net/jsgreenwood.

ROB HARROP is lead software architect of the UK-based development house Cake Solutions Limited. At Cake, Rob leads a team of six developers working on enterprise solutions for a variety of clients including the Department of Trade and Industry, the Metropolitan Police, and NUS Services Limited. Rob, and Cake, specialize in both .NET- and J2EE-based development, Rob having been involved with .NET since the alpha stages.

Rob is the author of *Pro Jakarta Velocity* (Apress, to appear) as well as coauthor of *Pro Jakarta Struts* (Apress, 2004) and *Oracle Application Server 10g: J2EE Deployment and Administration* (Apress, to appear).

In his limited spare time, Rob enjoys playing about with different technologies, his current favorites being Groovy and AOP. Rob is a committer on the open source Spring project (www.springframework.org), a Java and .NET application framework built around the principle of dependency injection. When not sitting in front of a computer, Rob usually has his head buried in a book and prefers the fantasy parodies of Terry Pratchett's Discworld.

COLT KWONG is a Microsoft MVP and addict in anything about .NET. He is currently a .NET developer and instructor with an IT solution provider in Hong Kong. He specializes in Microsoft technologies, including .NET, VB, C#, and ASP.NET. He is an ASPInsider and moderator of the official Microsoft ASP.NET and Windows forms community forums. He is the president of the #1 Hong Kong blogging community and Hong Kong .NET user group.

Colt speaks at several conferences each year and helps in managing the International .NET Association (INETA) for the Asia Pacific & Greater China region. He is coauthor of *Beginning Dynamic Web Sites with Web Matrix*, SAMS, and *ASP.NET Developer's Cookbook*. He can be reached at colt.kwong@ineta.org.

JAN MACHACEK is lead programmer at the UK-based software company Cake Solutions Limited (http://www.cakesolutions.net), where Jan has helped design and implement enterprise-level applications for a variety of UK- and US-based clients. In his spare time, he enjoys exploring software architectures, nonprocedural and AI programming, as well as playing with computer hardware. As a proper computer geek, Jan loves the *Star Wars* and *Lord of the Rings* series. Jan lives in Manchester in the UK and can be reached at jan@cakesolutions.net.

BRIAN BISCHOF, CPA, MCSD, is the author of the best-selling books *Crystal Reports .NET Programming* and *The .NET Languages: A Quick Translation Guide*. He is President of Bischof Systems, Inc. Brian discovered a marketing niche early in his career: Many software consultants were comfortable working with software applications but did not understand the corporate language through which they could discover a company's true needs. Conversely, business managers knew that they wanted to improve their business processes but did not know how to communicate this information to a computer techie. After spending years developing software and working in the accounting field as an auditor, Brian created a software development and training firm that provides a unique combination of business expertise and technical knowledge using Microsoft's .NET technologies. You can learn more about the author and Bischof Systems, Inc., by visiting the company's website at http://www.BischofSystems.com.

JON REID is the president and chief technology officer for Savitar Corporation, an independent software vendor and consulting company (www.savitar.com) developing database tools for the Microsoft .NET environment. He was editor for the C++ and Object Query Language (OQL) components of the Object Data Management Group (ODMG) standard, and has coauthored many .NET books, including *Beginning Visual C#, Fast Track to C# Programming, ADO.NET Programmer's Reference,* and *Professional SQL Server 2000 XML.* Jon would like to thank his family, coauthors, and the team at Apress for their support and encouragement.

KUNAL CHEDA is a senior analyst working with Syntel India Ltd. He is cofounder of the site www.dotnetextreme.com. He started his career with VB 5.0 in 1998, and since then he has used a variety of languages and platforms, including VB .NET, C#, Java, Remoting, web services, ASP, and ASP.NET, among others. Kunal was awarded the MVP for .NET and is currently a Microsoft India Communities Star. He enjoys teaching, programming, and architecting distributed solutions. His hobbies include playing guitar and listening to music. He can be reached at kunalcheda@hotmail.com.

About the Technical Reviewer

 **CHRISTOPHE NASARRE** is a development manager for Business Objects, which develops desktop and Web-based business intelligence solutions. During his spare time, Christophe writes articles for *MSDN Magazine* and *MSDN/Longhorn* and has reviewed books on Win32, COM, MFC, and .NET since 1996.

Acknowledgments

Most authors offer their thanks at the beginning of the book, but don't thank their readers in advance. Thank you, readers! In fact, after you have read the book, send the authors an email and let us thank you in person. We have put a lot of words on paper and a lot of code on the screen to bring this book to you, and we would like to know whether you liked it. This book was a long time in the making, and we think the wait was worth it.

Thanks to all of those who made this finally come together; all of the people at Wrox in England in the original version, Ian Blackham, Michelle Everitt, Darrin Murphy; and all of those at Apress who worked so hard to get it out under the Apress label, Gary Cornell, Julian Skinner, John Franklin, Dan Maharry, Dominic Shakeshaft, Sofia Marchant, Beckie Stones, David Kramer, and of course all of the authors. Also, I would like to thank all of my friends who read bits and pieces and commented, including Rex Mahel, Theresa Alexander, Mike Gallaugher, and Jim Andrews. Thanks to David Deloveh, whose prints are all over this book, and of course to Gabrielle, for that which she understands.

—Bill Sempf

My work on this book is dedicated to my mom, Mrs. Nirmal Cheda. You always have been a great inspiration to me. Thanks, Mom, for everything you have done for me.

—Kunal Cheda

Introduction

As I write this, Visual Studio .NET 2003 has been in the hands of developers for slightly over a year, and it has become one of the most popular development tools of all time for the Microsoft platform.

Visual Studio .NET 2003 is an incremental release of the Visual Studio IDE, and it includes a similarly incremental release of the .NET Framework, version 1.1. The significance of the changes in this release cannot be overlooked, although the basic philosophy has not changed from the original version. The differences in this release are a particular topic in this book, though we will also be reviewing some features that have changed little.

This book offers you the practical experience and wisdom drawn from a wide team of programmers who use Visual Studio .NET in their work every day. After a year of using Visual Studio .NET in a production environment, everyone has, of course, grown wiser in the use of this great product. This book brings you what we have learned across the depth and breadth of Visual Studio .NET.

Without further ado, then, let us dig into the depths of the Visual Studio .NET IDE, a look at the versions provided by Microsoft, and an overview of the rest of this book.

VS.NET Overview

Visual Studio .NET 2003 is, as it was with the original version, a single integrated development environment. Nearly all of the various types of development possible or reasonable on the Windows platform can be produced in Visual Studio .NET.

Throughout the late 1990s, we developers separated ourselves into camps. There were those who were InterDev developers, those who were Visual Basic programmers, those who were C++ coders. Now we are all Visual Studio .NET users.

There is more to that story. Visual Studio .NET comprehensively steps in at all points of the Software Development Life Cycle after requirements. With architecture tools and test tools, Visual Studio .NET 2003 is more of all things to all people than ever before.

One purpose of an overview is to ensure that everyone begins a book with the same background knowledge. To that end, let's look at the tools available in Visual Studio .NET as well as the problems that a single IDE occasionally encounters. Also, we will briefly look at the reasons to use Visual Studio .NET 2003 in preference to Visual Studio 6.0 and Visual Studio .NET 2002.

A Look at the Tools

As a developer toolbox, Visual Studio .NET is like one of those huge red tool cases one sees while watching the pits at an automobile race. The sheer number of features built into the software was staggering in the original versions, and it only got more comprehensive with the 2003 versions.

For example, we have the concept of server controls, very well implemented in Visual Studio .NET (see Figure 1). While all server controls, whether in ASP.NET or Windows forms, can be hand coded, the use of the Property Panel and the Visual IDE is a much faster way to get the same thing done.

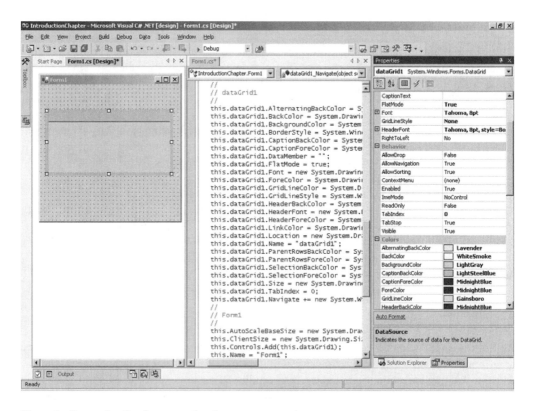

Figure 1. *Example of code generation in server controls*

While it could be argued that the use of code over the complexities of a RAD IDE reduces errors of omission and commission, there is no doubt that the combination of code and an IDE brings the most flexibility to the development of user interfaces. In previous versions of Visual Studio, code was available (as in Visual InterDev) or the IDE was available (as in Visual Basic), but the new Forms engine of VS .NET brings them together in a tremendously useful way.

While we are talking about the Property Panel, which we are all familiar with through Visual Studio 6.0 and most other development IDEs, the other RAD tools should be mentioned. The Server Explorer (Figure 2) allows unprecedented access to all of the tools of the common development server, with room for more.

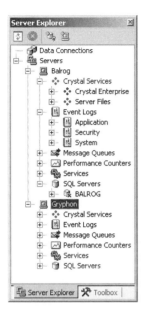

Figure 2. *Server Explorer*

Here we find expected access to things we have seen before, like SQL Server and the Event Viewer. Also, however, we see tools like the Performance Monitor, which would previously have required a separate application running. The services are shown as well, which would have previously been inaccessible to most developers. There is even space for third-party developers, as is shown by the Crystal Enterprise tools.

Part of the allure of a comprehensive IDE-like Visual Studio is the ability to extend or restrict the environment as needed. Add-ins and macros provide extensions to the IDE through a very powerful set of classes designed specifically for that purpose. Enterprise templates and project templates help to focus a developer's efforts by controlling the amount of information one needs to process at any given moment.

Macros in the Visual Studio .NET IDE are just as they have been in thousands of other applications throughout the history of computing. The principal benefit of Visual Studio .NET macros is the comprehensive access one has to the files and projects of the solution at hand. We'll cover macros in depth later in the book.

Add-ins, and the related Visual Studio Integration Program, are a much more permanent way to affect the usability of the Visual Studio .NET IDE. The entire interface is controllable: menus, templates, toolbars, even popup windows. Wizards can be developed using the add-in technology, and XML web services can even be accessed, searched, and published.

Project templates (Figure 3) are the application types we see every day when we create a new project: Windows forms, web forms, XML web services, and the like. These templates give us a needed starting point for our development efforts, providing the configuration files and code templates that help us most in our particular project type.

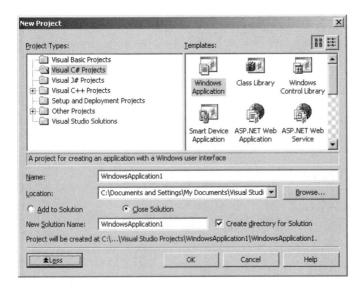

Figure 3. *Examples of project templates*

These features, while important, are familiar to those of you who have used the original version of Visual Studio .NET. There are more than a few new features as well, including cool new tools and several new project types.

New Stuff for 2003

The majority of the new features and tools were available as add-ons to the original Visual Studio .NET. The Mobile Internet Toolkit, for example, allows developers to easily write Internet applications for the plethora of devices showing up on the market. This is now part of the ASP.NET mobile controls.

Some of the new tools are really new. The Global XML architecture has been implemented as part of the XML web services project template as the WSDK class. This protocol implementation will bring significantly more reliability, security, and stability to XML web services developed using ASP.NET and the .NET Framework.

There are also additions to existing features. For instance, the new data connectors that work with the ADO.NET data infrastructure include Microsoft and third-party software by Btrieve and Oracle, among others.

Many of the other features found in Visual Studio .NET have been enhanced and improved, and the reader will find those enhancements and improvements highlighted in the book.

An in-depth look at features of the IDE will appear in the first chapter, *An IDE Tour*, and will continue throughout the book. We will look at significant tools like Macros in varying levels of depth throughout the book. RAD features will be covered at a professional level as well.

Why Migrate?

This isn't a book on migration, but it is understandable that one of the most pressing questions about Visual Studio .NET is, "why migrate?" The answer is primarily found in the speed with which one can develop if one has adequate knowledge of the features of the IDE.

Enter the New Microsoft Methodology

The New Microsoft Methodology is "Do it faster, better, with fewer errors and more maintainability. Oh, and do it your way, not our way." Visual Studio .NET is specifically designed to implement this methodology.

Many programmers favor the control that working directly with the code provides, and disapprove of the overhead of an IDE. Yet generating a 16,000-line class file that provides object-oriented access to a relational data source tends to make one lean toward the benefits of an IDE.

As an example, let's focus on web forms development for a moment. Many developers, present company included, use a text editor to develop ASP Classic code. Visual InterDev provides access to web project code through FrontPage Server Extensions, but other than that, it is just overhead.

ASP.NET is a different story. With server controls, we can use advanced ASP.NET tags to implement structures like DataGrids, and we can use the Design view and Property Panels to remind us of features that fall through the cracks when there are 1500 options. Additionally, multiple versions of browsers are supported at build time, thus providing a solution to the Microsoft only feel of the controls in Visual InterDev.

Making the Move from Visual Studio 6.0

So how about migration from Visual Basic 6, or ASP Classic? This is made necessary primarily by the advent of two things: the Internet and XML.

While the current incarnation of the Internet predates Visual Studio 6.0, it doesn't predate Windows DNA, the architecture that VS 6 is built around. Those of us attempting to build network tools using VB 6, for example, discovered how the classes that provide Internet access were clearly add-ons, not really integrated into the architecture.

The .NET Framework is designed from the ground up to include the Internet as the ultimate development platform. XML web services, implemented in Windows DNA as the Soap Toolkit, are a core feature of the Framework and Visual Studio .NET. The System.Net namespace provides intelligently designed access to all major Internet protocols, with room for more.

Extensible Markup Language, better known as XML, is the accepted language for relational data description. InterDev utilized classes built into Internet Explorer for most of its XML manipulation, an effective but messy solution to the problem. Much of the beauty of XML was lost in the translation, and many Microsoft developers fell behind in XML skills because of the ungainly implementation.

The .NET Framework is built from the ground up thinking in XML. When one saves an ADO.NET data set to the Session State variables, no manual translation takes place: the system transparently preserves the data as XML.

Visual Studio .NET implements this well in the IDE. The XML design tools in VS .NET are second to none, and they provide a strong argument to the text editor supporters above. Since XML defines relational data, it is easily described using an entity relationship diagram. Many of us have been using these to design SQL server databases for years, but now we can never leave the IDE and easily design XML schema definitions. See Figure 4.

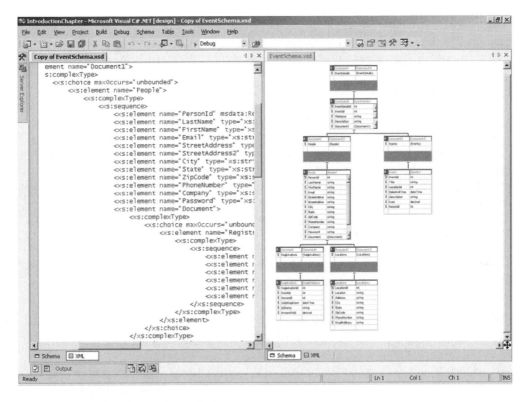

Figure 4. *Example of XML schema designer*

Aside from the new project types like mobile forms and the cool new languages like C#, one must seriously consider migration from Windows DNA in order to handle the Internet and XML more eloquently.

The Flavors of Visual Studio .NET 2003

In answer to the need for a development system that is everything to everyone, Microsoft has created a somewhat bewildering array of versions of their development software. While the marketing jargon can sometimes be confusing, the features really make the selection process quite easy.

Essentially, there are six different editions of the Visual Studio .NET install:

- Professional

- Enterprise Developer

- Enterprise Architect

- Academic Edition

- Standard Edition

- ASP.NET Web Matrix

Professional is made for the single developer in a small organization, or consultant perhaps. It is not designed to work in an enterprise as much as on a single machine. The core features only are included:

- The IDE

- The Compact Framework

- VB, C#, and C++

- Web, Windows, and Service development templates

Enterprise Developer is the appropriate version for the majority of programmers in large organizations. It includes the features of Professional, in addition to the following:

- SourceSafe

- Application Center Test

- The Data tools

- Enterprise Frameworks execution

Enterprise Architect is the complete version of the software. It is designed for team leaders and system analysts who need to model software visually and control the access of other developers. To the tools of Enterprise Developer, it adds these:

- Template authoring

- Biztalk

- Software and Data modeling with Visio

The Academic edition of the software has the full suite of tools available in Enterprise Architect, but it is not licensed to produce production software. The standard editions are for creating Windows forms in specific languages only. The ASP.NET Web Matrix is a free version of a development system for web pages that is available from the ASP.NET website, at `http://www.asp.net/webmatrix`.

How to Choose

Role Based Development (RBD) is at the heart of the New Microsoft Methodology. The existence of an architect in a Microsoft development pool has, until .NET, been something of a documentation position at the beginning of the project, and a coder at the end of the project. With Visual Studio .NET, architects will never need change their hats.

Selecting the right version for a specific environment is surprisingly simple. For a professional independent developer, creating ASP.NET websites and web services, or Windows forms for specific tasks, Professional edition will be just fine.

The larger development shop is where the RBD philosophy and the editions of the software really take their place. Small, tight teams of developers with specific roles and an architect in the center are armed with one Enterprise Architect edition and a set of Enterprise

Developer editions. Given the set of features in those editions, this is a remarkably efficient and cost-effective way to structure a development team.

Hobbyists can turn to the Standard edition for their language of choice for Windows forms development. Also, the ASP.NET Web Matrix fills that need well for Web hobbyists. Students can get the academic edition from school; just remember to upgrade upon graduation!

What's in This Book

Let's take a brief look at what's in the book, chapter by chapter.

Chapter 1: An IDE Tour

The *IDE Tour* chapter provides a tour of the IDE, so that we are all starting with the same basic set of knowledge as we dig into the more advanced features. As part of the IDE tour, we will cover the following topics:

- Start Page
- Windows
- Solution Explorer
- Server Explorer
- Class view
- Toolbox
- Properties window
- Resource window
- Task list
- Dynamic help

We will look at other topics, including these:

- Help
- Projects and solutions
- Migration

Chapter 2: Building Windows Applications

This chapter discusses the power and flexibility of Windows forms. It is a fast-paced, IDE-focused chapter that will cover topics like these:

- The controls
- Invisible and visible controls

- Adding components

- Adding references

- Menu editor

- Visual inheritance

- Component Designer

- Microsoft Active Accessibility

Chapter 3: Web Application Development

Since ASP.NET is based on the Common Language Runtime (CLR), it inherits all of the same language features as regular Windows applications. CodeBehind provides the speed of scripting with the ruggedness of compiled code. In short, web application programming is now largely modeled after the way Visual Basic programmers have been doing things for years. In this chapter, you'll find the following:

- Improved Drag & Drop web application development

- New tools in your toolbox

- Server controls

- Working with ASP.NET and CodeBehind

Chapter 4: Data Tool Orientation

This chapter takes some time to describe the advanced functionality of the data tools included as part of Visual Studio .NET. Here are some of the topics we'll cover:

- Server Explorer

- Property Window

- Object Browser

- Component Designer

Chapter 5: Mobile Client Development

The last in the series of project types, we will look at the capabilities for mobile development:

- Mobile web construction

- Working with the device SDK to build native applications

- Smart Device development, including .NET CE and the Pocket Platform

Chapter 6: Team Development with VS .NET

There are a number of current limitations related to Visual SourceSafe, and they are being addressed in version 6.0c. In addition, Visual Studio .NET has been updated to work with the VSS environment. We'll take a look at the following:

- New features

- Updated tools

- New IDE

- Pending checkins

- Enhanced Integration

Chapter 7: Performance Testing

Certainly one of the most fantastic development tools for the average enterprise programmer is the Application Center Test (ACT). This tool allows component developers to look for bottlenecks in the *n*-tier environment during development, thus supporting the RAD design effort. It is designed to simulate large groups of users by sending multiple HTTP calls through multiple connections to the server. This way, it stresses web servers and middleware, and then analyzes the results.

We will take a run through creating new tests with ACT, running them against some of the software built in other chapters. We'll look at dynamic testing, authentication, and other testing considerations.

Chapter 8: Project Deployment

Thanks to the Common Language Runtime (CLR), deployment of *n*-tier applications and other Windows applications is a different and simpler beast than it once was. Developers have more power and less to do than in Windows DNA. In this chapter, we'll cover the highlights:

- Types of projects explained

- Microsoft installer

- XCOPY deployment

- URL deployment

- Custom installers

- Handling COM+ easily

Chapter 9: Crystal Reports for .NET

Crystal Reports is finally an embedded Visual Studio tool, and none too soon. Windows and Web developers alike have been setting aside 25% of their development time to do reports for far too long. With the new integration and partnership between Crystal Decisions and Microsoft comes a host of new features, including these:

- Tight Web and Windows report integration

- Reports as a Web Service

- Runtime customization

Chapter 10: Customization

Here we start to get into in-depth features of Visual Studio .NET. This chapter looks at various settings used by the IDE and where they live:

- Environmental controls

- Compilation settings

- Configuration files

- Creating your own build configuration

- Customizing the toolbox

Chapter 11: Add-Ins

Here we find an overview of add-ins, noting that these can be used with a whole host of apps, including Word, Outlook, and the like. We'll be concentrating on Visual Studio .NET add-ins, and these topics:

- Add-in architecture

- Project file manipulation

- Add-in examples

Chapter 12: Macros

In this chapter we cover the .NET automation model in depth for the first time. We will dig into the object features, and building macros in general. The reader will also find a few useful prebuilt macros here that show the strength of the automation model:

- Automation object model

- Macro recording and editing

- The macro IDE

Chapter 13: Wizards

We'll cover all the tools provided to write a wizard and integrate it with Visual Studio .NET. We will check out a few practical examples, and some tips and tricks.

Appendixes

- A: Visual Studio .NET project files

- B: Visual Studio .NET directory structure

- C: Visual Studio .NET and certification

What Isn't in This Book

Ok, now we know what the book is about. Let's take a brief sojourn into what the book isn't about, to clear up any potential misunderstanding.

The .NET Framework

There is no question that the .NET Framework is going to change the way developers do their work in the Microsoft world. Even developers on different platforms are going to feel the pressure as their suppliers change things due to the marketing pressure applied by the Microsoft marketing juggernaut. In fact, Open Source proponents are replicating the logic of the .NET Framework for platforms like Linux. Even nondevelopers will see changes as their software allows for more network operations and provides more machine-to-machine interactivity. .NET will change many, many things.

Although everything in this book is about .NET, this will not be a .NET primer. You won't find a chapter explaining .NET.

This is a very fine distinction, but it bears making. What .NET is to COM, Visual Studio .NET is to Visual InterDev and the other software packages by Microsoft circa 1999. You will find COM references in an InterDev book, but little explanation of how COM works. The same is true here. This book won't provide a listing of Framework namespaces, but it will provide a description of various form components that use those namespaces.

Visual Basic .NET, C#, or Any Other Language

This book's text uses mostly C# in the examples, Microsoft's .NET specialized language. C# is a fantastic language, fixing many problems in C++ while maintaining the tight, easy-to-read code structure. It was born and bred for .NET work, and is now an open standard, managed by the ECMA. It is a good language for both academic writing, like this book, and production coding, like what we are all doing every day.

This book is not a C# reference guide. Everything in this book can be done in VB.NET, JScript.NET, and Perl, or any of the 20-odd other .NET languages. In fact, we will focus on visual tools instead of code where we can. This isn't necessarily because it is better to do things that way, but because that is what this book is about, the tools available to Visual Studio users.

You can code everything for a Microsoft Windows program in a text editor if you wish using the .NET Framework. We won't be doing that. In fact, we won't even be showing both ways to do things. If you want to get the job done with Visual Studio, this book is for you. We will use the tools to get the job done.

The .NET Servers

The third part of the .NET strategy is the multitude of server software available. Essentially, Microsoft has packaged all of the option packs, add-ons, and toys into stable server batches so that your organizations can build its servers just right. This is a reasonable though expensive strategy, and important to our cause.

Again, though, this book will not cover the installation, configuration, or management of any Microsoft servers. We will often use SQL Server 2000, and will mention BizTalk, Mobile Internet Application Server, and Application Center. In fact, we strongly recommend that readers have SQL Server 2000 installed before reading this book. An installation of Visual Studio will include the developer edition of SQL Server 2000, and this will work for our examples.

- For more information on the .NET servers, first look at Microsoft's web page. Their new layout for the .NET information is both easy to use and informative.

May we also suggest finding a test machine, installing the servers with the 120-day evaluation, and spending a weekend learning them. Since the topics covered by these servers are so specific, it is surprisingly easy to see how the software interfaces with existing functionality. We will avoid any examples in this book that require the installation of any specific servers other than SQL Server 2000, but we still advise taking a look at all of them.

This is because of Microsoft's commitment to the component model of server creation. One of the major complaints against NT in general was its density; a ton of functionality was never used. If you need a web server, one installs Windows 2000 and the ASP.NET components, for example. To increase scalability and portability, Microsoft has approached functionality from a divide-and-conquer perspective. Now you install only the server components you need, and leave the rest of the tools on the CD.

Methodology

Readers will find that this is not a book about how to develop software. While we do our best to design and code in a good rapid application development (RAD) style, please don't take them as examples of the "right" way to design software. Space considerations and time allowances in writing force us to take shortcuts in our code that most people wouldn't make in a production environment.

The Unified Modeling Language

Another point of clarity should be made about our architecture chapters. If you plan on using Visio 2002 for the creation of UML static structures for framework code, we suggest familiarity with the UML before you read that section. There is a lot to cover in a small space here, and much has already been written about UML.

If you need a short, excellent work about the language, not the methodology or process, we recommend *UML Distilled*, second edition, a brief guide to the Standard Object Modeling

Language, by Martin Fowler (2000). It provides an essential overview of the six primary diagrams and how to use them, and is only about 200 pages long.

Summary

There isn't much to summarize in an introduction. The rest of the book will provide both excellent educational reading, and a strong reference guide. We, the authors, hope that it will be a much dog-eared reference in the reader's library. Without further ado, let's start by looking at the basic usage of the Visual Studio .NET 2003 IDE.

CHAPTER 1

■■■

An IDE Tour

In order to make an integrated development environment (IDE) as useful as possible, you need to find your way around it. Part of developer production falls on the shoulders of the IDE producer, but part of it falls on the developer. The payoff for taking the time to learn about the IDE is all of the great labor-saving tools that are to be found within the deep recesses of the IDE.

I bring good news from the deep reaches of the Visual Studio .NET IDE. It is chock full of labor-saving, production-enhancing, really cool tools. In this first chapter, we'll talk in general about the IDE layout and definitions, and specifically about a few of the key features.

The IDE Tour

Let's start with an overview of the parts of the IDE, including the Windows layout, the menus and toolbars, and some of the specific tools to be found within.

Windows

To begin with, when Visual Studio .NET is launched, you immediately feel at home with the IDE, no matter whether you are coming from Visual Basic 6 or Visual Studio .NET 2002. Figure 1-1 gives the names of some of the pieces of the IDE.

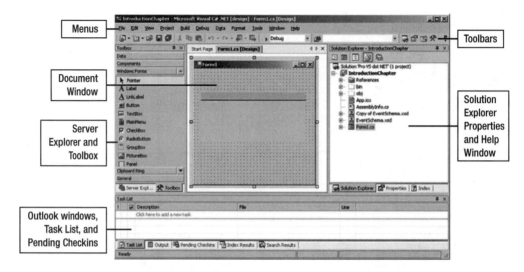

Figure 1-1. *Parts of the Visual Studio .NET IDE*

Laying Out Document Windows

The document windows you create for the files you open take up all the space not used by tool windows or the menu bars. As multiple windows are opened, they are placed on top of one another, each distinguished by a tab with its name (and mode) on it. By default, Visual Studio (VS) .NET uses a single horizontal *tab group* to make each document window available, but you can add more tab groups if you wish. The tab groups can be either horizontal or vertical, though not both at the same time, to create a split window effect. This can come in handy when the code you need to reference is split across separate files. It can also be helpful when you are trying to look at multiple forms to ensure that they share a consistent look and feel.

For example, in the screenshot shown in Figure 1-2, a new vertical tab group allows you to work on both the design and code behind your form at the same time.

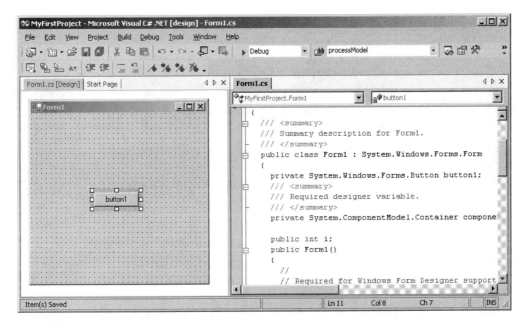

Figure 1-2. *A vertical tab group*

To start a new tab group in Visual Studio .NET, perform the following two actions:

1. Select a document window.

2. From the Window menu, select New Horizontal Tab Group or New Vertical Tab Group.

The order of tabs in a tab group can be rearranged by dragging them. Dragging tabs can also move them between groups. The main restriction on creating tab groups is that they can be created in only one direction. Remember, you cannot create both horizontal and vertical tab groups at the same time.

MDI Mode Versus Tabbed Windows

If you have used previous versions of Visual Studio, you will recall that rather than documents being herded together in a tab group, each document was given its own window, which could be maximized, minimized, or arranged as the developer wanted. This option is available to Visual Studio .NET users as well, as shown in Figure 1-3.

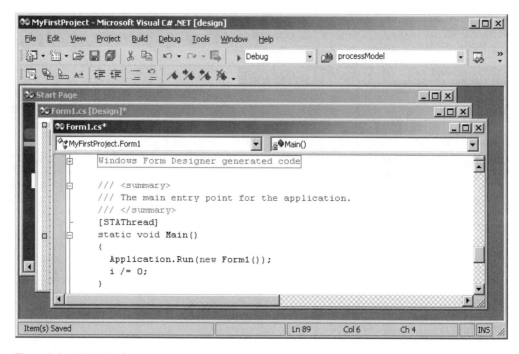

Figure 1-3. *MDI Windows*

To work with this configuration, do the following:

1. Select Tools ➤ Options.

2. In the resulting dialog box, select the Environment ➤ General pane from the left-hand side pane, and select the MDI Environment radio button at the top.

3. Visual Studio .NET will tell you that it must be restarted before MDI Mode can be used. Click OK, and then close and restart Visual Studio .NET.

To change back from MDI mode to using tab groups, follow these instructions again, but select the Tabbed Documents radio button rather than MDI Environment.

Laying Out Tool Windows

There are a few more ways to have your tool windows act and fill the screen than there are for document windows. The first thing to do, though, is to make sure that you have the windows you want actually onscreen. If you need to make a window available, either select it from the View (or Help) menu or use its keyboard shortcut.

If you want to close a window from view, do one of the following:

- Click on the close icon.

- Click on the window, and then choose Hide from the Window menu.

- Right-click on the window and choose Hide from the Context menu.

You might want to consider having available all the tool windows mentioned earlier, at least initially. It's easier to never to use a window that you can see than to figure out which window you need from among those that you can't see.

Floating Tool Windows

All tool windows have three "layout modes," namely, *dockable*, which is the default, *floating*, and neither of the above. The second of these, floating, is the easiest to demonstrate, in that it makes a tool window behave like any other application running Windows, rather than as a piece of Visual Studio.

To put a tool window in float mode, either:

- Right-click the window and select Floating, or

- Select the window and choose Floating from the Window menu.

Whichever you choose, you'll see the window detach itself from the Visual Studio .NET IDE window, and you are now free to drag it around the screen to wherever you want it to be. I exaggerated slightly by saying that the window is typical of all other applications. A floating window in VS .NET's case has only a "close" button and no "maximize" or "minimize" functionality. This window is still tied in with Visual Studio itself, and all floating windows will minimize and reappear when VS .NET does. As the mode name suggests, if you now maximize the Studio window, you'll see that the tool window continues to float on top of its parent application.

Dockable Tool Windows

The default state for a tool window is *Dockable*, which means that like any other window, you can select and drag it around your screen like a floating window. But when your cursor reaches an inside edge of the Visual Studio .NET IDE window, you'll see a ghosted outline in the IDE suggesting that the window can be attached to the IDE again.

▓**Tip** Note that you can also keep a tool window from docking by pressing Ctrl while moving it. Or if you need it docked immediately, you can dock a tool window instantaneously by double-clicking its title bar.

The Floating option tells a window to detach itself immediately if it is docked. If it is already floating, this option will keep the tool window from docking.

For improved use of available space, tool windows can also be *tab docked*. This refers to multiple tool windows sharing the same display area but displaying tabs at the bottom for selecting them. Figure 1-4 shows the Server Explorer and Solution Explorer docked in the picture on the left and tab docked in the picture on the right.

Figure 1-4. *Tab docking*

To tab dock a window with another one, select it and drag it so that your cursor is in a corner of the window you want it to share space with. The ghost outline you saw earlier will encompass the target window, and you can let go your mouse button, and voilà. If you drag the tab-docked window anywhere, you'll now take both windows with you. To un-tab-dock a window, double-click its tab.

Auto Hide

The Auto Hide option is new in Visual Studio .NET. It is applicable only to windows that are docked in the Visual Studio .NET IDE window. Making a tool window auto hide means that when it is not being used, the window "minimizes" itself to the edge of the IDE that it was docked to. It can then be brought back into view by moving the cursor over its tab.

There are several ways to make a docked window auto hide:

- Right-click on the window and select Auto Hide from the context menu.

- Select the window and choose Auto Hide from the Window menu.

- Left-click the "pin" icon next to the window's Close button.

Note that the pin icon will change from vertical to horizontal, signifying that the window is now in auto hide mode. You can also make every tool window auto hide at once by selecting any one tool window and then Auto Hide All from the Window menu.

When you build up a number of tool windows on any one side, the tabs will cover the descriptions, or they may be scrolled off the screen. To view a full list, right-click in any part of the tab area they use and a list will be displayed.

None of the Above

The last layout option occurs when a tool window is set to be neither Dockable nor Floating. This will cause a tool window to be placed in the tab group and act like a document window. That's it for laying out the IDE to your specifications.

Start Page

The *Start Page* (see Figure 1-5) provides quick access to many of the tasks you'll be performing on a daily basis. It is the foundation for the online community and support system that Microsoft has enhanced and is emphasizing with this release of the product. The functions of the Start Page are new for Visual Studio .NET 2003.

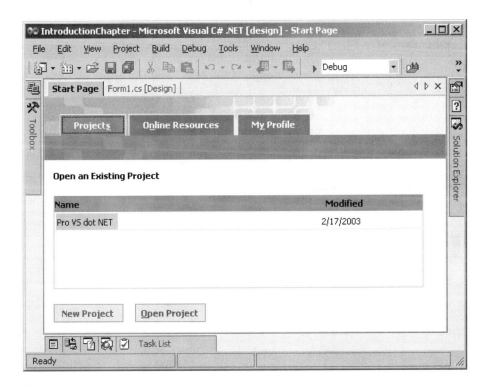

Figure 1-5. *Start page*

Information about the start page has been newly categorized into three useful tabs: Projects, Online Resources, and My Profile. The Projects tab is, confusingly enough, the primary harbor for solutions, as was the similar screen in the previous version. The Online Resources tab includes access to information in the MSDN, as well as UDDI searching and other cool Internet features. The My Profile tab allows each developer to set up a custom keyboard scheme and other properties based on previous versions of the development system.

Visual Studio .NET is actually running an instance of Internet Explorer (IE) 6.0 to display the Start Page and its associated pages. Try clicking through the titles in Online Resources with

IE working offline and you'll see the message, "This feature requires that you have connected to the Internet previously or are currently online," for all but Get Started and My Profile, unless you've already worked through them while online. In this case, these pages will have been stored in IE's cache and you'll see the last version of them that you downloaded (provided they're still in the cache). Quite a few pieces of Visual Studio .NET depend on your copy of IE (Netscape Navigator and Opera won't do here) being up-to-date and online. Don't worry if you forget, though; Visual Studio will tell you when this is the case.

Menus

While it isn't a good use of time to discuss every menu option in every situation and its implications, we should look at some of the more interesting options, and those that have changed since Visual Studio.NET 2002.

A number of the menu options change drastically with the type of file being viewed. Code alteration options appear in the Edit menu only when you are viewing code pages, such as CS and VB files. Many debug menu items often appear only when you are in debug mode, not surprisingly. If an option described in the following doesn't appear where expected, make sure you are viewing the type of file for which the option would be useful.

File

The file menu is as expected. There are functions to handle projects and individual files, with and without source control. Under Open... there is a newer function called Convert..., which brings up the Convert dialog, as shown in Figure 1-6.

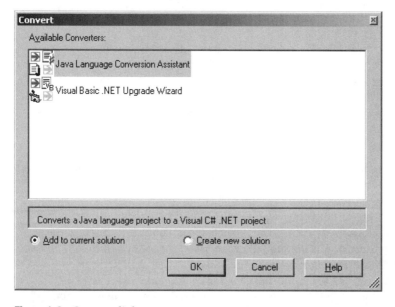

Figure 1-6. *Convert dialog*

These functions can also be brought to the forefront by attempting to open a project of the specified type, for instance, running VB 6.0 from within VS.NET. It is nice to know that you can easily get to the wizards, though, or write your own using the AddIn and Wizard project.

Another point of interest regarding the Open... submenus is the "From Web" option. This will allow you to open a project from a URL if Visual Studio detects that the Web can be accessed via Front Page Server Extensions or that files can be accessed via a shared drive specification. Keep in mind that using the From Web option will result in a project file being saved in the web directory, and an attempt will be made to save a Solution file in your local Visual Studio Projects folder.

When Saving projects, you may use the Advanced Save Options dialog, which allows for a variety of encodings for the ASCII text of source code, as well as line endings that match a variety of operating system requirements. See Figure 1-7.

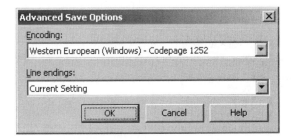

Figure 1-7. *Advanced Save Options dialog*

This is fantastic for those working in development shops where some of the workstations may be Unix (especially for C++ projects) or Macintosh (especially for HTML). Also, if you have multilanguage environments, the encoding could be a lifesaver.

Edit

The Edit menu, aside from the expected copy and paste functions, has a wide variety of code formatting options. Many of these are available on the Text Editor toolbar:

- Format Selection

- Tabify Selection

- Untabify Selection

- Make Uppercase

- Make Lowercase

- Delete Horizontal White Space

- View White Space

- Word Wrap

- Incremental Search

- Comment Selection

- Uncomment Selection

- Increase Line Indent

- Decrease Line Indent

Also note that several language-specific options are often available in the Edit menu, such as the Insert Script Block menu in HTML. This option exists to assist with a quick addition of a Client or Server script block, and is visible in the HTML editor but enabled only in HTML view.

Project

The Project menu essentially defines all the options that are available in the content menu shown when right clicking on a project in the Solution Explorer. Both Solution and Project properties are available. Generally speaking, the following options groups are available:

- Add a specific type of file to a project

- Copy a project

- Modify how a project is viewed in the Solution Explorer

- Modify the project properties, such as build order and references

Build

As expected, the Build menu gathers all of the Build options into one place for easy access. For the record, the keyboard shortcut for a Solution build is `Control+Shift+B`, but the option is also available in the menu selections and the Build toolbar.

The Build menu also provides easy access to the Configuration Manager, which is usually tough to get to, requiring a search through the Solution Property window. The Configuration Manager allows you to select the projects in the solution that get compiled in a default build, and also allows project-by-project selection of Release and Debug build configurations.

XML

There are only two significant options in the XML menu: Create Schema and Validate XML Data. Create Schema adds an XSD to the project. Validate XML Data is essentially a compile action for XML files; it adds errors and omissions to the Task list based on the validity of the XML file. An XML file must be open for you to view this menu.

Data

The Data menu appears when you have data objects—like adapters—in your current scope. As with the XML option, two main functions are available in the Data menu: Generate Dataset and Preview Data. Generate Dataset does as expected. If there is a DataAdapter on the current form, a DataSet object will be added to the form to match it using the Generate DataSet wizard. The Preview Data option is also as expected. If there is an adapter on the page, the data can be previewed, complete with parameter availability. Also note that you can preview the Schema of a dataset with the tool shown in Figure 1-8.

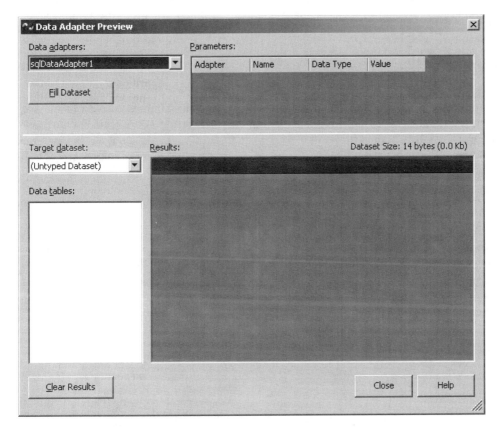

Figure 1-8. *Data Adapter Preview dialog*

When there are data options on the form, a number of configuration options appear that mimic the context-sensitive menus on the data objects themselves. Configure Data Adapter and DataSet Properties fall into this category. These options replicate functions in the context-sensitive menus of DataAdapters and DataSets, respectively.

Format

The Format menu has all of the nice layout options that you expect from a good word processing program. Colors, Fonts, Alignments, and the like are all available from this menu. Note that much of this is available from the Formatting menu, which comes up by default when you are working on a Web or Windows Form design.

For Web developers, there is one more thing of note: the Styles designer. This will be covered more in our Web Forms discussion in Chapter 3.

Table

The Table and Frames menus are for the Web folk among us. The functions available in the Tables menu are similar to those in the Microsoft Word table editor: the ability to add, delete, or modify a row, column, or table.

Also, the Merge Cells function is available, which works much as it does in Excel. When several cells are selected, they can be merged, and Visual Studio will insert the appropriate ROWSPAN or COLSPAN attribute in the appropriate table cells.

Frames

As with the Tables menu, this option gives the Web developer a tool to deal with the HTML-specific problem of FRAMESETs. You have the option to add new frames to an existing layout and to edit frames. One of the more difficult problems of frames in HTML is that of the frame source: the file that supplies the content for a given frame. Visual Studio gives us the Set Page for Frame option to assist with this issue, essentially making the source file a property of the frame entity.

Tools

The Tools menu is cool. This is where all of the neat stuff that Visual Studio does for you will appear. The content of this page is very individualized, because third-party tools and add-ins will appear in this menu as they are registered with each installation of Visual Studio. Some third-party tools will be included in every edition of Visual Studio, and they will be discussed later in the book. Create GUID, which generates unique strings on command, and Dotfuscator (Figure 1-9) are among these tools.

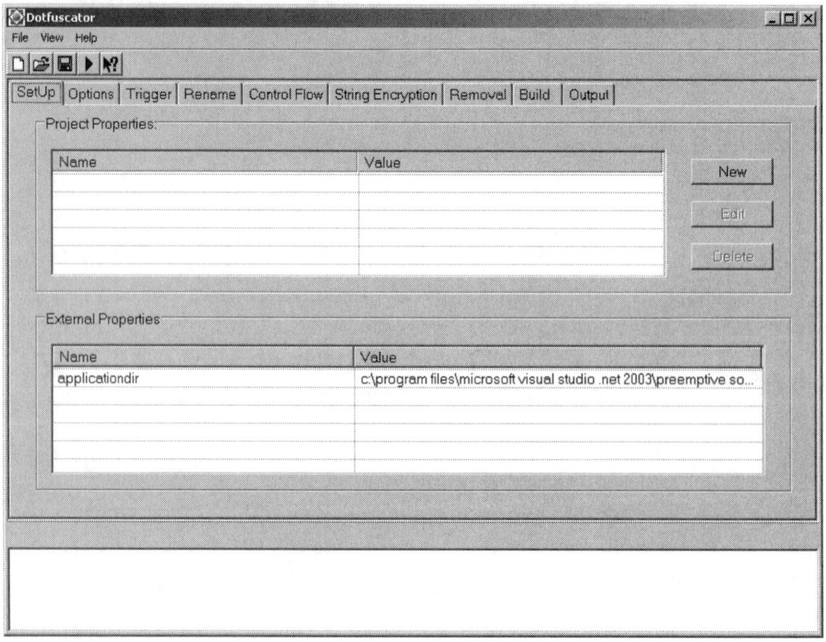

Figure 1-9. *Dotfuscator*

Dotfuscator is a third-party (i.e., not from Microsoft) tool that encrypts the binaries produced by the .NET build engine so that they cannot be reverse engineered. And software that uses a virtual machine, like Java JAR files or .NET, can be reversed into its base language if compiled normally. Dotfuscator makes this more difficult, and it is built right into Visual Studio .NET 2003.

Additionally, connections to external development sources, such as devices, databases, and servers are controlled from this menu. Add-in and Macro controls are available here, as well as from individual projects that use devices, databases, and servers. The Add-in Manager (Figure 1-10), for instance, shows what items are loaded for the developer's use.

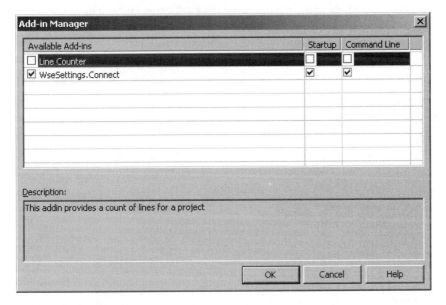

Figure 1-10. *Add-in Manager*

Most importantly, the Customize and Options managers are both found in this menu. These are so significant that we will cover them in depth later in this chapter.

Window

The IDE window controls are found in this menu option, as are many other Windows-based tools. We discussed more of the functionality of these controls in the Windows section. These are the controls:

- Splits

- Tab Groups

- Docking

- Hiding

- Floating

Help

As with the Windows menus, the Help menu is significant enough to command its own section in this chapter. The Help system is much improved in the .NET IDEs in general, and with Visual Studio .NET 2003 in particular. Easy access to tech support and filtering of the massive help files make this a powerful set of tools for developers.

Solution Explorer

One of the first tool windows to get familiar with is the *Solution Explorer*. Here you'll see a hierarchical listing of all the projects that your current solution contains and the files within each of those projects. Double-clicking on a container icon will either show or hide its contents, and double-clicking on a file will open a document window for that file. For our newly created project, the solution explorer will look like Figure 1-11.

Figure 1-11. *Solution Explorer*

The icons above the tree view represent the most common user options for the selected file and change according to the file selected. With form1.cs selected, for example, the icons from left to right represent View Code, View Designer, Refresh, Show All Files, and Properties. Moving your cursor over the icon will trigger a tooltip after a few seconds, and you can get a full set of options for the file, rather than the most common ones, by right-clicking on the file and choosing an option from the context menu that appears.

The solution explorer also tells you a few more useful pieces of information about our solution if you know what to look for:

- Files can be part of a solution, but not part of a project. These will be shown directly under the solution. A container called Miscellaneous Files may also appear in the window, the contents of which are files that are not part of either project or solution. For example, a file containing useful code snippets to reuse would be in Miscellaneous Files.

- If the name of a project is in bold (as in Figure 1-11), it is the *active project* in the solution. That is, when you compile, build, and run a solution, it is this project that will run initially. Any other projects in the solution will run only when called from this active one.

- File names suffixed with a red exclamation point in Solution Explorer denote that while the file is still part of the solution, it has been moved or deleted by someone outside of Visual Studio .NET, which cannot now find it.

- Whatever item is being worked with in the Design or Code view is now being selected in the Solution explorer. To change this behavior, uncheck Track Active Item in Solution Explorer in Tools ➤ Options ➤ Environment ➤ Projects and Solutions.

- Files with grayed-out icons denote that these files have been excluded from a project or solution and will not be included when it is compiled and built.

Server Explorer

The Server Explorer (Figure 1-12) is a sort of Microsoft Management console (MMC) that allows developers to see all available server resources on any network server. Server Explorer takes the MMC into the world of the middle-tier developer.

You can use Server Explorer to view and manipulate data links, database connections, and system resources on any server to which you have network access. Do you need an instance of the ASP.Net Requests Rejected perfmon counter? No problem. Do you need to intercept an eventlog message sent to the print log? It's right there for you to view or use in your programs.

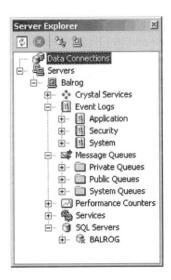

Figure 1-12. *Server Explorer*

As you can see in the figure, each category of tool appears as a top-level item. There can be a number of these, and we won't go over every one. We will look at the following:

- SQL Servers

- Services

- Data connections

- Performance Counters

- Message Queues

- Event Logs

Products like Crystal will have their own top-level item, which should be covered in the product documentation. We'll cover the concepts here, and the idea should hold true for middle-tier development with any of the tools.

SQL Servers

The SQL Server Explorer is where many RAD developers will spend their time. Are you tired of spending time in Enterprise Manager? Those days are gone. The SQL Server Explorer gives you access to everything Enterprise Manager does, at least from a development perspective. See Figure 1-13.

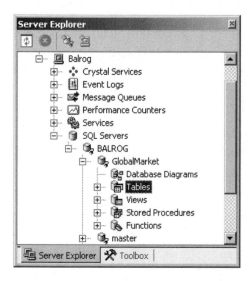

Figure 1-13. *SQL Servers in the Server Explorer*

The Tables and Views create SqlConnection and SqlDataAdapter objects, with properties specifying the object. Developers can further create a DataSet by right-clicking on an SqlDataAdapter. Another option that you have when you are working with a Server Explorer-generated SqlDataAdapter is to use the Data Adapter Wizard.

To access the data adapter wizard from an existing SqlDataAdapter, right-click and select Configure Data Adapter.... The wizard then allows you to do the following:

- Select an existing data connection, or create a new one.

- Determine how the adapter is to access the database.

- Specify the information to get from the database as part of the adapter.

- Determine what to name the statements used to interface with the data (update, delete, insert, and select).

The Data Adapter even allows you to specify that stored procedures are to be created rather than taken from inline SQL. After specifying the use of the SELECT statement to get information from the database, the wizard interpolates some pretty impressive SQL code to generate the procedures. Note that all four (UPDATE, DELETE, INSERT, and SELECT) statements are generated with unique names, which you get to specify. Here is some generated SELECT code, for example:

```
IF EXISTS (SELECT * FROM sysobjects WHERE name = 'NewSelectCommand'
    AND user_name(uid) = 'dbo')
  DROP PROCEDURE [dbo].[NewSelectCommand];
GO

CREATE PROCEDURE [dbo].[NewSelectCommand]
AS
  SET NOCOUNT ON;
  SELECT CustomerID, CustomerTypeID FROM CustomerCustomerDemo;
GO
```

On the visual side, the properties of a table or field are readily viewable in the Properties dialog, which we'll discuss later in more detail.

Stored procedures can also be dragged into the Component Tray—the area of the designer reserved for components—for visual and programmatic access. The stored Procedure creates an instance of the SqlCommand class. For instance, dragging the SalesByYear procedure out of the globalMarket Stored Procedure folder causes the following code to be created:

```
this.SalesByYear.CommandText = "dbo.[Sales by Year]";
this.SalesByYear.CommandType = System.Data.CommandType.StoredProcedure;
this.SalesByYear.Connection = this.sqlConnection1;
this.SalesByYear.Parameters.Add(new
  System.Data.SqlClient.SqlParameter("@RETURN_VALUE",
  System.Data.SqlDbType.Int, 4, System.Data.ParameterDirection.ReturnValue,
  false, ((System.Byte)(10)), ((System.Byte)(0)), "",
  System.Data.DataRowVersion.Current, null));
this.SalesByYear.Parameters.Add(new
  System.Data.SqlClient.SqlParameter("@Beginning_Date",
                        System.Data.SqlDbType.DateTime, 8));
this.SalesByYear.Parameters.Add(new
  System.Data.SqlClient.SqlParameter("@Ending_Date",
  System.Data.SqlDbType.DateTime, 8));
```

This is perhaps slightly more convoluted than it would be if we wrote it by hand, but certainly not bad for a RAD tool. It is certainly better than a hidden batch of compiled code, or a dependence on a group of included server-side JavaScript.

Services

The Services Server Control essentially gives us visual access to the System.SystemProcess.Servicecontroller object. We can actually drag an instance of a service controller, like the MSFTP service on a Windows 2000 Server in our network, onto the project and access it visually and programmatically. A whole host of properties are available to us in the properties window, including the name of the instance, and also these:

- CanPauseAndContinue

- CanShutdown

- CanStop

- Container

- DependentServices

- DesignMode

- DisplayName

- Events

- MachineName

- ServiceName

- ServicesDependedOn

- ServiceType

- Site

- Status

The Server Explorer shows us the state of the services: started, stopped, or paused. See Figure 1-14.

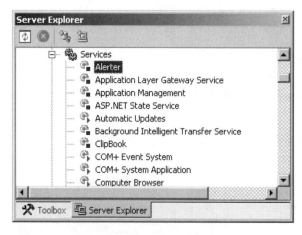

Figure 1-14. *Service states in the Server Explorer*

The Properties window (Figure 1-15) gives us access to the instance name, the service we are managing in that instance, the machine name, and other information.

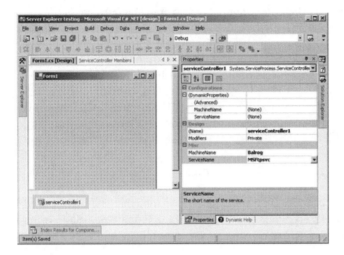

Figure 1-15. *Properties for a selected service*

Keep in mind that it is just an instance of the ServiceController. If you need two services at the same time, you will need two instances with two names.

As with other drag-and-drop tools in Visual Studio, all that is happening is that references are being added to your code. There is no magic here; you could hand code all of this if you wished. For instance, here is the code that is generated by the components just mentioned being added to your project:

```
public class Form1 : System.Windows.Forms.Form
{
  private System.ServiceProcess.ServiceController serviceController1;
  private System.ComponentModel.Container components = null;

  public Form1()
  {
    InitializeComponent();
  }
{...}
}
```

This kind of functionality lends itself to a number of possible uses, including but not limited to the following:

- Writing your own service controller application

- Checking for the state of a service before using it

- Easy stopping and starting for low-level changes during an install

- Executing a custom command to the service with the help of ExecuteCommand()

Did you ever want to create an SQL Server function inside your development environment? No problem. It is also possible to create tables and Stored Procedures, and do direct data editing. However, it is the functions that really are impressive for some reason. Like Stored Procedures, SQL Functions dragged to the Component Tray also appear as SqlCommands.

Data Connections

The Data Connections icon provides easy access to the Data Link Properties dialog.

There are a number of different ways to link to a database in .NET. We're not going to talk about all of them here, because this isn't a book about ADO .NET, but from a RAD perspective, the key is to visualize the data connections in a comprehensive yet compact way. Having access to all the different kinds of data connections for a project in one visual interface is the key.

To access the Data Link Properties dialog, right-click on the Data Connections icon and select Add Connection....

While in previous versions of Visual Studio it wasn't recommended that DSNs be created in development environments, now it is encouraged. The Data Link Properties dialog assumes that we want to connect to an SQL Server, but clicking the Provider tab gives us access to a list of installed data providers.

There are even a few more interesting connectors, like the Microsoft Project 9.0 OLE DB connector. Select the provider type from the Provider tab, and then click the All tab to edit other details. See Figure 1-16.

Figure 1-16. *The Data Link Properties dialog*

*If you choose a random project file from your hard drive and enter it in the flagged Project Name property, you can create a new way to get in touch with your project files from Visual Studio. See Figure 1-17.

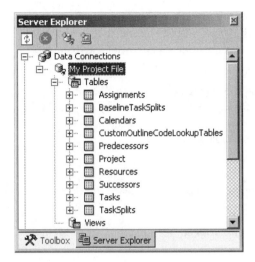

Figure 1-17. *Data Connections*

All of these tables act as in a similar manner to the tables from an SQL Server: You can view the data, edit properties, and in general get in touch with the environment. Right-click on the data connection and select Rename to rename the icon. Check out the *SQL Servers* section in this chapter for more detail.

Performance Counters

Another of the nice visual features of Windows servers is the performance monitor (PerfMon), software that reads continuous performance and error-tracking data produced by all of the system's hardware and software services. Everything from ASP.NET cache to the temperature of the processor is often available from the performance monitor. Most of us view it from PerfMon, the neat little graphing tool that comes with Windows operating systems. Few of us think of it as a development tool.

The fact is that if we could track every aspect of our program's function using the performance counter, wouldn't we? We would no longer have to write the number of corrupt images to a field commented out in HTML. We can now easily write performance information to a custom counter and leave it in, forever out of the user's way, but available to us as needed.

Another interesting facet of this is system tracking, which could be an essential part of maintenance applications. Imagine a desktop application that is smart enough to know when the rest of the system is taxed, and reduces its own needs in response. Or a server application that automatically carries out a cleanup after a certain kind of error. Watching the properties of the performance counters (Figure 1-18) makes it all possible.

Figure 1-18. *The performance counter icon*

Dragging an existing performance counter onto the Component Tray produces the familiar icon, and creates the underlying code that calls and configures the `System.Diagnostics.PerformanceCounter` object with properties set to set the instance to the counter chosen:

```
this.performanceCounter1 = new System.Diagnostics.PerformanceCounter();
((System.ComponentModel.ISupportInitialize)(this.performanceCounter1)).BeginInit();
this.performanceCounter1.CategoryName = "ASP.NET";
this.performanceCounter1.CounterName = "Application Restarts";
this.performanceCounter1.MachineName = "Balrog";
```

The instance of `performanceCounter1` gives us access to the properties of the class, including the following:

- `CategoryName`: the category name for this instance of counter, like ASP.Net or Memory

- `Container`: inherited from component

- `CounterHelp`: gets the description

- `CounterName`: gets or sets the name of the counter, like Request Wait Time

- `CounterType`: gets the type of counter for the instance, like Continuous or Instance

- `InstanceName`: the name of the instance, like performanceCounter1

- `MachineName`: the PC name being watched

- `RawValue`: the unmodified value of the counter

- `ReadOnly`: true for system counters, false for custom counters

- `Site`: inherited from component

To get into the really interesting stuff, you have to make custom counters for your namespace. This is an amazingly simple endeavor, never requiring you to leave Visual Studio. Simply do the following:

1. In Server Explorer, right-click on Performance Counters and select Create New Category.

2. Set the Category Name to `GlobalMarket`.

3. Click the New button.

4. Name the counter `Errors`.

5. Set the Type to `NumberOfItems32`.

6. Click OK.

7. From the Server Explorer, drag the new Errors counter you just created onto the designer.

8. Right-click on the `performanceCounter1` and select Properties.

9. Set the InstanceName to `errors`.

10. Set the ReadOnly attribute to `False`.

For instance, refer to the following code. It implements a performance counter as part of the Initialize event handler.

```
private void InitializeComponent()
{
    this.performanceCounter1 = new System.Diagnostics.PerformanceCounter();
    ((System.ComponentModel.ISupportInitialize)
                (this.performanceCounter1)).BeginInit();
    //
    // performanceCounter1
    //
    this.performanceCounter1.CategoryName = "GlobalMarket";
    this.performanceCounter1.CounterName = "errors;
    this.performanceCounter1.InstanceName = "errors";
    this.performanceCounter1.MachineName = "draco";
    this.performanceCounter1.ReadOnly = false;

    ((System.ComponentModel.ISupportInitialize)
                (this.performanceCounter1)).EndInit();


}
```

It is a simple operation to use the `performanceCounter1.Increment();` method to increment the value. After setting up a new counter, we can right-click on it and Add Installer to the project, which creates the C# code needed to install the counter on the computer running the software. This is the code, for instance, that would install the counter on an installation server:

```
using System;
using System.Collections;
using System.ComponentModel;
using System.Configuration.Install;

namespace Server_Explorer_testing
{
  [RunInstaller(true)]
  public class ProjectInstaller : System.Configuration.Install.Installer
  {
    private System.Diagnostics.PerformanceCounterInstaller
      performanceCounterInstaller1;
    private System.ComponentModel.Container components = null;
```

```
    public ProjectInstaller()
    {
      InitializeComponent();
    }

    private void InitializeComponent()
    {
      this.performanceCounterInstaller1 = new
        System.Diagnostics.PerformanceCounterInstaller();
      this.performanceCounterInstaller1.CategoryHelp = "None";
      this.performanceCounterInstaller1.CategoryName = "GlobalMarket";
      this.performanceCounterInstaller1.Counters.AddRange
        (new System.Diagnostics.CounterCreationData[] {
      this.Installers.AddRange(new System.Configuration.Install.Installer[] {
    }
  }
}
```

Event Logs

Event logs offer the same features as the performance counters: ease of responding to events or logging your own. Doing this in Visual Basic 6 was a hassle, requiring all kinds of hacks. Now with the RAD tools, it's a drag, drop, 'n' code kind of operation. Dragging the application, security, or system log to your application design window provides the following properties and methods (not a complete list):

Properties:

- EnableRaisingEvents

- Entries

- Log

- LogDisplayName

- MachineName

- Source

- SynchronizingObject

Methods:

- Clear

- CreateEventSource

- Delete

- DeleteEventSource

- EndInit

- Exists

- GetEventLogs

- LogNameFromSourceName

- Send

- SourceExists

- WriteEntry

Microsoft Message Queue (MSMQ)

We don't want to get into a discussion of message queuing in depth here. There just isn't space. Suffice it to say that you can easily create components to run on a server that watch a message queue and react when there is a message. More information is available on MSDN.

A possible use of message queuing is a fax server. When a client places an order, the application generates a fax document, then drops it in a queue with a Send method. The fax server is a component on another machine that checks every 5 seconds for a message. When one arrives, it passes it on to the fax transmitter.

Message queuing in .NET is easier than making a recordset in Windows DNA. Even without the Server Explorer, it's a four-line accomplishment, and with the Server Explorer, it's very easy. Figure 1-19 shows how simple it is.

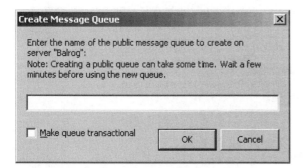

Figure 1-19. *Create a Message Queue*

Right-click on Public Queues in the Server Explorer and select Create New Message Queue. Now type in the name of the message queue you want to create and click OK. Keep in mind that workgroups can't manage public queues: Nondomain systems will pass errors if you try to view, edit, or make new public queues.

Go ahead and right-click on the Private Queues folder and select Create Queue. Name the queue TestMessageQueue. See Figure 1-20.

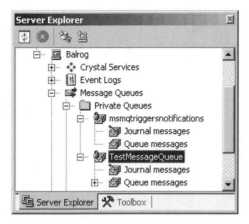

Figure 1-20. *Message queues in the Server Explorer*

Now drag the new queue to your designer. From here on it's code. To add a message to your queue, you need to add the following code to some event:

```
messageQueue1.Send("Hello World","Test Message");
```

This is clearly not the world's most complex code. But what has this done for you? It has left information in a waiting area for another program to pick up when it has time. Essential for stable scalable systems, message queuing is an important tool in the kit of the distributed application designer.

Run the Send method a few times by adding it to the event handler for a button, and you can view the independent messages in the queue using the Server Explorer, as shown in Figure 1-21.

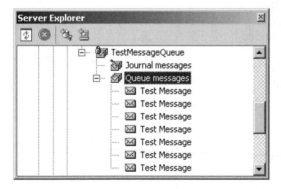

Figure 1-21. *Example messages in the Server Explorer*

Here is the code for a quick form with two buttons and a label to test this:

```
private void button1_Click(object sender, System.EventArgs e)
{
  messageQueue1.Send("Hello World","Test Message");
}

private void button2_Click(object sender, System.EventArgs e)
{
  System.Messaging.Message myMessage = messageQueue1.Receive();
  label1.Text = myMessage.Body.ToString();
}
```

Class View

Those of you who have used previous versions of Visual Studio will recognize the Class View window as unchanged and still present. For those of you new to this version, the Class View window is another hierarchical tree view representing an alternative view of the solution as a whole. Instead of files and resources, the Class View shows the projects in the solution as a collection of the classes and class members that are declared within them. Even our first project has a few things declared in it from the start, as you can see in Figure 1-22.

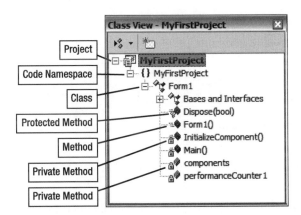

Figure 1-22. *Class View*

The Class View uses many different icons in its tree view to denote exactly what type of class member or class container that particular branch refers to. Although you can't see it, the icons for basic class members are also color-coded; methods are purple, fields light blue, and properties (not shown here) white rather than the various shades of gray that you'll see in the book. If you're not familiar with what an icon represents or cannot remember how a particular class or class member was declared, you can do either of the following:

- Move your cursor over the entry in the tree, and a tooltip will appear containing the member's declaration.

- Double-click the entry, and the code file containing that particular class will appear in a document window open at the point where the item is declared.

As with the other tool windows, right-clicking on any item will bring up a context menu allowing you to view the file containing its definition, the file containing the call to it (the reference), or its definition as given by the object browser, which we'll meet later. The Quick Find Symbol option will also run a search through the files in the project and return a list of definitions and references to it.

The Class View can get messy rather quickly. In .NET, everything is an object derived from the System.Object class, even the form in your project, albeit six nodes down. With the vast number of classes and members to deal with, Visual Studio .NET offers you five ways to sort Class View into a set of items you can navigate (see Figure 1-23). These options are available via the icons above the tree in the window and via the context menu.

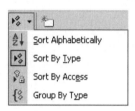

Figure 1-23. *Sorting the Class View*

- **Sort Alphabetically:** Orders the members of a class alphabetically

- **Sort By Type:** Groups class members into methods, fields, properties, and events first and then sorts those subgroups alphabetically

- **Sort By Access:** Orders class members by their access property—public, private, protected—and then alphabetically

- **Group By Type:** Emphasizes the Sort By Type options by creating virtual folders for each type of item in a container and placing that type of item within (see Figure 1-24)

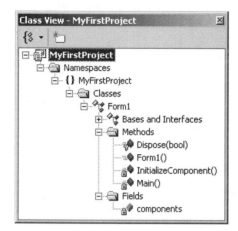

Figure 1-24. *Viewing classes by project*

The final option to make some sense out of a busy Class View window is to create a folder for your own purpose using the second icon in the Class View toolbar and drag copies of classes and class members into this folder for easy reference. For example, you could create a folder for the definitions you most commonly use and populate it accordingly, as shown in Figure 1-25.

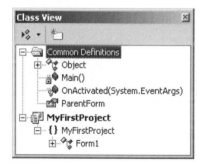

Figure 1-25. *A new folder in Class View*

Note that dragging icons to a new folder will not change where your code is declared or alter it in any way; it simply copies the reference to it.

Toolbox

Used in conjunction with a form's designer, which we mentioned previously and will look at in much more detail in the next chapter, the Toolbox window is probably the most frequently used window in Visual Studio .NET. Make sure you can see the toolbox window (Alt+Ctrl+X) and do a simple experiment. First of all, if it's not already open and visible, open the Form Designer for our simple project. If you closed it, double-click on form1.cs in the Solution Explorer, or if it's open but hidden in the main window, click on the tab labeled Form1.cs [Design]. Now look at the toolbar. You will see the Toolbox looking something like Figure 1-26.

Figure 1-26. *The Toolbox*

Now double-click the form in the designer to reveal the code that underlies the form. Note that the Toolbox becomes almost completely empty. The Toolbox contains a dynamically updated collection of controls and components (invisible controls) that are valid for use with the document that is currently active. So, when you make the form designer active, the Toolbox will adjust to show the components and controls that are used with this type of project, be it Windows or Web based.

What are components and controls? Bring the Form Designer for form1.cs into view again; then select and drag a Button control from the Windows Forms list in the Toolbox onto your Form. A Button will appear on your form, and if you switch to the form's code page, you'll see that the appropriate code for the button has been generated there as well. In this way, you can design the look of complete user interfaces for your solutions without writing a single line of code simply by dragging whichever controls you want onto your forms. The Toolbox is flexible as well in that once you are comfortable with the way things work, you can download or create your own controls and add them to the Toolbox for future use by adding a custom button to the toolbar.

As you can see from Figure 1-26, the controls in the Toolbox are divided into various categories according to what the controls are to be used for. If there are more controls available in a category than can be shown in the Toolbox, you can scroll through the full list by hitting the black arrows or selecting the Toolbox and using your mouse's scroll wheel.

By default, the Toolbox for a basic installation of Visual Studio .NET comes with the following category tabs, which you can see all at the same time by right-clicking on the Toolbox and selecting Show All Tabs:

- **General:** A catch-all tab for components not falling into the other categories. You can also add your own custom items here.

- **Clipboard Ring:** Stores a list of the most recent text items copied or cut onto the clipboard.

- **HTML:** Controls used for creating web forms.

- **Components:** Contains some components from the .NET framework and some third-party controls. Most of these are not visible to the user, but programmatic only, i.e., invisible things.

- **Windows Forms:** Controls used only in the development of windows forms.

- **Web Forms:** Controls used only in the development of web forms.

- **Dialog Editor:** Controls designed for creation of dialog boxes and forms.

- **XML Schema:** Controls used in working with XML Schemas or ADO.NET DataSets in XML Schema view.

- **Data:** Components relating to data access such as DataSet and SQLCommand.

- **Mobile Web Forms:** The ASP.NET controls for mobile web applications.

- **Device Controls:** Controls for windows forms on devices, like the Pocket PC.

- **Crystal Reports:** Components for use in building reports with Crystal.

You might see extra tabs here depending on what you've chosen to install and what edition of Visual Studio .NET you have.

Properties Window

Like the Toolbox, the Properties window allows you to change the code behind a form, a web page, and so on, without needing to actually write a line of code. Most useful when you're working within a designer document window, the Properties window automatically updates itself with a list of the properties (or events) for the element of the page—form, control, image, and so on—that is currently selected. For example, bring up the Designer window for the form in our little project and you'll see the Properties window populate itself with a very long set of properties as shown in Figure 1-27.

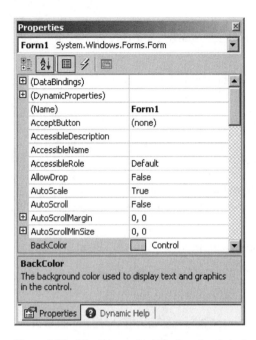

Figure 1-27. *The Properties Window in alphabetical order*

There's a great deal of information here, so let's walk through what's offered starting at the top and working our way down:

- The dropdown list at the top of the box displays all the items in the current designer that can be accessed and altered. These are listed alphabetically by name, and beside each name is the .NET object type of the item. Our empty form then is listed as **Form 1** System.Windows.Forms.Form. If you drag controls from the Toolbox onto the form, you'll find that entries for them appear here as well.

- The icons under the dropdown determine what will be shown here and how. From left to right, you can choose to view an item's events or properties grouped by category (shown in Figure 1-28) or alphabetically (the default view shown in Figure 1-27). The next two toggle between a view of the item's properties and its events. A third, visible only using VC++, toggles to a list of all Windows messages. The last item will give you access to a project's configuration properties when selected in Solution Explorer or Class View.

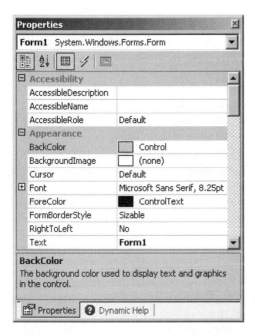

Figure 1-28. *The Properties Window ordered by type*

- The main area of the Properties window displays the item's properties, events, messages, and their current value, if any. You may change the value by clicking on the box opposite the property name and either choosing from the dropdown menu of choices or typing a value straight in. If an ellipsis button (...) is displayed at the end of the value property, then you'll make your choice using a dialog box that will appear when you click on it. Right-clicking on the property allows a reset to the defaults.

- When an expansion icon (+ or –) is displayed next to a property, you can expand and access multiple values underneath it. For example, the Font property in the screenshot of Figure 1-2 can be expanded to reveal properties for font name, size, unit of width, boldness, and so on.

- Finally, the textbox under the property selection area gives a user-friendly description of the property you've selected in case you don't understand what it does.

Working with properties in this window is fairly straightforward: You just select a property and change its value. If you've chosen to make use of it to add events to the form you're designing, however, you need to change tack slightly. In order to add a reaction to an event on your form or web page, you can do any of the following:

- Add the code directly in the Code window, and it will be displayed in the Properties/Events window accordingly.

- Double-click the event name that you wish to add, and Visual Studio .NET will create the stub for the event and take you to edit the code.

- Enter the name of an existing function to be used for this event. Selecting the property box will show all appropriate methods in the code-behind.

Note that while the Properties window becomes inactive when you are working directly with programming languages, it does work with markup languages such as HTML, reflecting the possible attributes and their values as the cursor is placed within the tag. In fact, it seems to work with any XML file whose schema Visual Studio .NET can access and parse. Likewise, this window will show properties for items selected in the Solution Explorer and a few of the other regularly used tool windows.

Resource Window

The Resource View window is sure to remind you of days of using Visual C++ 6 or earlier, when in order to create a windowed application, you would have to include a resource file containing uncompiled code such as cursor images and icons for the application to use. The Resource View allows those of you who need to revisit C++ applications written in previous versions to navigate through these resource files and see what lies within. It works in exactly the same way as in the previous version, presenting the resources in a tree view grouped by type of resource, as shown in Figure 1-29.

Figure 1-29. *The Resource View toolbox*

C# and Visual Basic .NET users will not need to use this window.

Task List

Once you've gone beyond creating trivial routines and started developing decent-sized applications, one of the things you'll inevitably need to do is to keep track of the things you have still to do and the ideas you have for improvement along the way. The Task List is the place to do this, and Visual Studio even helps by placing system messages for the developer here as well. See Figure 1-30.

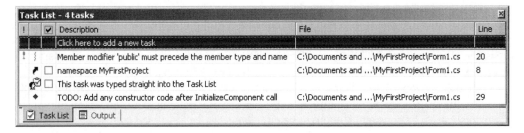

Figure 1-30. *The Task List*

In fact, quite a few different types of message can be found here. Here they are, in the order they appear in the screenshot in the figure:

- Warnings that Visual Studio .NET will add if its IntelliSense detects a syntax error in your code, telling you what it might be and where it thinks it might be located.

- Bookmarks to a specific line of code you create by right-clicking the line of code in the Document window and choosing Add Task List Shortcut.

- Notes written straight into the Task List.

- Comments written in the code prefixed with any of the following specified words: TODO, HACK, UNDONE. This can be edited in the Tools/Options/Task List dialog.

Two other types of error message will be displayed here should they occur:

- If you're building an application based on an Enterprise Template and a piece of code disobeys the template policy, an error stating as much will be shown here.

- If errors should occur at build time when you compile and build your code, you'll find the build error messages here in the task list.

For your convenience, double-clicking on any item in the Task List will activate a Document window containing the relevant code open to the specific line of code to which the task/error message is attached. If you're getting lost in the number of tasks, notes, and errors you've got in this window, you can also customize the view on this list. Right-clicking anywhere in the task list and bringing up its context menu will give you access to the Show Tasks and Sort By viewfinders. The former allows you to specify which types of message of the six previously named you wish to look at (singularly or all together), and the latter allows you to sort those messages by column (priority, category, checked/unchecked, description, and file).

One last note here. If you do get build errors when you try to make your project, the Task List will by default show only those errors. If you have other messages, you can retrieve them again by bringing up the context menu and choosing either Previous View or an option from the Show Tasks view filter.

Help

One of the first reasons to look at the use of an IDE is the Help integration that is available. When we were working in COBOL and Perl, with few words in the languages, it was possible to memorize all of the language. In those days, we could work in text editors.

Since the advent of object-oriented languages, this is no longer possible. There are 13,000 words in the .NET Framework and related libraries. No one is going to remember all of that. One must have a help system if one is to be effective.

Aside from the normal Contents, Index, and Search that the traditional Microsoft Help system provides, there are three options as part of Visual Studio .NET:

- Context-Sensitive Help

- IntelliSense

- Dynamic Help

Each of these can significantly speed your design and coding when properly used. Let's look at some of the details.

Context Sensitive Help

One of the most basic bits of help in the Visual Studio .NET IDE is the context help feature, and it is often the most helpful. Similar to tool tips in Internet Explorer, the context-sensitive help feature is hard to miss. Instantiate an object, and use it later in code. Then mouse over the code with the object name and you get Figure 1-31.

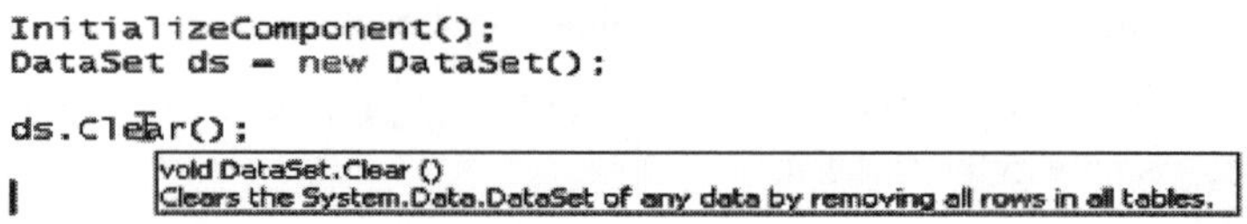

```
InitializeComponent();
DataSet ds = new DataSet();

ds.Clear();
        void DataSet.Clear ()
        Clears the System.Data.DataSet of any data by removing all rows in all tables.
```

Figure 1-31. *Context sensitive help example*

Keep in mind when writing comments for class files that the addition of remarks lines will add tool tips to even local methods and properties. Once text is added to the remarks section, that text will be displayed in the IntelliSense if the object is used, and will show in the Properties window for Events and Properties, as shown in the following code:

```
/// <summary>
///
/// </summary>
/// <remarks></remarks>
  public Form1()
  {
```

IntelliSense

IntelliSense is an autocompletion feature much like the one found in Microsoft's Office suite, only instead of proffering the correct spelling for the word it thinks you're spelling, it proffers a list of namespaces, classes, class members, and so on, basically, anything you might be trying to use. See Figure 1-32.

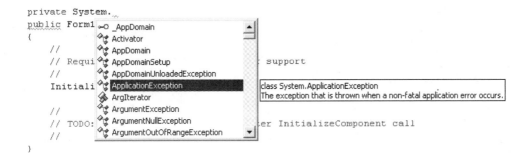

Figure 1-32. *IntelliSense help example*

In the figure we've opened the code behind `form1.cs` and started to declare a new private variable. As you type the period after `System`, IntelliSense realizes that you are going to be writing an object type and proffers an alphabetized list of the valid names you could use here. If you scroll down the list with cursor keys, a tooltip appears with a full name of the class and its short description.

The list that IntelliSense offers is dynamically generated, which means that if you type one or two more letters of the class name into the page, it will refine itself down to six or seven valid possibilities, which are then easy to select (double-click) from. This is an invaluable timesaving feature that eliminates the cost of a great deal of debugging for syntax errors and looking up the right name for a class or something in your project. In Visual Studio .NET 2003, this feature has further improved, taking a good guess at what item you may need from IntelliSense, and highlighting it.

Dynamic Help

One last window to make a swift but careful note of is the Dynamic Help window.

The default view, shown in Figure 1-33, dynamically updates itself with hyperlinks to help files relevant to the item, window, or codeword currently selected. The easiest way to come to grips with it is experimentation. Just click on different areas of the Visual Studio IDE and see the different hyperlinks appear. Each grouping has a slightly different context related to that selected item. Clicking on a hyperlink will open a new document window in the IDE containing that particular help topic.

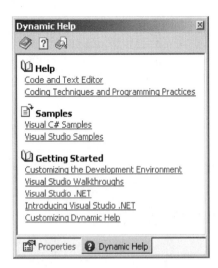

Figure 1-33. *Dynamic Help window*

The three icons at the top of the window offer you the traditional Windows Help style access to the full set of Visual Studio .NET help files. From left to right, they give you access to the help contents subject tree, the keyword index, and a search page to check the help files for phrases and words that may not be present in the other two. Each of these is useful, depending on the context of your query. Indeed, if you're just starting out, the Dynamic Help window will become your friend very quickly.

There are a number of options for the dynamic help system that can be beneficial, since it is something of a performance drain. If performance becomes a problem, it is possible to limit the number of links per category. See Figure 1-34.

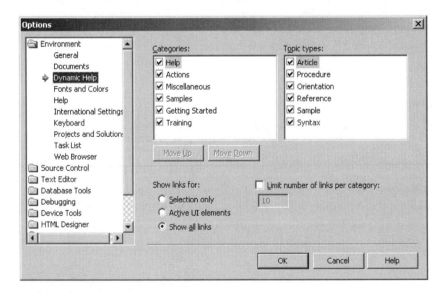

Figure 1-34. *Dynamic help options*

In the first version of Visual Studio .NET, the dynamic help system (`helpsvr.exe`) had an unchecked memory leak that would occasionally tie up massive amounts of resources. While this bug remains unfixed in the 2002 version, a change in the architecture in Visual Studio .NET 2003 seems to have solved the problem.

Projects and Solutions

Next let's have a quick look at the concepts of projects and solutions, two things you'll deal with every day you work with Visual Studio .NET. We've already seen that the Start Page asks you when you load whether to start a new project or load one already in progress; so let's start with that.

Invariably, as you continue to work with .NET, the applications you build will consist of more than one file: perhaps several C# class files, an icon or two, an ASP.NET page or a windows form, and so on. Visual Studio .NET lets you define a *project* as a container that holds all of the files that when compiled will contribute to your final executable file, DLL, or website. Thus when you open a project in Visual Studio .NET, all the files you have created so far toward your goal will also be made available should you need to access them.

Visual Studio .NET also makes life easy for you by autogenerating the files you will most likely need in your project when you first create one. As you'll see if you try to create a new project by clicking on the New Project button in the Start Page or File ➤ New ➤ Project, Visual Studio defines close to fifty different types of project in the New Project dialog box for you to choose from according to your needs. Each of these generates a different set of files to start with according to the templates Microsoft has predefined. You will see at the end of the book how you can create our own project templates, but that's getting ahead of ourselves.

The content of the majority of the windows surrounding the main one is determined by the project (or file) you have opened at the time, so let's create one for the first (but not the last) time. Bring up the New Project dialog box if it isn't still in view and select Visual C# Projects in the left-hand pane and Windows Application in the right-hand one. See Figure 1-35.

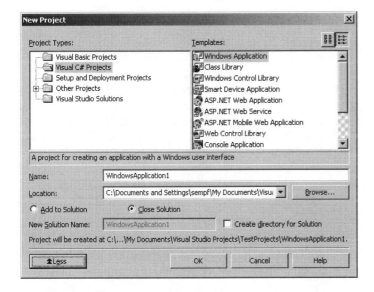

Figure 1-35. *New project options*

This dialog also lets us choose a name for our project and a location for saving it. The default name, `WindowsApplication1`, is pretty bland, so change it to `MyFirstProject`, and let the location stay at the default. Press OK. All being well, Visual Studio will work a few things out behind the scenes for a couple of seconds, generate a few files, display an empty windows form in the main window, and populate some of the surrounding windows with information. That was easy, wasn't it?

■**Note** Visual Basic 6 users should note that Visual Studio .NET contains an upgrade wizard that opens VB6 projects. It is discussed in greater detail in the Migration section of this chapter.

Before we go on, you should note that in creating a new project, we have also created a new solution. A solution is a container representing a larger development. It can contain more than one project, reflecting the fact that as development tasks grow, several smaller projects may be thought of collectively as a solution to the overall task. For example, in a classic three-tier development, an application is split into the user interface, business logic, and data access tiers. The Visual Studio solution for the whole development might well contain a project for each of these tiers.

This solution concept is the core of the workflow for the average developer. The files saved on the developer's machine might just represent a link to an external website, or might have all of the source files for a Windows Forms application. These folders can be changed, renamed, and moved as needed. Solution folders are best renamed within the IDE itself, but they can be reorganized if needed, in contrast to Visual InterDev, for instance.

As you work through the book, you will see what files each type of project generates and what they're for. Right now however, let's look at some migration issues with Visual Studio .NET 2003 and .NET 1.1.

Migration

The issue of moving applications from .NET 1.0, or even from Windows DNA in VB 6.0, is potentially significant. Much has been published, including the excellent *ASP to ASP.NET Migration Handbook*, by Richard Conway et al., and the Microsoft publication *Developers Guide to Upgrading to Microsoft .NET*.

Here we will cover a few points specifically with regard to Visual Studio .NET. Primarily, questions revolve around versions of the IDE and developer workflow, so we will handle those along with a few other points.

Migrate Settings

Upon installation of Visual Studio .NET 2003, the user is asked whether the settings should be migrated from the previous version of the development environment. These settings include largely those things that are in the Profile, such as keyboard layout. If the dialog was missed or ignored, the settings can be migrated later with the DOS command

```
devenv /migratesettings
```

Developer Workflow

Things change for the programmers in a large shop when they migrate to Visual Studio .NET 2003. As discussed in the Introduction, Role Based Development has changed the way developers work with the IDE.

For a comprehensive set of rules for working with .NET in a development environment, check out the Patterns and Practices website at `http://msdn.microsoft.com/patterns`. For the moment, there are a couple of points that are worth reviewing:

- The focus is on local development. Web authors use SourceSafe to download webs to local development boxes and work and compile locally, then load the changes back into SourceSafe for deployment. There is no longer a "local mode," nor a "local copy" to speak of.

- As we've seen, database work, DLL middle tiers, web applications, and even Web Services or mobile applications can be made part of a single solution. With the complex assembly property tools, a developer can determine what is built and what isn't.

- Web project files are saved with the web project itself. The solution file is saved locally, but if a developer is working on a remote project, the project files are on the remote web root.

Versions of the IDE and .NET

Let's settle one issue right away: You can run Visual Basic 6.0, Visual Studio .NET 2002, and Visual Studio .NET 2003 all at the same time. I am doing it now (see Figure 1-36).

Figure 1-36. *My startbar, with three versions of Visual Studio*

You cannot interchange projects or solutions between the versions of Visual Studio, however. If you try to open a 2002 solution in 2003 you get Figure 1-37.

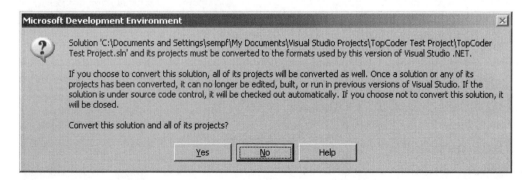

Figure 1-37. *Better dialogs make beter programming*

Dialogs from Visual InterDev 6.0 projects are getting better. When they are first opened, the message from 2002 appears, as in Figure 1-38.

Figure 1-38. *Project type conversion notification dialog*

Then the option is given to convert the project as discussed previously.

As regards compiling projects to various versions of the .NET Framework, it is all handled by the IDE. Web projects and windows forms alike will use the proper version of the framework based on the IDE in which it was compiled.

Crystal Reports

Crystal Decision's RPT files must also be upgraded to Crystal 9 format to use in the new IDE, though the version is the same throughout the two versions of Visual Studio .NET. When trying to save a report in VS .NET, the user is given the option to upgrade, as in Figure 1-39.

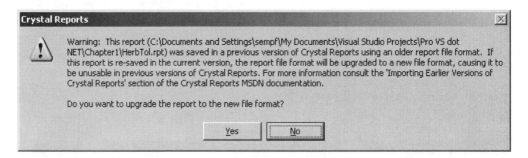

Figure 1-39. *Crystal warning*

Much more information about moving to Crystal 9 can be found in Appendix A of *Professional Crystal Reports*, by David McAmis.

Interoperability

Two other considerations in migrating to Visual Studio .NET are the death of VBScript in ASP.NET and the interoperability of COM components. We will go over both of these topics in much more detail throughout the book, but they deserve mention here. Macros are written in a scripting edition of VB.NET. All of the tools your organization has written in VBScript will still run in Windows, but they won't work within Visual Studio .NET. The COM components, however, will still work with COM Interop, and functions exported by legacy C/C++ DLLs may be called through P/Invoke (aka Platform Invoke) by your C# or VB.NET code. More information is in the MSDN library.

Summary

In a whirlwind tour, we have covered the majority of the bits and pieces of the Visual Studio.NET interface. We all should now be on the same page with regard to terminology and the use of these pieces. The information will be very useful throughout the remainder of the book. The next step is Windows and Web Forms, and the remainder of the major project types within Visual Studio .NET 2003. Then we will get into customization of the IDE, as promised.

CHAPTER 2

Building Windows Applications

While the Windows applications created in Visual Studio .NET look very similar to those created using earlier versions of Visual Studio, a great deal has changed behind the scenes. The main benefit that Visual Studio .NET brings to forms-based applications is the equal footing that developers are put on regardless of the language being used. The underlying classes used are now the same whether one is developing in VB.NET, C#, C++ .NET, or any other .NET language. This is a huge step forward from Visual Studio 6, where Visual Basic was dominant in many market sectors in comparison to Visual C++, and developers were faced with many intricacies involved in creating rich applications using Visual C++.

Over the past few years the focus of many developers, and the tools they have been provided with, has largely centered on the creation of distributed, stateless Web-based applications. With the creation of standards (such as Web Services, covered in Chapter 3) that aid in the development of distributed applications, regardless of the user interface provided, and certain features of .NET WinForms applications such as no-touch deployment, which will be covered shortly, it is fair to say that rich-client applications have been given a new lease on life.

In this chapter, we'll take a look at WinForms, covering the significant features provided by Visual Studio .NET. Specifically, we will

- See how a WinForms project works

- Look at the different controls in the toolbox to add to your forms

- Investigate the tools to make designing your form easier

- Work through a simple WinForms application from start to finish

However, before we delve into any of this, let's take a closer look at WinForms in general

General Overview

A whole class of applications is covered by WinForms projects; standalone SDI and MDI client-side applications, MMC snap-ins, full-screen games, and front-end interfaces to large remote systems. Regardless of what technology and environment a developer has been using for creating such Windows client applications in the past, Visual Studio .NET offers something new. For those coming to Visual Studio .NET from earlier versions of Visual Basic, everything superficially seems very similar, but since Visual Basic .NET is a first class language, it has access to all of the low-level interfaces that C# and the other .NET languages have, along with the associated performance optimizations. To developers migrating from other languages and tools, the transition will be more marked. The ease with which applications can be developed without relying on MFC and the associated headaches should be an especially great relief to C++ developers. However, for developers migrating from earlier versions of Visual Basic, the sheer size of the Framework and features the platform offers may seem daunting.

In designing the .NET Framework, one of the aims was to include high-level support for visual tools, a goal that has been achieved with WinForms. First of all, Visual Studio .NET includes a WinForms designer that allows forms to be created that contain all the standard controls: textboxes, buttons, dropdown lists, and so on. On top of this, there is built-in support for more advanced features such as menus, graphics, and a plethora of more advanced controls such as the DataGrid and TreeView controls. Third party controls can also be installed, and these have the exact same platform support as the built-in ones, as do further custom controls that can be created from within the development environment itself. Finally, Visual Studio .NET includes resource-editing functionality to allow developers to embed nonexecutable content such as graphics and sound files within their applications. While providing all of these features, Microsoft hasn't forgotten about backward compatibility with all the existing COM-based code that is still in use, with mechanisms built into the CLR to allow almost transparent use of COM components from within managed code.

While providing the power of the full .NET Framework to WinForms applications, allowing for access to system resources, peripherals, and so on, Visual Studio .NET also provides a rich means of visually and programmatically taking control over the creation of our applications. For instance, visual inheritance allows us to derive one form from another, allowing for both the logic and the controls present on a form to be reused, and removing the need for the repetitive application of the same settings to multiple forms and controls. This is possible due to the way in which the definitions for forms are built up: using standard programmatic declarations within the code for the form, rather than in a tool-specific format as with Visual Basic 6 or with dialog boxes defined in resource textual format, and other such mechanisms in earlier releases of Visual Studio. Further support built into .NET allows for our WinForms applications to support Print functionality with next to no effort, again making life far simpler for developers.

Just as with .NET applications created with other user interfaces, whether they are command-line or WebForm based, WinForms applications can be part of a larger whole, making use of the other types of project available within Visual Studio .NET. This includes class libraries, remote Web Services, and Windows Services. They can also be included in Setup and Deployment Projects that create professional, standardized installers for applications. However, a feature that has been introduced with WinForms applications is zero-touch deployment. This allows newer versions of Internet Explorer to access and initiate .NET applications from a remote URL. This can save huge amounts of deployment and systems maintenance time, since it means that rolling out a new version of an application can be as simple as copying a single file to a single location, with users accessing the new version of the application the next time they request it.

Creating a Project

As well as creating a firm foundation in the form of the .NET Framework upon which to build our WinForms applications, Microsoft has provided totally comprehensive support for their creation within Visual Studio .NET. Applications can be developed using any of the built-in .NET languages (such as C# and VB.NET), along with any third-party languages, all with almost identical support. WYSIWYG (What You See Is What You Get) support is provided for all the major controls that can be placed on forms, along with extensions to allow controls created by developers to exhibit the same behavior and features. Context-sensitive help and IntelliSense are available throughout, making it far easier to find the classes, methods, and variables needed to write an application, along with support on all of the built-in functionality of the .NET Framework.

In order to explore Visual Studio .NET and come to grips with everything it provides, we'll create a simple WinForms project to demonstrate the key concepts and features.

Creating a WinForms Project

First, load Visual Studio .NET, and select the New Project option from the Start Page that is presented. This will cause the dialog box of Figure 2-1 to be shown.

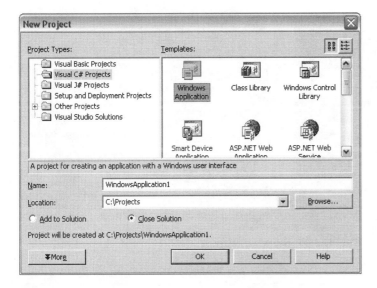

Figure 2-1. *New Project dialog*

After you have selected the Visual C# Projects option in the Project Types tree to the left, the Windows Application option can be chosen from the Templates pane on the right. When this is selected, you will be able to enter a Name and Location for the application. Note that if you always want to store your projects in the same folder, you can set things to run like this from the Tools/Options Environment/Projects & Solutions, in the "Visual Studio Projects Location" textbox.

Clicking OK will let Visual Studio provide default values for both of these settings, which will be fine for this demonstration.

After a short delay, a skeleton project should be created, the contents of which will appear in the Solution Explorer window (see Figure 2-2).

Figure 2-2. *Solution Explorer window*

This solution contains all of the files, code, and settings required for the application to compile and run. In the central portion of the environment, the Form1.cs file that is highlighted within the Solution Explorer will be open in Design View (Figure 2-3).

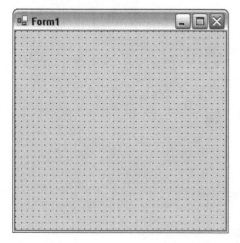

Figure 2-3. *Blank form*

This is the default form that is provided for us to place our controls on, and is the starting point for our application when it runs. By default, it is totally blank, with only an icon, title, and the standard minimize/maximize and close options present within the title bar. Pressing F5 or selecting Debug ➤ Start from the menu now will cause the application to compile and run. If at any point you want to run the application without debugging it, either pressing CTRL+F5 or selecting Debug ➤ Start without debugging will achieve this. As shown in Figure 2-4, the compiled form matches that shown by the designer precisely, with the exception of the design grid.

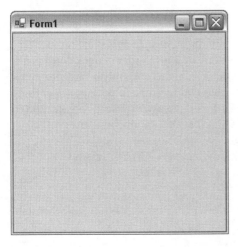

Figure 2-4. *Running an instance of a new WinForms project*

Since there is no functionality present within our application, there is little we can do for now, other than click the Close button to return us to the IDE.

Before moving on to adding to this application, now is a good time to take a look at the files that constitute a WinForms project, and how our application is actually functioning.

Solution Contents

As we saw when we created our project, several files were automatically generated for us and placed within the solution. These are as follows:

- `App.ico`: This is the icon file associated with the executable being created. This icon can be replaced or edited. It's worth remembering that Visual Studio .NET has an icon editor if you need this functionality.

- `AssemblyInfo.cs`: This file contains the metadata for our application, such as its version, culture, and private key. These are used by the compiler and assemblies that are built for this project.

- `Form1.cs`: This is the initial form to which we'll add controls in order to provide the user interface of our application.

In addition to the files within the project, the References folder can be seen within the Solution Explorer. This contains a list of all of the .NET class libraries that our application requires in order to function. These include System.Drawing and Systems.Windows.Forms, which are used mainly by WinForms applications, and more generic libraries such as System, System.Data, and System.XML, which are used throughout the development of many types of .NET projects.

How a Form Works

One of the main advantages to using a development environment such as Visual Studio .NET is its ability to allow applications to be *stepped through* line by line in order to track down problems and see what is going on under the hood. Since there shouldn't currently be any problems with our code, we'll step through it for the latter of these two reasons. To do this, select the Debug ➤ Step Into menu option, or press F11 on the keyboard. This will cause the application to start at the line shown in boldface in the special Main function declaration found in Form1.cs:

```
/// <summary>
/// The main entry point for the application.
/// </summary>
[STAThread]
static void Main()
{
    Application.Run(new Form1());
}
```

This function contains a single call to Application.Run, and it passes in a new instance of our class, Form1, as a parameter. Pressing F11 again will cause the debugger to continue to the next line of code being executed: the class-scoped declaration of components for the Form1 class. If there were any further class-scoped declarations, these would be handled next. Pressing F11 again causes the form's constructor to be processed, with a call to InitializeComponent being made. If we take a look at the source code around that point, we'll see that it's contained within a specific region, "Windows Form Designer generated code":

```
#region Windows Form Designer generated code
/// <summary>
/// Required method for Designer support - do not modify
/// the contents of this method with the code editor.
/// </summary>
private void InitializeComponent()
{
    this.components = new System.ComponentModel.Container();
    this.Size = new System.Drawing.Size(300,300);
    this.Text = "Form1";
}
#endregion
```

It is this function that Visual Studio interacts with whenever controls are added to, removed from, or edited on the form. For now, we can see that there are currently only two properties having values set: the Size and Text of the Form itself. In a finished application, additional controls will be defined here, their properties will be set, and any associated events will be wired up. We'll take another look at this function later on to see how additional functionality to the form is represented here. For now, it's enough to know that an application relies on the Main function to create a new form for display, and the on InitializeComponent routine to set up the form and its contents.

Pressing F11 a further six times will finish stepping through the code required in order to initialize the form. Once all the code has been stepped through, the close button can be clicked; one further press of F11 and the application will terminate and return us to the IDE. If we look closer at the Form1.cs file, we'll see that there's a Dispose method there, yet this wasn't called as we stepped through the code that created and destroyed the form. This is because it's called only by the garbage collector, and then only once the form has already gone out of scope and the resources it was using are being reclaimed. In a small application that doesn't continually instance new objects, etc., we cannot rely on the garbage collector ever calling the Dispose method before the application exits, and hence we shouldn't put code that is required to be run within it unless the time at which it occurs is irrelevant.

WinForms Controls

In addition to the Solution Explorer and the main design canvas/code view, the Toolbox and Properties windows, which are also displayed, are two of the main windows used in creating WinForms applications. Within the Toolbox are all of the controls necessary for building applications, from standard visual controls such as Buttons and TextBoxes to nonvisual items such as database connections and message queues. These items are all categorized under various tabs in the Toolbox, as shown in Figure 2-5.

Figure 2-5. *Toolbox window*

We can make use of the items in the Toolbox by dragging the icon representing the required control onto the design canvas. This will cause Visual Studio to automatically generate the code necessary to create an instance of the control; this code is inserted in the InitializeComponent method that we saw earlier.

While the first window allows us to add new controls to our forms, the second, Properties, allows us to configure all of the settings of these controls. If you drag a button control from the Windows Forms tab of the Toolbox onto the form, and then take a look at the Properties window, you'll see something similar to Figure 2-6.

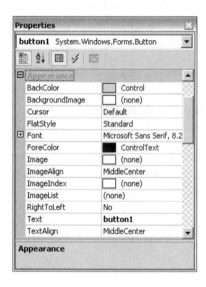

Figure 2-6. *Properties window*

Change the setting of the Text property to Search Now, and the Name property to btnSearch. If you view the source code of the form at this point, you'll see that in addition to a variable declaration for the btnSearch control, the following has also been added to the InitializeComponent method:

```
this.btnSearch = new System.Windows.Forms.Button();
this.SuspendLayout();
//
// btnSearch
//
this.btnSearch.Location = new System.Drawing.Point(104, 48);
this.btnSearch.Name = "btnSearch";
this.btnSearch.TabIndex = 0;
this.btnSearch.Text = "Search Now";
```

Try changing the Text property from Search Now to Search in code view, and then switch back to design view. You'll see that the text on the button has immediately been updated with the new value you set. Thus the designer is a two-way process: changes made on the form are shown directly in the code, and changes in the code are visible on the form. If you now double-click on the Search button, you'll be taken back into the code view, with the following method declaration added:

```
private void btnSearch_Click(object sender, System.EventArgs e)
{

}
```

In addition to this, an event handler has been added to the InitializeComponent method to ensure that the code within btnSearch_Click is called whenever the button is clicked:

```
this.btnSearch.Click += new System.EventHandler(this.btnSearch_Click);
```

The values that can be set using the designer aren't just limited to textual settings such as the caption displayed on the button. To demonstrate this, and to illustrate many other features of WinForms as we go along, we'll create a sample application that makes use of the Northwind database installed with the SQL Server, allowing us to search the Employees table within it.

Controlling Form Elements

The first thing we'll do for our application is to create the user interface by adding the necessary controls to the form. To do this, drag a Group Box onto the form, then a TextBox and a Label onto this GroupBox (all of these controls can be found under the Windows Forms tab). The TextBox and Label controls that we've added function in a very similar way to the Button we've already seen; they each have their own properties and settings that mainly affect their own behavior. The GroupBox, however, functions differently, acting as a *container* for other controls, grouping them together. If we had not created the controls within the GroupBox, we could associate them with it by either dragging them into the GroupBox itself after creating them or cutting and pasting them into it. Since we already had a Button on the form, we'll take the second option. Select the Button, Label, and TextBox controls by holding down the Shift key and clicking each of them in turn, and select Edit ➤ Cut from the menu. Then select the GroupBox, and select the Edit ➤ Paste menu option. The form will now look similar to Figure 2-7.

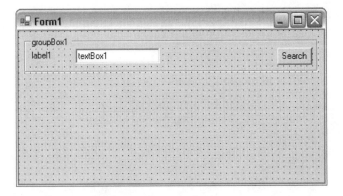

Figure 2-7. *Adding a fieldset of controls to the form*

Next, change the Text and Name values of the three newly added controls to those shown in Table 2-1 and set the Text property of the form itself to Employee Search.

Table 2-1. *Settings for the Control Properties*

Control	Name	Text
GroupBox	grpEmployee	Employee
Label	lblName	Name:
TextBox	txtEmployeeName	

Arranging and Formatting Controls

Now that we've created the controls that will make up our search form, we can take a look at one of the biggest improvements in form design with Visual Studio .NET: control arrangement. Anyone who has developed Windows applications in the past will be familiar with the problems associated with laying out controls so that they are properly aligned and can move and resize correctly when the form itself is resized. .NET provides us with the notion of *Anchoring* and *Docking*, which allows us to visually specify the behavior we wish our controls to exhibit when a form is resized, with the .NET Runtime handling all of the details for us. First, let's take a look at the simpler formatting options, such as alignment.

Basic Formatting

As with almost all properties of controls, setting the formatting options is simply a matter of selecting a control on the form and changing the appropriate value in the Properties window, allowing the environment to generate the necessary source code to effect this.

The properties to change for the most obvious effects are those governing the text and font of the controls on the form: Text, Forecolor, and Font. The Font property itself consists of nine values covering font type, size, boldness, italics, and so on, though oddly its color is left for the separate ForeColor property. As we've already seen, the Text property sets the text associated with the control on the form (or the form itself). Note that although the environment will allow you to specify any valid text size or font, it relies upon you to ensure that the chosen text fits within the confines of the space you've given it. For instance, if we were to increase the font size on our search button to 12 points, it simply wouldn't fit (Figure 2-8).

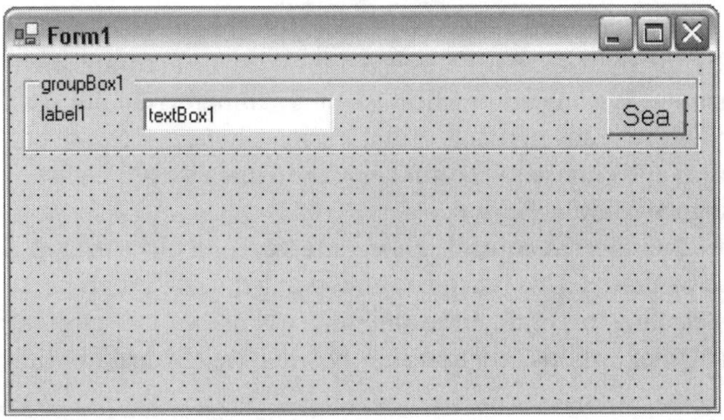

Figure 2-8. *Form with oversized button text*

If you want the same value to apply to multiple controls, there are shortcuts so that you don't have to set the values on each control independently. First, you can select multiple controls at once, as we did earlier, and then set properties that are common to all of them using the Properties window. Alternatively, you can select the form itself and set new default values for the controls it hosts, as you can with any container that hosts other controls. If a control hasn't already had that property explicitly altered, it will inherit the new values given from the form. Any further controls you add to the form will also inherit these new default values.

In addition to such visual properties, there are also several useful features of the IDE that allow us to perform operations across multiple controls to provide consistency across our forms. These are found on the Format menu and the Layout toolbar, and rely upon the fact that all controls have Location (reflecting the *x,y* coordinates), Size, and Locked properties.

If multiple controls are selected, then the options under the Align, Make Same Size, and other submenus become available (Figure 2-9).

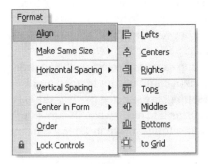

Figure 2-9. *The Format menu*

Using these options on the Align menu, the Location property of the controls is altered, aligning all of the selected controls in the manner indicated by the icons alongside the menu options. Similarly, the Make Same Size options cause the Size property of all selected controls to be given identical values. Setting a consistent spacing between controls can be accomplished by selecting the options in the Horizontal Spacing and Vertical Spacing submenus. To tidy up the layout of your search form if it doesn't already match that in the screenshots, you can select the three controls within the GroupBox and choose the Format ➤ Make Same Size ➤ Height option, followed by the Format ➤ Align ➤ Middles option.

The Lock Controls option causes the selected controls to become frozen in place to stop them from being accidentally moved or altered. This is achieved by setting the Locked property to True on all the selected controls. Selecting this option a second time will unlock the selected controls. We'll take a look at how the Order options function shortly, when we are dealing with docking controls.

Anchoring Controls

The Anchor property lets you specify which edges of a container (top, left, bottom, and right) a control is anchored to, defaulting to Top and Left for most controls. This can be seen by selecting the txtEmployeeName control, and clicking on the Anchor property (Figure 2-10).

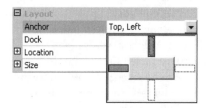

Figure 2-10. *Control anchoring options*

Being anchored to the top left corner means that wherever a control is placed on a form (or other container such as a GroupBox) it will remain at the same position inside its resized container. Technically, this means that the amount of space between the Top and Left edges of the control and the container will be maintained at all times. So, if the Left setting is replaced by Right by clicking on the rectangles to either side of the popup caused by selecting the Anchor property, the control will maintain its position from the right-hand border instead and be right-aligned (albeit with a margin). Now, if both opposite settings are selected (such as the Left and the Right), the control will be anchored to both sides, causing it to resize when its container is resized. In the case of the controls on our form, the Anchor settings shown in Table 2-2 need to be applied.

Table 2-2. *Settings for Control Anchoring*

Control	Anchor
grpEmployee	Top, Left, Right
lblName	Top, Left
txtEmployeeName	Top, Left, Right
btnSearch	Top, Right

Once all of these settings have been applied, and the controls have been positioned and stretched, our form should look like the screenshot of Figure 2-11.

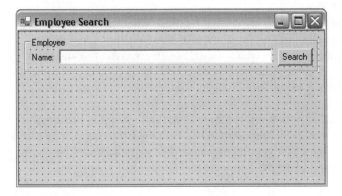

Figure 2-11. *Controls named and positioned correctly*

Note It should be noted, as mentioned, that Controls are anchored in relation to their parent control, not necessarily in relation to the form. In the previous example, the lblName, txtEmployeeName, and btnSearch controls are actually anchored to the grpEmployee GroupBox, and will maintain the same distance from the borders of this control at all times, rather than those of the form.

Docking Controls

While the Anchor property maintains the distance of a control from the border of its container, the Dock property butts the control up against that border. At the same time, it extends the width or height of the control to ensure that it fills up that entire edge of the container. To see how this works, drag a StatusBar control from the Toolbox onto the form. You will see that this control has the value Bottom set for its Dock property by default (Figure 2-12).

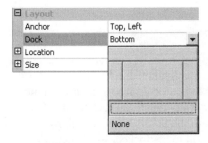

Figure 2-12. *Settings for control docking*

By clicking on any of the buttons around the edge of this popup, we can see how the control moves to the positions indicated by the buttons, fixing itself to that side of the form.

By clicking on the center of the popup, we cause the control to dock to all sides, filling the form up, while selecting None will stop the control from docking altogether. For our application we're happy with the default setting of Bottom, but let's change the Name of the StatusBar to sbStatus, and set the Text of it to be blank.

One of the more confusing aspects of docking is what happens when you have multiple controls with varying Dock and Anchor settings applied, and these settings seem to be in conflict with one another. The simplest case, in which a single control has Anchor and Dock settings that are in conflict, is resolved simply: whichever was set most recently takes precedence. To demonstrate the situation with multiple controls, drag a DataGrid onto the form from the Toolbox.

If you set the Dock on the DataGrid to Bottom, you'll see that it actually docks to the top of the StatusBar, rather than to the form. The alternative to this is to have the controls on top of each other, which isn't feasible, since every control that was docked to the same border would then be overlaid with all others. The way that .NET resolves this is with *control ordering*.

Control Ordering

If you right-click on the DataGrid, in the popup menu, you'll see two options near the top; Bring to Front and Send to Back (Figure 2-13).

Figure 2-13. *Context menu options*

These are the same two options that appear on the Format ➤ Order menu that we recently skipped over, and they normally control whether a control is displayed in front of or behind other controls that it overlaps with. But in the case of docked controls, it sets the precedence of the docking, i.e., which control is closest to the edge of the container. If you click Send to Back, you'll see the DataGrid move to the bottom of the form, with the StatusBar placed above it.

For our application, we actually don't need the DataGrid to be docked, so after changing its name to dgResults, set its Dock property to None and its Anchor property to Top, Bottom, Left, Right (Figure 2-14).

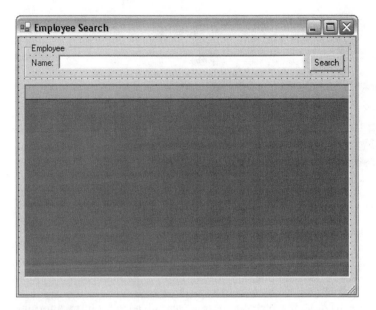

Figure 2-14. *Form with DataGrid and StatusBar positioned*

As should be apparent, Visual Studio has great integration with the code that defines our applications, even when we're interacting with them in a visual manner. This goes much further than the visual form controls we've looked at, however, as we'll see throughout the rest of the chapter.

Tab Order

Along with control resizing, setting the TabIndex of each control on a Form was one of the more frustrating tasks in creating an application in previous versions of Visual Studio. The TabIndex (or tab order) defines the order in which controls are highlighted when the user presses the *Tab* key. This is most useful in performing data entry on large or repetitive forms. Previously, whenever a new control was added to the form, we could end up having to go back and select each control in turn using the Properties window if a tab ordering had already been configured.

With Visual Studio .NET, things have improved greatly. We can now select the Tab Order option from the View menu, and view the current order for each control as a small numbered box in the upper left corner of the control. As shown in Figure 2-15, this even takes into consideration the fact that some controls can be grouped within others.

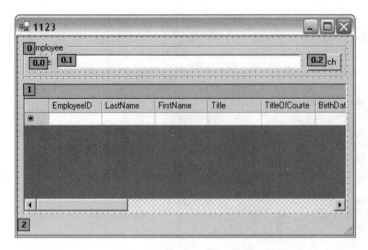

Figure 2-15. *Setting the Tab Order of controls on forms*

The initial tab order reflects the order in which the controls were added to the form. Altering the order is achieved by clicking on the controls in the order in which the tab focus should be given to them. As they are clicked, the number will change to show the new TabIndex, and the box containing the number will change color to show that a value has been assigned.

When all controls have been assigned an ordering, the box coloring will return to standard. Once the desired tab order has been assigned, selecting View ➤ Tab Order once again will return to the standard view, as will pressing the Escape key.

UI Controls and Components

All of the controls that we've just looked at are what are known as *visible* controls, those that are shown to the end user. As mentioned, all of the standard user interface controls fall into this category: CheckBoxes, TextBoxes, ListBoxes, etc. A second category of controls exists, however: *nongraphical controls*, or *components*. These are found in the other tabs on the Toolbox such as Data and Components, and include controls such as Database connections, DataSets, and EventLogs, items that are more closely associated with the logic and processing of the application rather than with user interaction.

Support for such invisible controls is a feature that is much improved in Visual Studio .NET over earlier offerings such as Visual Studio 6 for two main reasons:

- Invisible controls are now treated differently from visible ones, being displayed on a different part of the screen, rather than cluttering up the visual form itself.

- Rather than having a sparse set of unrelated invisible controls for handling specific functions as was previously the case, these controls now form collections that can interact with each other, allowing for much more flexibility in their use.

We'll now go about adding some functionality to our application using some of the commonly used invisible controls: *Data controls*.

Data Controls

With every new Microsoft platform comes a new data access technology. With the .NET Framework we have ADO.NET. As always, it builds on the technologies that came before it: ADO, RDO, DAO, and so on. However, it is much more closely integrated with the surrounding technologies than its predecessors were, through support for key components of ADO.NET, such as DataSets, which are prevalent throughout the Framework.

In the case of WinForms development within Visual Studio, this integration is largely through the use of Data Controls, and the way they can interact with standard form controls, such as the DataGrid that we have on our Employee Search form. If we switch to the Data tab of the Toolbox, we can see the options that we have available (Figure 2-16).

Figure 2-16. *Data options in the Toolbox*

Most of these options can be grouped into support for the four types of database supported: OleDB-compliant databases, SQL Server, ODBC-compliant databases, and Oracle. Each of these groupings contains three controls that match up to the three standard classes required for database operations: Connections, Commands, and DataAdapters. There are two further controls: a DataSet option to contain the data retrieved, and a DataView to filter and sort the data as necessary.

The first control we'll need for adding the required functionality to our form is an SqlConnection. This will handle all of the connections to the database that our form needs to make. Drag one of these from the Toolbox onto the form, and you'll see that the environment places it in a separate window, the *Component Tray*, as shown in Figure 2-17.

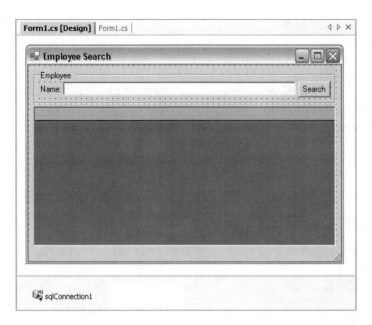

Figure 2-17. *Adding controls to the Component Tray*

This is much more convenient than earlier versions, where such controls ended up cluttering up the main form. If you select this control, you'll see that it has properties just like any other control. Change the name to connEmployees, and then select the ConnectionString property and click on the dropdown arrow to the right of the field and choose the <New Connection. . .> option. This launches the Data Link Properties dialog, which allows us to choose a database to work with.

The Connection tab of this dialog should be populated with the details for connecting to the Northwind database on your local SQL Server (or MSDE) installation. If the default installation options were selected, then the settings shown in Figure 2-18 should be correct. Clicking the Test Connection button will allow you to see whether the settings provided are correct.

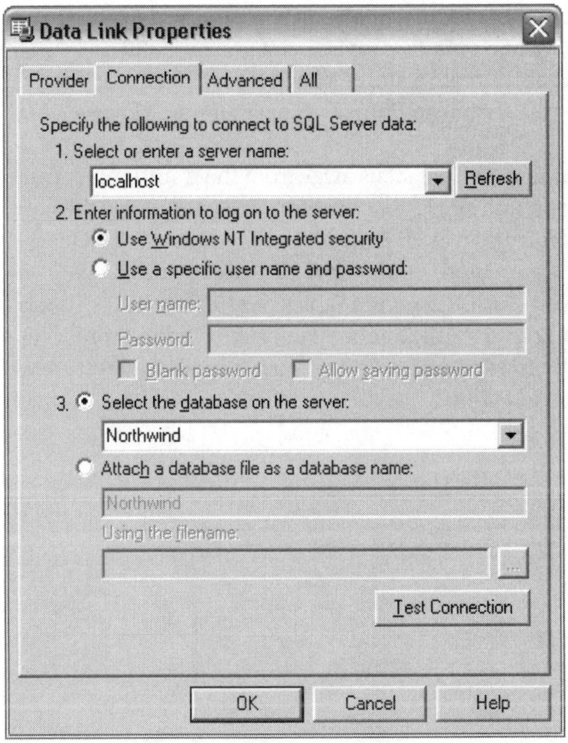

Figure 2-18. *Data Link Properties dialog*

Note Note that the SqlConnection, SqlDataAdapter, and other such controls will work only with the SQL Server and MSDE database servers. If you are using a Microsoft Access–based system, or other database provider, you will need to choose one of the other options available, most likely the OleDB controls. These differ in certain properties and settings, but the principles for their use remain the same.

Click OK on the Data Link Properties dialog once the correct settings have been entered, drag an SqlDataAdapter onto the form, and rename it daEmployees. This DataAdapter will retrieve the employee data to display in the DataGrid.

Right-clicking on daEmployees, and selecting the Configure Data Adapter . . . option from the context menu will introduce one of the other great features of Visual Studio .NET: wizards. These serve the same purpose as wizards used throughout Windows; simplifying commonly performed tasks within the environment. The Data Adapter Configuration Wizard is particularly useful, for it saves us from the laborious process of creating numerous similar SQL statements, writing SQL queries by hand, and more. Click the Next button on the first page of the wizard, and the Data Connection page will be displayed. The database connection we just created will be selected by default on this page, meaning that we can just click Next again. On the third page, Choose a Query Type, select the top option—Use SQL statements—and click Next. In a real-world application you would probably create a stored procedure in the database that would allow you to pass in the name you were searching for as a parameter. However, for this example it's not necessary.

The next page can be a bit daunting at first, since it steps away from the traditional format of just presenting checkboxes, dropdown lists, and single-line text entry, instead leaving the user to enter the full SQL query required in the form provided. Fortunately, we can click the Query Builder . . . button and visually select the data we require. Once you've clicked this, the Query Builder tool will launch. Select the Employees option from the Tables pane of the dialog that is shown, click Add, and then click Close. Check the * (All Columns) checkbox in the Employees table; then right-click on the bottom of the four panes and select Run. This should return all of the employees in the database, as shown in Figure 2-19.

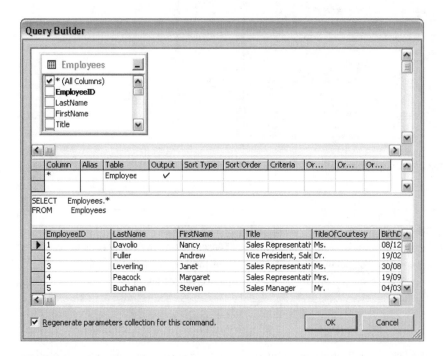

Figure 2-19. *Query Builder window*

One this has been done, click the OK button on the Query Builder, which will take you back to the wizard.

Click the Advanced Options button to see the Advanced SQL Generation Options dialog settings. In this dialog three options appear, which are all checked by default. The first, Generate Insert, Update and Delete statements, determines whether corresponding INSERT, UPDATE, and DELETE statements should be created, which can save a significant amount of time. The second option, Use optimistic concurrency, decides whether UPDATE and DELETE statements should be modified to prevent concurrency conflicts. The last option, Refresh the DataSet, specifies whether, after UPDATEs and INSERTs are performed, the DataSet is to retrieve new values that may have been generated by the SQL operations, such as identities, calculated values, and default values. We do not need any of these options for our application, since we are only retrieving data rather than amending it, but the settings can be left at their defaults in case of future additions.

Click the OK button to return to the wizard, and the Next button to complete the process. The wizard should now complete successfully, allowing the Finish button to be clicked. When the wizard completes, it does a lot of work for us: creating SqlCommand objects for Select, Update, Delete, and Insert statements, populating them with the necessary data. It has also populated the TableMappings collection with all of the columns that are to be retrieved from the database. Finally, if we hadn't created our own database connection beforehand, it would have even done this for us.

Now that we have our DataAdapter configured, we need a DataSet. We could create one using the same method as our other controls: dragging it onto the form and configuring it. However, it's often better to create a *typed DataSet*, since this allows us to ensure at compile time rather than runtime that the data it contains have no type errors, and perform other operations on it. We can create such a dataset by right-clicking on the daEmployees control in the component tray and choosing the Generate DataSet option.

We will now see the Generate DataSet dialog. Select the New option from the radio buttons at the top and enter the name dsEmployees in the textbox. In the middle pane, the Employees table will be listed and checked, shown along with the name of the DataAdapter it is associated with in parentheses. If we had created other queries with the wizard, these would also be displayed here. The option "Add this dataset to the designer" should be left checked, meaning that Visual Studio .NET should display the DataSet in the Component Tray when created (Figure 2-20).

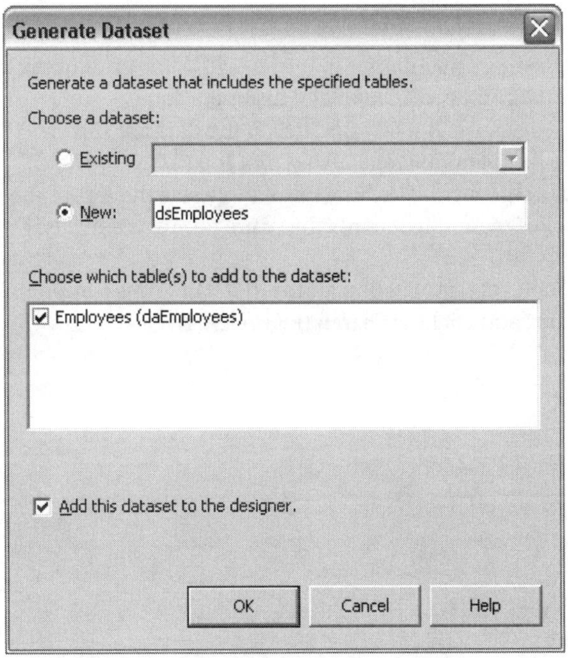

Figure 2-20. *Generate Dataset dialog*

Click OK to close the dialog; Visual Studio .NET will create and instantiate the dsEmployees DataSet as dsEmployees1, adding it to the Component Tray and also adding the dsEmployees.xsd XML schema to the solution.

Binding Data to the Grid

Now that we have all of our Employee data in a DataSet, we need to add the functionality that will display only the results matching the (partial) name typed in the textbox on our form. As stated earlier, in a real-world application we would let SQL Server do all the work involved in our search using an SQL stored procedure, but for the sake of staying on topic, we'll use a *DataView*, which can sort and filter the contents of a DataSet.

Drag a DataView component from the Toolbox onto the form and rename it dvEmployees. Next, set the Table property of the DataView to dsEmployees1.Employees by selecting it from the dropdown list, thus specifying what data the DataView will sort and filter. You can now set the DataSource property of the dgResults DataGrid to dvEmployees, the DataView, tying the data to the user interface. The form should now refresh, with the columns in the Employees table being shown on the DataGrid to highlight the data binding.

Finally, we need to actually write some code to perform the search. To do this, double-click on the Search button to take us into the code view and, more specifically, the btnSearch_Click method. Add the following three lines of code shown in boldface:

```
private void btnSearch_Click(object sender, System.EventArgs e)
{
    daEmployees.Fill(dsEmployees1);
    dvEmployees.RowFilter = "LastName LIKE '%" + txtEmployeeName.Text +"%'";
    sbStatus.Text = dvEmployees.Count.ToString() + " matching records found";
}
```

The first of these lines tells the daEmployees DataAdapter to retrieve all of the employees out of the database, and place them in the dsEmployees1 DataSet. This operation is performed each time the button is clicked to ensure that any updates to the data are shown. The second line then filters that data using the DataView, specifying that the LastName field should be *like* (similar to) the text entered on the form. The final line simply sets the text of the status bar to inform the user of the number of matching records that were found as a nicety. That's all there is to it!

Select the Debug ➤ Start option to compile the application and start it. Once it is running, try entering a few values in the Name textbox and clicking Search (Figure 2-21).

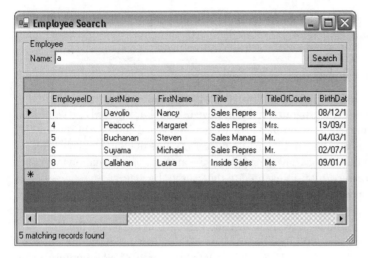

Figure 2-21. *The running application*

Given the minimal effort required to create our Employee Search form, it should come as no surprise to find out that it's lacking in many areas as compared to a real-world application. The main problems that our application currently suffers from, and those that we'll address in the rest of the chapter, are these:

- It has no menus.

- It has no toolbar.

- The icon doesn't give any clue as to the function of the form.

- There is no validation on the data entered in the textbox.

- There is no feedback to the user should an error occur, should no results be found, etc.

Menus, Toolbars, and Dialog Boxes

In addition to the standard form controls such as those that we've already looked at, there are three further common ways of providing interaction and options for end users when you are developing WinForms applications:

- **Dialog Boxes:** To inform the user of the result of operations, present choices to the user, and alert the user to unusual circumstances

- **Menus:** To present the user with a largely static set of commands and options that appear in standardized locations both within the application itself and across multiple Windows applications

- **Toolbars:** To present the user with the most common or most important options in a standard location (usually the top of the form)

In this section we'll cover all three of these items in turn, showing how our application can be extended and polished using them.

Message Boxes and Dialogs

Message boxes are, in effect, small forms that are usually presented to the user in a modal style: holding up the execution of the program until they have been acknowledged and closed. Rather than needing lengthy initialization routines to be written and called, forms to be designed, and so on, they can be created and shown in .NET using a single line of code for each. While this is a great labor-saving feature, it does have a drawback: the amount of information that can be displayed is limited, as are the options presented to the user in the dialog.

The first message box that we'll add to our application will inform the user if no results were found when the search was performed. Before writing the code to do this, we'll tidy up our existing search code in preparation for how it's to be used throughout the rest of the chapter. To do this, create a new, private method called PerformSearch; then cut and paste the existing three lines of C# from btnSearch_Click into it. Finally, update btnSearch_Click to contain a call to PerformSearch:

```
private void btnSearch_Click(object sender, System.EventArgs e)
{
    PerformSearch();
}

private void PerformSearch ()
{
    daEmployees.Fill(dsEmployees1);
    dvEmployees.RowFilter = "LastName LIKE '%" + txtEmployeeName.Text +"%'";
    sbStatus.Text = dvEmployees.Count.ToString() + " matching records found";
}
```

Once this is done, it is a simple addition to inform the user when no results are found, implemented by simply adding the following four lines to the bottom of PerformSearch:

```
if (dvEmployees.Count==0)
{
    MessageBox.Show("No matching records found");
}
```

The call to MessageBox.Show presents the user with a simple message box. This single line of code takes care of everything for us: initializing the message box, displaying the text, and waiting for a response. When entering the code, you should see that there are actually twelve overloads for the method, allowing for much more control over what is shown in it. The overload we've used is the simplest, just taking the main text to display as a parameter, and it simply displays an OK button to the user, as shown in Figure 2-22, when the application is run and a search for a nonexistent LastName is performed.

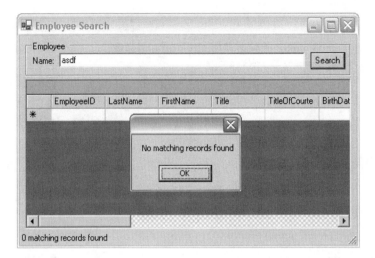

Figure 2-22. *MessageBox prompt*

Though they are quite useful for providing simple feedback, message boxes can be used much more effectively in some situations by making use of all of the settings that can be applied in making a call to MessageBox.Show:

- **Text:** The main text displayed in the message box, as shown in the previous example.

- **Caption:** The text shown in the title bar of the message box.

- **Icon:** An element of the MessageBoxIcon enumeration, which chooses an image to show to the left of the Text. This takes any of the familiar message box icons such as an Information symbol or stop sign.

- **Buttons:** An element of the MessageBoxButtons enumeration, allowing for the buttons displayed at the bottom of the message box to be chosen from the standard options available, such as OK, Yes/No, and Retry/Cancel.

- **Owner:** A reference to the window in front of which the message box is to be shown can be passed as a parameter, allowing the code displaying the message box to be located elsewhere than in the form itself.

To demonstrate a couple of these options, and to show how we can determine which of the buttons a user clicked when responding to a message box, we'll update the PerformSearch method to ask the user whether the search should be performed again when no results are found, rather than just informing the user of the situation. To do this, update the method so that it matches the following code:

```
private void PerformSearch()
{
    daEmployees.Fill(dsEmployees1);
    dvEmployees.RowFilter = "LastName LIKE '%" + txtEmployeeName.Text +"%'";
    sbStatus.Text = dvEmployees.Count.ToString() + " matching records found";
```

```
    if (dvEmployees.Count == 0)
    {
        string message = "No results were found. Attempt search again?";
        DialogResult result = MessageBox.Show(message,
                                        "Search Results",
                                        MessageBoxButtons.YesNo,
                                        MessageBoxIcon.Question);
        if (result == DialogResult.Yes)
        {
            PerformSearch();
        }

    }
}
```

The MessageBox.Show method returns a variable of type DialogResult that can be compared to values of the DialogResult enumeration to determine what option was selected. In our code, this is assigned to the rslt variable and used to determine whether to make an additional call to PerformSearch.

When the application is run again and no matching employees are found, the user will now be presented with the message box shown in Figure 2-23, in the hope that another user has updated the system since the previous search.

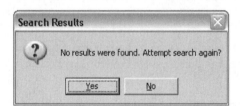

Figure 2-23. *MessageBox presenting a query to the user*

■**Note** In a live system, it is inadvisable to let the logic of an application cause a potentially infinite recursive loop as in the example above: if for one reason or another the dialog gets shown many, many times in a row, the system will eventually run out of memory and cause an error. In such a repetitive situation, iteration should generally be used, with a construct such as a while loop enclosing both the search itself and the question to the user.

As well as the general-purpose MessageBox, there are several other types of Dialogs that exhibit specific functionality and are generally used within applications by adding them as controls to a form, causing them to appear as items in the component tray. The following dialogs are available, and all appear in the Windows Forms tab of the Toolbox:

- **ColorDialog:** A (custom) color picker dialog

- **FontDialog:** Dialog that lists all the fonts installed on the machine

- **OpenFileDialog:** Standard dialog for selecting and opening a file

- **FolderBrowserDialog:** Standard dialog for selecting a directory

- **PageSetupDialog:** Standard dialog for setting the size of the page that will be printed on

- **PrintDialog:** Standard dialog for starting a print session

- **PrintPreviewDialog:** Standard dialog for displaying a preview of a printed document

- **SaveFileDialog:** Standard dialog for choosing a location and name for a file to be saved

Form Menus

Nearly all commercial Windows applications make use of menus, and for a good reason: they're a great way of collecting commonly requested functions together into one well-known location. There's no reason that our application shouldn't use them too, even if only to let the user know who wrote it and providing alternative ways of performing searching and quitting.

To add a menu, drag the MainMenu control onto the form from the Windows Forms tab of the Toolbox. The Menu control is a little different from the controls we've seen so far; it will appear both in the components window at the bottom of the main window and at the top of the form as an actual menu. Select it in the components window and rename it "menu"; then click the Type Here text on the control in the main window. When you do this, you will be presented with several further labels instructing you to Type Here, as shown in Figure 2-24.

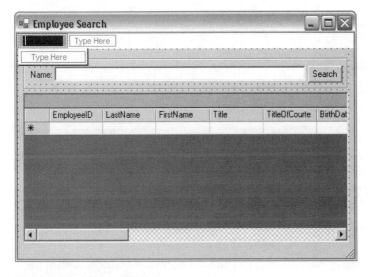

Figure 2-24. *Adding a MainMenu to the form*

For our application, we'll have two top-level menu options: File and Help. Select the Type Here in the top left, and type &File. Then select the Type Here to the right of it and type &Help. You'll see that for each entry you add, an extra option is added to allow for the addition of further items. The ampersands (&) before the words indicate the letter to be underlined as a shortcut (such as the F in File).

The same pattern applies to adding submenu options. Click on the Type Here beneath File, and type &Search; then again beneath that type &Exit. See Figure 2-25.

Figure 2-25. *Populated MainMenu control*

Finally, under the Help option, type &About to allow the addition of a dialog box giving details about the application.

Although we've configured the text that is shown on the menus, you will see in the Properties window that each menu entry has a name such as menuItemX, where X is a value from 1 to 5. This is because each menu item is itself a control that receives a default name provided by Visual Studio, just as Buttons and Textboxes do. These can be edited through the Properties window in the same way as other controls, but a quicker option is to right-click on the menu and select the Edit Names option. This will update the display to show the display text (grayed out) and allow the editing of the item's name. Update the name of each item as shown in Figure 2-26, with a value of mnuHelpAbout for the final, unpictured, option.

Figure 2-26. *Editing MenuItem names on a MainMenu control*

Tip Although there is no hard and fast rule for menu naming, taking a hierarchical approach such as the one above is very useful, since it allows you to see at a glance where a control sits within a menu, and can help to reduce the occurrence of conflicting names in a form.

Now that our menu is visually complete, we can add the necessary code for each of the menu items. Still in design view, double-click on each of the three menu options in turn. This will bring up the code editor, providing a blank method for you to fill in that's already wired up to the Click event of that menu item. You'll need to keep switching back to design view after each double-click. Once this is done, fill in the method stubs that have been created as follows:

```
private void mnuFileSearch_Click(object sender, System.EventArgs e)
{
    PerformSearch();
}

private void mnuHelpAbout_Click(object sender, System.EventArgs e)
{
    MessageBox.Show("Northwind Employee Search\r\n(c) 2004 APress");
}

private void mnuFileExit_Click(object sender, System.EventArgs e)
{
    this.Close();
}
```

The first of these methods simply calls the PerformSearch method that we've written, executing the same code as when the Search button is clicked. The code for the About option displays a dialog similar to those we've already covered. Note the use of the carriage return and line feed in the string. This splits the text across two lines when the dialog is shown. The final method terminates the application by calling the Close method on the currently running (and only) form.

Context Menus

In addition to the standard main menus displayed at the top of application screens, a second menu type can be utilized in .NET applications: context menus. These are the menus that appear when the right mouse button is clicked, and are known as context menus because the menu shown is dependent on the current context. That is, the menu shown when one control is right-clicked can differ from that of another in the simplest case, and multiple menus can even be attached to a single control if need be.

There's no real need for a context menu in our application, but we can add one in just a few mouse clicks to show how easily they are created, and how similar they are to standard menus. To start with, drag a Context Menu control from the Toolbox to the main form. As with a Main Menu control, it will appear both at the bottom in the components window and at the top of the form. When selected, you'll see that it actually replaces the Main Menu at the top of the form. As soon as it is deselected, the Main Menu control will reappear, meaning that for the Context Menu to be graphically edit, it first needs to be selected in the component window.

Ensure that the control is selected, and rename it cmSearch. You'll see that there is only one Type Here option, and that the top-level menu title is uneditable and set to Context Menu. This is because it appears as a single-menu popup, and hence doesn't have a title. Click on the sole Type Here option it displays, and type Search. We'll make our context menu provide the same functionality as the Button and Search Main Menu option we've already implemented. As with the Main Menu, you can select the Edit Names option from the context menu of the Context Menu, and ensure that appropriate naming conventions are applied (Figure 2-27).

Figure 2-27. *Editing a context menu*

Next, double-click on the cmSearchSearch option to switch to code view, and enter our usual method call:

```
private void cmSearchSearch_Click(object sender, System.EventArgs e)
{
    PerformSearch();
}
```

Now that the menu itself has been created, it needs to be associated with a control: our DataGrid in this example. This can be done most simply using the Design view; select the DataGrid and click the dropdown list on the ContextMenu entry in the Properties window (this appears under the Behavior heading). This will display a list of all Context Menu controls in the current form that can be associated with the DataGrid. Selecting the only entry in the list, our cmSearch control, will bind the menu to it.

When the application is now run, right-clicking on any of the controls other than the Textbox and the DataGrid will have no effect. The Textbox will continue to exhibit its standard behavior (showing the Cut, Copy, Paste, and other editing options), and the DataGrid will display our own (albeit small) menu. See Figure 2-28.

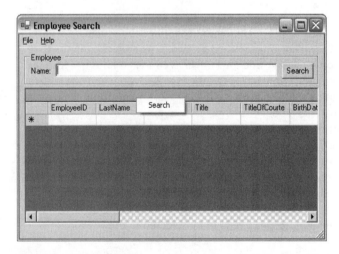

Figure 2-28. *Displaying a context menu when the application is running*

Toolbars

The last control type that we'll take a look at is the Toolbar, which allows us to group various user-initiated actions together in much the same way as in a MainMenu. Toolbars act as containers for the ToolbarButton items that display the text and images for each individual entry. Unlike MainMenu controls, Toolbars are visible controls, so they are shown on the form but not in the component tray.

To begin with, drag a ToolBar control from the Toolbox onto the form and rename it tbTop. You will see that it is automatically docked to the top of the form, causing much of the GroupBoxes contents to be hidden. Don't worry about this for now; we'll adjust this shortly.

In order to have standard toolbar buttons that have icons rather than just plain text, we'll need to make use of an ImageList control, which is a container for the icons to display on the toolbar buttons. Drag one of these from the Toolbox onto the form, causing it to appear in the component tray, and rename it ilToolbar. Next, click the ellipsis in the Images field for the control in the Properties window, causing the Image Collection Editor dialog to be shown. This dialog is used to configure the images contained within the ImageList. We'll add two images to the list that we'll assign to the Quit and Search options that we're going to create on the ToolBar. To do this, click the Add button and navigate to the Visual Studio installation folder (usually C:\Program Files\Microsoft Visual Studio .NET 2003), and then to the Common7\Graphics\icons\ subfolder. Select the Computer\MSGBOX01.ico file (a stop sign) and click OK. Then add a second image: Misc\BINOCULR.ICO (a pair of binoculars). Since the images are added to the control, they will appear in the left-hand pane, showing a thumbnail preview of the file added. Selecting any of these items will give the image's details in the right-hand pane (Figure 2-29).

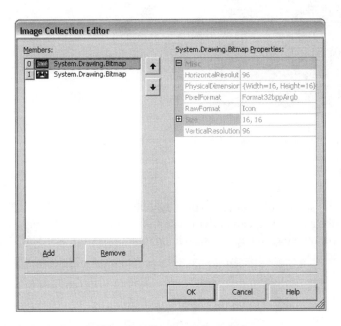

Figure 2-29. *The Image Collection Editor dialog*

Click OK to finish editing the ImageList.

With the ImageList configured, we can attach it to the ToolBar, making the images we've added available to the buttons we'll create. Do this by selecting the ToolBar, then choosing the ilToolbar control from the dropdown list of the ImageList property. Next, click the ellipsis on the Buttons property, causing the ToolBarButton Collection Editor to be shown (which looks surprisingly similar to the Image Collection Editor).

Create two new entries by clicking on the Add button. Set the Name of one to tbbClose and the other to tbbSearch, with ToolTip and Tag values for each of Close and Search, respectively. Following this, select the correct icon from the dropdown list of the ImageIndex property for each, and ensure the Text property is set to be blank. Finally, add an extra item to the list, set its Style property to Separator, and use the Up and Down arrows to place it between the two buttons. This will add a standard separator, a vertical bar, to the toolbar, which can be used to group buttons. Click OK to close the dialog now that we have finished editing our buttons.

Although we've done everything we need to create our ToolBar buttons before adding functionality to them, you may notice that the toolbar appears quite "out-dated," with 3-D buttons. This can be fixed by changing the Appearance property from Normal to Flat.

With our ToolBar now taking up the correct amount of space, resize the form and move the controls out from under it to ensure that it is displayed correctly when run. See Figure 2-30.

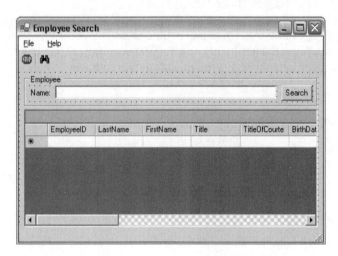

Figure 2-30. *Adding a toolbar to the form*

Handling events with toolbars is slightly different from dealing with menus; rather than having a separate event handler for each, a single handler is used, with the ToolBarButton clicked being passed through as a parameter. This can be seen if the toolbar is double-clicked on in design view, creating this handler:

```
private void tbTop_ButtonClick(object sender,

    System.Windows.Forms.ToolBarButtonClickEventArgs e)
{

}
```

To retrieve the button clicked, we use the **Button** property of the **e** parameter. As a **ToolBarButton** object doesn't have a **Name** property like most of the controls we've looked at, we need to come up with our own way of determining which button was selected. One common way is by making a call to:

```
tbTop.Buttons.IndexOf(e.Button)
```

This will return an integer value that we can perform a **switch** on. However, each time we reorder buttons, or add new ones between others, the code written will need to be changed. For this reason, an alternative method of using the buttons' **Tag** property can be used, although not with a **switch** statement due to the **string** values that are returned:

```
private void tbTop_ButtonClick(object sender,
    System.Windows.Forms.ToolBarButtonClickEventArgs e)
{
    if (e.Button.Tag.ToString() == "Close") {
        this.Close();
    } else if (e.Button.Tag.ToString() == "Search") {
        PerformSearch();
    }
}
```

When the application is now run, you will see a standard toolbar, as expected (Figure 2-31).

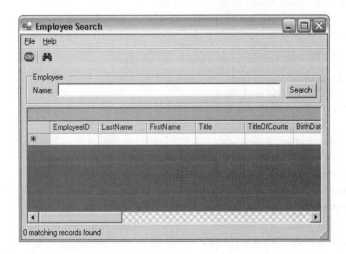

Figure 2-31. *Running an application with a ToolBar*

Creating Additional Forms

The majority of real-world applications require more than one form in order to provide all of their functionality, whether they're used to allow changes to configuration options, show a splash screen, or serve one of any number of other purposes. To demonstrate how easily an additional form can be added to and used within our solution, we'll create an "about" form that is displayed when the Help ➤ About menu option is selected.

The first step in doing this is right-clicking on the project node in the Solution Explorer and selecting the Add ➤ Add Windows Form. . . option. This will display the Add New Item dialog, with the correct Template item selected. Enter About in the Name textbox, and click OK (Figure 2-32).

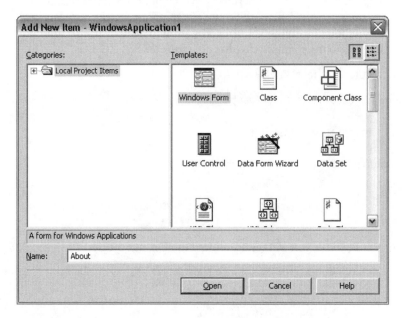

Figure 2-32. *Add New Item dialog*

An additional form will now be present in the Solution Explorer, with both a filename of About.cs, and a class name of About if the code is viewed.

To create the correct layout for the form, drag a Label and Button control from the Toolbox onto it, renaming them lblAbout and btnOK, respectively. Next, set the Text property of the button to OK, and that of the label to "Northwind employee search application (c) 2004 APress LP."

Since this form is to be used as a modal dialog, we can make use of some of the *Appearance* and *Window Style* properties it offers to alter how it's presented. Changing the MaximizeBox, MinimizeBox, and ShowInTaskbar properties to False will cause the window to have behavior more fitting a dialog, leaving the user with only the option of closing it. Also, changing the FormBorderStyle property to FixedDialog will cause the appearance of the form's edges to match that of a dialog (Figure 2-33).

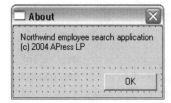

Figure 2-33. *Creating an About form*

The only functionality our form needs is to respond to a click of the OK button by closing. This can be achieved solely by setting form properties.

First, select the OK button and set its DialogResult property to OK. Next, select the About form itself, and set its AcceptButton property to btnOK.

Displaying this form when the Help ➤ About menu option is selected is simply a matter of updating the event-handler code to create a new instance of the form and then show it. Update the main form's code to do this as follows:

```
private void menuHelpAbout_Click(object sender, System.EventArgs e)
{
    About aboutForm = new About();
    aboutForm.ShowDialog(this);
}
```

The fourth line of this subroutine calls the ShowDialog method on the form instance, causing it to appear, with its owner being set to the main form (indicated by it being passed through as a parameter). This differs from the standard Show method on the form, since it causes our About form to appear modally: the main form remains disabled until the About form is closed.

Visual Inheritance

Before we move away from directly designing forms, there's one more handy and powerful feature for WinForms developers that is new to Visual Studio .NET: *visual inheritance*. We've already discussed how a control can inherit default property settings from the form or container it is on; this is one consequence of this new feature. The real power of visual inheritance comes when you realize that this simple principle extends to generating entire forms that inherit their initial layout and content from a single base form. To demonstrate this in action, we'll create a second About form that inherits from our existing one.

Make sure that the project build is up-to-date to begin with by either running the project or selecting the Build ➤ Build Solution menu option. Then right-click on the project name in the Solution Explorer (making sure to be in Design mode first), and choose the Add ➤ Add New Item option, bringing up the Add New Item dialog. Scroll through the templates pane on the right, and select Inherited Form. Type About2 in the Name Textbox, and then click Open to bring up the Inheritance Picker dialog (Figure 2-34).

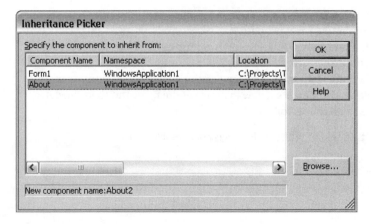

Figure 2-34. *Inheritance Picker dialog*

Select About from the list displayed and click OK to close the dialog. The new form, About2, will be added to the project and automatically opened in the designer (Figure 2-35).

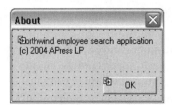

Figure 2-35. *Editing an inherited form*

As you can see, this new form is identical to the one it inherited from, down to the text on the Button and Label. The small blue icon on the top left corner of each control indicates that it is inherited and that we cannot make changes to it on this form. However, if we make changes to the About form, they will also be updated on About2 as soon as the project is rebuilt.

Debugging Applications

Although a few of the features present in pre-.NET Visual Basic IDEs are still missing, Visual Studio .NET 2003 builds upon the 2002 release by including additional runtime debugging features.

Setting Breakpoints

In code-view mode, click in the grey window border to the left of the first line of code in the PerformSearch subroutine. This will set a *breakpoint* in the code, which will be highlighted in red, as shown in Figure 2-36 (though without the color!).

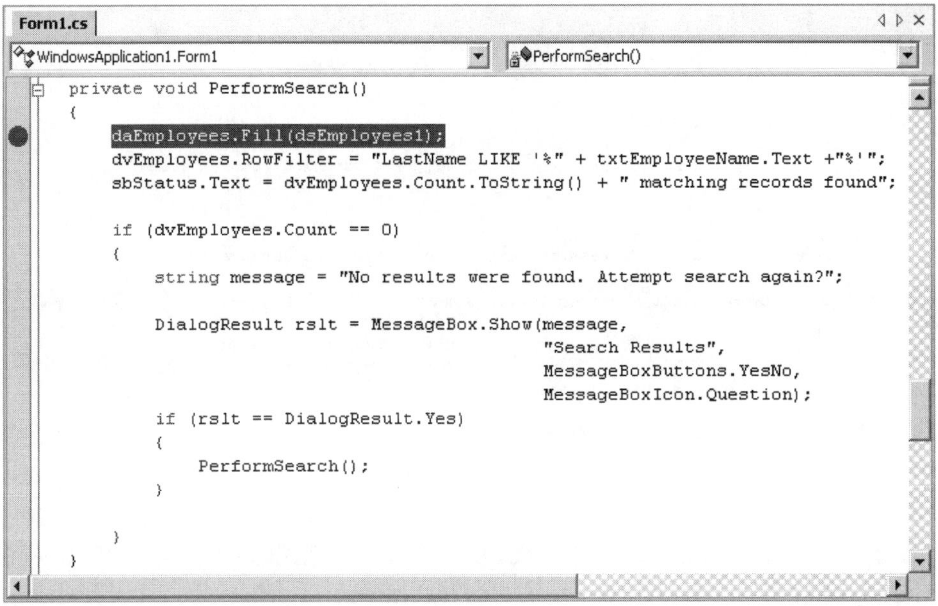

Figure 2-36. *Adding a breakpoint to an application*

This will cause the program to pause execution at the highlighted line every time it comes to it, allowing code paths to be followed and values to be examined.

On the Debug menu there are three options for setting breakpoints:

- **New breakpoint...:** This brings up a dialog that allows a breakpoint to be set. It is a more complicated way to achieve what we did above by clicking in the margin.

- **Clear all breakpoints:** This removes any breakpoints that have been set in the whole solution.

- **Disable/Enable all breakpoints:** This option toggles between disabling and enabling all breakpoints that have been set in the solution, allowing code to continue execution unabated for a time. This is signified by the breakpoints turning from a solid red circle to an outlined red circle.

Stepping Through Code

Press F5 to start the program, and you'll see that the application starts, and runs normally until the Search button is clicked on. Click the button, and Visual Studio will switch back to code view, showing the point of execution in yellow (Figure 2-37).

```
Form1.cs                                                                    ◁ ▷ ×
WindowsApplication1.Form1                          ▼    PerformSearch()              ▼
        private void PerformSearch()
        {
            daEmployees.Fill(dsEmployees1);
            dvEmployees.RowFilter = "LastName LIKE '%" + txtEmployeeName.Text +"%'";
            sbStatus.Text = dvEmployees.Count.ToString() + " matching records found";

            if (dvEmployees.Count == 0)
            {
                string message = "No results were found. Attempt search again?";

                DialogResult rslt = MessageBox.Show(message,
                                              "Search Results",
                                              MessageBoxButtons.YesNo,
                                              MessageBoxIcon.Question);
                if (rslt == DialogResult.Yes)
                {|
                    PerformSearch();
                }

            }
        }
```

Figure 2-37. *Stepping through code*

Assuming that the standard Visual Studio .NET key configurations have been selected, pressing F11 will advance the code one line, stepping into any subroutines encountered, etc. Clicking the Step Into button on the Debugging toolbar has the same effect (Figure 2-38).

Figure 2-38. *The Debug toolbar (with the Step Into button highlighted)*

This button, along with the button to the right of it—the Step Over button, which ignores any subroutines that are being called—and the left-hand Continue button are the most useful options for stepping through code.

Two of the debug windows can also be used for stepping through code: the Breakpoints window and the Call Stack window. Both of these are available from the Debug ➤ Windows menu.

Breakpoints Window

The Breakpoints window allows complete management of the breakpoints set within a solution, such as setting when to make use of breakpoints, letting new ones be added, and having existing ones maintained. The main options can be accessed through the toolbar at the top of the window (Figure 2-39).

Figure 2-39. *The Breakpoints toolbar*

In order, these buttons perform the following operations:

- **New (Breakpoint):** Opens the New Breakpoint dialog box, which gives you complete options for creating a new breakpoint.

- **Delete:** Removes the breakpoint that's currently selected.

- **Clear All Breakpoints:** Removes all breakpoints currently set.

- **Disable All Breakpoints:** Disables all breakpoints that are currently set. You can reenable the breakpoints by clicking the button again.

- **Go to Source Code:** Opens a source window, if necessary, and shows you the location where the breakpoint is set.

- **Go to Disassembly:** Shows the Disassembly window and the location where the breakpoint is set.

- **Columns:** Selects the columns that appear in the breakpoint list below the toolbar.

- **Properties:** Opens the Breakpoint Properties dialog, which allows you to edit the properties of the currently selected breakpoint.

In the breakpoints list, the following three columns are displayed by default (additional columns can be added from the Columns button in the toolbar, as mentioned earlier):

- **Name:** A descriptive name for the breakpoint, created by the debugger based on the breakpoint's location or other properties. A checkbox that can be used to enable or disable the breakpoint appears before each item's name.

- **Condition:** An optional property that determines whether your program breaks when the breakpoint is reached. The condition can be any valid expression recognized by the debugger that equates to a Boolean value. The debugger evaluates the condition and breaks execution only if the condition is satisfied (i.e., if it returns *true*).

- **Hit Count:** Another optional property that determines whether execution pauses when the breakpoint is reached. If this property is not set, the debugger stops each time the breakpoint is hit, assuming that the expression shown in the Condition column is satisfied. The value entered here is used to instruct the debugger to break after the breakpoint has been hit a certain number of times.

Call Stack Window

The Call Stack window enables you to view the names of functions on the call stack, parameter types, and parameter values. This information is shown only when the program being debugged is in a break state, that is, when execution is paused. The stack is listed in order, with the innermost code at the top of the list. Clicking individual entries will open up a code window if necessary, and show the associated line of code. The code for points on the call stack will be marked with a triangular arrow in the margin, and the text will be highlighted in green. Two columns are displayed within the window:

- **Name column:** This shows the name of each function on the call stack. To allow you to distinguish between various calls to functions of the same name (or actually the same function), each entry also shows such values as the parameters passed through to a function, the module containing the code, and the line number.

- **Language column:** The language column shows the language in which the code was written. If the language cannot be determined, this column will be blank.

Examining Values

Step over the code until the *if* statement is highlighted. If you hover over the Text property of the sbStatus control, a tooltip will be displayed showing its value. This same technique works for all variables, constants, and so on, allowing for quick checks on value assignment. In addition to this, there are several advanced ways of monitoring values using some of the debugging windows, all of which can be accessed from the Debug ➤ Windows menu option:

- **Locals:** This window displays all variables that are currently within scope, displaying columns for their name, value, and type.

- **Autos:** This window displays all variables that are referenced in the current line and previous line of code, updating automatically while stepping through code. The same columns are displayed as in the Locals window.

- **This/Me:** The Me window (in VB.NET) or the This window (in C#/C++) are one and the same, with different names purely to make them more relevant to developers. These windows show, in a tree control, all of the members of the This/Me object, using the same three columns as discussed previously.

- **Watches:** There are four identical *watch* windows. Each of these contains the same three columns again, but any valid programmatic expression can be typed into the Name column. For instance, we can copy the "dvEmployees.Count == 0" code from our *if* statement and paste that in the column (Figure 2-40).

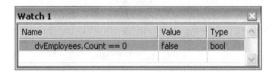

Figure 2-40. *The Watch window*

The Command Window/Immediate Window

This window is used for debugging purposes such as evaluating expressions, executing statements, printing variable values, and so forth. It allows you to enter expressions to be evaluated or executed by the development language during debugging. In some cases, you can change the value of variables. With the release of Visual Studio .NET 2003, this window now also supports IntelliSense, unlike the 2002 release.

As well as being able to enter expressions, you can prefix lines typed with either a question mark (?) or a greater-than sign (>). A question mark returns the value of the expression entered following it, whereas a greater-than sign allows Visual Studio .NET IDE commands such as *alias* to be executed while you are debugging code. To switch between Immediate mode (used for interrogating code) and command mode (used for controlling the environment), the string >cmd can be entered to switch to command mode and immed to switch back.

Processes

As well as debugging an application from the outset—by starting it up attached to the debugger—we can also debug an application once it's already running by attaching to its process. To do this, close the application if it is already running, and press Ctrl+F5 from within the IDE to start the application without debugging (this can also be done by selecting the Debug ➤ Start Without Debugging menu option).

Once the application has started, selecting the Debug ➤ Processes menu option will bring up the Processes dialog (Figure 2-41).

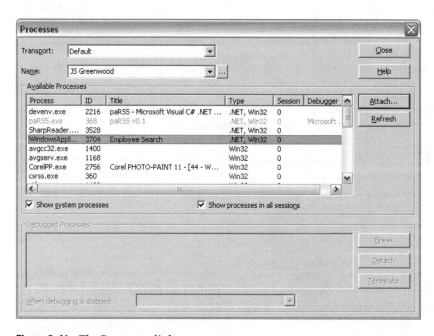

Figure 2-41. *The Processes dialog*

This dialog allows you not only to debug your own application, but also to attach to any other process, even across machines. Due to the usefulness of this form, it's worth going into a bit of detail about the available options:

- **Transport:** For remote debugging, this enables you to select a DCOM-based remote connection (default), Native-only Pipe, or Native-only TCP/IP. Native-only TCP/IP is less secure than Native-only Pipe, but is significantly faster, so it can be of use when you are debugging remote resources. Native-only Pipe is not supported on "consumer" versions of Windows: Windows 95, Windows 98, and Windows Me.

- **Name list box:** Specifies the local machine name or a remote machine name for attaching to a program for debugging.

- **Attach:** Attaches to the currently selected process, enabling debugging for it.

- **Refresh:** Updates the Available Processes list, taking into account any changes in the running processes.

- **Show system processes:** Displays processes created by the operating system.

- **Show processes in all sessions:** Displays processes running in all terminal server sessions.

The following options are enabled in the bottom half of the dialog when processes are attached from this instance of Visual Studio .NET:

- **Break button:** Clicking this will break execution of the program selected in Debugged Processes.

- **Detach button:** Clicking this will stop debugging the selected application and detach from it. This does not terminate the program. To enable native detach on Windows 2000 or Windows NT 4.0, enter the command `net start dbgproxy` on the command line.

- **Terminate button:** Click to terminate the program selected in Debugged Processes.

- **When debugging is stopped list box:** For the program selected in Debugged Processes, this setting determines whether the program terminates or merely detaches from the debugger and continues to run when you stop debugging.

A final point to note is the graying out of the paRSS process above. This means that the process can't be debugged. Looking in the Debugger column, you'll see that there is a value set, meaning that the application is already being debugged; only one debugger can attach to a process at a time.

Exceptions

A final topic to cover on debugging is the Exceptions dialog that's found under the Debug ➤ Exceptions. . . menu option. This option lets you change the way the debugger handles individual exceptions or categories of exceptions (Figure 2-42).

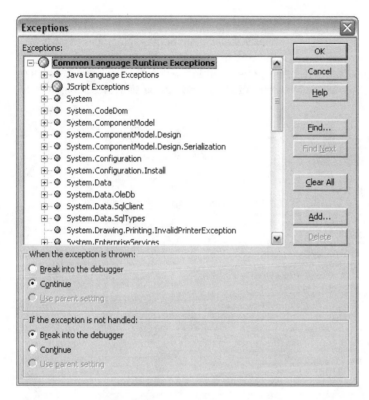

Figure 2-42. *The Exceptions dialog*

By default, execution actually continues when an exception is initially thrown; the debugger alerts the user to the error only if the exception is not handled (caught). This can be changed within the Exceptions dialog, causing the execution to pause as soon as an Exception is thrown. Selecting any of the Framework-defined exceptions from within the tree and amending the values within the "When the exception is thrown" and "If the exception is not handled" group-boxes will change this.

The Add. . . button allows for user-defined exceptions to be handled, too, by typing in their class names in the input box it presents.

Importing Additional Functionality

Although the .NET Framework provides us with a wealth of functionality previously unavailable with any other Microsoft development technology, there are times when it does not provide everything needed. Similarly, there are now many more user interface controls than there ever have been before, but they still may not provide for all situations. In such situations, developers may either want to create their class libraries and UI components to reuse throughout their applications, or they may choose to purchase third-party products that provide the functionality required. Whichever option is picked, such components and libraries can be used within Visual Studio .NET solutions in the exact same way as those provided by Microsoft.

Adding References

Since adding references to third-party assemblies is the same as adding references to parts of
the .NET Framework, we'll use part of the Framework itself as an example of doing this. To do
so, right-click on the References subnode of the project within the Solution Explorer, and select
the Add Reference. . . option. This will bring up the Add Reference dialog, as shown in Figure 2-43.

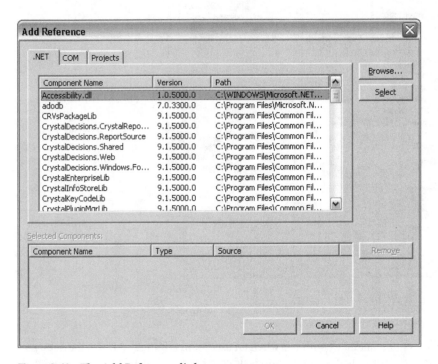

Figure 2-43. *The Add Reference dialog*

The three tabs on this dialog allow for the three different types of references to be added:

- **.NET:** This tab lists all of the registered, compiled .NET assemblies on the local
  machine, allowing for class libraries of managed code to be used within projects.

- **COM:** This tab lists all of the COM components registered on the local machine. These
  can be accessed from within .NET applications using *Interpol*. Whenever a COM component is referenced, a proxy class is created that provides a duplicate of the COM interface.
  It is this proxy class that our .NET code calls. This in turn interacts with the COM component invoking the underlying functionality.

- **Projects:** This tab allows for references to one project to be made from another, all
  within one solution. This feature is great for debugging, since code can be seamlessly
  stepped through from one project to another.

In addition to the three tabs present, the Browse. . . option allows assembly files containing functionality to be located and referenced.

Scroll down the list provided under the .NET tab, and double-click the System.Enterprise-eServices item, causing it to be displayed in the Selected Components pane. Clicking OK will close the dialog, add the reference, and update the Solution Explorer (Figure 2-44).

Figure 2-44. *Viewing references in the Solution Explorer*

Now, when in code view, you will find that there's a System.EnterpriseServices namespace that can be accessed that was not available prior to adding the reference.

Web References

A second type of reference exists, Web References, allowing for functionality present on a remote server to be called from applications. Making calls to the methods provided by the Web Services that can be referenced is identical to making calls to any other method present on a class library. As with COM references, this is achieved by the creation by Visual Studio .NET of a proxy class.

Adding Components

In the same way that we can add references to external class libraries, we can add additional components for use within the Toolbox, providing us with both additional user interface elements and invisible controls to be added to the component tray. To add a new component to the Toolbox, select the tab you wish it to appear on (use General for this example), right-click on it, and select the Add/Remove Items. . . option. This will cause the Customize Toolbox dialog to be shown (Figure 2-45).

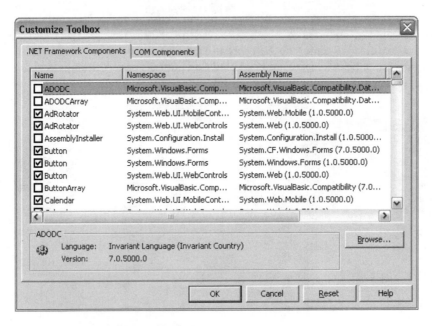

Figure 2-45. *The Customize Toolbox dialog*

This dialog functions similarly to the Add Reference one, providing tabs for both .NET Framework Components and COM Components, along with a Browse. . . button to locate further items not shown in the dialog. Check the box next to the DriveListBox option and click OK, closing the dialog and adding the selected item to the Toolbox (Figure 2-46).

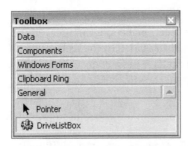

Figure 2-46. *Adding components to the Toolbox*

This control can now be dragged onto forms and used just like any other.

Component Designer

As well as being able to use the Windows Forms Designer within Visual Studio .NET, we can also use the same drag-and-drop metaphor when creating components using the Components Designer. These components represent nonvisual classes that contain the functionality that is utilized by the user interface forms, further classes, and so on. To add one, right-click on the project node in the Solution Explorer and select the Add ➤ Add Component. . . option. Change the component's name to TestComponent.cs and click OK. Opening the component by double-clicking on it will bring up the Component Designer, and prompt the user to add items to it by dragging them onto the design canvas (Figure 2-47).

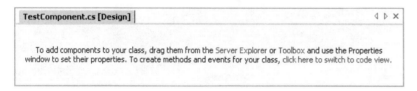

Figure 2-47. *The Component Designer window*

If an SqlConnection object is dragged onto the canvas from the Data tab of the Toolbox, you'll see that the component designer functions identically to the Component Tray in the Windows Forms Designer, creating an icon for each element. Behind the scenes, the exact same process is going on, too, with variables being declared, properties being set, and events being wired up for each item. When all of the required functionality is added to the component, it can be instanced and used from elsewhere in a .NET solution.

Summary

The world of Windows Forms has matured considerably since the first form design tools for Windows were released around a decade ago, especially when you consider that these early IDEs borrowed heavily from even earlier DOS development environments. Visual Studio .NET is a large step forward even from what was previously the premier IDE for developing such applications: Visual Studio 6. It should be especially welcome for those who do not come from a VB background, who can now work with forms with a speed and grace that were previously simply impossible. In the space of a single chapter we've put together a functional front end for querying the Employees data in the NorthWind database, managing to produce a working version of the application by initially writing only two lines of code.

In this chapter we've really covered only the very basics of working with Windows Forms applications, so that we can begin to get comfortable with the various pieces of the IDE, such as the Toolbox, form designer, Properties window, and Component Tray. And there are many other wizards and features present that can be utilized in creating an application.

With our whistle-stop tour of Windows Forms development complete, we can now move on to look at their counterpart, Web Forms. For further information on Windows Forms development, I recommend you check out Matthew MacDonald's book *User Interfaces in C#: Windows Forms and Custom Controls* (ISBN 1-59059-045-7), also from Apress. There's also a VB.NET version of this title (ISBN 1-59059-044-9).

CHAPTER 3
■ ■ ■

Web Application Development

Introduction

Today, all sorts of people have their own websites, from the home user to the director of a large corporation. There are about 945 million Internet users worldwide at present, and it is projected that this number will increase to 1.1 billion in 2005.[1] Therefore, the world is becoming increasingly dominated by the Internet, and the Internet is becoming more and more an indispensable tool in our lives.

A website can have practically an unlimited range of uses. You may already have a cool personal website—static or dynamic—which can be used to display items of interest, personal profiles, a résumé, or mementos of gatherings with your friends. Businesses will probably have a website for promotional or commercial use, such as building customer relationships or improving customers' experience with the company. You can also use Internet and web application to pay bills, do online banking, book services, shop, and on and on. Of course, one of the reasons for the increased use of web applications is the flexibility and popularity of the Internet, which means that once you create a web application, your family, customers, and actually anyone that you trust can use this application from anywhere on Earth.

Writing web applications is a great way to start your programming career. Microsoft provides a .NET Framework and its Software Development Kit (SDK) to developers, and one of the core materials from this framework is ASP.NET, a Microsoft technology and new standard for building web applications on its .NET framework. ASP.NET contains a large and powerful set of tools that developers use for creating dynamic websites easily. Using Visual Studio .NET, you can develop an ASP.NET web application visually and rapidly that can contain a great deal of functionality that was unavailable in previous versions of ASP. Most importantly, you can use Visual Studio .NET to build a reliable and powerful web application in an efficient and productive way.

Microsoft's Vision of Web Development

In the old days, applications were built around a central mainframe computer. Typically, a user interacted with the application on a central, large, and expensive mainframe computer through a *dumb terminal*. This scenario is called *centralized computing*. As hardware became cheaper

---

1. From http://cyberatlas.internet.com/big_picture/geographics/article/
   0,1323,5911_151151,00.html.

and personal computers became more powerful, a portion of the processing load was leveraged to the user. Thus was born the client/server model, which is the pioneer model of a Windows and web application. Early client/server systems buried the business logic inside the user interface on the client side or within the database, say in the form of stored procedures, or the business logic was divided between client and server. This is called a two-tiered model.

Minimizing the disadvantage of deployment and concurrent user limitations of two-tiered rich client/server systems (that is, systems of a standalone executable with a graphical interface comprising several user controls), the software giant Microsoft has shifted its attention to the Web architecture. Based on the introduction and utilization of distributed computing, client, business logic, and data storage can be separated logically into multiple tiers. The Web architecture can also be fully integrated with this model, so that an author can write and place web pages on a web server with business logic or processing that can also access data storage if necessary and then render the output to the client as HTML through the HTTP protocol. In fact, this is nothing new, since static HTML is ideal for displaying relatively static content all the time. The CGI-BIN interface was an early solution for launching processes on a server and generating a dynamic response based on user requests. Later, Sun and Microsoft invented the Java Servlet and Microsoft Active Server Pages technologies in order to hook in their own server and create interactive web pages while serving nearly unlimited client access.

Currently, web servers have increased in complexity to the point where the web server has become an application server in the sense of n-tier architecture, and the web page no longer has to be static. It can be dynamic, or even personalized to the individual user, so that a better user experience can be provided. At the same time, the web client is no longer a dumb user. It is a "glorified dumb terminal." Since there are unlimited uses of the Internet, and web technology can be applied to any kind of architecture, Microsoft created ASP.NET and Visual Studio .NET, and now developers can use this latest visual tool to develop reusable components, modules, and classes for writing n-tier ASP.NET pages to be hosted by Microsoft's Internet Information Server (IIS).

n-Tier Methodology

The presentation, application, and data layers are logically separated in an n-tier environment. In two-tier architectures, the business layer is rarely implemented as a separate logical entity, and it is mixed with the presentation logic. In n-tier architecture, all layers can be isolated, and they can be distributed.

For the presentation layer, a user interface can be deployed on the client side, and this is really limited to the interface level only. The data layer does what its name implies, which is working with the data store for data manipulation. The business logic layer, however, becomes more significant in this situation. Since the server hosting the business logic, which we called the application server, can be further partitioned across many application servers, sometimes each application server is dedicated to a particular business purpose.

All of the Windows and web applications can now be built on top of the rich .NET Framework, where flexible language options are supported, such as C#, VB.NET, and J#. These are fully object-oriented languages, and you can use these to write or design an ASP.NET web application with different classes, modules, components, etc. in an n-tier architecture.

Scalability, extensibility, and reusability play an important role in *n*-tier architecture. In the .NET architecture, there is a concept called Assembly, which works like a COM object as in the past. This increases the reusability and scalability of an ASP.NET application considerably, since each ASP.NET application works like a lightweight executable on a web server, and this "component-based" concept can be powered up by deploying more and more assemblies into a web application. These "components" can be distributed into multiple tiers as well.

The Death of ASP As We Know It

From Microsoft's point of view, the word "Active" has dominated the IT industry over the past 10 years. Microsoft introduced ActiveX control, ActiveX Documents, Active Data Objects, and, the most impressive one for us, the Active Server Page (ASP). Over the past four or five years, ASP has become a success story in web development and the marketing of dynamic websites. ASP is the predecessor of .NET, but ASP.NET is not merely the next generation of ASP. ASP.NET builds on the .NET Framework with fully object-oriented architecture, and ASP.NET can be used to build a more secure and efficient website, with better performance, than with ASP.

ASP normally relied on either JavaScript and/or VBScript with some HTML tags. Both JavaScript and VBScript are scripting languages, and using one or the other resulted in a page of "spaghetti" code. In a client/server model, a client types a URL and submits a request to a web server, which locates the ASP file and interprets the web page from the top to the bottom and then returns the resultant HTML to the client. Moreover, classic ASP web pages are not built in an event-driven manner. We have to write a great deal of code in order to determine what event was fired from the client side and then execute the corresponding methods, manually store and make persistent a few values, and generate the resultant content from the server side. In ASP.NET, everything is an object, and controls and pages are event-driven. Each web form will be "posted back" to itself by default, and we can write or consume different resources from local or remote machines.

The next generation of ASP, ASP.NET, is just a subset of the whole .NET architecture and is an evolution of the development of the Web. Using the rich functionalities and classes offered by the .NET Framework, many tasks that you can't do or even never imagined could be done on the Web now become possible. In contrast to classic ASP, you can now create a dynamic web application with more powerful features and functionality. For example, you can build a secure website based on different types of authentication and authorization mechanisms, increase the load and efficiency of a website by using the caching and threading architecture, improve performance by serving the client from a compiled "executable" assembly instead of reading spaghetti code, and provide a better user experience based on the concepts of globalization, personalization, and page templating.

The New Presentation Layer

Building a presentation layer is easy, fast, and fun in Visual Studio .NET. ASP.NET makes use of the concept of server controls for web forms. This means that a web form is basically composed of one or more server controls and their associated event handlers.

The presentation layer is the top layer among the layers in the *n*-tier architecture. It is also the interface that provides users the first "look and feel" of your application. The CodeBehind technique was used in Visual Studio .NET, and the presentation elements, that is, the ASPX file, form a standalone file separated from the business logic or event handlers. Therefore, web designers can focus attention solely on the interface design job, whether it be drawing a pretty icon or creating a flashy motion graphic, which many ASP.NET developers cannot do (more accurately, programmers like us don't know how to do it).

The presentation and business logic are separated for a web form, and the model shows that the interface and business layers can be isolated, which is why you will see something like what is shown in Figure 3-1 in the Solution Explorer of Visual Studio .NET.

Figure 3-1. *File listing in Solution Explorer*

You can see that there are two files with the same name (in this case, the name is "WebForm1"), but the two files have different extensions. The actual model of such an architecture is, for example, like that shown in Figure 3-2.

```
<%@ Page language="c#"
Codebehind="WebForm1.aspx.cs"
AutoEventWireup="false"
Inherits="WebApplicationIntro.WebForm1" %>

<HTML>
<form id="Form1" method="Post" runat="Server">

</form>
</HTML>
```

WebForm1.aspx (Presentation)

```
namespace WebApplicationIntro
{
  public class WebForm1 : System.Web.UI.Page
  {
    //Business Logic
  }
}
```

WebForm1.aspx.cs (CodeBehind)

Figure 3-2. *Presentation and CodeBehind file of an ASP.NET web form*

As you can see from the figure, the presentation and business logic are separated into two files for a single web form. The presentation file has a "directive" tag pointing to its CodeBehind file, while the CodeBehind file inherits from the Page object. You will see more details about this issue in the coming sections, while for now we will focus on the presentation file. It is an ASPX file, containing a large number of server controls. You can use the built-in ASP.NET server control, Internet Explorer server control, third-party control, or even your own custom server control.

Every web form contains at least three server controls once it has been created in Visual Studio .NET. Even if you don't put a server control onto the web form explicitly, there are two literal controls and one HTML Form control. Visual Studio .NET creates an HTML Form server control for you once you start a web form, namely Form1 with a Post method by default. You can drag and drop any server control to a web form, provided that all of these controls are placed "within" this HTML Form control. The HTML source code of a web form created by Visual Studio .NET looks like this:

```
<%@ Page language="c#" Codebehind="WebForm3.aspx.cs"
AutoEventWireup="false" Inherits="WebApplicationIntro.WebForm3" %>
<!DOCTYPE HTML PUBLIC "-//W3C//DTD HTML 4.0 Transitional//EN" >

<html>
  <head>
    <title>WebForm3</title>
    <meta name="GENERATOR" Content="Microsoft Visual Studio .NET 7.1">
    <meta name="CODE_LANGUAGE" Content="C#">
    <meta name=vs_defaultClientScript content="JavaScript">
    <meta name=vs_targetSchema
        content="http://schemas.microsoft.com/intellisense/ie5">
  </head>
  <body MS_POSITIONING="GridLayout">
    <form id="Form1" method="post" runat="server">
    </form>
  </body>
</html>
```

Dividing the Presentation Layer into Logical Segments

You can change the content of the interface or presentation elements dynamically and logically. In ASP.NET, there are many controls, such as user control and custom server control, that you can treat as a single control and container, into which you can drag and drop different controls to make a reusable unit. Commonly used, such units are navigation menus and user login modules. Thus an administrator may see more tabs in the menu than a normal user, or the entire login box in which you enter a user name and password will disappear after a successful login. Thus the content can change dynamically based on the actions of the user. Both of these controls—navigation menu and login module—may contain many other controls, such as TextBoxes, Buttons, and LinkButtons, and the visibility and functionality of these controls are controlled programmatically by your server-side code.

For example, you can use Visual Studio .NET to create a User Control easily by selecting the ASP.NET Web User Control from the Templates pane of Add New Item (see Figure 3-3).

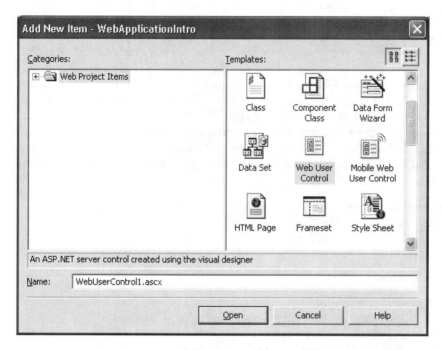

Figure 3-3. *Creating a User Control from the "web user control" template*

After creating the User Control, you can reuse it in any other web form by marking a reference at the top of a web form, or simply dragging the User Control from Solution Explorer onto a web form directly (Figure 3-4).

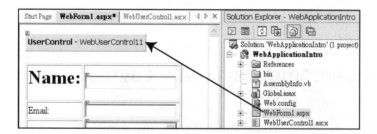

Figure 3-4. *Adding a User Control to a web form in Visual Studio .NET*

Web Page Development Using the ASP.NET Web Application Template

There are a few things that have to exist for every ASP.NET web application. This includes the web page or user interface files, configuration files, a BIN folder with your project assembly, a virtual directory (configured as a web application), and the CodeBehind files. Visual Studio .NET will do all of these necessary tasks and create the necessary files for you automatically once you create a new ASP.NET web application.

Visual Studio .NET 2003 and ASP.NET Version 1.1

Visual Studio .NET runs on .NET Framework Version 1.1 by default. In Visual Studio .NET 2002, the web application developed is supposed to be run on .NET Framework Version 1.0, while Visual Studio .NET 2003 is supposed to run on Version 1.1. Therefore, you may see the following error message shown in Figure 3-5 if you have not installed .NET Framework Version 1.1 or have not yet configured your Internet Information Server (IIS) to recognize the ASP.NET Version 1.1.

Figure 3-5. *Visual Studio .NET cannot open an ASP.NET 1.1 web application.*

You should not have this problem if you installed Visual Studio .NET 2003 properly. But what exactly do we mean by "properly"? If you install the IIS after the installation of Visual Studio .NET, then this problem will probably occur.

In order to solve this problem, you have to manually register the assembly file for the reorganization of ASP.NET Version 1.1 in IIS. Therefore, you are required to go to the command prompt under the folder of the .NET Framework, which would normally be placed in the system root:

(*%sysroot%*\Microsoft.NET\Framework\[*VersionNumber*])

For example: C:\WINDOWS\Microsoft.NET\Framework\v1.1.4322.

Then, you can manually register the required assembly by running the regsvr32.exe command, as shown in Figure 3-6.

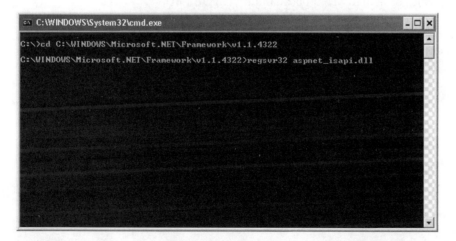

Figure 3-6. *Registering an assembly with a specific version of .NET Framework*

Files in the Project

To see what will be created by Visual Studio .NET when you are building an ASP.NET web application, let's walk through the development of a simple such application:

1. Choose File ➤ New ➤ Project from the menu, or click the New Project button at the bottom of the Start Page (Figure 3-7).

Figure 3-7. *Creating a new project in Visual Studio .NET*

2. When the New Project dialog appears, select Visual C# Projects and ASP.NET Web Application in the left and right panes, respectively.

3. Change the Location to WebApplicationIntro (Figure 3-8).

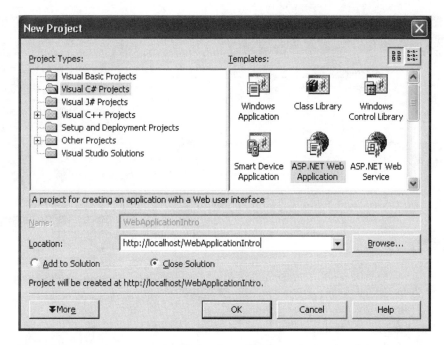

Figure 3-8. *Creating a new ASP.NET web application (C#) in Visual Studio .NET*

4. Click OK.

After you have clicked the OK button, Visual Studio .NET will create a new folder with the name of the Project at the IIS Server, for example C:\Inetpub\wwwroot, by default. Visual Studio .NET will also configure the newly created project as a web application in the IIS as well. Apart from creating an application in the local machine, you can change the location and point it to a remote web server, provided that you have sufficient privileges to create a project on that remote machine. After the web application has been created by Visual Studio .NET, a few of the basic required files, assemblies, references, and a default web form were all created, and from that point on, you simply use the design environment to drag controls onto the design grid (see Figure 3-9).

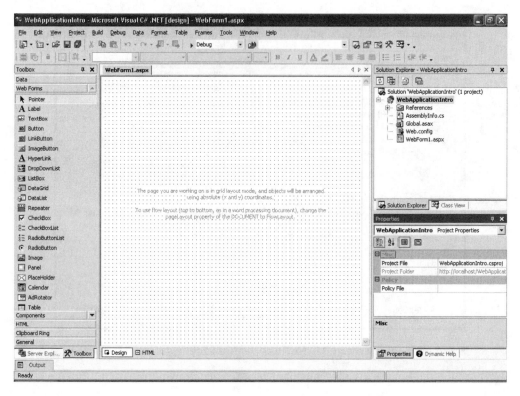

Figure 3-9. *Working with a newly created web form in Visual Studio .NET*

Once the new project is created and a few references have been set up, you can also click the Show All File button in order to view an additional and hierarchical structure of the handful of files in Solution Explorer (Figure 3-10).

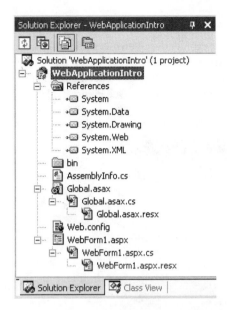

Figure 3-10. *File listing after clicking the "Show All" button*

Table 3-1 provides a brief description of each file.

Table 3-1. *Description of Files Shown in Solution Explorer*

File Name	Description
AssemblyInfo.cs	Contains attributes stored in the metadata about the assemblies assembly built by the project, such as name, version, and culture
Global.asax and Global.asax.cs	Contain CodeBehind declaration <%@ Application Codebehind="Global.asax.cs" Inherits="WebApplicationIntro.Global" %> and codes for handling application-level events
Web.Config	Contain configuration data for the project web application in XML format
WebForm1.aspx and WebForm1.aspx.cs	Contains CodeBehind tag <%@ Application CodeBehind="Global.asax.cs." Inherits="WebApplicatioinIntro.Global"%> and codes for handling application-level events
WebForm1.resx	Contains localization information and data in XML format

Working on the Page

Looking at the default web form, WebForm1.aspx, in your application, you can see that this is definitely not enough for you to build a powerful ASP.NET web application. You can add more web forms by right-clicking on the application name in Solution Explorer, choosing Add, and then adding a new item as web form or selecting Add Web Form directly (see Figure 3-11).

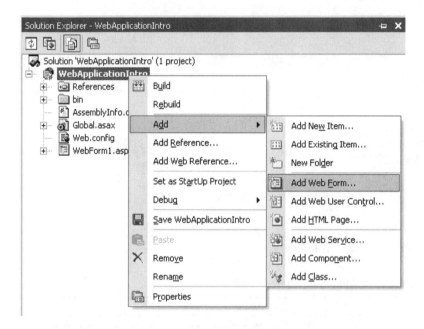

Figure 3-11. *Adding a new web form in Solution Explorer*

For every web form, there are three editing modes:

- **Design Mode:** The central pane of a web form displayed in Visual Studio .NET by default

- **HTML Mode:** HTML of a web form generated by Visual Studio .NET to produce the layout for Design Mode

- **Text Mode:** CodeBehind file containing the event handlers and classes for the web form

Grid Mode

When you start working on a web form by double-clicking on a file in Solution Explorer, you will see the design mode of this web form immediately by default. The HTML/XML Editor with Encoding was used as default, but you are also able to open files with a different editor or change the default editor by the following steps in Server Explorer:

Right-click the file name ➤ Open With ... ➤ Select a program to open ➤ Set as default ➤ OK. See Figure 3-12.

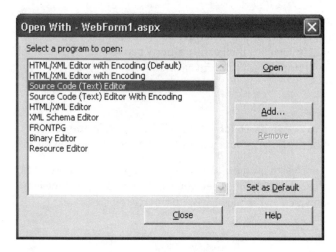

Figure 3-12. *Opening a file with a different editor in Solution Explorer*

If you open up a web form in Visual Studio .NET, you may notice that a couple of properties of the web form are displayed that are modifiable.

Properties of a Document

Whenever you open a new or existing web form, you can right-click and select the Property option from the Context menu. Then you can pop up a property dialog for this document (Figure 3-13).

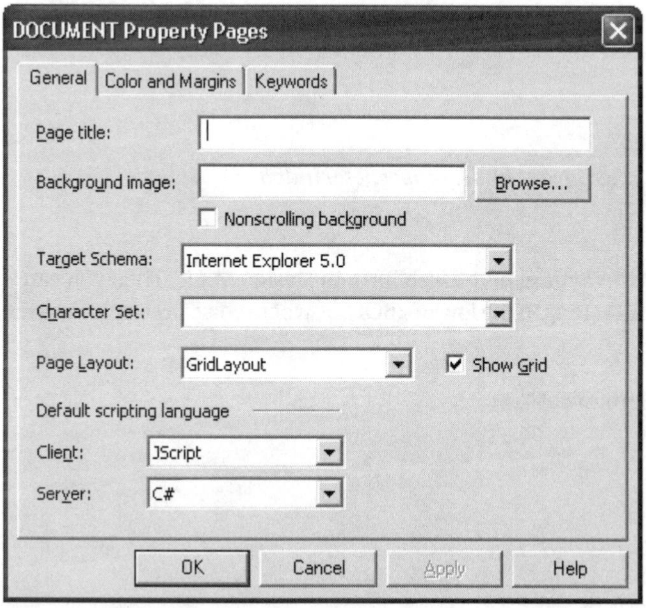

Figure 3-13. *Property pages of a document*

In these property pages, you can customize and set the properties of a document, such as the title of the page, target schema, or color of the text. You can also configure the properties in the Properties window, while the point is you can change the property of a web form in a visual way in Visual Studio .NET so as to customize your web form easily.

Page Layout

There are two different ways for you to design a web form in Visual Studio .NET, and you can change it from either the properties of the HTML document or HTML mode of the web form:

1. Single-click on the web form in Design mode, and you can either press F4 or right-click to select the property from the context menu. Then you can find and toggle between the two options in the dropdown list of the pageLayout property (Figure 3-14).

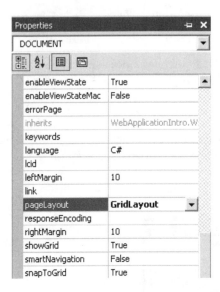

Figure 3-14. *Changing the page layout in the properties window*

2. Click the HTML button at the bottom of the web form in Design Mode. Then you can see that there is a page layout setting in the line of <BODY>, where you can switch between

```
<BODY MS_POSITIONING="GridLayout">
```

and

```
<BODY MS_POSITIONING="FlowLayout">
```

What is the difference between grid layout and flow layout?

- **Grid layout:** Developing a web form with the grid layout is just like working in a Windows Form application environment, since it uses absolute positioning to place the HTML or web server control, which means that you can drag a control from the Toolbox and drop it anywhere in a web form. Moreover, you will find that each element on the web form in grid mode will have a style and positioning attributes if you look at the HTML code of the web form. The values of the Top and Left attributes indicate the position of an element being displayed on a web form. So wherever you drag a control onto a web form, it will be displayed at this "specific" location when a user views this page.

- **Flow layout:** This is a common way of placing elements on a web form, with each element arranged in the logical order that it occurs on the page, sequentially from the top to the bottom, and so the page can be edited as a word processing document.

The major difference between flow layout and grid layout is that in flow layout, you cannot drag elements across the design view surface or use the positioning grid, and the element will not display at a specific location, even if you have set the positioning attributes. However, there are certain HTML elements that do not flow in this way, and they cause the layout of a page to be disrupted. One of the most obvious examples of inefficient use of flow layout is a guest book. You will probably want to line up the controls, for example, to get all descriptions and TextBoxes to align vertically instead of placing these items without formatting them properly. In this case, a borderless HTML Table control will normally be used to line up the web page neatly. The result of a sample guest book inside an HTML table with FlowLayout, without the need to specify the locations of the web controls, is shown in Figure 3-15.

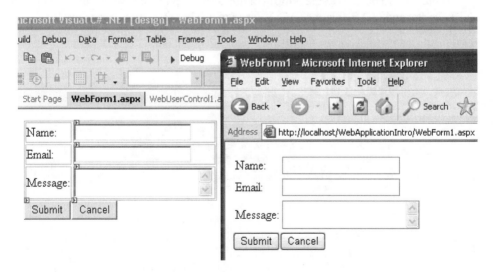

Figure 3-15. *Aligning controls on a web form inside an HTML table*

As you can see from the figure, the web form was built using the "FlowLayout" property. The descriptive text and textboxes are properly aligned because an HTML table was used to arrange and contain the corresponding text and textbox. (The border of the HTML table was set to 1 pixel for easier viewing. You may set it to zero in production.) However, if you use FlowLayout without the HTML table, the control is simply placed from left to right and from top to bottom, as shown in Figure 3-16.

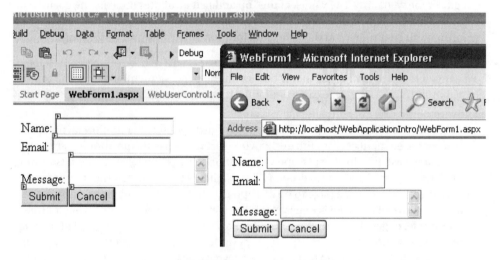

Figure 3-16. *Aligning controls on a web form without using an HTML table*

There are two buttons at the bottom of the designer pane of a web form in Visual Studio .NET: Design and HTML (Figure 3-17). You can toggle between these two views for web form editing:

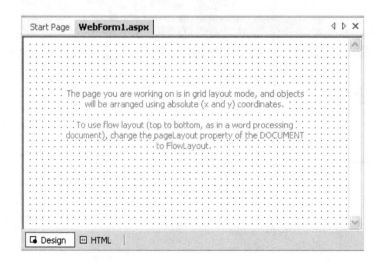

Figure 3-17. *Toggling between design and HTML modes for a web form in Visual Studio .NET*

- **Design Mode:** Design mode provides a graphical viewing surface for creating and editing web forms. You can add and remove elements and text, and position and format properties using drag-and-drop techniques in this WYSIWYG environment. In this mode, you can see the web form much as it will appear in a browser, since most of the controls are transformed and displayed instantly in this mode by Visual Studio .NET.

- **HTML Mode:** HTML mode provides a text-editing environment that enables you to edit the HTML markup directly with the aid of "Intellisense" in Visual Studio .NET to insert elements and properties as you edit, format, and debug.

Target Schema

You can name a web browser for the targetSchema property in order to indicate a validation schema used for designing an HTML document, an XML document, or web forms pages. You have to use a browser that supports HTML 4.0 or later if you want to use CSS styles.

The targetSchema property shows a uniform resource identifier (URI) of the schema, known as the targetNamespace. Different documents may have different representations for this property:

- **Web Form or HTML document:** Add at the ‹meta› tag, for example:

```
<%@ Page language="c#" Codebehind="WebForm1.aspx.cs"
    AutoEventWireup="false" Inherits="WebApplicationIntro.WebForm1" %>
<!DOCTYPE HTML PUBLIC "-//W3C//DTD HTML 4.0 Transitional//EN" >
<HTML>
  <HEAD>
    <title>WebForm1</title>
    <meta name="GENERATOR" Content="Microsoft Visual Studio .NET 7.1">
    <meta name="CODE_LANGUAGE" Content="C#">
    <meta name="vs_defaultClientScript" content="JavaScript">
    <meta name="vs_targetSchema"
        content="http://schemas.microsoft.com/intellisense/ie5">
  </HEAD>
    <body ms_positioning="GridLayout">
      <form id="Form1" method="post" runat="server">

      </form>
    </body>
</HTML>
```

- **ASP.NET User Control:** Add at the Page directive, for example:

```
<%@ Control Language="c#" AutoEventWireup="false"

Codebehind="myUserControl.ascx.cs" Inherits="WebApplicationIntro.myUserControl"

TargetSchema="http://schemas.microsoft.com/intellisense/ie5"%>
```

- **XML/XSL Document:** Add at the XMLNS attributes to the root element, for example:

```
<xsl:stylesheet xmlns:xsl="http://www.w3.org/1999/XSL/Transform" version="1.0">
```

Error Page

In case any unhandled page exceptions exist, you can redirect the requesting browser to a specific web page by setting the ErrorPage property for a web form page. You can set up a custom error page, and then redirect your user to this page in the event of an unhandled exception by stating an ErrorPage at the Page directive, for example:

```
<%@ Page language="c#" Codebehind="WebForm1.aspx.cs"

    AutoEventWireup="false"

    Inherits="WebApplicationIntro.WebForm1"

    ErrorPage="WebForm2.aspx" %>
```

Note Note that this is not the only way to handle exceptions in ASP.NET. In fact, there are many different ways to handle exceptions in ASP.NET. For example, the Try...Catch block is one of the greatest enhancement introduced in ASP.NET for structured exception handling, or you can also make use of the Application_Error event handler in Global.asax for global exception handling, so that you can use redirection in the event of an exception.

Trace

Outputting the trace information of a web form is useful in debugging. In the Properties window of a web form, you can find the option Trace, which you can set to True or False. The trace information will then be output if you have set the option to True (Figure 3-18).

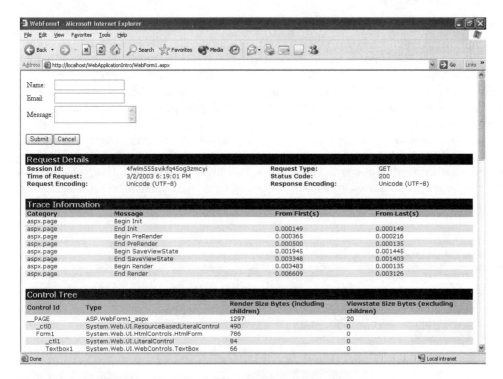

Figure 3-18. *A web form with Trace enabled displayed in the browser*

You can also set the option to False, and then the trace information will not display on the screen at runtime. This means that you can switch tracing on and off without removing or rewriting any of the trace statements in your CodeBehind page. This is a good technique, and it saves time in developing and debugging.

If you do not want to control the tracing functionality in Design mode of Visual Studio .NET, you can also toggle this option by placing Trace attributes in your Page directive:

```
<%@ Page language="c#" Codebehind="WebForm1.aspx.cs"

    AutoEventWireup="false"
    Inherits="WebApplicationIntro.WebForm1" ErrorPage="WebForm2.aspx"
    Trace="True"%>
```

Coloring

When you switch to HTML mode in the designer, you can see that there are different colors for different elements. For example, in the `<meta>` tag in the `<head>` section, there are three colors for this line: Maroon, Red, and Blue. The word "meta" appears in Maroon, while "name" is in Red, and the value is in Blue. This feature is provided by the Visual Studio .NET environment runtime, and you cannot see it in other text editors, such as Notepad, though you can use these tools for editing an HTML or web form.

This coloring of code is a very nice feature. It gives a better experience to developers, since they can distinguish different portions of the HTML tags and elements easily. Features like this are configured using the Options dialog. To access this dialog from the menu bar, select Tools ➤ Options. When the Options dialog appears, select Environment and its subitem Fonts and Colors in the left pane to display a list of option pages (Figure 3-19).

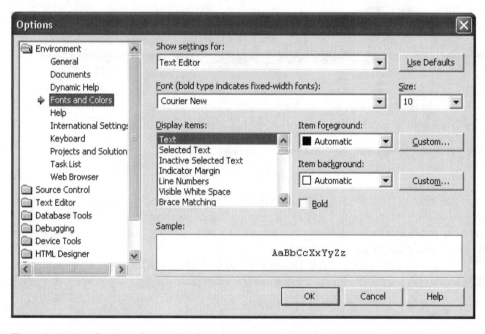

Figure 3-19. *Configuring font and color properties under the Tools menu*

As you can see in the figure, you can customize the color and fonts in different areas and items, or you can simply click Use Defaults and use the original settings.

After diving into the code coloring in your HTML or CodeBehind file, let's take a look at the user interface. If you want something on a web page to stand out, you can change its size and color. To do this, move your cursor and select the text. When the text is highlighted, select Heading 1 from the style list on the formatting toolbar, as shown in Figure 3-20.

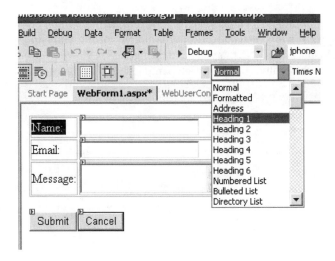

Figure 3-20. *Changing style and format for text in the designer pane*

This formats the selected text, just as you would do in a word processor (Figure 3-21).

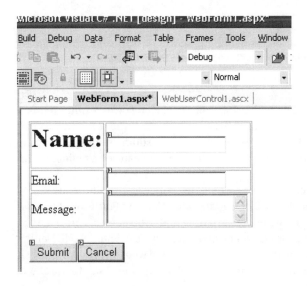

Figure 3-21. *Result of formatting text and style in the designer pane*

In addition to formatting the text, you can also change its color and size, or make it bold, for instance, and change the font face and color of any control in its properties window.

Tools in the Toolbox

Recall the Toolbox section in Chapter 1, which is a collection of available components and controls located in the left pane of Visual Studio .NET. If you have opened or are viewing a web form page in Design mode, you can see the Toolbox tab on the left pane, as shown in Figure 3-22.

Figure 3-22. *The Toolbox is located at the left pane of Visual Studio .NET by default.*

There are actually several menu headers in this Toolbox: Data, Web Forms, Components, HTML, Clipboard Ring, and General. The menu headers work in much the same way as the Outlook Bar works in Microsoft Outlook, where there are different sliding menus, and only one section is visible at a time. In the Toolbox for this web form, you can see a collection of available web form controls by default.

ASP.NET comes with a host of new controls with which developers can easily create stunning web applications. Working with them is just like working with Windows Form counterparts. The controls in the Toolbox allow ASP.NET developers to drag and drop controls onto a web form directly, and the corresponding code or tag will be generated by Visual Studio .NET automatically. This means that developers can just drag the controls to the web form, and then each control will be smart enough to detect and render the best HTML output or result to the client browser window automatically.

Alternatively, you can create and manage a server control programmatically by creating an instance of the control and then adding it to the control tree of the web form. We cannot go into the details here. A number of such controls, ranging from a checkbox to a DataGrid control, can be found in the Web Form tab of the Toolbox, as shown in Figure 3-22.

Based on the controls available in the Toolbox of Visual Studio .NET, those related to ASP.NET can be placed in five categories:

1. **ASP.NET Web Form controls:** This is the major set of controls for a web page, equivalent to normal HTML controls such as <select>, <input>, and <form> after rendering. You can see more of this kind of control in the next section.

2. **ASP.NET Rich controls:** ASP.NET comes with a few rich controls such as Calendar and Ad Rotor, which required a great deal of hand coding to produce the same output in the classical ASP age.

3. **ASP.NET List controls:** One of the major types of web application is the data-driven application. ASP.NET provides several data binding controls, such as DataGrid, DataList, and Repeater, to which data can easily be bound.

4. **ASP.NET Mobile controls:** A full set of mobile controls is available in Visual Studio .NET without any additional toolkit download or installation, which was necessary with Visual Studio .NET 2002. These controls are the extension to the ASP.NET web form controls, but they can be rendered and displayed correctly on mobile devices, such as mobile phones.

5. **ASP.NET Validation controls:** This is a set of form validation controls, which can be run on the client and/or server side, depending on your choice of its properties and the capabilities of the requesting user.

Table 3-2 presents a few of the ASP.NET controls available in the Web Forms tab of the Toolbox.

Table 3-2. *Names and descriptions of a selection of web form controls in the Toolbox*

Control Icon	Control Name	Characteristic
A	Label	Rendered as a <div> element and able to display text on a web form.
abl	TextBox	User can enter information to a web form with this control, and data can be bound to this control from a DataSource.
ab	Button	A pushbutton control with two types: Submit and Command buttons. The former type will post the web form back to the server side, while the latter one will fire an event handler on the server side.
ab	LinkButton	Acts like a button but looks like a hyperlink. It returns the user to the same page.
🖾	ImageButton	Functions like a button control but displayed as an image, so that clicking on the image produces the function of a normal button control.
A	HyperLink	A navigational tool with which you can change the displayed text or linked URL through server-side code.
🗏	DropDownList	A dropdown listbox with only one element visible at a time, which is actually a <select> list in HTML.

Continued

Table 3-2. *Names and descriptions of a selection of web form controls in the Toolbox (continued)*

Control Icon	Control Name	Characteristic
	DataGrid	Generates a <Table> that can be bounded with data. Other features, such as pagination, editing, selection, and sorting are supported.
	DataList	Generates a <Table> and bound with data on your customized appearance of each row.
	Repeater	Repeats the contents that you define once for each source item.
	RadioButton or RadioButtonList	A single selection can be made in a control array, and can also be bound to a list of data.
	CheckBox or CheckBoxList	Functions like the RadioButton or RadioButtonList to allow selection from a list, but more than one element can be chosen in this list, which can also be bound to a list of data.
	Image	Displays an image on a web form. The path of the image and other properties can be set in server-side code.
	Panel	A Container control, used to group different controls together. Can be used as a parent for static text or other controls.
	Field Validation	A set of validation server controls providing client- and server-side validation appropriate to the viewing browser to test user input.

■**Note** Visual Studio .NET is built on .NET Framework V1.1, with a number of new features compared with the old V1.0. For example, list controls such as DropDownList, RadioButtonList, CheckBoxList, and ListBox, have a new property, called SelectedValue, which is much like the *ControlName*.SelectedItem.Value property in the old V1.0. You can see all of the properties of controls in the Properties window or through IntelliSense of Visual Studio .NET 2003.

Another type of control that you can use in a web form is an HTML Control. Since you do not always want to use the powerful but expensive ASP.NET Server controls, the HTML tab of the Toolbox offers another collection of simple HTML controls that are familiar from classic ASP (Figure 3-23).

Figure 3-23. *HTML controls in the Toolbox of Visual Studio .NET*

These HTML controls are merely counterparts of ordinary tags that generate standard HTML in your web form. As standard HTML controls, these do not tailor their output for the requesting client, nor do they require any server-side processing. You can, however, explicitly attach a Runat="Server" property to the HTML controls, which means that certain properties of the control can be manipulated in server-side code.

Please bear in mind that both the Server and HTML controls ultimately represent the same thing, since a Server control will be rendered as an HTML element or tag on a web page and will then be delivered to the client browser for interpretation and display.

Since ASP.NET Server Controls provide much the same features as HTML controls, you may wonder why ASP.NET doesn't replace all HTML controls with ASP.NET Server controls. In particular, why does Visual Studio .NET provide two sets of controls/tools in two separate tabs?

Visual Studio .NET tries carefully to minimize the resources of a web application or website, since the Server control can be rendered in optimal format when targeting a specific user, and the performance of this rendered process is more expensive than simply rendering and delivering the HTML code of an HTML control to the client. Therefore, we have to choose and use controls wisely; that is, we must use Server controls only when the interaction and processing of server-side code is involved.

HTML and Server controls have visual differences in Visual Studio .NET. Apart from the overhead issue and that you have to use Server controls selectively, as mentioned in the previous paragraph, there is a visual difference between these two types of controls in Visual Studio .NET. Apparently, they are the same thing. For instance, you can drag and drop a Button server control and Button HTML control onto the Designer pane, as shown in Figure 3-24.

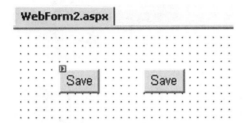

Figure 3-24. *ASP.NET button and HTML button controls placed on a web form*

Let's play a game of "PhotoHunt." Can you tell the difference between the two buttons in Figure 3-24. and in particular, which one is the Button Server control? That's right, the left one. If you look at them carefully, you may notice that every server control in Visual Studio .NET has a small arrow at the top left-hand corner by default. This icon is called a Glyph, which is a feature provided by Visual Studio .NET that enables users to distinguish server and HTML controls easily. This visual feature can be controlled to display the icon from Tools ➤ Options ➤ HTML Designer ➤ Display. In the right pane for this option, there is a checkbox called Show glyphs for server control, and you can toggle its visibility in Designer mode by checking it.

The Wonderful World of Server Controls

ASP.NET comes with a collection of new and smart server controls, which are able to detect and determine, and then render, the optimal output to the client side. A frequently asked question is, Why do you need an HTML control if all of the functionality and interface of the HTML control are covered in the Server control? While all of the functionality in HTML controls can be found in the Server controls, the reverse is not the case. Visual Studio .NET still has two sets of controls in the Toolbox, because HTML has its value: We do not have to use a Server control if the control does not involve any interaction with the server or any server-side events.

Use a Server control only if you really need it. Server controls are much better and smarter than HTML controls, but if you want to display a static element, such as displaying text on the screen, you do not actually have to use the Label web control. You can simply use a <div> to obtain the desired effect. The reason is as simple as the performance. Server controls provide lots of functionality and allow you to work with them programmatically. You can use the methods and properties for a server control in server-side code, which would involve a PostBack or a certain amount of server resources to detect and render the control on the screen. Moreover, the ASP.NET Server control offers a flexible and consistent interface and rich functionality, such as the Calendar and DataGrid controls, which generate complex and well-structured tables containing calendar data and spreadsheet-like data, respectively.

One of the nice features in Visual Studio .NET is that you can easily drag and drop Server controls and HTML controls onto a web form. You simply select the web form or HTML tab in the ToolBox, and then it is easy to drag and drop different kinds of controls.

When a page is sent to a client, values representing the current state of the page's control persist, and all information is stored in a hidden form field by the viewstate mechanism. For example, when you complete a Registration form and post the data back to the server, the web form will cause a postback, and the data previously entered will persist after this postback. That is because all of the values are stored in the viewstate temporarily, and the value on the TextBox is restored after the postback action. In this case, you can selectively use the Server and HTML TextBox controls to meet your requirements. The ViewState property can be applied at the application, page, or control level. Thus you can disable the viewstate property of a Server control by setting its EnableViewState property to False, or by changing it in the Properties window of the document (see Figure 3-25).

Figure 3-25. *Toggling the EnableViewState property in the properties window of a document object*

HTML Mode

HTML mode of Visual Studio .NET allows you to edit elements in web forms manually just as with classic ASP. Note that there is a pair of buttons located at the bottom of the design mode of a web form. These are the Design and HTML tabs. If you click on the HTML button, then the HTML code generated by Visual Studio .NET will be displayed.

In this kind of edit mode, you cannot see the server control in the Toolbox. If you have experience in developing classic ASP, then you may use your text editing tool, say Notepad, and you can type everything you need or want to see on a web page. For example, if you want to use a textbox with some text, then you have to type the following statement completely:

```
<input type="TextBox" Value="Professional VS.NET 2003">
```

However, if you use Visual Studio .NET, you can simply type a "less-than" sign (<) in HTML mode, and then you will see that a ListBox has popped out showing a list of available elements for you to scroll through to pick out the most suitable one. Let's try to add a TextBox Server Control in HTML mode of Visual Studio .NET (Figure 3-26).

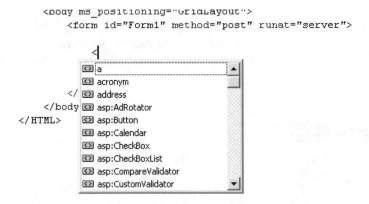

Figure 3-26. *Inserting elements in the designer pane under HTML mode*

If you continue typing after you type the "<" sign, the selected index of the ListBox will immediately locate the closest match, as shown in Figure 3-27.

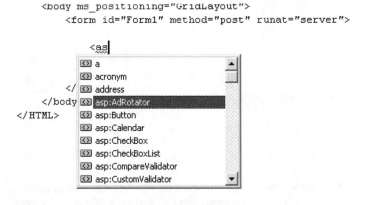

Figure 3-27. *Inserting elements with the aid of "IntelliSense" features in the designer pane*

If you find the selected index point to your desired item even before you have finished typing the complete element, you can press the space bar, and the text will be completed by Visual Studio .NET automatically (Figure 3-28).

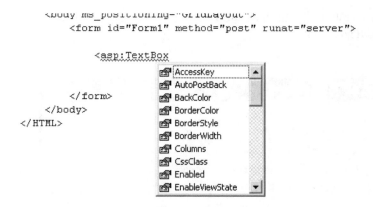

Figure 3-28. *Inserting elements with the aid of the "AutoComplete" feature in the designer pane*

After you press the space bar, the name of the element will be completed, and after you type one more space, the available properties for that element will pop out as well.

When you type the "greater than" sign (>) at the end of a declaration, the corresponding closing tag will be inserted by Visual Studio .NET (Figure 3-29).

```
<body ms_positioning="GridLayout">
    <form id="Form1" method="post" runat="server">

        <asp:TextBox id="txtName" Runat="server"></asp:TextBox>


    </form>
    </body>
</HTML>
```

Figure 3-29. *Insertion of a closing tag when entering the greater than sign (>) in the designer pane*

This is one of the nice features provided by Visual Studio .NET. It is called *AutoComplete* in HTML Mode. If you have fairly good knowledge or background in programming ASP.NET, then coding a web form in this HTML mode is sometimes simpler than using Design mode. The AutoComplete feature of Visual Studio .NET's IntelliSense, along with coloring, applies to different types of elements, greatly simplifying your work.

▓**Note** For your information, another ASP.NET development tool by Microsoft is called ASP.NET Web Matrix (Version 0.6, Build 812). This is a free Visual Studio .NET-like development tool. It has code coloring, but it does not have the AutoComplete and IntelliSense functionalities. You can go to http://www.ASP.NET/WebMatrix/ Download.aspx to evaluate it.

If you want to modify, enable, or disable the features of AutoComplete, you can go to the Options in the Tools menu (Figure 3-30).

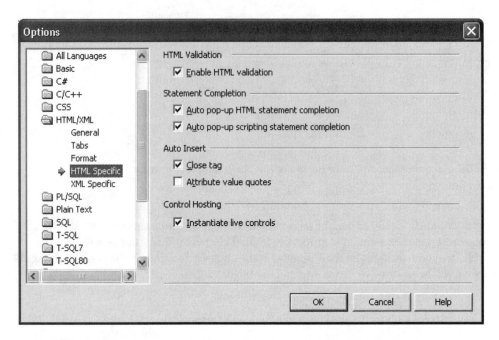

Figure 3-30. *Configuration of the AutoComplete feature in Visual Studio .NET*

In the Options dialog, you can select Text Editor and its subitem HTML/XML in the left pane to display a list of option pages as shown in the figure. This list of options is obviously specific to the HTML mode of Visual Studio .NET when you are editing your HTML or XML document. You can see that the statement completion list has popped out, because "Auto pop-up HTML statement completion" was checked in the Statement Completion block.

Two of the options in this dialog are worth being highlighted here:

- **HTML Validation—Enable HTML validation:** This feature will highlight and let you know where you are typing and point out potential errors in your code. When this option has been enabled, you can see a curly underline for any incomplete or invalid tag in the web form, as shown, for example, in Figure 3-31. If you are sure that you can type a web form precisely and find the red curly underline disturbing, you can uncheck the checkbox in the Options dialog. When you were typing a document in Microsoft Word, you may see a red curly line under any word that may be misspelled or be involved in a grammatical error. This validation works similarly. It will validate your web form as you type and alert you if an error is detected. This curly and red underline will disappear once you type a line break that completes an error-free line.

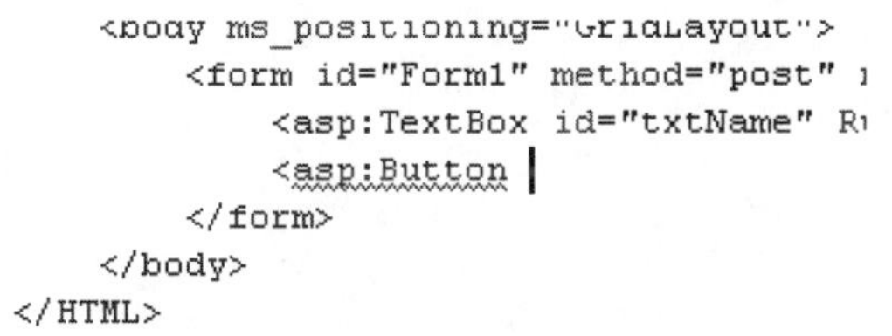

```
<body ms_positioning="GridLayout">
    <form id="Form1" method="post" ı
        <asp:TextBox id="txtName" Rı
        <asp:Button |
    </form>
</body>
</HTML>
```

Figure 3-31. *HTML validation feature in the designer pane*

- **Auto Insert—Attribute value quotes:** This feature applies to any place in your web form, once you create an attribute and set its type. This will let Visual Studio .NET automatically insert a pair of double quotes around the value of your attribute. This can also enhance compatibility with protocols like XHTML.

This will not edit or modify your existing code once you turn it on, but it will affect any future additions or changes, for example, if you want to create a TextBox and type something like what is shown in Figure 3-32.

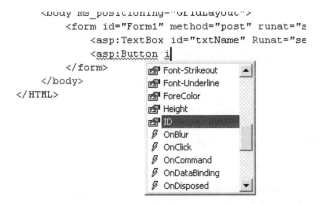

Figure 3-32. *Insertion of a TextBox control in a web form*

The IntelliSense shows all of the properties available for the Button server control, and the selected index will point to ID if you type i. If you now press the space bar, you will see that a pair of double quotes was inserted, and the cursor will be placed between them, ready for your declaration. (For this to work, you need to change the options in Tools/Options/TextEditor/ "HTML/MXL"/HTML Specific and select "Attribute value quotes."). See Figure 3-33.

```
<body ms_positioning="GridLayout">
    <form id="Form1" method="post" r1
        <asp:TextBox id="txtName" Rui
        <asp:Button ID="|"
    </form>
</body>
</HTML>
```

Figure 3-33. *Automatic insertion of double quotes around the value of an attribute*

If you create a Button control in a web form, you will probably have something like this:

```
<asp:Button id="btnSave" Runat="server"></asp:Button>
```

If you want to add some text to this button control, you can place the cursor in the Button control tag just before the "greater than" sign and press the space bar once. A list of available properties for a Button control will pop out, and you can select any one of them, as before.

If you type only part of a word but want to finish it automatically or see a list of the possible words associated with this object, you can use the Complete Word feature. For example, you might type te only and then ask Visual Studio .NET to fill in the complete word on your behalf. See Figure 3-34.

```
<body ms_positioning="GridLayout">
    <form id="Form1" method="post" runat="server">
        <asp:TextBox id="txtName" Runat="server"></asp:TextBox>
        <asp:Button id="asdf" Runat="server" te|</asp:Button>
    </form>
</body>
</HTML>
```

Figure 3-34. *Entering a portion of a word in editing a web form*

Then, you can select Edit ➤ IntelliSense ➤ Complete Word and press Alt+Right Arrow or Ctrl+Space, with the result shown in Figure 3-35.

```
<body ms_positioning="GridLayout">
    <form id="Form1" method="post" runat="server">
        <asp:TextBox id="txtName" Runat="server"></asp:TextBox>
        <asp:Button id="asdf" Runat="server" Text|</asp:Button>
    </form>
</body>
</HTML>
```

Figure 3-35. *Enabling the AutoComplete feature in editing a web form*

Alternatively, if you type one or two characters and want to view all available properties, you can select Edit ➤ IntelliSense ➤ List Members and press Ctrl+J or Ctrl+Space, and you will see the list shown in Figure 3-36.

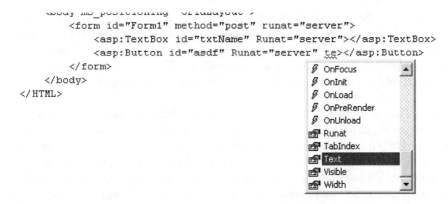

Figure 3-36. *Display of available methods/properties for a specific element*

As you can see, all the properties have popped up for your selection. If you find the selected index point on your desired item, you can press the "=" button to type the attribute value directly, or you can press Enter and let Visual Studio .NET complete the word for you. Thus you can some-times complete a line of code by actually typing only one or two characters. These IntelliSense features work in most text scenarios such as writing code or XML and Cascading Style Sheet editing.

Even when you are editing an HTML control, you can also use these features provided by Visual Studio .NET. For example, when you are trying to create a Submit HTML button, you can type a few words and then let IntelliSense complete it for you (Figure 3-37).

Figure 3-37. *Insertion of HTML Submit button with the aid of the "AutoComplete" feature in Visual Studio .NET*

There are three ways to select a control when you want to alter its properties:

- Single-click on a control in Design mode.

- Select a control from the dropdown list of controls at the top of the Properties window in Design mode.

- Place a cursor within the tag in HTML mode.

Typing in HTML mode of Visual Studio .NET is not really typing. Using the features of AutoComplete and IntelliSense provided by Visual Studio .NET, you can type or edit a web form, XML, or Cascading Style Sheet document quickly and easily. Since most of the words, properties, attributes, etc., can be completed with a press of the space bar, Equal button, Enter button, or the like, typing in HTML mode of Visual Studio .NET is no longer like typing in HTML mode of Notepad.

If you are used to hand coding for your web forms and switching between the Design and HTML modes frequently, Visual Studio .NET will apply formatting for you automatically. Your web form may involve some manual or intentional formatting in your code, and some tags like <td> and line break will be removed if they do not meet the standard of Visual Studio .NET. You may feel uncomfortable about this change, or lose some code when switching between these modes frequently. This option can actually be turned on or off in the Tools menu: Tools ➤ Options ➤ HTML/XML ➤ Format. Then, you can (un)check the checkboxes to meet your personal preference, and you will end up with the result shown in Figure 3-38.

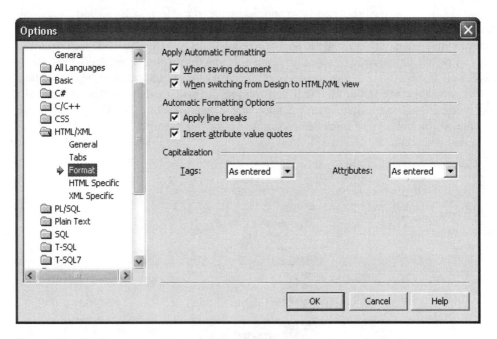

Figure 3-38. *Configuration of the automatic formatting function in the Tools menu*

Text Mode

Many websites are written by a team of programmers, mixing together the interface design and programming logic. However, today, ASP.NET uses an object-oriented and event model, in which the server-side programming logic is separated from the HTML interface code, avoiding the mixing of processing code with HTML code in a page. One of the major characteristics of using Visual Studio .NET to write ASP.NET code is the CodeBehind feature.

The CS (or VB) File

As mentioned earlier, we can now have two types of model in coding an ASP.NET page, that is, the inline and CodeBehind approaches. The inline code model involves putting all server-side processing procedures and event handlers in a section in the web form, which will use a single ASPX file to contain both the server- and client-side script. The CodeBehind approach can be found in Visual Studio .NET only. It separates code from content, and the code is completely removed into a separate file. The content or interface file has a special Page directive to tell the Common Language Runtime (CLR) that the current page inherits its code from the named file, which looks like this:

```
<%@ Page language="c#" Codebehind="WebForm1.aspx.cs"
      AutoEventWireup="false" Inherits="WebApplicationIntro.WebForm1" %>
```

For the default web form created in a web application, WebForm1.aspx, the files are as listed in Table 3-3.

Table 3-3. *Characteristics of a web form*

File Name	Characteristic
WebForm1.aspx	Contains the HTML for the web form, or you might put Javascript and/or Cascading Style Sheet code over here. This is directly displayed when you select the HTML tab in Design mode.
WebForm1.aspx.cs	Contains the event handlers for the web form, which will be executed on the server-side only.
WebForm1.aspx.resx	Contains localization data or information in XML format.

The CodeBehind and resource files are hidden by default. To show them, you can click the Show All Files button in Solution Explorer, as shown in Figure 3-39.

Figure 3-39. *Display of files by clicking the Show All Files button in Solution Explorer*

You can see the content of a web form in Visual Studio .NET only by default, while there are four ways for you to view the content of the CodeBehind file:

- Right-click on a web form in Design or HTML mode and then select View Code.

- Double-click on a CodeBehind file in Solution Explorer.

- Right-click on a web form file in Solution Explorer and then select View Code.

- Click on the first (Code) button in the Solution Explorer mini toolbar with the web form selected.

Note that Visual Studio generates a couple of event handlers, initializations, or XML comments once you create a web form automatically. If you expand the hidden region labeled "Web Form Designer generated code," you would see something like this:

```
using System;
using System.Collections;
using System.ComponentModel;
using System.Data;
using System.Drawing;
using System.Web;
using System.Web.SessionState;
using System.Web.UI;
using System.Web.UI.WebControls;
using System.Web.UI.HtmlControls;

namespace WebApplicationIntro
{
/// <summary>
    /// Summary description for WebForm1.
    /// </summary>
    public class WebForm1 : System.Web.UI.Page
    {
        private void Page_Load(object sender, System.EventArgs e)
        {
            // Put user code to initialize the page here
        }

        #region Web Form Designer generated code
        override protected void OnInit(EventArgs e)
        {
            //
            // CODEGEN: This call is required by the ASP.NET Web Form Designer.
            //
            InitializeComponent();
            base.OnInit(e);
        }
```

```
        /// <summary>
        /// Required method for Designer support - do not modify
        /// the contents of this method with the code editor
        /// </summary>
        private void InitializeComponent()
        {
            this.Load += new System.EventHandler(this.Page_Load);
        }
        #endregion
    }
}
```

CodeBehind Versus the DLL File Versus ASP.NET

The principle of CodeBehind is that you can create a class for your code, and this class inherits from the ASP.NET Page type. In contrast to classic ASP, you have the HTML content page mixed with inline scripts scattered throughout, and this file will be parsed and interpreted by the ASP engine (asp.dll) in IIS. With the ASP.NET Framework, the state and model for a web application are changed; the ASP.NET web form is no longer being interpreted; and the entire web form page is in effect an executable assembly running on the web server, and a different engine (aspnet_isapi.dll) was dedicated for this job.

Once you have written the web forms and the associated CodeBehind files have been built, a single assembly will be created, and a DLL file can be obtained and run on the server. This assembly file will be placed in a folder named BIN, and it will dynamically emit the required HTML code and page output, so it can be downloaded to the client browser upon request. This assembly will be compiled on the first hit from the client, and further requests to the same page will be served by the assembly file again. This provides increased speed and a better user experience.

The CodeBehind class actually inherits from the ASP.NET Page type, which will give your class access to the page intrinsic, and allow it to interact with the postback architecture. You can find this information in the Page directive of a web form, since the CodeBehind file is inherited from the Page type.

Namespace, Class, and Function

After Visual Studio .NET has created the CodeBehind class, the required namespaces are referenced automatically. This can be found from the code sample that we just saw. At a minimum, these need to be the System and System.Web.UI namespaces, though you can see that there are additional ones automatically included. If you need to reference controls on the page and to define the control types, you should reference System.Web.UI.WebControls. You can also include any other namespaces that you require. For example, if you want to access the SQL 2000 Database Server or Microsoft Desktop Engine (MSDE), you can use and import the System.Data.SqlClient namespace; or if you want to create or do manipulation in imaging, you can use the System.Drawing namespace.

In the class of your CodeBehind file, you have to declare public or protected instances of the ASP.NET Server control that corresponds to the control declared on the web page, using the same name (Property of ID) for the variables that the Web Control has. This will create a link between the actual server control and the CodeBehind class. If you have a button on a web form, then the code snippet for this issue is like that shown in Figure 3-40.

```
namespace WebApplicationIntro
{
    /// <summary>
    /// Summary description for WebForm1.
    /// </summary>
    public class WebForm1 : System.Web.UI.Page
    {
        protected System.Web.UI.WebControls.Button Button1;

        private void Page_Load(object sender, System.EventArgs e)
        {
            // Put user code to initialize the page here
        }

        #region Web Form Designer generated code
        override protected void OnInit(EventArgs e)
        {
            //
            // CODEGEN: This call is required by the ASP.NET Web Fo
```

Figure 3-40. *Controls and events are declared and wired in the CodeBehind file.*

Within the CodeBehind class you can create event handlers, procedures, methods, and properties, just as you would with any class. Perhaps you can expose those properties as in an object-oriented manner as well. The events can be event procedures named on server controls in the web page, for example

```
<asp:Button id="btnSave" Runat="Server" onclick="btnSave_Click"></asp:Button>
```

Alternatively, events can be wired in the InitializeComponent() method in the CodeBehind file in C# or with the use of the Handles keyword in VB.NET projects (see Figure 3-41).

```
        /// <summary>
        /// Required method for Designer support - do not modify
        /// the contents of this method with the code editor.
        /// </summary>
        private void InitializeComponent()
        {
            this.Button1.Click += new System.EventHandler(this.Button1_Click);
            this.Load += new System.EventHandler(this.Page_Load);
        }
```

Figure 3-41. *Event wiring in the CodeBehind file in C#*

If you don't let Visual Studio .NET add the event handler for a control, especially when you want to create a dynamic web page or inherit from a master base page, you can add the event handler programmatically:

```
[C#] this.Button1.Click += new System.EventHandler(this.Button1_Click);
[VB.NET] AddHandler Button1.Click, AddressOf Button1_Click
```

Designer Templates

Visual Studio .NET creates a few lines of code for you in your presentation and CodeBehind files. Once you create a new item in Visual Studio .NET, for example, you suppose you want to add a new web user control for your web application. Then you would probably right-click the application name in Solution Explorer, after which you can either Add ➤ Add New Item ➤ Web User Control or Add ➤ Add Web User Control. After that, you can see the screens shown in Figure 3-42, if you turn to Text mode.

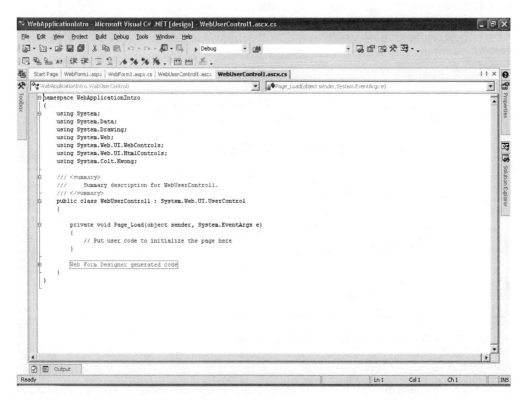

Figure 3-42. *CodeBehind file of a web user control*

This is a basic web user control with only a few lines of code, including the namespace of this application, class name, import of namespaces, the base from which this control inherits, and a Page_Load event handler.

This is very convenient, since we can start coding immediately. In order to further customize the control and tailor it to your needs, there is a trick involving the Designer Template of Visual Studio .NET. For example, suppose you have your own assembly and want to import System.Data.SqlClient in every newly created page automatically. You can modify the base file of the Designer Template, and then add these two things, so that Visual Studio .NET will parse and include them automatically in the next run.

The Designer Template of Visual Studio .NET is stored at (C# Application) *%sysroot%*\Program Files\Microsoft Visual Studio .NET 2003\[*Language*]\DesignerTemplates\[*LocalID*], for example, C:\Program Files\Microsoft Visual Studio .NET 2003\VC#\DesignerTemplates\1033.

Let's look at the previous example in action: Open `NewWebUserControlCode.cs` in the Designer Template folder with Notepad, and the result will look like Figure 3-43.

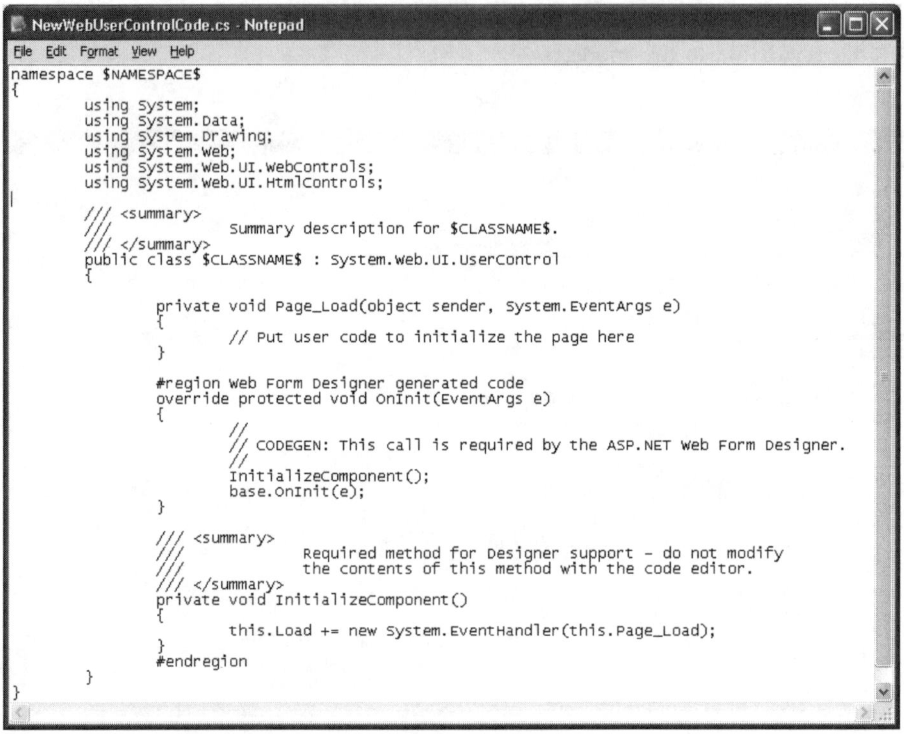


```
namespace $NAMESPACE$
{
	using System;
	using System.Data;
	using System.Drawing;
	using System.Web;
	using System.Web.UI.WebControls;
	using System.Web.UI.HtmlControls;

	/// <summary>
	///		Summary description for $CLASSNAME$.
	/// </summary>
	public class $CLASSNAME$ : System.Web.UI.UserControl
	{

		private void Page_Load(object sender, System.EventArgs e)
		{
			// Put user code to initialize the page here
		}

		#region Web Form Designer generated code
		override protected void OnInit(EventArgs e)
		{
			//
			// CODEGEN: This call is required by the ASP.NET Web Form Designer.
			//
			InitializeComponent();
			base.OnInit(e);
		}

		/// <summary>
		///		Required method for Designer support - do not modify
		///		the contents of this method with the code editor.
		/// </summary>
		private void InitializeComponent()
		{
			this.Load += new System.EventHandler(this.Page_Load);
		}
		#endregion
	}
}
```

Figure 3-43. *Designer template file of a web user control*

This code contains the basic material for a blank web user control. The variables are enclosed between "$" signs; for example, the name of the namespace for the control is $NAMESPACE$, which will be automatically replaced by your actual application name in Visual Studio .NET. In the importation of namespace lines of code, you can modify it as follows:

```
using myApplication.myAssembly;
using System;
using System.Data;
using System.Data.SqlClient;
```

```
using System.Drawing;
using System.Web;
using System.Web.UI.WebControls;
using System.Web.UI.HtmlControls;
```

After that, start up Visual Studio .NET and add a new web user control to your application. Then, when you view the source code of the CodeBehind file in Text mode of Visual Studio .NET, you can see that two more lines have been included in the user control (Figure 3-44).

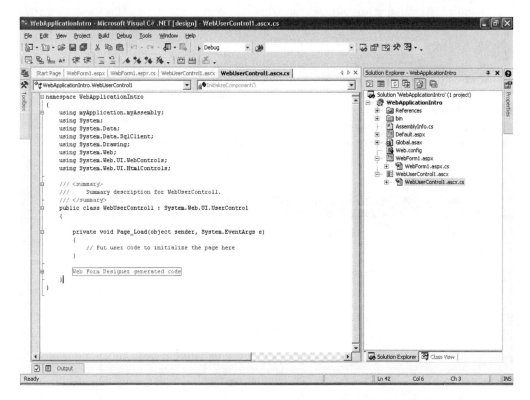

Figure 3-44. *Source of a CodeBehind file after modification of the designer template file*

Cascading Style Sheet

In every web application, the front end is what our visitors see first. In order to make a good impression on our visitors, stable and efficient server-side processing is a must, but we also have to pay attention to the user interface design. Therefore, a cascading style sheet is widely used in web applications, because we can apply it to any web form, and by writing or changing this cascading style sheet file once, a consistent look and feel can be provided for the web application. Using the cascading style sheet is as easy as dragging and dropping the cascading style sheet file onto any web form in the Solution Explorer of Visual Studio .NET.

Let's take a simple example of the creation and use of a cascading style sheet in Visual Studio .NET. Assume that you have a guest book submission web form, with many descriptive texts and textboxes, and two buttons (Submit and Cancel). You would like to change the buttons to a "Flat" look, which is similar to what you see in the Windows XP environment. You can do this in two ways:

- Click on a Button and then press and hold the Shift key, click on another button, and then go to the Properties window and set its BorderStyle to Solid and its BorderWidth to 1px.

- Define a Class in the Cascading Style Sheet and set the border style, width, and color, and add a reference on your web form that you want to make use of the Cascading Style Sheet, and then set the CssClass property of the control(s) accordingly.

In this section we will look at the second approach. The first one is covered in the section on the Properties window; it is limited to changing the property of a control in a single web form. You have to repeat the process if you want to create a consistent look and feel for all controls in all your web pages.

There is no cascading style sheet file in your web application by default, but you can right-click your application name in Solution Explorer, and then look for the Cascading Style Sheet item in the right pane in Add New Item ➤ Style Sheet. See Figure 3-45.

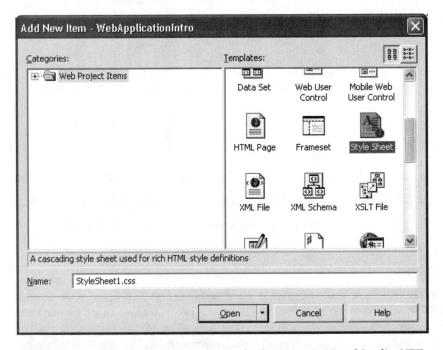

Figure 3-45. *Creation of a new Cascading Style Sheet item in Visual Studio .NET*

After creating the Cascading Style Sheet in your web application, you can see that an element called "body" with empty content was created by Visual Studio .NET, but it is not what you want for this example. You can right-click on the Classes node in the CSS Outline in the left pane of the Designer, and then select Add Style Rule. You can enter FlatButton as the Class name and click OK. See Figure 3-46.

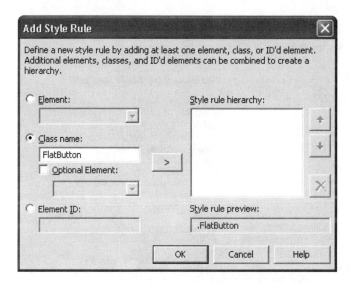

Figure 3-46. *Adding a new style rule in Visual Studio .NET*

After clicking the OK button, you can now define the Style of a Flat Button. In order to make a button look flat, you have to set the top, bottom, left, and right border widths to 1px. One point you should notice is that you can also enjoy the features of AutoComplete and IntelliSense even in writing the Cascading Style Sheet file, so that you can press Enter or the space bar and type only a few words. The result will look like this:

```
body
{
}

.FlatButton
{
    border-top: solid 1px black;
    border-bottom: solid 1px black;
    border-left: solid 1px black;
    border-right: solid 1px black;
}
```

Then, you can drag the cascading style sheet file, StyleSheet1.css, onto your web form in Solution Explorer, and a reference to this cascading style sheet will be created by Visual Studio .NET automatically:

```
<LINK href="StyleSheet1.css" type="text/css" rel="stylesheet">
```

In order to see the cascading style sheet in action, what you should do now is highlight the two Button server controls and then mark the CssClass property of the Buttons to "FlatButton" in the Properties window (Figure 3-47).

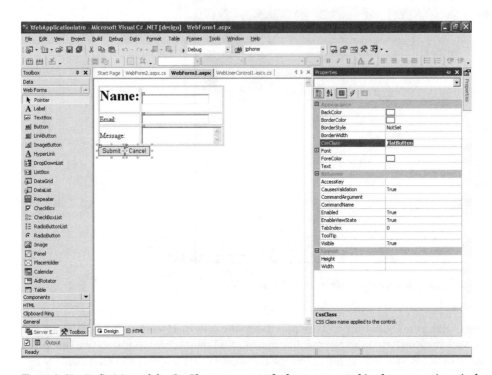

Figure 3-47. *Definition of the CssClass property of a button control in the properties window*

ASP.NET Mobile Web Application

Did you ever think that you would be able to log into an online banking system, retrieve and edit your personal investment plan, or monitor the stock market while traveling or even sitting in a boat on a lake? Using today's mobile/wireless technology, such a situation has become an everyday affair. The most interesting feature about ASP.NET mobile web applications is that you can write your application once, and then you can use your mobile devices, say a mobile phone, to connect to this application and modify your data at your backend database, and all of these changes will be synchronized when you return to your desk in your office. In fact, you could use any of more than 200 different types of mobile devices to do this. (The number of targeted and tested devices with ASP.NET mobile web applications was about 200 at the time of this writing, and this number is continually increasing.)

ASP.NET mobile web applications are an extension of ASP.NET that target mobile devices. You may have experience in developing mobile web applications in ASP.NET with the use of the Mobile Internet Toolkit in Visual Studio .NET 2002, which is a separate download and installation from the Microsoft Software and Developer Network (MSDN) website. The "Mobile Internet Toolkit" no longer exists. It has been integrated into Visual Studio .NET 2003, and now you can select and create an ASP.NET mobile web application from the New Project Template directly (see Figure 3-48).

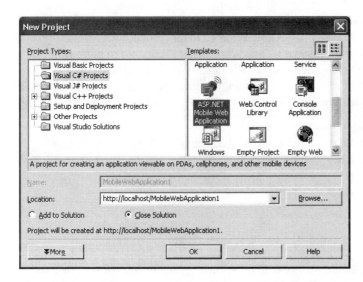

Figure 3-48. *Creation of an ASP.NET mobile web application in Visual Studio .NET*

After creating a new mobile web application, you can see that there is a mobile web form on the Design mode pane of Visual Studio .NET. A big difference between mobile web forms and normal web forms is that you can put more than one mobile web form on a single page, as shown in Figure 3-49.

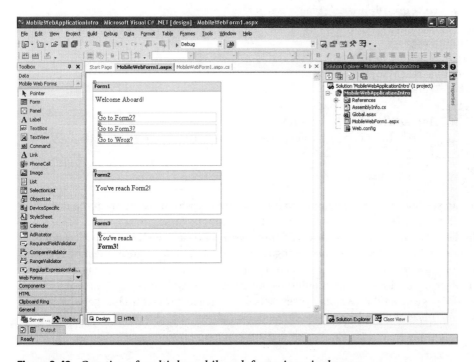

Figure 3-49. *Creation of multiple mobile web forms in a single page*

Mobile controls are an extension of ASP.NET Server controls, which are a collection of controls that can be placed in ASP.NET pages and rendered to different outputs according to the requesting browser. The output may be HTML, WML, or cHTML. You can place multiple mobile web controls on an ASP.NET page because the mobile web form is basically a kind of ASP.NET server control (recall that an ASP.NET web application is composed of server controls and event handlers). You can see this fact from the HTML source code of the mobile web page:

```
<%@ Page language="c#" Codebehind="MobileWebForm1.aspx.cs"
            Inherits="MobileWebApplicationIntro.MobileWebForm1"
            AutoEventWireup="false" %>
<%@ Register TagPrefix="mobile" Namespace="System.Web.UI.MobileControls"
            Assembly="System.Web.Mobile" %>


<HEAD>
    <meta name="GENERATOR" content="Microsoft Visual Studio .NET 7.1">
    <meta name="CODE_LANGUAGE" content="C#">
    <meta name="vs_targetSchema" content="http://schemas.microsoft.com/Mobile/Page">
</HEAD>
<body Xmlns:mobile="http://schemas.microsoft.com/Mobile/WebForm">
    <mobile:Form id="Form1" runat="server">
        <P>Welcome Aboard!</P>
        <mobile:Link id="Link1" runat="server"
                NavigateUrl="#Form2">Go to Form2?</mobile:Link>
        <mobile:Link id="Link3" runat="server"
                NavigateUrl="#Form3">Go to Form3?</mobile:Link>
        <mobile:Link id="Link2" runat="server"
                NavigateUrl="http://APress.com">Go to APress?</mobile:Link>
    </mobile:Form>
    <mobile:Form id="Form2" runat="server">
        You've reach Form2!
    </mobile:Form>
    <mobile:Form id="Form3" runat="server">
        <mobile:TextView id="TextView1"
                runat="server">You've reach<br><b>Form3!</b></mobile:TextView>
    </mobile:Form>
</body>
```

You can see that there is a reference to the `System.Web.Mobile` assembly at the top of the directive of the ASP.NET page. This means that every mobile form control `<mobile:Form/>` is basically a server control from the ASP.NET framework, and each such control will render the correct code to the client browser, according to the server variable of the requesting browser, such as `HTTP_USER_AGENT`, `HTTP_ACCEPT`, and a couple of others related to device capabilities.

Moreover, if you view the CodeBehind file for this mobile web page, you will also find that this ASP.NET page now inherits from `System.Web.UI.MobileControls.MobilePage`, which is the base class for any mobile web page:

```csharp
using System;
using System.Collections;
using System.ComponentModel;
using System.Data;
using System.Drawing;
using System.Web;
using System.Web.Mobile;
using System.Web.SessionState;
using System.Web.UI;
using System.Web.UI.MobileControls;
using System.Web.UI.WebControls;
using System.Web.UI.HtmlControls;

namespace MobileWebApplicationIntro
{
    /// <summary>
    /// Summary description for MobileWebForm1.
    /// </summary>
    public class MobileWebForm1 : System.Web.UI.MobileControls.MobilePage
    {
        protected System.Web.UI.MobileControls.Form Form1;
        protected System.Web.UI.MobileControls.Form Form2;
        protected System.Web.UI.MobileControls.Link Link1;
        protected System.Web.UI.MobileControls.Link Link3;
        protected System.Web.UI.MobileControls.Form Form3;
        protected System.Web.UI.MobileControls.TextView TextView1;
        protected System.Web.UI.MobileControls.Link Link2;

        private void Page_Load(object sender, System.EventArgs e)
        {
            // Put user code to initialize the page here
        }

        #region Web Form Designer generated code
        override protected void OnInit(EventArgs e)
        {
            //
            // CODEGEN: This call is required by the ASP.NET Web Form Designer.
            //
            InitializeComponent();
            base.OnInit(e);
        }

        /// <summary>
        /// Required method for Designer support - do not modify
```

```
        /// the contents of this method with the code editor.
        /// </summary>
        private void InitializeComponent()
        {
            this.Load += new System.EventHandler(this.Page_Load);

        }
        #endregion
    }
}
```

Mobile Controls in the ToolBox

If you open the Design mode of a mobile web form, you can see that there is a list of mobile controls available in the ToolBox in Visual Studio .NET (Figure 3-50).

Figure 3-50. *Mobile web controls available in the ToolBox*

As with a normal ASP.NET web application, you can drag and drop any mobile control from the ToolBox onto a mobile web form, or you can switch to HTML mode by clicking on the HTML button at the bottom of the Designer of the mobile web page, and then do your hand-coding on the mobile web form. Features like AutoComplete and IntelliSense are all totally supported in the mobile web page (Figure 3-51).

Figure 3-51. *Writing a mobile web form with the aid of IntelliSense*

Table 3-4 shows a few of the mobile controls available in the Mobile Web Forms tab of the Toolbox.

Table 3-4. *Names and descriptions of a selection of mobile web controls in the Toolbox*

Control Icon	Control Name	Characteristic
	Mobile Form	A container object that contains other objects for the application's use; more than one mobile form can exist in an ASP.NET page, and it works like a card in a deck.
	Label	Display text to a browser, which can be changed at server side programmatically.
	TextBox	Enable user to input data and allow input of plain text, numeric, or password.
	TextView	A control that works like a literal web control and displays text with HTML tags.
	Command	A control to interact with the user by clicking, resulting in an execution of an event handler at server side.
	Link	Create a simple hyperlink for navigational use.
	PhoneCall	A control allowing the user to call a phone number or to display a hyperlink if the requesting browser does not support this feature.

Continued

Table 3-4. *Names and descriptions of a selection of mobile web controls in the Toolbox (continued)*

Control Icon	Control Name	Characteristic
	Image	Embed an image on the form. A careful declaration on the sources of the image must be made for different devices, because many devices are able to display only a two-color image.
	List	A list of text, commands, or links can be displayed. Navigation or a server-side event handler will be invoked upon clicking. This control can be bound with data from DataSource.
	SelectionList	Similar to a List control, but it has five types: DropDown, ListBox, Radio, MultiSelectListBox, and CheckBox. The selection made on this control does not have to fire a PostBack.
	ObjectList	A more complex list compared with a List control. Each item in this ObjectList is the visual representation of an object. Additional and multiple object information can be defined.
	Calendar	A control that enables the user to select a date. Similar to the Calendar web control but has a much simpler interface.
	TextView	A control that works like a Literal web control. It displays text with HTML tags.

Mobile Capabilities

Once you create a mobile web application that has inherited the characteristic of an ASP.NET web application and put it on the Internet, you have to bear in mind that an unknown number of visitors can visit your site and access your application, and each of them may be using a different device with a different configuration and input mechanism. Therefore, you have to try programmatically to favor as many of the incoming clients as you can. Visual Studio .NET provides a friendly and visual environment for you to do so.

With the entries in the Web.Config file, you can use <DeviceSpecific> and <Choice> elements to customize the output of mobile controls on a mobile web form. This list of capabilities, which is too long to be covered here, is stored in the file machine.config. The elements in machine.config contain information and characteristics of devices such as its screen dimensions and acceptance of cookies. For more information about the configuration of device-specific rendering, please visit: http://msdn.microsoft.com/library/en-us/mwsdk/html/mwcondevicespecificrendering.asp.

Device Filtering

Once you understand the list of mobile devices and their capabilities, you can work on a control and dynamically determine and set customized output for a specific device. Let's take the mobile Image control as an example. If you click on an Image control and look at the Properties window, you will see the screen displayed in Figure 3-52.

Figure 3-52. *Properties of Image mobile web control in the properties window*

You can see that there is an AppliedDeviceFilters property. If you click on the button, the Applied Device Filters window will pop up, as shown in Figure 3-53.

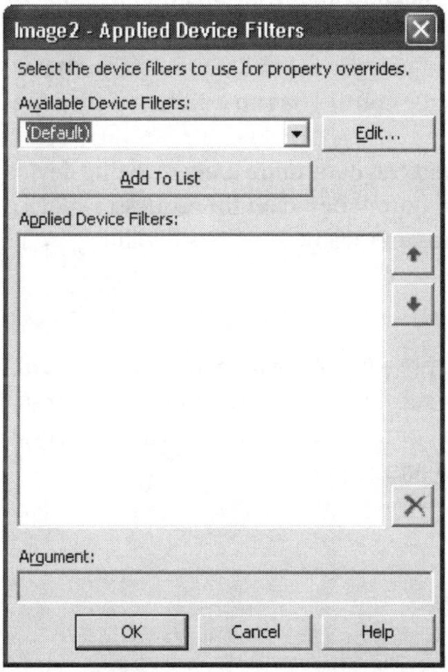

Figure 3-53. *Applied Device Filters per Image mobile web control*

In this window, you can select an item from the current Available Device Filters dropdown list and define the argument for this device. Alternatively, you can click on the Edit button to edit the Type and Argument of the existing filters (Figure 3-54).

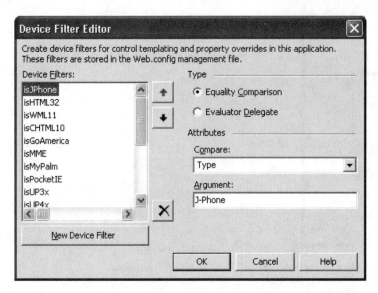

Figure 3-54. *Modification of device filter in device filter editor window*

In addition to the list of the existing device filters, you can also create your own type of filter by clicking on the New Device Filter button. After clicking on it, you can enter a name for that device filter and the values of the attributes of Compare and Argument. If you now click OK and refer to your Web.Config file from Solution Explorer, you can see that a new element has been added. Thus, for example, the imageUrl of the Image control has an additional filtering choice when displaying the image for a new device.

Let's take the Mobile Image control as an example. You can determine the requesting device and force the mobile image control to render customized output based on the requesting device with the tested list in Web.Config, or you can do it programmatically.

DeviceSpecific Controls

With the use of the DeviceSpecific control, you can apply a filter to a form or panel control. Thus you can select a schema to use if the device meets the filtering criteria. In order to do so, you can drag a DeviceSpecific control onto a container control, and then right-click on it and select Templating Options to select a filter, as shown in Figure 3-55.

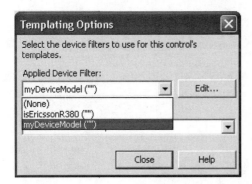

Figure 3-55. *Application of different device filters for a DeviceSpecific control*

Templates

Mobile controls can be displayed using templates, but the display can also be based on the specific device. You can apply different templates to controls from the TemplateOptions as shown in Figure 3-55. There are eight available templates for different controls. We shall not go into them here; additional information can be found in *ASP.NET Mobile Controls Tutorial Guide* (ISBN 1-861005-22-9).

Summary

This chapter presented some historical facts about the web development cycle and *n*-tier architecture. It also covered the properties of web forms and mobile web forms, which are an important focus of Microsoft. You also saw how to utilize the unique characteristics of Visual Studio .NET, such as AutoComplete and IntelliSense.

In summary, this chapter contains the following highlights:

- Composition of a web form

- Files organized in Visual Studio .NET for a web application

- Three working modes for developing a web form: Grid, HTML, and Text

- Creation and use of Cascading Style Sheets

- HTML and Server controls in the ToolBox and the difference between these two types of controls

- Use of the device filtering in Visual Studio .NET to write for a mobile web form target according to various specifications.

CHAPTER 4

■■■

Data Tool Orientation

Introduction

Dynamic applications use a variety of data sources: relational databases, XML data files, or even text files. When we start to write an application, data storage is undoubtedly important. Not only is it used to store company data, but it also contains valuable information about our clients or customers. In order to maximize the performance and efficiency of the application, suitable data storage has to be chosen and partitioned carefully.

Most applications are data-driven. No matter whether you are building a personal home-page, user group portal, online shopping cart, or workflow application, you have to use data storage for your application. Many applications rely heavily on database systems. These include such applications as guest books for a personal homepage, accounting or invoicing, address books, calendars or scheduling applications, blogs, event logging, and online shopping.

Dynamic applications save a great deal of human interaction. It is well known that data sources are used to store information or data, but it is also interesting to note that we can also store our application in the data source. In the world of Internet applications, ASP.NET is the current technology used for building Internet web applications in the .NET Framework. A starter kit provided by the ASP.NET Product Team is called Community Starter Kit. It is an open source application that can be used to run and administer a portal site for user groups. In this application, everything is established dynamically, which means that we can customize default web pages, add modules and functions to this starter kit, or remove them. Even the content or structure of the portal developed by this application is stored in a Microsoft SQL or MSDE database. Therefore, it is highly flexible and customizable for any user group or ISP administrator, so that they can store data, for example upcoming user group activities, in the database, and they can also delete a module by just deleting a record in a database table, because the layout and content of the application are established by reading the data and structure information from the database at runtime. You may be currently working on a project other than this kind of application, but what I want to point out is that a data-driven application or data-driven content can be extremely useful in our daily work.

Therefore, if we want to build an application and utilize the rich ADO.NET infrastructure, a powerful and easy-to-use development tool for data sources is very important for developers like us. Visual Studio .NET provides many useful features, and we can leverage its power to build our applications, often without writing a line of code, or with minimal coding. Thus, our output and performance are greatly enhanced, while development time and cost decrease.

In this chapter, we will walk through the data-related resources and features provided by Visual Studio .NET, and then we can see how we can use Visual Studio .NET to build our data-driven applications in a visual way.

Data Access in .NET

Before we see how we can use the data tool of Visual Studio .NET to facilitate our programming, we can start looking at some basic information about what are we actually working with within the .NET Framework. With this background information, we can understand how Visual Studio .NET is working for us behind the scenes. However, since we will go rather rapidly in the coming sections, you should refer to your .NET documentation, and look particularly for the ADO.NET section, since discussion of ADO.NET is outside the scope of this book. If you want more information on this subject, `http://msdn.microsoft.com/library/en-us/cpguide/html/cpconadonetarchitecture.asp` is a good starting point, and `http://samples.gotdotnet.com/quickstart/howto/doc/adoplus/adoplusoverview.aspx` provides a good introduction through examples.

No matter what database servers you are currently using—perhaps you are using a relational database, or you may be using an XML file as storage only—Visual Studio .NET provides a single way for you to access these database servers easily, and it can save time in development or data manipulation, because Visual Studio .NET normally generates a large amount of code for us. Moreover, we can access different data sources in ADO.NET transparently through Visual Studio .NET.

ADO.NET has several advantages over previous versions, including greater extensibility. ADO.NET takes the existing ADO architecture model and extends it by using the XML model and separating the presentation and data objects into two separate layers. The ADO.NET object model is shown in Figure 4-1.

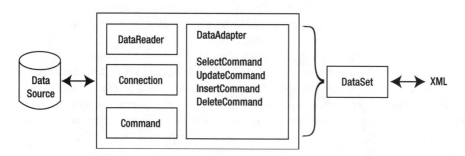

Figure 4-1. *ADO.NET object model*

With the increasing importance of distributed computing, we can use a separate class or library to access the data source in an application. There are three logical layers for a system: the presentation, business, and data layers. If you were using a client/server architecture, you could combine the business and data layers, or you could separate them or even further partition these layers to form a multitiered application. We are going to describe how we can use Visual Studio .NET to manipulate the data in the third layer, that is, how we can work on access to and operations with data for adding, updating, and deleting operations. For instance, we may want to retrieve customer information and display it on a browser. Then the DataReader object will normally be used for data retrieval and display. Or we may want to retrieve a log of messages for reading, in which case we can use the Microsoft Message Queuing (MSMQ) technology to access the message queue for display.

An Overview of ADO.NET

ADO.NET is a set of libraries that comes with the .NET Framework, and we can use it to communicate with various data stores in a .NET application. The ADO.NET classes can be found in the System.Data.dll assembly, which provides interoperability by closely integrating with XML. We can also use it to communicate with Microsoft SQL Server, Oracle, or AS400. The .NET Framework data providers are composed of four core objects. You may not know what exactly each of these objects is or just how they work when you are operating with a Data Source, and although there is only a brief description and a few lines of code here, more detail will be presented in the subsequent sections of this chapter. Visual Studio .NET basically generates all of the necessary code for you with full summary comment. You will see a couple of lines of code in the following paragraph, but it is not necessary for you to memorize or care about this code, since most of it is generated and provided by Visual Studio .NET when you drag and drop the corresponding objects onto the designer pane or customize them through the properties window.

The four core objects in the .NET Framework Data Providers are as follows:

- **Connection Object:** A Connection object provides a connection to the data source with your specific type, location, and other attributes. You can retrieve or update the data source over this connection, and you can declare and initialize it by using

```
Dim myConnection As New _
     SqlConnection("server=COLT;database=Northwind;
                    uid=myUser;pwd=myPassword")
```

- **Command Object:** After connecting to a data source, you can execute commands in the form of an SQL statement or a stored procedure in an SQL Server. Visual Studio .NET allows us to create stored procedures on the fly when we are creating the Command objects with a wizard. This will be covered in the next section. The code would be

```
Dim myCommand As New SqlCommand("SELECT * FROM Products", myConnection)
```

- **DataAdapter Object:** Another option for executing an SQL statement or stored procedure is to use a DataAdapter object. DataAdapters serve as a bridge between the data source and the disconnected objects in ADO.NET, known as DataSets. You can execute the Fill() method of a DataAdapter object to open a connection to the data source and also to move the result into a DataSet or a DataTable for offline use. Here is the necessary code:

```
Dim myDataAdapter As New _
    SqlDataAdapter("SELECT * FROM Products", myConnection)

Dim myDataSet As New DataSet
myDataAdapter.Fill(myDataSet)
```

- **DataReader Object:** a fire-hose-like approach for fetching data. You can retrieve your data or move it to a desired row directly with this object, which uses a lightweight mechanism to retrieve data. Moreover, it will discard the data in the previous row. It is also the underlying working mechanism for the DataAdapter object. Here is the code:

```
Dim myDataReader As SqlDataReader
myDataReader = myCommand.ExecuteReader()
```

.NET Data Provider

.NET Data Provider provides services to ADO.NET. In the age before Visual Studio .NET 2003, if we wanted to connect to a MS SQL Server 7.0 or above, we could have used the native SqlClient Data provider to do so, while we had to use the providers of SQLOLEDB, MSDAORA, and Microsoft.Jet.OLEDB.4.0 for SQL Server 6.5 or earlier, Oracle, and MS Access Database.

If you want to connect to a database through ODBC, you can use the ODBC.NET Data Provider, but this is a separate downloadable package from the Microsoft website. Moreover, we have to use the MSDAORA Data Provider if we want to access an Oracle Database server, but you can forget all these things if you wish, since Visual Studio .NET 2003 now provides all the native and managed providers for these databases.

Recall from the previous section that you cannot find the information about a provider in the connection string when declaring the Connection object, but we could create a new instance of, for example, the SqlConnection class when we wanted to connect to an MS SQL Server. Moreover, you can see that there are different kinds of objects available in the ToolBox of Visual Studio .NET. If it does not appear on your screen, you can press Ctrl+Alt+X to display it in Visual Studio .NET.

You can simply drag the required object and drop it onto the designer pane in Visual Studio .NET, and you can see that the object will be placed in the component tray, and then you can start accessing the database server directly. We don't have to care what kind of provider we are using or download any additional data providers, since all .NET Data Providers ship with Visual Studio .NET 2003, which helps us to carry out all connections and declarations in the background.

A First Taste of Visual Studio .NET

To obtain an understanding of the basic concepts and background information about ADO.NET, and the robust, hierarchical, and disconnected data cache from the .NET Framework, let's try a quick demo showing the use of Visual Studio .NET with a data source. I put this demo in the first part of this chapter because not only does it serve to attract your attention and show how you can connect to a data source and retrieve and display data, but it also demonstrates and reviews the concepts that we discussed in the previous sections. (I would prefer not to build an application from scratch, but instead to read and follow examples in books or the starter kit.)

Let us consider the following situation: You are a high school principal, and you are preparing for an event involving the students and their parents. After obtaining two lists containing information about the students who are to attend this event, you want to make the data available to all the students and their parents. You finally decide to create a web page hosted on your school web server on the Internet and allow public access.

In this example, an MS SQL or MSDE database will be used, and two hierarchical and relational tables will be created. You have a list containing the name of the school and its corresponding classes, and another list showing which class each student belongs to. The design and structure might look something like what is shown in Figure 4-2.

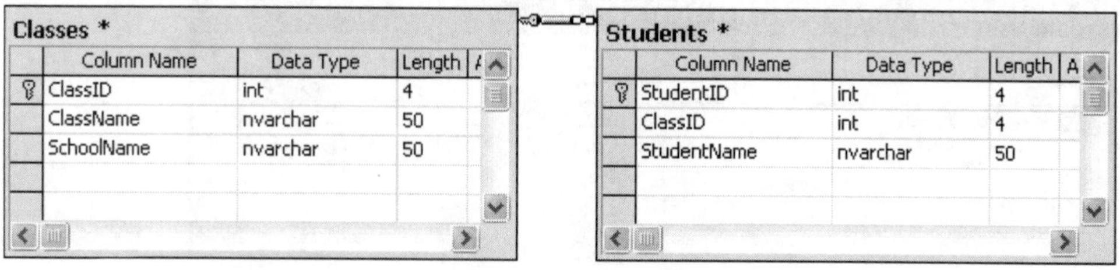

Classes *			
Column Name	Data Type	Length	A
🔑 ClassID	int	4	
ClassName	nvarchar	50	
SchoolName	nvarchar	50	

Students *			
Column Name	Data Type	Length	A
🔑 StudentID	int	4	
ClassID	int	4	
StudentName	nvarchar	50	

Figure 4-2. *Relationship and structure of Classes and Students tables*

In order to start creating this web application, you can open Visual Studio .NET and create a new project by selecting File ➤ New ➤ Project ➤ Visual Basic Projects ➤ ASP.NET Web Application and then entering "http://localhost/StudentInformation" in the location and then clicking OK. The screenshot should look like Figure 4-3.

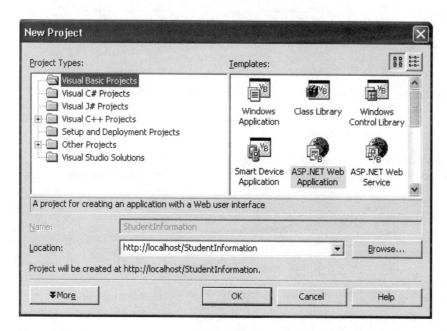

Figure 4-3. *Creation of a new ASP.NET Web application in Visual Studio .NET*

After creating the web application in Visual Studio .NET, you can remove the default web form, `WebForm1.aspx`, and select Add ➤ Add New Item ➤ Data Form Wizard (see Figure 4-4) with its default file name, `DataWebForm1.aspx`, from Solution Explorer.

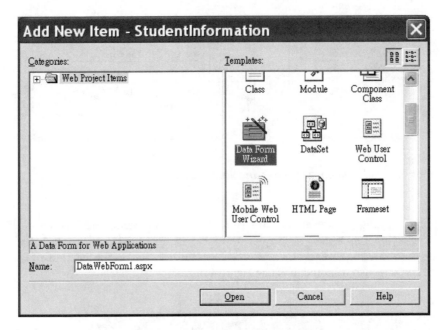

Figure 4-4. *Creation of an item using the Data Form Wizard*

You are now ready to build a complicated Master–Details web form with the help of a DataForm Wizard in just a couple of steps:

1. Click Next in the welcome page.

2. Enter a name for the DataSet that will be used for the data binding of the resultant DataGrids. For instance, you can enter `dsStudentInformation` (see Figure 4-5).

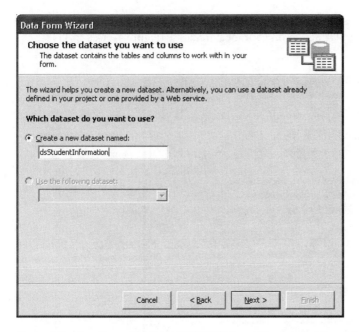

Figure 4-5. *Creation of a new ASP.NET Web application in Visual Studio .NET*

3. Before accessing the database, we first have to create and open a Connection, so we can click New Connection and let Visual Studio .NET create a connection for you, as shown in Figure 4-6.

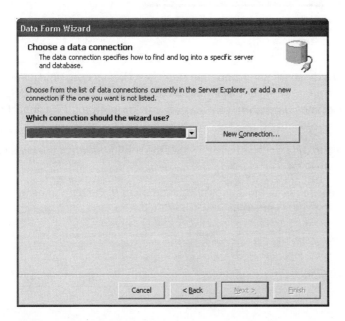

Figure 4-6. *Creation of a new connection for the Data Form Wizard*

4. After that, you can enter the name of your server, or you can enter " . " (for localhost) if you have an MS SQL Server on your local machine (Figure 4-7).

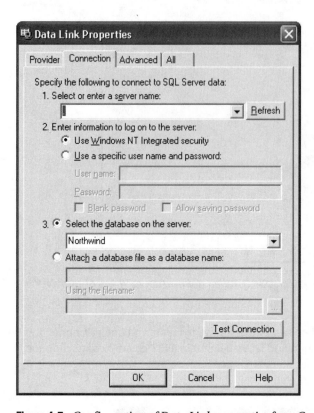

Figure 4-7. *Configuration of Data Link properties for a Connection object*

5. You can now select a database name and then click "Test Connection," and a "Test Connection Success" message will be displayed if there is no problem with the connection. You can also enter a Timeout period or configure another property for this connection by clicking on the Advanced and All tabs.

6. You will be returned to the DataForm wizard when the configuration of the Data Link properties is completed.

7. You can select the two tables in the database and add them to the right pane by clicking on the right arrow (Figure 4-8).

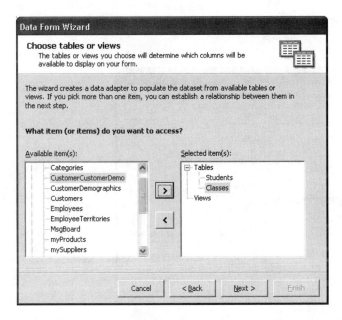

Figure 4-8. *Selection of database tables from the Connection object*

8. You can define the relationship between the two selected tables. First, you should give a name to the relation, then select the value from the dropdown lists and add it to the right pane as shown in Figure 4-9.

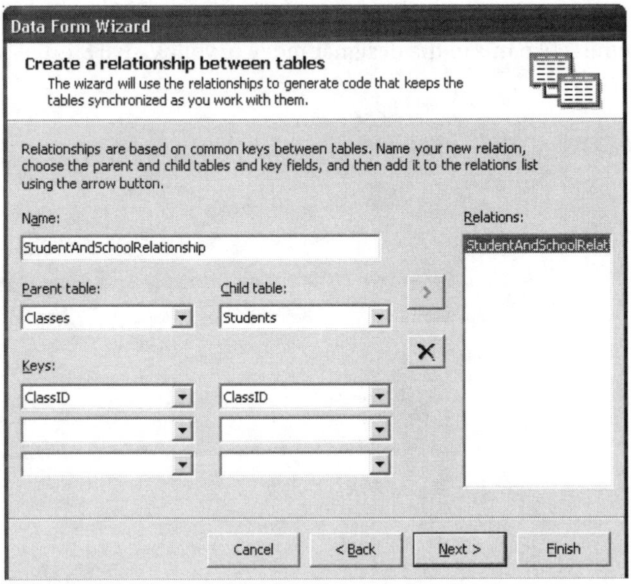

Figure 4-9. *Creation and definition of a relationship between selected database tables*

9. Click Next, and then you can customize the columns to be displayed on screen later (Figure 4-10).

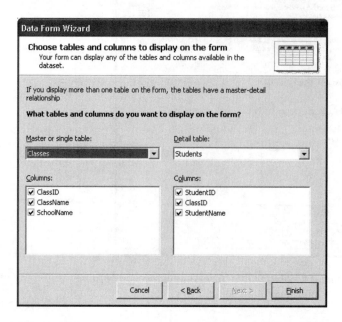

Figure 4-10. *Customization of tables and columns displayed on a form*

10. Click Finish.

That's it. Our Master–Details relational web form for students, classes, and schools is complete. You can see something like this in the designer mode of your Visual Studio .NET now, as shown in Figure 4-11.

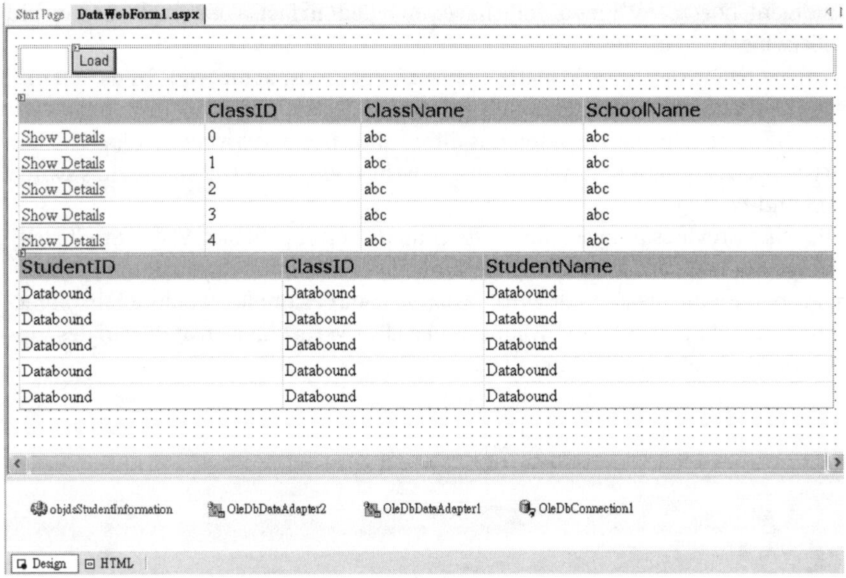

Figure 4-11. *Design layout of Master–Details web form developed by the Data Form Wizard*

Right-click this file name (DataWebForm1.aspx by default) in Solution Explorer, set it as Start Page, and press F5 to see it in action! The result will be like that shown in Figure 4-12.

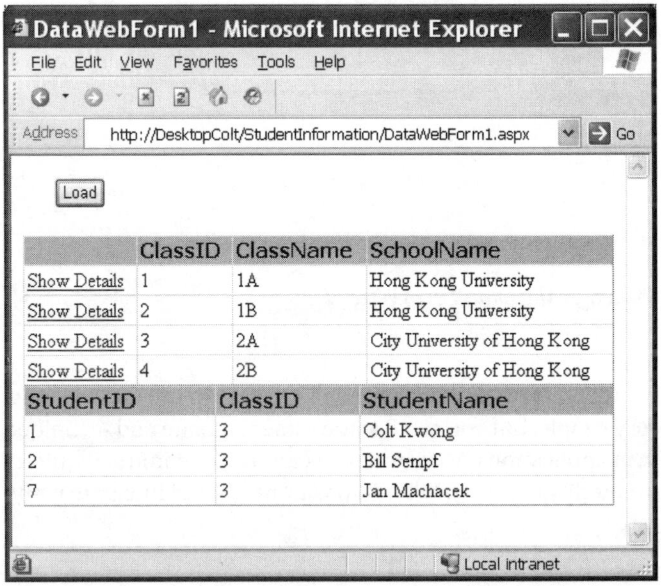

Figure 4-12. *Displaying the Master–Details data web form using the Data Form Wizard*

Up to this moment, how many lines of code have you typed? In fact, a better question would be, how many clicks have you made?

As mentioned in previous sections, Visual Studio .NET does most of the work for us. You may question the value of obtaining a result without typing any code. You may think that you haven't learned anything and your value as a developer is diminished because Visual Studio .NET has automated everything. As a programmer, I also like to write code, and I will sometimes switch to Text mode for hand-coding.

Visual Studio .NET provides many channels for human learning. In fact, Visual Studio .NET does not hide everything and does not endanger our means of livelihood. If you double-click on the generated code behind the file (DataWebForm1.aspx.vb in our example) in Solution Explorer, you can see all the code (Figure 4-13), and what is especially nice is that a great deal of descriptive comment is provided between the lines of code.

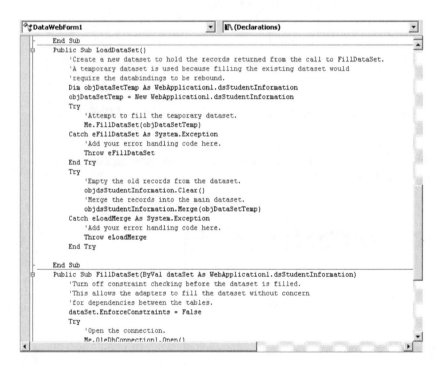

Figure 4-13. *Code behind file generated by the Data Form Wizard*

Customizing and modifying the existing code will hasten your development and learning curve. The previous example is very simple, but you can use the same template and technique in both the Windows and Web Form applications. Moreover, you can see the comments and code, and then further enhance or modify it so as to tailor it to your needs and integrate it into your application.

Data Components in the ToolBox

You can drag and drop data components onto the designer pane and let Visual Studio generate the code for us. The ToolBox in Visual Studio .NET has a Data tab, in which we can drag components onto the designer pane. This would generate the necessary code and event handler for us automatically. For instance, you can create a new web form, name it WebForm1.aspx, and then just drag a database table and a DataGrid control onto it, and you will probably see something like Figure 4-14.

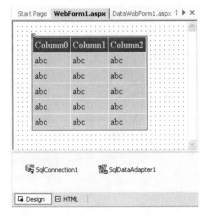

Figure 4-14. *A Database table and DataGrid control were dragged and dropped onto the designer pane.*

The drag-and-drop action eventually generates the code in the code behind the file. The code snippet is shown in Figure 4.15.

```
#Region " Web Form Designer Generated Code "

    'This call is required by the Web Form Designer.
    <System.Diagnostics.DebuggerStepThrough()> Private Sub InitializeComponent()...
    Protected WithEvents SqlSelectCommand1 As System.Data.SqlClient.SqlCommand
    Protected WithEvents SqlInsertCommand1 As System.Data.SqlClient.SqlCommand
    Protected WithEvents SqlUpdateCommand1 As System.Data.SqlClient.SqlCommand
    Protected WithEvents SqlDeleteCommand1 As System.Data.SqlClient.SqlCommand
    Protected WithEvents SqlConnection1 As System.Data.SqlClient.SqlConnection
    Protected WithEvents SqlDataAdapter1 As System.Data.SqlClient.SqlDataAdapter
    Protected WithEvents DataGrid1 As System.Web.UI.WebControls.DataGrid

    'NOTE: The following placeholder declaration is required by the Web Form Designer.
    'Do not delete or move it.
    Private designerPlaceholderDeclaration As System.Object

    Private Sub Page_Init(ByVal sender As System.Object, ByVal e As System.EventArgs) Handles MyBase.Init
        'CODEGEN: This method call is required by the Web Form Designer
        'Do not modify it using the code editor.
        InitializeComponent()
    End Sub

#End Region

    Private Sub Page_Load(ByVal sender As System.Object, ByVal e As System.EventArgs) Handles MyBase.Load

    End Sub

End Class
```

Figure 4-15. *Code generated by Visual Studio .NET after the drag-and-drop action*

We can drag and drop any data component to suit our different system and application requirements. This is because different data components are available for us in the ToolBox, with functionality and features as shown in Figure 4-1 and Table 4-1.

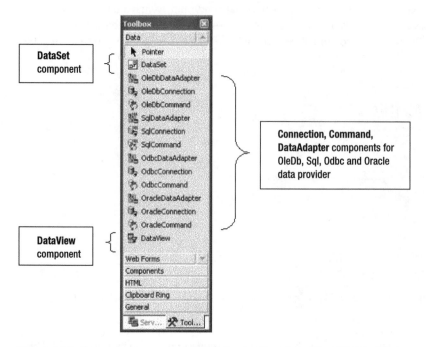

Figure 4-16. *Data components available in the Visual Studio .NET ToolBox*

Table 4-1. *Names and Characteristics of Data Components in Visual Studio .NET*

Data Component Icon	Data Component	Characteristic
	DataSet	A disconnected and cached data object containing multiple DataTable objects
	OleDbDataAdapter	A set of commands and connections used for data query and submitting changes to a data source through OLE DB
	OleDbConnection	An open connection to a data source through OLE DB
	OleDbCommand	An SQL statement or stored procedure to execute operations to a data source through OLE DB
	SqlDataAdapter	A set of commands and connections used for data querying and submitting changes for SQL database server 7.0 or above
	SqlConnection	An open connection to an SQL database server 7.0 or above
	SqlCommand	An SQL statement or stored procedure to execute an operation on an SQL database server 7.0 or above

Table 4-1. *Names and Characteristics of Data Components in Visual Studio .NET (continued)*

Data Component Icon	Data Component	Characteristic
	OdbcDataAdapter	A set of commands and connections used for data query and submitting changes to a data source through ODBC
	OdbcConnection	An open connection to a data source through ODBC
	OdbcCommand	An SQL statement or stored procedure to execute an operation on a data source through ODBC
	OracleDataAdapter	A set of commands and connections used for data query and submitting changes for an Oracle data source
	OracleConnection	An open connection to an Oracle data source
	OracleCommand	An SQL statement or stored procedure to execute an operation on an Oracle data source
	DataView	An object that allows you to view data in different ways (sorted or filtered)

Based on Table 4-1, five major components can be classified: *Connection, Command, DataAdapter, DataSet, DataView.* (Pointer is ignored, and Connection, Command, and DataAdapters of different data providers, with different prefixes, were grouped together, since their functionality and features are the same).

Connection Data Component

In order to access and work with data in a data source, a connection has to be made in advance of any operation. In order to make a connection to a data source, a Connection object first has to be created and instantiated, and Visual Studio .NET provides a couple of ways for us to do this.

Data Connection in Solution Explorer

You can use a Data Connection to create a Data Link with your data source in a wizardlike way. There is a Data Connection node in the Server Explorer of Visual Studio .NET. You can press Ctrl+Alt+S to display it if you cannot see it on the screen.

You can create a Data Connection to your data source by first right-clicking on Data Connection ➤ Add Connection.... Then you can see the screen for editing the Data Link properties, and you can enter the information of your server, such as the server name, login credentials, default database, timeout value, and data provider, as well as other properties (Figure 4-17).

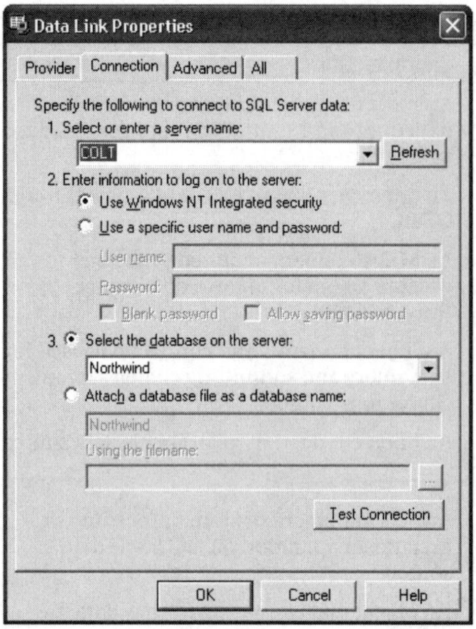

Figure 4-17. *Configuration of a connection in the Data Link properties window*

If you switch to another tab in this screen, you can also select a data provider, for instance, Microsoft.Jet.4.0, Microsoft OLE DB Provider for SQL Server, or Microsoft OLE DB Provider for Oracle (Figure 4-18).

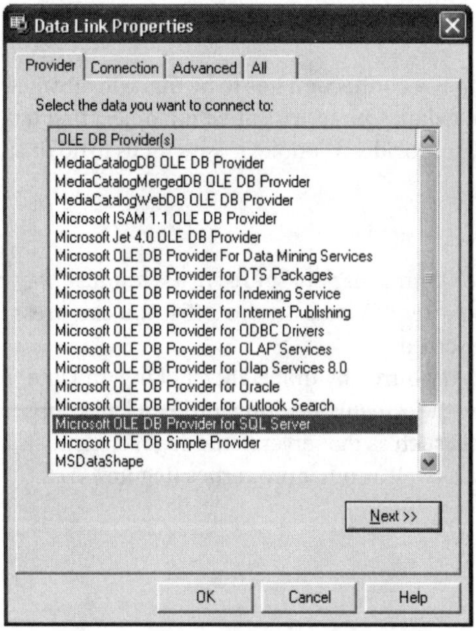

Figure 4-18. *OLE DB Provider for the data source*

After customizing the data link properties, you can test the connection and see whether it is available to use in Solution Explorer (Figure 4-19).

Figure 4-19. *Connectivity from/to data source in Server Explorer*

Connection Object in Solution Explorer

Apart from creating a reusable data link connection object, you can drag and drop data connection objects for different data providers directly from Server Explorer. There are four connection objects for four data providers: OleDbConnection, SqlConnection, OdbcConnection, and OracleConnection. Each of them can be dragged and dropped onto the designer pane of Visual Studio .NET so that it can generate the necessary code automatically.

For example, if you create a Windows form and/or web form with the name "Chapter5Demo1" and then drag an SqlConnection object to the designer, you will see something like what is shown in Figure 4-20.

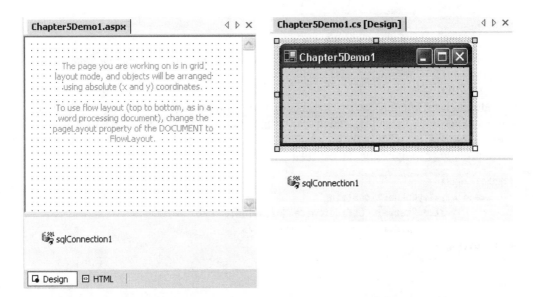

Figure 4-20. *SqlConnection object in Web and Windows Form application designer pane*

An SqlConnection object appears in the Component Tray right under the designer whether you are working with a Windows or web form. This is because the data connection object is an invisible object, and all invisible objects are placed at the bottom of the designer in Visual Studio .NET. This is similar to a Timer control in Visual Basic 6.0 under Visual Studio 6.0.

Connection String of a Connection Object

Configure the connection string of Connection object in the properties window or hand code it. After dragging the Connection object onto the designer, you can customize and work against it in order to open a connection to your data source. You have two ways to configure its properties:

- **Programmatically:** Use as with Visual Studio .NET to generate the following code for a Connection object, for example:

```
Me.SqlConnection1 = New System.Data.SqlClient.SqlConnection
Me.SqlConnection1.ConnectionString = _
        "server=COLT;database=Northwind;uid=myUser;pwd=myPassword"
```

- **Properties Window:** You can set the connection string in the properties window for this Connection object. If you right-click on the Connection object and then select Properties from the Context Menu, then you can see the properties window and specify a connection string such as that shown in Figure 4-21.

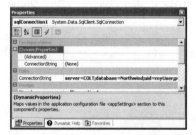

Figure 4-21. *Connection string for a Connection object in the properties window*

Alternatively, not only can you hardcode a connection string for that object, but you can also reference it to a variable stored in the configuration file Web.Config (Web Form) or *ApplicationName*.exe.config (Windows Form). Assume that you have a key–value pair in the XML-formatted configuration file like this:

```
<appSettings>
    <add key="myConnectionString"
        value="server=COLT;database=Northwind;
                uid=myUser;pwd=myPassword" />
</appSettings>
```

After defining a key–value pair in the configuration file, you can right-click on Connection object ➤ Properties window ➤ Dynamic Properties ➤ Connection String and then enter the key of your connection string, for example myConnectionString in the previous example (see Figure 4-22).

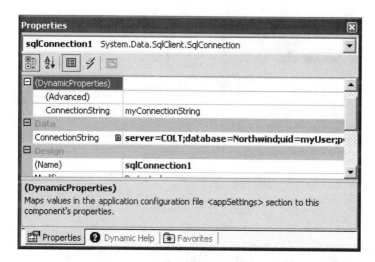

Figure 4-22. *Configuration of connection string of dynamic property for the Connection object*

Visual Studio .NET will look for that key from the configuration file, and then display it in the ConnectionString property under the Data tab, since Visual Studio .NET will generate the code for us behind the scenes:

```
Dim configurationAppSettings As System.Configuration.AppSettingsReader = _
    New System.Configuration.AppSettingsReader
Me.SqlConnection1.ConnectionString = _
    CType(configurationAppSettings.GetValue("myConnectionString",
                        GetType(System.String)), String)
```

If you have defined a Data Link object in Server Explorer, you are able to see and select it from the dropdown list of the Connection String in the Properties Window directly, or create a new one immediately. A screenshot showing the use of a previously created Data Link connection is shown in Figure 4-23.

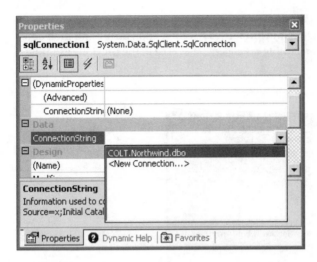

Figure 4-23. *An existing or new connection is available in the properties window of a connection object.*

Event of a Connection Object

Click on the Connection object and define its event in the properties window. You can click on the events button in the properties window to see all events exposed by the Connection object easily, and we can *double-click* on InfoMessage and OnStateChange to write the event handler for these events of a Connection object directly, since Visual Studio .NET generates the following code:

```
Private Sub SqlConnection1_InfoMessage(ByVal sender As Object,
        ByVal e As System.Data.SqlClient.SqlInfoMessageEventArgs)
        Handles SqlConnection1.InfoMessage
...
End Sub
```

Note Alternatively, you can programmatically write an event handler, and then attach it to the Connection object by code, or you can select an object and its associated event handler from the dropdown list at the top of the editor if you are using VB.NET in Visual Studio .NET. See Figure 4.24.

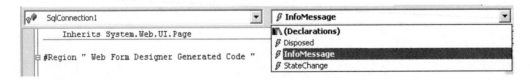

Figure 4-24. *Creation of event handlers with the use of dropdown listboxes at the top of the window*

Command Data Components

A command operation is executed to query and update changes to a data source after establishment of a data connection. If you want to submit a query or update of a data operation to a data source, an established data connection has to be made in advance. There are two classes available that use the Connection object, as shown in Figure 4-25.

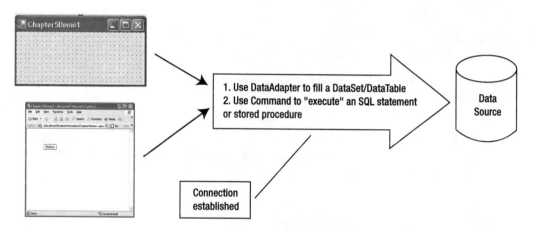

Figure 4-25. *Working with the data source after establishing a connection*

Visual Studio .NET provides four types of Command object for four different data providers: SqlCommand, OleDbCommand, OdbcCommand, and OracleCommand. After establishing a connection to the data source successfully, you can create and instantiate one of these command objects; which one depends on your data provider. Then you can drag the corresponding command object from the ToolBox onto the designer, and two lines of code will be generated by Visual Studio .NET automatically:

```
Me.SqlCommand1 = New System.Data.SqlClient.SqlCommand
Protected WithEvents SqlCommand1 As System.Data.SqlClient.SqlCommand
```

CommandType of a Command Object

For any kind of Command object, there are three types of CommandType (see Figure 4-26):

- **Text (default):** a plain SQL text command

- **Stored Procedure:** a single-execution plan programmed in Transact-SQL

- **TableDirect:** returns rows and columns of table(s) but supported for OLE DB Data Provider only

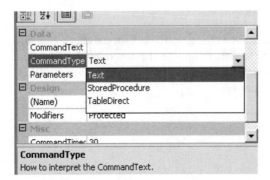

Figure 4-26. *Enumeration of the CommandType property, specifying how a command string is interpreted*

In order to tell this command object which connection it can use, you can select an existing Connection object or create a new one in the properties window, which will pop out the edit of the Data Link properties screen again (Figure 4-27).

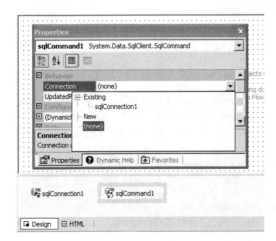

Figure 4-27. *Definition of a connection for the Command object*

Now, you can define your query statement and let it work with the data source. You can do it programmatically, in the way that the corresponding Command and Connection objects were declared, or you can type it in the CommandText field in the properties window. You have two ways to set the CommandText with CommandType's Text mode in the properties window:

- **Manual Typing:** You can type your SQL statement into this field in the properties window. It will look something like Figure 4-28.

Figure 4-28. *Specification of a CommandText in the properties window*

- **Query Builder:** You can pop out a Query Builder in Visual Studio .NET, which is basically much like the Query Analyzer in SQL Server or the query wizard in MS Access database. In order to call it out, you have to click the ellipsis button at the end of the CommandText input box and enter your database server login credentials. Then, you can create a command text from this tool by adding your required database table to the designer, and the relationship will be automatically created for you visually if it exists. You can also select the column in which you are interested, defining the query criteria, sort order, etc. This is much like working in the Enterprise Manager of an SQL Server, where you have to drag and drop in addition to making a couple of "clicks." Then the Query Builder will generate a query for you without any manual coding. The working screenshot is shown in Figure 4-29.

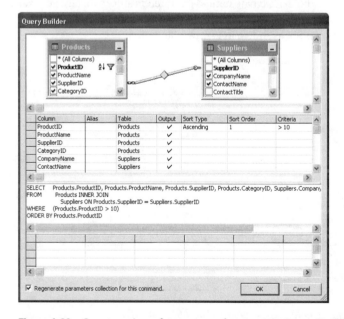

Figure 4-29. *Construction of a command text using Query Builder*

As previously mentioned, you can create a relationship between tables by executing the INNER JOIN instruction between the tables' identity fields, selecting the column(s) (checking the CheckBox), defining an alias to determine which column(s) are to be displayed, setting the WHERE clauses in the criteria field, and setting the direction of data output in the sort type and sort order. You can therefore do everything visually, such as viewing the table relation, by dragging and dropping in the top pane, modifying the SQL statement in the second pane, hand-coding the actual SQL statement in the third pane, and previewing the data in the bottom pane.

Parameterized Query of Command Object

Parameterized queries and parameter collections are another way to represent a query command. No matter whether you use manual typing or the Query Builder to build up your SQL statement, a frequently asked question is, "Why does the database server sometimes interrupt the query and throw an exception?" You obtain an SQL query from either of the two approaches, and your user may enter a string that your application will concatenate into the SQL statement. A frequent occurrence is that of a user entering a single quotation mark, resulting in an exception being thrown. The database server will consider the quotation mark as the first of two, and will look for the second one to complete the SQL statement. When it is unable to find the second single quotation mark, it throws an exception due to an incomplete or invalid SQL query. This kind of exception is by design. However, we can use a parameterized query to avoid this problem, and Visual Studio .NET provides an easy way for us to do so.

Visual Studio .NET provides a wizardlike parameter collection tool. If you want your application to create a query that can be used many times, but with a different value each time, then you may set the criteria of the WHERE clause with a placeholder in the command text and reuse it by passing one or more parameters to this query. A placeholder is a location of the parameter in the query that will be replaced by the values entered by users. You can insert a placeholder (?) into the CommandText, or let Visual Studio .NET create named parameters automatically. For example, if you want to construct an SQL query with two parameters, you can put named parameters in the criteria column in the Query Builder, as shown in Figure 4-30.

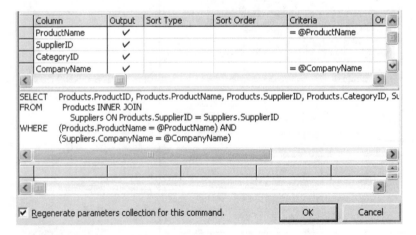

Figure 4-30. *Creation of a parameterized query in Visual Studio .NET*

You can see that the auto-generated SQL statement in the lower pane will generate a WHERE clause with your named parameters, and the CheckBox in the lower left-hand corner indicates that the parameters collection will be regenerated by Visual Studio .NET automatically when you click the "OK" button. If you want to view the parameters collection, you can click OK and go back to the Properties Window (Figure 4-31).

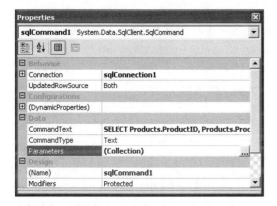

Figure 4-31. *Parameters collection per command object can be viewed in the properties window*

When you create a query with Query Builder, this query will then be displayed in the CommandText field in the properties window. You can click the ellipsis button, and an SqlParameter Collection Editor will pop out, as shown in Figure 4-32.

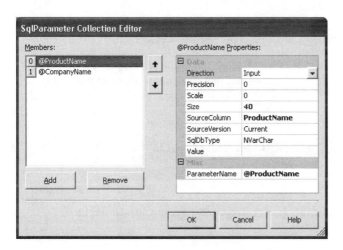

Figure 4-32. *SqlParameter Collection Editor in Visual Studio .NET*

You can add, modify, or delete parameters at this screen, and this parameters collection will be updated to reflect any changes made in the Query Builder if you have checked the "regenerate parameters collection for this command." (Figure 4-33).

☑ R̲egenerate parameters collection for this command.

Figure 4-33. *Checkbox instructing Visual Studio .NET to show the latest query after amendment of the query*

■**Note** For MS SQL queries, you can use "?" as an unnamed parameter and use a parameter beginning with "@"for a named parameter, while you have to use a parameter beginning with ":"for an Oracle database server. Parameterized queries are better than concatenated user-entered values with the Command-Text from both performance and security points of view.

Stored Procedures

A stored procedure is a batch of code programmed in Transact-SQL (T-SQL). It offers better performance than plain SQL statements.[1] Creating a stored procedure requires knowledge of T-SQL, and we can normally "execute" the stored procedure and/or pass parameters to it, so that it can run a batch of commands and then generate a result for the .NET application. Let's say you have a stored procedure in the MS SQL Server to query the Customer Orders information in the Northwind Database. Here is the code for this stored procedure:

```
ALTER PROCEDURE CustOrdersOrders @CustomerID nchar(5)
AS
SELECT      OrderID, OrderDate, RequiredDate, ShippedDate
FROM        Orders
WHERE       CustomerID = @CustomerID
ORDER BY    OrderID
```

You have two approaches to executing a stored procedure in Visual Studio .NET:

- As mentioned in the previous section, you can set the name of the stored procedure as the CommandText with a CommandType equals Text, and then work exactly as in a Query Analyzer, for example:

```
sqlConnection1.Open()
sqlCommand1.CommandText = "EXEC CustOrdersOrders 'HILAA'"
sqlCommand1.CommandType = CommandType.Text

DataGrid1.DataSource =
            sqlCommand1.ExecuteReader(CommandBehavior.CloseConnection)
DataGrid1.DataBind()
```

---

1. You will be able to create database objects in C# or VB.NET in the next version of SQL Server, code-named "Yukon." More information on this can be found at http://www.microsoft.com/sql/yukon/productinfo/top30features.asp

- Set the CommandType to Stored Procedure and set the name of the stored procedure to the CommandText property. An example is shown in Figure 4-34.

Figure 4-34. *Definition of CommandText and CommandType property for the command object in the properties window*

As with a parameterized SQL query, you can input the value of parameters in the SqlParameter Collection Editor directly

---

Note A faster way to use a stored procedure in your application is to drag and drop the name of the stored procedure from Server Explorer in the ToolBox onto the Designer of Visual Studio .NET (Figure 4-35). This will generate a Connection object and a Command object automatically. The Connection object will connect to your SQL server, as when you worked with Server Explorer, and the Connection property of the Command object will be set to point to the Connection object automatically. All you have to do is configure the value of the parameter.

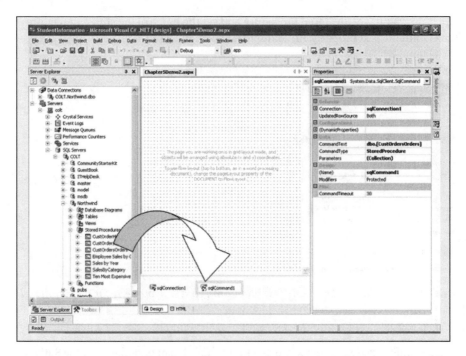

Figure 4-35. *Dragging a stored procedure from Server Explorer onto the Designer pane*

The DataAdapter Data Component

A DataAdapter is able to submit a query and update modified data back to a data source. Acting like an intermediate agent between a data source and a DataSet, A DataAdapter fills data into a DataSet for a query operation so that further data manipulation can be processed in the DataSet without a direct and open connection to the data source and without the need to reestablish a connection with the data source. A DataAdapter can also submit any modification in a DataSet and update the original data source. When the DataAdapter is called, it will create an underlying connection with the data source automatically.

Configuration of a DataAdapter Component

Working with a DataAdapter with a query or update operation can be done graphically, without the necessity of writing code manually. In order to use a DataAdapter to fill a DataSet or update a data source, you can select and drag a selection of column(s) or a table name directly (Database View can also be used if you're using an MS SQL server) from the ToolBox of Server Explorer, and then drop it onto the designer pane, as shown in Figure 4-36.

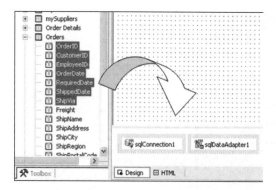

Figure 4-36. *Selection of column(s) of a desired database table from Server Explorer*

You will then see that Connection and DataAdapter objects were created and placed in the Component Tray by Visual Studio .NET automatically. If you look at the code, you will see that Visual Studio .NET had generated the SelectCommand, UpdateCommand, InsertCommand, and DeleteCommand with the default connection and CommandType for you behind the scenes (Figure 4-37).

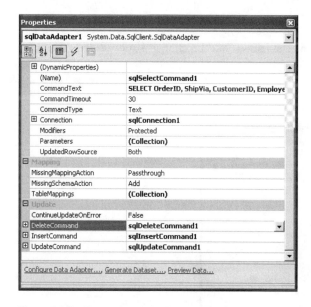

Figure 4-37. *Generation of SelectCommand, UpdateCommand, InsertCommand, and DeleteCommand by Visual Studio .NET.*

You can now configure the DataAdapter and its operations by right-clicking on the DataAdapter object or clicking "Configure Data Adapter ..." in the properties window, which will cause a wizard to appear.

After skipping the welcome screen, you can select an existing Connection object or create a new one by editing the Data Link properties, which is what we covered in the beginning of this chapter (see Figure 4-38).

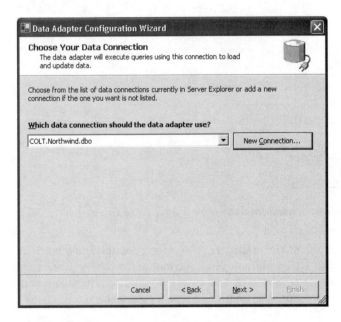

Figure 4-38. *Data Adapter Configuration Wizard*

When a connection object has been established, you can choose a query type in the next screen (Figure 4-39).

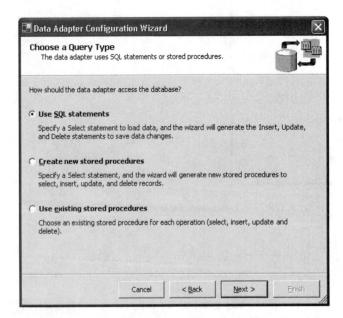

Figure 4-39. *Selection of query type for the Data Adapter object to access the database*

There are three choices of Query Type for your selection:

- **Use SQL statement:** You specify an SQL select statement in this option. You can do so by manually typing or through the Query Builder. The Insert, Update, and Delete statements can also be generated automatically.

- **Create new stored procedure:** A stored procedure will be created in your database by Visual Studio .NET if you choose this option, and no SQL statement in your business logic, but if your database does not support stored procedures, MS Access for example, this option will be disabled by default.

- **Use existing stored procedures:** Here you select an existing stored procedure to select, delete, insert, and update records.

Query Type of DataAdapter Object

If you select the first and second options, you can see a text area in which you can enter an SQL statement or select from the Query Builder (Figure 4-40).

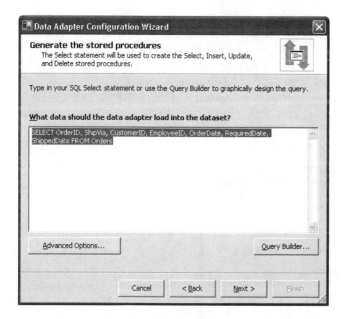

Figure 4-40. *Construction of a query for the DataAdapter object to load data into a DataSet*

This will generate the insert, update, and delete SQL statement or stored procedure according to your choices in the "Advanced Options" (Figure 4-41).

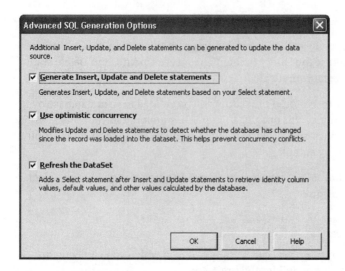

Figure 4-41. *Advanced SQL Generation options of the Data Adapter Configuration Wizard*

If you select the first option, a couple of SQL statements or stored procedures will be created. Select the second option for optimistic concurrency for the operation. You can see a WHERE clause appended to the statement or a stored procedure if this option is checked. The second and third options will be disabled if you uncheck the first one, since it is nonsense to deal with the concurrency issue when users just want to "view" the same set of data.

If you select the "Create New Stored Procedure" option and check the "Generate Insert, Update and Delete statements" option in the Advanced Options dialog, you can then enter the names for these newly created stored procedures, as shown in Figure 4-42.

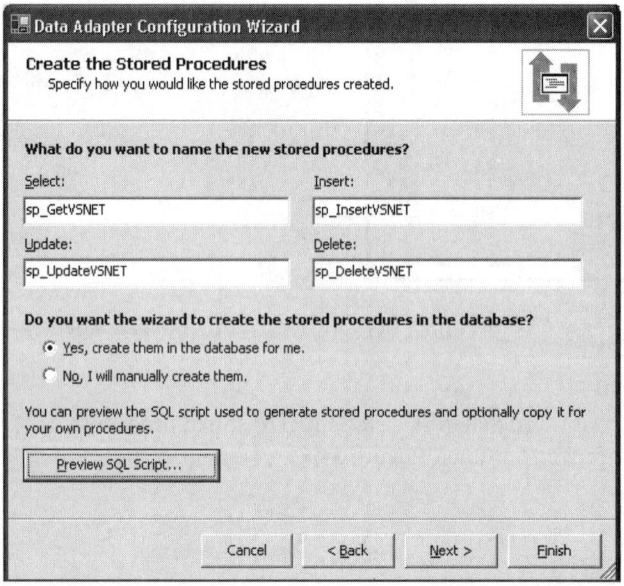

Figure 4-42. *Naming of stored procedure(s) if you want the wizard to create it for you*

You can preview the script generated by Visual Studio .NET by clicking the "Preview SQL Script…" button (Figure 4-43).

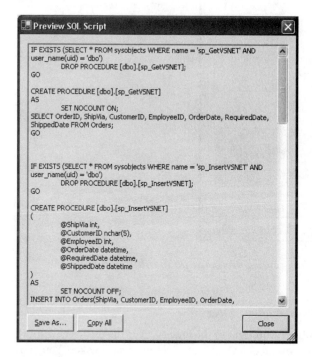

Figure 4-43. *Preview of content of the SQL script by clicking the Preview SQL Script button*

If you have an existing stored procedure in your database server, you can use the third option in the Query Type selection screen. What you have to do in this step is to specify the name of an existing stored procedure for the corresponding operation, and specify the required field for the parameters if necessary (Figure 4-44).

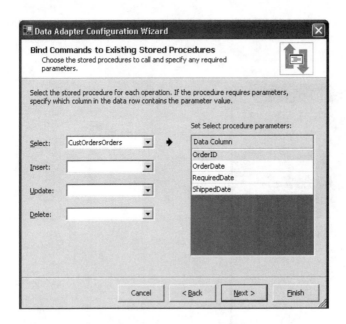

Figure 4-44. *Use and definition of an existing stored procedure for the operation*

Previewing the Data Filled from the DataAdapter Object

After configuration of the DataAdapter object, you can use the Preview Data dialog box to display data or report errors when the SelectCommand of a DataAdapter object was invoked. You can right-click the DataAdapter object to select the "Preview Data..." button, or simply click "Preview Data" in the properties window. Then, you can fill the DataSet that you are using and/or specify the required parameter(s) at the top right-hand corner. This preview action will pop up an alert box if an error occurred in the *fill* process of the DataAdapter. The most frequently occurring problems when a DataAdapter is filling a DataSet are the mismatch of a column name in the database and DataSet, syntax errors in the SQL statement or stored procedure, and data type mismatch. Eventually, the result can be displayed in the Result pane by clicking the "Fill DataSet" button (see Figure 4-45).

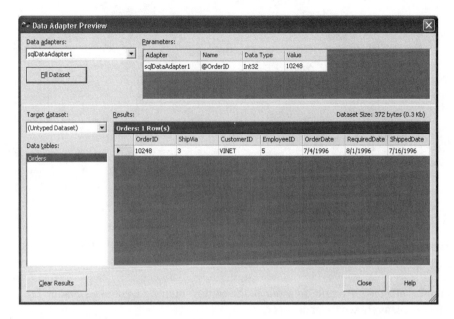

Figure 4-45. *Filling the DataSet and its data*

The DataSet Data Component

A DataSet is a *set* of disconnected and cached *data*. A DataSet contains a set of cached data representing the data physically stored in a relational database. It is stored in memory and has the same structure, name, data type, and data information as in the database. Data can be filled into a DataSet from a physical database, and multiple DataTables are allowed in a single DataSet, in which the constraints, or relationship, between DataTables can be established once the connection has been made. What is nice about DataSets is that once you fill in a DataSet in a connection, you can close the connection at once. The data in the DataSet persist, and you can manipulate these data afterward. Therefore, you can perform any operation on the DataSet, such as deleting a row or modifying a column value, by actually working with the data in active memory and not the database itself.

There are four different types of data provider, each of them with its own Connection, Command, and DataAdapter objects, while there is only one DataSet object in the Data tab of the ToolBox, since you can place data from any data provider in this object into your Windows/web form or Component Designer directly. You may query this set of data or make changes to it, provided that you eventually "update" this DataSet against the actual data source. There are two ways for you to create a DataSet in Visual Studio .NET.

The first way is to generate a DataSet from DataAdapter Objects. When you use a DataAdapter to fill a DataSet, the structure of the data will also be returned, and Visual Studio .NET lets you create a DataSet object based on the DataAdapter objects either by right-clicking the DataAdapter object and selecting Generate DataSet in the context menu, or clicking the Generate DataSet... button in the properties window. A screenshot is shown in Figure 4-46.

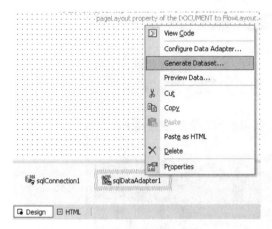

Figure 4-46. *Generation of a DataSet from the context menu by right-clicking the DataAdapter object*

After you have selected Generate Dataset... in the context menu, a Generate DataSet dialog box will pop up, as shown in Figure 4-47.

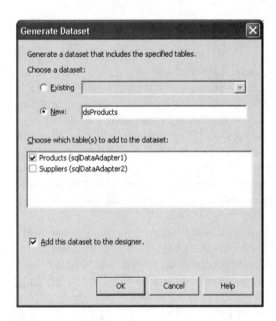

Figure 4-47. *Configuration of a DataSet in the wizard*

The dialog box allows you either to create a new DataSet or to modify an existing one, and the name of the DataAdapter object(s) created in your designer will be displayed, too, which lets you know which DataAdapter object you want to use to build your DataSet. You can use a CheckBox located at the bottom of the dialog box to let Visual Studio .NET create a visual instance of the DataSet on the component tray of the designer pane, so that you can configure the properties of the DataSet through properties window easily.

A file with the name of your DataSet but with a .xsd extension will be created and included in your project by Visual Studio .NET automatically. This file actually contains the schema information of the DataSet. You can double-click this file and use the Visual Studio .NET XML Schema Designer to edit it (see Figure 4-48).

Figure 4-48. *A DataSet with extension XSD generated by Visual Studio .NET*

The .xsd file actually contains the schema information for the DataSet. The data in the DataSet can persist without a direct connection to the data source because of the XML file, which stores the schema information of the DataTable(s) in the DataSet, so that you can add, update, or delete data in/from the DataTable(s) correctly. You can see that the letter E appears in the .xsd file, which represents a DataTable as an element of the DataSet, while the DataColumns such as ProductID, ProductName, ... are elements of the DataTable. This forms a hierarchal structure of the DataSet, and you can add, update, or delete any elements in this DataSet through the properties window by highlighting any element (Figure 4-49).

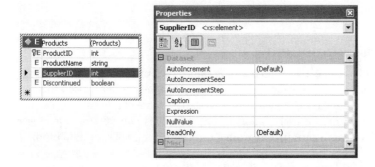

Figure 4-49. *Element of the DataSet indicating the structure of the DataTable*

The second way to create a DataSet in Visual Studio .NET is to create a DataSet from the Toolbox or Solution Explorer. Apart from creating a DataSet based on a DataAdapter object, you can also create a DataSet by double-clicking or dragging a DataSet component from the Data tab of the ToolBox onto the designer pane. Then an Add DataSet dialog box will pop up, as shown in Figure 4-50.

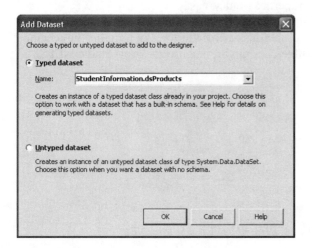

Figure 4-50. *Typed and untyped DataSets in the wizard*

You can create a typed or untyped DataSet from this dialog box. Typed DataSets inherit from the DataSet class and provide strongly typed methods, events, and properties, in which you can access tables and columns by name instead of using collection-based methods. For example,

```
myDataSet.Products.ProductName;
```

Another nice feature that Visual Studio .NET provides is "IntelliSense" for strongly typed DataSets when you are hand coding; an untyped DataSet is an instance of the DataSet class without schema information.

The DataView Data Component

A DataView object is a view of the data of a corresponding DataTable. After filling a DataSet from a DataAdapter object, we obtain a set of data at that moment. A DataSet acts like a disconnected mode of a relational database, and a DataTable acts like a database table of this database, while a DataView object acts like a view in a normal relational database; that is, you can use a DataView object to view, filter, sort, and search certain data from a DataTable for display or data binding to controls.

You can create a DataView object for DataSet from the ToolBox. Unlike a DataSet, you cannot create a new DataView object by selecting and adding a new item in Solution Explorer. You have to click on the Data tab of the ToolBox, and then double-click or drag a DataView object onto the designer pane. Assume you have previously dragged a certain number of columns from a database table onto the designer pane, and you have already created a DataSet object from the DataAdapter object. You can now drag a DataView object, which will be placed in the Component Designer again (Figure 4-51).

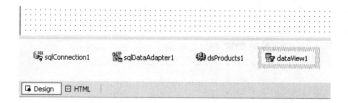

Figure 4-51. *Dragging a DataView object from the ToolBox onto the designer pane*

As DataView is a kind of "view" of data based on a corresponding DataTable, and a sample DataTable (dsProducts in the previous example) has been filled by the DataAdapter object (sqlDataAdapter1 in the previous example), so that you can select a DataTable with which the DataView object will be used from the properties window (Figure 4-52).

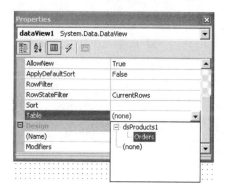

Figure 4-52. *Composing a table member from a DataSet object*

After the DataAdapter object has filled the DataSet object, you can sort, filter, or search data in the DataView object directly, or you can bind it to a List Control, as shown, for example, in Figure 4-53.

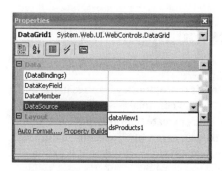

Figure 4-53. *Binding a DataView object to a list control*

■Note There are two options when you click the dropdown list for DataSource in the properties window. You may feel confused from the previous sections, since a DataSet can contain multiple DataTables, but how can you bind a DataSet to a single list control? The reason is that there is a shorthand way of writing the binding of a DataSet object to a list control, such as a DataGrid control, whereby the first DataTable in this DataSet will be used and bound to the DataGrid control by default.

Like other controls, you can customize the DataView object's properties programmatically or through the properties window by entering static or dynamic properties from a configuration file (Figure 4-54).

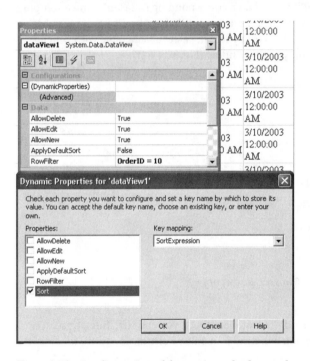

Figure 4-54. *Configuration of dynamic and advanced properties for a DataView object*

Using Third-Party Data Access Components in Visual Studio .NET

Easy compilation and deployment of reusable components is one of the key features in the .NET environment. Using Visual Studio .NET, you can develop custom controls, assemblies, or components in a visual and easy way, since VS .NET will compile and/or create self-descriptive metadata for assembly, so that we can use XCOPY methods to deploy an assembly. Therefore, a number of commercial control and data access components are available in the market. It is extremely easy to purchase and integrate these kinds of components in Visual Studio .NET, and we will see how this can be done in the next section.

It is fairly simple to add a reference to a third-party data access component and let it become a part of Visual Studio .NET. The ASP.NET Product Team develops a free development tool for ASP.NET developers, which is called ASP.NET Web Matrix. There is a data access component in this tool, called SqlDataSource control, that is available only in Web Matrix. By using this control, ASP.NET developers can connect to an MS SQL server and bind it directly to any databinding control. I will highlight and go through the use of this control quickly, since it is beyond the scope of this book, but you can take a look at *Beginning Dynamic Websites with ASP.NET Web Matrix* (ISBN: 1-86100-792-2) for a detailed description and explanation of ASP.NET Web Matrix.

Connecting to a Data Source Through an SqlDataSource Control in Visual Studio .NET

If you want to use the SqlDataSource control from Web Matrix in Visual Studio .NET for your ASP.NET web application, which actually comes from a DLL in the Web Matrix installation path, for example `C:\Program Files\Microsoft ASP.NET Web Matrix\v0.6.812\Framework Microsoft.Matrix.Framework.dll`, then you can use this control in Visual Studio .NET and bind data to a list control in three steps. That's right, three steps with drag-and-drop action only:

1. Drag the control file to the ToolBox in Visual Studio .NET (Figure 4-55).

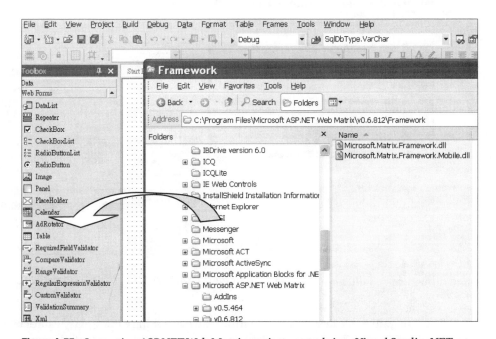

Figure 4-55. *Importing ASP.NET Web Matrix project controls into Visual Studio .NET*

2. You can see that there are three new controls available for use in the ToolBox. You can drag one of the new controls named "SqlDataSourceControl" and also an MxDataGrid control onto the designer pane (Figure 4-56).

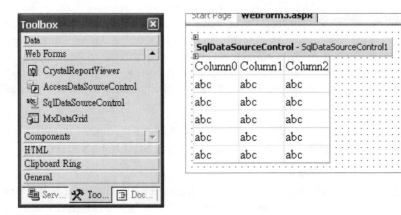

Figure 4-56. *SqlDataSource and MxDataGrid controls are available in the ToolBox and designer pane*

3. Now you can see that the SqlDataSource control is ready for you, and you can configure the properties like Connection String and Select Command and then bind the configuration to the DataGrid control (Figure 4-57).

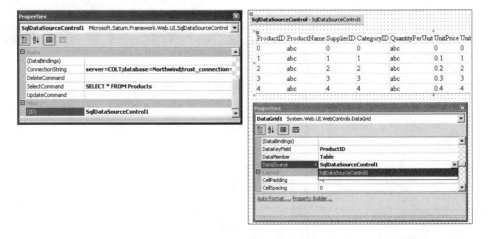

Figure 4-57. *Configuration of properties for the SqlDataSource and MxDataGrid controls*

There is considerable flexibility in importing and consuming a third-party data access control in Visual Studio .NET. You can manually register any third-party control/component by right-clicking the Reference node in Solution Explorer, followed by browsing and selecting the third-party assembly. See Figure 4-58 for an example.

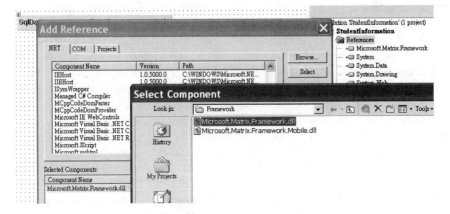

Figure 4-58. *Adding a reference to a third-party control/component*

You can also create a new tab for easy navigation and customization of components in your Toolbox. You can right-click in any tab of the Toolbox and select Add/Remove Item, and then you can select and see your component in the Toolbox immediately.[2] For an example, see Figure 4-59.

Figure 4-59. *A new component and tab in the ToolBox*

---

2. For more information about creating and using third-party controls in VS .NET, you can take a look at the MSDN Library at `http://msdn.microsoft.com/library/en-us/dnaspp/html/ ASPNet-NewSrvrCntrls-WebMatrix.asp`, `http://msdn.microsoft.com/library/en-us/dnaspp/html/ aspnet-usingtreeviewiewebcontrol.asp`, and `http://msdn.microsoft.com/library/en-us/dnaspp/html/ aspnet-buildmenuservercontrol.asp`.

Visual Studio .NET = Rapid Application Development

Not only does Visual Studio .NET provide an integrated development environment for developers; it is also a Rapid Application Development (RAD) tool. We know how to use Visual Studio .NET to access a commonly used database server, such as a relational database or file-based database, but the functions and features of Visual Studio .NET are far more extensive than this. We can use it to create an application rapidly and thereby greatly improve our productivity. Since the cost of hardware is no longer a major consideration for application development or production and today there are highly educated and highly skilled developers throughout the world, there is great competition as to who can complete and deliver the best software product. Visual Studio .NET is an effective tool in this competition, since it can provide a visual and integrated environment for building applications in different languages and for working with any objects on top of the Common Language Runtime (CLR), especially if we are working in the enhanced .NET Framework v1.1. Moreover, we have available the Data Access and component tools in Visual Studio .NET, which provide plenty of easy-to-use tools, including Server Explorer, Object Browser, Component Designer, and Properties Window.

Server Explorer

Working with the Server Explorer is similar to dragging and dropping controls from the ToolBox onto the designer pane. Server Explorer is basically a kind of Microsoft Management Console, which allows us to see all the server resources on any network server, whether connected or disconnected. A screenshot of a Server Explorer is shown in Figure 4-60.

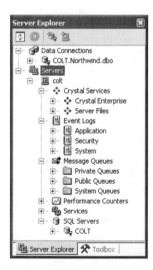

Figure 4-60. *Server Explorer in Visual Studio .NET*

You can use Server Explorer to make a data link to a database, which is what we covered earlier in the chapter, and you can also use it to consume system resources on a local or a remote server, provided that you have the IP number or computer name of the remote server. You can obtain a tree view of the services, tools, or resources as in Figure 4-60. With the use of this

Server Explorer, it is not necessary to open multiple tools and windows and then hide an uncontrollable number of windows in the task bar, or switch between Query Analyzer, development tool, and snap-in of the management console repeatedly. You can expand the Server Explorer and control most of the resources on your local and remote machines. The data connection was covered in the early sections. The first node under the Server node is called Crystal Services, for which you are referred to the documentation from Crystal Decision for more information. The other items will be covered in the following sections. All of the objects found in the Server Explorer are invisible objects, which means that they will appear in the Component Tray under the designer pane only.

Event Logs

You can create and generate an event log programmatically for investigation and notification purposes regarding your system and applications. Scanning a log file for a server in order to monitor network traffic and the health of your system, you can open the Event Viewer to see the event log of your system and trace what has been going on in your system. Formerly, if your application generated an error or hung up the system, you could dump this event and relevant information into a text file for further investigation or at most send an email to notify the system administrator. Now you can view the event log by clicking and highlighting an entry of the Event Log in Server Explorer, and then you can see the properties of the log in the properties window (ReadOnly), as depicted in Figure 4-61.

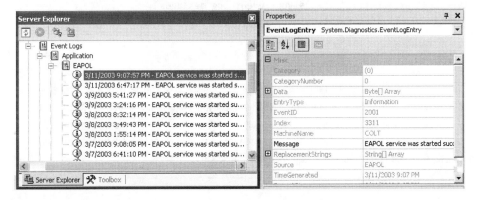

Figure 4-61. *Event logs and their entries are available in the Server Explorer and Properties Window, respectively*

Moreover, you can drag an Event Log object from Server Explorer and drop it onto the designer pane, and you can now write code to work with it inside your application, so that you can record any event into the system event log from your application programmatically. This is one of the nice features about error handling in .NET applications, whose use can be summarized as follows:

1. Drag an event log entry from Server Explorer to the designer pane.

2. Programmatically configure the properties of an event log object such as the machine, source, and log name, or configure it in the properties window as shown in Figure 4-62.

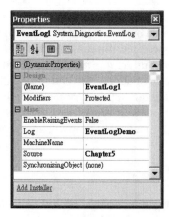

Figure 4-62. *Configuration of properties of an event log object in the properties window*

3. You are able to write an entry in the system event log in your application:

```
If Not EventLog.SourceExists("Chapter5") Then
        EventLog.CreateEventSource("Chapter5", "EventLogDemo", ".")
End If
EventLog1.WriteEntry("Here is your event log messages", _
                        EventLogEntryType.Information)
```

> **Note** I used an ASP.NET web application as an example, since it requires special handling compared with a Windows form application, since every incoming HTTP request will use a weak account—ASPNET—to access the application, which might show an "Access Denied" message if you use this account with the previous code by default, and a modification of a user account or an impersonation will have to be made if you want to use the Event Log object for an ASP.NET web application.

Message Queues

A message queue is a stack of messages that you can store or send as a batch. One possible use of message queues is in an online forum. You may subscribe to a thread in which you are interested, and then you will be able to receive notification of any reply posted. Normally, the forum application may make use of the message queue to store the notification messages in a folder, which are then picked up by another process asynchronously, so that there is no blocking or delay in sending email. Such an arrangement would have yield better performance and minimize your system's overhead, since it won't have to loop through the tables of subscribers and send out a notification message to each of them in the event of a new message being posted. You can use an existing folder or create a new one for message queuing in the Server Explorer or programmatically insert or send out a message for a queue. If you choose to drag a message queue to the designer pane, a new instance of a MessageQueue object will be created for you automatically. See Figure 4-63.

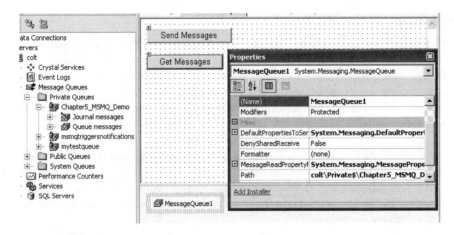

Figure 4-63. *Creation of a MessageQueue object from the drag-and-drop feature*

As shown in the figure, a new instance of a MessageQueue object named MessageQueue1 was created when you dragged a queue from the Server Explorer onto the designer pane, so you can send and receive messages from the queue programmatically by using something like the following:

Send messages in the message queue:

```
If MessageQueue1.GetAllMessages.Length > 0 Then
    MessageQueue1.Delete("colt\Private$\Chapter5_MSMQ_Demo")
End If

Dim counter As Integer
For counter = 0 To 9
    MessageQueue1.Send("Demo Message " & counter.ToString, "Chapter5 MSMQ Demo")
Next
```

Retrieve messages from the message queue:

```
Dim Messages As System.Messaging.Message
Dim myStringBuilder As System.Text.StringBuilder

If MessageQueue1.Exists("colt\Private$\Chapter5_MSMQ_Demo") Then
    For Each Messages In MessageQueue1.GetAllMessages
        myStringBuilder.Append(Messages.Body.ToString)
    Next
End If

Response.Write(myStringBuilder.ToString)
```

Performance Counter

Monitoring performance is extremely useful for both the pre- and postrelease of an application, and it provides good user experience. Apart from just focusing on what the application has to accomplish, an application must exhibit good performance, and that's why developers normally have to monitor and stress test an application during development, on both the staging server and the production server. Since users or visitors may abandon your application and choose another one if yours is extremely slow or unresponsive, no matter how powerful and full of features it is otherwise.

Performance monitoring and collection of such data can be applied at the level of the system or of the application. There is a PerformanceCounter object in the Server Explorer of Visual Studio .NET, and you can use it to keep track of the status of your system or application. Expanding the node of the performance counter, you can see many objects available for investigation and monitoring (see Figure 4-64).

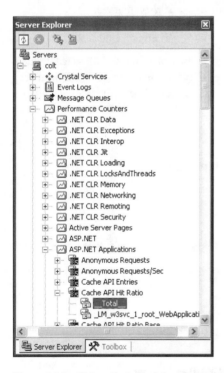

Figure 4-64. *Object listing of the performance counter*

If you want to monitor a particular application, you can open and drag the object, as shown in the figure, and then drop it onto the designer pane, resulting in a new instance of this PerformanceCounter object being created by Visual Studio .NET automatically. Next, you can configure it through the properties window or programmatically work with it.

Let's say you want to monitor a web server by monitoring the total number of occurrences of "Request Not Found" (Error 404). You can drag the object from Server Explorer onto the designer pane, as shown in Figure 4-65.

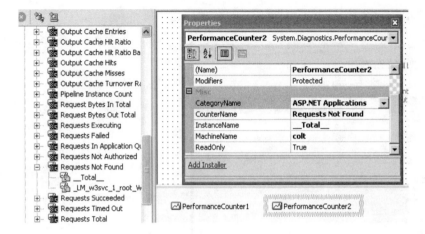

Figure 4-65. *Creation of a PerformanceCounter object by using the drag-and-drop feature in VS.NET*

You can view the properties of each PerformanceCounter object in its properties window, or you can write code to work and display its value for your reference, like the following:

```
Private Sub Page_Load(ByVal sender As System.Object,

ByVal e As System.EventArgs) Handles MyBase.Load
    lblMessage.Text = "Total Number of ""Request Not Found"" occurred: " & _
                        PerformanceCounter2.NextValue.ToString()
End Sub
```

The result of this counter will be displayed if the client attempts to access a nonexistent URL (Figure 4-66).

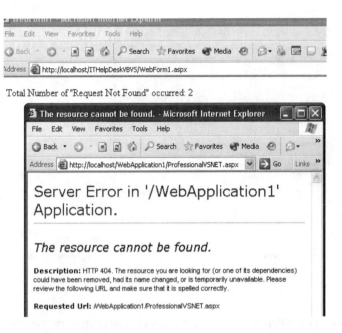

Figure 4-66. *A screen shot and result of the occurrence of the "Request not found" counter*

Properties Window

Everything is an object in .NET. Since .NET prefers an *n*-tier architecture with an object-orientated approach, everything can be treated as an object. Each object has its own methods and properties, which is what we learn in school. But how in fact can the properties window be applied in this context? The details of the properties window were mentioned in Chapter 1 of this book, so I will just highlight a couple of points that every developer can use for application development.

Every method and property can be adjusted or triggered in the properties window. Let's say you have a DataGrid for data access in an ASP.NET web application and you want to customize its appearance. You may switch to HTML mode and write an HTML tab with style and color for your DataGrid manually, or you could actually do it in a faster and more convenient way through the properties window. In the designer pane of Visual Studio .NET, you can click on the DataGrid, and the properties will show all the available properties for that DataGrid, as shown in Figure 4-67, and then you can apply a formatting style or define the column or properties for your DataGrid by clicking the Auto-Format button.

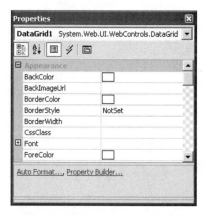

Figure 4-67. *Configuration of property of DataGrid control, for example "Auto Format" with the use of the properties window*

In addition, you may want to fire the ItemDataBound event of the DataGrid so as to fire an event handler after an item is data bound to the DataGrid control. In this situation, there are three approaches that you can use:

- Mark the event handler inline with the declaration of the control:

```
<asp:DataGrid id="DataGrid1" Runat="Server"
            OnItemDataBound="DataGrid1_ItemDataBound" .../>
```

- Register the event manually by switching to the code behind page and then manually entering the following:

```
Private Sub DataGrid1_ItemDataBound(ByVal Sender As Object,
                          ByVal e As DataGridItemEventArgs)
                          Handles DataGrid1.ItemDataBound
...
End Sub
```

- Trigger an event handler in properties window. Honestly, the result of this approach is the same as with the second approach, while the point is that the code is done by Visual Studio .NET automatically. Since we would not want to memorize all the available events and properties of all controls, or we might somehow forget the event arguments even if we remember the events, Visual Studio .NET therefore allows you to view all the available events and properties of a control in the properties window. You can click on the flash icon, and then you can view the available event handler for that control (see Figure 4-68).

Figure 4-68. *Manipulating with event handlers in the Properties Window*

You can double-click an event name, for example "ItemDataBound," so that an event handler with the name *ControlID_EventHandlerName* (for example DataGrid1_ItemDataBound) will be created and registered on the page by Visual Studio .NET automatically, and the generated code is as follows:
[VB.NET]

```
Private Sub DataGrid1_ItemDataBound(ByVal Sender As Object,
                            ByVal e As DataGridItemEventArgs)
                            Handles DataGrid1.ItemDataBound
...
End Sub
```

[C#]

```
private void DataGrid1_ItemDataBound(object sender,
                    System.Web.UI.WebControls.DataGridItemEventArgs e){
...
}

this.DataGrid1.ItemDataBound += new
System.Web.UI.WebControls.DataGridItemEventHandler(this.DataGrid1_ItemDataBound);
```

Object Browser

The object browser shows you detailed information about objects and base classes. If you choose View ➤ Object Browser from the menu, click the icon, press the shortcut key Ctl+Alt+J or double-click on an assembly in the Reference subfolder in Solution Explorer, an object browser will be opened in the designer pane. This object browser shows all the objects and their members, for instance namespaces, classes, interfaces, types, events, methods, and properties. The object browser will show not only the objects in the .NET Framework, but also the structure and information about the component of your project, referenced component, or third-party components. A screenshot of an object browser is shown in Figure 4-69.

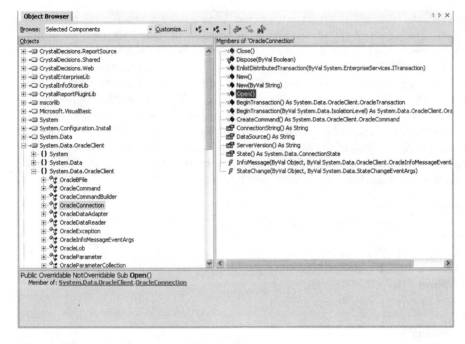

Figure 4-69. *Object Browser available in VS.NET*

There are three main panes for the object browser

- **Objects pane:** The available namespace and objects

- **Members pane:** The member belonging to the selected object in the objects pane

- **Description pane:** The syntax, usage, and description of the selected objects or members in the objects or members panes

The object browser allows you to browse, search, and learn. As I mentioned in the previous section, no one is able to know all of the namespaces, classes, and interfaces in the .NET Framework, since the whole .NET Framework is made up of several thousands of classes.[3] Therefore, a tree view showing all available objects in the object browser is extremely useful for developers, especially for Control Developers. For instance, a control developer may write a custom control that inherits from a DataGrid control, from which he can get the benefit of all the existing control work, as well as being able to override those features that should be changed. At this time, the developer probably wants to know the underlying interface and all the available methods and properties of the control that should be inherited, while the object browser is definitely a great reference tool.

Searching for similar items and XML documentation files can be done in the object browser, whereas XML comment results can be displayed in a tooltip at runtime through reflection.

---

3. Lutz Roeder created a tool called "Reflector for .NET," which is a class browser for .NET components. You can view it at http://www.aisto.com/Roeder/DotNet. Reflector Add-Ins are maintained at http://workspaces.gotdotnet.com/reflector.

When you select and highlight an object in the object and member panes, you can right-click this object and do a search on any similar item(s) by selecting the Quick Find Symbol option from the context menu. You can also write a summary comment in your code, and these comments will be displayed in the Description pane in the form of an XML Documentation file. This is a really cool feature provided by Visual Studio .NET, but you can see it in action only for applications written in C#.[4] The result and configuration of this XML Documentation file can be found at the menu of Project ➤ Properties or by right-clicking your project and selecting "Properties" in Solution Explorer. You can then go to Configuration Properties ➤ Build, and then you can specify the path of the XML Documentation file to be processed. If you have something like the following in your code, you can see the comment in the description pane of the Object Browser if you browse to your application (see Figure 4-70):

```
/// <summary>
/// This method is used for evaluating the ranking based on the score
/// </summary>
private string Ranking(int score) {
    if ( score > 50 ) {
        return "foo";
    }
    else {
        return "bar";
    }
}
```

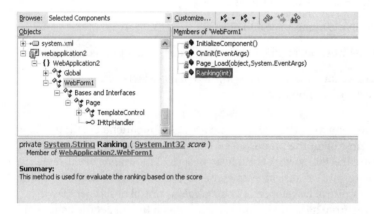

Figure 4-70. *Comments in code are available in the description field in the object browser.*

Component Designer

Designing and partitioning business logic in components is a universal rule for application architecture. The .NET Framework v1.1 and CLR provide rich functionality for application

---

4. You can apply XML comments to your VB.NET code by using VBCommenter (http://www.gotdotnet.com/team/ide) of the PowerToys, and this feature will be officially available in VS.NET Whidbey. Please refer to the chapter on "Whidbey Preview."

developers. Since using component-based architecture is not a new thing, you may have applied this approach in your pre-.NET applications. With components in an application, not only can you benefit from encapsulation of code and structure, but you can also reuse these components across applications or perhaps with different languages.

One can develop methods and properties for components in Visual Studio .NET visually. One of the nice features of Visual Studio .NET is the Component Designer, which you can use for designing and programming in the designer pane of Visual Studio .NET, which means that you can easily connect to a data source with any .NET data provider from Server Explorer, drag and drop an object out of the ToolBox, configure the object through the Properties Window, and double-click to write code for that object. You can use the component designer in Visual Studio .NET by, for example, adding a new component to your project. Right-click your project in Solution Explorer, select Add Component in the context menu, and select Component Class, or you may select Add Component from the Project menu. See Figure 4-71.

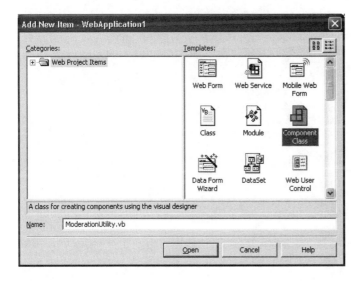

Figure 4-71. *Creation of a Component Class in VS.NET*

Summary

This chapter has covered the orientation of data tools in Visual Studio .NET, which provide a visual and drag-and-drop technique for programming. We introduced data access in the .NET environment, ADO.NET, and its data provider, including a quick demo showing a hierarchical data structure in Visual Studio .NET through a couple of clicks.

This chapter also explained the major data components found in the Data tab of ToolBox in Visual Studio .NET:

- Connection Data Component

- Command Data Component

- DataAdapter Data Component

- DataSet Data Component

- DataView Data Component

In showing how to integrate a third-party data access component in Visual Studio .NET, we also saw the resources and services listed in the Server Explorer of Visual Studio .NET. The Server Explorer includes the resources on your local or remote machine, and items that we mentioned are as follows:

- Event Log

- MSMQ

- Performance Counter

- Properties Window

- Object Browser

- Component Designer

CHAPTER 5

■ ■ ■

Mobile Client Development

Visual Studio is filled with mobile development tools. In this chapter, I'll explore with you two key areas of mobile development:

- Mobile Web application development

- Smart device development

In the first part of this chapter, I'll run you through mobile web applications, which are much more like ASP.NET applications than anything else. Many controls work in both the standard and mobile worlds, and program much the same as well. Mobile Web refers to websites, deployed on IIS, that are viewable by a variety of devices, from cell phones to Pocket PCs. To work with these sites, mobile devices need to have Internet access to the server on which the application is deployed, just as PCs need to have access to ASP.NET web applications.

In the second half of the chapter, I'll discuss Smart Device development with you. Smart Device development is tightly integrated, and the documentation clearly states what is and isn't included in the mobile .NET Framework. Smart Device applications are programs built directly for Smart Phones or Pocket PCs using the .NET framework, just as we would write Windows Forms applications for a PC running Windows XP.

The mobile tools didn't quite make it into the 1.0 release of Visual Studio, except in the ill-fated MIT and SDE add-ons. The 2003 release, however, does mobile development right. Mobile web forms, formerly MIT, and mobile windows forms, formerly SDE, are much better represented this time around.

In this chapter, you'll learn the following elements of mobile development across both Mobile Web applications and Smart Device development:

- ASP.NET controls for the mobile browser

- Windows forms controls on different devices

- Debugging mobile device applications

- Special problems of mobile development

- Security in the mobile world

- Accessibility aspects of mobile applications

- Creating a Smart Device application

- Key differences between .NET CF and the main .NET Framework

- Pocket PC platform development and .NET CE

When you finish this chapter, you'll be able to make a strong determination about the format your mobile application needs to take. Then, you'll be able to use the power of .NET to develop mobile applications with the approach that works best for your projects.

Mobile Web Development

Websites for mobile devices are just like websites for PCs. They reside in IIS, on a Windows server. They have navigation, controls, and images. They are even viewable in a regular web browser, though they usually aren't very pretty. The only effective difference is in the controls themselves, which are designed to render properly in a number of mobile devices' built-in browsers. This is because of the ASP.NET Mobile Framework.

The .NET Mobile Framework

Let's get started talking about the ASP.NET Mobile Framework by looking inside. The lifecycle of a mobile ASP.NET page is not much different from a normal page. Remember, the pages are still generated from a normal IIS server, but they have to handle the intricacies of the mobile controls.

First, let's review the lifecycle of the ASP.NET model, as outlined in Figure 5-1.

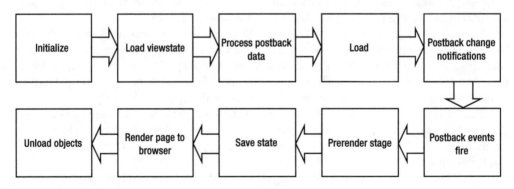

Figure 5-1. *The ASP.NET lifecycle*

The differences are slight, but very important. Let's take a look at them one by one:

- The **Initialize** stage is focused on choosing the DeviceAdapters. The ASP.NET components review the details of the header sent by the client browser, and set all baked-in and customized device code.

- **Load** is essentially the same as Initialize, but the device-specific controls (which include essentially all of them) have specific overloads to handle the differences in browsers. This happens behind the scenes, but it is important to know about it. If you plan on overriding the OnLoad method of the page, know that you may need to handle the Adapter.OnLoad method as well.

- In the **PreRender** stage, mobile form pagination is "automagically" performed.

- **Render** has essentially the same differences as Load. The DeviceAdapters Render method is called for each control, to ensure correct rendering in each browser for each control.

- **Unload** is also device-specific.

Another important behind-the-scenes detail is the concept of containers and adapters. Let's start with containers.

Mobile web forms are divided conceptually into three parts. The page is the traditional ASPX file collection. The Form is like a Panel in normal web applications. It represents a navigational or organizational structure that we can use to handle the fact that mobile pages often don't scroll, especially when we are dealing with mobile phones. Finally, we have the control itself, which is the textbox or calendar in the form, on the page. See Figure 5-2.

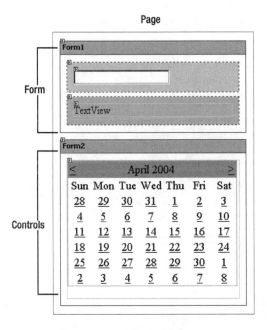

Figure 5-2. *Parts of the Mobile Web form*

Adapters are classes that sit between your ASP.NET code and the mobile controls and provide device-specific rendering. There are (as of May 2004) 265 tested devices, and creating new adapters is easy to accomplish.

Adapters are relatively transparent to us as developers. However, if you are working on an unusual platform, or trying to do something that is not supported by the framework out of the box, you must first turn to the adapter to make your changes. Envision the adapter as a proxy, sitting between your ASP.NET code and the final application that is delivered to the client device.

Microsoft has accomplished partnerships with the vast majority of device and browser manufacturers. You can find detailed lists on `http://www.asp.net/mobile`. The device manufacturers are shown in Table 5-1.

Table 5-1. *Device Manufacturers Supported at Press Time*

Device	Manufacturer
@Migo	NetFarm
Alcatel	Nokia
Audiovox	NTT DoCoMo
Benefon	OKWap
BenQ	Openwave
Casio	Orange
Compaq	Palm
Cyberbank	Panasonic
DoCoMo	Pantech&Curitel
DOPOD	Personal
Ericsson	Philips
Fujitsu	Psion
Handspring	RIM
Hitachi	Samsung
HP	Sanyo
IBM	Sharp
Jataayu	Siemens
JTEL	Sony
Jungle	Sony Ericsson
Kyocera	Sony Ericsson
Legend	Sprint Denso
LG	Sprint LG
Microsoft	TCL
Mitsubishi	T-Mobil
Motorola	T-Mobile
NEC	Toshiba

The browsers, which differ tremendously, include those shown in Table 5-2.

Table 5-2. *Browsers Supported by ASP.NET Mobile Controls*

Browser	Supplier
ACCESS	Microsoft
AU-Systems	NATE Browser
AvantGo	Nokia
Blazer	NTT DoCoMo
Ericsson	OEM
EZOS	Omnisky
GoAmerica	Openwave
Grand	Opera
Handspring	Original Equipment Manufacturer
ilinx	Palm
Infraware	Panasonic
i-page master	Qualcomm
Jataayu	Sony Ericsson
J-Sky Viewer	Symbian

New device adapters can be added by Microsoft and its partners through Device Updates, available from http://www.asp.net, or you can roll your own with the new Mobile Internet Toolkit. The <mobileControls> section of Web.Config helps to define adapter sets:

```
<mobileControls
    allowCustomAttributes="true➤false"
    sessionStateHistorySize="historySize"
    cookielessDataDictionaryType="System.Web.Mobile.CookielessData"➤"">
    <device
        name="name"
        inheritsFrom="parentAdapterSet"
        predicateClass="predicateClass"
        predicateMethod="predicateMethod"
        pageAdapter="pageAdapterClass"
    >
    <control name="controlClass" adapter="adapterClass" />
        <!--More adapter classes can be added-->
    </device>
</mobileControls>
```

I don't have space to cover device adapter development here, but if you are working outside the range of browsers or manufacturers specified in the tables, search MSDN for "asp.net device specific adapter code" for more information.

Designing for Mobile Devices

We have a lot of thinking to do on the topic of design before we ever start to develop for this platform. There is no keyboard, no mouse. Users are on the move, and working on wireless networks. There is no browser with 90% of the market, as there is on PCs. Essentially, everything is different.

Yet, Visual Studio hides much of this from us with the device adapters, as we have just seen. The complexity of various browsers and manufacturers isn't our problem until we get under the hood. For most of what we do, it is only the traditional design issues we need to deal with.

Navigation

By far the most important consideration in mobile development is navigation. Before an application can be built, a comprehensive site map must be constructed. This site map needs to take into consideration the platform.

If you, as the developer, don't have a mobile device, get one. If you have one, use it. There is nothing like standing on a bus trying to navigate a mobile web application that requires you to click on a four-pixel square to commit a transaction.

Mobile webs need to be small and flat (Figure 5-3). A site map can have as many as nine outgoing navigation points on any page, as long as they make sense to the user in the context of the page. The trick is to make the site no more than three levels deep, which leaves us with 9^3 potential pages in the site, which is really too large for the platform, but it's a reasonable upper limit. If you can't do it in that, don't do it.

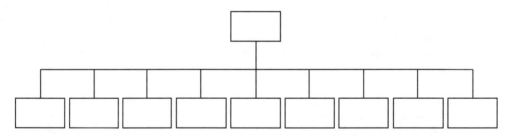

Figure 5-3. *Wide and flat navigational schemes*

Visual Studio doesn't have many baked-in navigational controls for mobile forms. When building applications, you are left with the ItemPager class, the ObjectList, and a roll-your-own solution as the only options.

The ItemPager is used to move between pages of items in a control. On a phone screen, which might be only 30×40 pixels, pagination needs to occur automatically. In the prerender phase of the lifecycle, pagination gets sorted by each control that needs to consider it; often the Form objects top that list, also Lists, LiteralText, and ObjectList, which we will cover soon.

If you need to handle custom pagination, the `ItemPager`, in coordination with `ObjectList`, is the tool of choice. To handle pagination manually, set the Paginate property of the containing Form to False. Once that is complete, it works very similarly to a datagrid, with `PageCount`, `CurrentPage`, and `PagerStyle` properties as specified by the device adapter in question.

The ObjectList (Figure 5-4) is essentially a List class with delusions of grandeur. As a templated control:

- It is databound only.

- It allows the view of multiple properties of an object, as opposed to a control like a DropDownList.

- It handles multiple commands per object, as in the user pressing 1, 2, or 3 while an object is selected.

- It supports pagination, per the ItemPager.

Figure 5-4. *The ObjectList icon*

You also have the opportunity to roll your own solution. Aside from just relatively simple links between pages and good design, you have the option to make User Controls just as you do in web forms.

Another roll-your-own concept is the linked form. There is no NAME reference in an anchor tag in mobile web, so we have to carefully consider the linking of our forms. The MobileLink (Figure 5-5) is the key to this.

A Link

Figure 5-5. *The Link icon*

In the NavigateUrl parameter, just as we would do with an HTML page, we can refer to the form and control using a pound sign:

```
#control:formName
```

Within a given page, then, we would link between two forms with this Link control:

```
<mobile:Link runat="server" NavigateUrl="#Form2">Next</mobile:Link>
```

If we needed to link to a subcontrol, as a name reference would, we use a colon in the URL:

```
<mobile:Link runat="server" NavigateUrl="#Form2:Panel2">Next</mobile:Link>
```

Figure 5-6 shows how this looks in the designer.

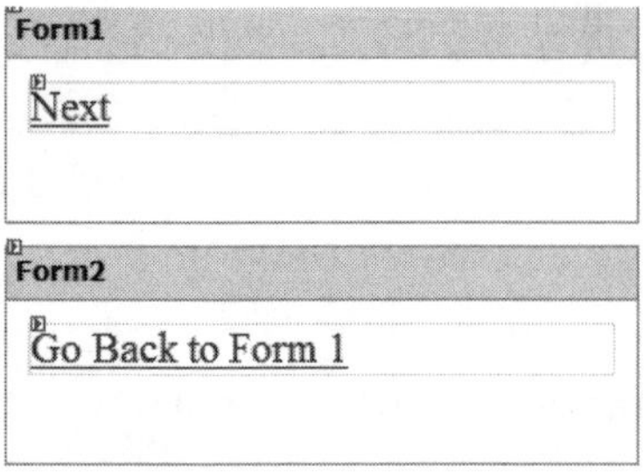

Figure 5-6. *Navigation with forms*

In the same line as the linked form is the Panel (Figure 5-7), which you can use to organize your content, especially when it comes to hiding and showing information. This works just like a traditional web application.

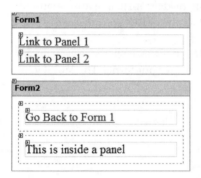

Figure 5-7. *Navigation with Forms and Panels*

The key to navigation, though, is design. Don't get lazy; map your site. Lay out every inter-action with the user, every page. Ask yourself, "Is this really necessary?" See whether there is a better way to get there from here. Review the design of the site. Take the time to go over it with users. They will thank you later.

Input Considerations

How a user gets input into your application isn't your concern as a web developer, but catering to those input methods is a concern. Here are a few rules of thumb:

- Don't make the user input things more than once. If they have to type in an email address to log in, remember it next time.

- Once they have logged in to an application, don't ask them for stuff you know. Make a round trip to the database and look it up.

- Don't put more than four related fields on a page. If there is only one field of a particular type, put it by itself.

- All multipage input needs to be in wizard format. Tell your users how far they are in the process, and change pages for them when you can.

There are a few classes that meet your development needs here. The first is the most basic: the Mobile Form. We have covered the Form ad nauseam, and will do again later, so I won't cover it again here.

Another class that is of interest is the CookielessData class, excellent for storing information about a session when the platform doesn't support cookies, as is the case with most phones.

Highly Selective Features

When you are developing a PC web application, often the users want everything and the kitchen sink. Sometimes they are right.

When developing a mobile web application, use Occam's Razor everywhere. Question every feature, twice. To keep the total number of pages to 729 or fewer, and the total number of steps to fewer than three, you must filter every feature to the bare minimum.

There are no Visual Studio features to assist with filtering features; it is a scope issue. If you need inspiration, look at the total number of controls in a default install of the Mobile Web, about a fourth of what is available for traditional Web development. Mobile devices simply do less.

A Look at the Mobile Controls

The mobile controls are what make Visual Studio the tool it is for mobile development. Some of these controls are truly awe-inspiring in their complexity, with the way they handle multiple devices with such ease. Let's look at a few examples.

Mobile Input Controls

The input controls accept input from the user other than just an event. The mobile web controls very closely match the corresponding controls for the full browser ASP.NET, but of course take device into consideration. For this reason, the choices are relatively limited.

We will focus on most of the differences, rather than the functionality. These controls inherit the vast majority of their functionality from the ASP.NET controls of the same name, so much of what they do is the same. To allow custom attributes, say for a feature on a device that is not normally supported by a web application (like a camera, perhaps), set the appropriate property to true in the `System.Web` section: `<mobileControls allowCustomAttributes="True" />`. Here is a description of the available mobile input controls:

Textbox: Text in the Title property is displayed on phones. Single line only. Size property is number of characters. Phones support a Numeric property.

Selection List: Pagination not supported in this class. DataBinding is supported. Multiple selection is supported also, like the ListBox.

Calendar: Varies tremendously based on browser. HTML browsers look like what one would expect from an ASP.NET control; phones give user option to type date, or select each portion separately.

Command: Essentially a button for submission events. HTML renders an input tag with a BR, and phones render an anchor with an onClick handler. Avoid special characters in the URL, especially spaces.

Validation

The validation controls, and the validation classes represented by the controls, are almost exactly as in ASP.NET. Because of polymorphism, the various methods that make the validation classes a reality work against a true variety of input: if you use the same method against a different object, you get a polymorphic result:

Required Field Validator: This control works exactly like the parent control in System.Web.UI.WebControls. The Command event triggers client-side validation.

Compare Validator: This control works exactly like the parent control in System.Web.UI.WebControls. Empty fields validate, so use a RequiredFieldValidator if a value is required.

Range Validator: This control works exactly like the parent control in System.Web.UI.WebControls.

Regular Expression Validator: This control works exactly like the parent control in System.Web.UI.WebControls.

Custom Validator: This control works exactly like the parent control in System.Web.UI.WebControls.

Validation Summary: Essentially the same as the similarly named control in the WebControls namespace, except that the Validation Summary for mobile web derives from the MobileControl class. For that reason, we cannot directly use the validation summary to handle back-end error reporting, since the properties are not available.

Data Controls

Practically all of the controls in the mobile library are data-aware, because they derive from the complementary classes in the web library. There are very few classes, however, that are specifically designed for mobile web data presentation. The ObjectList, described above, can be used with any collection of objects up to and including a collection of rows in a table. The TextView control is also data-aware, and provides rather interesting pagination and viewing capabilities.

You cannot just write text to the page in a mobile control. Text must, if it is to be viewed accurately, be contained somehow. The TextView control is the container of choice. TextView is similar to a label, except that since it derives from PagedControl, it supports automatic pagination for mobile devices. If we view a page control in the designer,

And then on the screen of a phone, with data,

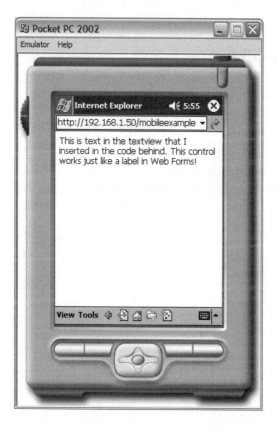

the usefulness of the control becomes more obvious. Use this control to output text to the screen. Its ability to handle paging on small phone screens is a must for mobile applications.

Special Controls

There are a number of mobile-specific controls in the mobile library as well. These controls take specific advantage of the mobile platform, sometimes enhancing existing functionality:

PhoneCall: Devices with telephony can use this link to place a call to the number in the PhoneNumber property.

DeviceSpecific: DeviceSpecific is the class that allows you to directly touch, or even bypass, the DeviceAdapters. The context menu for the DeviceSpecific control includes Templating Options, which gives you the ability to control display on a given device that is specific to your needs.

Stylesheet: This control is akin to a CSS file in a normal web application. Drag it onto the page, not the form, and select Edit Styles in the Context menu to assign fonts and colors as appropriate to the device's capabilities.

Image: The mobile image class doesn't convert images for different devices. It allows the programmer to define multiple images for multiple platforms. This does indeed mean that some research will need to be done about the target devices, and the image types they expect.

Debugging Mobile Web Applications

The reason to use Visual Studio for a web application is the debugger. You can write ASP.NET with a text editor all day long, but only in Visual Studio can you press F5 and see the website appear with the code available for browsing.

Mobile web isn't quite that easy. Debugging for the mobile web is much like debugging for Web Services, but it includes the complexities of the device. Nonetheless, it is significantly more user-friendly than the alternative.

To debug a mobile web, you need to start in the IE browse installed on your local machine. If you load a Mobile project and press F5, IE will run, with the mobile web within it, just as with any other ASP.Net project. Debug your logic there, as shown in Figure 5-8; it is easier than dealing with the emulator anyway.

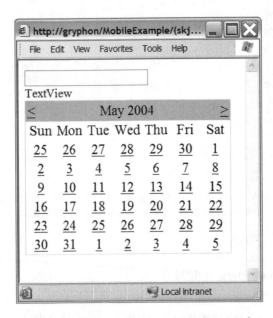

Figure 5-8. *Example mobile web application form*

Then we need to test in emulators. It is easy to download emulators for almost every manufacturer listed previously by going to the MSDN Mobile page, or the manufacturer's developer website. For PocketPC or SmartPhone, you need the PocketPC SDK, which is required for the emulator for Windows Mobile 2003.

When debugging for an emulator, we are stuck attaching to the ASP.NET worker process, just as if we were debugging a web service. Open the Processes dialog from the debug menu (Figure 5-9).

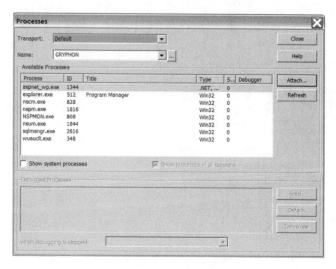

Figure 5-9. *Processes dialog*

Double click on `aspnet_wp.exe` and make sure Common Language Runtime is selected. Then click OK, and you will enter debug mode. When you run the application in the emulator, Visual Studio will run as if it were attached to IE if you press F5 (see Figure 5-10).

Attach to Process

Process:

[1344] C:\WINNT\Microsoft.NET\Framework\v1.1.4322\asp

Choose the program types that you want to debug:

☑ Common Language Runtime
☐ Microsoft T-SQL
☐ Native
☐ Script

OK

Cancel

Help

The following programs will be debugged:

.NET application
/LM/w3svc/1/root/MobileExample-9-127288158396815760
/LM/W3SVC/16/Root-4-127283415835163824
DefaultDomain

Figure 5-10. *Attach to Process dialog*

Then we can run the application in our emulator, in debug mode, as a normal website. If you are working with a Pocket PC SDK emulator, they integrate nicely with Visual Studio. Just go to Tools / Connect To Device ... and select your emulator. See Figure 5-11.

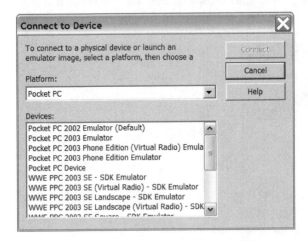

Figure 5-11. *Connect to Device dialog*

Figure 5-12 shows the application running in a Windows Mobile 2003 emulator.

Figure 5-12. *Our application in the PocketPc emulator*

Security for Small Screens

Often, security is a last-minute effort, an afterthought that is tacked on because we needed role-based access anyway, so why not secure the application while we were thinking about it? Mobile applications are no different in security designs than larger applications, but they are often much more significant. While an intruder needs to have significant technical knowledge to access your intranet, they only need to steal the mobile device to have access to the mobile web.

Browser Considerations

Realistically, there are two threat matrices to be drawn for mobile webs: one for Pocket PCs and one for phones. Pocket PCs are essentially desktop machines today; the mobile version of IE is the mirror image of the desktop version. Phones are a different matter entirely, with browsers that speak variants of HTML, and questionable security protocols. Let's take a look at both.

Pocket Internet Explorer is capable of using up to 128-bit security in both the PCT and SSL protocols, and will do so when requested by the user or the link selected. However, the 2002 versions of the browser report themselves as Internet Explorer 3.2 in the header of requests, so sites that check such things will fail the browser for 128-bit encryption much of the time. Keep this in mind when developing secure sites for Pocket IE.

Also, Pocket IE and Pocket PC operating systems in general have support for secure certificates as distributed by Verisign and other providers. In short, anything you can do with certificates on a PC browser, you can do with Pocket IE.

Phone browser security is another matter entirely. Much of the security is built into the protocol, Wireless Transport Layer Security, similar to HTTPS. It is more or less invisible to us as developers, providing encryption of the information only as it passes from tower to phone.

So, what are we as developers to do? If the need is for general user-level security, the basis is the same as for web applications: use SSL or WTLS, and require strong passwords. If the need is for nonrepudiation and comprehensive authentication, then user certificates are needed, and WML is probably out of the picture. Have your users acquire certificates and block WML browsers from using the site.

Watching WiFi

WiFi is a security disaster. During a recent extensive airport tour (courtesy of the airlines), the author made an extremely unnerving discovery. With a Compaq 3850, running CE 3.0, he was able to walk though the file system of every single airport at which he landed, using no hacking techniques, simply with a file browser.

So we need to watch access methods. That is no news to a administrator, but rarely does the average developer consider the intricacies of a wireless device.

Encryption

Like wireless access, encryption on a wireless device rarely enters a developer's scope. When a black hat steals a wireless device, access to the cookies collection and the entire cache is freely available. It is imperative to encrypt information before storing it.

Encryption is handled elsewhere in the book, but we should cover the design principles here. The process we are looking at is encryption of state information before it has stored the cookies collection. Looking at the lifecycle above for mobile devices, we have something like Figure 5-13.

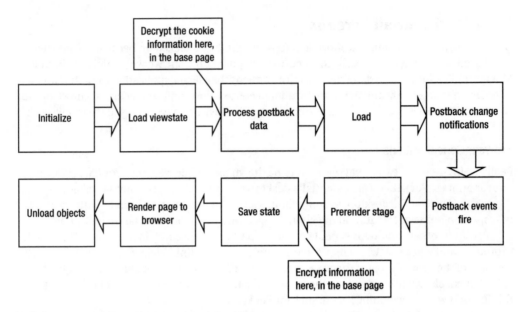

Figure 5-13. *Mobile ASP.NET security lifecycle*

Another thing to keep in mind is the viewstate. A user can view the source for an HTML rendered page and get to the viewstate on a mobile device just as easily as on a normal PC. Viewstate can be decrypted easily. Don't store secrets in there. The viewstate is as plain on a mobile browser as it is on a PC browser:

```
<html><body>
<form id="Form1" name="Form1" method="post"
action="MobileWebForm1.aspx?__ufps=700043">
<input type="hidden" name="__VIEWSTATE"
value="aDxfX1A7QDw74ZKjoIDig4Tgo4csMDs+Oz4=">
<input type="hidden" name="__EVENTTARGET" value="">
<input type="hidden" name="__EVENTARGUMENT" value="">
<script language=javascript><!--
function __doPostBack(target, argument){
  var theform = document.Form1
  theform.__EVENTTARGET.value = target
  theform.__EVENTARGUMENT.value = argument
  theform.submit()
}
// -->
</script>
<input name="TextBox1"/><br>
TextView<br>
<br>
</form></body></html>
```

Authentication

Authentication is fairly simple on mobile devices. Just as with web browsers, everything supports basic and form-based authentication, and Windows devices support Windows (formerly NTFS) authentication. Forms-based authentication is built into your application, and Basic and Windows use IIS for their setup and the web application level. Look for the setup in the Properties panel for a website, in the Directory Security tab. See Figure 5-14.

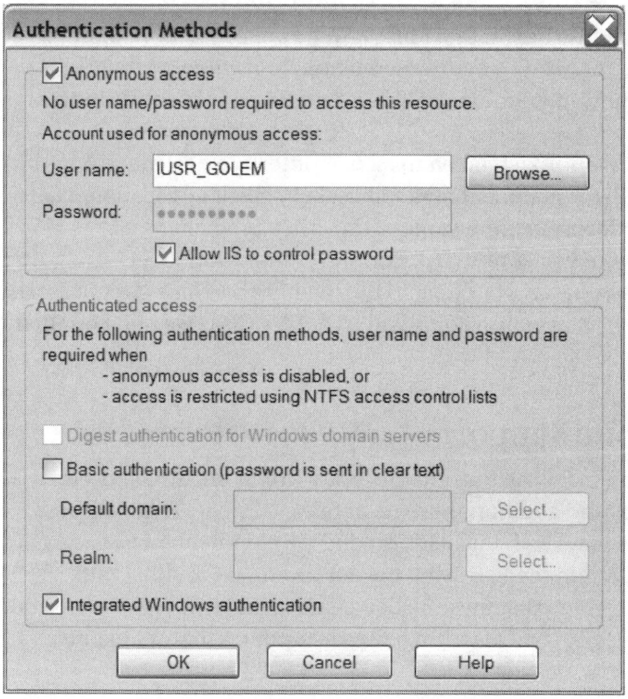

Figure 5-14. *Authentication Methods dialog*

Other Mobile Security Elements

I am more or less assuming that you are already taking the following elements into consideration in your application development:

- Generate strong passwords for your users.

- Use the Password textbox type in the mobile control. It is supported on practically all browsers.

- The ASP.NET Mobile Templates assumes that you want cookieless sessions. Therefore, if you use session state at all, the session information will be cached on the server and referred to by URL.

- If something is very secure, consider not putting it in a mobile format at all.

- Validate user entry on the client and server side to prevent attacks. Mobile webs are just as susceptible to attack as public webs.

- Use VPNs. Most phones and all PocketPCs will support them.

Smart Device Development

Let's now move our discussion of mobile client development on to Smart Device development, through now to the end of this chapter.

Since I've already pointed out in this chapter that Mobile Web application development is rather like ASP.NET development, you won't be surprised when I tell you now that Smart Device application development in Visual Studio .NET is rather like traditional Windows Forms development.

This is due both to the common approach taken to all user interface designs within the environment, and the similarity with development for a full desktop client application. There are differences, however, and I'll be focusing us on some of those in a moment.

First, though, I want to share with you some .NET Compact Framework (CF) installation details, and offer you a comparison between .NET CF and the main .NET Framework. This will provide a good basis for you to grasp what we are doing with the .NET CF as we build our first Smart client application.

Installing Windows Mobile Support

Although the .NET CF, device emulator, and all the other necessary tools are installed with this Visual Studio, several major updates and additions have been released since. These address a number of important glitches and flaws with the platform and development tools, such as the inability to debug code correctly from the IDE using the device emulator, along with adding further functionality. It is suggested that these be downloaded and installed before you develop any mobile applications. At the time of writing, the key updates that should be installed as a minimum are:

- .NET Compact Framework Service Pack 2

- Windows CE .NET Utilities v1.1

Further tools, such as the Windows Mobile Developer PowerToys, are also worthwhile downloads. All of these are available free of charge from http://msdn.microsoft.com/mobility/downloads/default.aspx. If mobile device applications are intended to connect to a standard Win32-based SQL Server, ensuring that it is updated with the latest service pack is also advisable (currently service pack 3).

Similarities Between .NET CF and the .NET Framework

Before taking a look at the details of creating a Smart Device Application, it's prudent to have an overview of the similarities and differences between the .NET Compact Framework and its desktop equivalent.

As you'd expect, the fundamentals of the Compact Framework don't deviate from those of the original desktop release, and in particular, the following key concepts remain:

- **Common Language Runtime:** The common language runtimes in both Frameworks benefit from managed code execution, just-in-time (JIT) code compilation, and garbage collection. They support the Common Language Specification (CLS). The .NET CF common language runtime is approximately 12% of the size of the full .NET Framework CLR.

- **Assemblies and file formats:** Applications for both Frameworks use assemblies. Both Frameworks access portable executable (PE) files, which contain the Microsoft intermediate language (MSIL) and metadata that define a .NET Framework application. A PE file can refer to a programming namespace defined and shared by other assembly files. Although the file formats of both Frameworks are identical, you cannot take a binary component compiled in the .NET CF and run it in the full .NET Framework or vice versa. This is due to the strong binding rules: .NET CF assemblies are signed with different strong-name key pairs from their .NET equivalents. You can, however, recompile your application to target either Framework. It is possible that with future releases of Visual Studio and the .NET Framework, true interoperability will be provided.

- **Multiple language support:** Cross-language interoperability is built into the .NET CF. Visual C# and Visual Basic .NET are the first supported languages. Currently, there is no J# implementation for the CF.

- **Common type system:** Both Frameworks have built-in primitive types as well as other types that you can use and derive in when building applications.

- **Model:** Both Frameworks provide a multithreaded programming model that uses the scheduling mechanism of the host system.

Differences Between .NET CF and the .NET Framework

Given the difference in nature between the underlying hardware and operating systems, and the size differences between the Frameworks as mentioned above, there are inevitably numerous differences between the two Framework implementations. For full details of all discrepancies, refer to the MSDN documentation. The most important points are these:

- **ASP.NET:** ASP.NET features (found in the System.Web namespace) are not available in the Compact Framework. This is because it was designed for creating client applications, not hosting Web-based applications. The exclusion of this functionality helps contribute to the comparatively small size of the .NET CF.

- **COM interop:** COM interop is not supported in the .NET CF. Calling COM-based functionality can be achieved indirectly by writing custom wrappers that call specific DLL entry points.

- **Current directory:** Pocket PC devices don't have the concept of a current directory, hence the methods in the Framework that make use of this: GetCurrentDirectory and SetCurrentDirectory aren't supported.

- **Data:** The System.Data classes support the key features of ADO.NET, including DataSets, DataViews, and the associated relationships that they contain, but strongly typed DataSets aren't supported. The System.Data.OleDb namespace and SQL Server support for connection pooling, distributed transactions, and encrypted connections are also not present. Finally, the System.Data.SqlServerCe namespace has been developed to add support for connecting Microsoft SQL Server 2000 Windows CE Edition 2.0 (SQL Server CE) databases hosted on the devices themselves.

- **Exceptions:** Exceptions themselves function much the same as on the desktop Framework. The descriptive strings associated with each exception are kept separately in the System.SR assembly to save space. If this DLL is installed onto devices, the Framework will automatically locate the correct description for an Exception. For debugging purposes, it can be very useful to include this assembly, since it is only 100 KB in size.

- **Framework Classes:** The majority of .NET CF classes are identical to their desktop counterparts. However, as mentioned earlier in the case of ASP.NET, not all of the standard classes are present. Additionally, the IrDA classes, System.Data.SqlServerCE namespace, and certain UI features such as the InputPanel control are in the .NET CF but not the desktop edition.

- **I/O:** The majority of File I/O works the same on both versions of the Framework. Certain features are not supported, though, most notably, file-change notifications and file/directory attributes. Path resolution is also different within the Compact Framework. One of the Compact Framework Quickstart applications provided by Microsoft demonstrates working with files: http://go.microsoft.com/fwlink/?LinkId=8734.

- **IrDA:** The Compact Framework supports additional classes within the System.Net.Sockets namespace to enable IrDA communication as found on many mobile devices. These classes are within the System.Net.Irda assembly, as discussed on MSDN: http://msdn.microsoft.com/library/en-us/dv_evtuv/html/etconinfraredconnections.asp.

- **Performance testing:** At the time of writing, there are no comprehensive tools available for performance testing of .NET applications on smart devices. Microsoft is currently working on developing such tools, though.

- **Reflection:** For the most part, Reflection with the .NET CF performs identically to its desktop counterpart. The major exceptions to this are the lack of the System.Reflection.Emit namespace and classes, and the omission of the == operator for instances of many of the classes.

- **Remoting:** Remoting support isn't present in the Compact Framework, largely due to the infeasibility of developing distributed applications on mobile devices.

- **Serialization:** Object serialization is not supported in the .NET CF. Since DataSets implement serialization using a custom mechanism, this is still supported in this version, making it possible to pass structured data between applications and web-service calls.

- **Timers:** The System.Timers.Timer class is included in the .NET CF, but the Timer.Enabled Boolean property must be used for enabling and disabling the timer; the Timer.Start and Timer.Stop methods aren't available.

- **Windows Forms:** As described earlier in the chapter, graphical application development is tailored to mobile devices; the .NET CF has its own controls, which, while similar to their desktop counterparts, are tailored and optimized to the Pocket PC platform. Other small differences also exist, such as the Compact Framework not supporting Activated and Deactivated events. The GotFocus and LostFocus events are still present, however.

- **XML:** While the .NET CF does support the XML DOM, it does not support X-path querying, XSLTs, schema validation, or the XmlDataDocument class.

Creating a Smart Device Application

To create a new application, select the Smart Device Application icon from the C# projects in the New Project dialog. After entering a name for it (SmartDeviceApp is used as an example throughout this chapter), clicking OK will bring up the application wizard, the first difference you will find in mobile development. See Figure 5-15.

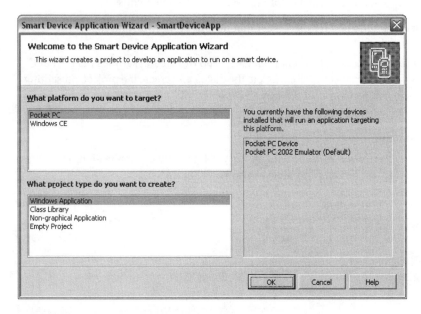

Figure 5-15. *Smart Device Application Wizard dialog*

Pocket PC and Windows CE Platforms

The first choice to make when developing an application is whether to target the Pocket PC or Windows CE platforms, as shown at the top of the dialog in the figure. The relationship between the Pocket PC platform (or rather the Windows Mobile for Pocket PC as it is now called) and the Windows CE platform is that Windows CE underpins them both. The Pocket PC platform builds on Windows CE, adding new functionality, UI, and applications to create an optimized computing platform for mobile devices, whereas Windows CE is targeted at all embedded systems. More specifically, Pocket PC 2002 is based on the Windows CE 3.0 platform, while Windows Mobile 2003 relies on Windows CE .NET 4.2.

Project Types

The project types that are available for smart-device applications are very similar to those of traditional client systems:

- **Windows Application:** For developing applications with GUI features.

- **Class Library:** For developing class libraries to be used in a Smart Device Application.

- **Nongraphical Application:** For creating applications that don't need a user interface; usually for applications that run in the background. This option is available only for Pocket PC devices.

- **Console Application:** This option is applicable only to the Windows CE .NET platform. It creates an application that runs within the Windows CE .NET console.

- **Empty Project:** For creating a new project that doesn't contain any files.

In the example used throughout the chapter, we'll keep the default settings of Pocket PC and Windows Application. Clicking OK will complete the dialog and create the project, presenting the user with the usual design canvas and Solution Explorer.

Deploying to the Emulator

Pressing F5 or selecting the Debug ➤ Start menu option will first build the application, as expected, and then bring up the Deploy dialog, as shown in Figure 5-16.

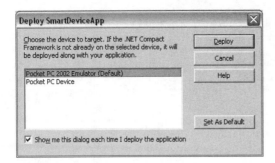

Figure 5-16. *Choosing the device to target*

This dialog allows the target device for the build to be selected; although the application is compiled within Visual Studio running on Windows, it must then be deployed to either a real or virtual Pocket PC (or Windows CE) device before being run or debugged. If the checkbox at the bottom of the dialog is unchecked, this dialog will be ignored for subsequent debugging sessions. Select the Emulator and click Deploy to start the emulator and deployment process.

As soon as the emulator (or real device, should that be selected) is started up and connected to, Visual Studio will copy the executable and any other necessary satellite assemblies, resources, etc. to the device. The files will be placed in the following folder:

`\Program Files\<ApplicationName>`

If this is the first time the emulator has been used, the standard Pocket PC device-initialization process will be carried out; the user will be taken through the basics of using the OS, and will have to configure the time zone for the device.

Once the application has been deployed, Visual Studio will check to see whether the .NET CF is deployed. If not, then it will be installed automatically (see Figure 5-17).

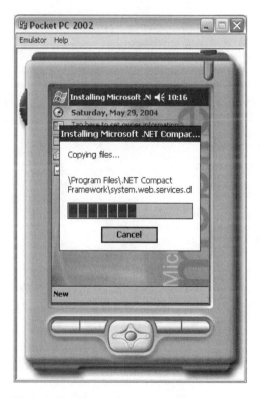

Figure 5-17. *The Pocket PC emulator*

Immediately following the installation of the Framework (if necessary), the application itself will then run.

■Note If the deployment of the application succeeds, but Visual Studio can't start the application following this, a common cause of the problem is running an unpatched development environment. Installing the updates discussed at the start of this section should remedy the situation. Further information on such problems is available from MSDN: `http://download.microsoft.com/download/c/d/b/cdbff573-73fb-4f9f-a464-c5adc890e1ae/Readme.htm`.

As soon as the application starts, you'll see that it appears much as you'd expect: a blank form just as in the IDE, with the standard Pocket PC look and feel (Figure 5-18).

Figure 5-18. *A blank form in the IDE*

As with all Pocket PC applications, clicking the X button at the top right of the screen does not actually end the process; it makes use of the *Smart Minimize* functionality to hide the application but leave it running. This is important, since it means that a further deployment cycle by Visual Studio cannot be carried out straightaway; the files that will need to be overwritten will be locked by the Pocket PC OS. There are three options available to prevent this situation from arising:

- **Stopping the application from Visual Studio:** Pressing the Stop button from the Debug toolbar (or selecting the Stop Debugging option from the Debug menu) will close the application.

- **Terminating the process manually:** On the device, selecting the Start Menu ➤ Settings menu option, then selecting the Memory option on the System tab will bring up the Memory dialog. On the Running Programs tab of this, all of the loaded applications are listed. Selecting the relevant .NET application and clicking Stop will end the process.

- **Turning the Emulator off:** Clicking the Close button on the emulator itself will bring up the Shut Down dialog (Figure 5-19). This provides two options; Save Emulator state and Turn off Emulator. The former of these options is akin to putting the device in Standby mode: when the emulator restarts, the memory contents will be kept intact and execution of the emulator will resume from where it left off. The latter option, turning off the emulator, is like taking the batteries out of a real device and clearing it completely, including shutting down applications. This will require the time zone, etc. to be entered before the device can be used, and the .NET CF will be installed again as part of the next deployment.

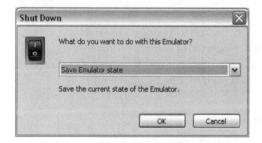

Figure 5-19. *Shutting down the emulator*

Restarting the Emulator

Just as there are two different ways to shut down the emulator, there are two variations on restarting the emulator. These can also be used for closing the currently running applications. Most real devices have a reset button located at the bottom or on the sides of the casing, making them easy to reset, and have batteries that can simply be removed if that fails. To reset the emulator, there are two choices:

- **Hard reset:** Restarts the emulator and restores the emulator to its original state. All programs that you have installed will be gone. In particular, the assemblies for the .NET CF will need to be reinstalled the next time you run your application from Visual Studio .NET 2003.

- **Soft reset:** This just restarts the emulator, retaining all of its previous settings.

Invoking the Emulator Manually

When you choose to run your smart-device application in Visual Studio using the emulator, the emulator will be automatically launched. However, there are times when you will want to launch the emulator without using Visual Studio, to test the appearance of an application on multiple devices alongside each other, for instance. In this case, you can invoke the emulator manually, running it as a standalone application.

The emulator is located in the following directory: `C:\Program Files\Microsoft Visual Studio .NET 2003\CompactFrameworkSDK\ConnectionManager\Bin`. The `emulator.exe` application supports these options:

- **/Video:** Sets the resolution and bit depth of the Emulator for Windows CE display. Must be in `<width>x<height>x<bit-depth>` format with width, height, and bit depth as integers.

- **/Ethernet:** Enables or disables the Ethernet controller in Emulator for Windows CE. Use values of none, shared, virtualswitch, or the MAC address of the Ethernet adapter to use.

- **/Skin:** Indicates which skin to use with Emulator for Windows CE. Requires an XML file-name describing skin.

- **/CEImage:** Indicates which Windows CE kernel image to use.

For instance, to launch the emulator for Pocket PC 2002, navigate to the subdirectory where the emulator is located and issue the following command: `start emulator /CEImage images\PocketPC\2002\1033\PPC2002.bin /Video 240x320x16`.
And for a Windows CE .NET Web pad emulator, use the following command: `start emulator /CEImage images\windowsce\webpad\1033\wce4webpad.bin`

Note that using the start command runs the emulator and immediately returns control to the command prompt, rather than leaving it hanging while the emulator runs.

Visual Studio Device Controls

Back in the Visual Studio IDE, looking at the Toolbox will show that although there are plenty of familiar controls present, there are also many of the desktop edition's controls missing, while some additional entries, such as InputPanel, are present and functional in ways you would expect from desktop development (see Figure 5-20). The dragging and dropping of controls works just the same as with standard WinForms development, as can be seen by dragging the controls shown in Table 5-3 onto the form to recreate an interface (as you saw in Chapter 2).

Figure 5-20. *The Smart Device toolbox*

Table 5-3. *Some Smart Device Controls*

Control	Name	Text
Label	lblEmployeeName	Employee Name:
TextBox	txtEmployeeName	
Button	btnSearch	Search
DataGrid	dgResults	

As well as having a white background to the form to show the difference between mobile and desktop development, when the controls are dropped onto the canvas, they are also shown with a flat appearance, in-line with how they'll appear on the device itself. Other than that, the paradigm, again, remains similar to traditional application development (see Figure 5-21).

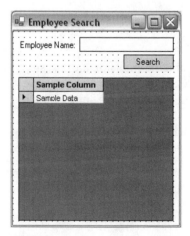

Figure 5-21. *The employee search screen in the designer*

One of the slight limitations of .NET CF development can be seen if the application is run on the emulator as it stands; controls don't line up quite as they did in design view due to the difference in fonts, etc. This manifests itself in the screenshot of Figure 5-22, with the colon after "Employee Name" being hidden.

Figure 5-22. *The Employee Search screen in the emulator*

.NET CF in VS.NET: The Internals

With all of the controls appearing on both the design canvas and the emulator, the next step is to add the functionality behind the Search button. If you look at the Toolbox in Design View now, you'll see that there is no Data tab. Even if you select the Show All Tabs option from the context menu, all of the data items will be grayed out.

This is due to the fact that we're not actually developing against the standard .NET Framework. If you expand the References in the Solution Explorer, the standard items will seem to be present, as shown in Figure 5-23.

Figure 5-23. *Smart Device project references*

Similarly, if the Search button is double-clicked to create an event handler, then using clauses in the code will look as though they were a standard WinForm-based .NET application. What we're actually doing is developing against a completely different set of assemblies that just happen to occupy the same namespace as the standard Win32 ones; the .NET CF is just a separate implementation of the vast majority of the normal Framework. This can be seen if the Add Reference dialog is opened up for the project and the columns expanded: the Path to the Microsoft assemblies includes a CompactFramework subdirectory (Figure 5-24).

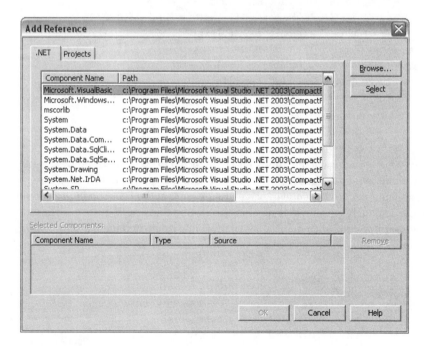

Figure 5-24. *Add a Reference dialog*

While on this dialog, select the System.Data.Common and System.Data.SqlClient assemblies, since we'll need the functionality they provide for our example.

Data Access in Smart Device Applications

As we just saw, when developing smart device applications, we're actually working with a completely different version of the Framework. When you consider that the Compact Framework is roughly only 10% of the size of the desktop version, there are clearly going to be certain items missing, not only enterprise runtime features such as System.EnterpriseServices and System.Messaging, but also further design-time items, such as designer-enabled data components.

In order to wire our DataGrid up to show search results from the Northwind database (as in Chapter 2), we'll need to write all of the code ourselves, creating our own connection string, manually crafting the SQL query, and tying all of the controls together, as shown in the following code, which should be inserted in the event handler that is created when the btnSearch control is double-clicked, with the Data Source address being replaced with the reference to localhost or the IP Address or name of the local machine. Otherwise, the device will try connecting to itself:

```
private void btnSearch_Click(object sender, System.EventArgs e)
{
    string connectionString = "Data Source=localhost;Initial"+
                    "Catalog=Northwind;User ID=sa;Password=";
    string query = "SELECT * FROM Employees WHERE LastName LIKE '%{0}%'";
    query = string.Format(query,  txtEmployeeName.Text)
    DataSet results = new DataSet();
    new SqlDataAdapter(string.Format(query, txtEmployeeName.Text),
                connectionString).Fill(results);
    dgResults.DataSource = results.Tables[0];
}
```

To determine the IP Address of the SQL Server, open up a command prompt on the machine running SQL Server (usually your local machine), and type ipconfig /all, followed by Return. This should display details about the machine's IP address configuration and its host name.

Running the application with this code in place (assuming that the SQL Server username and password are as previously) should give no surprises; when the Search button is clicked, the DataGrid should be populated with the test data almost immediately (Figure 5-25).

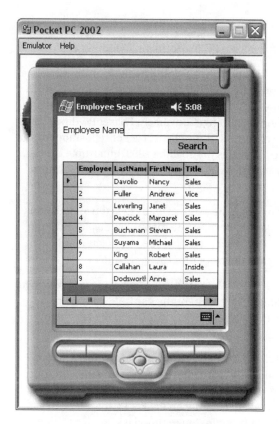

Figure 5-25. *Running the Employee Search screen*

Debugging Database Connections

If there is a long pause after the search button has been clicked, followed by an SqlException being raised, it is likely that either the SQL Server credentials are not correct, or that the Pocket PC device cannot locate the SQL Server. If the latter is the case, the network connection properties of the Pocket PC device can be configured by selecting the Start ➤ Settings menu option, followed by the Connections option on the Connections tab.

Browsing to IIS on the remote machine (assuming that it's enabled) from within Pocket Internet Explorer on the device (or emulator) is a good way of seeing whether a network connection can be established.

CE .NET Versus Pocket PC Development

As I mentioned earlier, the Pocket PC platform is based on Windows CE. There are several differences in development for both platforms, however, as summarized in the following.

Graphical Application Differences

These are the graphical differences between the Pocket PC platform and Windows CE:

- **Sizing & positioning forms:** Windows CE supports multiple screen resolutions; hence CE .NET applications are allowed to create forms of any size, appearing anywhere on the desktop, much as desktop Windows applications can. These can be resized and repositioned at will while the application is running. Conversely, Pocket PC devices all have a fixed screen size of 240 px × 320 px; forms cannot be resized or repositioned, and each form fills the screen. Newer devices, such as the Toshiba e800, quadruple this to 480 px × 640 px, but only for certain applications, due to the original fixed-resolution design of the platform.

- **Menus:** Windows CE displays the menu-bar in the same place as desktop applications – at the top of the form. However, on Pocket PC devices, the menus are displayed at the bottom of the screen. Another difference is that a menu is added by default for Pocket PC applications, but has to be added by the developer for CE applications.

- **Tab control:** Windows CE.NET allows tab controls to be placed anywhere on the screen, with the tabs themselves being positioned at the top of the control. On the Pocket PC, the .NET CF places TabControls at the top edge of the form, with the tabs being rendered at the bottom of the control.

- **Input panel:** Pocket PC devices generally do not have any form of a keyboard, largely relying on a stylus for input. For data entry, a "software-based input panel" (SIP) is available to simulate a keyboard onscreen. This functionality is implemented by the InputPanel class in the .NET CF, but it is available only on Pocket PC-based devices. Applications can be compiled for CE that try to instance this class, but a runtime exception will be raised when the code is reached.

Other Differences

There are various other differences between the Pocket PC platform and the Windows CE platform, as detailed here:

- **Application lifecycle:** Windows CE applications support both minimize and close application functionality, allowing for the traditional buttons to appear at the top right of the screen. Disabling minimize functionality can be achieved by setting the MinimizeBox property of a form to false. Pocket PC devices make use of the "smart minimize" functionality, however, which keeps an application running when the close icon in the top right of the screen is clicked, allowing it to be restored quickly. Setting the MinimizeBox property to false on Pocket PC applications changes the X icon that is displayed to an OK icon that does actually close the application.

- **Debugging:** In addition to the interactive debugging available from both mobile platforms, Windows CE .NET provides the familiar Debug.Write and Debug.WriteLine methods, which output data to the Console window on the local device (as opposed to the Visual Studio output window). Since Pocket PCs don't support a console window, the Debug.Write and Debug.WriteLine methods are not valid on this platform. Making use of these methods will not cause an error; it will merely lose the output, meaning that debugging the same application on both mobile platforms doesn't require editing the Debug calls.

- **Nongraphical/console applications:** Depending on whether a Pocket PC- or Windows CE-based project is chosen from the Smart Device Application Wizard, either the option to create a nongraphical application or a console application will be present, as shown earlier in the chapter. The Pocket PC platform doesn't have the concept of a console window, with nongraphical applications functioning similarly to console applications, but without the associated UI. Nongraphical applications can be used similarly to desktop *service* applications to perform background processing, etc. Because Windows CE .NET does support a console window, console applications that make use of text-based I/O (through the Console class) can be created. However, these applications still can't receive windows messages.

For comparisons between the differing runtime platforms as opposed to the development issues discussed above, Microsoft has produced a document that's available from the MSDN site at http://www.microsoft.com/downloads/details.aspx?FamilyID=111fe6d5-b0e1-4887-8070-be828e50faa9&DisplayLang=en.

Summary

This chapter has been a brief foray into the world of Mobile Client development, branching out into Mobile Web applications and Smart Device applications. My aim has been to introduce you to these branches, and to show you some of the similarities and key differences with more traditional desktop application development.

I've taken you through some first examples of designing and building Mobile Client applications, looking at the controls available and some of the design considerations that are specific to Mobile rather than desktop applications.

I then took you through a few installation notes for the .NET CF and comparison of the CF to the main .NET Framework, before launching you into your first Smart Device application. We also took a comparative look at the Pocket PC platform and the Windows CE platform options in this sequence.

This chapter has taken you through the two key branches of today's Mobile Client development technology; I hope that I have presented you with a helpful introduction to some of the options, considerations, devices, and techniques available for your mobile client development with VS.NET.

CHAPTER 6

■■■

Team Development with VS .NET

Visual Studio .NET is an excellent platform for an individual developer to build any kind of application for the Microsoft platform. Most of us, however, spend our time in teams of two or more, building larger applications that require the skills of multiple developers.

In order to make team development work, project management, architectural oversight, and good communication are required. One topic that is commonly overlooked is source control. A nod in the direction of versioning and code check is the norm in many development shops.

Source control is the secure storage of versions of files. A source control system is like a library of editable books. A developer can check out a book, change it, and check it back in. When subsequent developers check out the book, they can see the original or the changes, as they wish. This is helpful in development, because a baseline can be set for a stable version, and the code can be "rolled back" to that point.

The source control integration in Visual Studio .NET 2002 was a great start, but the new features and new patterns and practices that have been published by the Microsoft architecture team make source control integration simpler, finally. Everyone should take a moment to reconsider their source control strategy.

In this chapter on Team Development we'll consider both Microsoft's recommended strategy for source control and the specifics of using Visual SourceSafe with Visual Studio .NET. Some of the topics we'll consider include:

- Getting Started with Source Control

- Team Development Strategies

- Solutions and Projects

- Web Application Development

- Windows Application Development

- MSSCCI and using other source control packages

In order to show the ins and outs of source safe integration into a team development environment, we'll follow Bill, our intrepid project manager. Bill is facing a lot of the problems that many of our readers face: deciding on a source control strategy, migrating projects to the new strategy, and setting up servers.

Bill works in an environment that looks a lot like the team programming shops many of us work in. There are seven developers, who divide their time among five projects. These projects include some that are in maintenance, some that are in design, and some that are in development.

We'll focus on watching Bill handle all of the project-management-type duties that relate to file management and source control integration. In the process we'll learn that Visual Studio .NET brings enterprise source control integration to a new level on the Microsoft platform.

Getting Started with Source Control

Before we talk strategy, philosophy, or advanced techniques, let's get the basics down pat. In order to use Visual Studio effectively with a source control system, a few things have to happen:

1. A computer must have the source control server software installed.

2. There must be some kind of source control database accessible to the development computer.

3. The source control client tools must be installed on the development computer.

In order to meet these requirements, we should accomplish the following tasks:

1. The file server or the development server must have Visual SourceSafe—or another source control system, though we will be using SourceSafe—installed. If you are concerned about security, keep in mind that the default Admin user account does not have a password.

2. The SourceSafe install will create a directory called VSS that has the data files and the client tools. Share that folder with the development group; it is the easiest way to see to it that everyone has access to the needed data files and the installer for the client tools.

3. From each development machine, run the setup for the client tools by executing netsetup.exe in the VSS directory. Note that all users will need the CD key to do this installation.

Once the client tools are installed on the development workstations, you'll notice that the Source Control options are enabled in the File Menu, whereas before they were shown but grayed out (see Figure 6-1).

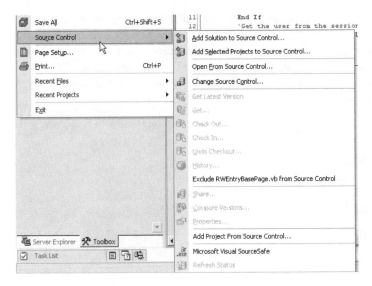

Figure 6-1. *SourceSafe menu options in the file menu*

Add Solution to Source Control and Add Selected Projects to Source Control have similar functionality: that of adding an existing project to the Source Control database. Open from Source Control and Add Project from Source Control, on the other hand, are for opening files and projects already in the Source Control database and making working local copies.

Change Source Control and Microsoft Visual SourceSafe are commands that assist with running the client tools, which won't happen very often. In fact, developers using Visual Studio shouldn't have to run the client tools at all for development projects. All source control operations should be run from within Visual Studio's IDE.

If you have a project open, or just want to create a quick Windows Forms application for the sake of education, go ahead and add the solution to source control, even better if there are two projects in your solution. You'll get the ubiquitous SourceSafe Login box (Figure 6-2).

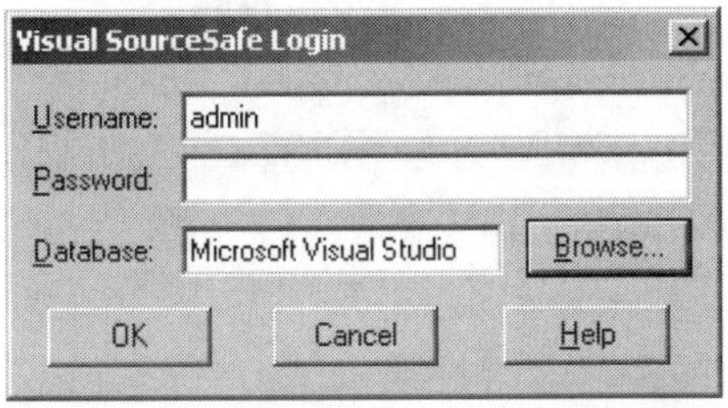

Figure 6-2. *The ubiquitous SourceSafe Login box*

This is an immensely confusing dialog with not enough information, considering how important it is. First, you have to make sure the login information is correct; because that is how everyone tells who has what checked out. Second, the database location is very important, yet it doesn't seem so here. Do you recall when we shared the VSS folder in our Source-Safe server? That's where we are going to point this dialog. In my case, my file server has the SourceSafe server, and that machine is called Draco (Figure 6-3).

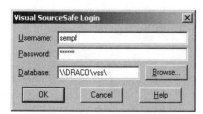

Figure 6-3. *Selecting the database*

From here, click OK. The next window you see will allow you to add the project to the directory tree in SourceSafe (Figure 6-4). Then, you'll find a complete section on strategies for naming directory structures, and every one will be different. You can place the solution in the $/ directory, make a new directory, or create a complete structure if you like. We'll talk options later.

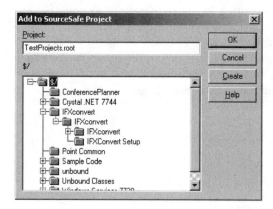

Figure 6-4. *Adding a project by selecting the folder*

As you can see, it didn't do a very good job of adding my solution. The solution I added was IFXConvert, and I now have two nested identically named structures in my directory tree. This is OK for now, but we'll learn how to better this system later, in Solutions and Projects. Both projects in the solution were added, however, in the second nested structure, and Visual Studio decided what specific files should and should not be added to the source control database.

Before we start to work, we'll need to check out the items. This is handled very well by the Check Out dialog, as seen in Figure 6-5.

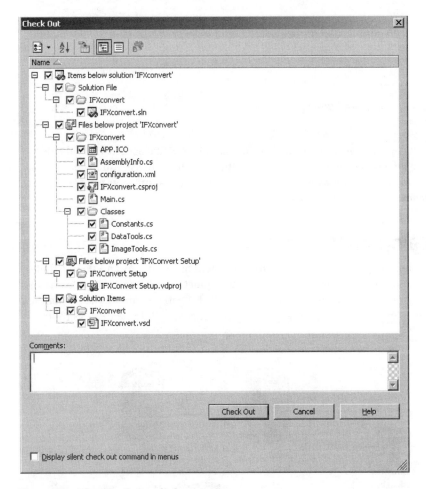

Figure 6-5. *The Check Out dialog*

Even my Solution Items document, a Visio diagram in this case, is correctly handled by Visual Studio. It should be noted that this document is stored in the main directory for the application, and Visual SourceSafe correctly stores it with the rest of the project files. However, Visual Studio knows that it isn't part of the solution, and doesn't keep it in the solution.

This all leads to the most important lesson of this chapter. Don't use the Visual SourceSafe client tools to do your checkout work. Visual Studio .NET and Visual SourceSafe are meant to be used in an integrated fashion, and only the tools within Visual Studio really know how to get the files out correctly. Don't use the client tools to check out your projects, as you may have done under Visual InterDev, or even Visual Basic 5.0 and 6.0.

The last simple task you will need to master before moving on is check in. You'll notice that the checked out items have a checkmark with an exclamation point next to them (Figure 6-6). This means that they are checked out in shared mode, and will be merged on check in. This is by far the most underrated and neatest feature of source control integration with Visual Studio. You can bypass this with the Check Out Exclusive command, but we'll chat more about that a bit later, in Strategy.

Figure 6-6. *Sample check out checkboxes*

To check in you'll use a similar dialog to check out as above. Visual SourceSafe will determine whether any changes need to be merged, and if there are, it might ask you to choose the particular changes to keep. This makes team development much simpler, as we'll see in the next section on Team Development Strategy.

Team Development Strategy

The Team Development environment is made up of a system of computers and people that have to depend on communication to turn out a decent product. Developers and workstations, servers and processes need to be understood by all in order to keep the environment functioning smoothly. We'll use Figure 6-7 to help us keep the parts in order while we discuss their implications.

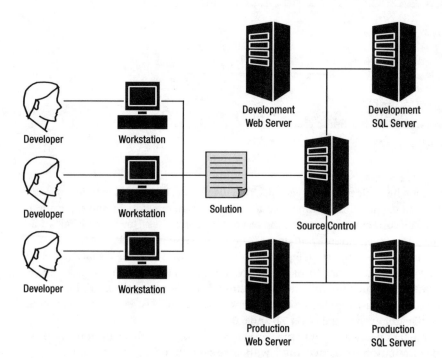

Figure 6-7. *The team development environment*

So what do we have here? Well, we know that we have a set of developers, and their individual workstations. These workstations have a similar set of characteristics in Bill's world.

Development Workstations

- They are all running an Enterprise class Microsoft operating system, like Windows 2000 or Windows XP Professional.

- They are all running Visual Studio .NET 2003.

- They are all connected to the same LAN, running the same domain.

- They all have the Visual SourceSafe 6.0d client components, SQL Server 2000 developer edition, and the MSDN Library.

- Most importantly, they all have IIS running. Keep in mind that IIS is not installed by default on Windows XP Pro machines.

All of these workstations are set up using an imaging process. Using Ghost or a similar program to create an image of a standard developer drive not only ensures similarity between the workstations, but saves time in setup as well. Sysprep.exe can be used to create an image of an existing machine as well, and that image can be deployed using Norton or another image deployment system.

Server Environment

The next thing to look at is our server environment. We have a Build server, an SQL Server, a Visual SourceSafe server, and a resources server. All of these servers are enterprise class Microsoft servers running Windows Server 2000 or 2003. The build server holds the key to our final implementation of the project. It has the build scripts and the attachment to the VSS server to allow for builds of our final product. The SQL Server is the normal test database server we are used to. The Visual SourceSafe server is a file server running the Visual SourceSafe components. The resources server is optional, and runs web services, BizTalk, COM+, or any other application that might be being used by the development workstations and build server.

That gives us an environment. It is a fertile ground in which to grow a development process, but without the procedures, and the technical details of how to implement those procedures, we are still in the dark. Visual Studio .NET makes source control integration easy, but not so easy that procedures and communication fall by the wayside. To begin handling the issue of Visual Studio .NET integration, let's start with a look at the terminology of source controlled projects.

Solutions and Projects

Solutions and projects are such a misunderstood part of Visual Studio .NET that they command two later appendices. Because they are so tightly integrated with the Source Control features of Visual Studio .NET, we will cover the basics of strategy here, and let the appendixes handle the details.

Visual Studio .NET Solutions

Solutions are designed to hold projects. The kicker is that they can be any kind of project you need, from web services to class libraries. A lot of the detail about solutions will make more sense after projects are completely understood, but first things first.

Visual Studio gives us a significant amount of control over what part of what solution is controlled by what source control system. For instance, the solution understands which of its projects are source controlled. We can see the details of what a solution knows about the source control system by glancing at a portion of the solution file in a text editor:

```
GlobalSection(SourceCodeControl) = preSolution
    SccNumberOfProjects = 3
    SccProjectName0 = \u0022$/IFXconvert/IFXconvert\u0022,\u0020CHAAAAAA
    SccLocalPath0 = ..
    SccProvider0 = MSSCCI:Microsoft\u0020Visual\u0020SourceSafe
    CanCheckoutShared = false
    SccProjectFilePathRelativizedFromConnection0 = IFXconvert\\
    SolutionUniqueID = {7C921640-DDC9-40BC-88E6-829B4DA003F7}
    SccProjectUniqueName1 =
                ..\\IFXConvert\u0020Setup\\IFXConvert\u0020Setup.vdproj
    SccLocalPath1 = ..
    CanCheckoutShared = false
    SccProjectFilePathRelativizedFromConnection1 = IFXConvert\u0020Setup\\
    SccProjectUniqueName2 = IFXconvert.csproj
    SccLocalPath2 = ..
    CanCheckoutShared = false
    SccProjectFilePathRelativizedFromConnection2 = IFXconvert\\
EndGlobalSection
```

There are three projects in this solution (from a little program called IFXconvert that I found on my laptop). In the solution file, Visual Studio stores source control information about the provider and the ability for that project to exist in shared mode, as well as a global Unique ID assigned by Studio.

The first thing we learn about source control and solutions is that we can have several source control systems for several projects within any given solution. This gives us extreme flexibility, seeing as how we can distribute projects over diverse systems in an enterprise-style environment.

The information stored about the projects just gives us a view into the inner workings of the source control system in Studio; it is very much like a database, and we should treat it as such.

On that topic, we have one major lesson: the Solution is the parent object. When dealing with solutions and projects, create the solution first, separately, as you would the parent table in a database. Then create the projects. While Visual Studio will let you create a solution with a project, don't let it. Create an empty "umbrella" solution, and then build all of the projects you need underneath.

Visual Studio .NET Projects

Projects are more specific than Solutions; they define what tools Visual Studio will use to compile the code stored within. For code, project files store information about the build settings, references, and files. For source control, details are stored in the *proj.vspscc file:

```
{
"FILE_VERSION" = "9237"
"ENLISTMENT_CHOICE" = "NEVER"
"PROJECT_FILE_RELATIVE_PATH" = "relative:IFXconvert"
"NUMBER_OF_EXCLUDED_FILES" = "0"
"ORIGINAL_PROJECT_FILE_PATH" = ""
"NUMBER_OF_NESTED_PROJECTS" = "0"
"SOURCE_CONTROL_SETTINGS_PROVIDER" = "PROVIDER"
}
```

Most of this information is of little interest to us, but you can see that again we have a common pattern: several source control providers supported, and future functionality available (in terms of the NUMBER_OF_NESTED_PROJECTS property).

Outside of the Source Control features, we have to understand that there are essentially two kinds of projects: Web and Local. Web projects are stored on the server supporting the web, which might be the local development machine, or a remote Front Page server. Local projects are stored inside the project directory, and are for non-web types of projects, like Windows Forms and Class Library projects.

All project files have a common problem in Visual Studio: they are stored in the source control system. Some information that might be of interest to a number of users finds itself controlled by SourceSafe, and suddenly we can't change the things we need to change.

Consider a common example: We have five developers on a project: one DBA, one business tier developer, two web developers, and a report writer. The business tier developer needs to add a page to test a DLL she has created, so she creates a directory and file in the web project in Visual Studio. Then the project file and web file are checked in.

After lunch, our intrepid report writer needs to create a new report. He checks out the project file, adds a report, and checks everything back in. But we have a problem. Now the report writer can't compile, because he has a reference to a file that doesn't exist in his project!

This all points to the need for a Team Development Strategy. We need to develop a system for who adds files, when everyone gets a copy of the project, and who compiles final versions. This whole chapter is leading up to this idea, and we'll cover a possible strategy at the end of the chapter.

Handling References

An important part of project control in Visual Studio is the storing of reference information. References are handled differently under .NET than under Windows DNA, since the files are copied from referenced locations at build time. This causes some interesting problems, because obviously, the files referenced by one programmer may well not be in the same place as on other machines. Additionally, things may change from development through test to deployment, and use of a dynamic reference can make this easier.

This harks back to the core problem of Project files in source control, just as the addition of new files did previously. The primary way around this problem is the use of Project References. Project References are driven by the relationship between projects in a given solution, all of whose information is stored in the Project and Solution files handled by the source control (see Figure 6-8). Assuming that we are developing the assemblies we are referencing, this is the best way to reference them in child projects.

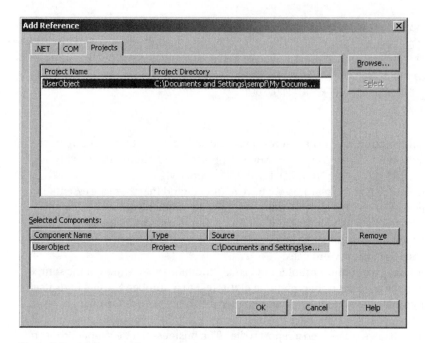

Figure 6-8. *Adding a reference*

The figure shows an example of adding the output of the UserObject project as a reference to a current project. This will cause changes within the Project file of the current project, and it will reference the project as specified within the solution. Because everyone on the team has the same solution file, we can guarantee the location of the original assemblies.

We can see in this extract from the current Project file that the Project reference uses a GUID to reference the added assembly, while the System assembly uses a UNC path. The GUID reference is much more mobile:

```
<!—This is the Project reference we just added.-->
<Reference
    Name = "UserObject"
    Project = "{B5527212-B4A1-4225-B34C-7DB8C490EBA2}"
    Package = "{FAE04EC0-301F-11D3-BF4B-00C04F79EFBC}"
/>
<!—This is a traditional File reference. -->
<Reference
    Name = "System.XML"
```

```
      AssemblyName = "System.Xml"
      HintPath = "..\..\..\WINDOWS\Microsoft.NET\Framework\v1.1.4322\System.XML.dll"
/>
```

When there is no choice but to use a File reference, the trick is to make sure that all developers have the assembly referenced in the same place. Otherwise, when the project files are loaded, Visual Studio won't be able to find the assembly.

Web Services references bring a whole new host of problems. In most applications, web service references are just added using the Add Web References... dialog in Visual Studio. In a team environment, however, a Web service should be treated like a database. The reference is likely to change from development to deployment.

We manage this just as we do a database connection string: the information for the web service should be stored in the application's configuration. Add a File attribute to the appSettings element of the *.config file, and point it to a separate Config file that is not source controlled:

```
<configuration>
    <appSettings file="user.config">
    </appSettings>
</configuration>
```

Of course, you can put <Add> statements within the appSettings block as usual, but developer-specific configuration options can now go in the new User.Config file. Specifically, add a key that is pointing to the service you are referencing:

```
<appSettings>
    <add key="thisApp.remoteServer.service"
      value="http://localhost/webService/Service.asmx"/>
</appSettings>
```

Make sure this User.Config file isn't checking into SourceSafe by excluding it from the project. You can still edit the file as needed in Visual Studio, but other developers won't get it with a normal Get From Source Control operation. Everyone can have an individual service reference.

This will slightly change the way in which web services are built as part of your host application. We are essentially giving up on the automatic building of reference DLLs for your services in exchange for the ability to use the dynamic behavior feature of web services.

Every web reference class in a project interacts with a proxy DLL used to access the web service as if it were a regular assembly. Normally, the URL to reference the service, called the UrlBehavior, is compiled into the DLL. With the UrlBehavior property set to Dynamic, the appSettings element we set in the Config file is used to get the URL instead of the original referenced DLL.

Types of Files in Source Control

In handling source control operations, Visual Studio .NET adds some files to the source control database and reserves others. The information as to which files are reserved and which files are included is useful, but not necessary for day-to-day operations. The fact is that developers should always use Visual Studio for all source control operations. Table 6.1 covers the types of files in consideration by the source control system, as well as their disposition.

Table 6-1. *File Types in Source Control*

Source Controlled files	Independent files
Solution files: The solution file, as we saw above, collects project information.	**Solution User Option files:** The Option file stores solution information about a given workstation that relates to a solution and its collection of projects.
Project files: Project files collect information about files and references.	**Project User Option files:** Project Option files work like Solution Option files, storing information specific to a given workstation.
Config files: These files form system templates. The Config files are programmer modifiable and used to store application-level static information. ASPX applications use Web.Config, and Windows applications are called <appname>.Config.	**Webinfo files:** The WebInfo file allows individual workstations to have different virtual roots, but this is inadvisable.
Source files: The basis of any project, these are the CS, VB, ASPX, and other files that make up the program we are writing. This group constitutes the vast majority of files.	**Build output:** This is what the compiler makes out of our source code.

What it all comes down to is this: Don't use Visual SourceSafe explorer, or the file explorer with any other source control package for that matter. Use Visual Studio for source control operations. It knows all of the files that should and shouldn't be added, and it stores important metainformation about the source control of the solution, as we saw before.

Naming Conventions

Naming conventions are not required or enforced by Visual Studio or Visual SourceSafe (though tools like FXcop assist with this). It just makes sense to have them. Because the Solutions and Projects in Visual Studio are similar to Solutions in Visual Studio, folders in the file system, and the hierarchy of the .NET Framework, we should endeavor to keep the naming similar. Here are some suggestions for naming conventions:

- Use a common root namespace. Use the Namespace property. Make your company name part of a root namespace. MyCompany.MyDivision.MyProject.MyClass is a great reference for future development.

- Namespaces and assembly names should be similar. For the class just given, try MyCompany.MyDivision.MyProject.dll as an assembly name.

- Ensure that VSS Solutions and local folders match the structure of the project, as shown in Figure 6-9.

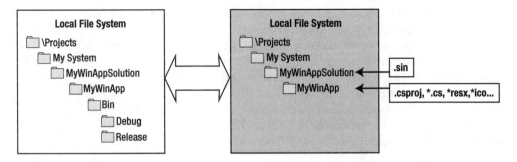

Figure 6-9. *Comparison between the file system and the Source Control*

Web Forms

With the advent of ASPX, writing Internet applications in the Microsoft world is even more popular than it was in the Windows DNA world. Due to the wide variety of skills required, it is also often a team development fiasco, with four or five developers trying to determine how best to utilize source control to get the job done.

Collaborative Development

Because of this difficulty, it is best to have a strategy for tackling group development. There are a number of patterns we can follow, which are derived from the isolation of the developers. In general, the more isolated the developers are, the more smoothly the source control will function. No matter how isolated the development is, however, there are a few bits that should be considered:

- Determine roles before development begins. Decide who has the final word on the ASP files, the report files, the database, the business objects. Determine who is the team leader, and who has the final say on the source control system.

- Create all of the files you will need at the beginning of the project. After that, adding files should be a big event, not something just casually done as needed. Plan the file adds, have everyone check their files in, and get a fresh copy of the project after the add is complete.

Semi-isolated Models

Two kinds of semi-isolated environments are possible given our environment. To enable either one, we use a central server for storage of source files and refer to the URL of the remote project. Each developer can have an individual virtual root and use a local copy of that application. This prevents them from having to have the complete server environment on their workstations, but it has its problems.

First of all, we have the problems of network latency. Working on the server, as is required in a semi-isolated model, requires that the user upload a complete version of the DLL to the server on every compile. With a number of people working on the server, this will eventually be a drag on development. Also, it is amazingly easy to affect another developer's environment. A change to the project of one developer can modify global IIS attributes fairly easily.

The most significant problem, though, is debugging. First, keep in mind that this is remote debugging. The client computer has to attach to the remote machine's ASP.NET process via DCOM or Remoting. This is a very slow process. Most importantly, however, once one client has attached the IIS process, *no other user can access the IIS process at all on the web server*. The significance of this cannot be underestimated. Once one developer is in debug mode, no one else can even access the web server at all.

Working in an Isolated Development Model

Web development in an isolated environment is the way to go. In this system, every developer gets a full copy of the application and works on it independently of everyone else. When a developer has compiled a section, tested it, and checked it back into source control, the lead developer gets a complete copy of the application, compiles it, and deploys it to a test server.

This requires that all of the developers have a complete development system, more or less. If this is an ASP.NET application, everyone has to have at least Windows 2000 or XP Pro, in order to run IIS. If there is Crystal involved, those developers must have the development environment for Crystal Enterprise. In short, the developers must be somewhat empowered to work in this environment.

Even considering the complexities of isolated development, it is by far the better model considering the alternative. Debugging on the client is much preferable to debugging on the server. Control of one's environment is much preferable to joint access. Developers can use File access rather than Front Page access to author the web in question. In short, all of the problems of semi-isolated development are mitigated by using an isolated model.

Some Final Thoughts

Planning is the key to source control, but there is more to the process than just creating a plan: there is carrying it out. Tools have been provided throughout Visual Studio to make the simplest or the most complex source control scenario manageable.

There is a lot to the APIs for source control, more than we can discuss in this chapter. .NET provides a sophisticated automation model that we will discuss, but we should discuss Microsoft's generic Source Control API as well, Microsoft Source Control Command Interface (MSSCCI).

MSSCCI and Other Source Control Packages

As you might have guessed by now, Visual SourceSafe is not the only source control package that we can use to provide document control. Visual Studio .NET subscribes to Microsoft's source control integration API, called Microsoft Source Control Command Interface (MSSCCI). Source-Safe, PVCS, and a host of providers subscribe to this API, just as they do to Visual Studio, Power-Builder, and a host of IDEs. In fact, the list is getting quite long:

- Microsoft Visual C++ 4.0, 5.0, and 6.0

- Microsoft Visual Studio 97 (C++, Basic, J++, etc.)

- Symantec's Visual Café (version 2.0 and later)

- Oracle Developer 2000

- Powerbuilder (versions 5 & 6)

- IBM Visual Age for Java (v2.0, at least)

- Allaire ColdFusion Studio and Allaire HomeSite

- Sun NetDynamics

- Microsoft Visual SourceSafe 4.0 (and later)

- Starbase Versions

- MKS Source Integrity

- Perforce P4 Version Control System

- IBM VisualAge TeamConnection (version 3.0)

- CS-RCS from Component Software

- ClearCase

Setting up the connection between Visual Studio and any other source control package is likely to be the same as setting up a connection to SourceSafe. There is, in fact, a Web-based source control system on the GotDotNet workspaces that is as completely different from Source Safe as one can get, and the setup in Visual Studio is the same, because setup of source control is defined by the IDE in MSSCCI, where the document management is controlled by the source control package.

The trick is changing from one SCC-managed source control package to another. This is very poorly handled by Visual Studio, and requires a registry modification, as defined in Knowledge Base article 319318:

1. Click Start, click Run, type regedit, and then click OK to open Registry Editor.

2. In Registry Editor, expand the following registry key: HKEY_LOCAL_MACHINE\SOFTWARE\ SourceCodeControlProvider\InstalledSCCProviders.

3. In the right pane, double-click the registry key of the source control provider that you want to use (for example, Microsoft Visual SourceSafe), and then copy the data of this key to the clipboard (for example, Software\Microsoft\SourceSafe).

4. In the left pane, click SourceCodeControlProvider.

5. In the right pane, double-click ProviderRegKey.

6. In the Edit String dialog box, replace all of the text in the Value Data box with the contents of your clipboard, and then click OK.

7. Close the registry editor.

8. Restart your application for the changes to take effect.

Using document control under MSSCCI is rather simple, with the majority of source control systems implemented under Visual Studio working very much as defined in the above sections.

Automation

The second minor breakthrough of Visual SourceSafe 6.0c is bringing the SourceControl object to the realm of the people. Though it has previously been accessible (however badly documented the APIs were) from C++, it is now part of the DTE namespace in the Script for the .NET Framework. This means that we can now include source control features in our automation macros.

As part of the DTE.SourceControl property, which returns a SourceControl object, we have six methods:

- **CheckOutItem:** Checks out the specified item

- **CheckOutItems:** Checks out the specified items

- **ExcludeItem :**Excludes the specified item from source control

- **ExcludeItems:** Excludes the specified items from source control

- **IsItemCheckedOut:** Retrieves a Boolean value that indicates whether the specified item is checked out

- **IsItemUnderSCC:** Retrieves a Boolean value that indicates whether the specified item is under source control

Checkout

CheckOutItem and CheckOutItems are exactly what they seem. The principal use for these is to add source control capabilities to existing macros. For instance, if we have a macro that adds text to selected files, we may want to check them all out first. This could be accomplished with a macro similar to the following:

```
Imports EnvDTE
Public Module Module1
  Sub CheckOutSelectedFiles()
    Dim OurFile As SelectedItem
    For Each OurFile In DTE.SelectedItems
      DTE.SourceControl.CheckOutItem(OurFile.Name.ToString())
    Next
  End Sub
End Module
```

Exclude

The ExcludeItem and ExcludeItems methods perform as expected as well. If we needed to remove all images from the source control package, we could run a macro to do so:

```
Imports EnvDTE
Public Module Module1
  Sub RemoveImagesFromSS()
    Dim OurProject As Project
    Dim OurProjectItems As ProjectItem
    OurProject = DTE.ActiveSolutionProjects(0)
    For Each OurProjectItems In OurProject.Collection
      If InStr(OurProjectItems.Name.ToString, ".gif") <> 0 Then
        DTE.SourceControl.ExcludeItem(OurProject.FullName.ToString(), &_
                OurProjectItems.Name.ToString)
      End If
    Next
  End Sub
End Module
```

IsItem

There are two different IsItem methods. They complement the above series of methods. The first is IsItemCheckedOut(). This determines whether source control is required to check out an item. We could use it, pretty much as expected, to determine whether a check out operation would be required at all:

```
Public Module Module1
  Sub CheckOutSelectedFiles()
    Dim OurFile As SelectedItem
    For Each OurFile In DTE.SelectedItems
      If Not DTE.SourceControl.IsItemCheckedOut(OurFile.Name.ToString()) Then
        MsgBox(DTE.SourceControl.CheckOutItem(OurFile.Name.ToString()).ToString())
      End If
    Next
  End Sub
End Module
```

The second, IsItemUnderSCC, could be used in a similar manner in conjunction with the Exclude methods.

Summary

We've covered a lot in a short time. Team development is a big part of working in the Microsoft world, and source control is a big part of team development. We've looked into the following topics, and there is still more to cover that we haven't gotten to here:

- Getting started with Source Control

- Team development strategies

- Solutions and projects

- Web application development

- Windows application development

- MSSCCI and using other source control packages

For more information, using MSDN or the USENET and searching for SCC or MSSCCI would point you in the right direction. Also, there is a great primer on using Visual SourceSafe with Visual Studio as part of the MSDN library installed with Visual Studio. It can help with questions about basic SourceSafe functions, database repairs, and the like.

The most import part of source control, however, is planning. Make sure everyone on the team understands how the system works, and works within the protocol. Create a source control strategy as part of the design documentation. And remember that the purpose of source control is code safety, so treat it as such and the project will move along smoothly.

CHAPTER 7

■ ■ ■

Performance Testing

When people talk about application testing, they mostly talk about testing the software to discover bugs and prove the correctness of the application's behavior. We often refer to this kind of testing as functional testing. On the other hand, there's the fact that sometimes you run up against performance problems that need to be rectified in order to make your applications viable. Consequently, we also need to test applications in order to discover performance problems and prove that the application performs as expected or required. The software industry has developed many test strategies, techniques, and tools to combat the potential bugs and performance bottlenecks in software. In this chapter, we will take a close look at one performance testing tool, namely, Application Center Test, which comes with Visual Studio .NET Enterprise Editions.

Different types of applications demand different types of performance testing techniques and tools. As one of the most commonly used development environments, Visual Studio contains a wide range of debugging and testing tools such as integrated debuggers, profiler, and remote debugging tools. As we are developing more and more Internet and intranet applications, we find that Visual Studio has sadly been lacking a web application performance testing tool, and so we often need to use other tools.

With the release of Visual Studio .NET, things have changed. VS .NET Enterprise Editions include Application Center Test, or ACT, which provides powerful features to make web application performance testing easy to create and operate.

In this chapter, you will learn the following:

- What ACT can (and can't) do

- How to create and configure ACT projects and tests

- How to run tests

- How to analyze test results

- How to customize test scripts

In the following sections, we'll have an overview of performance testing issues and ACT. Later in the chapter, we'll then go into more detail to explain the tasks involved in testing web applications using ACT.

Performance Testing

Web applications typically support a large number of concurrent users. It is critical that development teams understand the capacity of both the web servers and the applications themselves in order to deliver successful applications that perform well under all conditions, especially during peak periods. Performance testing of a web application provides us with concrete and quantified data to measure how well the application performs under heavy load, and to identify any potential problems that may affect the application's performance.

A successful web application should have the following three performance characteristics:

- **Low response time**: The response time is often measured as the delay between the time when a request is sent by a client and the time the client receives the full response to the request. Technically, the application response time is the sum of the response times of all components including the web server, database server, network connections, and so on. In general, response time increases as the number of client requests increases. When the system's resource is under a low load, the response time increases slowly because the system has the capacity to serve more clients. When the system is under heavy load, response time increases sharply, since the system lacks the resources to serve additional clients.

- **High throughput**: The web application throughput is the number of client requests the system can process in a unit of time, normally a second. It measures the practical throughput that can be achieved in normal operation, not the theoretical maximum capacity. When the system load is light, throughput increases proportionally to the number of client requests. As the number of client requests continues to rise, it eventually reaches its peak and then starts to degrade.

- **High scalability**: Scalability is measured by how well the application performs when the number of requests increases, and how much the application's performance increases when the system is upgraded. It is common for a business to outgrow its supporting applications. For instance, a business may anticipate that it will have 10,000 customers per day, but soon finds that it now attracts 100,000 customers per day. A good application should be able to be scaled up by simply upgrading its system hardware without significant redesign and recoding. For instance, it should be able to increase the throughput proportionally with faster or more processors and more memory. We should also be able to scale up applications that may serve a very large number of users concurrently, and therefore are designed to run on a web farm environment, by simply adding more servers to the farm without changing the application code.

In most applications, system requirements normally include the first two measurements. For instance, an online bookshop application's requirement specification may be to provide up to 1000 concurrent users the ability to search the catalog with an average response time of 5 seconds. Development teams must then design and build the applications to satisfy such requirements. While the high scalability measurement is not always clearly stated, it's still a real requirement in most applications.

During the development cycle, the development team must conduct numerous performance tests with different objectives. At the early design stage, performance testing provides data for the team to decide on hardware and software requirements. At the implementation phase, developers execute performance testing to ensure that the application will provide the required performance with the given hardware and software. If the application fails to achieve the performance target, developers must investigate the problem, normally by identifying and resolving the bottlenecks of the application. In the testing phase, testers and customers also execute performance testing to prove that the system performs as required.

With proper performance testing, we can measure the application performance, discover existing and potential problems, and improve the application performance. A good performance testing tool provides us with statistics about not only the performance of applications, but also any potential problems. ACT is one such performance testing tool.

Overview

ACT is the second incarnation of a web application performance testing tool created by Microsoft. In 1999, Microsoft released the Web Application Stress tool (WAS), a tool that can simulate multiple requests to web application pages. ACT builds on WAS and includes most of the useful features available in WAS.

■**Note** If you don't have ACT included in your version of VS .NET, you can download WAS from `www.microsoft.com/technet/archive/itsolutions/intranet/downloads/webstres.mspx`. Note that Microsoft has not made any new improvements to WAS since early 2000, and it is not clear whether it will continue to make WAS available, now that ACT has been released.

ACT comes in two editions. The ACT Enterprise Edition is included with Application Center 2000, a deployment and management tool for web applications. The Developer Edition is shipped with Visual Studio .NET, and is also called ACT for Visual Studio .NET. The latter has a subset of the features available in the former. In this chapter, we will be looking at the Developer Edition, and the term ACT will always denote this edition unless explicitly stated. If you'd like to learn more about the ACT Enterprise Edition, please read the Application Center 2000 documentation or go to the Application Center website at `http://www.microsoft.com/applicationcenter/default.asp`.

ACT is a simulation tool that can be used to stress test any web applications compliant with the HTTP 1.0 and 1.1 protocols. Since the primary purpose of stress testing is to discover and analyze application performance and scalability issues, ACT provides a valuable tool for web application developers to test their applications against their performance requirements. In addition to normal testing features like the ability to generate test scripts, automate testing, and collect and report test results, ACT provides other features that are more specific to web applications.

As I mentioned earlier, web applications typically support a large number of concurrent users. ACT allows us to create multiple simultaneous connections to simulate such situations. It records, collates, and presents test results, which can be analyzed to work out the performance of many web application elements and pinpoint any potential problems. By their nature, web applications are open to misuse, hacking, and so on. As businesses have become increasingly aware of security issues, especially those associated with web applications, more and more web applications are being protected with security mechanisms such as the Secure Sockets Layer (SSL) in combination with user authentication. ACT supports testing incorporating both of these, but with some limitations. Before we get into detail about how to use it, it is important to understand what ACT can do and what it can't do.

What ACT Can Do

ACT provides a set of functionalities sufficient to most common web application stress testing requirements. The following is a list showing ACT's features:

- ACT is a web application performance testing tool. It is designed (and should be used) to test how well applications perform.

- ACT can create a number of simultaneous browser connections for each test run, and it is therefore capable of collecting realistic result data that reflect the server performance under heavy traffic.

- ACT supports both 40-bit and 128-bit SSL encryption. You can test URLs with HTTPS.

- ACT supports all four Microsoft Internet Information Server (IIS) authentication methods: anonymous access, basic authentication, integrated Windows authentication, and digest authentication for Windows domain servers.

- ACT supports the simulation of a large number of unique user connections. You can create test users and user groups.

- ACT stores test results for later analysis and comparison.

- ACT provides simple graphic representations of test data.

- ACT supports browser session recording. You can generate test scripts by recording activities performed in a browser session and rerun the test at a later time.

- ACT can collate test data for pages on the same or different web servers. If your test script sends requests to pages on different web servers, ACT can log performance statistics for each of them and calculate various average results.

- ACT supports test automation and scheduling by providing two well-designed object models: Application and Test. You can use any programming language or script capable of instantiating COM objects and invoking COM methods to automate ACT or to execute tests.

What ACT Can't Do

It's important to know right up front what ACT can't do, at least so you can start to try to find alternative ways around certain things. The following list shows the features I feel would be great but that aren't in the current version of ACT:

- ACT is not a functional testing tool. That is, it doesn't provide you with the ability to verify the correctness of the target applications. In situations in which you need to perform functional testing, you should use functional testing tools such as Rational TeamTest.

- While ACT can run on both client and server machines, it doesn't provide the ability to coordinate multiple test client machines to execute tests. While it's possible to use high performance test client machines to create and execute tests, in most cases test clients are less powerful than target web servers. Therefore, you often need to run tests simultaneously using multiple test clients in order to stretch the web server. The lack of test client coordination is rather surprising given that the older WAS does offer this capability, although it's not always easy to set up the clients, and it may take some time to configure all test clients properly. You can work around this limitation by distributing tests to multiple client machines and running them simultaneously. However, you will have either to manually coordinate them or write your own program to do so.

- Although ACT supports SSL, it can't send client certificates or verify server certificates.

- ACT can't simulate different network bandwidths between the test client and web server. Users of web applications normally use different connection media: Some use a corporate network, some use broadband Internet connections, and others use dialup through analog modems. Users on low-speed connections normally generate fewer requests than those on high-speed connections. When you test a web application under development, you typically run tests across the high-speed corporate network. The test result may not always be a true reflection of real-world scenarios. This is also a surprising omission considering it was implemented in WAS.

- ACT does not support the form-based authentication used by most Internet applications.

What the above list implies is that if you already use WAS or other tools for web application performance testing, you should not abandon them yet, because they still provide a few features you can't get from ACT. I know that until ACT catches up, I'll keep WAS handy alongside ACT for my own work. In addition to WAS, there are other tools that offer more sophisticated functional and performance testing features, including those missing from ACT. Such tools include LoadRunner by Mercury Interactive (http://www.mercuryinteractive.com), Rational TeamTest by Rational (http://www.rational.com), Web Performance Trainer by Web Performance Inc. (http://www.webperformanceinc.com), and e-Load by Empirix (http://www.empirix.com).

A First Look at ACT

ACT is available as a part of both Visual Studio .NET Enterprise Architect and Visual Studio .NET Enterprise Developer Editions. If you selected to install ACT during the installation of Visual Studio .NET, you can find the shortcut to the ACT program in the Visual Studio .NET Enterprise Features folder. When it runs for the first time, it loads a sample project entitled ACTSamples. If this project does not appear, you can find it in the ACT program folder and open it. By default, it's installed in Program Files\Microsoft ACT\Samples\ACTSamples.

ACT provides a well-organized integrated development environment (IDE) that allows you to easily create and execute tests as well as to analyze the test results. Figure 7-1 illustrates an example of viewing test results in the ACT IDE.

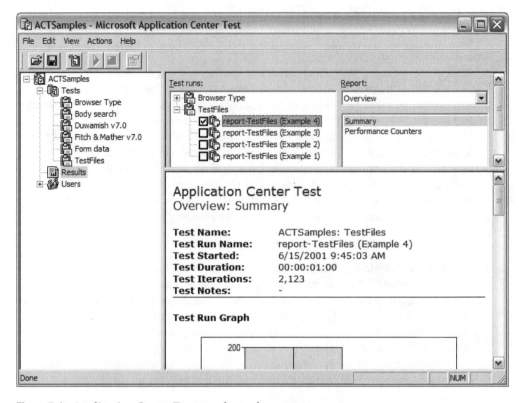

Figure 7-1. *Application Center Test sample results*

The left pane shows a tree view of tests, users, and test results in the currently open project. I will use the term Project Explorer, if only to be consistent with the Visual Studio .NET terminology, to refer to this pane. The ACTSamples project contains several preconfigured sample tests that can be used to demonstrate the capabilities and features of ACT.

Of the six included sample tests, you can run the following four to test against a set of test pages shipped with ACT:

- Browser Type: Sends different HTTP headers with each request, mimicking access by a range of different browsers

- Body Search: Checks to see whether a specified string is in the body of the response

- Form Data: Pulls query string data from a text file and passes it in a POST

- TestFiles: Performs a dynamic test that uses the sample test files provided

You can see full descriptions about each test in the header comments of the test script. The target test pages are in the Program Files\Microsoft ACT\Samples\TestFiles folder. In order to access and test them, you need to set up the TestFiles folder in IIS in one of two ways:

- Copy the TestFiles folder to the root directory of your web server.

- Create a virtual root in your web server to point to the TestFiles folder. The default Read and Script permissions are adequate.

Once you have done this, you can access the test files through http://localhost/TestFiles/. Note that the sample tests all reference the web server using localhost. Therefore, if your web server is on a different machine from the one you run ACT on, you will need to manually modify the test scripts. We'll look at writing test scripts in more detail in later sections. If you need to change the target web server now, simply follow these two steps:

1. Open each test by clicking it in the Project Explorer. The right pane should then show the test script for the selected test.

2. Change the value of g_sServer from localhost to your web server address.

Now you can run a test by first selecting a test and then either clicking the Start Test button on the toolbar, or the Start Test command in the Actions menu, or, simply pressing Ctrl+F5. The test status dialog will appear as shown in Figure 7-2.

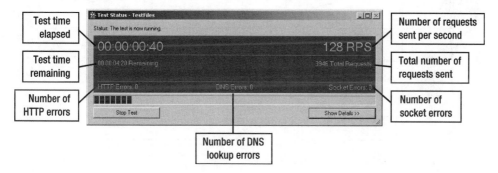

Figure 7-2. *Testing in Progress*

The Show Details button expands the dialog to show the above results in a chart, as illustrated in Figure 7-3.

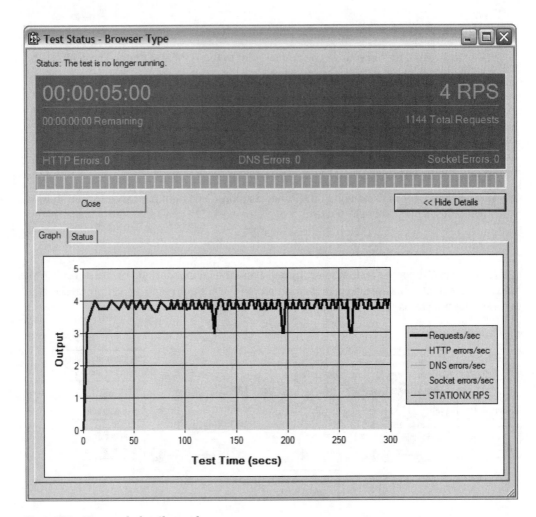

Figure 7-3. *Test result details graph*

During the test, you can also click the Stop Test button to stop the test. Once a test has been stopped, you can restart it only from the beginning. That is, you can't pause and resume a test. After the test finishes, you can view your test results by clicking the Results node in the Project Explorer. Figure 7-4 shows an example.

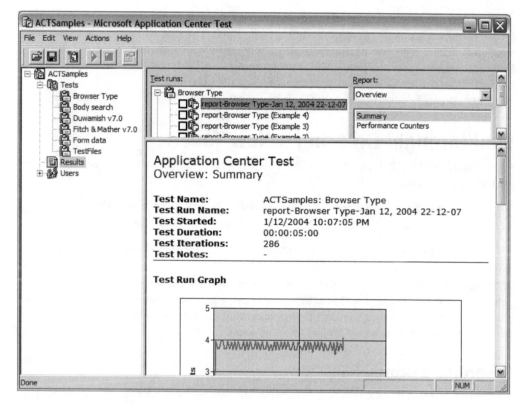

Figure 7-4. *Test results*

In the right-hand pane, you can see a list of tests and the reports from each run. Later sections explain the test results in more detail. For now, just try running a few to get a feel for the process.

The other two tests, Duwamish v7.0 and Fitch & Mather v7.0, target the Duwamish Online and F&M Stocks sample applications shipped with Visual Studio .NET. Because the Visual Studio .NET installer does not automatically install those sample applications, you will need to install them yourself if you want to try these tests. By default, the Visual Studio .NET installation copies the Windows Installer package for both sample applications to the Microsoft Visual Studio .NET\Enterprise Samples folder. Please read the Readme.htm files for each application for installation instructions.

As with other Microsoft applications, the ACT IDE offers a toolbar for you to quickly perform some common tasks (see Figure 7-5).

Figure 7-5. *The ACT toolbar*

The first two buttons let you open another project and save the current project. The third button is for you to create a new test in the current project. The next two allow you to run and stop a test. If no test is running, the stop button is grayed out, as shown in the figure. The last button allows you to see the properties of the currently selected test. These actions are all available from the menu, which also provides a few more functions.

Once you are familiar with the ACT IDE, it's time to create a simple test to get started.

Walkthrough: Creating a New Test

An ACT test is a script that uses the ACT Test object hierarchy to specify the test process. There are two ways to create a new test in ACT:

- Create a new test by recording a browser session. You can then modify the generated script if required.

- Create a new test by manually entering test scripts using either VBScript or JScript.

Once you are familiar with the Test object model, you can create tests by writing scripts yourself. However, it's often more productive to record a browser session and let ACT generate a script for you. You can then modify the generated script to suit your needs. So, let's start from the beginning by creating a new project and a new test.

Recording a Browser Session

Recording a browser session in ACT is fairly straightforward. The following steps show the whole process.

1. In ACT, select File and then New Project from the menu to create a new project.

2. Click the New Test button on the toolbar to create a new test.

3. In the New Test Wizard, select the Record a new test option. While ACT supports both VBScript and JScript for writing test scripts, recording creates test scripts only in VBScript.

4. In the Browser Record dialog, click the Start recording button. ACT will start a new instance of Internet Explorer.

5. In Internet Explorer, type in the URL http://localhost/TestFiles/ad_test.asp and click Enter. This opens the page in Internet Explorer. In the background, ACT records the requests sent to the web server. When you run the test later on, ACT will be able to re-create those requests.

Switch back to ACT, click the Stop recording button and then the Next button. Name the test `AdTest` and click the Next and then the Finish buttons to close the wizard. ACT will automatically generate a test script that will set up page requests when you run the test later on. The test is now ready. The next step is to run it to ensure that it works properly. By default, the test will run for five minutes.

On your web server, open the Windows Task Manager and click the `Performance` tab to watch the CPU usage. If you run the test from another machine, do the same there as well. You should see that the CPU usage on both machines is much higher than normal. CPU usage is an important indicator of the website performance and the test's effectiveness. We will explain this in more detail in a minute. Let's now turn our attention to configuring and running tests.

Creating a Test Manually

Whether you are an experienced programmer or just starting out, you probably have a love for code writing in your blood. Once you have run through the Test object model reference in the ACT help files, you may feel the temptation to actually write some code yourself. After all, wizards are for nonprogrammers, and automatically generated code is unlikely to be as good as your own code. You might want to modify a prerecorded test to get a feel for what can be done in test scripts first.

If you want, you can create an empty test by selecting `Create an empty test` in the New Test Wizard (no, you can't avoid the wizard here). You can then select the script language and assign it a name. ACT will still generate one line of code, `Test.SendRequest("http://localhost")`, for you, but I really can't see why it shouldn't be deleted. The rest, of course, is up to you. But don't despair! We'll look at testing in more detail so you can get a better idea of the sort of thing you will need to write.

Project Properties

Before we go any further, let's take a look at the settings you can configure for each test project. Right-click the project in the Project Explorer and select `Properties`. The project properties dialog presents all configurable projectwide settings.

General Properties

The `General` tab in the project properties dialog allows you to set whether any objects on the web server should be excluded from tests in the project. You can also set proxy server properties if the test clients connect to the web server through a proxy server. Figure 7-6 illustrates the configurable general properties.

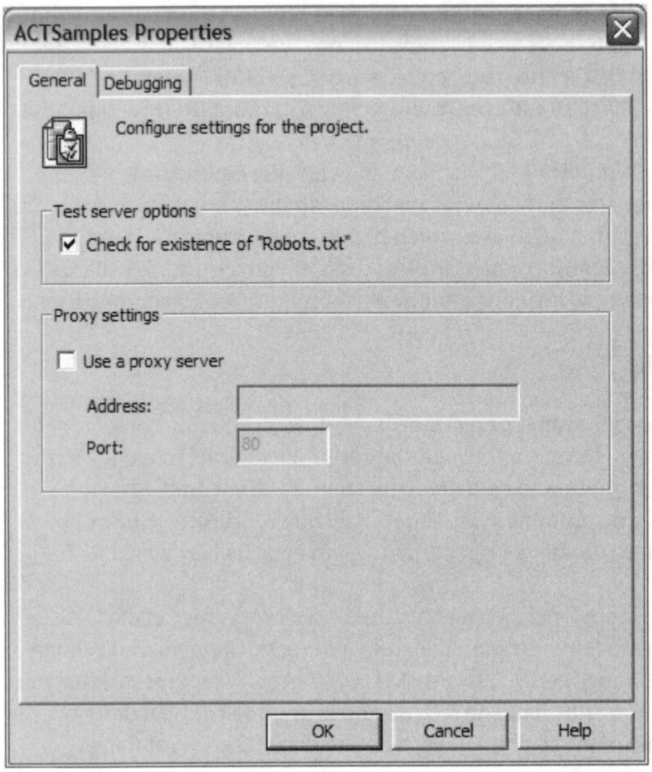

Figure 7-6. *ACT general properties page*

Since search engines became popular to help Internet users find information on the Web, system administrators use the web robot exclusion list to instruct the search robots to bypass certain sites or pages that they do not want to be searchable. They usually create a robots.txt file on the root directory of a website to specify a list of pages, or the whole site, that should not be indexed. ACT can check this file to decide whether certain objects on the target web server should be excluded from the tests as well. ACT enables this checking by default, but you can turn it off by clearing the Check for existence of "Robots.txt" checkbox. Since ACT ignores all META tags in target HTML pages, it doesn't pick up any exclusion instructions specified in the ROBOTS META tags. Therefore you must use a Robots.txt file to specify what pages should be excluded. You can find more information about the Robots.txt file at http://www.robotstxt.org/wc/robots.html. A good resource for the robots exclusion protocol can be found at http://www.robotstxt.org/wc/exclusion.html#robotstxt.

Many corporate networks use proxy servers to cache frequently accessed web content to reduce the traffic between the network and the Internet. If you test a website outside of the company network, you may have to follow the company policy to go through a designated proxy server. In such cases, you can enable the Use a proxy server option and specify the proxy server address and port.

However, you should be aware of the implications of using proxy servers for stress testing. The first is that you may be getting test responses from the proxy server rather than the actual web server, and this will obviously invalidate the test results. Second, the proxy server itself may become the bottleneck during the stress testing, so you won't get a true indication of the target web application performance.

Debugging Properties

You can also configure the test tracing properties for a project. Figure 7-7 illustrates the possible settings.

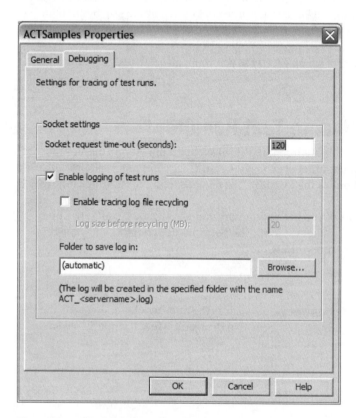

Figure 7-7. *ACT debugging properties*

If a connection has been idle for a long time, you may want to close it so that inactive connections don't eat up valuable system resources. You can specify the `Socket request time-out` value to instruct ACT to drop a connection if the specified number of seconds has elapsed since the last request or response.

While ACT already collects useful test data during a test, you may also want to log extra information about the test status or error conditions in your script. You can instruct ACT to write textual data to a log file by enabling test logging in this dialog and calling the Trace method of the global ACT Test object when required. By default, ACT writes the log data to the `ACTTrace.log` file located in the `Program Files\Microsoft ACT` directory. However, you will generally want to store project-specific data in a separate log file by specifying a folder where the log should be placed. ACT will then write the log data to `ACT_<ServerName>.log` in that folder, where `<ServerName>` is the name of the target web server.

> **■Caution** The log file is cleared each time a test is run. If you intend to review the log files between runs, be sure to rename the file after a test is finished.

If your script writes a large amount of data to the log file, the size of the file may increase rapidly. To prevent it from growing too large, you can restrict its maximum size by enabling log file recycling and specifying a threshold size. Once the log file reaches this size, it will be cleared before new data are added to it.

Now that you have your project set up exactly as you want, give it a run. This time, let's take a closer look at the results.

Reading and Analyzing Test Results

For each test, ACT presents three different reports. The *overview* report shows the summary of test statistics and major errors encountered during the test. The *graphs* report allows you to generate graphical representations of the test data. The *requests* report lists various test results related to each request.

The overview report consists of two parts: summary and performance counters. The summary shows statistics related to the test itself. The performance counters show the readings of selected performance measures during the test.

Overview Summary

The overview summary shows various test results such as the number of requests sent and the average response time. Figure 7-8 illustrates the IDE in the results view. It contains seven sections. Let's look at each section in more detail.

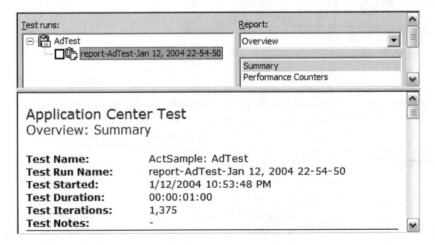

Figure 7-8. *Test result summary*

Header

The lower pane in Figure 7-8 shows the header of the overview summary. The results are fairly self-explanatory. The only item that may not be quite so obvious is Test Iterations. This value shows the number of passes the test has run through. This is different from the total number of requests, because a test can generate multiple requests in each pass. The test we created with the wizard is quite simple, since each pass generates exactly two requests: one to the ad_test.asp page and another to an image file, logo.gif, used in that page.

Test Run Graph

This graph is almost identical to the one shown in the details view of the Test Status dialog. The only difference is that by default it shows only the number of requests sent during the test, as illustrated in Figure 7-9.

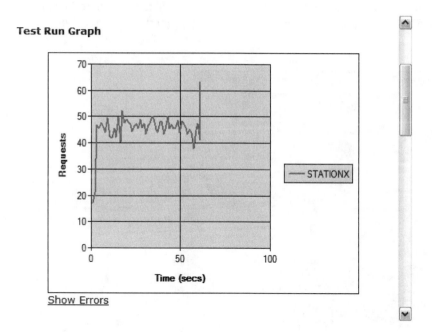

Figure 7-9. *Test run graph*

To see the number of socket, DNS, and HTTP errors, you can click the Show Errors link below the graph. We saw those statistics earlier, on the Test Status screen while a test was running.

Properties

This section shows the test type and other configurable properties for the current run, as illustrated in Figure 7-10.

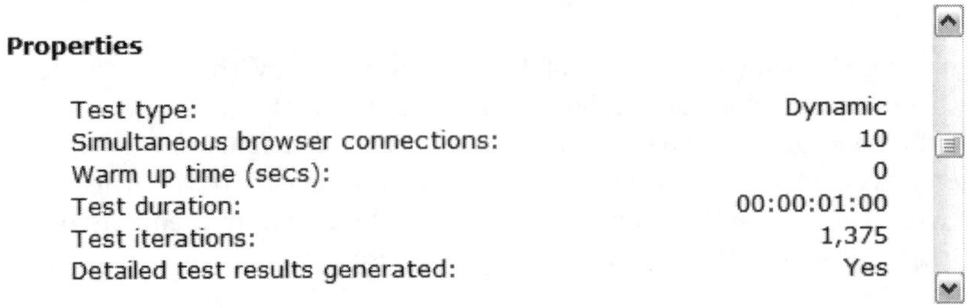

Properties

Test type:	Dynamic
Simultaneous browser connections:	10
Warm up time (secs):	0
Test duration:	00:00:01:00
Test iterations:	1,375
Detailed test results generated:	Yes

Figure 7-10. *Test properties*

ACT supports only dynamic tests. A dynamic test is either a bit of VBScript or JScript that sends requests to a web server. When a dynamic test runs, it can change many aspects of the test such as the target URLs and the order in which the requests are sent.

You can configure other properties by right-clicking the test in the project explorer and selecting Properties from the context menu to open the test properties dialog as shown in Figure 7-11.

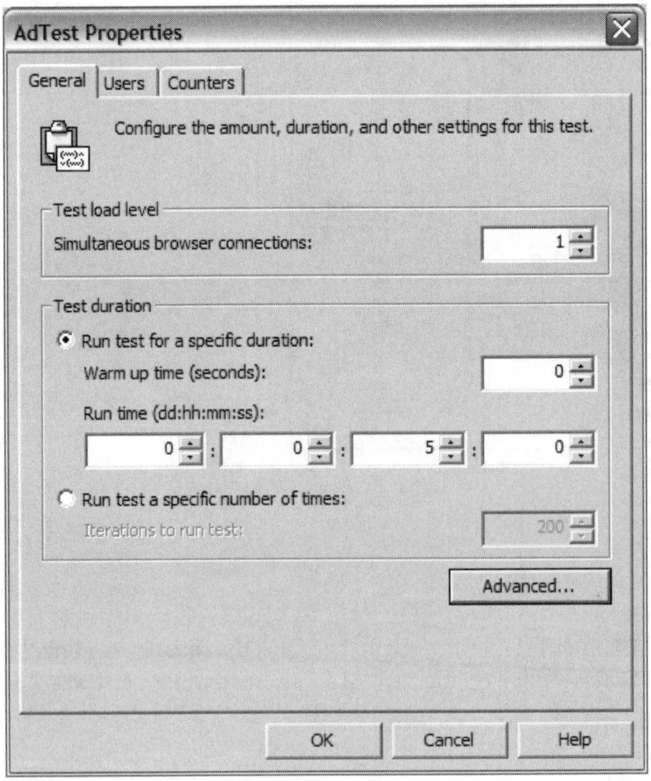

AdTest Properties

General | Users | Counters

Configure the amount, duration, and other settings for this test.

Test load level

Simultaneous browser connections: 1

Test duration

● Run test for a specific duration:

Warm up time (seconds):   0

Run time (dd:hh:mm:ss):

0 : 0 : 5 : 0

○ Run test a specific number of times:

Iterations to run test: 200

Advanced...

OK   Cancel   Help

Figure 7-11. *General test properties dialog*

The simultaneous browser connections figure shows the number of concurrent connections to the web server. This test uses only one connection. While HTTP itself is a connectionless protocol, HTTP 1.1 offers the keep-alive feature. A web browser and a web server supporting this feature will establish one connection between them, send multiple requests through the connection, and close it once all requests have been sent.

Since web servers typically serve many simultaneous connections, a test with multiple connections more accurately represents the real-world situation. ACT is capable of opening up to 2000 simultaneous connections, although you would usually use considerably fewer, because such a large number of connections would overload the client machine running the test. If the client machine is powerful enough, you can configure it with the maximum number of concurrent connections your web application is designed to support. In most cases, however, the client machine may not be able to support that maximum number of connections. In such cases, you start with one connection and increase it gradually in each subsequent test until the CPU usage at the client machine reaches about 80% during the test. In general, when the CPU usage is above 80%, the client machine can't generate requests fast enough and therefore becomes the performance bottleneck itself. The test results then don't accurately reflect the server performance. You can either watch the CPU usage using the Windows Task Manager, or record it by adding a CPU performance counter to the test. We will cover the latter method in the Performance Counters section.

The warm-up time specifies the number of seconds after the test starts and before ACT starts to collect the test results. If you have worked with databases before, you probably know that it takes much longer to open the first database connection than to open subsequent connections because of the connection pooling feature used to cache database connections. As a result, when you access a web page that needs to open database connections for the first time, the response time may not be representative if included in the test result. Another factor that may cause false long response times is that a page may need to instantiate COM+ components, again due to the COM+ object pooling feature. There are other factors such as connection to other systems via Web Services or SOAP requests.

The test duration specifies the length of time the test should run. Instead of specifying the test duration, you can also specify the number of test iterations in order to run a test for a particular number of passes. Setting those figures allows you to test the system in continuous operation.

There is another setting, `Generate detailed test results`, which is accessible by clicking the Advanced button. Figure 7-12 shows the Advanced Settings dialog.

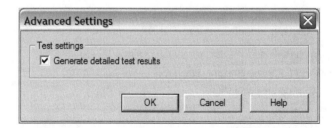

Figure 7-12. *Advanced test settings*

When you enable this setting, ACT will generate statistics for each request, shown in the detailed request statistics report. If this option is disabled, ACT will generate only the average overall requests during the test. While enabling this option will create a more detailed report, it also takes more time to record the data and therefore reduces the test client's ability to generate more requests.

The other two tabs, users and counters, allow you to assign users and add performance counters to tests. We will cover adding users in the Authentication and Users section, and performance counters in the Performance Counters section.

Summary

This section contains the test result summary. It shows the total number of requests and the total number of connections in fairly obvious fashion, as illustrated in Figure 7-13.

Summary

Total number of requests:	2,753
Total number of connections:	2,751
Average requests per second:	45.88
Average time to first byte (msecs):	91.07
Average time to last byte (msecs):	102.74
Average time to last byte per iteration (msecs):	205.70
Number of unique requests made in test:	2
Number of unique response codes:	1

Figure 7-13. *Test results summary*

Since each test run produces two requests in our example, one to the page and another to the GIF image file, you would probably expect that the total number of connections should be exactly half of the total number of requests. The report, however, shows that they are the same.

The reason for this seemingly unexpected result is that the New Test Wizard generates a script by which it creates a new connection for each request. It also posts requests only in HTTP 1.0 format. In order to test the server performance with the HTTP 1.1 keep-alive feature, you will have to change the script manually. You will see how this can be done later in the chapter.

■**Note** The total number of connections may be less than the total number of requests (as shown in the figure). This is because when the test finishes at a specific time, the test may not have a chance to close and record the connection after it sends a request using the connection.

The average requests per second (RPS) figure is also quite obvious; it's just the total number of requests sent divided by the test duration in seconds. The next two figures, though, are more interesting.

The time to first byte (TTFB) shows the time difference, in milliseconds, between sending out a request to the server and receiving the first byte of the response from the server. The time to last byte (TTLB), on the other hand, shows the time between sending out a request and receiving the last byte of the response. The average TTFB and TTLB therefore show the average measurements obtained during the test run.

Both TTFB and TTLB figures measure the *latency*, or response time, of the web server to serve out a page. When the server is heavily in use, the latency increases rapidly. A long TTFB usually indicates a combination of server and application performance problems:

- The web server may be under stress; that is, the request may be held in the request queue on the server for a long time before it gets processed. If the web server is shared between your applications and others, it is possible that there is a problem with the server itself rather than your application.

- Or your application may be slow. Since TTFB indicates when the browser receives the first response byte, it may indicate that your application may take a long time to render the response HTML.

The difference between TTFB and TTLB shows how long the application takes to process a request, and therefore is a good indication of how the application performs under heavy load.

The average time to last byte per iteration shows the difference between the time when the first request in a pass is sent and the time when the last byte of the last response is received. Since this test sends out two requests per pass, this figure is roughly double the average TTLB.

The number of unique requests made in this test is two: the ad_test.asp page and the logo.gif image file. The number of unique response codes reports the response code received from the web server. Note that it reports only HTTP errors. If you stop the web server or pull out the network cable on your development machine, ACT can't record any more response codes, because it isn't receiving any HTTP response from the server at all. The Response Codes section shows all HTTP response codes in greater detail.

Error Counts

This section shows the number of HTTP, DNS, and socket errors, as shown in Figure 7-14.

Figure 7-14. *Test error counts*

We've already seen these, so I won't go into any more detail about them now.

Additional Network Statistics

As the title suggests, this section reports aspects of the network status that aren't reported in previous sections. Figure 7-15 shows a sample result.

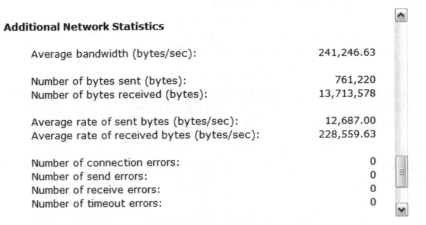

Additional Network Statistics

Average bandwidth (bytes/sec):	241,246.63
Number of bytes sent (bytes):	761,220
Number of bytes received (bytes):	13,713,578
Average rate of sent bytes (bytes/sec):	12,687.00
Average rate of received bytes (bytes/sec):	228,559.63
Number of connection errors:	0
Number of send errors:	0
Number of receive errors:	0
Number of timeout errors:	0

Figure 7-15. *Network statistics during testing*

The average rate of sent bytes and average rate of received bytes show the respective numbers of bytes sent and received per second during the test. The average bandwidth shows the sum of the above two quantities. Note that this figure is generally lower than the actual network bandwidth because it measures only the bandwidth actually used by the test. The number of bytes sent and the number of bytes received show the total number of bytes sent and received during the test.

To accurately measure the server performance, suspend as many programs and services as possible that may use the network on the client machine to maximize the network bandwidth available to testing. If the average bandwidth used by the test approaches the actual network bandwidth, the test result may not be accurate, since the bottleneck may now be the network connection between the client and server machines. You can add network performance counters to obtain the total network usage during testing in order to compare them with the bandwidth consumed by the test.

The number of connection errors shows the number of times the test client fails to connect to the web server. Such errors may indicate that the web server is offline, but it can also be caused by the inability of the web server to establish connections under heavy load, a bad router, and so on. The number of send errors and the number of receive errors show the number of times the test client fails to send out a request or receive a response. The number of timeout errors indicates the number of times the test client times out between sending out a request and waiting for the response to come back. The default timeout is 120 seconds, which you can change manually in the test script by setting Test.Properties.Item("TestProperties:Timeout").Value. You can find a list of all configurable test properties under the TestProperty object in the MSDN Library. Since most web applications require a faster response time than 2 minutes, you should change it in most cases. A good timeout value should represent the threshold of acceptable server response time. For instance, if a web application requirement specifies that users should get a response within 30 seconds, setting the timeout value to 30 will help you identify how often this requirement has not been met during testing.

Response Codes

This section lists all response codes that the test client received from the server. The Count figure shows the total number of times a particular response code was received, while the Percent figure shows the percentage of a response code count against the total count of all response codes.

Requests

If you have enabled the Generate detailed test results option for the test, you can investigate detailed results for each unique request made in the test. To see the test result for a request, select Requests in the report list and then click the request target, as illustrated in Figure 7-16.

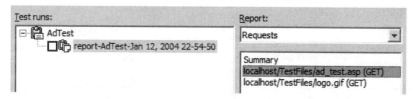

Figure 7-16. *Checking a request*

The request details report header is the same as that of the overview report. The report contains four sections. Three of them will be very similar to the corresponding sections in the overview:

- The Request Information section shows the server name and the request target path on the server. It also displays the request method, which is either GET or POST.

- The Additional Network Statistics section shows the network statistics related to the request. Each result has the same meaning as its counterpart in the Summary and Additional Network Statistics sections of the Overview report, except that it reports only the test data collected for the particular request.

- The Response Codes section is also similar to the corresponding section in the Overview report. Again it also shows the response code received from the response to the request.

The Request Performance section, however, is where you can get more detailed information about the request. The request number shown here is the number of this particular request sent during the test. The meaning of the request content length is clear enough. While you already know what TTFB and TTLB mean, the detailed statistics for each of them and the request content length need some more explanation, since they show some statistically significant results.

Statistics Review

To understand the importance of your data, it helps to know a little bit of statistics theory. While we won't be able to cover nearly enough here, it is a good idea to understand a few terms. A graph will also help.

Figure 7-17 shows a distribution of results known as a *normal distribution* of response times. As you can see, in a normal distribution most results are close to an "average" time in the middle of the graph, while a smaller number of requests have been delivered really quickly, and a few have taken a bit longer.

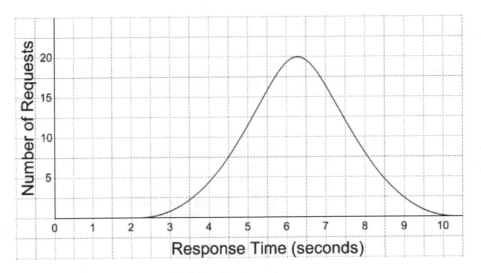

Figure 7-17. *Response time normal distribution*

Let's make sure we understand a few terms:

- Minimum: The lowest individual value in our distribution. Here the minimum is about 3 seconds, with one request achieving the minimum response time.

- Maximum: The highest individual value in our distribution. Here the maximum is about 9.5 seconds, also with one request achieving the maximum response time.

- Median: The "middle" value in our distribution. If we have, say, 99 requests, the median is about 6.5 seconds, which is the response time for the 50th fastest (same as the 50th slowest) request. In other words, the median is the value for which half the responses are faster, and half are slower.

- Mean: What most people just call the "average." It's the sum of all the response times divided by the total number of requests. In a perfectly "normal" distribution, the value of the median and the mean are identical. Most real distributions are actually slightly skewed, so the median and the mean are most likely different. (For example, if the slowest response time were doubled, the mean response time would increase, but the median would be unchanged.)

- Percentiles: The 25th percentile (for example) is the value below which 25% of the results fall. In our response example, 25% of the requests took less than roughly 5 seconds to answer, so the value of the 25th percentile is 5. Similarly, the 75th percentile is roughly 7.5 seconds. Therefore, 50% of the requests received a response between 5 and 7.5 seconds.

And again, in a perfect world, the 50th percentile would have the same value as both the mean and the median. Although the world is not perfect, in most cases these three values are very close.

- Standard Deviation: This is a tricky one. This is a measure of how tightly or loosely the results are spread about the median. A smaller number indicates a sharper curve, and means that most of our results are quite close to the mean. A curve with the same mean and a much bigger standard deviation would mean that our average speed is the same, but that we're getting a spread of really fast and really slow responses. A standard deviation of zero would mean that every response took exactly the same time.

There's more to statistics than this, and if you get into testing in a real way you'll need to study it a little so you know what your numbers are telling you.

Request Performance

Now that we understand a little statistics, it's a matter of applying the knowledge when reading the request performance data in the request details report. Let's look at a sample set of TTFB statistics as shown in Figure 7-18.

```
Time to first byte - TTFB (msecs)
    Minimum:                    0.00
    Maximum:                  110.00
    Average:                   18.17
    Standard Deviation:         9.37
    25th Percentile:           10.00
    50th Percentile:           19.99
    75th Percentile:           20.04
```

Figure 7-18. *TTFB statistics*

The minimum TTFB is 0.00 milliseconds, which is rather strange, since it's very unlikely that you would actually receive a response in less than a hundredth of a millisecond. A reasonable guess as to the cause of this anomaly is that the response came so quickly that ACT couldn't properly record the time difference. This abnormality can occur if you are running a test against a web server located on the same machine as the client. Regardless of the cause, this is more of an exception, and we won't concern ourselves much about it.

The maximum indicates that the longest wait for a response during the test was 110 milliseconds. What's labeled here as "average" is really the mean of the test results. The standard deviation of 9.37 indicates a rather sharp distribution. Looking at the value alone won't tell you much about how sharp the distribution is, though, so you should also look at the percentiles: As always, half of the data are found between the 25th and 75th percentiles.

Therefore, half of our requests lie in a 10-millisecond range between 10 and 20 milliseconds, and a further 25% of our requests are faster than 10 milliseconds.

The other 25% lie somewhere between 20.04 and 110 milliseconds, which is quite a spread, which is shown in the broad shallow tail on the slow side of the curve. The diagram in Figure 7-19 shows a possible curve representing the distribution of response times in this test run.

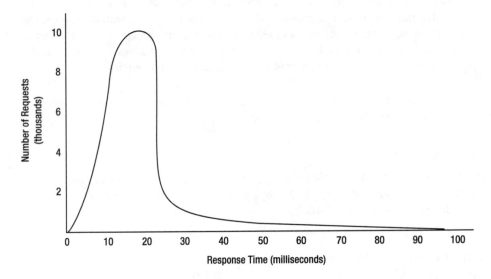

Figure 7-19. *Response time distribution graph*

An interesting observation is that the 50th and the 75th percentiles are very close to each other, indicating that the TTFBs for the vast majority of requests are very close to the 50th percentile value of 19.99 milliseconds. In fact, considering that the mean is 18.17, which is also very close to the 50th percentile, you can quite safely work out that most requests receive a response between 16 and 20 milliseconds. While all this might not be obvious from the quick pass through statistics we've taken, it illustrates that with a bit of practice you can get quite a lot from a set of seven figures like the ones in the figure.

Graphs

Graphs are a useful tool for analyzing website performance across different conditions. In order to create a good comparison, you need to run the test several times. Each time, you should generally change only one test property. For instance, you can run the test three times, each with a different number of simultaneous browser connections. You can then create a graph comparing the number of requests per second for each run to see how well your web server handles heavy traffic.

To see how this works, run the test three times with 10, 20, and 30 connections. Then select all three tests and report on RPS and TTLB against connections, as illustrated in Figure 7-20.

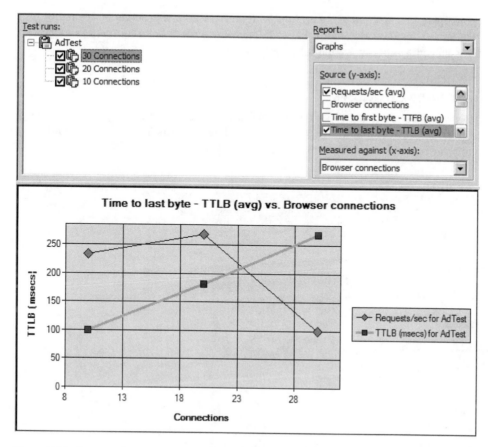

Figure 7-20. *Test results by number of connections*

The graph in the figure shows that the best performance seems to be achieved when you open 20 simultaneous browser connections to the server, because in this configuration, you get the highest RPS count. Obviously, you may want to try a few more runs, possibly with the number of connections set to 15 and 25. The graph will show more accurately when the performance peaks and when it starts to suffer. On the other hand, the TTLB increases with the number of connections, as we might expect. In this way, you can better configure your setup to work at its peak performance across all the factors that affect it.

There are too many useful combinations to be covered fully here. In a production project, you should try to play with various test settings to stress your web server and to see how many concurrent users it can satisfactorily support. For instance, if a performance requirement is to support 100 concurrent users with the average response time of 30 seconds, you can try to run 100 simultaneous connections and check the average TTLB. If the average is more than 30 seconds, you reduce the number of simultaneous connections until the TTLB falls to less than 30 seconds. You now know that the current configuration of your application can support, say, only 80 concurrent users.

Such test results provide quantified support to decide whether you need to fine tune your application, or whether you should consider upgrading or adding new hardware. Note that a hardware upgrade is just one of the options for increasing your web server performance. You will often find other software bottlenecks by adding some performance counters to your reports for collecting other types of information.

Performance Counters

To add performance counters to your test, select the Counters tab in the test properties dialog. By default, ACT does not include any performance counters in tests. You can click the Add button to bring up the Browse Performance Counters dialog.

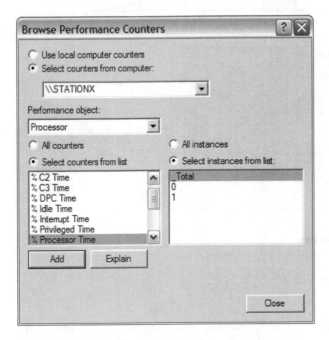

Figure 7-21. *Add performance counters*

You can add performance counters from both the web server and the test client machines. The reason for collecting server performance data should be obvious, because that's what tests are generally designed to do: test the server's performance. However, a less obvious consideration is that you want to ensure that your test really does test the server by removing extraneous bottlenecks that are not related to the performance of the target web server.

The Client Machine

One such bottleneck is the test client machine. If the client machine is overloaded, it will not be able to generate as many requests during the test. In such cases, the collected test result will not truly represent the performance of the server. For instance, if the test client manages to send only 50 requests per second, the test result will show 50 RPS even though the server may have no problem handling 200 RPS.

A good indication of the client machine's ability to generate as many requests as possible is its CPU usage, which is the Processor Time of the Process object. If the CPU usage by ACT is very close to 80%, the client machine may be overloaded and therefore unable to generate requests fast enough. Other useful performance counters for the client machine are as follows:

- Memory – Available Bytes: This shows the available physical memory. If the CPU usage is not very high, but you run out of physical memory, the machine will still not be able to generate many requests.

- Network Interface – Bytes Total: This shows the network volume during the test. If it is close to the network bandwidth, you are reaching the limit.

There are several methods to increase the client machine's performance:

- Suspend unnecessary processes by stopping some inessential services and other programs on the test client.

- Reduce the number of simultaneous browser connections used in the test.

- Upgrade hardware, for example by adding more memory and replacing your network card if its capacity is below the network bandwidth.

- Use multiple client machines.

Because test client machines are generally less powerful than the server, the best you can get by applying the first three techniques is normally still not enough to really stress test the server. Therefore the realistic solution is to use multiple clients. Unfortunately, ACT as shipped with Visual Studio .NET does not have the ability to coordinate testing among multiple machines.

A workaround is to install ACT on multiple client machines. Once you have created and run a test on your development machine, you can distribute the test script to all client machines. You can then start the test on all client machines manually. To automate the process, you can write scripts to start a test using the ACT application object model and then add it to the Windows Task Scheduler for each test client so that they can all run at the same time.

Useful Performance Counters

There are many factors that can affect application performance. Each application has its own technical characteristics, requiring you to collect a range of test data in order to identify the potential bottlenecks and other issues. While performance analysis is a big subject that warrants its own book, the web server system resources are usually the bottlenecks in many applications. Here are some of the most significant performance counters.

The CPU usage (Processor: %Processor Time: _Total) tells you when, and by how much, the processor or processors on the web server become the bottleneck. If the processors run constantly above 90%, you should consider replacing them with faster processors. Another indicator is the amount of available physical memory (Memory: Available Bytes). If it is constantly low, the system will have to perform a great deal of memory paging, which is very slow. In such a case, you should also add the Memory: Pages/sec counter, which reports the paging rates. If the paging rates are high, you will want to increase the system memory size.

The IIS itself can also be a bottleneck. If many incoming requests are being queued (Active Server Pages: Requests Queued), the server may be overloaded. While this sometimes relates to CPU usage, you should keep an eye on this as well because it may be caused by other factors such as COM+ component overload. If a COM+ component is getting more requests than it can handle, it may block the web server and prevent requests from being processed as fast as the server can normally handle. There are more important performance counters than I can possibly cover here. Fortunately, you can find an excellent article on MSDN that discusses in great detail the performance counters that you should monitor: "ASP.NET Performance Monitoring, and When to Alert Administrators" (http://msdn.microsoft.com/library/en-us/dnaspp/html/monitor_perf.asp).

Since most web applications use a database to allow for persistent data, you should watch the database server statistics. ACT can collect this kind of test data only through performance counters. If you use SQL Server, you can get most database-related statistics this way. However, using the SQL Server Profiler may provide you with more detailed information. Furthermore, since not all database servers make their performance data available through the Windows Performance Monitor, you have to use database-specific tools separately to monitor their performance.

Authentication and Users

If the target web server requires authentication, the test client will need to be able to log on. ACT supports all three authentication methods used by the IIS: basic, integrated, and digest. It also supports anonymous access, in which case no login is required. You can provide a list of users for ACT to use for tests, as explained in the next section. Once you have selected users for a test, ACT can automatically detect the web server authentication methods and manage the HTTP authentication with the web server.

On the other hand, ACT does not support form-based logon methods. If the target web server uses such methods, you will need to edit the script manually to specify the username and password.

User and User Groups

ACT allows you to create users and user groups, which are available for all test projects. In ACT, each user can belong to one group only. Although you can create identical user name/password pairs in different groups, a user in a group does not relate in any way to another user with the same user name and password in another group. Furthermore, you can create multiple users with identical user names and passwords in the same group.

By default, ACT provides a default user group containing 200 users with arbitrary names and passwords. You will usually want to create your own user groups containing users on the target web servers. To create a user group, right-click the Users node in the Project Explorer and select Add from the context menu. You can then rename the group by right-clicking it and selecting Rename from the context menu. To add users to a user group, simply select the group in the Project Explorer and type in the user name and password in the right-hand pane. If the target web server requires domain information, you need to enter user names in the DomainName\UserName format as illustrated in Figure 7-22.

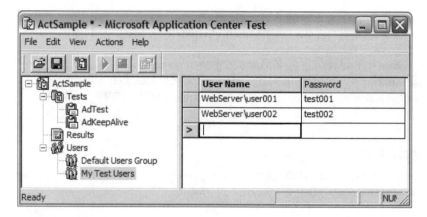

Figure 7-22. *Test users*

For each test, you can select users in one or more groups. To select a group for a test, select the Users tab in the test properties dialog. The first option, Automatically generate users, allows ACT to automatically generate users during the test. However, it is not clear what rules ACT uses to generate user names and passwords, and it is generally not possible for ACT to create application-specific users. To use your own group or groups of users, select the Specify users option and check all groups you wish to use in the test. When you run a test, ACT cycles through all users in the selected groups and uses them to log on.

If you configure a test with more than one simultaneous browser connection, ACT requires that you use at least one user for each connection. For instance, if you use one user group for a test using five simultaneous browser connections, you need to ensure that there are at least five users in that group. If you use two groups, the total number of users must be five or more. If you don't use enough users, ACT will report an error: the number of users must be at least as large as the number of connections.

Cookies

Many web applications use cookies to store certain application data locally. Once a test creates a cookie for a user, other tests can share this cookie whenever the user is used and the web server requires a cookie. ACT lets you edit or delete cookies between test runs. To edit or delete a cookie for a user, select the user in a group and the Edit Cookies command from the Actions menu item. You can then edit or delete cookies in the Edit User Cookies dialog.

That's it for analyzing data; now let's see how we can get deeper into the realms of customizing our own test scripts.

Customizing Test Scripts

While the ACT browser recording feature does well to construct test scripts that simulate browser requests, there are times when you will want to further customize a test. In general, I'm quite happy with the wizard-generated scripts and have not found many things that I definitely need to change yet. But among the things I have found, one really stands out.

As I mentioned in a previous section, ACT supports HTTP 1.1. However, the wizard generates scripts to create requests only with HTTP 1.0 headers by default. As a consequence, the keep-alive feature available in HTTP 1.1 is not used in the generated scripts. Since IIS supports the keep-alive feature and many browsers are capable of generating HTTP 1.1 requests, the recorded scripts may produce test results that do not quite match the real-world performance of the web server.

This presents us with a good reason for customizing the test scripts. If you know VBScript, the required changes to the generated scripts are quite simple. Let's look first at the structure of the wizard-generated script and then see how you can change it to use HTTP 1.1's keep-alive feature.

Test Script Structure

A typical recorded test script contains a `Main` procedure, several `SendRequest` procedures, and a single global statement that simply invokes the `Main` procedure:

```vbscript
Sub SendRequest1()
  ' code to send the first request
End Sub

Sub SendRequest2()
  ' code to send the second request
End Sub

'...

Sub SendRequestN()
  ' code to send the Nth request
End Sub

Sub Main()
  Call SendRequest1
  Call SendRequest2
  '...
  Call SendRequestN
End Sub

Main
```

The `Main` procedure is effectively the entry point of the script. You can certainly customize the script in any way you want, or make it adhere to your existing coding conventions. Once you have gained a good understanding of the ACT Test Object Model, you can write powerful test scripts. Both the ACT documentation and the MSDN Library provide good references to the object model.

Modifying Test Scripts

The script for `AdTest` created in the section Walkthrough: Creating a New Test creates two requests in each pass, one for the `ad_test.asp` page and the other for the `logo.gif` file. It creates a connection for each request, and closes the connection after the request has been sent. To simulate a keep-alive browser session, you should change it to create a connection and use it to send both requests. Here is how you do it.

In the `ActSample` Project created in the walkthrough, add a new empty test using VBScript and name it something like `AdKeepAlive.vbs`. Next, delete the one statement generated by the wizard, and then copy and paste the script from `AdTest.vbs` to `AdKeepAlive.vbs`. Now you have a script to work with.

First, define a script-level object, `oConnection`, and add two procedures to the script, as follows:

```
Option Explicit
Dim fEnableDelays
fEnableDelays = False

Dim oConnection

Function OpenConnection()
  Set oConnection = Test.CreateConnection("MyWebServer", 80, false)
    If Not oConnection is Nothing Then
      OpenConnection = True
    Else
      Test.Trace "Error: Unable to create connection to MyWebServer"
      OpenConnection = False
  End If
End Function

Function CloseConnection()
  If Not oConnection Is Nothing Then
    oConnection.Close
  End If
End Function
```

Remember to replace `MyWebServer` with the name of your web server, or localhost if the web server is on the same machine as the test client. Now that you have a script-level connection object and separate procedures to open and close it, you should remove the local connection objects and their corresponding open and close calls in both `SendRequest1` and `SendRequest2` procedures. The following code snippet shows the changes made to `SendRequest1`. Changes to `SendRequest2` are identical. Note that we're commenting out some lines and replacing them with others:

```
Sub SendRequest1()
'  Dim oConnection, oRequest, oResponse, oHeaders, strStatusCode
  Dim oRequest, oResponse, oHeaders, strStatusCode
  If fEnableDelays = True then Test.Sleep (0)
'  Set oConnection = Test.CreateConnection("MyWebServer", 80, false)
'  If (oConnection is Nothing) Then
```

```
'    Test.Trace "Error: Unable to create connection to MyWebServer"
'  Else
     Set oRequest = Test.CreateRequest
     oRequest.Path = "/testfiles/ad_test.asp"
     oRequest.Verb = "GET"
'     oRequest.HTTPVersion = "HTTP/1.0"
     oRequest.HTTPVersion = "HTTP/1.1"
     set oHeaders = oRequest.Headers
     oHeaders.RemoveAll
     oHeaders.Add "Accept", _
           "image/gif, image/x-xbitmap, image/jpeg, image/pjpeg, */*"
     oHeaders.Add "Accept-Language", "en-us"
     oHeaders.Add "User-Agent", _
       "Mozilla/4.0 (compatible; MSIE 6.0; Windows NT 5.1;.NET CLR 1.1.4322)"
'     oHeaders.Add "Host", "MyWebServer"
     oHeaders.Add "Host", "(automatic)"
     oHeaders.Add "Cookie", "(automatic)"
     Set oResponse = oConnection.Send(oRequest)
     If (oResponse is Nothing) Then
       Test.Trace "Error: Failed to receive response for URL to " + _
         "/testfiles/ad_test.asp"
     Else
       strStatusCode = oResponse.ResultCode
     End If
'     oConnection.Close
'  End If
End Sub
```

Note that while it's still normally valid to check whether the connection is alive in SendRequest1, it's neither necessary nor desirable. Since you usually want the client to be able to generate as many requests as possible, you should minimize the amount of work the client needs to perform. Apart from removing the connection-related statements, the only other change is to specify the HTTP 1.1 protocol for the request so that the connection will be kept alive between the two requests. The last change you need to make is obviously to explicitly open and close the connection in the Main() procedure, as follows:

```
Sub Main()
  If OpenConnection Then
    Call SendRequest1()
    Call SendRequest2()
    Call CloseConnection()
  End If
End Sub
```

That's it. If you run the test now, you should see that ACT creates one connection for every two requests by examining the Summary section in the Overview report. Figure 7-23 shows a sample test result.

Summary

Total number of requests:	1,710
Total number of connections:	855
Average requests per second:	5.70
Average time to first byte (msecs):	13.62
Average time to last byte (msecs):	166.06
Average time to last byte per iteration (msecs):	332.11
Number of unique requests made in test:	2
Number of unique response codes:	1

Figure 7-23. *Sample test result summary*

ACT in Visual Studio .NET

In addition to the standalone ACT program, Visual Studio .NET also offers an integrated ACT UI that allows for creating ACT projects directly in Visual Studio .NET IDE. You can add a new ACT project to an existing solution such as one containing a web application, or create it in a new solution. ACT projects created in ACT and in Visual Studio .NET use the same underlying technology for creating and executing tests, and to collect results. The integrated ACT UI also provides you with the ability to run tests and view test results in the Visual Studio .NET IDE.

Creating a Test

Visual Studio .NET provides a special type of project for creating ACT projects and tests. To create a new ACT test, follow these steps:

1. In Visual Studio .NET, create a new project. In the Add New Project dialog, select `Application Center Test Projects` under `Other Projects`. There is only one project template: `ACT Project`. Just select it and give it a name like `VsNetActProject`.

2. Add a new item to the newly created project. As in the standalone ACT program, you can create a browser recording test or an empty test in either VBScript or JScript. For this exercise, select `Browser Recorded Test` and name it `AdTest.vbs`.

3. In the `Browser Record` dialog, click the `Start recording` button. Visual Studio .NET will start a new instance of Internet Explorer.

4. In Internet Explorer, type in the URL `http://localhost/TestFiles/ad_test.asp` and click Enter. This opens the page in Internet Explorer.

5. Switch back to Visual Studio .NET, click the Stop recording button and then the OK button. You may also simply close the browser, which automatically terminates the test.

The project file and the script generated by Visual Studio .NET are identical to those in the standalone ACT program. In fact, you can open a Visual Studio .NET ACT project in the standalone ACT program, and vice versa.

Configuring Test Properties

In the Visual Studio IDE, you can also configure project and test properties. However, compared to the set of properties you can configure in the standalone ACT program, the configurable ACT properties in the Visual Studio .NET IDE are rather limited. Table 7-1 lists the configurable properties in Visual Studio .NET.

Table 7-1. *Configurable ACT Properties*

Property	Visual Studio.NET
Proxy server address/port	Configurable
Checking robots.txt	Always enabled
Socket request timeout	Always enabled (default to 120 seconds)
Test logging	Always enabled
Simultaneous browser connections	Configurable
Test run time	Configurable
Test iterations	Configurable
Warm-up time	Configurable
Generate detailed test results	Always enabled
Creating and using users and user groups	Not configurable (default to define 200 users)
Performance counters	Not configurable (default to none)

The standalone ACT program lets you configure all of these options. Therefore, in order to fine-tune settings that are not configurable in Visual Studio .NET, you should open the project (ProjectName.act) in the standalone ACT and modify the settings.

Reading Test Results

You can also view and compare ACT test results in Visual Studio .NET. Again, the set of result data is also limited. Once a test finishes, the result from the current test run is displayed in the output window, as illustrated in Figure 7-24.

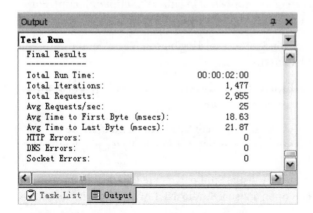

Figure 7-24. *Test results output in Visual Studio .NET*

You can also see a list of results from all previous runs by right-clicking the test node in the Solution Explorer and selecting View Results.

Summary

In this chapter, you've learned how to create ACT projects and tests. When a test runs, ACT collects various performance data. You can interpret the standard set of test data presented to you by ACT. You can also use ACT to collect other performance data that are more relevant to your applications by adding performance counters to tests.

A complex web application has many potential hot spots contributing to good or poor performance. Different applications have different performance characteristics, and therefore require different sets of test data to help in identifying the problems and their causes. You have seen that there are also issues that may affect the accuracy of tests. One of the common traps is that test clients may be overloaded and inadvertently become the bottleneck. It is critical to configure the test settings to avoid such traps.

In the past, we have seen applications that perform well under light load but do not scale well enough. By using ACT, you can discover such dangers early by stress testing your applications. Doing so helps you to identify the cause and resolve the problem before it gets too late. With ACT and other tools, you can develop applications that meet not only functional requirements, but also performance and scalability requirements.

CHAPTER 8
■■■

Project Deployment

In the highly competitive Windows application market, every little detail will impact the overall success of a product. A user's first impression of an application is formed when the application is installed, and so we should never overlook this first step. A professional and coherent installation process will give our users the confidence in an application that they require.

Back in the days when DOS was king, installing an application was simply a matter of copying all files—usually from a floppy—over to the hard disk. You would then simply run the executable, and that was that. When Windows came along, things changed. Installing Windows applications generally requires not only copying required files, but also registering libraries and creating shortcuts in the Start menu or on the desktop, to name just a couple of requirements. Microsoft first bundled setup creation tools with Visual Basic and Visual C++, and other companies have made a big business out of creating powerful and flexible application installation tools.

Microsoft's Windows Installer first appeared with the release of Office 2000, and it represented a quite new Windows application installation mechanism. Later versions of Windows Installer were released with Windows 2000 and Windows Millennium Edition. Microsoft also integrated the Visual Studio Installer developer's tool into Microsoft Visual Studio version 6 and above. As the Windows Installer evolves, third party installation toolmakers also update their products to allow the creation of Windows Installer packages.

With the advent of the .NET Framework and Visual Studio .NET, Microsoft's Windows Installer 2.0 has now entered the scene. Visual Studio .NET has a project category called Setup and Deployment Projects that contains templates for creating different types of projects for the deployment of other applications. In this chapter, you will see how to use these projects to deploy applications, looking at how to:

- Deploy Windows applications using the setup project

- Distribute the .NET Framework runtime with application installation packages

- Deploy applications manually

- Package component assemblies in merge modules

- Deploy component assemblies in merge modules using setup projects

- Create cab projects for deploying applications and components through the Internet

- Create web setup projects for deploying Internet applications

The next section presents an overview of the Windows Installer and Visual Studio .NET deployment projects. In the following sections, we will create several small, focused setup and deployment applications in order to explore the different types of setup and deployment projects and demonstrate the correct techniques for producing user-friendly installation packages for different types of applications.

Windows Installer and Visual Studio .NET

An installation package performs a set of tasks, such as copying files to specific locations on the target machine, registering components, and creating shortcuts for program executables and other application elements.

Traditionally, Windows installation is carried out according to a procedural model; that is, the installer typically performs these tasks in a sequential manner. While installation tools should hide the low-level details from application developers, they all create a predefined sequence of steps for the installation of the target application(s). When creating installation packages, then, we must attempt to devise a clear sequence that will result in the installation of the application elements required for the options selected by the user. We need to think about when and how an element should be installed. If any program files should become corrupt later on, the user will generally have to reinstall the whole application.

The Microsoft Windows Installer is a step beyond this model. From the developer's point of view, it is a Windows application deployment service that is data driven. Rather than specifying the exact sequence of steps to follow, we specify what files need to be installed, where they should go, what registry entries need to be created or modified, any other operations that need to be executed, and so forth. The Windows Installer then handles the execution of tasks itself: our focus is on the installation data rather than the process.

The Windows Installer also supports self-repairing applications. If some files become corrupt or destroyed, our application has the ability to detect and repair those files automatically. In most cases, the user will need to have the installation package, such as the distribution CD, at hand in order for the self-repair to work, but such a requirement is not too surprising. However, rather than leaving it to the user to detect and diagnose runtime errors, software installed using later versions of Windows Installer is more proactive in detecting and fixing potential problems. For instance, if one of the application files is corrupt, Windows Installer will step in when the application starts and try to repair it from known installation sources, e.g., from a network share where the setup package was originally run. If it can't find the source, e.g., if it was installed from a CD but the CD is not in the drive, it will prompt the user to insert the installation CD or specify an alternative source.

The deployment projects available in Visual Studio .NET provide tools for application developers to quickly create installation packages based on this Windows Installer technology. If you have used Visual Studio (6.0) Installer, you know already that it offers the aforementioned features because it uses the Windows Installer engine behind the scene. What Visual Studio .NET deployment projects offer are tighter integration with target Windows applications developed with Visual Studio .NET and extra features such as web setup projects. We can create and test an installation package in the familiar and feature-rich VS .NET IDE. Visual Studio .NET offers five types of deployment project templates:

- Setup Projects allow us to create installation packages for deploying Windows desktop applications.

- Web Setup Projects create installation packages that can deploy ASP.NET applications on Microsoft Internet Information Servers. However, in conjunction with Setup Projects, they can be used to deploy desktop applications over the Internet or an intranet.

- Merge Module Projects are for the prepackaging of application components. Setup and Web Setup projects can then use merge modules to include the components in the installation packages.

- Cab Projects allows us to create Internet download packages for ActiveX controls.

- Setup Wizard provides a, well, wizard to create any one of the above four types of projects. It simply presents you with a choice for creating one of the setup projects, but doesn't go much further to help you customize the projects. Therefore, its usefulness is very limited, and you will have no problem understanding what it does. For this reason, I will not discuss it further.

Each of these project types requires an application that it can deploy, so in this chapter, we'll create a couple of simple applications to illustrate how we can create setup and deployment projects for them in Visual Studio .NET. It's a fairly simple matter to swap these for any other application that you may have created already, should you so wish.

We'll start with the Visual Studio .NET Setup project type for desktop applications and a general discussion on basic features common to all setup and deployment projects. After that, we'll go on to examine the other types of setup and deployment projects.

In addition to creating Visual Studio .NET deployment projects using Windows Installer, Microsoft also introduces a new deployment technology, namely, no-touch deployment. I will briefly discuss this later in this chapter.

The Setup Project Type

The Setup project type creates the files required to successfully deploy an application on client machines. In this section, we'll see how to create Setup projects for various types of Windows applications and take a good look at the features common to all setup and deployment projects.

Setup projects can be simple when the applications to be deployed are small, but they can become complex and involved as the target applications increase in size.

A Simple Windows Application

First of all, we'll create a simple application to use as the deployment target application for our projects in this chapter. Open Visual Studio .NET and create a new Visual C# Windows application project called HelloWorld. Rename the automatically created form GreetingForm and change the form's Text property to Greetings. Next, drag a button from the Toolbox, and name it btnSayHello. Set its Text property to Say Hello and double click it to enter the following code in its Click event handler:

```
private void btnSayHello_Click(object sender, System.EventArgs e)
{
    MessageBox.Show("Hello World!", this.Text);
}
```

That'll do for our working sample application, so we'll now move on to create our first Setup project. As usual, you should test it before moving on, but I'll leave that to you. If you prefer to use your own project, just replace references to the HelloWorld application with your own application.

Creating the Installer

To create a Setup project for the HelloWorld project, right-click the solution name in Solution Explorer, and select Add ➤ New Project. In the Add New Project dialog box, select Setup and Deployment Projects in the Project Types list and select the Setup Project Template (see Figure 8-1).

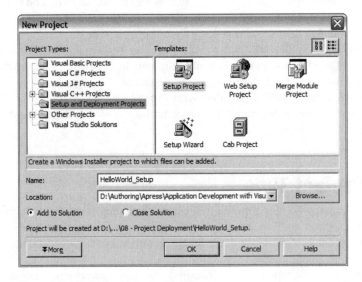

Figure 8-1. *Creating a setup project*

In this example, name the new project HelloWorld_Setup. Once you click the OK button, the Visual Studio .NET IDE adds the project to the solution as seen in Solution Explorer. In addition, the toolbar specific to Setup projects appears at the top of Solution Explorer, as shown in Figure 8-2. These buttons invoke the Visual Studio Editors for various setup tasks, and we'll cover each later. You can of course move your mouse over each button to see a tooltip specifying which editor that button opens.

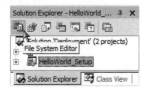

Figure 8-2. *Setup project toolbar*

When Visual Studio .NET creates a Setup project, it opens the File System Editor shown in Figure 8-3. You can also click the first button on the Solution Explorer toolbar to display it. Figure 8-3 shows a screen shot of the editor.

Figure 8-3. *The file system editor*

The left pane shows a list of certain key locations for the installation, each location representing a folder on the installation target machine. For instance, the Application Folder represents the folder where your application will be installed, and you can probably deduce what the other two represent from their names. We can also add other folders by right-clicking the top File System on Target Machine node, and selecting Add Special Folder. For instance, if you'd like your application to run when the user logs on to Windows, you can add the User's Startup Folder and create a shortcut to the application in the folder. You will see how you can create shortcuts in a moment.

If we select a folder in the list, all files we want to create in that folder will be shown in the right pane. Since we have just created a new Setup project, all folders are empty. We specify which files are to be installed in a given folder by adding those files to each folder, as we will see shortly.

So, we use the Application Folder (or its subdirectories) to store files directly relating to our application, such as the executables and help files. To place the HelloWorld executable in there, right-click the Application Folder item in the left-hand pane, and select Add ➤ Project Output to bring up the Add Project Output Group dialog box shown in Figure 8-4.

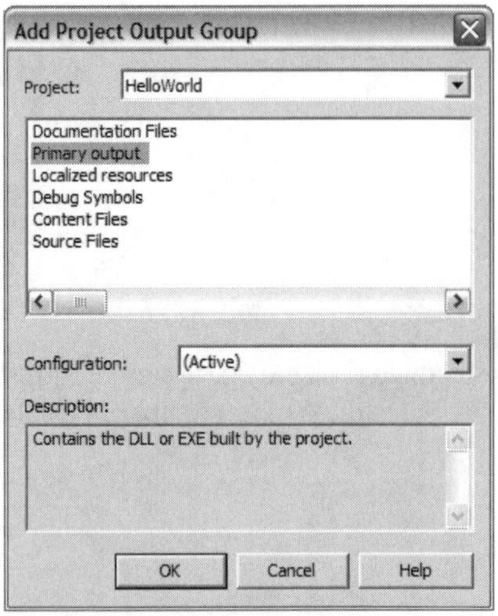

Figure 8-4. *Add Project Output Group*

Here, Project Output refers to the target application, that is, the application for which this setup project is created. A project output is any file, such as an EXE for a Windows application or a DLL for a Class Library or ASP.NET Web Application, created when the target application is built. The Project dropdown at the top of this dialog lists all application projects in the current solution, and so it shows only the HelloWorld project in this case. Note that deployment projects themselves are naturally not included in the list. In the pane below, which lets us select which file types from the application we're dealing with, select Primary output to indicate the build output of the selected application, which will be HelloWorld.exe in this case. The Primary Output of the application project corresponds to its Output File (for C#) or Output Name property (for Visual Basic .NET), as you can see in the Properties Window for the HelloWorld project shown in Figure 8-5.

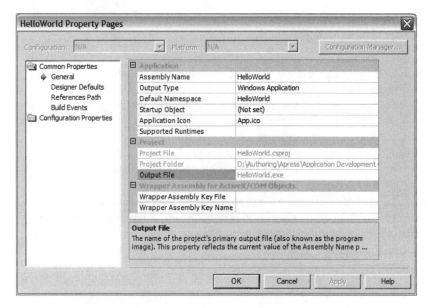

Figure 8-5. *Project Output property*

You can add multiple project outputs to a Setup project by repeating this process for each project. Furthermore, you can also package applications that are not in the solution by selecting Add ➤ Assembly. I will demonstrate these options in more detail later in this chapter.

Note that by default, the Setup project uses the HelloWorld.exe file produced by the currently active configuration of the HelloWorld project. For instance, if the active configuration is Debug, it will use HelloWorld\bin\Debug\HelloWorld.exe. If you in fact want to deploy the release version, for instance, you can select that from the Configuration dropdown box.

■**Caution** Be careful about which configuration you choose. If, for instance, you specify a release version of the primary project output, but only the debug version of the application has been built, Visual Studio .NET won't automatically perform a release build for you to create the required output. In fact, it will simply create the setup package without even warning you of the lack of the required project output. When the setup package is then run, however, it will fail with error code 2709, which indicates that the application executable file is missing from the package.

Please also note that during the build process, Visual Studio .NET skips the newly created setup project by default. This prevents the setup project from being built each time you rebuild the solution while working on the main project. To rebuild the setup project, you will need to select the project and build it explicitly. You can force Visual Studio .NET to include the setup project in the solution build process using the Configuration Manager.

Click OK, and you can now go ahead and build the Setup project.

Testing the Setup Project

Once the Setup project is built, right-click the Setup project in Solution Explorer and select Install from the context menu. We are now taken through the series of steps that installs the HelloWorld application. Although the installation process is smooth enough, it looks a little plain, to say the least, so we'll add a little polish in the next section.

Once the project has been installed, we can test the uninstall functionality by right-clicking on the setup project in Solution Explorer and selecting Uninstall. A nice feature of Visual Studio .NET is that you don't have to explicitly uninstall a previous installation before installing a new version. When you select Install from the context menu, Visual Studio .NET automatically detects whether a previous installation exists. If one does, it will be automatically removed before the new version is installed.

Alternatively, you can run the Setup.exe file in your Setup project's output folder—either the Debug or the Release subfolder depending on the configuration—to perform the installation procedure. In this case, you can specify that it should remove the previous installation before installing it again if that is desirable. By default, Setup projects don't force an uninstallation, but you can change it by setting the RemovePreviousVersions property of the Setup project to True (see Figure 8-6).

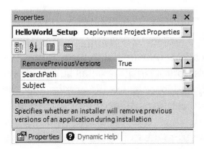

Figure 8-6. *Setting the* RemovePreviousVersions *property*

You can also explicitly uninstall a previous version if one exists before starting a new installation.

Ideally, you should test the final Setup project on a variety of operating systems before you roll out your application. Unless you are absolutely certain that the user machines will always have the .NET Framework runtime installed, you should also test on machines with and without that component. At the moment, our setup package for the HelloWorld program will work only on machines that already have the .NET Framework. The .NET Framework Runtime Package section later in this chapter introduces some of the ways we can include the .NET Framework redistributable in setup packages.

Additional Setup Features

The way we've installed the HelloWorld program, if we wanted to run it, we'd have to find the HelloWorld.exe file, perhaps using Windows Explorer, and then run it directly. This isn't an ideal solution, unless of course it's an application that will not be started by the user manually.

Normally, we'd want to at least create a shortcut to HelloWorld.exe in the usual places, such as the Programs menu or the Desktop.

It isn't difficult to set this up. In the File System Editor, open the Application Folder and right-click the Primary output from HelloWorld (Active) node in the right-hand pane. Then from the context menu, select Create Shortcut to Primary output from HelloWorld (Active). This will create the shortcut file in the Application Folder. This is still not quite what we want, which is to put it in the user's Programs menu. We need to drag and drop the shortcut into the User's Programs Menu folder in the left-hand pane. Similarly, we can add a shortcut to the user's desktop by creating another shortcut in the Application Folder and moving it to the User's Desktop folder.

Alternatively, we can create a shortcut directly within a folder by first selecting a "virtual folder" in the left-hand pane of the File System editor, and then right-clicking anywhere in the right-hand pane. From the context menu, we choose Create New Shortcut to open up the Select Item in Project dialog, where we specify the target of the shortcut, which in this case will be the project's primary output file.

Note that however you create it, the name of the shortcut file is Shortcut to Primary output from HelloWorld (Active) by default, so we want to rename it to something more suitable, such as Hello World, by right-clicking the shortcut file and selecting Rename.

If we're going to create several shortcuts in the user's Program menu, for instance one for the main program file and another for the user documentation, it's a good idea to create a subfolder in that virtual folder and place all the shortcuts there. This simply requires us to right-click the User's Programs Menu folder and select Add ➤ Folder. Once the subfolder has been created and named, we can create as many shortcuts as we need inside it.

We can further improve things by replacing the shortcut icon with an application-specific design. Note that even if we've already set up an icon for our main app, the setup project will still use the vanilla Windows executable icon rather than "inheriting" the application's icon. So, to assign the shortcut a smiley face icon perform the following actions:

1. Right-click the Setup project and select Add ➤ File.

2. Browse to the new icon file. Normally, you'd want to use the same icon as the application you are installing, which would generally be located in the application's project folder. The smiley face icon is named Face02.ico, in the Microsoft Visual Studio .NET 2003\Common7\Graphics\icons\Misc folder. It will be added to the virtual Application Folder.

3. Select the Icon property of the shortcut, click the down arrow, and select Browse. In the Icon dialog box, click Browse and then open the Application Folder. Select the Face02.ico file that should be listed there.

We can now build the setup project and install the HelloWorld program to check that the shortcut to HelloWorld.exe appears with a smiley icon in the target machine's Programs menu.

During the installation, you'll notice a few things that don't look very professional and are a little confusing. For instance, the installation title is Welcome to the HelloWorld_Setup Setup Wizard, and the default application folder is [*YourCompany*]\HelloWorld_Setup (where *YourCompany* is the company name you entered when Visual Studio .NET was itself installed). We can modify such settings by changing the corresponding properties of the Setup project.

Table 8-1 shows the minimum set of properties that we should set for a reasonable-looking setup process:

Table 8-1. *Configurable Installation Elements*

Installation Elements	Purpose and Value
Dialog Title	The value of the ProductName property appears as the title of setup dialogs.
Application Name	The ProductName is also displayed as the name of the application in dialogs.
Default Installation Folder	When the installation is created, application files will be placed in a folder named after the ProductName property value, within a folder that takes its name from the Manufacturer property value. This will be created inside the user's Program Files directory.

If you entered your full company name when installing Visual Studio .NET, you may want to change the Manufacturer property to be something shorter. For instance, we might prefer to use Apress rather than Apress L.P.

Figure 8-7 shows the welcome dialog after the ProductName property has been set to Hello World Program.

Figure 8-7. *The* Hello World *program setup welcome dialog*

Link Up the Setup and Application Projects

Now you have learned to create setup packages for .NET applications using the Visual Studio .NET Setup project. Before we move on to other topics, let's look at one small but handy feature in Visual Studio .NET.

After following the previous steps, you should now have a single Visual Studio Solution containing both the application and the Setup projects. There's no reason why we can't continue to modify the application project after having created the Setup project for it, and many developers do this. You just need to remember to rebuild the Setup project once you have made any changes and rebuilt the primary application.

However, we can automate the build process so that both are built together, in the correct order. When we create a Setup project for an application project in a solution, Visual Studio .NET automatically creates a dependency for it. That is, it marks the Setup project as dependent on its target application project, because the Setup project contains the primary output of the application project. It also configures the build order so that the application project is built first, followed by the Setup project. Therefore, you can select Build Solution in the Build menu, or click the Build Solution button on the Build toolbar if you have it displayed, to have Visual Studio .NET automatically build both projects in the correct order for you.

You can check out this feature by right-clicking the Solution node in Solution Explorer and selecting Project Dependencies, as illustrated in Figure 8-8.

Figure 8-8. *The Hello World program setup welcome dialog*

Since the Setup project depends on HelloWorld, Visual Studio .NET will build HelloWorld before building HelloWorld_Setup. We can check the order by clicking the Build Order tab in the dialog shown above. Note that although Visual Studio .NET can build both projects in the correct order, you don't have to build both all the time. If you need to build only one of them, just right-click that particular project and choose Build. Selecting the Build Solution command from the Build menu or the Build toolbar will build all projects.

Further Customization

In addition to the File System Editor, a Setup project has a number of other editors, accessed by clicking the buttons on the Setup toolbar at the top of Solution Explorer or through the View ➤ Editors menu command. These offer a range of further configuration options that we'll look at next.

The User Interface Editor

The User Interface Editor allows us to customize the dialogs and other visual elements that will be presented to the end user during the installation process. Figure 8-9 shows the default elements.

Figure 8-9. *The User Interface Editor*

The Install section defines the dialog boxes to be displayed when an end user installs the application by running Setup.exe. The Administrative Install section defines the dialog boxes to be displayed when a system administrator installs the application on a network share by running Setup.exe with the /a switch. An administrative installation copies the Windows Installer package for the application to the network share. End users can then install the application on their workstations by running the Windows Installer package from the network installation.

Both sections can contain several dialog boxes. By default, an installer created by a Setup project consists of the following five dialogs:

1. Welcome screen

2. Select installation folder screen

3. Confirm installation screen

4. Installation progress indicator

5. Setup complete screen

The User Interface Editor provides a way to add our own dialog boxes or even remove some of the default ones. To see the available dialog boxes, right-click the Start node and select Add Dialog.

Let's create a checkbox-based dialog to allow users to specify whether the installer should create a registry entry on the user's machine. You will see how to add registry entries in the next section. If our HelloWorld program could display random greeting phrases, say, then we could use this dialog to offer several related choices to the user.

First, right-click the Start node under Install root in the User Interface Editor and select Add Dialog. An installation can include at most three checkbox-type dialogs, each containing up to four checkboxes. Select Checkboxes (A) in the Add Dialog dialog box, and it will be presented after the Confirm Installation dialog. It makes sense to move it up to before the Confirm Installation dialog. You can do so by right-clicking Checkboxes (A) and selecting Move Up to move it one place up. You may also simply drag-and-drop it to its desired location.

However, if you leave the newly added dialog where it is, you will get this warning when you build the Setup project:

```
All custom dialogs must precede the 'Installation Folder' dialog
```

To me, such an arrangement just isn't logical, because it's better to present such actions after the user has chosen the installation folder. Fortunately, it's just a warning and doesn't prevent you from building the package. I haven't encountered a case in which an installation package misbehaves because of the placement of custom dialogs, so you can just ignore this warning, but be wary in case you encounter any strange behavior later on.

Now change the properties listed in Table 8-2.

Table 8-2. *Configuring Custom Dialog Controls*

Property Name	Description	Value
BannerText	Dialog title	Greetings
BodyText	Dialog text appearing before the checkboxes	Please select the optional greeting phrases
Checkbox1Label	Label of checkbox 1	Hello .NET
Checkbox1Property	Unique identifier of checkbox 1. If you use more than one dialog, each element must have an installation-wide unique ID.	GREETING_DOTNET
Checkbox1Value	Whether or not checkbox 1 should be selected by default	unchecked
Checkbox1Visible	Whether or not checkbox 1 is visible	True
Checkbox2Label	Label of checkbox 2	Hello Universe
Checkbox2Property	Unique identifier of checkbox 2. If you use more than one dialog, each element must have an installation-wide unique ID.	GREETING_UNIVERSE
Checkbox2Value	Whether or not checkbox 2 should be selected by default	unchecked
Checkbox2Visible	Whether or not checkbox 2 is visible	True
Checkbox3Visible	Whether or not checkbox 3 is visible	False
Checkbox4Visible	Whether or not checkbox 4 is visible	False

If you build and run the install, you will see the dialog box showing two checkboxes. In the next section, you will see how you can pick up the user choice and create the corresponding registry entries.

Registry Editor

The Registry Editor provides a tool to add application-specific entries to the system registry on the target machine. You can create registry entries in the same way as you would with the system registry editor, `regedit.exe`, to edit the registry.

While the preferred place for application settings in .NET is now shifted from the system registry to application configuration files, there are still cases in which the system registry is a more appropriate choice for certain things such as user-specific settings. I prefer not to go any further on the merits of each approach, because such debates are not really relevant here. Let's just focus on understanding how we can update the system registry in setup projects.

You can add entries to any of the four registry hives:

1. **HKEY_CLASS_ROOT:** COM registration information

2. **HKEY_CLASS_ROOT:** Settings specific to currently logged on user

3. **HKEY_LOCAL_MACHINE:** Machine-wide settings

4. **HKEY_USER:** Default settings for new users

You should follow the standard convention when adding entries to the registry. For instance, add user-specific settings to `HKEY_CURRENT_USER\Software\YourCompany` and system-wide settings to `HKEY_LOCAL_MACHINE\Software\YourCompany`.

Let's create two registry entries based on what the user selects from the checkbox dialog created in the last section, so that when the installer runs, it will pick up the entries specified here and merge them into the system registry on the user machine.

Expand the `HKEY_CURRENT_USER` node, and right-click the `[Manufacturer]` node appearing under `Software`. In the context menu, select New and then `String Value`. Change the new entry properties as shown in Table 8-3.

Table 8-3. *Create New Registry Entries*

Property	Description	Value
(Name)	Registry entry name	Greeting #1
Condition	An expression indicating whether this registry entry should be created	GREETING_DOTNET
Value	Registry entry value	Hello .NET

Repeat the above process to create a second entry, but this time with the value `Hello Universe`. Before you go, go back to the `[Manufacturer]` node and change its `DeleteAtUninstall` property to `True`. This will delete the registry entries when `HelloWorld` is uninstalled. Now build the setup project and verify that it will create registry entries only when you check the corresponding checkboxes.

File Types Editor

The File Types editor offers you the ability to associate your applications with certain file types. For instance, if you are writing an XML editor, you could associate all files with the extension .xml or .xsl with your application. Once you have added a file type and provided it with a descriptive name, such as Greeting Vocabulary File for this case, you can specify its extension and associate it with an executable file in your application.

When the installer runs, it will create the association as specified here on the user's machine. It's always preferable, particularly if the file type is a standard one, such as .xml, .txt, or .jpg, to ask your users whether they wish to associate those files with your applications before doing so. Unfortunately, Visual Studio .NET Setup projects don't let you set such a condition for file associations, and you will have to use the Windows Installer SDK if you wish to have such a feature. You can read more about the Windows Installer SDK in the MSDN Library or the Platform SDK documentation.

Custom Action Editor

In addition to customizing the installer using the aforementioned editors, we can also specify additional operations the installer should perform. A custom action can run one of four types of files:

- Executable file (.exe)

- Library file (.dll)

- VBScript file (.vbs)

- Jscript file (.js)

Let's create a custom action that invokes a VBScript file to display a thank-you note at the end of the installation. Custom actions using other file types work in the same way.

Create a new VBScript file, RunProgram.vbs, in the HelloWorld_Setup project folder with just one statement:

```
MsgBox "We hope you enjoy the program", , "Thank you"
```

Next, add it to the project by right-clicking the HelloWorld_Setup project node in Solution Explorer and selecting Add ➤ File. Follow these steps to create a custom action to run this script:

1. Open the Customer Actions Editor

2. Right-click the Install node and select Add Custom Action

3. In the Select Item in Project dialog box, open the Application Folder and select RunProgram.vbs.

4. A custom action will appear under Install. Rename the action to something suitable, such as Run Program.

Build and run the Setup project, and you should see the message box pop up right before the installation finishes. All custom actions under Install are executed at the end of the installation process. Files used by custom actions, such as RunProgram.vbs, will not be installed on the target machine by the installer, unless specifically set to do so in the file system editor.

We may also add custom actions for deinstallation, and we can also specify a condition for a custom action. Finally, we can pass parameters to the action file by assigning them to the CustomActionData property.

Launch Condition Editor

The Launch Condition Editor allows you to specify the installation prerequisites. If a user's machine doesn't meet those conditions, the installation will stop. You will see how to add and customize launch conditions using the Launch Condition Editor in the next section.

This concludes the introduction to creating Setup projects. In the next section, you will see how to deploy your application using Setup projects.

Deploy Applications

Once we have built an application setup project, we can deploy it on any machine running Windows 98, ME, NT 4 with Service Pack 6, 2000, XP, or Windows 2003 Server using the files created by Visual Studio .NET in the HelloWorld_Setup project's output folder, as described in Table 8-4.

Table 8-4. *Setup Output Files*

File Name	Description
HelloWorld_Setup.msi	The Windows Installer package for the HelloWorld project. We can change its name to something more conventional by modifying the Output file name property in the setup project's Property Pages dialog.
Setup.exe	The setup bootstrapper file, which reads Setup.ini to determine the required installation tasks. This is the file that is run to start the installation. Setup.exe will check for the required .NET runtime and prompt users to download it if it is not found on the target PC.
Setup.ini	The initialization file used by Setup.exe to perform the required operations. In a simple setup project like this, Visual Studio .NET creates a reference to the MSI file containing the application's Windows Installer package along with a reference to the required .NET Framework runtime. In more complex installations, it may contain other application-specific information.

Windows Installer

To distribute an application, we usually should include all three of these files in our installation package. The user can run Setup.exe, which checks whether the target machine has the correct version of the .NET Framework runtime installed. If not, it will prompt the user to download the runtime from Microsoft's website and install it. Once it is satisfied that the required runtime is installed, it then invokes HelloWorld_Setup.msi to install the HelloWorld program.

If you are certain that your users will have the correct version of the CLR, such as in a controlled corporate environment, you can get away with distributing only the application installation .msi file (such as HelloWorld_Setup.msi). In such case, you can change your setup project's Bootstrapper property so that it does not create any bootstrapper files. To do this, right-click the project node in Solution Explorer and select Properties to open the Property Pages dialog shown in Figure 8-10.

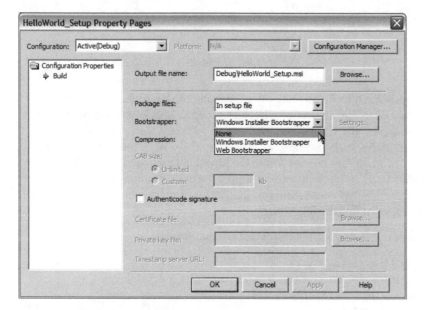

Figure 8-10. *Setup bootstrapper configuration.*

By default, a setup project will create a Windows Installer Bootstrapper as determined by the Bootstrapper dropdown. A bootstrapper, i.e., Setup.exe, checks whether the target machine has the correct version of the .NET Framework as just explained and satisfies other installation conditions. You will see more on the latter in a moment. Change the Bootstrapper property to None to have Visual Studio .NET only build the application installation MSI file and skip all other files. Now you can distribute just this file to users for them to run directly and install the application.

The third option, Web Bootstrapper, is normally used to create Setup packages for deployment over the Web, as discussed in the section "A Web Oriented Setup Project" later in the chapter.

The other option, Package Files, specifies how the application files should be packaged. The default is in the setup file, which means that all application files in the installation package are embedded in the MSI file. You can also choose for the files to be packaged in cabinet file(s) or as loose uncompressed files. The former creates one or more CAB files, determined by the CAB Size option, containing all application files. The latter simply copies all application files, alongside the MSI file, to the setup project's output folder.

The .NET Framework Runtime Package

There is a catch to the .NET installation process, though. If we run Setup.exe on a machine without the correct version of the .NET Framework Runtime, we see a message box like that shown in Figure 8-11.

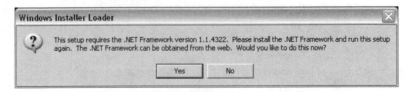

Figure 8-11. *.NET Framework checking*

The installation process terminates after you click either the Yes or the No button. If you click Yes, you will be taken to the Microsoft MSDN Download Center. You can then proceed to download and install the .NET Framework, after which you must restart Setup.exe to complete the installation. Because the Framework download is over 20 megabytes, this will take a long time if a user has a slow connection to the Internet. However, the .NET Framework runtime is freely distributable, and you can supply the .NET Framework as the single Dotnetfx.exe file with your setup package for installation on users' machines. You can obtain it from several sources, including the following:

- The Visual Studio .NET CD, in the \WCU\DotNetFramework folder.

- Microsoft MSDN Download Center
  (http://msdn.microsoft.com/library/default.asp?url=/downloads/list/
  netdevframework.asp); select Microsoft .NET Framework version (version number,
  e.g., 1.1) Redistributable.

Dotnetfx.exe contains the Windows Installer 2.0 redistributable. If the target machine does not already have this version of the Installer, Dotnetfx.exe will install it first, and then install the .NET Framework runtime. On some versions of Windows, such as Windows 98, Windows Installer 2.0 installation may require a reboot. In such case, Dotnetfx.exe will need to be invoked a second time after the restart.

Now, since the default message shown by Setup.exe when the target machine doesn't have the correct version of the .NET Framework runtime asks users to download the file from the Internet, we need to customize the message accordingly. To do so, right-click the Setup project in Solution Explorer, and select View ➤ Launch Conditions. Alternatively, with the Setup project selected, click the Launch Conditions Editor button on the Solution Explorer toolbar (see Figure 8-12).

Figure 8-12. *Select the Launch Conditions Editor*

Either way, the Launch Conditions editor and .NET Framework then appear in the Launch Conditions folder. If you click on it, you will see that its Message property has the value [VSDNETMSG], which represents the default message shown in the previous figure. Simply replace this with your own message text, and build and run the setup package again. The customized message should then appear on any machine without the runtime installed, such as the one shown in Figure 8-13.

Figure 8-13. *Display of the custom .NET Framework requirement message*

This kind of message is much more helpful to users, and we can be more confident that they will be able to install and run our applications correctly.

Install with Microsoft Bootstrapper

Asking users to manually install the .NET Framework runtime is workable, but most situations call for better than this. We can incorporate the process of detecting and installing the correct .NET Framework runtime into our installation package so that users can install our applications in a single pass, regardless of whether they already have the runtime on their machines.

If you expand the Detected Dependencies folder under the HelloWorld_Setup node in Solution Explorer, you'll see that Visual Studio .NET lists a dependency to dotnetfxredist_x86.msm, which is a merge module (we will look at merge modules in more detail later in the chapter) containing the .NET Framework runtime, as shown in Figure 8-14.

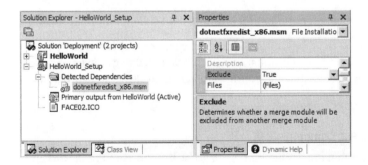

Figure 8-14. Dotnetfx *redistributable dependency*

The problem, however, is that Setup projects (or any other deployment projects for that matter) created using Visual Studio .NET can't include dotnetfxredist_x86_enu.msm, even though the Setup project identifies it as a dependency. Therefore its Exclude property is True, meaning that it will not be installed by the Setup project. If you try to change its Exclude property to False, you will get another error when you build the Setup project.

dotNETFXRedist_x86_enu.msm must not be used to redistribute the .NET Framework. Please exclude this merge module.

Therefore, we must leave its Exclude property set to True. So are we stuck?

Realizing this problem, due to the inability to integrate the .NET Framework runtime and Visual Studio .NET Setup projects, Microsoft has released a freely redistributable Setup.exe bootstrapper. This program will check whether the host machine has the .NET Framework runtime. If it can't find the runtime, it will install Dotnetfx.exe before running your application installation file. You can obtain this file and associated Settings.ini file on the same .NET Framework downloads page on MSDN:
http://www.microsoft.com/downloads/details.aspx?FamilyId=BF253CFD-1EFC-4FC5-BA7E-6A6F21403495&displaylang=en.

Because the Visual Studio .NET Setup project creates its own Setup.exe bootstrapper by default, we need to remove it from our project in order to use the new bootstrapper. We also have to modify the downloaded Setup.ini file to include your installation files:

1. Change the Bootstrapper property of the HelloWorld_Setup project to None because we will be using the custom bootstrapper instead. Once you rebuild the project, the output directory should contain only the HelloWorld_Setup.msi file.

2. Copy Dotnetfx.exe to the HelloWorld_Setup output directory.

3. Copy the downloaded Setup.exe and Setup.ini files to the HelloWorld_Setup output directory.

4. Modify the Settings.ini file as follows:

```
[Bootstrap]
Msi=HelloWorld_Setup.msi
ProductName=Hello World Program
DialogText=Do you want to install Hello World?
CaptionText=Hello World Installation
FxInstallerPath=.\
```

If you now run Setup.exe on a machine without the .NET Framework Runtime, it will invoke Dotnetfx.exe to install the required runtime files silently without user intervention before installing the HelloWorld program. Of course, on machines that already have the runtime, the setup will of course detect that and continue to install the HelloWorld program straight away.

Check for Microsoft Data Access Components (MDAC)

HelloWorld is a simple program that doesn't depend on anything but the .NET Framework runtime. Most real-world applications, on the other hand, deal with some kinds of data storage. If your applications need to use MDAC such as OLE DB or ADO, you will need to ensure that the correct version of MDAC is installed on your users' machines. Because the .NET Framework requires MDAC 2.6 (2.7 on servers) or later, you should check the presence of MDAC version 2.6 or later as a prerequisite to installing a client application. Note that although MDAC 2.6 is a .NET data access requirement, Dotnetfx.exe does not include the MDAC redistributable, and we must handle these ourselves if required.

The latest version of MDAC installed on a machine is indicated by the system registry key HKEY_LOCAL_MACHINE\SOFTWARE\Microsoft\DataAccess\FullInstallVer. Your Setup project can query this value to decide whether the installed version is adequate.

To check for the installed version of MDAC, you create an installation launch condition using the Launch Condition editor. In the editor window, right-click the Search Target Machine node and select Add Registry Search. You can change the search name to something more meaningful such as Search for MDAC Version and set its properties as shown in Table 8-5.

Table 8-5. *MDAC Registry Search Settings*

PropertyName	Value	Description
Property	MDACVERSION	The launch condition name
RegKey	Software\Microsoft\DataAccess	The registry key path
Root	vsdrrHKLM	A constant that denotes the HKEY_LOCAL_MACHINE registry group
Value	FullInstallVer	The registry value name

The next step is to add a launch condition to check the MDAC version returned from the search. In the Launch Condition Editor, right-click the Launch Conditions node and select Add Launch Condition. You may rename it something more descriptive, such as MdacSupport. Next, change its Condition property value to MDACVERSION >= "2.6", where MDACVERSION specifies the above search. Of course, if your application uses a higher version, you will use a correct version number string here.

If the launch condition is not satisfied, the installation will display the message specified by the value of the launch condition's Message property, and terminate. Therefore you should enter clear instructions in this property.

Now you can rebuild the setup project. If you followed the instructions in the last section, just remember to reset the Bootstrapper property to Windows Installer Bootstrapper before you build. When you run the setup on a machine without the required MDAC version, you should see a dialog box containing the text entered for the Message property. The installation will then terminate.

Your users will then have to install the correct MDAC version manually, probably by following your instructions. For instance, they can run Mdac_Typ.exe from the distribution CD. You can automate the process, just as we did for distributing the .NET Framework runtime, although there is no ready-made solution such as the one we used in the last section to install the .NET Framework runtime. So you will have to make your own using either the Windows Installer SDK or a third-party installer tool. This is one of the major annoyances of Visual Studio .NET Setup projects. Let's hope Microsoft acts to remedy it soon.

Applications with Dependent Assemblies

It is common to create applications that use custom assemblies not included in the .NET Framework. A Visual Studio .NET Setup project for an application can automatically detect and include any dependent assemblies. To see how this works, we'll create two projects in Visual Studio .NET.

A Server Library

First, create a Visual C# Class Library project and name it DotNetServer. Next, change the name of the automatically generated class from Class1 to DotNetClass and create a new function as follows:

```
using System;
namespace DotNetServer
{
    public class DotNetClass
    {
        public string GetInfo()
        {
            return this.GetType().AssemblyQualifiedName;
        }
    }
}
```

The one and only custom function, GetInfo, simply returns a string containing the fully qualified assembly name including its version. This helps us to verify that we are using the correct version of the library in later exercises. After we have built this project, we will have an assembly for other projects to use.

The Client Application

Create a client application by the following steps in a new solution:

1. Create a Visual C# Windows Application and name it DotNetClient.

2. Change the name of the automatically generated form from Form1 to ClientForm, and then change its Text property to .NET Client Form. You might also need to change the Startup Object to ClientForm in the project property dialog because VS .NET does not automatically change the StartUp Object when you rename the form.

3. Add a reference to the DotNetServer assembly: in Solution Explorer, right-click the References node in the DotNetClient project, and select Add Reference. In the Add Reference dialog, click the Browse button and find and select DotNetServer.dll. The DLL file will appear in the Selected Components list. Click OK to close the dialog.

4. Add a button to ClientForm.cs in the Designer. Then change its Name property to btnCall and its Text property to Call .NET Server. Double-click that button to set up a click handler, and enter the following code:

   ```
   private void btnCall_Click(object sender, System.EventArgs e)
   {
       DotNetServer.DotNetClass obj = new DotNetServer.DotNetClass();
       MessageBox.Show(obj.GetInfo(), this.Text);
   }
   ```

5. Build and run the project to verify that it runs correctly.

Create a Setup Project

Now that you have both the client application and its dependent assembly, add a Setup project named DotNetClient_Setup to the solution. You can add the primary output of the DotNetClient project to the Application Folder of the DotNetClient_Setup project. This time you will notice that Visual Studio .NET automatically detects that DotNetClient uses DotNetServer, and so it adds the DotNetServer.dll into the Application Folder.

If you prefer, modify the relevant Setup project properties as you did with the HelloWorld_Setup project. Once you are happy with the settings, build the project and install it. As you would expect, the installation will also copy DotNetServer.dll to the application folder.

This example shows how Visual Studio .NET Setup projects detect dependencies and create a Windows Installer package that correctly ensures that our applications are installed with all required dependent assemblies. Those dependencies are listed under the Detected Dependencies node of the setup project. If you find, for whatever reason, that the list is not correct, you can right-click the node and select Refresh Dependencies to force Visual Studio .NET to regenerate the dependency list.

A Setup Project for Applications Using COM

Creating brand new applications that use only .NET-managed components is fun. However, there are many unmanaged code applications that were created before .NET was released. If you have been developing applications on Microsoft platforms for more than a couple of months, it's likely that you already have a library of useful and fully tested COM and COM+ components. Unless your company has a lot of money to burn and plenty of time to kill, it makes sense to reuse these tried-and-trusted components in new .NET applications to maximize your company's investment.

The .NET Framework provides COM interop service to enable managed objects to communicate with COM objects. If you have already played with COM interop, you'll know that it's fortunately very easy to use existing COM components in a .NET application. When it comes to deployment time, creating setup projects to deploy applications that use COM components is just as easy. This section will guide you through the process.

If you already have a favorite COM DLL, you can use it for this exercise. Otherwise, you can use a simple COM DLL, ComServer.dll, included in the download for this book. The following text will reference ComServer.dll and use a class, ComClass, in the DLL, so substitute them with your own DLL and class if you wish. We need to register the DLL on our development machine before we can use it, by opening a Command Prompt window and changing to the directory where the DLL resides. For ComServer.dll, we then enter the command

```
Regsvr32 ComServer.dll
```

Now we are ready to create a client application for this DLL, and a setup project for that client application. Please note that the setup package will handle the registration of COM DLL on the target machine for us, and therefore no manual intervention is required during the installation process.

The Client Application

First, create a Visual C# Windows Application project and name it ComClient. On the automatically generated form, add a button. Table 8-6 lists the properties to set for the form and button.

Table 8-6. *COM Client Form Controls*

Object	Property Name	Property Value
Form	Name	ClientForm
--	Text	COM Client Form
Button	Name	btnCall
--	Text	Call COM Server

In order to use ComClass in ComServer.dll, you need to add a reference to the DLL file to the project. In Solution Explorer, right-click the References node in the ComClient project and select Add Reference from the context menu. In the Add Reference dialog box, click the COM tab and select Sample COM Server from the list. Click OK to close the dialog box, and you should see the registered ComServer listed in the References list.

Next, double-click the btnCall button in the Designer, and enter the following code:

```
private void btnCall_Click(object sender, System.EventArgs e)
{
    ComServer.ComClass obj = new ComServer.ComClassClass();
    MessageBox.Show("The COM Server is " + obj.GetVersion(), this.Text);
}
```

Now build and run the project. When you click the button, a message box should appear as shown in Figure 8-15.

Figure 8-15. *Displaying the COM Server version*

The next step for us is to create a Setup project that will deploy this application.

Creating a Setup Project

Add a new Setup Project named ComClient_Setup to the solution. As usual, add the primary output from ComClient to the Setup project. This time, you might see a message box similar to the one shown in Figure 8-16.

Figure 8-16. *COM component dependency warning message*

This is because in the COM world, a DLL may use other COM DLLs, and therefore all the dependent files must exist and be registered if necessary for the main DLL to work correctly. Consequently, it may be necessary to include all dependent files in the setup project. Such dependencies are in general included in a .DEP file. Since in this example we don't have this dependency file, Visual Studio .NET is unable to detect the dependent files and add them to the setup project automatically. Since this sample COM DLL doesn't depend on any other files, just click OK to close the message box. You should then see that it automatically adds two dependent classes, the original DLL, ComServer.dll, and Interop.ComServer.dll, which is a Runtime Callable Wrapper (RCW) generated in ComClient by Visual Studio .NET.

Perform any routine configuration setting changes as in the previous sections, and build the Setup project. It generates the same three files, the bootstrapper, the INI file, and the MSI file, in the output directory, just as before. And that's pretty much it. Try installing it on another machine to verify that it works, and that Visual Studio .NET has indeed made it very easy to use and deploy COM components by managing the registration process.

When You Don't Need Setup Projects

We've now seen the basics of creating and using Setup projects to deploy applications. Before moving on to learn more, let's hold back a little. The three setup projects essentially copy the application files to a user's file system. For example, HelloWorld_Setup copies HelloWorld.exe, while DotNetClient_Setup copies DotNetClient.exe and DotNetServer.dll to the HelloWorld application folder. There may be more files to copy for other projects, but the principle will be the same.

One feature of .NET is that assemblies are self-descriptive through their assembly meta-data manifests. That is, the .NET Framework runtime can retrieve relevant information from each assembly when it's loaded. This means that unlike COM and COM+ components, which need to be registered in the system before they can be used, .NET assemblies do not have to be registered. Therefore, there is no automatic registration process involved in the registration process. In other words, for simple applications, we can in fact just copy the required files to the user's machine without needing to go through the trouble of creating setup projects for them. This is what is known as XCopy Deployment.

XCopy Deployment

The term XCopy deployment may sound either futuristic or spooky, especially if you're a fan of "The X Files." However, it really just refers to using the trusty DOS XCopy command of old. The XCopy command is used to copy a file system folder, along with all its files and subfolders, to another location. We can of course achieve the same result using Windows Explorer, and a simple drag-and-drop.

With XCopy deployment, we can distribute all our application files using any media, so long as they are properly organized in the same directory hierarchy to be used on the target machine. We can burn them onto CD, compress them as a ZIP or CAB file for download off the Internet, or copy them to an internal file server for installation from the company network. In the last case, internal users can even run the application directly off the file server if they like. You can try out these different XCopy Deployment methods on the DotNetClient program to see how simple it can be.

Another good use of the XCopy installation approach is for deploying ASP.NET web applications and Web Services. A typical web application consists of middle-tier components, mostly DLLs, and UI elements such as HTML or ASP pages. Since .NET assemblies need not be registered, you can deploy the whole web application by simply copying the files to the web server.

As promising as XCopy deployment sounds, it has its limitations:

- An obvious drawback of XCopy is that it won't automatically create shortcuts on the desktop, in the Start menu, and so on. Users have either to run the application directly or manually create shortcuts themselves.

- If an application uses folders that don't belong to a single top-level folder, your users will need to run XCopy multiple times.

- If your application uses COM or COM+ components, you still have to register those components. This is a task you definitely don't want your users to do.

- You can't install components in the Global Assembly Cache (GAC). We cover this process in the section below.

- For web applications, you need to manually configure the web server to create any necessary virtual directory, set access privileges, and so on.

So, we still need the Setup projects. However, there are other deployment tasks that can't be achieved using the simple Setup project type or XCopy, so we'll now take a look at the tools Visual Studio .NET offers for those tasks.

Merge Module Projects

The whole process of creating Setup projects, or using XCopy deployment, to install applications seems fairly simple and well designed. However, if you are a savvy developer, you probably have noticed one missing piece. DotNetServer.dll is installed in the application folder, that is, as a private assembly. Therefore, it can't easily be used by other applications. What if you have designed DotNetServer.dll as a public assembly, that is, to be used by more than one client application, and want to distribute it as a shared component?

What the `DotNetClient_Setup` project does is to make a copy of the current dependent assembly, `DotNetServer.dll`, and install it as a private component of the target application. If you have another application that also uses it, the setup project for that application may make another copy of it and install it as a separate private component of the second application, resulting in two copies of `DotNetServer.dll` on that machine.

If this approach seems inefficient at first, that is intentional. It is designed to address the infamous Windows "DLL Hell" problem, that two applications may install different versions of the same COM DLL on one machine. The later version would overwrite the earlier one because there is only one registry entry for any given COM DLL. If the new version is not binary compatible with the older version, applications that rely on older versions may not work properly or even at all once a new version is installed. Being able to install a private copy for each application removes the hidden dependencies among applications that use the same DLL.

On the other hand, the shared DLL technique has some advantages over having multiple copies of the same DLL. As long as you keep each version of the DLL binary compatible with a common interface, applications that were built against an older version should continue to work with the latest version. Updating a single copy of the DLL is much easier and less error-prone than updating each copy separately. If a new DLL is released with a bug fix, we need to install it only once for all applications to benefit from it.

This same logic also applies to .NET assemblies. If we plan to have one assembly shared by many applications, installing it in a common area accessible to all applications is a good idea (but we'll then have to ensure that it remains backward compatible, of course). To do this, we can package the server assembly separately and link it into the client application setup packages. The first client application will install the server assembly, which will then be accessible to other client applications. The Visual Studio .NET Merge Module Project provides the functionality we require to package one or more shared server assemblies.

Furthermore, you can also create merge module projects to package server assemblies that are not to be shared. In essence, a Merge Module project provides a way for you to package any server assemblies. You can reuse a Merge Module project in many other deployment projects no matter how they intend to deploy the server assembly: shared or private.

In order to allow client deployment projects to decide how they want to deploy the server assembly, you configure the merge module project to allow client application setup packages to dynamically specify the installation location of the server assemblies. For instance, they can install a server assembly to the application folder, making it private to the application. Similarly, they can install a server assembly to the global assembly cache (GAC) and therefore allow it to be shared by other applications. This section provides a walkthrough to create a Merge Module project and use it in a Setup project.

A Merge Module Project

Add a new Merge Module Project to the solution used in the previous section, and name it `DotNetServer_Package`. As usual, add the primary output from the `DotNetServer` project to `DotNetServer_Package`. Notice that `Primary output from DotNetServer (Active)` is added to the `Module Retargetable` folder. Placing a component in this folder makes the installation location of `DotNetServer.dll` configurable by client installers. We will see how a client deployment packages does that in a moment. For now, we can build the project, which creates a file called `DotNetServer_Package.msm` in the `Debug` or `Release` subfolder.

Unlike Windows Installer files, which can be run to install target applications, we can't run a merge module to install its target components. We must merge it into other installer files that use its target components. To test how the Merge Module project works, create a new Setup project, and call it DotNetClient_Setup2. You will use this project to package the DotNetClient project and the DotNetServer_Package Merge Module project.

As you did when creating the DotNetClient_Setup project, add the primary output from the DotNetClient project to the DotNetClient_Setup2 project. Since we will now install DotNetServer.dll using DotNetServer_Package, we need to exclude this DLL file from the project by right-clicking it and selecting Exclude. Alternatively, you can select it and change its Exclude property to True.

Next, add the DotNetServer_Package merge module by right-clicking the DotNetClient_Setup2 project in Solution Explorer, and selecting Add ➤ Project Output. In the Add Project Output Group dialog box, select DotNetServer_Package from the Project dropdown box. This time only Merge Module appears in the list.

Click OK to close the dialog box. We can now build the project and install it with no problem. Once installed, run it to verify that it now works.

Installation Locations for Client Projects

The idea behind setting the target destination of a merge module to retargetable is that we don't always know at design time where future client projects will want to install them. For instance, a client project may need to include an assembly in a merge module as a private component and therefore want to install it in its own application folder. Visual Studio .NET provides an easy means for client installers to decide where to install components based on their own requirements, even long after the merge module was created.

Installing in the Application Folder

Select the Merge Module from the DotNetServer_Package (Active) node in Solution Explorer and find the Folder property in the Properties window. Its value will be Application Folder, which is the default setting for Setup projects. Since this is exactly what was configured when we created the installation package in the last section, you should see that DotNetServer.dll is installed in the application folder of the installed version of DotNetClient.

Installing in the GAC

All assemblies installed in the GAC must have a strong name so that the .NET Framework runtime can uniquely identify and load any assembly. It's not practical to explain the reason here, but you can look up MSDN or read other books on this subject. In order to install DotNetServer.dll in the GAC, we must assign DotNetServer a strong name. If you haven't created strongly named assemblies before, follow the steps below to assign DotNetServer a strong name:

1. Open a Visual Studio .NET 2003 Command Prompt window, which can be found under Visual Studio .NET 2003 | Visual Studio .NET tools, and change the current directory to the DotNetServer project folder.

2. Type in the command sn -k DotNetServer.key and click Enter. This creates a key file called DotNetServer.key in the current directory.

3. Go back to Visual Studio .NET IDE and double-click the AssemblyInfo.cs class in the DotNetServer project. Scroll to the bottom of the file and enter the path to the key file for the AssemblyKeyFile attribute, as follows:

```
[assembly: AssemblyDelaySign(false)]
[assembly: AssemblyKeyFile("..\\..\\DotNetServer.key")]
[assembly: AssemblyKeyName("")]
```

4. Rebuild the DotNetServer, project.

The next step is to add the GAC to your target folder list in the File System editor for the DotNetClient_Setup2 project. First, right-click the File System on Target Machine node in the File System editor, and select Add Special Folder ➤ Global Assembly Cache Folder. This adds the GAC to the list of target folders in the left pane. Next, click the Merge Module from DotNetClient_Setup2 (Active) node in Solution Explorer, and then change its Folder property to Global Assembly Cache Folder. This makes the GAC serve as the installation folder for DotNetServer.dll.

However, there is one more twist. If we build the project, we get this error message:

▪**Caution** Unable to build project output group 'Merge Module from DotNetServer_Package (Active)' into the Global Assembly Cache; the outputs are not strongly named assemblies.

Visual Studio .NET seems unable to detect that the DotNetServer_Package project contains a strongly named assembly. The workaround is to reference the compiled version of both the server assembly and the merge module as follows:

1. Remove the Primary output from DotNetServer (Active) component from the DotNetServer_Package project.

2. In the File System Editor for the DotNetServer_Package project, right-click the Module Retargetable Folder. Select Add ➤ Assembly to open the Component Selector dialog box. Then click the Browse button and find DotNetServer.dll. Once you have selected the DLL, click OK to close the dialog box.

3. Rebuild DotNetServer_Package.

4. Remove `Merge Module` from `DotNetServer_Package (Active)` from `DotNetClient_Setup2` project.

5. In Solution Explorer, right-click the `DotNetClient_Setup2` project node. Select Add ➤ Merge Module to open the `Add Module` dialog box. Locate the entry for `DotNetServer_Package.msm` and click Open to close the dialog box and add the file to the project.

6. In Solution Explorer, click the `DotNetServer_Package.msm` node under the `DotNetClient_Setup2` project and expand the `(MergeModuleProperties)` node in the Properties window. Click the `Module Retargetable Folder` and then the down arrow on the right. In the dropdown list, select `Browse`.

7. In the `Select Folder` dialog box, select `Global Assembly Cache Folder` and click OK to close the dialog box.

8. Rebuild the `DotNetClient_Setup2` project.

As usual, run the setup and verify that `DotNetServer.dll` is installed in the GAC and that `DotNetClient` works as expected. The DLL will also be removed from the GAC when you uninstall `DotNetClient`, provided that you haven't installed any other programs that also use that DLL.

That pretty much wraps up our introduction to merge module projects. In the next section, we will look at the Cab Project, which packages assemblies for distribution over the Internet.

Cab Projects

The primary objective of the Cab project type is to provide a means for downloading ActiveX controls from the Internet or an intranet via a web browser. The CAB file type takes its name from the word *cabinet*, because it is used to store multiple files and folders, and is pretty much like a ZIP file in concept. To see how the Cab project type is used, let's walk through an example.

The ActiveX Control

First, we need an ActiveX control to play with. You may use any ActiveX control that you've already written, or use `ClockControl.ocx` as provided in the code download for this book. We'll refer to this `ClockControl` ActiveX control in this section, so substitute this with the name of your own ActiveX control if you'd rather do that. Either way, you need to ensure that the ActiveX control is registered on your development machine.

To register `ClockControl`, open a Command Prompt box, and change to the directory where you placed the `ClockControl.ocx` file. Then enter this command:

```
Regsvr32 ClockControl.ocx
```

The `ClockControl` contains a control called `FlashingClock`, which displays a digital clock on the hosting web page. It refreshes the time and changes its background color every second, as illustrated in Figure 8-17.

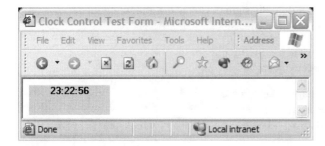

Figure 8-17. *A flashing clock control*

Now we're ready to create a CAB file to distribute this control.

Placing the Control within a Cab Project

In Visual Studio .NET, create a new Cab Project and name it ClockControl. Then right-click the project node in Solution Explorer, and select Add ➤ File. In the Add File dialog box, locate ClockControl.ocx and click Open. This should now appear under the ClockControl project.

There is not much to configure for the Cab project type, so just go ahead and build it and we are done. In the project output directory, you should see the file ClockControl.cab. We now need to create a web interface to install this control on a user's machine.

A Simple ASP.NET Project

Create a new Visual C# ASP.NET Web Project with Visual Studio .NET and name it ClockControl_Web. Next change the name of the automatically created web form from WebForm1.aspx to ClockControlForm.aspx and double-click it to display the form in design mode if it's not already open. Then follow the following steps to complete the project:

1. In Solution Explorer, right-click the project node and select Add ➤ New Folder. Rename the new folder Downloads. Next, right-click the Downloads folder node, and select Add ➤ Add Existing Item. In the dialog entitled Add Existing Item – ClockControl_Web, find ClockControl.cab created by the ClockControl cab project in its output directory, and click Open. The file ClockControl.cab will now appear under the Downloads folder node.

2. Right-click the Toolbox in Visual Studio, and select Add/Remove Items. Check ClockControl.FlashingClock on the COM Components tab in the Customize Toolbox dialog box, and click OK. The FlashingClock control should now become available right at the bottom of the Web Forms tab of the Toolbox.

3. Double-click the ClockControl.FlashingClock control to add it to the web form.

4. Click the control on the web form, select the codebase property in the Properties pane, and set it to Downloads/ClockControl.cab.

5. Build the project. If you run it on your development machine and the Initialize and script ActiveX controls not marked as safe option for Local Intranet is disabled in Internet Explorer, you may see a warning message about the page containing unsafe information. For simplicity, the ClockControl is not by default marked as safe for

initialization or scripting, nor is it digitally signed. Check out the following articles on MSDN for more information on these subjects:

- Signing and Checking Code with Authenticode (http://msdn.microsoft.com/workshop/security/authcode/signing.asp)

- Creating, Viewing, and Managing Certificates (http://msdn.microsoft.com/library/en-us/security/Security/creating_viewing_and_managing_certificates.asp)

- Safe Initialization and Scripting for ActiveX Controls (http://msdn.microsoft.com/workshop/components/activex/safety.asp)

- Microsoft Knowledge Base Article Q182598 - HOWTO: Implement IObjectSafety in Visual Basic Controls (http://support.microsoft.com/default.aspx?scid=KB;en-us;q182598)

6. For this exercise, just click OK, and the clock will display because the FlashingClock control is already registered on your local machine.

7. On another machine that has not had ClockControl registered, you will need to enable the following Internet Explorer security settings:

    Download unsigned ActiveX controls, and

    Initalize and script ActiveX controls not marked as safe

8. Open ClockControlForm.aspx in Internet Explorer. The control will be downloaded to the Downloaded Program Files subfolder in the Windows or WinNT directory. The web page then will display the clock.

So that's the procedure for creating Cab projects to deploy ActiveX controls. Don't forget to reset your IE settings to their previous values if you've had to change them.

Limitations

If you have already developed web pages utilizing ActiveX controls, you know that the concept of CAB file deployment is not new. The Visual Basic 6 Package and Deployment Wizard provided a convenient way of creating CAB files that package ActiveX controls for distribution. You can even mark your controls as safe for initialization and scripting when you create the distribution CAB file. Sadly, such an ability is as yet absent from the new Visual Studio .NET Cab project.

Only Microsoft can explain the exact reasons for such a limited Cab project type. A good guess is that with the release of the .NET Framework, ActiveX controls are on their way out. We should perhaps view ActiveX as a legacy technology that Microsoft would rather we no longer use.

The Cab Project as a Compression Tool

Another use of the Cab project type is simply as a compression tool. For instance, we can package all our Setup project output files in a CAB file so that users can download it over the Internet. They can then extract the setup files and install the application locally.

This isn't difficult to try out if you wish. Open the `DotNetClient_Setup` project in Visual Studio .NET, and create a new Cab Project. Next add the project output from the `DotNetClient_Setup` project to the new Cab project. When we now build the Cab project, all setup files created by `DotNetClient_Setup` will be packed up into a single CAB file. You can put this CAB file on a web server so that users can download it.

There is also another way of making Windows applications available for installation over the Internet, but I'll come back to that later in the chapter. For now, let's turn our attention to the Web Setup Project.

Web Setup Project

The primary purpose of creating a Web Setup project is to deploy a web application to other web servers. Like the Cab project, the concept of deploying web applications from a development machine to a server is not new in .NET. For instance, we could deploy a web application on the fly in Microsoft Visual InterDev. As stated earlier, we can also use XCopy to install web applications. So before we move on to the Web Setup project type, let's look at how to use XCopy to install a web application.

XCopy Deployment for Web Applications

If we wish to use XCopy to copy a web application to a new server, the first thing we need is write access to the drive or parent folder where we wish to place the web application. For instance, if we want to install the web application to `C:\Inetpub\wwwroot\ClockControl_Web`, we must have write access to either the wwwroot folder or at least the `ClockControl_Web` folder, assuming it already exists.

Assuming that the wwwroot folder on the web server is shared as wwwroot and that we have the required write permission, we would perform an XCopy installation by the following steps:

1. Copy the `ClockControl_Web` folder from your development machine to the `C:\Inetput\wwwroot\ClockControl_Web` folder on the web server. You can either use drag-and-drop and Windows Explorer, or enter the following XCopy command at a Command Prompt window:

   ```
   xcopy ClockControl_Web "\\WebServer\wwwroot\ClockControl_Web" /i /e /y
   ```

   Note that you'll need to substitute WebServer in the above command with the name of the machine where the web application is to be installed.

2. On the web server containing the new installation, open the Internet Information Services MMC snap-in. Under `Default Web Site`, right-click the `ClockControl_Web` folder and select `Properties`.

3. In the ClockControl_Web Properties dialog box that now opens, click the Create button toward the bottom to configure the folder as an application accessible as a website, and click `OK`.

That's the minimum required to deploy a web application using XCopy. If we don't carry out the third and final step above, users will be unable to browse to our web pages. We may wish to set other properties, such as the default start page or the application's protection settings, in which case there will be a few more things to do manually.

Note that the XCopy method copies all files, even though many of them (such as the project files) are not required at runtime. In a production environment, we should really remove such files manually. Needless to say, if your web application uses tried-and-trusted COM+ components, you also have to manually install those. Web Setup projects can automate such tasks, and more.

Deploy a Web Application

In this section, we'll create a Web Setup project to deploy the ClockControl_Web application. Before we start, make sure that the ClockControl_Web project is loaded in Visual Studio .NET.

Add a new Web Setup project to the solution and name it ClockControl_Web_Setup. In Solution Explorer, right-click the ClockControl_Web_Setup project node, and select Add ➤ Project Output from the context menu. In the Add Project Output Group dialog box, select the ClockControl_Web project and then select Primary Output and Content Files. Click OK to close the dialog box.

The Web Setup project will create a virtual directory on the target web server for the target web application (the ClockControl_Web project). By default, the virtual directory takes the name of the Web Setup project. Normally we'd want it to be named differently, for instance, to have the name of the web application. To do that, click the Web Application Folder in the File System editor and change its VirtualDirectory property value to ClockControl_Web. While you can change the name of the virtual directory when you actually install it, it's a good practice to specify a meaningful name here. As I said, Web Setup projects also allow us to change other web settings such as the default starting page and the application protection level. For this example, change the ApplicationProtection property value to high using the Properties window.

Now build the ClockControl_Web_Setup project. The last step is to copy all files from the project output directory to the web server, and run Setup.exe there. Once the setup is completed, our web application is all ready to go.

Deploy a Windows Application

In the Setup Project section, we saw how to create Setup projects to deploy Windows applications. The Setup project creates a set of files that can be distributed using CDs or a network. In addition to such "traditional" media, we can also distribute such applications over the Internet, expanding our potential user base to pretty much the entire planet.

A simple way of distributing a Windows application on the Internet is to package its setup program in a single ZIP or CAB archive. Users can then download this file, uncompress it, and run Setup.exe to install it. However, this method has the same drawbacks as creating standard Windows Setup packages, most notably distribution of the .NET Framework runtime. In order to allow users who don't have the correct version of the runtime on their machines to install our applications, we need to do one of the following:

1. We can choose to include the .NET Framework runtime redistributable and the Microsoft Bootstrapper in the application distribution package, as discussed earlier. This increases the size of the package dramatically, and users who have already installed the .NET Framework runtime on their machine will also have to download those files, even though they don't need them.

2. We could create two setup packages, one with the .NET Framework runtime redistributable and the Microsoft Bootstrapper and the other with the Windows Installer (MSI)
file only. Users with the runtime can choose to download the smaller package, while
others would need to download the full package. However, this puts the responsibility
on our users to know what .NET Framework runtime version they have on their
machines.

3. We can choose to exclude the Windows Installer redistributables from our package and
make them available for download separately. If the setup process detects that the
latest installer version is not present on the host machine, it would need to display
a message like that shown in the .NET Framework Runtime section earlier to instruct
them to download the Windows Installer redistributables. However, this is an inconvenience to users, who may give up and choose a competitor's product that makes
things simpler for them.

There are other options, such as using third-party tools, but they are beyond the scope
of this book. However, Visual Studio .NET has a much better way, based on a combination of
Setup and Web Setup projects. We create a Setup project for an application, and then create
a Web Setup project to deploy the Setup project output files to a web server. Users can then
install the target application directly from your web server. We'll have a go at doing this now.

A Web-Oriented Setup Project

First, create a Setup project for the DotNetClient application just as we created the
DotNetClient_Setup project. This time name it DotNetClient_Setup3. Before you build it,
change its Bootstrapper property to Web Bootstrapper, which will open the Web Bootstrapper Settings dialog box shown in Figure 8-18.

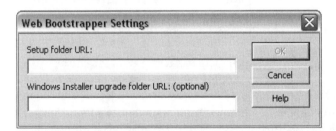

Figure 8-18. *Web Bootstrapper Settings dialog*

As discussed in the earlier Deploy Applications section, the bootstrapper Setup.exe
performs some preinstallation checks and then loads the application MSI file to install the
application. For normal installation, the application MSI file is located in the same folder as
Setup.exe, and there is no problem for Setup.exe in finding the application MSI. In a web
installation scenario, the user downloads and runs Setup.exe, which obviously needs to know
where it can find the application MSI file. You specify the location of the application MSI file
by entering the URL of the folder containing the application MSI file in the Setup folder URL

box. For this example, enter http://*MyServer*/DotNetClient_Setup, where *MyServer* denotes your deployment web server.

On the other hand, if Setup.exe detects that the user's machine does not have the required Windows Installer runtime during the preinstallation check, it will try to find the correct Windows Installer redistributable and update the user's machine by looking in the URL given in the Windows Installer upgrade folder URL box. If this is in the same folder as the application MSI file, just leave this field blank.

Close this dialog box now, and build the Setup project. If you look at the project output folder, you will see these two files:

- DotNetClient_Setup3.msi: The application installation Windows Installer package

- Setup.exe: The web-oriented setup bootstrapper

Comparing this list with the output files created by the regular Setup project, DotNet-Client_Setup, we see that this Setup project doesn't produce the bootstrapper initialization file, Setup.ini. Instead, it includes the locations of the setup MSI file and the Windows Installer redistributable files within the Setup.exe bootstrapper itself. This allows Setup.exe to run without having to look up details in Setup.ini.

Note that it is possible to simply copy those two files to a folder on your web server, à la XCopy. Knowing the limitations of the XCopy method, however, let's create a Web Setup project to fully automate the deployment process.

Deploying Installation Files with Web Setup Projects

By now, you should be quite familiar with creating Web Setup projects, so we can skip the walkthrough this time. Just create a new Web Setup project, call it DotNetClient_WebSetup, and add the Build Output of DotNetClient_Setup3 to its Web Application Folder.

One setting you should change is the Web Application Folder's VirtualDirectory property, which must match the Setup folder URL value entered in the Web Bootstrapper Settings dialog box shown in the last section. In the example, you must enter DotNetClient_Setup. You may also change other settings as you wish.

When you point your browser to http://MyServer/DotNetClient_Setup/Setup.exe, you will see a File Download dialog asking whether you would like to open or save the file to your computer. You can either open and run the Setup.exe file directly, or save it locally and run it later. The result is the same: in both cases Setup.exe will run and automatically try to download and run DotNetClient_Setup3.msi to install the application. Because this file is not digitally signed, your browser might not download it, or it may display a security warning.

For this exercise, just ignore the warning and let the installation start. In a production environment, we really do need to digitally sign it so that our users will feel comfortable installing it. An alternative would be to provide users with the option of downloading all setup files, including DotNetClient_Setup3.msi, and installing locally. You can package them all up together in a CAB, as described earlier, or a ZIP file, and create a link for users to download them all.

No-Touch Deployment

So far, we have learned how Visual Studio.NET provides built-in support for the deployment of Windows and web applications. Compared to previous versions of Visual Studio, the new Setup projects not only offer more powerful and flexible tools, but also greatly simplify the process of creating installation packages.

Modern businesses invest heavily in web-based applications, even after the popping of the dot-com bubble. One of the most powerful reasons in favor of web applications is the simplicity of deployment. Although there are issues when we are required to support multiple browsers, the Web presents an arena in which potential users require little setting up to use our applications. As long as they have a suitable browser version, they can just type in the URL for our application and start using it straightaway. If we need to update a web application, we simply update the files on the server and all clients start using the new code immediately.

Nevertheless, we can sometimes be frustrated by the primitive interface offered by standard Internet protocols. There is still no comparison in terms of user interface richness between Windows and web applications. It's a dilemma facing business decision makers and application architects: you go for either the much richer user interface and robustness offered by Windows applications, or the substantial advantage of virtually zero client-side setup and support cost, but not both.

The Web Setup project type aims to bring a little of the Web's ease of deployment to the world of Windows installation packages, but users still have to manually install them once downloaded. If the application changes, users must download and install the new installation package.

Microsoft attempts to take the idea a few steps further, to combine all the deployment advantages of the Web with the robustness and the rich user interface of Windows applications. The result is what is called *no-touch* (or *zero-touch*) *deployment of smart clients*.

The idea behind this is quite simple. Instead of installing a Windows Forms application and running it from the local hard disk, users run it remotely without installing it first. For instance, if we put `HelloWorld.exe` onto a web server, the user can just run `http://www.company.com/apps/HelloWorld.exe`.

Thus the user will always run the latest version of the application as soon as it appears on our web server. The infrastructure for this is already in place. On the server side, Microsoft Internet Information Server (IIS) can serve .NET assemblies over HTTP. On the client side, Microsoft Internet Explorer can download assemblies to its cache, and then execute them on demand. Each time you make a request to run the application, the .NET runtime checks whether the cached copy matches the latest on the web server. If they are the same, it will just run the cached copy from the browser cache. Otherwise, the latest copy is downloaded to the cache and then executed. You can try this out by copying `HelloWorld.exe` to a virtual directory on your web server and then running it through a browser on a remote machine.

Things are a little more complex when an application consists of multiple assemblies. While Internet Explorer can run the main assembly remotely, it isn't yet smart enough to figure out the dependent assemblies and download them automatically. For instance, if you copy `DotNetClient.exe` and `DotNetServer.dll` to a web server and run `DotNetClient` from a remote machine, you will receive an error as soon as `DotNetClient` tries to instantiate the `DotNetClass` in `DotNetServer.dll`. There are also security issues that may further complicate this – the assembly may be run in a more strict security context depending on how you configure the .NET Runtime Security Policy.

This leaves us with two options: convert `DotNetServer` to a web service and modify `DotNetClient` to consume the web service, or use .NET Remoting to remotely load `DotNetClass`, most likely when running in an intranet. Both are viable techniques, but detailed descriptions about them are beyond this chapter. For more information, read No Touch Deployment in the .NET Framework on MSDN, at `http://msdn.microsoft.com/library/default.asp?url=/library/en-us/dv_vstechart/html/vbtchNo-TouchDeploymentInNETFramework.asp`.

Rockford Lhotka's *Expert One on One VB .NET Business Objects*, published by Apress, ISBN 1-59059-145-3, contains an excellent working example of no-touch deployment with .NET Remoting. You can also read the whitepaper ".NET Client Applications: .NET Application Updater Component" at `http://windowsforms.net/articles/appupdater.aspx`.

Summary

Deploying applications has traditionally been less than straightforward and has required a lot of groundwork. Visual Studio .NET provides a collection of setup and deployment project types that make it easy for us to package and deploy applications. This chapter has attempted to introduce those project types, discussing along the way the commonly used techniques for creating different setup and deployment projects.

Setup projects offer application developers the power and flexibility to package Windows applications and customize their installation behaviors. Web Setup projects let us deploy and update web applications across multiple web servers. We can also combine the two project types to distribute Windows applications over the Internet.

Visual Studio .NET also includes the Merge Module project type, which allows application developers to create setup packages for individual system components and assemble them in Setup and Web Setup projects. The Cab project provides an easy way to make components and applications available for download via the Internet.

Knowing that we can create deployment packages easily for an application, and that we can synchronize the setup and deployment projects with the application during its development cycle, lets us focus more on producing high-quality software, confident that our applications will be deployed successfully. We can rest assured that our users will enjoy a hassle-free professional-quality installation process, setting them up to fully appreciate the quality of our .NET applications.

CHAPTER 9

■■■

Crystal Reports for .NET

Writing reports is part of many software applications. Every day you probably come across some type of report that was generated by an application. This could be business reports you get at work, utility bills you receive in the mail, or even something as simple as a receipt for groceries you purchased. For most applications this is a required part of the specification. An application that lets a user enter and manage data, but not print it out, lacks functionality that most end users expect. It's very important for developers to know how to use some type of report writing tool to integrate reports into their applications.

Fortunately, Visual Studio .NET comes with Crystal Reports as part of the default installation. The report writing tools are integrated into the IDE, so that you can write reports along with the rest of your application without leaving Visual Studio .NET. Prior releases of Visual Studio did come with Crystal Reports, but it was not part of the standard installation, and it was run separately from Visual Studio as a third-party application. Reports had to be created independently of your application and later integrated into it. Microsoft's first attempt at creating an integrated reporting component was called Data Reports, and it was released with Visual Studio 6. Everyone quickly realized that this was useful only for the most simplistic reports, and Microsoft dropped it from Visual Studio.

With the release of Visual Studio .NET, Microsoft gives developers an unprecedented level of report integration included as part of the Visual Studio suite of tools. This book shows you the different features and options available to you and how to quickly implement them. You will find that writing professional reports has never been more convenient.

.NET Integration Features and Options

There are many new features included with this latest release of Crystal Reports for .NET. These features give you many improvements over the prior options for report writing:

- **Default Installation:** When you install Visual Studio .NET, Crystal Reports is listed as one of the installation options alongside of VB.NET and C#.

- **IDE Integration:** Adding a report to your application is as simple as right-clicking on the Solution Explorer window and selecting Add New Item. You can design the report and test how it works without ever leaving the Visual Studio environment.

- **Typed Reports:** Reports are created as a class within your application. Upon compilation, the class is included within your application and no separate report file is necessary. This makes it easier to use the code editor's shortcuts and simplifies report deployment.

- **Untyped Reports:** As in previous versions of Crystal Reports, you still have the option to save a report as a separate file. This lets you call the report from multiple applications and update it independently of the application.

- **Web Services:** .NET makes writing platform-independent software much easier. Crystal Reports makes it possible to deliver reports to clients via these web services. With just a few clicks of the mouse, a report can be converted to a web service and delivered to a variety of client systems.

- **Language Independence:** Crystal Reports can be used with any .NET language. The developer gets to use the language of his or her choosing without restrictions.

Concepts and Terms

Crystal Reports uses new terminology to describe how reports are designed and processed. It's important to be familiar with this terminology so you can make decisions on the best way to write reports. This terminology is also used in the help files provided with Crystal Reports. If you need to access help, and all of us do at some point, then after reading this section you will have a better grasp of the concepts you need to understand the help files. This section defines terms you need to be familiar with and explains why each one is important.

Two-Pass Processing

Crystal Reports processes reports in two passes. Each pass is restricted to only a certain type of data, and each pass builds on top of the data from the previous pass. Each pass also restricts the types of functions that can be performed on the data. This pyramiding of data enables the generation of complex reports that wouldn't be possible with just a single pass. Knowing the details of what happens in each of the two passes lets you write advanced reports. You can use special keywords in a formula, known as Evaluation Time keywords, that allow you to specify that a formula should be evaluated at a certain time.

First Pass

During the first pass of report processing, the detail records are read from the data source. The records are used for creating the data that appear in the report, calculating formulas, and applying filters. Most of the data will be shown in the Details section of the report designer. Only formulas that reference this raw data (not subtotals or summary information) are processed during this pass. As the records are processed and the formulas are calculated, the data is grouped and sorted.

When this pass is finished, the data is stored in memory and to temporary tables to be used in the second pass. The database is not referenced again.

Once you start writing formulas, this pass is referred to by the evaluation time keyword "WhileReadingRecords."

Second Pass

Any formulas that couldn't be processed during the first pass are calculated during the second pass. These are primarily formulas that reference subtotals and running totals, including selection formulas that filter data based on groups. Charts and subreports are processed during this pass as well.

Formatting the report fields is performed during the second pass. Since formatting is completely visual, the report engine doesn't format every page prior to printing a report. Instead, it does so on demand. In other words, the page isn't formatted until it is shown to the user. This gives the user the impression that the report was generated very quickly, when in reality only the first few pages have been created.

Once you start writing formulas, this pass is referred to by the evaluation time keyword "WhilePrintingRecords."

■**Caution** If a report uses a group selection formula in combination with subtotals, grand totals, and summary data, then the report information could be incorrect. This is because data that is used to calculate subtotals and grand totals could get filtered out after the totals have been calculated. This is probably a little confusing, so let's look at a quick example. During the first pass, a grand total is calculated as the result of the subtotal of three groups. This grand total is stored in a temporary table to be used later. During the second pass, one of the groups gets filtered out, and now only two groups will be shown on the report. But the grand total was saved during the first pass, and it doesn't get recalculated. So its value is incorrect. To get around this problem, use running total fields on reports that have a selection formula for group values.

The final step of the second pass is to calculate the total page count. This is important, because it can have a big effect on report performance. Reports that include the total number of pages in the report footer, e.g., "Page X of Y," will print more slowly than reports that don't show the total page count in the footer. By putting the total page count in the page footer, the formatting of every page must be performed so that the number of pages in the report can be determined. This slows down the second pass, because it can't utilize the page-on-demand optimization techniques. To get optimal performance, don't include the total page count in the report.

Strongly Typed Reports

When you create a report using Visual Studio .NET, it is included in the project as a fully qualified ReportDocument class. You can access the properties and methods of the class as well as bind to the events of a report. This gives you a high degree of runtime integration and customization of reports.

Strongly Typed reports give you the benefit of having your reports included as part of your application. There isn't a separate file to install or keep track of. The drawback is that if you wanted to update only your report and not the rest of the application, then you would have to recompile and redistribute the complete application.

Untyped Reports

There are times when you want to load reports that are external to the application. For example, you could be writing reports that will be used by multiple applications or you might want to store them in a centralized location to optimize processing. Crystal Reports gives you the functionality to save reports as individual files and load them into the application when necessary. Such reports are called *Untyped*.

ReportDocument Class

Every report belongs to the ReportDocument class. It has properties to load, export, and print a report. Learning the properties and methods of this class gives you the ability to perform runtime customization of reports. This gives you the highest level of report customization and lets you seamlessly integrate reports with your .NET applications.

CrystalReportViewer Controls

Letting a user preview a report before it is printed requires adding a viewer to your application. There is a version of the viewer that can be added to Windows forms and a version for use with ASP.NET web forms. The viewer has built-in capabilities for viewing, exporting, and printing reports. If you don't use one of the viewers, you can still export and print the report, but you will have to do so by using the methods of the ReportDocument class.

Binding Reports

Binding a report is the process of telling the application how to load the report into memory, connect to the data source, and preview/print the report. Learning the different ways to bind a report is one of the key factors to writing an efficient reporting solution. Crystal Reports gives you an enormous number of options for binding reports, and each option changes depending on whether you are using the Crystal viewer control and whether you are writing an ASP.NET or WinForms application. Learning all the different options can be overwhelming at first, but once you use each one a couple times, you will find that it is easy enough to repeat.

Pull Model

The Pull Model is the easiest method for binding a report. It lets Crystal do all the work for you. You simply add a viewer control and a ReportDocument component to a form and tell the ReportDocument component which report to print. When the form loads, it automatically loads the report into memory and previews it.

The Pull Model doesn't require any coding on your part. Within a report file, all the data connectivity information is stored. The ReportDocument component knows how to take this information and automatically connect to the data source. The viewer then displays the report to the user. You don't have to write any code to implement this.[1]

■**Caution** When you save a report, the data source information that your report uses to connect and retrieve data is also saved. But even though the User ID is saved, the password you used to connect to the database is not. This is for security reasons in case someone decided to hack into the report's binary files. Reports that connect to a secure data source require you to write code to pass the password to the data source.

---

1. In ASP.NET there are a couple of lines of code you have to write, but it is very trivial.

Push Model

The Push Model of binding a report involves manually loading the report into memory and connecting to the data source. This is done by creating a report object variable and instantiating it. Set the properties of the object and call the appropriate methods to perform report functions such as exporting and printing.

Although the Push Model requires more work on your part than the Pull Model, it gives you greater control and lets you implement connection sharing for better performance.

Creating Reports with the Crystal Designer

When you install Visual Studio .NET, Crystal Reports is one of the items listed on the install tool. It is checked by default. After Visual Studio .NET is installed, you can design reports using the Crystal Designer. The same designer is used for writing reports that are used within Windows applications, web pages, or web services. Although each type of application connects to the report in a different way, they all use the same ReportDocument class for working with reports.

The following steps walk you through creating a simple report in an application. This report is used throughout the remainder of the chapter to illustrate the different ways that applications use reports:

1. Open an existing Windows application that you are working on or create a new Windows Application project.[2]

2. Move the mouse over the project name in the Solutions Explorer window and select Add | Add New Item. This opens the Add New Item dialog box.

3. In the Templates listbox on the right, move the scrollbar down till you find the Crystal Reports item. Click on it and then enter the name "Customer List" in the lower textbox. Click Open.

4. This opens the Crystal Report Gallery dialog box (see Figure 9-1). It lets you choose how you want to create the report. You can choose to create a new report using one of the report experts, create a blank report, or create a report using an existing report. For this example, leave the default selections unchanged and click the OK button. This opens the report expert for a new standard report type.

---

2.   If you prefer to create a new ASP.NET application instead, these steps will work with that as well.

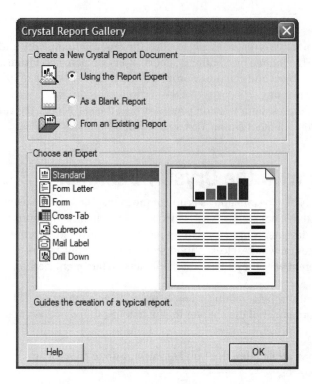

Figure 9-1. *Creating the Customer List report*

Note For the majority of your reports you will choose to use the Report Expert to create the first draft of the report. Although the Report Expert doesn't create a perfect report, it does a great job of doing most of the initial tedious work for you. For easier reports, sometimes the only work you have to do is rearrange the report fields and set formatting options.

One of the benefits of the Report Expert is that it is very easy to follow. The Report Expert uses tabbed dialog box format to prompt you for all the most common options that can be used with a report.

The tabs listed in the dialog box are different according to what type of report you selected in the Crystal Report Gallery, but the most common tabs you will see are Data, Links, Fields, Group, Select, and Style.

The Data tab is the most important because it sets the report's data source (Figure 9-2). You can choose whether to connect using ODBC, OLE DB, Data Sets, or other tools.

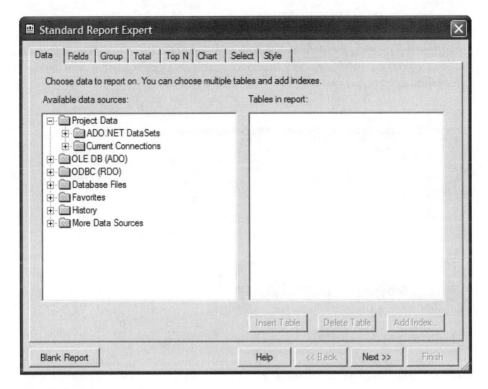

Figure 9-2. *Selecting a data source*

■Tip Although you can choose from different types of data sources for your report, some are better than others. For the best performance, choose either ODBC or OLE DB connections. You might be tempted to choose ADO.NET datasets because they were written specifically for .NET development. But datasets give you very poor performance, because the report engine is responsible for processing all the data on the client side. Using ODBC or OLE DB lets Microsoft's technologies process the data, and this results in a huge improvement in performance. If you decide to use datasets, you will quickly see how report performance is adversely affected.

5. For this example, expand the OLE DB option and select Microsoft Jet 4.0 OLE DB Provider. Follow the wizard to find the Xtreme.mdb database that is installed in the Crystal Reports folder within the Visual Studio .NET installation folder.

6. When you get back to the Report Expert dialog box, select the Customer table and click the Insert Table button.

7. Click the Next button to go to the Fields tab. Select the fields Customer ID and Customer Name.

8. Click the Next button multiple times until you get to the Style tab. For the title, type "Customer List" (see Figure 9-3). Click the Finish button to have the report created. Notice that the report is listed in the Solution Explorer as Customer List.rpt. It is stored as a separate "RPT" file, and it is also a class file that can be instantiated and accessed using an object variable.

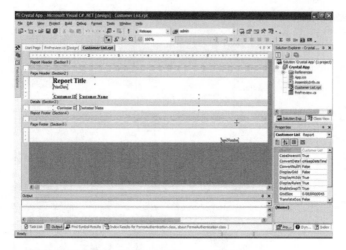

Figure 9-3. *The Customer List report in the designer*

Customizing Reports

The Report Expert does a good job of creating a report with all the fields formatted properly. But the reports that it creates should only be considered drafts to get you started in the right direction. You want to customize the first version so that it fits in with the look and feel of the rest of your application and follows your company's standards.

There are four primary areas of the Visual Studio IDE that you need to be aware of when customizing reports (Figure 9-4). The first is the report designer. It has sections for each part of the report: Report Header, Page Header, Group Header (optional), Details, Group Footer (optional), Page Footer, and Report Footer. The section in which you place fields and report objects determines where on the report they are shown.

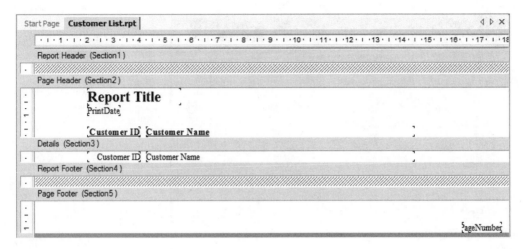

Figure 9-4. *The report sections*

The Field Explorer window (Figure 9-5), docked on the left side of the IDE, lets you add fields to the report, create formulas and parameters, and select special report fields such as the current page number or the print date. To add one of these objects to your report, drag and drop it onto the report in the proper location. You can right-click on most of these objects to see a popup menu for various options for using them.

Figure 9-5. *The Field Explorer window*

Each report field has many formatting options that can be set. Right-click on the field to change and select Format. This opens the Format Editor dialog box (see Figure 9-6). The formatting options within this dialog box change for each type of object. For most objects you will be able to change properties such as the font, border, and whether or not it is suppressed.

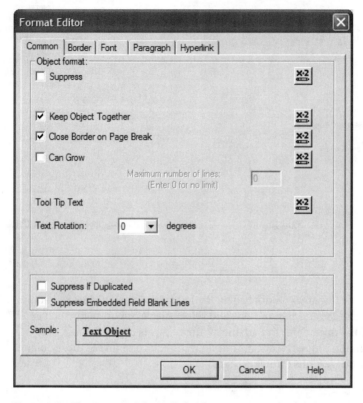

Figure 9-6. *The Format Editor dialog box*

Crystal Reports gives you the ability to apply conditional formatting for each property. Rather than always formatting a field the same way for every line on the report, you can change certain properties to show relative importance. For example, if a report shows the current amount of inventory on hand, when an item needs to be reordered you can change the font to red italics. Conditional formatting is added by clicking on the Formula button to the right of each property. When you click on it, the Formula Editor (Figure 9-7) opens, and you can enter a formula to customize the field's format.

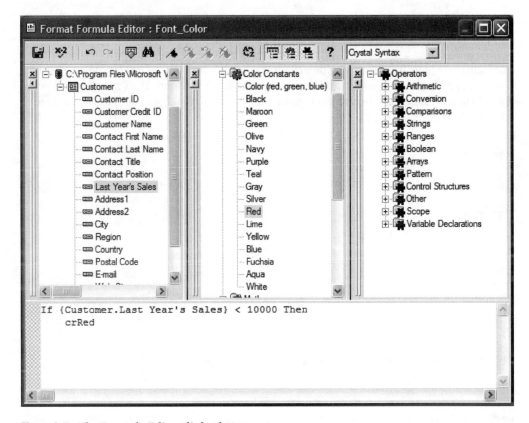

Figure 9-7. *The Formula Editor dialog box*

Integrating Reports into Applications

Crystal Reports gives you many ways to write .NET applications that print and preview reports. Each of these alternatives has its own strengths and weaknesses, and you need to be aware of these issues when writing the project specifications. Although reporting isn't the primary focus of most applications, it is important enough that certain limitations may force you to exclude some approaches to designing the application. The following sections show you how to integrate reports into different types of applications. It tells you which reporting aspects you need to consider when using each type of application.

WinForms Applications

Windows applications give you the most robust and feature-rich toolset to use. From a reporting standpoint, there are no limitations you have to worry about. You are only limited by the issues that are inherent for Windows applications (deployment issues, client machines must be Windows based, etc.). One drawback to designing reports within a Windows application is that you can't preview the report during design mode. You have to run the application to see what the report looks like. Of course, this isn't something that would affect your decision whether to write a WinForms application, but you should be aware of it.

To add a report to a Windows application, you need to add a CrystalReportViewer control to a form (see Figure 9-8). You can either create a new form that is used just for the purpose of previewing the report, or you can add the viewer to an existing report. The CrystalReportViewer is found in the Toolbox as the very last control. Scroll down to find it and double-click on it to add it to the form.

Figure 9-8. *The CrystalReportViewer component in the Toolbox*

By itself, the viewer doesn't do anything. You have to bind it to an existing report. This can be done in numerous ways, and each method is explained in the following section.

Adding a ReportDocument Component

Adding a ReportDocument component to the form lets you bind a report to the viewer without writing any code. In typical point-and-click fashion, you just click on different properties and set their values.

The ReportDocument component is found in the toolbox under the Components group (Figure 9-9). Double-click on it to add it to the form. You are immediately presented with a dialog box with a dropdown box for selecting which report to bind to. After selecting the report, click the OK button.

Figure 9-9. *The ReportDocument dialog box*

The last step is to bind the ReportDocument component to the viewer. In the Properties window, click on the viewer's ReportSource property and select the name of the ReportDocument component from the dropdown list.

When you run the application and open the form, it automatically previews the report.

Previewing with Report Files

Some applications need to be flexible enough to print any report. Your application can have a menu option that lets a user browse to the file location of the report that is to be printed. An application could also go out to a report server and dynamically list all reports it finds. Implementing this functionality requires using Untyped reports and performing binding at runtime.

To preview an Untyped report, add a CrystalReportViewer control to your form as before, but don't add the ReportDocument component.

Double click on the form so that the Code window opens and the Form_Load() event is created. Inside the Load event, type the following code:

C#

```
private void frmPreview_Load(object sender, System.EventArgs e)
{
    //Untyped report
    CrystalDecisions.CrystalReports.Engine.ReportDocument myReport;
    myReport = new CrystalDecisions.CrystalReports.Engine
    .ReportDocument();
    try
    {
        myReport.Load(@"..\..\Customer List.rpt");
        crystalReportViewer1.ReportSource = myReport;
    }
    catch(CrystalDecisions.CrystalReports.Engine.EngineException ex)
    {
        MessageBox.Show("Can't create report due to following error: "
        + ex.ToString());
    }
}
```

The code creates a new ReportDocument object, myReport, and calls the Load() method. This loads the report from a specified file location. The myReport object is assigned to the viewer's ReportSource property.

Notice that the file path for this example is relative to the Debug folder that the application runs from when you are developing your report. I did this so that this example will run on your computer with no code modifications. For production applications, you should replace this with the file location that is the central repository for all the reports. Another option is to add an OpenFileDialog control to the form so that the user can choose which report to preview.

Printing the Report Without Previewing It

The previous two examples showed two different ways to preview a report. But there are times when you want to print the report directly to the printer without previewing it. This could be when you are running a batch of reports that don't have any user intervention. Reports are printed directly by calling the PrintToPrinter() method of the ReportDocument class.

To print a report without previewing it, add a button to a form and double-click on it to open the Code window. In the Click event, type the following code:

C#

```
private void button1_Click(object sender, System.EventArgs e)
{
    Customer_List myReport = new Customer_List();
    myReport.PrintToPrinter(1,false,0,0);
}
```

This declares a report object that is an instance of the Customer_List report class. This class was created for you automatically when you added the report to your project.

Note The Customer_List class is the report that you created at the beginning of these examples. In your application you can substitute this class for the report that you want to print.

The PrintToPrinter() method is passed the number of copies to print, whether to collate the pages (print the entire report before printing the following report), and the start and end pages (enter zeros to print every page).

ASP.NET Applications

Crystal Reports is integrated into ASP.NET applications to provide robust reports over the Internet with a minimal amount of work. The biggest drawback to using ASP.NET is that the user experience is not as smooth as a WinForms application. For example, web reports don't have a print button. You either have to print the report from the browser window (which also prints all the controls shown in the browser and the URL at the bottom of every page) or to export the report to a PDF file and have it printed on the client side. One benefit that the developer gets when using ASP.NET is that the report can be previewed during design mode. You don't have to run the application to see what the report looks like.

To preview reports in an ASP.NET application, add a CrystalReportViewer (see Figure 9-10) to the web form by opening the Toolbox and double-clicking on the viewer control, which is usually at the bottom of the list.

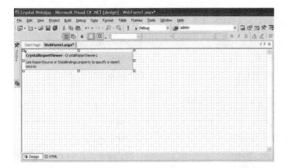

Figure 9-10. *CrystalReportViewer in an ASP.NET page*

This viewer is similar to the viewer in a Windows application in that by itself it doesn't do anything. A report has to be bound to the viewer before it can be displayed.

Adding the Report to the Project

Earlier in the chapter you saw how to create a new report with the Crystal Report designer. Creating a report with an ASP.NET project uses the same steps (e.g., right-clicking in the Solution Explorer and selecting Add | Add New Item). A second way of adding a report to a project is to use an existing report that has already been written. This lets you share reports between projects. Since you already created the Customer List report in the previous example, let's use it to demonstrate how to add an existing report to a project.

To add an existing project to a report, move the mouse pointer to the Solution Explorer window and right-click on the solution name. Select Add | Add Existing Item (see Figure 9-11). This opens the File Open dialog box.

By default, the File Open box selects files with an extension of `.cs`. You need to tell it to look for report files only. Click on the File Type dropdown box and select "`.rpt`."

Figure 9-11. *Selecting an existing report*

Browse to the location where you originally created the Customer List report and select it. Then click the Open button to add it to your project.

Adding a ReportDocument Component

The ReportDocument component is used to bind a report to the viewer without having to write any code. The Web version is the same as the one used in the Windows application. Just double-click on it from within the Toolbox and select the report to preview from the drop-down box.

The steps to bind the ReportDocument component to the web viewer are different than the steps for binding to the Windows viewer. Bind the component to the viewer by clicking on the viewer's DataBindings property to open the property dialog box (Figure 9-12).

Figure 9-12. *The DataBindings dialog box*

Click on the ReportSource property and then click on the Page node to display the customer_List1 component under it. Click on the component name and then the OK button.

Notice that the form now shows you a preview of the report. Only a small sample of data is shown, but this is enough to give you an idea of what the report looks like. This wasn't possible when using the viewer in a Windows application. See Figure 9-13.

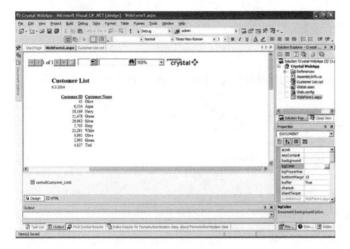

Figure 9-13. *Previewing the report in design mode*

Even though you can see a preview of the report in design mode, you still need to add one line of code to your web page so that it knows to bind to the live data when the application is run. Do this by calling the DataBind() method of the viewer:

C#

```
private void Page_Load(object sender, System.EventArgs e)
{
    CrystalReportViewer1.DataBind();
}
```

■**Tip** When you print a report using ASP.NET, the "Powered By Crystal" logo is always printed in the top right-hand corner. You can get rid of this logo, or even replace it with your own, by deleting or overwriting the GIF file on your computer. You can find it within the Visual Studio .NET installation folder under ..\crystalreports\ viewers\images\toolbar\logo.gif.

Previewing with Report Files

You can also show reports to the user by binding the file location to the report viewer during runtime. This lets you use one web form to view any report. This is referred to as an Untyped report.

To preview an Untyped report, add a viewer to the web form as before, but this time don't add the ReportDocument component. Instead, type in the following code to the Page_Load() event handler:

C#

```csharp
private void Page_Load(object sender, System.EventArgs e)
{
    CrystalDecisions.CrystalReports.Engine.ReportDocument myReport;
    myReport = new
    CrystalDecisions.CrystalReports.Engine.ReportDocument();
    myReport.Load(Request.PhysicalApplicationPath +
    "/Customer List.rpt");
    CrystalReportViewer1.ReportSource = myReport;
}
```

Just as in the Windows example, this code creates an instance of the ReportDocument class and loads the report. Then it sets the viewer's ReportSource property to this object.

The drawback to binding the report during runtime is that you don't get to see a preview of it in design mode. But this is a small price to pay for the additional flexibility you get. As you start writing more advanced reports that require runtime customization, this code will be the basis of every report.

■**Tip** A problem I frequently see posted on the newsgroups is that sometimes this code doesn't display the report when the web form opens. This will happen when a programmer mistakenly adds a call to the Data-Bind() method after manually setting the ReportSource property. This is because when manually binding the report to a report object, you didn't modify the DataBindings property and set a value to the ReportSource property. Calling the DataBind() method overrides the ReportSource property that you manually set with the programming code. You have either to call the DataBind() method prior to where you set the ReportSource property or not to call it at all. With most ASP.NET reports, all the necessary viewer properties are already set with code and there is no reason to call the DataBind() method at all.

Printing a report from a browser gives you a less than professional report. The browser can't differentiate between what is part of the report and the other HTML objects shown on the web page (e.g., the navigation buttons). It prints everything. Unfortunately, the web version of the viewer control doesn't have a print button that can be displayed on your form. As an alternative, Crystal Decisions has posted a workaround for this problem on their website. They suggest that you export the report to a PDF file and then load the PDF file into the browser.

■**Caution** The normal method of viewing an ASP.NET report is very efficient because pages are generated as they are displayed, and this conserves resources. This isn't the case when you export to a PDF file. The entire report has to be generated to create the file, and then it has to be sent to the user's browser to be displayed. For large reports your users might have a longer than normal delay.

The following code listing demonstrates how to export a web report to a file on the web server and transfer it to the user's browser as a PDF file.

C#

```
private void Button1_Click(object sender, System.EventArgs e)
{
    String FileName = request.physicalapplicationpath +
    "\\CustomerList.pdf";
    //Instantiate the object that controls where the file is exported to
    CrystalDecisions.Shared.DiskFileDestinationOptions DestOptions;
    DestOptions = new
    CrystalDecisions.Shared.DiskFileDestinationOptions();
    DestOptions.DiskFileName = FileName;
    //Set the Export Options
    Customer_List myReport = new Customer_List();
    myReport.ExportOptions.ExportFormatType =
    CrystalDecisions.Shared.ExportFormatType
    .PortableDocFormat;
    myReport.ExportOptions.ExportDestinationType =
    CrystalDecisions.Shared.ExportDestinationType.DiskFile;
    myReport.ExportOptions.DestinationOptions = DestOptions;
    myReport.Export();
    //Display the PDF file in the current browser window
    Response.ClearContent();
    Response.ClearHeaders();
    Response.ContentType = "application/pdf";
    Response.WriteFile(FileName);
    Response.Flush();
    Response.Close();
}
```

The first step instantiates a DiskFileDestinationOptions object that stores the destination PDF file's fully qualified file path.

The second step sets the export options of the ReportDocument object. This sets the PDF format and the information that it is a disk file. You also assign the DestinationOption property so that the file is saved in the correct location.

Call the Export() method to save the report to the PDF file.

After the file is exported, you have to display it to the user. The last lines of code use the Response object to load the PDF file and stream it to the browser window.

Tip It is very common for you to get an error stating that the temporary report file is not accessible. This is a confusing error message because it is written to make you think that you can't load the actual report file. But this isn't the case. Instead, what the error message should have said is that you do not have write permissions to the directory where you are storing the export file. You need to make sure that the ASPNET user has proper permissions to the folder in which the PDF file is to be stored. A simple way to test whether this is your problem is to write the PDF file to the Path.GetTempPath() folder. The ASPNET user has full access to this folder by default. If you make this change and your report exports with no errors, then you know that you need to set the proper permissions on the output folder.

Web Services

Creating reports as web services enables you to deliver reports using SOAP via an HTTP protocol. There are no issues with worrying about the report being blocked by security or network constraints.

Fortunately, Visual Studio .NET makes creating and consuming web services almost trivial. Two steps must be performed: First create a web service application that publishes the report. Second, write an application to consume the web service.

To publish the report as a web service, create a new application using the Web Service template. Then add the Customer List report to the project as you did in the other examples.

After the report has been added to the project, right-click on it and select Publish as Web Service.

That's all there is to it! Now run the application so that the web service can be consumed.

To create an application that consumes the web service, open a new instance of the Visual Studio IDE and create a new Windows application.

Right-click on the project and select Add Web Reference.

You are prompted to enter the location of where to look for the web service (see Figure 9-14).

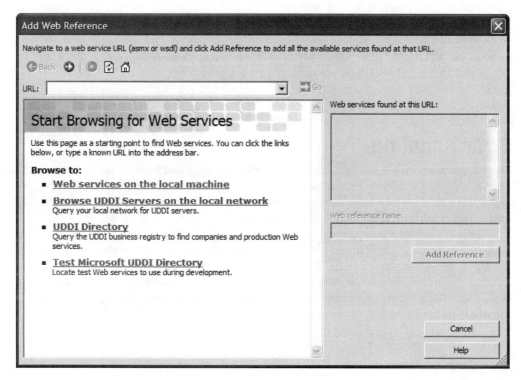

Figure 9-14. *Adding a web reference*

Click on the option Web Services on the local machine.

This shows you a list of the available web services that have been installed on your computer.

Select the web service Customer List Service.

Click the Add Reference button to close the dialog box and create the web reference in your project.

Add a CrystalReportViewer control to your form and bind it to the web service. The following code performs the binding:

C#

```
private void Form1_Load(object sender, System.EventArgs e)
{
    crystalReportViewer1.ReportSource = new
    localhost.Customer_ListService();
}
```

Tip Make sure that the web service application is running whenever you run the consumer application. A web service isn't like an ASP.NET application that is assumed to be always running. A web service is an independent application that must be running for its service to be available.

Error Handling

Every application should have proper error handling incorporated into it. Without it, applications might give the user cryptic messages when something goes wrong or just crash altogether. Crystal Reports is designed to make it easy for you to trap any errors that are triggered during report processing and handle them effectively.

There are two times when errors can occur. The first is when you are setting the properties of the ReportDocument object and calling it. The second is when the viewer is previewing the report to the user. Errors are handled differently depending upon what stage you are at.

The CrystalDecisions.CrystalReports.Engine class provides you with custom exception classes. Use these classes to pinpoint exactly what went wrong and handle it appropriately. They are listed as follows:

- DataSourceException

- EngineException

- ExportException

- FormattingException

- FormulaException

- InternalException

- InvalidArgumentException

- LoadSaveReportException

- LogOnException

- OutOfLicenseException

- ParameterFieldCurrencyValueException

- ParameterFieldException

- PrintException

- SubreportException

The first part of working with reports is to create the report object and set its properties. At this stage you need to use the standard try...catch method of error handling. Within the catch statement you can either treat the exception object as a general exception or use the Crystal Report error classes to trap for specific errors.

C#

```csharp
private void frmPreview_Load(object sender, System.EventArgs e)
{
    CrystalDecisions.CrystalReports.Engine.ReportDocument myReport;
    myReport = new
    CrystalDecisions.CrystalReports.Engine.ReportDocument();
    try
    {
        myReport.Load(@"..\..\Customer List.rpt");
        crystalReportViewer1.ReportSource = myReport;
    }
    catch(CrystalDecisions.CrystalReports.Engine.EngineException ex)
    {
        MessageBox.Show("Can't create report due to following error: "
        + ex.ToString());
    }
}
```

Once a report has been loaded and passed to the viewer, you can use the viewer's built-in exception event, HandleException, to trap for errors.

C#

```csharp
private void crystalReportViewer1_HandleException(object source,

    CrystalDecisions.Windows.Forms.ExceptionEventArgs e)
{
    MessageBox.Show("While generating your next report page,
    the following error occurred: " + e.ToString);
}
```

Web Resources

http://support.BusinessObjects.com

This is the generic support site that is provided by Business Objects. It has various links to FAQs, support documents, and hot fixes.

http://support.BusinessObjects.com/forums

The user forums on the Business Objects website is very helpful for posting questions and searching to see whether your problem has already been answered. This is a user-supported site, and Business Objects doesn't monitor it to answer your questions. However, some of their support engineers browse through the questions on occasion and answer them.

http://www.CrystalReportsBook.com

This website has a free PDF for download that walks you through the steps of integrating reports into your .NET application. It also gets you started with making runtime report modifications via your .NET application.

NNTP:microsoft.public.vb.crystal

This is the Microsoft newsgroup for posting all questions related to Crystal Reports. Although it has "VB" in its name, C# programmers should still use it. Most of your questions will be report-based and not language-specific. In addition to that, many .NET programmers are becoming fluent in both languages and can answer questions for either language.

http://groups.yahoo.com/group/CrystalReportsDotNet

This group is open to the general public. There are thousands of members, and there is a good response rate to questions posted.

http://www.Experts-Exchange.com

This is an independent site that encourages people to answer questions by awarding points for correct answers. As a result, it gets a lot of traffic, and most of the Crystal Reports questions do get answered by someone. You can find the Crystal Reports section by clicking on the DB tab.

http://www.tek-tips.com

This is another independent site that gets a lot of traffic as well. Most questions posted do get answered.

Newsgroup Tips

I see that many programmers post Crystal Reports questions to the newsgroups, and the questions go unanswered. Many times this is because the question wasn't phrased properly. You have to give everyone enough information to debug your problem. The most important information to post is the version of the tools you are using. For example, you could say that you are using CR.NET 2003. Or you might say that you are using Visual Studio 2003 with CR10. Secondly, state whether you are creating a Windows app or an ASP.NET page. Third, if you are getting error messages, post the code that triggers the error messages. There are dozens of ways to do something in Crystal Reports, and unless you give complete details about what causes the problem, no one will know what to tell you. If you follow these steps, you will get a much better response rate.

CHAPTER 10

■ ■ ■

Customization

Out of the box, Visual Studio .NET provides an excellent mechanism for creating both web and Windows applications rapidly. However, you will often find that the user interface is, perhaps, not configured quite to your liking, or that the menus aren't in the right place. During this chapter, we are going to take a look at the various ways of customizing the Visual Studio .NET IDE to increase productivity. We will address the following customizations:

- **Environment Settings:** This section will demonstrate changes that can be made to the IDE environment, along with some general tweaks that can be used to make working with Visual Studio .NET more pleasant.

- **Window Control:** You will learn how to manage the windows within Visual Studio .NET to simplify finding the tools and commands you need.

- **External Tools:** Visual Studio .NET often works best when combined with other tools and applications. This section addresses how these tools can be made easily accessible from within the IDE.

- **Menus and Toolbars:** Most of the commands that we use are available from either a menu or a toolbar. This section demonstrates how these menus and toolbars can be customized to your liking and also how to create new ones populated with the commands of your choice.

- **Dynamic Help:** The last section of this chapter will show how to add content to the dynamic help feature of Visual Studio .NET to allow easier access to custom information.

Visual Studio .NET Customization Options

Most of the configuration options in Visual Studio .NET are controlled from either the Options dialog or the Customize dialog. Both dialogs can be accessed from the Tools menu. The Options dialog is split into eleven main areas, each with a set of subcategories:

- **Environment:** Controls generic options that apply throughout the IDE

- **Source Control:** Changes the settings for Visual SourceSafe integration

- **Text Editor:** Edits the behavior of the text editor on a language-by-language basis

- **Analyzer:** Controls Visual Studio Analyzer integration options

- **Database Tools:** Controls the behavior of the database designer and the Server Explorer

- **Debugging:** Manages the settings for the Debugger

- **Device Tools:** Configures new and existing mobile devices

- **HTML Designer:** Changes the behavior of the HTML designer

- **Projects:** Modifies various defaults for projects within Visual Studio .NET

- **Windows Forms Designer:** Sets defaults for the Windows Forms designer

- **XML Designer:** Sets defaults for the XML Designer

The Customize dialog provides three tabs for customizing the Visual Studio .NET user interface:

- **Toolbars:** This tab allows you to manipulate the toolbars that are displayed and also to create new ones.

- **Commands:** This tab has two purposes: managing the commands that are shown on menus and toolbars and creating new menus.

- **Options:** This has generic options governing aspects such as the animation method of the menus.

When the Customize menu is active, you are also able to manipulate the menus on the menu bar, by changing their positions and removing them from the bar altogether. You will see an example of this later in the chapter.

During this chapter the features exposed through these dialogs will be used to customize the Visual Studio .NET development environment.

Environment Settings

Visual Studio .NET has a wide variety of options for customizing the IDE environment. In this section I will show you how to configure the environment to your liking and will also show you a collection of simple tweaks that can be made to the IDE to make your life easier.

Developer Profiles

When Visual Studio .NET starts, you are presented by default with the Start Page. As well as allowing recent Projects to be opened and Online Resources on .NET to be viewed, there is also the My Profile tab. This, shown in Figure 10-1, allows for the selection of a default profile to apply to the development environment and the alteration of some of the most immediately noticeable and far-reaching changes to the IDE.

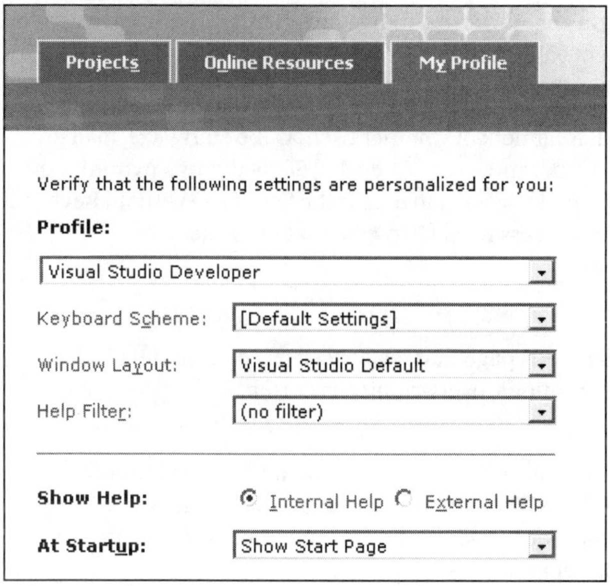

Figure 10-1. *Visual Studio .NET Start Page*

Most of these options are self-explanatory and don't need too much coverage given to them. For completeness, though, here they are:

- **Profile:** The Profile dropdown list populates the options below it with the default values for each of the other options provided, such as Student Developer. Each of these is tailored to developers from a specific background, such as Visual Basic or C++, making the transition to the Visual Studio .NET environment as natural as possible.

- **Keyboard Scheme:** Selecting an option from the Keyboard Scheme dropdown list other than [Default Settings] assigns the shortcuts that were used in environments such as Visual C++, or Visual Studio 6, rather than the updated ones used by Visual Studio .NET by default.

- **Help Filter:** By selecting one of the options in the dropdown list for the Help Filter, you can tailor the help topics that are presented to you through Dynamic Help, the Index, and so on. This reduces the chance of having suggestions made that are unrelated to the current area of development, and is especially useful in working with distinct areas of .NET, such as the Compact Framework. Custom filters can be added by selecting Edit Filters from the Help menu.

- **Internal Help:** If the default value of Internal Help is selected for the Show Help option, then whenever a dynamic help link is selected, F1 is pressed, and so on, the relevant Help page will be displayed within the Visual Studio .NET environment. Conversely, if the External Help option is selected, all help pages will be displayed using the *Microsoft Document Explorer*, the application associated with the MSDN library. Selecting

External Help can be useful if you generally have many documents open at once within the IDE and find the environment cluttered with Help in there as well.

- **At Startup:** The options in the At Startup dropdown list allow the user to select what action the IDE takes whenever it is launched: whether to show the Start Page, load a previous solution, create a new one, and so on. Choosing Show Empty Environment causes the IDE to load much faster. If you wish to access the Start Page without having to show it at startup time, you can access it via Help ➤ Show Start Page.

Window Layout

The Window Layout is the only option on this page that really needs its options detailed. It lists the possible default window configurations, overwriting any current settings whenever one is selected and applied:

- **Visual Studio Default:** This layout places the Server Explorer and Toolbox windows auto-hidden along the left side of the IDE, with the Solution Explorer and Class View tab-docked on the right. The Properties window and Dynamic Help window are tab-docked below the Solution Explorer and Class View.

- **Visual Basic 6:** This layout places the Server Explorer auto-hidden along the left side of the IDE with the Toolbox docked on the left. The Solution Explorer and Class View are tab-docked on the right, with the Properties and Dynamic Help windows tab-docked below.

- **Visual C++ 6:** This layout places the Solution Explorer, Class View, and Resource View windows tab-docked on the left. The Properties and Dynamic Help windows are tab-docked beneath these, also on the left.

- **Student Window Layout:** This layout places the Solution Explorer and Class View windows tab-docked on the left with the Dynamic Help window below. The Task List and Output windows are tab-docked on the bottom.

- **No Tool Windows Layout:** This layout displays the edit space only, with no tool windows open.

None of the Window Layout settings that are provided prevents the developer from adding or hiding interface components to customize the environment to his or her needs. Through the following sections in this chapter, we'll see how not only simple settings such as those discussed previously, but also more complex ones such as the automatic creation of code, can be tailored to the preferences of the individual developer.

Start-Up Behavior

When you load Visual Studio .NET, the default behavior is to load the Start Page. However, for many developers, this is just an extra step to open a project, which also happens to load Internet Explorer into memory. In the Options dialog, under Environment ➤ General page, you are able to change this behavior to one of five options:

- **Show Start Page:** This is the default behavior.

- **Load last loaded solution:** With this option the IDE immediately loads into the last solution you were working on, which is very handy if you work on a single, long-running project.

- **Show Open Project dialog:** This will automatically load with the Open Project dialog displayed. My developers use this often, since they never create projects or solutions; they simply open them up from either the source control server or the local machine cache.

- **Show New Project dialog:** This will automatically load with the New Project dialog displayed. I can see no benefit from this, since it implies that you are starting, and indeed finishing, a new project in every development session.

- **Show empty environment:** This option offers the fastest loading time and is the best choice if you are constantly creating new projects and working on a variety of projects at the same time.

From the descriptions above I'm sure you can see which behavior is ideal for you. If you work on a lot of different projects, but rarely create new ones, you should opt for the Show Open Project dialog option. If you work on a single project at any time, go for the Load last loaded solution option. Finally, if none of these fits, then the best way to load the IDE is empty, since you don't incur the overhead of loading in Internet Explorer.

Speeding Up Dynamic Help

The dynamic help feature of Visual Studio .NET is a fantastic addition that wasn't present in any of the earlier versions of Visual Studio. However, having dynamic help displayed all the time on slower machines can cause the machine to slow down dramatically. The reason for this is that by default, dynamic help will show all links relevant to the context of either the mouse cursor or the text caret.

You can change this behavior in the Options dialog under Environment ➤ Dynamic Help to one of two options:

- **Active UI Elements:** This will display the dynamic help in relation to the currently active user interface element only. This has a major drawback in that the help for the code window no longer functions.

- **Selection only:** This option will display the dynamic help for *any* selection, not just user interface elements. The difference between this and the default behavior is that in the code editor, help is displayed only for selected code, not for the code at the current caret position.

I use the second option, since I don't want to disable code help, but at the same time, I don't want to have help displayed for every item as I am typing. Selecting a piece of code is as easy as double-clicking the appropriate word, so getting access to the help is simple.

Learning Keyboard Shortcuts

One of my development colleagues is an absolute Delphi guru. The main reason for this is that he has mastered as many of the keyboard shortcuts in the Delphi IDE as he can humanly remember. In fact, he knows so many that he won't touch the mouse for at least three or four hours at a time when working in Delphi.

There is no doubt that by learning the keyboard shortcuts for an IDE you can increase your productivity tenfold. This section doesn't contain a list of common shortcuts, although some are pointed out during the rest of the chapter. Instead, I will show you a simple tip to make learning and accessing keyboard shortcuts easier.

All of the keyboard shortcuts can be accessed from the Environment ➤ Keyboard page in the Options dialog, but, the quickest way to find out a shortcut for a command is to enable shortcut tool tips. Under the Options tab of the Customize dialog you will see an option to "Show ScreenTips on toolbars." Make sure this is checked. This option also has a suboption: "Show shortcut keys in ScreenTips." If you check this, the shortcut for a command will be displayed in its toolbar button ScreenTip.

Creating Keyboard Shortcuts

Some of the commands in Visual Studio .NET do not have a keyboard shortcut, but you can easily create one. In the Environment ➤ Keyboard page of the Options dialog, scroll through the list of commands until you find the command you are looking for. Then you can enter the shortcut you want. The IDE will tell you if this shortcut clashes with any other shortcut for another command.

Source Code Readability

My biggest gripe with Visual Studio .NET out of the box is the source code highlighting. The font used by default is, in my opinion, horrible. Fortunately, you can change all this in the Environment ➤ Fonts and Colors page of the Options dialog.

From this dialog you are able to change how each piece of your code will be displayed. I would definitely recommend changing the default style for String and number literals, because by default these look just like plain pieces of code and can be quite confusing.

Ultimately, you can customize this to your heart's content, making the source code as readable as you like.

Default Project Location

When you create a new project, the default location is set to be the My Projects folder in your My Documents folder. However, you may not wish to store any of your projects there at all. You can easily change the location every time you create a new project, but after a while it gets a little irritating.

To change the default location, simply edit the Visual Studio project location value, in the Environment ➤ Projects and Solutions page of the Options dialog, to your desired path and click OK.

Task List Tokens

For those of you not familiar with the Task List tokens, they are specially formatted comments that will subsequently be added to the Visual Studio .NET Task List. These comments look something like this:

```
' HACK: I've done a hack
DoHack()
```

By default, Visual Studio .NET comes with four tokens defined: HACK, TODO, UNDONE, and UnresolvedMergeConflict. However, it is possible to add more of these tokens, which can prove quite useful.

New tokens are added in the Environment ➤ Task List page of the Options dialog. Simply type in a new name, set the priority, and click Add.

One of the things I have done using this functionality is to set simple bug tracking facilities in place. I have defined two tokens, BUG and FIX, and then in code I simply add the following:

```
' BUG - This method causes a StackOverflowException 08/03/2003 - RH
MyBuggedMethod()
```

As soon as this bug is fixed I add a FIX token:

```
' FIX - This method is now fixed 09/03/2003 - JM
' BUG - This method causes a StackOverflowException 08/03/2003 - RH
MyBuggedMethod();
```

At any time, my team can open the solution in Visual Studio .NET and view a list of the BUG or FIX tokens from within the Task List, enabling them to find and fix bugs within the application easily.

Auto-Reload Externally Changed Documents

If you use any external applications with Visual Studio .NET, then you will be familiar with the concept of round-tripping. Round-tripping is the process of opening a file in one application, making some changes, opening the same file in another application, and making some changes, before returning to the original application. During this process, you don't want to lose changes made in either application; otherwise, the whole process would be pointless.

To facilitate this, Visual Studio .NET will sense whether a file has been changed by an external application and prompt you to reload it before making any changes. Now this is fine, because you may also have made some changes in Visual Studio .NET, which would be overwritten if the document were reloaded, but more often than not, the document will not have changed within Visual Studio .NET.

Fortunately, you can change this behavior so that you are prompted to reload only if the document has changed within Visual Studio .NET as well as in the external application. To make this change, open the Environment ➤ Documents page in the Options dialog and check the Auto-load changes option.

Managing Help

By default, Visual Studio .NET will display all help documents internally, but you can change this so that help is displayed externally, using the Microsoft Document Explorer. To do this, modify the appropriate setting in the Environment ➤ Help page of the Options dialog. Changing help to external does not stop dynamic help working, so if you prefer to use the Document Explorer rather than the built-in functionality within Visual Studio .NET, you can do so without losing the benefits of dynamic help.

If you have installed new applications that integrate with Visual Studio .NET, or if you have multiple versions of MSDN installed on your machine, or if you just didn't install MSDN at the same time as Visual Studio .NET, then the chances are that the internal help will not be working as you like. Help documents are split into collections. Visual Studio .NET 2003 has a component called the Combined Help Collection Manager, which will manage which help collections are included in the Visual Studio .NET 2003 Combined Collection (VSCC). You can access the Combined Help Collection Manager by searching for VSCC in the internal help. If Help is not installed, then the error message displayed when you try to access help contains a link to the Combined Help Collection Manager.

Once you have loaded the Combined Help Collection Manager, it displays a list of those help collections that are installed on your machine and those that are included in the VSCC. You can add and remove help collections within the VSCC by checking or unchecking the boxes next to them in the list and clicking the Update VSCC button (see Figure 10-2). You will need to close all instances of Visual Studio .NET and the Document Explorer before reopening Visual Studio .NET for the update to succeed.

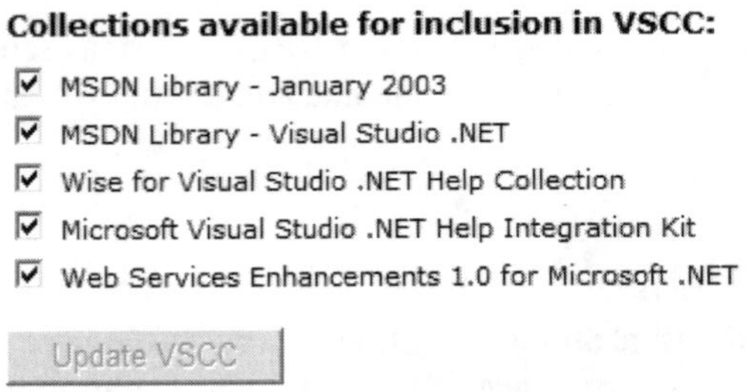

Collections available for inclusion in VSCC:

☑ MSDN Library - January 2003

☑ MSDN Library - Visual Studio .NET

☑ Wise for Visual Studio .NET Help Collection

☑ Microsoft Visual Studio .NET Help Integration Kit

☑ Web Services Enhancements 1.0 for Microsoft .NET

    Update VSCC

Figure 10-2. *Managing Help Collections*

Custom Keywords in Visual C++

In Visual C++, it is possible to define a list of user-defined keywords that will be highlighted differently within the code editor from the standard code. To create the list, first you need to create a plain text file called usertype.dat and save it in the same directory as the Visual Studio .NET executable. Add any keywords you want to define, one per line, to this file. Once you have created the file, close and restart Visual Studio .NET for the changes to take effect. Now in every Visual C++ project you will notice that your user-defined keywords are high-lighted just like standard keywords.

You can change the style for user-defined keywords by modifying the User Keyword style in the Environment ➤ Fonts and Colors page of the Options dialog.

You can add extra keywords to the file at any time, but the file is uneditable when Visual Studio .NET is open, so you will need to close the IDE before you make any changes.

Customizing the Text Editor

Customizing the Text Editor, perhaps the most widely used part of any IDE, to your liking is a must if you want to get a real productivity gain out of Visual Studio .NET. Under the Text Editor node in the Options dialog you will see a wide variety of options, perhaps more than in any other node. This is largely due to the fact that Visual Studio .NET supports so many languages out of the box, and is designed to support an even larger number of third-party languages.

For each language there are two default property pages: General and Tabs. The General page allows you to configure statement completion, word wrap and display settings. On the Tabs property page you can control various settings for code indentation and tab behavior. With the Indentation settings you are able to choose from None, Block, and Smart. Using None will place the caret at the beginning of the next line when you press Return, whereas Block will place you at exactly the same indentation as the line you are just leaving. The Smart indentation option will automatically indent your code based on language settings, so starting a For loop in C# and pressing Return will automatically indent the code by one extra level. Another interesting option on the Tabs page is the ability to insert spaces in place of tabs for indentation; if you work cross-platform (e.g., with the Mono Project), then this option will prove useful for platforms that don't handle tabs very well. It is also possible to convert tabs into spaces in a text selection using Edit/Advanced/Tabify(Untabify) Selection.

Besides these very general options, each language presents its own individual options, with Basic, C#, C/C++, and HTML/XML.

Basic

When the option **Automatic insertion of end constructs** is enabled, end constructs such as End If, End Property, and Next are added to the code automatically whenever an opening construct such as If or For is entered—a great preventive mechanism against RSI!

- **Pretty listing (reformatting) of code:** This option allows the editor to reformat code whenever it is entered into the editor, reindenting text, adding parentheses and quotation marks where needed, adjusting the case of keywords, methods, and variable names, and making other such changes.

- **Enter outlining mode when files open:** This option determines whether outlining mode is enabled by default when a file is opened.

- **Automatic insertion of Interface and MustOverride members:** When this option is selected and an Implements or Inherits statement is completed, prototypes for the methods that must be implemented are added to the source code automatically.

- **Show procedure line separators:** When this option is selected, Visual Basic 6 style separators are placed between each method declaration.

C# (and J#)

Although VB.NET is a first-class language in Visual Studio .NET, it still doesn't have quite the variety of options available to it that C# (and now J#) has. These features include the smart comments that make use of XML fragments to document code (JavaDoc in J#), and *Intellisense* preselection of the most commonly used members.

- **Leave open braces on same line as construct:** The code editor moves the open brace for a construct, such as an If statement, to the line after the statement declaration, aligning the open brace with the first character in the declaration. When this option is selected, the code editor does not move an open brace from the declaration line.

- **Indent case labels:** When this option is selected, the code editor indents the case statements from the switch statement that contains them.

- **Automatically format completed constructs and pasted source:** When this option is selected, the code editor formats and aligns text that is typed or pasted in. When unselected, the formatting that the developer enters is left unchanged.

- **Smart comment editing:** When using code comments with XML Documentation, the editor can add the <summary> start and end tags after you type the /// comment prefix. When this option is selected, the text editor will insert the <summary> start and end tags.

- **Enter outlining mode on file open:** This option performs the same operation as in Visual Basic .NET.

- **Collapse #region blocks when files open:** This option specifies whether #region blocks present within the code are collapsed or left expanded whenever a file is opened.

- **Intellisense preselects most frequently used members:** This feature is new to Visual Studio .NET 2003, and allows Intellisense (the popup List Members box) to automatically select the item that is used most often.

- **Clear history:** Clears the history of members that have been used during automatic object name completion.

C/C++

Both C and C++ are still fully supported in Visual Studio .NET. There are not quite as many parameters to control the C and C++ editors as there are for the C# and J# editors, but they are still useful nonetheless:

- **Enable automatic Quick Info ToolTips:** This option allows you to enable or disable Quick Info, that is, the tool tips that pop up when you hover over an identifier in your code.

- **Enter outlining mode when files open:** Outlining mode allows you to take advantage of the collapsible code editor within the C and C++ editors. Use this option to enable or disable this feature as appropriate.

- **Indent braces:** Use this option to control whether opening braces are indented or aligned with the first character of the preceding statement.

HTML/XML

Due to the highly structured nature of HTML and XML documents, there are many labor- and time-saving features provided by the environment that can be managed in this section:

- **Enable Validation:** Since elements in HTML documents follow a standard hierarchy (`<html>` containing `<body>`, `<body>` containing `<p>` tags, etc.), the editor can determine whether the tags entered match the HTML schema. For instance, a `<table>` tag can't have a child of `<p>` without it being within a cell (such as `<td>` or `<th>`). Similarly, XML documents that follow schemas can only have specific tags and attributes appearing as children of others. When this option is selected and an invalid tag or attribute is entered, it is underlined with a red wavy line, just as a spelling error in Microsoft Word would be.

- **Auto pop-up statement completion:** Similar to the Enable Validation option, this makes use of the schemas that documents being entered are supposed to adhere to. When an element, attribute, or attribute value is being entered, the editor displays a dropdown list of available options that match the text that has already been entered.

- **Close tag:** When enabled, this option allows Visual Studio .NET to insert matching closing tags automatically to any opening ones that are entered, such as `<table>` and `<asp:textbox>`.

- **Attribute value quotes:** This option lets the editor insert quotation marks around the values specified for attributes, so that rather than having an attribute of `width=40`, it is automatically updated to `width="40"`. This amendment is applied while you are typing, when the editor reformats the document (which can be done when switching to and from Design view), and when saving.

- **Capitalization:** The Capitalization options allow the editor to amend the case of tags and attributes automatically to Uppercase, Lowercase, or leaving the format as entered. While this is very useful for HTML, it should be used with great care in editing XML documents, since these are case-sensitive. Documents could become invalidated when data is entered or when it is automatically reformatted.

Other Settings

Besides the main editor options already covered, there are three other sections worth mentioning: one is new to this version of Visual Studio .NET, and two allow you to change some of the more important options:

- **HTML Designer:** The HTML Designer options allow for some of the most noticeable changes that can be made in the development environment, whether HTML, traditional ASP, and ASP.NET pages are opened in Design view or HTML view. If the code is opened in Design view, it will be reformatted by the editor when certain operations are performed, such as double-clicking on controls to set up events, and adding or removing controls from the page. If specific formatting of the page is required, then being able to disable the default option of Design View is invaluable.

- **Device Tools:** This section is a new addition to Visual Studio .NET 2003. Previously, it was available only by installing the Smart Device Extensions (SDE). The General and Devices property pages provided under this heading allow integration with Pocket PC and Windows CE devices, as well as emulators for testing and debugging applications written for these platforms.

- **Projects:** The Projects pages allow for the setting of default VB compiler values, such as Option Strict, that alter how the VB.NET compiler functions and can improve performance in applications. These settings can be overridden in individual projects. The Web Settings page that is also available in this section allows the Web Server Connection method to be specified, choosing from either File Share or FrontPage Extensions. The advantage of File Share mode is that it allows for integration with Visual Source Safe, while FrontPage Extensions can be used for development of web applications on remote servers more readily. Using the VC++ Directories tab you can specify a collection of folder paths that are used in searching for executable files, source files, include files, library files, and reference files. This is useful if you want to use the same set of directories across many different projects. Using the VC++ Build page you can turn build logging on and off, and also control whether the environment variables are included in the log.

Build Configurations

As well as being able to customize the work environment in order to improve productivity during development, you can customize the way in which the projects are compiled in order to make testing and deployment easier. This can be done through the use of *Build Configurations*. These provide a way of selecting which projects will and won't be compiled, whether they will be built for testing or as a final release, and which platform they will be built for. By doing this, and making it possible to save multiple configurations along with each project or solution, you can switch easily between customized configurations, tailored to the task that is being undertaken. Build configurations consist of two types of configuration, *project configurations* and *solution build configurations*, both of which are detailed in the following sections.

Project Configurations

Project configurations, as their name suggests, specify the parameters that are applied to a project whenever it is compiled. The settings that can be applied depend on the type of project. If it's a Windows Application, an application icon can be specified; if it's a web project, then a start page can be defined, and so on. The project configuration dialog can be viewed by selecting the Properties option from the context menu of a project node in the Solution Explorer, or from the View ➤ Property Pages option when a project is selected within the Solution Explorer. When this is done, the property pages window will be shown (see Figure 10-3).

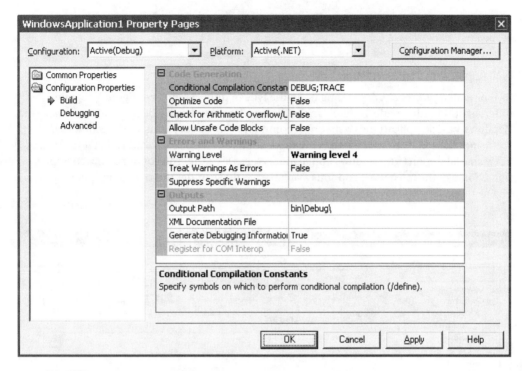

Figure 10-3. *Project Properties dialog*

In the screenshot shown in the figure above, the Build option is shown for a WinForms application. This is one of the more useful pages, since it makes it possible to customize the code that is generated, which types of errors cause the compilation process to abort, etc. The top option, Conditional Compilation Constants, allows you to define values that will be tested by the compilation preprocessor in statements such as those seen in Chapter 7:

```
#if (DEBUG)
  Console.WriteLine("This application is in debug mode");
#else
  Console.WriteLine("This application is NOT in debug mode");
#endif
```

These constants can be especially useful if an application is connecting to external resources that may not be available, or may be in a different format when in a development environment. By defining such a constant, sample data could be used for testing:

```
XmlDocument objXml.= new XmlDocument();
#if (DEBUG)
  objXml.LoadXml("<rootNode><someData value='something' /></rootNode>");
#else
  objXml.Load("http://www.tempuri.org/somefile.xml");
#end if
```

Entering a constant in this dialog is the same as making a call to a #define in C#, or #Const in VB.NET.

Web Application Configurations

As mentioned previously, depending upon the type of project being configured, slightly different options are made available in the dialog. These can largely be split into two: those for Windows-based applications (WinForms, command-line applications, and Windows services), and those that are web based (web applications and web services). While there are only a few special options for Windows applications, there are numerous options for web applications. Some of the most useful options available are those under the Debugging heading (see Figure 10-4).

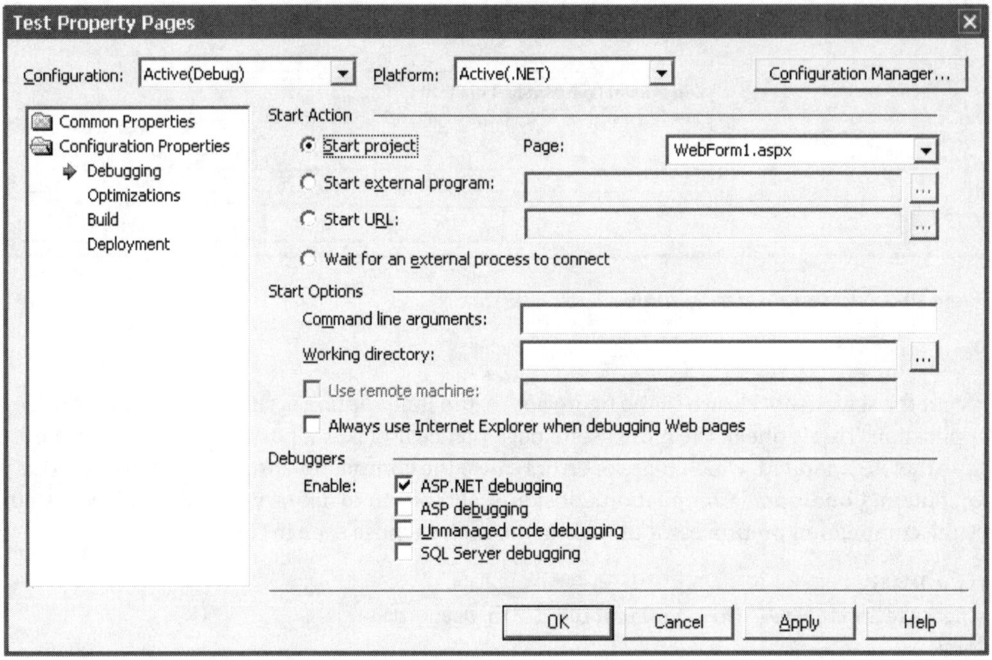

Figure 10-4. *Property page for web application projects*

This view allows us to specify which actions are performed when the application is started. By default, the Start Action is set to run the project, displaying the document that has been set up as the *Start Page*. While this is useful for beginning the application at a single specific page, it does not allow for more advanced testing situations. For instance, we may want to debug the site in a different browser, such as Netscape or Opera. If this is the case, then we can specify an external program to start. We could even call a batch file that launches the site in multiple browsers at once, allowing us to compare them side by side. Another use for this view is in the context of complex interaction processes being carried out by the application, such as integrated authentication. With this view enabled, debugging on the local machine may not be useful due to the account currently being used. Instead, the Start external program radio button can be selected, and an alternative workstation can be specified in the "Use remote machine" textbox.

Debug, Release, and Standard Configurations

You may have noticed that at the top of the Property Pages, there is a Configuration dropdown list. It is this list that allows us to save the settings that have been customized in the dialog to one or more named configurations. By default, the list has five entries in it:

- **Debug:** This is one of the standard configurations, representing one end of the spectrum: a project that is in development and testing. With their initial settings, projects in this configuration include all of the debugging information necessary in order to step through code, and don't include optimizations that increase compile time and improve runtime performance. For this reason a debug build usually runs slower. Also note that even though the debug build doesn't include the optimizations, it is usually slower than the release build, because it has to generate the debug information. The DEBUG compilation constant is also declared as standard in this configuration.

- **Release:** Release configurations represent the opposite end of the spectrum to Debug configurations. The default settings include build optimizations and exclude debug information, both of which can lead to improvements in performance and reduce the size of compiled applications. However, you may want to consider using both optimizations and debug information. Debugging an in-production application is a real pain without the debug information. Additionally, the DEBUG compilation constant is not declared as standard in this project configuration.

- **All Configurations:** Changes made to this configuration will affect all other configurations, unless overridden on a configuration-by-configuration basis.

- **Multiple Configurations:** Similar to the All Configurations option, this one allows changes to be applied to more than one configuration at once. When it is selected, a dialog will be presented to the user, displaying a list of available configurations, with a checkbox next to each. Whichever of these configurations is selected will have its settings updated by the changes made in the Property Pages.

- **Active:** The Active option does not store configuration settings itself. Instead, it inherits the values of one of the others that has been defined. The actual configuration depends on a solution-wide configuration setting. As well as being able to pick and configure a build for an individual project, you can also do this on a solution-wide basis. So, selecting Active in a project's Property Pages will take on the value of Debug, or any other value that is selected for the solution as a whole. Whichever value is selected for the solution will be displayed in parentheses after the Active prefix: for instance, Active (Debug).

Note It is important to note that projects in Debug configurations also have other subtle differences from Release builds that can affect testing, largely due to compiler optimizations. Once a solution has been thoroughly tested in Debug mode, it should undergo further testing in Release mode.

Custom Configurations

In addition to making use of the standard Debug and Release configurations, you can define your own. These are defined on a solution-wide basis, and will be covered shortly. These configurations can be selected from the dropdown list in the same manner as those that come predefined.

Language-Specific Options

One final point to note about project configurations is that depending on the language that is being used to develop a project (C#, VB.NET, JScript.NET), the options that will be present within the Property Pages will differ. As an example of this, VB.NET projects give options for setting the `Option Explicit`, `Option Strict`, and `Option Compare` defaults across an entire project. Like many of the settings that can be controlled within this dialog, these options can be overridden at the individual class level.

Solution Build Configurations

A solution build configuration specifies which projects within a solution should be built and (if enabled) deployed. These configurations are managed from within the *Configuration Manager*, which can be viewed by selecting either the Configuration Manager... menu option from the context menu of the root node in the Solution Explorer, or the Build ➤ Configuration Manager... menu option. The dialog that is displayed when this option is selected is similar to that shown in Figure 10-5.

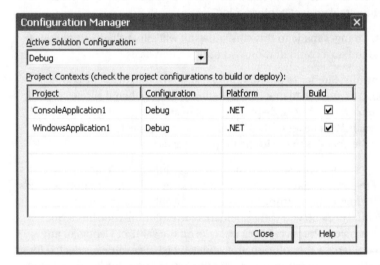

Figure 10-5 Build Configuration Manager

In this dialog there are two main sections: the Active Solution Configuration dropdown and the Project Contexts grid. The active configuration dropdown allows you to select from the configurations that have been defined, create new ones, and edit or remove existing ones. As we have already seen, when a solution is first created, two solution configurations are predefined: *Release* and *Debug*.

Debug and Release Solution Configurations

In their initial state, each of these configurations builds all of the projects within the solution, targeting the default platform and using the project configuration name that matches the solution configuration (either Debug or Release). These settings can be modified by the developer to represent the current status and requirements of the solution. For instance, if a setup and deployment project were part of the solution, it could be omitted from a debug build if it was never to be installed beyond the local machine (or if a manual installation was going to be performed).

Creating Build Configurations

There are many reasons that a developer might want to create custom build configurations in addition to those that are predefined. Whether this is relevant or necessary for a project depends largely on the way that the solution is managed or implemented, with the following three main categories:

- **Multiple Developers:** When there are multiple developers working on an application, there is a choice as to how they work on the projects within it simultaneously: they can either each have an individual Solution file, with Debug and Release configurations set according to the areas of the system that they are working on, or they can each have a custom solution configuration within a single solution. If a developer does not have an individual solution or configuration, then it is likely that many projects that are unchanging will continually be recompiled, with projects that are not in a buildable state causing further issues. Picking the most appropriate of these options depends on whether it is more important that developers be able to test each others' configurations, or whether source control is being used, preventing multiple users from amending solution settings at once.

- **Development Stages:** It can be helpful to create a build configuration for each stage of the development cycle. The number of stages will depend upon the methodology used and the application being developed. For instance, if a Smart Devices application were being developed, separate *Emulator Debug* and *Device Debug* configurations may be created in order to help track down issues relating to the compatibility of the two testing platforms.

- **Large Projects:** With a particularly large project the compile time can become unwieldy, slowing down the build/test cycle and thus reducing developer productivity. In this case it can be useful to split the project into different build units that can be compiled and tested separately. A typical example of this is that of a web application in which there is a customer-facing website and an administrator-facing management site.

■**Tip** The Debug and Release configurations that come predefined do not actually have any special properties that can't be defined in custom configurations. They are merely provided as a convenience and can be edited or deleted just as with any that you define yourself.

To create your own solution configuration, select the <New...> option from the Active Solution Configuration dropdown list. This then shows the New Solution Configuration dialog (Figure 10-6).

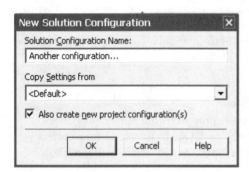

Figure 10-6. *New Solution Configuration*

As well as specifying a name for our new configuration here, we can also select which existing configuration we want to copy our settings from. This dropdown list contains all of the configurations that we've already defined, along with the special option <Default>, which applies the system default settings to the solution configuration, such as building all of the projects within the solution. The checkbox below this list lets the user specify whether to create a new configuration for each project as well as for the solution as a whole. If this option is unchecked, then the Configuration dropdown list at the top of the Property Pages dialog will not contain an entry for this solution. This limits the settings that can be applied to those that are in the Configuration Manager dialog: the Selected Project Configuration, Platform, and whether or not to Build the project.

Dependencies and Build Orders

Whenever a reference is added within a project, whether it is to a built-in .NET assembly such as System.Web.dll (which contains the System.Web namespace), a third party assembly, or another project within the solution, a *dependency* is created. If the reference is to an external resource, then we generally don't need to worry; the built-in namespace DLLs change only with a new release of the Framework, and even then the old ones execute side by side on the system. When references are added to projects that are within the same Solution, this is generally not the case; the other assemblies may well change just as often as the project that you are concerned with. This causes problems, since you have to ensure that when you are performing a build of the solution, the project that is being referred to is built first. If this doesn't happen, and your code makes use of new or updated methods that haven't been compiled yet, then errors will be thrown. When we have many projects in a solution, ensuring that the *build order* is correct so that projects are compiled in the right order is of paramount importance.

Visual Studio .NET makes ordering a build much simpler than was the case with previous versions. When references are added between projects, the environment can calculate in which order the solution needs to be built. This ordering can be examined from within the Project Dependencies dialog, viewable by selecting the Project Dependencies... option from the context menu of the root node in the Solution Explorer (see Figure 10-7).

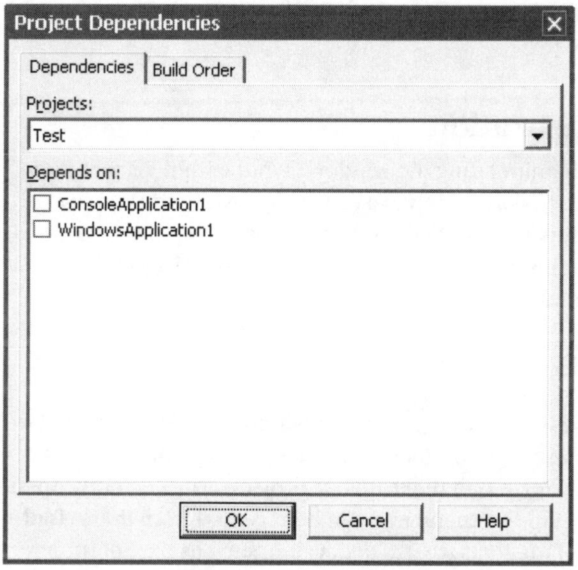

Figure 10-7. *Project Dependency Manager*

The main advantage that this dialog provides over adding references is that it makes it possible to add a dependency to a project that isn't actually referenced in order to alter the build order. This is a useful feature, since references can be added only to projects that have a DLL output. When a project is selected from the Projects dropdown at the top of the dialog, a list of all the other projects is displayed within the "Depends on" pane. Checkboxes are shown next to each project, allowing dependencies to be added and removed. Any references desired can be added, with two caveats:

- A dependency can't be removed from a project that is referenced; the only way that this can be done is by removing the reference itself.

- A dependency can't be added to a project if it creates a circular dependency, one in which a series of projects form a loop, such as Project A depending on Project B, and Project B depending on Project A.

If there is a need for two projects to make use of functionality provided by the other, the available options include moving all of the classes from both projects into a single one, and, more frequently, using *Late Binding* and *Reflection* to instantiate objects and call the methods in another project programmatically.

Once the dependencies have all been configured, switching to the Build Order tab will display the order in which the projects will be compiled whenever the solution is built.

Window Control

A big part of the productivity gains that can be realized in Visual Studio .NET is through being able to access the correct tools at the correct time. Visual Studio .NET has an extremely advanced windowing system, allowing individual developers to configure the IDE to their liking. In this section, we will look at the different types of windows in Visual Studio .NET and how they can be configured to gain maximum efficiency.

Restoring the Default Configuration

It is entirely possible that while you are manipulating the window layout within Visual Studio .NET, you make a mess of it (it is very easy!). Fortunately, we can easily restore the window layout to the factory settings. Under the Environment tab in the Options dialog there is a section called General. This section contains a button labeled "Reset Window Layout" that will restore the window layout to the default.

Window Types

Visual Studio .NET has two different types of window: document windows and tool windows. Document windows are the windows in which we do most of our work. They hold the code, Windows Forms, XML, WebForms, and so forth that make up our projects. The currently open document windows are listed under the Window menu and can be accessed from there. Tool windows are the windows that contain all the tools we use to develop, such as the Solution Explorer, the Server Explorer and the Object Browser. All of these windows can be accessed from the View menu.

Window Modes

You can choose to display document windows in one of two ways:

- **Tabbed:** This is the default, and each window is a tab within the designer.

- **MDI:** This is similar to Visual Studio 6.0 in that each window is separate from the designer and free-floating.

You can change the window mode in the Environment ➤ General page of the Options dialog.

Window Manipulation

The two different types of window can be manipulated differently.

Tool Windows

Visual Studio .NET allows for very flexible manipulation of the tool windows. Each tool window can exist separately or as part of a group with other tool windows. When tool windows are grouped together, they take the space of one window, but have tabs at the bottom, so you are able to choose which window in the group is displayed. As you can see in the dialog shown in Figure 10-8, there are four tool windows grouped into one free-floating window. The tabs at the bottom allow you to select which window you want to move.

Figure 10-8. *The Solution Explorer inside a Tool window*

Each group or window can be free-floating, as in the figure, hovering above the design area, or it can be docked to any of the four sides of the main IDE window. It is possible to dock more than one group or window to a single side of the IDE, allowing each side to display more than one window at a time. Windows can be docked either by dragging them to the appropriate side of the IDE, at which point you will see a faint outline displayed where the window will be docked, or by double-clicking on the window title bar. Manually docking the window in the correct group can be tricky, especially if there are already some windows docked at that edge of the IDE. For this reason you should opt to use the double-click method of swapping between docked and undocked, since this will dock the window into its last known docking position.

When a window or group is docked, you have the option of keeping it onscreen permanently, or having it slide offscreen until you hover over its label to bring it back. Having your windows slide off the screen will allow you to free up valuable real estate within the application. You can see in the screen shot shown in Figure 10-9 that the same four tool windows have been docked as in the example of Figure 10-8 to the right-hand side of the IDE, thus having them hidden offscreen.

Figure 10-9. *Docking Tool windows*

You can change the docking mode of a window by clicking on the pin icon in its top right-hand corner. When the pin is pointing down, the document will remain on the screen when you move away, whereas when the pin is pointing to the left, the window will slide out of view.

Document Windows

As mentioned earlier, document windows can exist in one of two forms: MDI and Tabbed. When your document windows are in MDI mode, they will float around inside the IDE. When you maximize an MDI window, it takes up the whole of the available real estate within the IDE. This means that any other maximized windows are stacked behind the current document. You can access the documents stacked behind the current one by using the Window menu.

In tabbed mode, documents are split into tab groups. By default, one tab group exists, and all documents are contained within this tab group. Each document within a tab group has a tab at the top, allowing you to move quickly through the available documents within the group.

When you have more than one document in a tab group, you can create another tab group by right-clicking on a documents tab and choosing either "New Horizontal Tab Group" or "New Vertical Tab Group." Using tab groups, you can view multiple documents at one time; this is especially useful when working on ASP.NET projects, since you can display the WebForm in one tab group and the code behind in another.

Window Configuration (Normal, Debug, Full Screen)

When you close and reopen Visual Studio .NET, you will notice that the layout of your Tool Windows has been remembered. What you may not notice is that Visual Studio .NET in fact remembers three different Tool Window configurations: one for normal editing, one for use during debugging, and one for full screen mode.

Using these different configurations, you can set up the IDE so that the appropriate information is displayed at the correct time. For instance, when I am in debug mode, I have set up the IDE to display all the debug windows that I need and nothing else. The whole of the IDE is taken up by the debug windows, and the rest of the windows are hidden. However, when I switch out of debug mode, the IDE is returned to its normal state.

You should really take the time to set out the windows as you like for debugging and as you like for developing and be assured that Visual Studio .NET will remember the different configurations.

Using Full Screen Mode

When developing, I always prefer to use full screen mode. In this mode, Visual Studio .NET takes up the *whole* of the screen, including the area normally occupied by the Start menu and the Visual Studio .NET window caption bar. You can switch in and out of this mode easily by pressing Shift+Alt+Enter. Visual Studio .NET also maintains a specific window configuration for full screen mode as well as for normal mode, so you can set up a different environment for full screen mode than you would for normal mode.

I have found it useful to have the Toolbox, Properties, Server Explorer, and Solution Explorer windows all docked and hidden at the right of the window, allowing me to have as near a full screen for editing as possible. A handy keyboard shortcut I found is that you can make the Properties window pop up and get to the last set property in it by pressing F4.

External Tools

Although Visual Studio .NET provides an excellent coding environment, it is often useful to use it in conjunction with other applications. For instance, I often use Macromedia Dreamweaver and Fireworks when building ASP.NET applications, so that I can lay out my pages and create new images. Normally, you would have to switch into these applications manually, but with Visual Studio .NET you can create new menu buttons to load these applications automatically and at the same time, pass in some command line arguments to load the current file automatically.

Adding External Tools

External tools are added using the External Tools dialog, which is accessible from the Tools menu. Once you have the dialog open, click the Add button. This will add a new external tool item to the Tools menu. You can now specify a name for the tool and the path to the executable file. The executable file can be any file ending with one of the following extensions: exe, com, bat, cmd, and pif. As you can see in Figure 10-10, I have specified the path to Dreamweaver MX on my machine and given my new tool item a name.

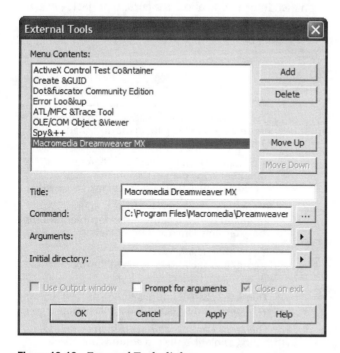

Figure 10-10. *External Tools dialog*

Using the Move Up and Move Down buttons, you can reorganize the order in which the external tools appear on the Tools menu.

Removing External Tools

You can also remove an existing external tool reference using the External Tools dialog. Simply select the tool you want to remove and then click Remove. This feature will allow you to remove the external tools that are included in Visual Studio .NET by default. Before you do this, it may be worth taking a note of the settings in case you want to restore that tool at a later date.

Passing Command Line Arguments

If you have Dreamweaver installed on your machine, then set up the external tool as specified in the last two steps and try it out. If you don't have Dreamweaver, you can either download a trial version from http://www.macromedia.com or use another HTML editor.

If you click on the new Macromedia Dreamweaver command on the Tools menu, you will see that it opens up Dreamweaver, but nothing else happens. To make this command even more effective, we want to be able to load the active document within Visual Studio .NET straight into the new instance of Dreamweaver. To do this, we need to pass in the file name as a command line argument. Look back at the previous screen shot of the External Tools dialog and you will notice that we can specify arguments to pass to the executable for our command.

To make things easier, Visual Studio .NET has a preset collection of dynamic arguments that we can pass to the executable that match information about the current project. You can quickly access these arguments by clicking on the arrow button next to the arguments text box. The available arguments are shown in Table 10-1.

Table 10-1. *Arguments for External Tools.*

Argument Name	Argument	Description
Item Path	&(ItemPath)	If a document window is active, then this argument is the full path to the document. Otherwise, it is blank.
Item Directory	&(ItemDir)	If a document window is active, then this argument is the path to the directory containing the document. Otherwise, it is blank.
Item File Name	&(ItemFilename)	If a document window is active, then this argument is the filename of the document without the extension. Otherwise, it is blank.
Item Extension	&(ItemExt)	If a document window is active, then this argument is the file extension of the document. Otherwise, it is blank.
Current Line	&(CurLine)	This is the current line position in the text editor, or blank if the text editor is not selected.
Current Column	&(CurCol)	This is the current column position in the text editor, or blank if the text editor is not selected.
Current Text	&(CurText)	This will return either the word after the cursor in the text editor, or the single line of selected text if there is one. If neither is available, this argument is blank.
Target Path	&(TargetPath)	This argument returns the path to the target.
Target Directory	&(TargetDir)	This argument returns the directory where the target will be placed.

Table 10-1. *Arguments for External Tools. (continued)*

Argument Name	Argument	Description
Target Name	&(TargetName)	This argument returns the name of the project target.
Target Extension	&(TargetExt)	This argument returns the extension of the project target.
Project Directory	&(ProjDir)	This argument is the path to the directory of the currently active project. For ASP.NET applications, this will be the URL of the virtual directory.
Project File Name	&(ProjFileName)	This argument is the filename of the currently active project.
Solution Directory	&(SolutionDir)	This argument is the path to the directory of the current solution.
Solution File Name	&(SolutionFileName)	This argument is the filename of the current solution.

Most Windows applications accept the path to a file to open as the first command line parameter. To pass the path of the current file to Dreamweaver, we simply need to set the arguments to &(ItemPath) to pass in the path of the current item.

Once you have done this, try clicking on the Macromedia Dreamweaver MX menu item when you have a file active in the IDE. You will see that Dreamweaver will open it (provided that it supports the particular file type) and that it is ready for editing.

Toolbars and Menus

If you are able to access easily the tools that you need within Visual Studio .NET, you will work more effectively. The toolbar and menu system in Visual Studio .NET is extremely advanced, allowing you to reorganize the existing toolbars and menus, as well as the commands contained in them, in addition to creating your own new toolbars, menus, and commands.

Organizing Toolbars

Organizing the display of toolbars can help make working with Visual Studio .NET much easier. There is a glut of features contained within Visual Studio .NET, with some of the more useful ones being hidden away below a collection of less useful ones.

To make accessing these features simpler, it is often beneficial to rearrange the toolbars that are present when Visual Studio .NET is first installed. With Visual Studio .NET, there are well over 30 default toolbars that are displayed at different times. You can change the toolbars that are displayed by using the Toolbars submenu of the View menu or by using the Toolbars tab of the Customize dialog. You can also drag and drop Toolbar items by holding down the ALT key.

Toolbars don't have to stay docked to the top of IDE; you can dock them at any side of the IDE you choose, or you can have a Toolbar floating free on the screen. To undock a Toolbar from the main IDE screen, move your mouse over the grip icon on the left-hand side of the Toolbar (or any separator), and hold down the mouse button to drag the Toolbar. By dragging the Toolbar using this icon, you can move it to any side of the screen you wish, where it will dock either against the side of the IDE or with any toolbars that exist there already. Alternatively, you can drop the Toolbar in the middle of the IDE to have it float freely above your document windows. To return a free-floating toolbar to the docked position, you can either drag it to the desired side of the IDE or double-click the Toolbar caption to have it return to its previous dock position.

Using free-floating Toolbars means that you have less distance to cover using the mouse when you want to access commands, since you can place the Toolbar near where you are working. This is especially useful for the Layout toolbar, since you can place it near the controls you want to lay out and then access the features directly.

Organizing Menus

Toolbars are not the only elements of the default IDE that can be changed. With the Customize dialog open, you have the ability to move any of the menus or menu items that are present in the IDE to a new location. This can involve changing the order of the menu bar, making one menu such as the Help menu a submenu of another menu such as the Edit menu, or removing the menu altogether.

You can rearrange the menus by simply dragging them around when the Customize dialog is open. When you are dragging a menu and you hover over another menu, it will pop open, allowing you to drop the menu you are dragging into its contents. By dragging a menu off the menu bar and dropping it into the IDE, you remove it from the menu bar altogether.

Under the Commands tab of the Customize dialog, you can find a categorized list of the available commands. You can drag any of these commands onto any menu or toolbar that is already present in the IDE.

Creating Toolbars

Visual Studio .NET provides the ability to create new toolbars to supplement the features available by the default toolbar set. To do this, first open up the Customize dialog. Under the Toolbars tab, click on the new button and enter a name for your toolbar, such as My Toolbar (Figure 10-11).

Figure 10-11. *Creating a new toolbar*

The new toolbar will appear in the IDE immediately, floating above the work area. To add some buttons to it, switch to the Commands tab of the Customize dialog and find the command you want to add to your new toolbar. When you have found the command, drag and drop it onto the new toolbar. You can add as many buttons to the new toolbar as you like.

To dock your toolbar, simply close the Customize dialog and double-click the toolbars caption. It will be automatically docked at the top of the IDE.

To remove this toolbar, simply open up the Toolbars tab of the Customize dialog again, select the toolbar, and click Delete.

Creating a Macromedia Studio MX Toolbar

The ability to create new toolbars really becomes useful when it is linked with the ability to add external tools to the IDE. When you set up a new external tool, you are actually creating a new command within the IDE. This command is accessible from the Customize dialog, so we can easily add it to a toolbar.

To highlight this, I am going to create a toolbar to link my copy of Visual Studio .NET with the three main applications from Macromedia Studio MX: Dreamweaver, Fireworks, and Flash.

To start, we need to add the external tool links. Open up the External Tools dialog by selecting External Tools from the Tools menu. Next, add a new external tool for each of the three external applications. For Dreamweaver you will want to pass in the &(ItemPath) argument so that the current file will be loaded into Dreamweaver.

Once you have added the three tools, open up the Tools menu to verify that they have been added correctly. Now we need to create the toolbar. Open up the Customize dialog and switch to the Toolbars tab. Click the New button to create a new toolbar and call the toolbar Macromedia Studio MX.

The next step we need to take is to add the external tool commands to the toolbar. Switch into the Commands tab of the Customize dialog and look under the Tools category. Scroll down until you find the external commands. You will notice that all the external commands are named "External Command" with a sequentially increasing number appended to the end. You may find it easier to identify which commands match the Macromedia MX ones by opening up the Tools menu while still in Customize mode and dragging the appropriate menu items off the menu onto the toolbar. Repeat this process until all the Macromedia commands have been added to the Macromedia toolbar.

When you close the Customize menu, you will notice that the toolbar is displaying the buttons as text. What we want to do now is add icons to the toolbar so that the buttons match all the other buttons in Visual Studio .NET.

Let's start with the Dreamweaver button. To get the icon for Dreamweaver you can open the executable file directly in Visual Studio .NET and copy the icon to the clipboard. Once you open the executable in Visual Studio .NET, you will be presented with the Resource Browser, allowing you to view and manipulate all the embedded resources within the Dreamweaver executable, as shown in Figure 10-12.

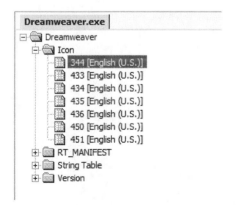

Figure 10-12. *Icons in the* Dreamweaver.exe *file*

Collapse the Icon node and browse through the icons until you find the one you want. Each icon will be available in different sizes and colour depths. You can switch through these settings by right-clicking in the editor and choosing the appropriate icon type from the Current Icon Image Types menu. With the icon editor open, right-click anywhere within the editor, *except* on the icon itself, and choose Copy to copy the icon to the clipboard.

Now open up the Customize dialog and switch the IDE into customization mode. Right-click on Dreamweaver MX button in the Macromedia Studio MX toolbar and choose Paste Button Image to set the button image with the icon data from the clipboard. With the button image set, you will notice that it now displays the image as well as the button text. To rectify this, right-click on the button again and choose Default Style from the popup menu to display just the image.

If you want to edit any of the images, just right-click on the button and choose Edit Button Image. To reset the button image at any time, just select Reset Button Image from the button context menu.

Repeat this process for the remaining two buttons, taking the icons from the appropriate executable file. When you have finished, the toolbar will look something like Figure 10-13.

Figure 10-13. *The Custom Macromedia Studio MX toolbar*

Creating Menus

Not only can we create new toolbars in the IDE, but we also have the ability to create completely new menus as well. To create a new menu, simply open up the Customize dialog and switch to the Commands tab. At the bottom of the Categories list you will find the New Menu category. Select this, and the New Menu command will appear in the Commands list. Drag this new menu onto the menu bar, as either a top-level menu or a submenu of another top-level menu (Figure 10-14).

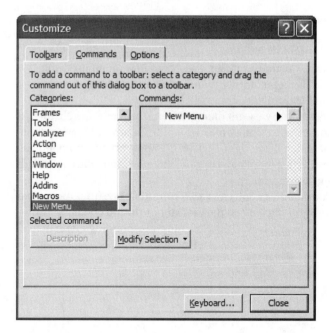

Figure 10-14. *Customizing menus*

Once you have dropped the menu onto the menu bar, you can right-click it to set various options. Rename the menu My Tools. Now drag some commands from the Customize dialog and drop them onto your menu. To split the menu into groups, right-click the *first* item in the group and choose Begin a Group. When you have finished, your menu will look something like Figure 10-15.

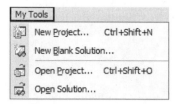

Figure 10-15. *A custom menu*

You can add as many commands to the menu as you like, and Visual Studio .NET will automatically manage the hiding of items that are used infrequently.

Creating a Macromedia Studio MX Menu

Now that we have seen how menu creation works, let's create a menu for your Macromedia Studio MX commands so that you have both a menu and a toolbar. You are going to create the menu so that it is a submenu of the My Tools menu you just created.

First, clear all the menu items from the My Tools menu by opening the Customize dialog, opening the My Tools menu, and dragging the items off the menu. Now we need to add another menu as a submenu of the My Tools menu.

Switch to the Commands tab of the Customize dialog and drag a new menu up to the menu bar. If you hover over the My Tools menu, it will expand, and you can drop your new menu onto it. Rename the new menu Macromedia Studio MX.

Now we need to drag the commands that we want onto the menu. As mentioned before, external commands have fairly nondescriptive names, making it difficult to identify which one matches your commands. To make it easier, if you right-click on the appropriate command on the toolbar, it will show you the name of the command. Drag the three Macromedia commands onto the new menu and rename them appropriately.

By default, the items have no icons on them. You can easily copy the icons from the toolbar buttons that we created previously by right-clicking on the toolbar button and choosing Copy Button Image to add the icon to the clipboard. Now right-click the corresponding menu item and choose Paste Button Image to set the button image. See Figure 10-16.

Figure 10-16. *A custom menu for Macromedia Studio MX*

It's that simple. You can add as many items as you wish to the My Tools menu, and I have found it very useful to link all the tools I use most often into the Visual Studio .NET IDE.

Customizing the Toolbox

The Visual Studio .NET toolbox is where all the components and controls available for use within your particular project type appear. The toolbox itself is split into tabs, allowing for components to be organized into logical groupings. For instance, when working on an ASP.NET web application, you get the Data tab for components such as SqlConnection and OracleDataAdapter, the WebForms tab for controls such as Label and DataGrid, and the Components tab for server components such as FileSystemWatcher and MessageQueue. See Figure 10-17.

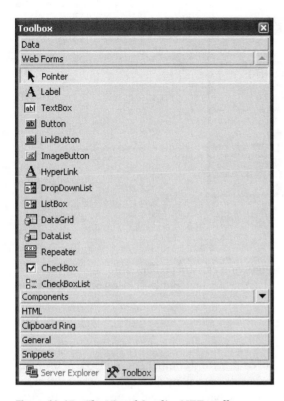

Figure 10-17. *The Visual Studio .NET toolbox*

Like most parts of the Visual Studio .NET IDE, the toolbox is not fixed, and it can be modified and manipulated in a variety of ways.

Using Snippets

One of the most useful features of Visual Studio .NET is the ability to store snippets of code, in any language, that can later be reused by simply dragging the snippet onto the text editor window. Snippets are created by highlighting a portion of code within the text editor and dragging the code onto the Snippets tab of the toolbox. You should note that Snippets can be stored on any tab of the toolbox, even those that you create yourself, but storing them on the Snippets tab provides some degree of organization. See Figure 10-18.

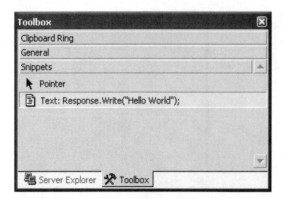

Figure 10-18. *Storing code snippets in the toolbox*

Once a snippet has been stored in the toolbox, you can drag it back onto any text editor window, where the stored code will be inserted at the cursor. Double-clicking on a snippet will insert it at the current cursor position.

Managing Controls

The .NET Framework contains a great number of controls and components right out of the box. However, as you progress in your development projects you will no doubt come across others, be they ones you have created yourself or ones that you have purchased from a third party. To enable easier access to these controls and provide support controls that can work with the visual designer, you are able to add your own controls to the toolbox. Achieving this is extremely simple. You simply right-click on a tab and choose Add/Remove Items... (Figure 10-19).

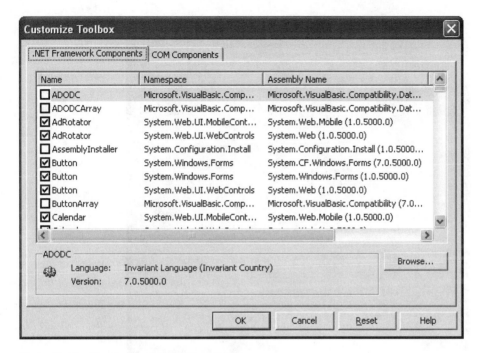

Figure 10-19. *The Customize Toolbox dialog*

Listed in the .NET Framework Components tab are all components that are registered in the Global Assembly Cache (GAC). To add your own components to the toolbox, you can either register them in the GAC or browse using the Browse button to the assembly containing the component.

In Figure 10-19, you will also notice the option to add COM components to your toolbox. This tab will list all the COM components listed on your machine, any of which can be added to your toolbox. When you add a COM component from the toolbox to your project, Visual Studio .NET will generate the appropriate Interop assembly automatically.

Manipulating Tabs

Adding new controls to the existing tabs on the toolbox will eventually render the tabs unwieldy and unorganized, making controls difficult to find and use. Fortunately, we have the ability to create our own tabs, to which we can add our components. To add a new tab you simply have to right-click on the toolbox and click Add Tab. A new tab will appear at the bottom of the toolbox window, and the caret will be placed there ready for you to enter your tab name. Once you press Return, your new tab is created (see Figure 10-20).

Figure 10-20. *Creating a custom tab*

To remove or rename an existing tab, simply right-click the appropriate tab and choose either Delete Tab or Rename Tab respectively. To reorganize tabs, simply hold down the ALT key and drag and drop them within the Toolbox.

Creating an Infragistics NetAdvantage Suite Tab

Now for a practical demonstration. Anyone who knows me will tell you that my graphic design skills leave a lot to be desired. Naturally, this reflects in my programming work, resulting in the most hideous graphical controls you can imagine. To circumvent this limitation, I use prebuilt graphical controls made by people with some degree of style! My preference in this area is the Infragistics NetAdvantge Suite, which I use in the majority of my .NET projects. To speed up my development time I have built myself a custom toolbox tab, containing all the Infragistics controls in a single, easy-to-access place. To try out this demo you can download a trial of the NetAdvantage suite from http://www.infragistics.com.

The first thing to do is create the tab, so right-click on the toolbox and choose Add Tab. Give the new tab a meaningful name such as "Infragistics NetAdvantage Suite" and then press Return to create the tab. Now that we have the tab, it is time to add the Infragistics controls to it. Right-click on the newly created tab and choose Add/Remove Items. Fortunately, when you install the NetAdvantage suite, all the controls are added to the GAC, so there is no need to go browsing for them. In the Add/Remove Items dialog, scroll down to the NetAdvantage controls (they are usually named Ultra<something>), and check the controls you want to add to your tab. Voilà! You have a nice, shiny new toolbox tab containing all the controls for easy access. See Figure 10-21.

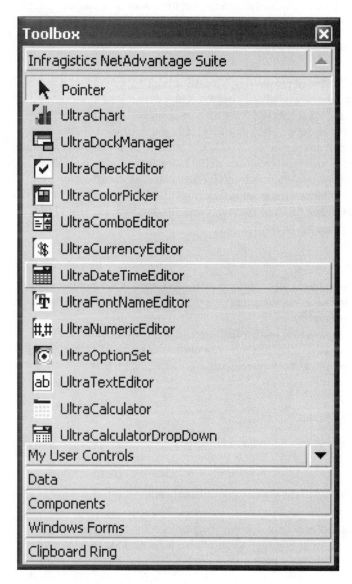

Figure 10-21. *The Infragistics NetAdvantage Suite tab*

Dynamic Help

One the best features of the Visual Studio .NET IDE is Dynamic Help. When Dynamic Help is visible, it suggests links to help content based on the current context of the IDE. Dynamic Help works in a variety of contexts in the IDE, providing help not just when you are coding, but also when you are manipulating the menus and toolbars of the IDE.

In this section, we are going to look at a feature of Visual Studio .NET called the *XML Help Provider*. The XML Help Provider allows you to define your own links to be displayed within the dynamic help window. This will be especially helpful if you are distributing a class library or a Visual Studio .NET add-in to your customers and you want to provide true context-sensitive help.

XML Help Provider

The XML Help Provider (XHP) is a service provided by Visual Studio .NET that makes it possible to extend the set of links that is available by default in the dynamic help window. Each time Visual Studio .NET loads up, it checks for the `HTML\XMLLinks\<lcid>` directory under the directory where the executable is stored. The value of `<lcid>` is determined by the locale of your machine. For the English locale, the locale Id (LCID) is 1033, so on an English machine, Visual Studio .NET would check in the HTML\XMLLinks\1033 directory.

If this directory exists, and it will by default, it looks for files with an `.xml` extension that matches the XML Help Provider schema. This schema describes a set of keywords and a set of links that match these keywords. Using this information, Visual Studio .NET will extend the information set available in the dynamic help window.

XML Help Provider Context

The XML Help Provider organizes content topics into *contexts*. A context is the combination of programming language, UI elements, selected items, project types, etc. that Visual Studio .NET uses to narrow the display of topics.

By default, all the keywords you specify will be displayed, in any context, provided that the keyword exists in that context. To reduce the scope of a particular keyword, you associate *attributes* with it. These attributes allow you to specify various elements, such as

- Current Programming Language

- Current IDE Mode (Design/Code)

- Project Type (Web, Windows Forms, Command Line, etc.)

- Current Selected Item

- Current Active Product (Visual Basic, Visual C#, third-party app)

These can be used to limit the visibility of your dynamic help links. A full list of the attributes can be found in the Visual Studio Help Integration Kit, available for download from MSDN.

XML Help Provider Documents

The XML Help Provider defines a set of ten XML tags that make up a dynamic help extension document. Rather than reiterate the list of tags, which in any case is contained in the MSDN documentation, I will run through the creation of a trivial example to highlight the different tags and then progress to a more useful example to end the chapter.

To start, open up a new XML file in Visual Studio .NET and add the following XML to it:

```
<?xml version="1.0" encoding="utf-8" ?>
<DynamicHelp xmlns="http://msdn.microsoft.com/vsdata/xsd/vsdh.xsd">

</DynamicHelp>
```

Every XHP document starts with the DynamicHelp tag. The tag needs to have the appropriate namespace specified to avoid any name clashes that might arise in the future. As mentioned in the previous section, each help topic you want to add is organized into a context. To create a new context, add a Context element to the XML:

```
<DynamicHelp xmlns="http://msdn.microsoft.com/vsdata/xsd/vsdh.xsd">
    <Context>

    </Context>
</DynamicHelp>
```

You can add as many Context elements as you like to each XHP document, allowing for a document to support multiple topics. We are going to add two topics to our document: one for the System.Collections.ArrayList class and one for the Macro Explorer window.

Before we look at actually creating the rest of the XML file, let's take a quick look at a useful utility to help us debug our dynamic help files. Visual Studio .NET allows us to trace the attributes of the current help context, along with the appropriate keywords that Visual Studio .NET is displaying content for, at the bottom of the dynamic help window. To activate this, open up RegEdit and navigate to the HKCU\Software\Microsoft\VisualStudio\7.1\Dynamic Help key. This key has a value, Display Debug Output in Retail, which is set to NO by default. To enable the debug information, set the value to YES. When you next open up Visual Studio .NET, you will see a set of trace information at the bottom of the dynamic help window, as shown in Figure 10-22.

Figure 10-22. *Debugging Dynamic Help*

If you are unaware of the keywords you want, you can simply place the IDE in the state you want and check out which keywords the IDE is looking for. It is also useful to do this in both Visual Basic and Visual C#, since they both provide different keywords for the dynamic help to look at. The most notable example of this is in the code editor. For instance, check out the following code snippets:

```
// C#
ArrayList al = new ArrayList()
```

```
''VB
Dim al As New ArrayList
```

If you selected the ArrayList definition in C#, the dynamic help will look up content matching the keyword ArrayList. However, if you selected the ArrayList definition in VB, the keyword that is used is actually System.Collections.ArrayList. Visual Basic always uses the fully qualified type name, whereas C# will always use the short type name. This should be taken into consideration when you build the keyword list.

Now let's move straight on to creating the help entries for the ArrayList class. To add the keywords, you need to add a Keywords node to the Context node. The Keywords node then contains one or more KItem elements that define a single keyword. In the case of the ArrayList, we will need two keyword entries: one for VB and one for C#:

```
<Keywords>
    <KItem Name="ArrayList"/>
    <KItem Name="System.Collections.ArrayList"/>
</Keywords>
```

This defines the keywords that match our context, but does not define any links for the context. Links are added to a Links node, which itself is added to the Context node. Each Links node can contain one or more LItem elements to define a link:

```
<Links>
    <LItem URL="http://www.asptoday.com" ToolTip="CSharpToday">ASPToday</LItem>
    <LItem URL="http://www.apress.com" Priority="700">Apress.com</LItem>
</Links>
```

This code specifies two links for the keywords, one to link to http://www.asptoday.com and one to link to http://www.apress.com. In addition, there is a tool tip for the ASPToday link and a priority for the APress link. The priority is a relevant numeric ranking for each link.

Now try saving this into your HTML\XMLLinks\1033 directory and restarting the IDE. After you restart, fire a project that references the ArrayList class and place your cursor on the reference. You will see that the two links we defined now appear in the dynamic help window under the default group Help. Now change your file so that you can define your own link group instead of using the default one.

The first thing you need to do is add a LinkGroup element to the dynamic help XML. This element comes directly under the DynamicHelp node:

```
<LinkGroup ID="ApressHelp" Title="Apress Help">
    <Glyph Expanded="vs:/ctxhelp_opn.gif" Collapsed="vs:/ctxhelp_cls.gif"/>
</LinkGroup>
```

Two attributes have been specified in the LinkGroup tag above: ID and Title. The ID attribute uniquely identifies the link group, and the Title attribute defines the text that will be displayed in the dynamic help window. The Glyph tag is used to define two images for the group: one for the group in its collapsed state and the other for the group in its expanded state. I have used two images that are built into Visual Studio .NET, but you are free to use any image whatsoever.

Now you have to associate the links with this link group. This is done by adding a LinkGroup attribute to the LItem elements that define the links. The value of LinkGroup is the ID of the link group you wish to use:

```
<Links>
    <LItem URL="http://www.asptoday.com" ToolTip="ASPToday"
                    LinkGroup="ApressHelp">ASPToday</LItem>
    <LItem URL="http://www.apress.com" Priority="700"
                    LinkGroup="ApressHelp">Apress.com</LItem>
</Links>
```

Now save the document again and reopen Visual Studio .NET. Navigate to the definition of ArrayList again, and you will see that the help links are now specified in a group of their own.

Now restrict the scope of your context so that these links are displayed only for projects that build an executable, not a DLL. To do this, you need to define some attributes for your context. This is done by adding an Attributes node to the Context node and adding to this a list of AItem tags, defining the different attributes you want in your context:

```
<Attributes>
    <AItem Name="Project" Value="Exe"/>
</Attributes>
```

This attribute defines that the project should be an EXE project. Save the XML file again and restart the IDE. Try out some different project types, and you will find that the links will display only for projects that generate an EXE.

Now let's create the help entry for the Macro Explorer. All the windows in Visual Studio .NET have their own keywords that the dynamic help provider uses when that window is currently selected. You can find out the keywords for each window by selecting it and checking the keywords in the dynamic help debug information. The keyword for the Macro Explorer window is VS.MacroExplorer.

To create the help entry for the Macro Window, first you need to add a new Context element to the DynamicHelp node. Then, as before, you add the Keywords and Links nodes. The resulting XML looks like this:

```
<Context>
    <Keywords>
        <KItem Name="VS.MacroExplorer"/>
    </Keywords>
    <Links>
        <LItem URL="http://www.asptoday.com"
                    LinkGroup="ApressHelp">ASP Today</LItem>
    </Links>
</Context>
```

Save the XML file and reboot the IDE. When the IDE reloads, select the Macro Explorer, and you will see that the new help topic is displayed in the dynamic help window.

As you can see, adding new content to the dynamic help window in Visual Studio .NET is quite a trivial task. In large projects, this type of customization can really help boost performance, especially if individual teams are providing dynamic help content for other teams. Imagine the team working on data access components providing dynamic help content about the components to the business logic team.

Extensibility Options

While Visual Studio .NET can take you far, you may, and indeed probably will, find that sometimes you just have to do some tasks yourself. Fortunately, when you reach this point, there is still something in Visual Studio .NET to help. Visual Studio .NET provides three mechanisms that allow you to automate tasks that you would otherwise have to perform manually. In this section we will look at the three main mechanisms provided out of the box with Visual Studio .NET and also at the Visual Studio Integration Kit (VSIK), which is available for download from MSDN.

Macros

Most of you will already be familiar with macros, since they have been around in Microsoft Office for years and were also available in Visual C++ 6.0. Macros are ideally suited to automating repetitive tasks such as code formatting, documentation generation, and other simple tasks that require little user input.

Macros can be created in two different ways, both of which are accessible from the Tools ➤ Macros menu. The first way of creating a macro is to have Visual Studio .NET record the actions that you are taking within the IDE so that they can be replayed at a later date. This is useful if the task you want to perform involves using multiple tools or options that are accessible through the Visual Studio .NET user interface.

The second and more flexible mechanism for macro creation is to code them. Provided along with Visual Studio .NET is the Visual Macro IDE, which while aesthetically similar to Visual Studio .NET itself has some noticeable functional differences. The most apparent of these differences is the lack of a visual designer and the limitation (in a nice way!) of using only VB.NET to create your macro code. Creating macros in code gives you full control over the tasks the macro performs and will also give you the ability to perform tasks that have no associated user interface elements within the IDE.

Macros are covered in more detail in Chapter 12.

Add-Ins

While macros are extremely useful for reducing the work needed to perform repetitive tasks that require little or no input, they are not ideal when you want to build custom tools that are run interactively with the user and the IDE. In this case you can leverage Visual Studio .NET add-ins to create custom tools that run within the IDE, providing a user interface and a more interactive approach.

As with macros, you use the Visual Studio .NET IDE to build add-ins, in this case via a special add-in project type available from the New Project dialog, as shown in Figure 10-23.

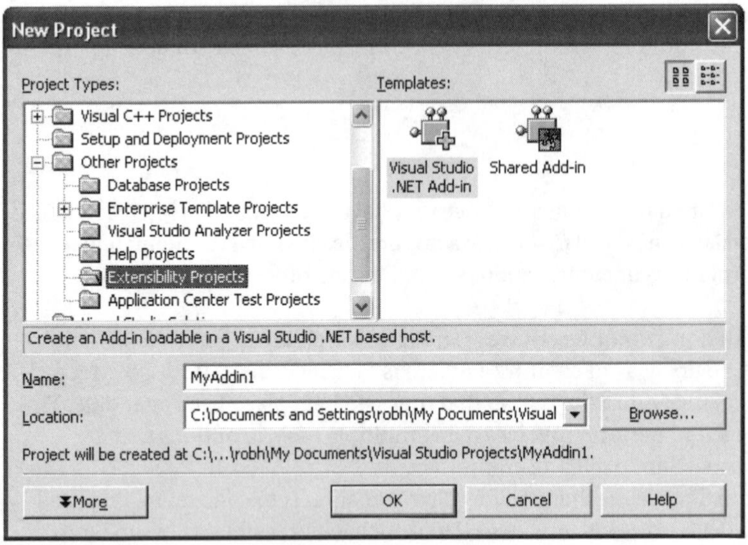

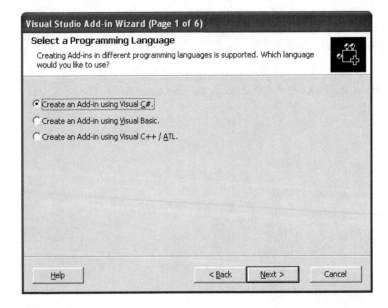

Figure 10-23. *Creating an add-in project*

Notice also that you can create an add-in that can be hosted in Microsoft Office applications as well as in the Visual Studio .NET IDE. This can be useful when your add-in provides a service that does not require specific interaction with Visual Studio .NET. Unlike macros, add-ins can be created in both VB.NET and C#, as well as using C++/ATL, making them much more flexible if you or your team are more comfortable with C# or C++ (see Figure 10-24).

Figure 10-24. *Choosing the language for your add-in*

I won't go into any more detail on add-ins here, since we have dedicated the whole of Chapter 11 to the discussion of add-ins.

Wizards

Macros and add-ins are great for automating tasks, and they provide additional functionality for use within your projects, but what if you want to provide a way to automate project or file creation? For instance, you may have an application of your own that has an extensibility model and you want to be able to automate the creation of a new extensibility project for your application. Using wizards allows you to build a wizard to walk your users through this process and then add your wizard to the New Project dialog. The add-in wizard that we saw in the last section is a classic example of this.

■**Note** If you are considering building some wizards for your team to use, then you might want to consider building a wizard to automate wizard creation (that is, a wizard wizard). Strangely, Microsoft neglected to include this in the standard Visual Studio .NET release.

A wizard is a standard DLL project, with a class that implements the IDTWizard interface accompanied by either a VSZ or a VSDIR file. The IDTWizard interface and the format of the VSZ and VSDIR files is discussed in much more detail in Chapter 13.

Visual Studio .NET Integration Kit

Out of the box, Visual Studio .NET provides a great deal of extensibility with macros, add-ins, and wizards. However, if you want to manipulate the actual design area, link into the debugger, or manipulate the IDE user interface, then none of these solutions is adequate. Fortunately, we now have access to the full Visual Studio .NET Integration Kit (VSIK), available free to registered users. Originally, the VSIK was available only to licensed users, with the license coming in at a hefty $10,000. To obtain the VSIK you will need to register for the download at http://www.vsipdev.com.

The VSIK is split into four separate Software Development Kits (SDKs): the Help Integration SDK, the Environment SDK, the Debugger SDK, and the Data Source Reference SDK. Each SDK provides a level of integration above and beyond what is available with the standard Visual Studio .NET extensibility model, and you will find that most commercial products that are integrated into Visual Studio .NET have been built using the VSIK.

Help Integration SDK

The Help Integration SDK comes in two parts: the authoring tools and the integration tools. Using the Help Integration SDK, you can build help content using Microsoft Help 2.0, compile it, and integrate it into the IDE. Microsoft Help 2.0 provides much more functionality than previous versions, such as sophisticated support for context-sensitive help (more so than with XHP) and better support for localization and multiple languages.

Using the Help Integration SDK is outside the scope of this book, and it shouldn't pose much of an obstacle for anyone who is familiar with HTML or HTML Help. More details on the Help Integration SDK can be found in the VSIK documentation.

Environment SDK

The Environment SDK is perhaps the most used of all the SDKs in the VSIK. It provides access to the Visual Studio .NET IDE, allowing you to manipulate all the existing user interface elements as well as providing mechanisms for creating additional user interface elements. Using the Environment SDK, you have full control over your user interface. You can create new tool windows that operate exactly like the Visual Studio .NET tool windows, with full support for docking and hiding. You also get access to the entire design window, allowing much more flexibility than that available with add-ins or macros.

The core of the Environment SDK is the notion of VSPackages. A VSPackage is a COM component that can be installed on the target system to extend the Visual Studio .NET IDE. A VSPackage contains all the user interface elements, project type definitions, and editors/designers required for your extension. The actual functionality of Visual Studio .NET such as Visual C++.NET and Visual Basic.NET has been written as a set of VSPackages that are "plugged in" to the Visual Studio .NET host.

Creating VSPackages is much more involved than creating add-ins, and requires that the developer have a good grasp of C++ and COM concepts.

You can find more information on the Environment SDK in the VSIK documentation, and there are plenty of fully featured examples that you can use to familiarize yourself with the Environment SDK.

Debugging SDK

The Debugging SDK provides a mechanism for you to hook into various parts of the Visual Studio .NET debugger, either to provide your own custom debug engine or to manipulate the way an existing debug engine functions. Anyone who is planning on integrating a language into the Visual Studio .NET IDE will need to provide debugging support as well as editors and designers.

The Debugging SDK has a fairly complex API and requires some degree of knowledge of C++, ATL, and COM, but if you want to build your own language, then you will find this SDK invaluable.

Data Source Reference SDK

The Data Source Reference SDK is used to transfer database metadata from the Server Explorer to the Clipboard, to another application, or from an external application into Visual Studio .NET via drag-and-drop operations. Essentially, the Data Source Reference SDK uses the DSRef in-process COM object to act as a container for the database metadata, which can then be accessed from your Visual Studio .NET extension. You can see an example of how this works if you try to drag a database table from the Server Explorer and drop it onto a Windows Form; Visual Studio .NET automatically generates the required connection and data adapter components required to load that table's data into your application.

To use this SDK you will need to be familiar with C++, COM, and OLE2/Compound document format, but you will find this extremely useful if your extension manipulates a database in any way.

Overall, the VSIK is a very effective mechanism for extending Visual Studio .NET, and it provides all the features necessary for commercial-level integration with the IDE. Most of the actual Visual Studio .NET functionality was created using the VSIK, and a selection of successful commercial components that use the VSIK are available on the market.

Summary

As you can see, the Visual Studio .NET IDE allows for a massive amount of customization, ranging from simple tweaks to full .NET plug-ins. Specifically, we have looked at how to

- Customize the IDE's appearance to your liking

- Modify the behavior of the all-important code editor

- Add content to the dynamic help menus

- Link Visual Studio .NET with external tools

Also, we have taken a quick look at the three extensibility options available to you in Visual Studio .NET. Over the course of the next three chapters, we will take a much more in-depth look at each of these extension methods, allowing you to really come to grips with Visual Studio .NET customization.

CHAPTER 11

■ ■ ■

Add-Ins

Now we will continue our examination of how to customize the Visual Studio .NET environment by looking at add-ins. Visual Studio add-ins are similar to Visual Studio macros, which will be covered in detail in the next chapter, but they differ from them in several ways:

- Macros are primarily intended for automating repetitive tasks that can be accomplished by a series of commands. Add-ins, on the other hand, can be used for a wide variety of general purposes, including tasks that cannot be accomplished by any sequence of existing Visual Studio .NET commands, for example, calling the COM library of a non-Microsoft source code configuration tool to check in your project, or carrying out some other task specific to your development environment.

- Add-ins can be seamlessly integrated into Visual Studio .NET menus so that they look like built-in commands.

- Macros have a simple structure and can be stored in a text file; add-ins are compiled binaries that can be written in any Visual Studio .NET language.

- As compiled binaries, add-ins can be distributed as a commercial product without their source code being revealed.

There are similarities between add-ins and macros as well. Since both macros and add-ins can freely access the Visual Studio .NET Development Tools Extensibility (DTE) automation model, DTE objects are used in both macros and add-ins, and they behave in exactly the same way in each case.

Visual Studio .NET DTE

The DTE is Visual Studio's built-in object model for accessing itself; it contains objects for accessing Visual Studio commands, tool bars, and settings, the current project a developer is working on, the setting and options for the project, and the source files that are contained in the project, right down to the individual code elements. A complete reference for all the classes, properties, and methods of this complex object is beyond the scope of this book, but such information can be found in the Visual Studio .NET help under "Developing with Visual Studio .NET," in the section "Common Environment Object Model Objects," under the "DTE" topic.

Because this model is the same across all Visual Studio extension facilities, an example of the use of a particular DTE object in an add-in may also be used to illustrate a macro, and vice versa. The overview and examples for the DTE automation model in the preceding and following chapters apply to add-ins also, so we will just describe the specific classes and objects we are using in this chapter's examples as we go.

Add-In Architecture

Technically, an add-in is a Component Object Model (COM) module that implements the IDTExtensibility2 interface. It may seem ironic that Visual Studio .NET uses a legacy COM interface for extending itself, but because .NET has complete interoperability with COM, this preserves compatibility with older add-ins and still allows add-ins to be built with .NET languages, since a .NET program can be wrapped as a COM object.

Furthermore, the use of COM preserves the same extensibility interface used by other Microsoft products including the Office product line (Word, Excel, Outlook, etc.) as well as Visual Studio .NET. If you're familiar with making add-ins for Office products, then some of what we're going to cover here will be similar to what you have seen. However, we're going to concentrate on Visual Studio .NET as a target.

Changes from Visual Studio .NET 2002

There are no significant changes to the add-in architecture and DTE objects of Visual Studio .NET 2003 compared to previous versions of Visual Studio .NET, except for some additions specific to Visual C++ ; indeed, the file containing the DTE objects, EnvDTE.DLL, is exactly the same for both the 2002 and 2003 editions of Visual Studio .NET! Consequently, if you've used add-ins in Visual Studio 2002, you'll be quite at home in Visual Studio 2003. We'll describe the changes for Visual C++ projects later in this chapter after we've covered the basics.

COM Objects for Add-Ins

When we said that the add-in is a COM object, did you feel a bit let down? If you're using Visual Studio .NET, it would really be preferable to create .NET components, not legacy COM components. However, this isn't a problem, since we can develop add-ins in Visual Studio .NET as true .NET managed-code assemblies; there is no need to use unmanaged code unless you are doing something in the add-in that would normally require unmanaged code, such as using a legacy DLL written in C or interfacing with a device driver (though it is unlikely that you'd do this in an add-in!).

You then expose your .NET managed code add-in to COM via the standard .NET interop technique of creating a COM-Callable Wrapper (CCW) for your .NET managed assembly.

■**Note** You may be familiar with the Runtime-Callable Wrapper (RCW) for wrapping a COM object to call from .NET; instead, we're going in the opposite direction, wrapping .NET code in order to give it a COM interface. This is described under CCW and RCW in the .NET framework online help, but the Add-In Project Wizard in Visual Studio .NET automatically creates the wrapper for you, so you don't have to worry about the details.

When you build your .NET assembly, you create a type library (TLB) to make the .NET managed code in your add-in available to COM. You also register the add-in as a COM object, and save information about your add-in in the Add-Ins key under the Visual Studio .NET section of the Windows system registry, which tells Visual Studio .NET what add-ins are installed.

Figure 11-1 attempts to explain this a little more. Visual Studio .NET is shown on the left, and the IDTExtensibility2 interface defines the set of methods that Visual Studio .NET will call, via COM, to load and invoke an add-in. The optional IDTCommandTarget interface defines a set of COM routines that let the menus inside Visual Studio .NET execute commands in your add-in.

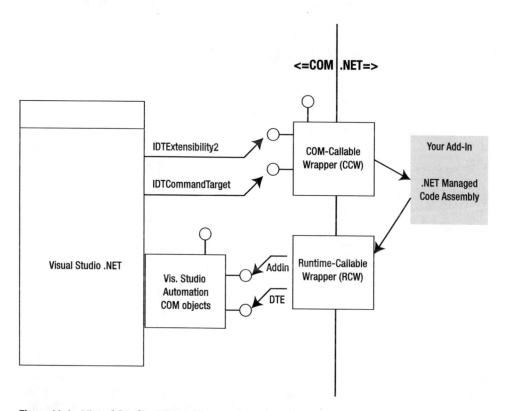

Figure 11-1. *Visual Studio .NET Add-In architecture*

Your add-in may need to call back into Visual Studio .NET to access information about loaded projects or other add-ins. Visual Studio .NET exposes this information to your add-in as a set of COM objects that the add-in accesses just as any other .NET application would reference a COM object: through a Runtime Callable Wrapper (RCW). Visual Studio .NET exposes information about itself and loaded projects via the DTE interface, and information about other add-ins is exposed via the AddIn interface. When Visual Studio .NET connects to an add-in, it passes a pair of objects that implement these two interfaces, which the add-in can use to call back into Visual Studio .NET as needed.

Luckily, there is an Add-In Wizard that automates setting up an add-in project to implement the correct interfaces and registering it with COM. Let's try this out now.

The Visual Studio Add-In Wizard

Let's start with a simple add-in that lets us explore the .NET classes that let us access the different parts of a Visual Studio .NET solution. We'll use the Visual Studio Add-In Wizard to make the project.

To make a Visual Studio add-in with the wizard, choose the Visual Studio .NET Add-in template under Other Projects ➤ Extensibility Projects in the New Project dialog (Figure 11-2).

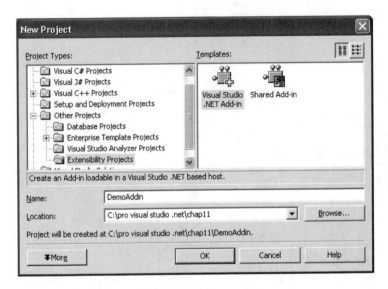

Figure 11-2. *Visual Studio .NET Add-in template*

Visual Studio .NET add-ins specifically target the development environment itself, while the shared add-in template is for creating generic add-ins for multiple Microsoft applications, such as Excel, Word, and/or Visual Studio .NET. While many add-ins are specific to Visual Studio .NET, such as code-editing aids, a generic feature enhancement such as the Multiple-Line Find-and-Replace add-in, an example coming up later in this chapter, could conceivably be useful in Word or Excel as well.

Next (Figure 11-3) we choose the programming language for the add-in.

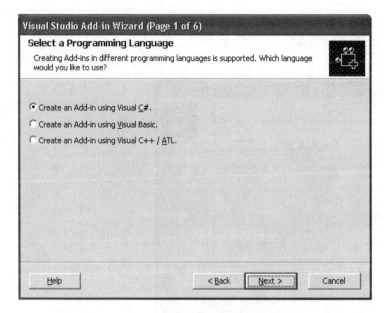

Figure 11-3. *Visual Studio .NET Add-In Wizard "Select a Programming Language"*

We're going to choose C# as our programming language for the examples in this chapter, but note that VB.NET and C++ are also perfectly fine for add-ins.

Next (Figure 11-4) the wizard asks whether the add-in is for the Visual Studio Macros IDE (as shown in the next chapter) or Visual Studio .NET. By default the wizard enables the add-in for both, but because this not a macro add-in, uncheck the VSMacros IDE box; this saves slightly on add-in size.

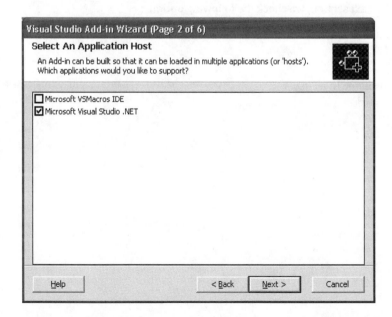

Figure 11-4. *Visual Studio .NET Add-In Wizard, page 2*

Next (Figure 11-5) we give the add-in a name and description. By default, these are set to No Name and No description.

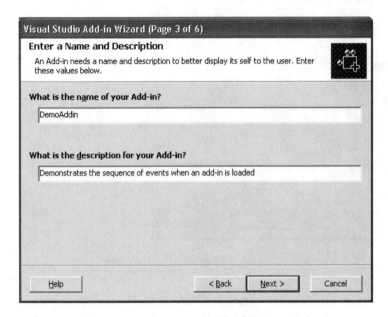

Figure 11-5. *Visual Studio .NET Add-In, page 3*

The next screen (Figure 11-6) presents several add-in options. Make sure to check the options on this page to match those shown in the screenshot. Specifically, to see the effect of these options on the code in the next section, we check the following options:

- Create a Tools menu item so the user can start the add-in.

- Load the add-in on startup.

- Make the add-in available to all users.

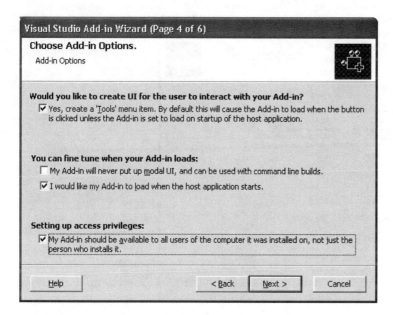

Figure 11-6. *Visual Studio .NET Add-In, page 4*

The "Tools" menu item option generates code that we can use as is or modify to show our add-in menu choice in another location, such as in the "Edit" menu, where we will place the menu item for the Multiple-Line Find and Replace example coming up later in this chapter.

Most commercial add-ins normally load when the host application (Visual Studio .NET in this case) is started, so we will check this box; this overrides the load behavior noted in the first option, but preserves the presence of the "Tools" menu. Most commercial add-ins are also installed for all users, so we'll check that box as well.

One box we didn't check deserves some extra explanation: The choice that says "My Add-in will never put up modal UI ..." indicates that the add-in will have no user interface, and so is suitable for command-line builds. This is for add-ins intended to be used from batch files that automatically do some task that does not require input from the user, such as formatting code consistently throughout a project.

The next page (Figure 11-7) lets us specify information for the About box that most commercial products have, such as website information and a customer support phone number. We'll enable that as well; in your own add-ins make sure to update the text with appropriate information about your company or product.

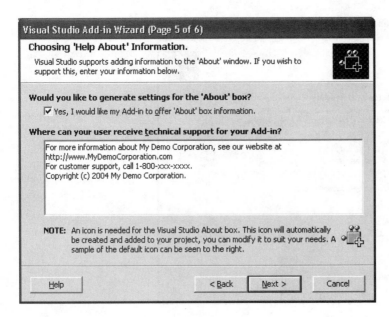

Figure 11-7. *Visual Studio .NET Add-In, page 5*

The last screen (Figure 11-8) summarizes all the options we've picked for verification before code is generated. Click on Finish to accept them.

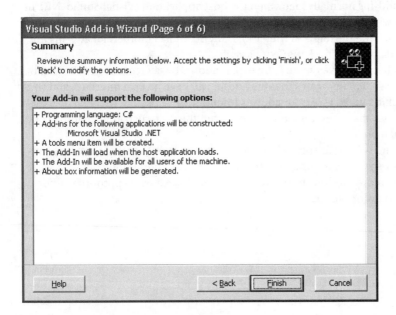

Figure 11-8. *Visual Studio .NET Add-In, page 6*

Now the Visual Studio Add-In project has been created. Note that the wizard has created a solution with two projects. The first is the add-in itself, in the DemoAddin project. The second is the DemoAddinSetup project, which produces a self-contained installer for deploying your add-in on other machines. You do not need to build this setup project during the development of the add-in, however. The add-in project contains a single source file called Connect.cs, which contains all the code that the wizard has created for us.

The Default Connect.cs Code

The screen you see in Visual Studio .NET after finishing the wizard is shown in Figure 11-9.

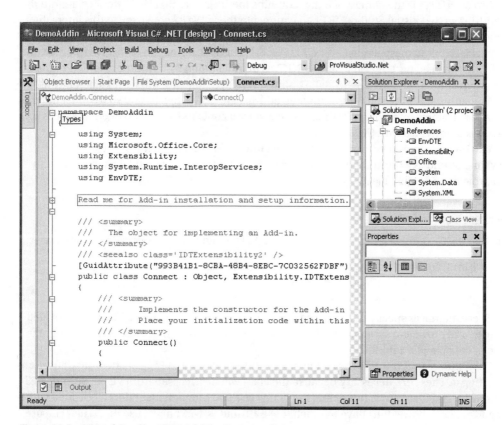

Figure 11-9. *Visual Studio .NET Add-In Connect class*

The Connect Class Namespaces

If we expand the References node for the DemoAddin project in Solution Explorer, we see extra references for the EnvDTE, Extensibility, and Office namespaces. Also, the Connect.cs file uses four namespaces:

```
using Microsoft.Office.Core;
using Extensibility;
using System.Runtime.InteropServices;
using EnvDTE;
```

The Microsoft.Office.Core namespace contains classes and interfaces for Office user interface objects such as command bars: Add-ins for VS.NET are built on the same basic code as add-ins for products in the Office family. This code is contained in the Office reference, which refers to the Office.dll file, in the same directory as the standard .NET framework assemblies (C:\WINDOWS\Microsoft.NET\Framework\v1.1.xxxx).

Extensibility is the namespace that contains the IDTExtensibility2 interface, required for add-ins so that Visual Studio .NET can connect to them. We'll come back to this later when we look at the inheritance hierarchy of the Connect class. The Extensibility reference supplies the objects in this namespace, in Extensibility.dll. This DLL is not part of the .NET framework itself, but is instead part of Visual Studio .NET, as demonstrated by its location, at C:\Program Files\Microsoft Visual Studio .NET 2003\Common7\IDE\PublicAssemblies\Extensibility.dll.

As mentioned at the start of the chapter, add-ins are COM objects, and so we must import the System.Runtime.InteropServices namespace, since it contains classes and interfaces for .NET programs to interface with COM.

The EnvDTE namespace is perhaps the most interesting of these namespaces. It contains the Visual Studio .NET automation model classes and interfaces, which let us work directly with projects and code objects.

Inheritance of the Connect Class

Note that the Connect class inherits the IDTExtensibility2 and the IDTCommandTarget interfaces:

```
public class Connect : Object, Extensibility.IDTExtensibility2,
                       IDTCommandTarget
```

These interfaces specify the methods that our add-in must implement. The code provided by the wizard provides a skeleton implementation for each of these methods, and we'll examine these in detail in just a minute.

First, notice that the class has a big hairy GuidAttribute and ProgId attribute definition preceding it. These are necessary because the class will be accessed from Visual Studio .NET using COM, and these attributes define the COM class and program identifiers associated with our add-in. Luckily, we don't have to touch these attributes, we can just use the GuidAttribute and ProgId that the wizard provides and move on to the real work of implementing our add-in.

Methods of the Connect Class

The Connect class comes with eight methods. The first is Connect(), the constructor for the Connect class. The next five implement the IDTExtensibility2 interface, and are invoked by Visual Studio .NET at various points when the add-in is loaded and unloaded in the IDE:

- OnConnection(): Called by Visual Studio .NET on first connecting to the add-in.

- OnDisconnection(): Called by Visual Studio .NET on final disconnection.

- OnAddInsUpdate(): Called by Visual Studio .NET when the list of add-ins is changed.

- OnStartupComplete(): Called when Visual Studio .NET's startup is finished.

- OnBeginShutdown(): Called by Visual Studio .NET as its begins its exit processing.

The next two methods implement the IDTCommandTarget interface:

- QueryStatus(): Called when Visual Studio .NET checks to see whether an add-in is available. This is a good place to check conditions to see whether your add-in should be grayed-out (if, for example, the add-in requires a solution to be open).

- Exec(): Called by Visual Studio .NET when a user clicks on the add-in's menu or toolbar item. This is where the main work of the add-in is done.

If you look through the wizard-generated code, you'll notice that five of the eight methods generated by the wizard have empty bodies: Connect(), OnDisconnection(), OnAddInsUpdate(), OnStartupComplete(), and OnBeginShutdown(). These methods must be defined to satisfy the requirements of the IDTExtensibility2 interface, but they do not need to contain any code unless your add-in has its own actions that need to be performed when connecting, disconnecting, starting up, and shutting down. It's acceptable to leave them empty unless you need them.

Three of the methods generated by the wizard contain a fair amount of code: OnConnection(), Exec(), and QueryStatus(). These also happen to be the Connect methods most used by add-ins. We'll examine the code in these methods in detail shortly, but first let's modify the code so the add-in will output information to let us see how these methods are called from Visual Studio .NET.

Modifying the Add-in Code

The first thing we need to add to the wizard-generated code is a Using statement for the Diagnostics namespace, so we can use the objects it contains to write messages to track events and exceptions in our add-in, such as Debug.WriteLine(). I am a big fan of this method, especially when other programs are interacting with my code:

```
using System.Diagnostics;
```

Now we can use Debug.WriteLine() and its relatives without excessive typing.

The next modification that we want to make is to put in trace message calls to tell us when these methods are called. At the beginning of each of the eight methods in the Connect class, insert a Debug.WriteLine() call such as the ones shown here:

```
public Connect()
{
  Debug.WriteLine("DemoAddin: Connect() constructor called");
}

public void OnConnection(Object Application, . . . )
{
  Debug.WriteLine("DemoAddin: OnConnection() method called");
```

```
    applicationObject = (_DTE) application;
    .
    .
    .
}
```

Be sure to put this Debug.WriteLine() call at the very start of each method before any conditions are checked; we want to see where (and why) each method is called and in what order.

The messages from Debug.WriteLine() will show up in our debugger output window, which is handy for tracing the execution of programs that have no user interface or readable output as of yet. While we're at it, set a breakpoint (press F9) at each Debug.WriteLine() call as well; this will not change the flow of events and will let us see what happens at each step.

Tracing Add-In Methods in the Debugger

Now we're ready to try out our add-in. Debugging an add-in is a bit weird, because we need to start a new instance of Visual Studio .NET to provide a host in which to run the add-in. The add-in project is already set up to do this, and will automatically start a second "host" session of Visual Studio .NET. The original copy of Visual Studio .NET runs as a debugger for the second host instance, so debug output and any breakpoints you set will naturally occur there.

We'll try this out now. Make sure there's a breakpoint at each Debug.WriteLine() call and press F5 to build and start the add-in. If the add-in doesn't load as described, verify that you've used the exact same steps described, and see the following section on using the Add-In Manager to load the add-in.

The first thing that will happen is that you will hit the breakpoint for the Connect() constructor. This is where the add-in constructs anything it needs for initializing the Connect class. This will happen only for class variables you've added, since initialization for class variables generated by the VS.NET wizard is taken care of in OnConnection(), as we'll see in the next section.

Press F5 to continue, and you will now hit the OnConnection() breakpoint.

■**Note** If you get an error message about the class not being registered, build and start the debug session again. A code change is required for repeated debug sessions; in the OnConnection() method, change the line

```
if (connectMode == Extensibility.ext_ConnectMode.ext_cm_UISetup)
```

to read as follows:

```
if (connectMode == Extensibility.ext_ConnectMode.ext_cm_Startup)
```

The ext_ConnectMode value checked for in the wizard-generated code, ext_cm_UISetup, is a one-time-only value that occurs once the add-in is first installed on a user's computer. This code is discussed in more detail in the examination of the code in the OnConnection() method ahead in this chapter.

Press F5 two more times to take you up to the `OnStartupComplete()` breakpoint.

At this point, the second Visual Studio .NET instance hasn't appeared yet, and messages in the Output window indicate that Visual Studio .NET is loading another copy of itself along with various DLLs, including your add-in DLL:

```
'DefaultDomain': Loaded 'c:\windows\microsoft.net\framework\v1.1.x\mscorlib.dll',

No symbols loaded.'DefaultDomain': Loaded 'c:\pro visual studio .net

\chap11\DemoAddin\DemoAddin\bin\debug\DemoAddin.dll', Symbolsoaded.
'DefaultDomain': Loaded
'c:\windows\assembly\gac\extensibility\7.0.xxxx\extensibility.dll', ...
'DefaultDomain': Loaded 'c:\windows\assembly\gac\envdte\7.0.xxxx\envdte.dll',
No symbols loaded.
    . . .
DemoAddin: Connect() constructor called
'DefaultDomain': Loaded 'c:\windows\assembly\gac\office\7.0.xxx\office.dll'
DemoAddin: OnConnection() method called
DemoAddin: OnAddInsUpdate method called
'DefaultDomain': Loaded 'c:\program files\microsoft visual studio .net
 2003\common7\ide\microsoft.visualstudio.dll', No symbols loaded.
.
.
.
```

We don't see the message from `OnStartupComplete()` yet because our breakpoint precedes its execution. Press F5 again, and the second Visual Studio .NET session appears, blocking your view of the debugger. Go to the Tools menu in the second session, and you will hit the `QueryStatus()` breakpoint. Press F5 again, and we hit that darned `QueryStatus()` breakpoint again!

`QueryStatus()` gets called multiple times in order for Visual Studio .NET to compose the contents of the Tools menu, to make sure disabled add-ins are grayed out or do not appear. OK, that's enough! Disable this breakpoint by pressing F9, and then hit F5 again. Now we see our add-in on the Tools menu (Figure 11-10).

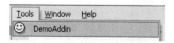

Figure 11-10. *Add-In menu added to Tools menu*

■Note If you don't see the DemoAddIn icon, it may be because of the issue with the `ext_cm_UISetup` test in the wizard-generated code mentioned previously; change the test in `OnConnection()` to `ext_cm_Startup` as recommended.

Who picked the smiley face icon? I didn't ask for that, did I? Actually, you did, since it is one of the parameters to the AddNamedCommand() method call in OnConnection(). But no problem, we'll show you how to change that.

Choose the DemoAddin choice from the menu, and we'll hit the breakpoint in Exec(). This is where the add-in's actual work is done. We need to add a call to our add-in's user interface or main function in Exec(), which we'll do in a moment. Press F5 again.

Now in the host or second Visual Studio .NET session, choose File ➤ Exit to see the shutdown sequence. Press F5 for all remaining breakpoints. You should see OnBeginShutdown() followed by OnDisconnection(), and then Visual Studio .NET exits.

The Output window in the first Visual Studio .NET session contains a record of all the calls to the various methods; we see many calls to QueryStatus(), one call to Exec() for each time we chose our add-in's menu item, and then on exit a call to OnBeginShutdown() (where you would place code to close any add-in windows still open, prompt for saving files before closing, and so on), followed by OnDisconnection() (where you would place code to dispose of or delete resources).

Using the Add-In Manager

If your add-in doesn't load or appear on the menu, select Add-In Manager from the Tools menu (Figure 11-11) to see whether it is listed.

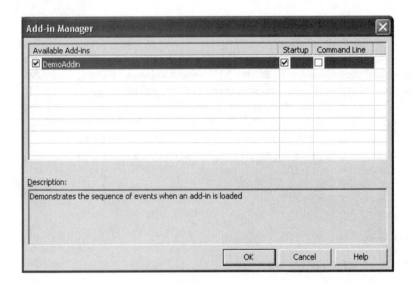

Figure 11-11. *Visual Studio .NET Add-In Manager*

This tool lists the available add-ins and lets you choose which are always loaded when Visual Studio .NET starts. When you create an add-in, and tell the wizard to load the add-in on startup, you are in effect pre-checking these boxes. If the boxes aren't checked, check both the box at the far left for DemoAddin and also its Startup item, and then exit Visual Studio .NET and try again. You don't need to check the command-line box, since we are not presently making a command-line add-in.

The Connect Class in More Detail

Now that we understand the flow of calls from Visual Studio .NET into our add-in, let's look in more detail at the code within the Connect class methods.

Executing Your Command with the Exec() Method

We saw that when we actually picked our add-in option from the menu, the Exec() method was called to execute it. Let's look at that method in the wizard-generated code. I've added a comment and another trace statement to show where we would execute the code for a functional add-in:

```
public void Exec(string commandName,
   EnvDTE.vsCommandExecOption executeOption,
   ref object varIn, ref object varOut, ref bool handled)
{
   Debug.WriteLine("DemoAddin: Exec method called");

   handled = false;
   if(executeOption ==
                   EnvDTE.vsCommandExecOption.vsCommandExecOptionDoDefault)
   {
     if(commandName == "DemoAddin.Connect.DemoAddin")
     {
       handled = true;

       // insert main entry point for executing add-in here
       Debug.WriteLine("DemoAddin Command was executed by user!");

       return;
     }
   }
}
```

The handled variable, passed in by Visual Studio .NET, is set to True to indicate that the add-in action we chose was executed correctly.

The default command action (vsCommandExecOption.vsCommandExecOptionDoDefault) is all that is needed by most add-ins. The other options in the vsCommandExecOption enumeration, such as vsCommandExecOptionShowDefault, seem to imply that Visual Studio .NET could indicate alternative actions to the add-in, but I haven't found a way to get anything other than the default.

Using QueryStatus() to Indicate Add-In Availability

We saw the QueryStatus() method being called repeatedly from Visual Studio .NET. As I mentioned, this method can be used to indicate the status of your add-in to Visual Studio .NET. Let's look at the default code for QueryStatus():

```
public void QueryStatus(string commandName, EnvDTE.vsCommandStatusTextWanted
                  neededText, ref EnvDTE.vsCommandStatus status,
                  ref object commandText)
```

```
{
    Debug.WriteLine("DemoAddin: QueryStatus method called");

    if(neededText ==
        EnvDTE.vsCommandStatusTextWanted.vsCommandStatusTextWantedNone)
    {
        if(commandName == "DemoAddin.Connect.DemoAddin")
        {
            status = (vsCommandStatus)vsCommandStatus.vsCommandStatusSupported
                                | vsCommandStatus.vsCommandStatusEnabled;
        }
    }
}
```

The method sets the status variable, passed in by Visual Studio .NET, to a combination of vsCommandStatus flags to indicate the add-in's status. We see that by default the add-in is both supported and enabled.

We can insert code in this method to enable the add-in only if certain conditions are true. For instance, if the add-in examines classes or code, a solution must be open, or else there is nothing for the add-in to work on. We could code this like so:

```
if(commandName == "DemoAddin.Connect.DemoAddin")
{
    // Don't enable menu choice if no solution open
    if (applicationObject.Solution.IsOpen)
    {
        status = (vsCommandStatus)vsCommandStatus.vsCommandStatusSupported
                            | vsCommandStatus.vsCommandStatusEnabled;
    }
    else
    {
        status = (vsCommandStatus)vsCommandStatus.vsCommandStatusSupported;
    }
}
```

If no solution is loaded, the command appears on the menu (vsCommandStatusSupported) but is grayed out (not vsCommandStatusEnabled). Code like this is used in the CodeModelWalker sample, later in the chapter, which requires a solution to be loaded.

Note that if status is set to vsCommandStatusUnsupported, the command does not appear on the menu at all.

You may now be wondering how to get the solution information in the first place, and what the applicationObject variable that we use here is. We'll look at these matters next.

Connect Class Variables

As generated, the Connect class contains two private class variables that give your add-in a pair of objects it can use to call back into Visual Studio .NET to get data or perform an action. These are private _DTE applicationObject and private AddIn addInInstance.

The applicationObject variable is perhaps the most important variable supplied by the wizard-generated code. This is the root object used in all calls to the various methods in the EnvDTE namespace, providing access to a project's files, code, status, outputs, and so on. We'll examine its usage in some detail a bit later in this chapter.

The addInInstance object gives access to system information about the add-in. For example, we can get the COM ProgID for the add-in from one of the properties of this variable, which we'll demonstrate in one of the upcoming examples. It typically isn't used as much as the applicationObject, but it is handy when you need to reference the instance of your add-in loaded by Visual Studio .NET.

■Note If you're wondering what I'm talking about because you don't see these variables in the Connect class, look at the very end of the code created by the wizard. We're used to seeing class variables at the start of a class, but probably because these are private variables, the wizard puts their declarations at the end of the class.

The OnConnection() Method

Now let's take a look at the OnConnection() method. This is one of the first methods called when the add-in is initialized, and its first job is to set the applicationObject and addInInstance variables we just mentioned in the previous section. Visual Studio .NET passes the values for these variables to the add-in via the application and addInInst parameters to OnConnection():

```
public void OnConnection(object application, Extensibility.ext_ConnectMode
                    connectMode, object addInInst, ref System.Array custom)
{
  applicationObject = (_DTE)application;
  addInInstance = (AddIn)addInInst;
```

The next section of code sets up a menu choice for our add-in in the Visual Studio .NET Tools menu. First it checks to see how Visual Studio .NET is connecting to the add-in by testing the connectMode parameter:

```
  if (connectMode == Extensibility.ext_ConnectMode.ext_cm_UISetup)
```

You'll recall the earlier note about the use of ext_cm_UISetup causing problems when you debug an add-in, since it assumes that the code to set up the menu is fully debugged and finalized, and that the add-in menu is never removed once it is added. You may have made the suggested change to use ext_cm_Startup instead:

```
  if (connectMode == Extensibility.ext_ConnectMode.ext_cm_Startup)
```

The help for ext_ConnectMode tells us that it is an enumeration that has several possible values, including ext_cm_Startup, ext_cm_AfterStartup, and so on. Each of these refers to a different time that Visual Studio .NET may load the add-in after startup.

When I see one of these unfamiliar enumeration values from the Extensibility or EnvDTE namespaces for the first time, I usually explore it a bit by using the IntelliSense feature. For example, position the cursor immediately following ext_ConnectMode in the previous line of code and type a period (full stop) to see the possible values pop up. Then delete the extra period to restore the code to its original state.

Another alternative is to remove the connectMode check altogether, and always reset the IDE on connection. We'll look at this approach in the Icon Explorer sample coming up soon.

Let's look at the complicated code inside the if block that sets up the choice in the Tools menu. I've reformatted it in a probably vain attempt to make it more readable:

```
{
            object []contextGUIDS = new object[] { };
            Commands commands = applicationObject.Commands;
            _CommandBars commandBars = applicationObject.CommandBars;

            // long comment about setup here.
            try
            {
              Command command = commands.AddNamedCommand(addInInstance,
                                "DemoAddin", "DemoAddin",
                                "Executes the command for DemoAddin",
                                true, 59, // <- icon number
                                ref contextGUIDS,
                                (int)vsCommandStatus.vsCommandStatusSupported+
                                (int)vsCommandStatus.vsCommandStatusEnabled);

              CommandBar commandBar = (CommandBar)commandBars["Tools"];
              CommandBarControl commandBarControl = command.AddControl(
                                                    commandBar, 1);
            }
```

The command and commandBar objects are instances of EnvDTE.Command and EnvDTE.CommandBar, respectively. These objects provide access to the menu and command bar system inside Visual Studio .NET. The third and fourth arguments to AddNamedCommand set the command name and tooltip that the user sees, while the second argument is an internal name. Note also where the Tools menu in the commandBars collection is specified; you can change this to another top-level menu by specifying a different location to insert the command (["Edit"], for example).

Here we can see where the names of the menu choices are set and also the smiley icon that we saw in Figure 11-10; the icon number is the ID of a bitmap in the Office DLL. We'll show you how to experiment with this in the Icon Explorer sample coming up in just a bit.

Modifying the Connect() Exception Handler

Let's look at the catch block following the menu insertion code:

```
catch(System.Exception /*e*/)
{
}
```

I really don't like that empty exception handler; you can hit an exception while debugging and never have any idea what's happening. It is there to handle the case in which the command already exists in the menu, which generates a System.ArgumentException from the underlying COM routine.

Unfortunately, this handler will mask other types of exceptions, and moreover, the same ArgumentException can be generated by other conditions that you should deal with.

I recommend putting something in that exception handler, at the very least a debug message so you can see when you've hit an unexpected exception while developing:

```
catch(System.Exception e)
{
    Debug.WriteLine("Exception in DemoAddin.OnConnection():" + e.Message);
}
```

This can prevent a great deal of frustration.

The Icon Explorer Add-In

The Icon Explorer add-in aims to show how to force the AddNamedCommand() method to reload the menu item every time it is invoked. It also changes its icon each time its menu choice is made, cycling through all the four-hundred-plus icons in the Office DLL (if you're patient enough to click that many times). This is handy if you're fickle, as I am, and decide to change the icon for the add-in several times or even load the add-in menu choice into a different menu each time.

■**Tip** For a commercial add-in, you may want to make a custom icon. For help in doing this, search for "Custom Bitmap Add-In" on the MSDN Automation Samples page at http://msdn.microsoft.com/vstudio/downloads/samples/automation.asp

---

While you can get Icon Explorer by downloading the sample code for this book and looking in the directory for this chapter, it is easy enough to create it with the Add-In Wizard. Create an add-in project named IconExplorerAddIn using the same choices in the wizard as shown in the earlier sample.

The Connect Class

Open the Connect.cs file, and add a class variable to hold the icon number at the end of the class, where applicationObject and addInInstance are declared as shown here:

```
private _DTE applicationObject;
private AddIn addInInstance;
private int iconNumber;        // private member variable added so that
                               // we can increment it between calls to Exec()
```

Next, modify the `Connect()` constructor:

```
public Connect()
{
  iconNumber = 2;  // Start at 2 because one, zero, or negative do not work
                   // (throw exceptions or give blank menu)
}
```

Now, change the `OnConnection()` method like this:

```
public void OnConnection(object application, Extensibility.ext_ConnectMode
                   connectMode, object addInInst, ref System.Array custom)
{
    applicationObject = (_DTE)application;
    addInInstance = (AddIn)addInInst;

    try {
      AddCommand.ReplaceCommandInMenu(addInInstance, applicationObject,
              iconNumber, "IconExplorerAddIn.Connect",
              "IconExplorerAddIn",
              "Icon Explorer: this is #" + iconNumber.ToString(),
              "Icon will change to Icon #" + Convert.ToString(iconNumber+1)
              + "next time you click this command",
              "Tools");
    }
    catch(System.Exception e)
    {
      Debug.WriteLine("Exception in OnConnection: " + e.Message);
    }
}
```

The `AddCommand` class containing the ReplaceCommandInMenu() method is a new class that we will add to the project. It wraps the Microsoft `AddNamedCommand()` method with some support routines that you can use in both these examples and your own add-ins.

In Icon Explorer, the `Exec()` method will contain the same call to ReplaceCommandInMenu() as well, since we want to replace the menu item each time it is invoked with a new command using a different icon. `Exec()` is shown in the following code; as usual, change the code in boldface:

```
public void Exec(string commandName, EnvDTE.vsCommandExecOption
                   executeOption, ref object varIn, ref object varOut,
                   ref bool handled)
{
    handled = false;
    if(executeOption ==
                    EnvDTE.vsCommandExecOption.vsCommandExecOptionDoDefault)
    {
      if(commandName == "IconExplorerAddIn.Connect.IconExplorerAddIn")
```

```
    {
      handled = true;
      try
      {
        iconNumber++; // increment icon number and replace it
        AddCommand.ReplaceCommandInMenu(addInInstance, applicationObject,
                                        iconNumber,
                                        "IconExplorerAddIn.Connect",
                                        "IconExplorerAddIn",
                              "Icon Explorer: icon #" + iconNumber.ToString(),
                    "Icon will change to icon #" + Convert.ToString(iconNumber+1)
                    + " next time you click this command.",
                    "Tools");
      }
      catch(System.Exception e)
      {
        Debug.WriteLine("Exception in Exec(): " + e.Message);
      }

      return;
    }
  }
}
```

The AddCommand Class

Now we can add the AddCommand class. Add a new class to the project called AddCommand.cs, and add the following two static methods to the generated code. First, add the ReplaceCommandInMenu method that we have already seen in use:

```
public static EnvDTE.Command ReplaceCommandInMenu(
  EnvDTE.AddIn addInInstance,
  EnvDTE._DTE applicationObject,
  int iconNumber,
  string progID,
  string commandName,
  string commandButtonText,
  string commandDescription,
  string commandBarName)
```

The method is static, so it doesn't require a class instance before it can be called. Here is the body, which looks a lot like the wizard-generated OnConnection() code you've seen a couple of times already:

```
{
  object []contextGUIDS = new object[] { };
  Commands commands = applicationObject.Commands;
```

```
_CommandBars commandBars = applicationObject.CommandBars;
try
{
 Command command = FindCommand(commands, progID + "." + commandName);
 if (command != null)  // if we found one
 {
  command.Delete(); // delete it, since we're going to replace it
 }
 // call commands.AddNamedCommand to add it
 command = commands.AddNamedCommand(
  addInInstance, commandName, commandButtonText,
  commandDescription, true, iconNumber, ref contextGUIDS,
  (int)vsCommandStatus.vsCommandStatusSupported+
  (int)vsCommandStatus.vsCommandStatusEnabled);

 CommandBar commandBar = (CommandBar)commandBars[commandBarName];
 CommandBarControl commandBarControl = command.AddControl(commandBar, 1);

 return command;
}
catch(System.Exception e)
{
 MessageBox.Show("Exception in ReplaceCommandInMenu: " + e.Message);
 return null;
}
}
```

The basic idea is that FindCommand() looks up the command in the commands collection. If found, the command is deleted with command.Delete(). This Delete() method must be used on a command instance, since there is no method to delete commands on the container. Then we call AddNamedCommand() to add the new command, just as in OnConnection().

The change made from the default code generated by the wizard code is the forced lookup and deletion of the command before it is added again. The code for FindCommand() is shown here:

```
public static EnvDTE.Command FindCommand(EnvDTE.Commands commands,
                                         string commandName)
{
 // first find this command if it exists, then delete it
 System.Collections.IEnumerator enm = commands.GetEnumerator();
 while(enm.MoveNext())
 {
  Command cmd = (Command) enm.Current;
  if (cmd.Name == commandName)
  {
   return cmd;
```

```
    }
  }
  return null;   // command not found
}
```

We get an enumerator from the `commands` collection, and then look for the command name. This is crude but effective: The `Index()` method on the commands collection looks more efficient, but it is not easy to use, and it throws an exception if the requested item is not found. The above method works consistently, but it should be used judiciously, because it is expensive, since it iterates through all the commands. However, for our purposes here it does the job well enough.

Build and run the solution now. Under the Tools menu in the host Visual Studio .NET session that opens, you will see the first icon (Figure 11-12) (For some reason, Visual Studio .NET assigns this ID #2; there is no #1).

Figure 11-12. *Icon #2 on Tools menu for Icon Explorer*

Click to choose the add-in, and now go back to the Tools menu to verify that the icon and menu text have changed (Figure 11-13).

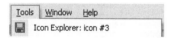

Figure 11-13. *Icon #3 on Tools menu for Icon Explorer*

Repeat as many times as you want. The icon number shown in the menu is the valid ID that you can pass to `AddNamedCommand()` if you wish to use a particular icon in another add-in.

Exploring the EnvDTE Automation Model

We've been putting a lot of work into exploring the surface features of an add-in, but we really haven't gotten into the guts of what a Visual Studio .NET add-in does, and how it lets us work with solutions, projects, and code. We'll now build an add-in that works with the `DTE` object to analyze some project code and do something useful with it.

The CodeModel Walker Pattern

A fairly common situation that add-ins are written for involves walking through all the classes in a project, doing something with the class variables, properties, methods, parameters, or whatever. To determine the structure of a project loaded in Visual Studio .NET, we use the DTE's CodeModel classes.

The Shapes Class

We'll need a set of classes to show off our CodeModel Walker. We'll knock together a quick set of classes to represent various geometric shapes. There will be a parent Shapes class that contains attributes common to all two-dimensional shapes, such as *x* and *y* coordinates. Classes for specific shapes such as circle, triangle, and square will inherit from this parent class, adding their own specific attributes, such as radius for the Circle class and base and height for the Triangle class. The Shape class will have an abstract Area() method, which each subclass must implement.

These sets of classes are pretty straightforward, and there shouldn't be any need to go into detail through the source code here (look in the download if you need to). The screenshot in Figure 11-14 shows the Shapes project loaded into Visual Studio .NET.

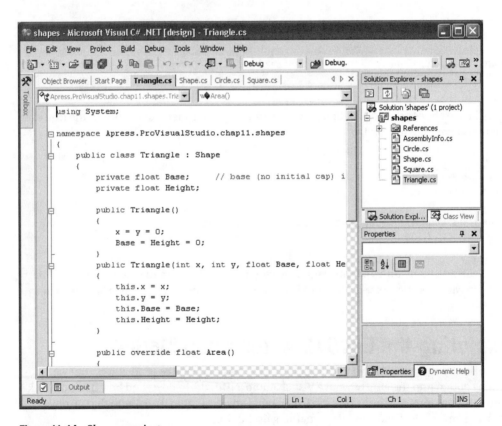

Figure 11-14. *Shapes project*

The CodeModelWalker

To create the add-in, use the Add-In Wizard to create an add-in called CodeModelWalker, with similar parameters to those used for the previous add-in example. I like icon #172 for this one, which shows a magnifying glass examining a document that could be code.

Add a class to this project, and call it CodeModelWalker.cs. We'll call a method in this CodeModelWalker class from the Exec() method of the Connect class. We'll call this method WalkDTE(), since it starts with the top-level DTE object and walks its way down through the Solution, Project, CodeModel, and CodeClass hierarchy:

```
public void Exec(string commandName, EnvDTE.vsCommandExecOption
                executeOption, ref object varIn, ref object varOut,
                ref bool handled)
{
  handled = false;
  if(executeOption ==
     EnvDTE.vsCommandExecOption.vsCommandExecOptionDoDefault)
  {
   if(commandName == "CodeModelWalker.Connect.CodeModelWalker")
   {
    handled = true;
    CodeModelWalker.WalkDTE(applicationObject);
    return;
   }
  }
}
  private _DTE applicationObject;
```

We pass the _DTE object to WalkDTE() (it's called applicationObject), which is in CodeModelWalker.cs. We'll look at this in some detail in a bit, but there is a lot of code, and rather than typing it all in, it's better if you use the downloaded sample code, and we'll discuss what's going on once we've built and run it.

Running CodeModelWalker

Open the CodeModelWalker project, and press F5. When the host Visual Studio .NET instance opens, you will see CodeModelWalker grayed in the Tools menu (see Figure 11-15). This is because our code in QueryStatus() has detected that there is no open solution and therefore has not enabled the menu item.

Figure 11-15. *CodeModelWalker grayed out*

Open a solution with some kind of class hierarchy, such as the Shapes class library, also included in the code download. You'll see that the menu choice is now enabled, as shown in Figure 11-16, because QueryStatus() has detected the open solution.

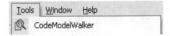

Figure 11-16. *CodeModelWalker enabled*

Click on the CodeModelWalker option now, and watch the output appear in the Output window of the first (debugging) Visual Studio .NET session (yes, there I go using Debug.WriteLine() again!) . We'll look at a more sophisticated implementation of this add-in that actually performs a task after we see how this works.

The relevant output begins immediately after the call to Exec(), which executes when we choose CodeModelWalker from the menu:

```
.
.
.
CodeModelWalker: Connect.QueryStatus() called.
CodeModelWalker: Connect.Exec() called.
DTE applicationObject: Microsoft Development Environment
Solution - FullName:C:\pro visual studio .net\chap11\shapes\shapes.sln
.
.
.
******Project Name:shapes**********
----- project item:AssemblyInfo.cs ------------
walking FileCodeModel...
no code elements in this FileCodeModel
----- project item:Circle.cs ------------
walking FileCodeModel...
namespace:shapes
...class:Circle
...inherits from:Shape
......variable: radius type: float
......function: Circle() returns: void
......kind: vsCMFunctionConstructor
.
.
.
```

As you can see, we are recursively navigating our way through the class structure in each file, examining the contained methods, parameters, and so on. We look at the code model in each file, and then, at the end, display the code model for the entire project as a unified whole, showing all contained namespaces:

```
======== Walking Project.CodeModel for: shapes =========
==== code model language is: {B5E9BD34-6D3E-4B5D-925E-8A43B79820B4} =======
namespace:Apress
...namespace:ProVisualStudio
......namespace:chap11
.........namespace:shapes
............class:Circle
...........inherits from:Shape
...............variable: radius type: float
...............function: Circle() returns: void
...............kind: vsCMFunctionConstructor
.
.
.
```

What is the hexadecimal gobbledygook shown as the code model language output? Some of the properties in the EnvDTE namespace are not what they appear. The CodeModel.Language property is of type String, which you might think contains human-readable content. However, it contains a GUID corresponding to the vsCMLanguageCSharp enumeration value (see the "CodeModelLanguageConstants Enum" topic in the Visual Studio .NET online help if you want to see where I found this). If we wanted to use this property, we would have to enhance our code to check for this explicitly, with code such as the following:

```
If (CodeModel.Language==vsCMLanguageCSharp)
```

If this condition evaluated to true, we could display a readable string such as C#.

Now that we've seen the CodeModelWalker run, let's take a look at the code itself.

Methods in CodeModelWalker.cs

Let's start with the WalkDTE() method in CodeModelWalker.cs , which as you'll recall was invoked by the Exec() method of the Connect class. Note the use of the EnvDTE and System.Diagnostics namespaces at the top of the file:

```
using System;
using System.Diagnostics;
using EnvDTE;
  .
  .
  .

  public static void WalkDTE(EnvDTE._DTE applicationObject)
  {
   do_DTE(applicationObject);
   WalkSolution(applicationObject.Solution);
  }
```

The parameter passed to WalkDTE() is an EnvDTE object – here it is the applicationObject itself – which we first pass to a do... method. After this, we call a Walk... method on one of the parameter's properties, which is a different EnvDTE class. We will see this pattern repeated throughout our CodeModel Walker, for example in the next method, WalkSolution():

```
public static void WalkSolution(EnvDTE.Solution solution)
{
 doSolution(solution);
 WalkProjects(solution.Projects);
}
```

These are implemented as static methods to make the code simpler and avoid allocating instance objects that we don't need. This method goes down to the next level, which is the project. These do... methods are found at the bottom of the CodeModelWalker class in a separate program block of their own:

```
//----------------------- "do" methods separate from "walk" methods here
public static void do_DTE(EnvDTE._DTE applicationObject)
{
 Debug.WriteLine("DTE applicationObject: {0} ", applicationObject.Name);
}
public static void doSolution(EnvDTE.Solution solution)
{
 Debug.WriteLine("Solution - FullName: {0}", solution.FullName);
}
```

We call the methods doXYZ because they are intended to be generic templates; you can modify them to do anything you want done to the code in a project. OK, there I go with umpteen Debug.WriteLine() calls again; I did warn you! A single pattern is repeated in all these methods: Walk through the EnvDTE class properties to get to an object of interest, then call a do... method to perform some action on it (in this case, to display some information with Debug.WriteLine()). For almost every object, the sample code displays the Name property. Most objects in the EnvDTE classes have a Name property, including the top-level DTE object itself, which is called the Microsoft Development Environment, as we shall see when we run the code.

■**Note** I am not showing you all of the "do" methods, since they are quite repetitive; please download the sample code to see these details.

This process can be repeated through all the levels of the DTE hierarchy to get to whatever object your add-in needs to read or manipulate. You can substitute your own actions in the do... methods, though I suggest leaving some Debug.WriteLine() calls in, since they help to indicate what is going on.

Note This example demonstrates only a small subset of the methods and properties available in the DTE namespace. Explore MSDN or use IntelliSense in Visual Studio .NET to see what else you can do beyond what is shown here! Also see the examples in the preceding and following chapters of this book.

Collections in the EnvDTE Properties

Many of the DTE properties are collections, which we can examine with a ForEach loop as in WalkProjects():

```
public static void WalkProjects(EnvDTE.Projects projects)
{
 foreach (EnvDTE.Project proj in projects)
 {
  doProject(proj);
  foreach (EnvDTE.ProjectItem projItem in proj.ProjectItems)
  {
   doProjectItem(projItem);
   WalkFileCodeModel(projItem.FileCodeModel, "");
  }
  WalkCodeModel(proj.CodeModel, "");
 }
}
```

The WalkProjects() method has a doubly nested ForEach loop to run through the projects and project items. I could have put in a WalkProjectItems() method to keep the code neater, but using this method allows me to point out both CodeModel objects in the project easily in the last couple of lines of the method. These are the FileCodeModel and project CodeModel objects.

EnvDTE CodeModel Objects

CodeModel contains a hierarchy of all the namespaces, classes, interfaces, inheritance, constructors, methods, functions, parameters, return types, and almost every other construct in the code.

Note that there are two CodeModel objects: the FileCodeModel object, which has the CodeModel for the code in a single file (project item); and the project CodeModel, which contains the unified code model for all the code in the project in a single hierarchy. There are separate classes to walk through the hierarchy of these CodeModel objects:

```
public static void WalkFileCodeModel(EnvDTE.FileCodeModel fileCodeModel,
                                     string indent)
{
 doFileCodeModel(fileCodeModel);
 WalkCodeElements(fileCodeModel.CodeElements, indent);
}
public static void WalkCodeModel(EnvDTE.CodeModel codeModel,
                                 string indent)
```

```
  {
   doCodeModel(codeModel);
   WalkCodeElements(codeModel.CodeElements, indent);
  }
```

The difference between these two objects is mainly their Parent property, which in the FileCodeModel case is a project item, while for the CodeModel object its parent is the project itself. Both kinds of CodeModel objects have a CodeElements collection, which we navigate using the same WalkCodeElements() method in both cases:

```
public static void WalkCodeElements(EnvDTE.CodeElements codeElements,
                                     string indent)
{
  foreach (EnvDTE.CodeElement codeElem in codeElements)
  {
   if (codeElem.Kind == EnvDTE.vsCMElement.vsCMElementNamespace)
   {
    // walking System/Microsoft namespaces generates too much output
    if (codeElem.Name != "System")
     if (codeElem.Name != "Microsoft")
      WalkNamespace((EnvDTE.CodeNamespace) codeElem, indent);
   }
   else
   {
    doCodeElement(codeElem, indent);
   }
  }
}
```

Here we see some interesting things beginning to happen. Many EnvDTE objects have a Kind property, which is nice (ahem). It contains an enumeration defined in the EnvDTE namespace to identify different kinds of objects, in this case vsCMElementNamespace. Here we check for a namespace object as the top-level code construct with which to begin our walk through the code model.

We do not walk through any of the System or Microsoft namespaces; these are present in all .NET projects' CodeModel instances, but are outside the scope of what we want to examine. (Normally, at least, although for fun you can try removing the check for the System namespace and walking through it; make sure to reserve a few hours to read through the output from this exercise!)

You will need a check like this in an actual add-in that uses the project CodeModel to avoid wasting time walking through the system classes.

The CodeNamespace.InfoLocation property can tell you whether a namespace is external to the project, but unfortunately, it classifies nested namespaces like the Apress.chap11 namespace we use in these examples as external, so it is not foolproof. This is a reason to use the FileCodeModel, since it contains only the code inside its parent project item.

WalkNamespaces Method

Let's look at the WalkNamespaces() method next:

```
public static void WalkNamespace(EnvDTE.CodeNamespace cns, string indent)
{
 doNamespace(cns, indent);

 foreach (EnvDTE.CodeElement codeElem in cns.Members)
 {
  switch (codeElem.Kind)
  {
   case EnvDTE.vsCMElement.vsCMElementNamespace:
    WalkNamespace((CodeNamespace) codeElem, indent+"...");
    break;
   case EnvDTE.vsCMElement.vsCMElementClass:
    WalkClass((CodeClass) codeElem, indent+"...");
    break;
   case EnvDTE.vsCMElement.vsCMElementInterface:
    WalkInterface((CodeInterface) codeElem, indent+"...");
    break;
   default:
    doCodeElement(codeElem, indent);
    break;
  }
 }
}
```

Again we use the vsCMElement enumeration to distinguish between the kinds of objects we are encountering. Since a namespace can be contained inside another namespace, we need a recursive call back to WalkNamespace() to handle these nested namespaces.

WalkClass and WalkInterface Methods

Here, as you might expect, we need to look at a wider variety of property collections, including inheritance, properties, class variables, and methods. The name of the property collection of interest in each of these methods varies—Bases for inheritance, Members for properties, variables, and methods—so you need a specific method for each type of EnvDTE class you are processing. Unfortunately, the generic Children property throws a "not implemented" exception; apparently, it applies to Visual C++ only:

```
public static void WalkClass(EnvDTE.CodeClass cls, string indent)
{
 doClass(cls, indent);
 foreach (EnvDTE.CodeElement codeElem in cls.Bases)
 {
  doInheritsFrom(codeElem, indent);
 }
 foreach (EnvDTE.CodeElement codeElem in cls.Members)
```

```
  {
   switch (codeElem.Kind)
   {
    case EnvDTE.vsCMElement.vsCMElementVariable:
     doCodeVariable((CodeVariable) codeElem, indent);
     break;
    case EnvDTE.vsCMElement.vsCMElementProperty:
     doCodeProperty((CodeProperty) codeElem, indent);
     break;
    case EnvDTE.vsCMElement.vsCMElementFunction:
     WalkFunction((CodeFunction) codeElem, indent+"...");
     break;
    default:
     doCodeElement(codeElem, indent);
     break;
   }
  }
 }
```

The WalkInterface() method is exactly the same as WalkClass(), except that it does not need a class variables case, and of course its input parameter type is an interface, not a class. Passing an object and casting it to CodeClass or CodeInterface would probably work, but you need to be careful with this. For instance, casting FileCodeModel to CodeModel causes an exception!

```
public static void WalkInterface(EnvDTE.CodeInterface ifac, string indent)
{
 doInterface(ifac, indent);
 foreach (EnvDTE.CodeElement codeElem in ifac.Bases)
 {
  doInheritsFrom(codeElem, indent);
 }
 foreach (EnvDTE.CodeElement codeElem in ifac.Members)
 {
  switch (codeElem.Kind)
  {
   // no EnvDTE.vsCMElement.vsCMElementVariable case for interface
   case EnvDTE.vsCMElement.vsCMElementProperty:
    doCodeProperty((CodeProperty) codeElem, indent);
    break;
   case EnvDTE.vsCMElement.vsCMElementFunction:
    WalkFunction((CodeFunction) codeElem, indent+"...");
    break;
   default:
    doCodeElement(codeElem, indent);
    break;
  }
 }
}
```

The WalkFunction() Method

Finally we get to the bottom of the tree, at least as far as we are going in this example. The
WalkFunction() class does not do any further navigation, so it contains only a couple of do...
methods to print out the function information:

```
public static void WalkFunction(EnvDTE.CodeFunction func, string indent)
{
  doFunction(func, indent);
  doParameters(func, indent);
}
```

CodeWalker do... Methods

As I said at the start, I am omitting many of the do... methods in the book text to avoid repeti-
tion. There are a couple of interesting examples that I'd like to look at here, however. The
doFileCodeModel() method checks that the Count property of its collection parameter is posi-
tive, because we want to see an explicit message if a file has no code. This might often be an error,
but it is true of the AssemblyInfo.cs file in all projects that define assembly-level attributes only:

```
public static void doFileCodeModel(EnvDTE.FileCodeModel fileCodeModel)
{
  Debug.WriteLine("walking FileCodeModel...");
  if (fileCodeModel.CodeElements.Count <= 0)
  {
   Debug.WriteLine("no code elements in this FileCodeModel");
  }
}
```

The doParameters() method called by WalkFunction() performs a similar explicit check.

Modifying Code and Text with the Automation Model

While I've used these methods only to print out information in this example, you can also modify
a project's code or text using the classes I've shown so far to navigate to the point of interest, and
then perform an operation on the code. Here is an alternative implementation of doFunction()
that will insert a skeleton XML comment above the function containing the actual parameter
names and other info, instead of the xyz name you see when the IDE inserts a skeleton XML
function comment:

```
public static void doFunction(EnvDTE.CodeFunction func, string indent)
{
    doCreateXMLDocumentForFunction(func);
}
```

I probably could use some of the XML support built-into .NET to create the XML text, but
it is simple enough to do manually. The first part of the method constructs the comment using
the EnvDTE class objects to determine what to put in each section:

```
public static void doCreateXMLDocumentForFunction(EnvDTE.CodeFunction
                                                    func)
 {
```

```
// use of StringBuilder here would improve performance/memory use, but for
// readability we are using string operations.
    string xmlComments = "";

    xmlComments += "\t\t/// <summary> " + func.Name+ "()";
```

So we have now added the method name. Next we say whether it is a constructor:

```
switch (func.FunctionKind)
{
 case vsCMFunction.vsCMFunctionConstructor:
  xmlComments += " constructor"; break;
 case vsCMFunction.vsCMFunctionDestructor:
  xmlComments += " destructor"; break;
 default: break;
}
```

Now we put in an explicit note in the summary description if there are no parameters:

```
if (func.Parameters.Count <= 0)
{
 xmlComments += ". No parameters";
}
xmlComments += ". </summary> \n";
```

Then we loop through the EnvDTE.CodeFunction.Parameters collection to create a note for each parameter:

```
foreach (CodeParameter param in func.Parameters)
{
 xmlComments +=
  "\t\t/// <param name=\""+ param.Name + "\"> type: " +
  param.Type.AsString + "</param> \n";
}
```

Finally, we add the <returns> tag for the return type, and display the complete comment in the debugger so we can make sure we're constructing it correctly:

```
. . .
xmlComments += "\t\t/// <returns> " + func.Type.AsString
               + "</returns>\n";
Debug.WriteLine(xmlComments);
```

The EnvDTE TextPoint and EditPoint Functions

To place this comment in the code, we use the DTE Comment property for the function; however, we cannot simply assign to this property. This is documented as not working for Visual Basic.NET, and it doesn't seem to work for C# either, at least not in the general extensibility model. Instead, we can get an EditPoint object to actually edit the code.

First, we check to see whether a DocComment already exists: We don't want to overwrite one that someone has already entered by hand. Next, we get a TextPoint object that is located at the start of our function, using the GetStartPoint() method:

```
if (func.DocComment.Length <= 1)
{
// this does not work: func.DocComment = xmlComments;
// editing does work, however
Debug.WriteLine("writing XML comments to source file...");
EnvDTE.TextPoint tp =
    func.GetStartPoint(EnvDTE.vsCMPart.vsCMPartWholeWithAttributes);
```

From a TextPoint object, we can get an EditPoint object with CreateEditPoint():

```
EnvDTE.EditPoint ep = tp.CreateEditPoint();
```

EditPoint exposes methods to move around in the document, moving up and down lines, and so on. The start point of the function is located at the first non-white-space character in its declaration. We move to the start of the line in case the function is indented:

```
ep.StartOfLine();
```

Now we simply call the Insert() method to insert our comment string into the document:

```
ep.Insert(xmlComments);
```

That's all there is to it! To try this out, simply remove the comment in front of doCreateXMLDocumentForFunction() in CodeModelWalker.cs in the sample code and try adding XML comments to a copy of the Shapes class library or other code that you may have.

Language-Specific Features of EnvDTE

So far, we've described the general extensibility model that is not language-specific. However, several .NET languages have special objects in the EnvDTE namespace that have capabilities specific to that language.

Visual C# and Visual Basic .NET

Visual Basic .NET and C# both have additional properties accessible via the VSProject object, described in full in the Visual Studio .NET online help in "Developing with Visual Studio .NET," under the topic *Introduction to the VSProject Object.*

Visual C++

The language-specific features for Visual C++ are the only significant changes to Visual Studio .NET 2003's automation model from the previous version. These changes bring Visual C++ language support more in line with Visual Basic .NET and Visual C#. For example, when files are added to Visual C++ projects through DTE, the hierarchical structure created now matches that of the other .NET languages. Other enhancements take the model for Visual C++ beyond what is available for other languages. For example, five new property pages have been added for Visual C++ projects:

- Managed Resources

- XML Data Generator Tool

- Managed Wrapper

- Auxiliary Managed Wrapper

- Primary Interop

The automation model support for these new property pages is contained in the `Microsoft.VisualStudio.VCProjectEngine` (VCProjectEngineLibrary) namespace, within the `VCProjectEngine.dll` file, and includes the new classes `VCManagedResourceCompilerTool`, `VCXMLDataGeneratorTool`, `VCManagedWrapperGeneratorTool`, `VCPrimaryInteropTool`, and about half a dozen others. See the *Objects* topic under *Visual C++ Project Model* in the Visual C++ Extensibility Reference on MSDN for detailed information on these classes.

Now let's look at a general-purpose add-in with a user interface that uses another set of `EnvDTE` objects for editing text.

A Multiline Find & Replace Add-In

Here is a small but useful add-in. The Find and Replace function built into the Visual Studio .NET editor is very useful for making massive, repetitive changes to a project, except in one respect. It cannot handle multiple-line find and replace strings, since the dialog limits you to entering one line of text.

For certain changes to projects, such as changing the style of `try...catch` blocks or changing the comments and attributes of multiple methods throughout a project, multiline find and replace is a very handy capability.

When I started to implement this example, I was afraid I would have to write a lot of tedious code to search through lines of text in each document. The DTE has a `Documents` collection that lets us get an `EditPoint` object on a document and then access the text lines directly.

The DTE also has a `Find` object with a `FindReplace()` method that performs a find/replace operation without our having to implement all the dirty details of opening document files, searching for matching lines, and replacing them. The signature for this method is as follows:

```
public vsFindResult FindReplace(vsFindAction Action, string FindWhat,
                                int Options, string ReplaceWith,
                                vsFindTarget Target, string SearchPath,
                                string FilesOfType,
                                vsFindResultsLocation ResultsLocation);
```

This method accepts multiline find/replace string parameters, so implementing our add-in consists mainly in setting the various options for the find/replace operation and passing them to this routine. Let's begin by finding out about the DTE enumerations for find/replace, support for editing documents, and how to add a user interface to an add-in while building an add-in that implements multiline find and replace.

Starting the Add-In Project

First, we'll use the Add-In Wizard to generate our project as before. Choose the same options as before, but with these differences:

- Name the project `MultiLineFindReplace`.

- For the friendly name and description, use Find and Replace (Multi-Line) and Multiple-Line Find and Replace.

The project is generated by the wizard, with a `Connect.cs` file as we saw in our first project.

We're going to add a Windows Form to the `MultiLineFindReplace` project, which will constitute the user interface, by selecting Add ➤ Add Windows Form. Rename the form `FindReplace` (Figure 11-17).

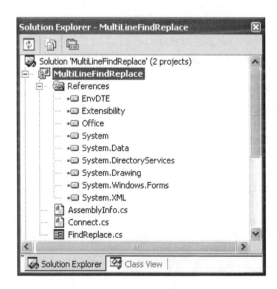

Figure 11-17. *MultiLineFindReplace solution*

As happens when we choose a Windows Forms project in the New Project wizard, Visual Studio .NET has automatically added the `System.Windows.Forms` reference, along with the `EnvDTE`, `Extensibility`, and other references we've seen before.

Now we will design our form. We use the standard Windows Forms designer toolbox to create and place controls on our form. Arrange controls on the form as shown in Figure 11-18.

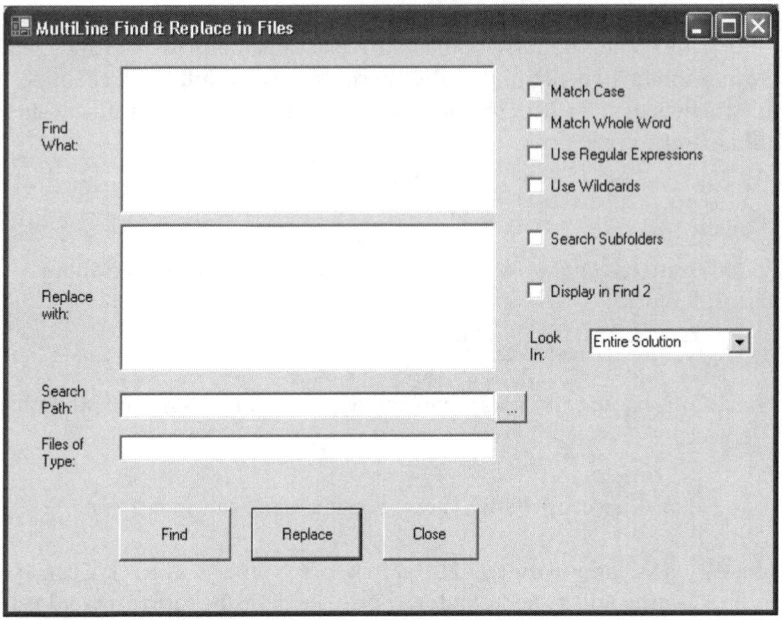

Figure 11-18. *MultiLineFindReplace main dialog*

The dialog has two multiline text boxes for the Find and Replace text, called findBox and replaceBox. Also, we have two regular text boxes for an optional search path and file type specifier called searchPathBox and filesOfTypeBox.

The dialog has a Find button, a Replace button, and a Close button called findButton, replaceButton, and closeButton, respectively. The separate Find and Replace buttons give us the option either to find our multiline search text or to replace it.

We also have a set of checkbox controls offering the standard find and replace options most such features offer, such as case-sensitivity, and whether regular expressions or wildcards are allowed. The checkbox controls are named checkMatchCase, checkMatchWholeWord, checkRegularExpression, checkSearchSubfolders, checkDisplayFind2, and checkWildcards.

Make sure to set the Multiline property of findBox and replaceBox to True, since that is more or less essential for multiline find and replace!

OK, now let's look at what we need to do to our add-in to hook it up to our form.

Changes to the Connect Class

Let's look at the changes we need to make to Connect.cs to use this form:

```
public void Exec(string commandName, EnvDTE.vsCommandExecOption executeOption,
    ref object varIn, ref object varOut, ref bool handled)
{
    handled = false;
    if (executeOption ==
        EnvDTE.vsCommandExecOption.vsCommandExecOptionDoDefault)
```

```
    {
        try
        {
            if (commandName ==
                "MultiLineFindReplace.Connect.MultiLineFindReplace")
            {
                handled = true;
                FindReplaceForm frm = new FindReplaceForm(applicationObject);
                frm.Show();
                return;
            }
        }

        catch (System.Exception e)
        {
            MessageBox.Show(
                "Exception from MultiLineFindReplace Connect():" +
                e.Message);
        }
    }
}
```

Implementing Find and Replace

Now we'll see the changes we need to make to FindReplace.cs. First, we need to add the DTE namespace at the top the file so that we can declare the DTE object:

```
using EnvDTE; // needed to reference Add-In DTE object.
```

We have to pass the applicationObject into the form so the event handler can call DTE methods. We'll add a private class variable to the form called applicationObject, to be consistent with the name in the Connect class, and make the applicationObject a parameter to the form constructor so that it can be set by the Connect class:

```
private _DTE applicationObject = null;
public FindReplaceForm(_DTE applicationObject)
{
 //
 // Required for Windows Form Designer support
 //
InitializeComponent();
 //
 // TODO: Add any constructor code after InitializeComponent call
 //
this.applicationObject = applicationObject;
}
```

Modifying the Form Event Handlers

We are going to use the Find support built into the DTE to actually make the changes to the documents. We'll write a method called doFindReplace() to call the method in the DTE that does the work. There are several enumerations in the DTE that support the different find and replace options. The first time we use these is when we make our Find and Replace buttons each do something different. We set the appropriate find action as a parameter when we call our doFindReplace method in the click event handlers for these buttons:

```
private void FindButton_Click(object sender, System.EventArgs e)
{
    doFindReplace(EnvDTE.vsFindAction.vsFindActionFindAll);
}
private void ReplaceButton_Click(object sender, System.EventArgs e)
{
    doFindReplace(EnvDTE.vsFindAction.vsFindActionReplaceAll);
}
```

Now we need to take care of the doFindReplace() method itself:

```
private void doFindReplace(EnvDTE.vsFindAction findAction)
{
    EnvDTE.vsFindResultsLocation findResultsLocation;
    int findOptions = 0;
```

The local findOptions variable is an integer, individual bits of which may be set or cleared to represent various combinations of options. Each of the checkboxes on the form is processed with a similar if statement that sets or clears the corresponding option bit, using the EnvDTE.vsFindOptions enumerations. Here is the code for the Match Case checkbox:

```
if (checkMatchCase.Checked)
{
    // set this bit in findOptions
    findOptions |= (int) EnvDTE.vsFindOptions.vsFindOptionsMatchCase;
}
else
{
    // clear this bit in findOptions
    findOptions &= ~ (int) EnvDTE.vsFindOptions.vsFindOptionsMatchCase;
}
```

Note the use of OR-equals (|=) to set the bit and AND-equals followed by NOT (&= ~) to clear it. A similar if statement follows for the checkboxes for checkMatchWholeWord, checkRegularExpression, and checkWildcards. See the sample code for the complete listing.

The FindReplace() method can optionally put its results in the Find Results window 1 or 2, or not at all, as specified by the findResultsLocation parameter rather than findOptions, so the code to set this is a little different. It doesn't seem to make sense not to display the results, so we won't worry about that option (although it could be set easily enough through use of the EnvDTE.vsFindResultsLocation.vsFindResultsNone enumeration value):

```
if (checkDisplayFind2.Checked)
{
 findResultsLocation = EnvDTE.vsFindResultsLocation.vsFindResults2;
}
else
{
 findResultsLocation = EnvDTE.vsFindResultsLocation.vsFindResults1;
}
```

Next we actually do the work by calling the DTE FindReplace() method, passing all the options we've selected from our dialog:

```
// this method does all the hard work for us
 applicationObject.DTE.Find.FindReplace(
findAction, findBox.Text,
findOptions, replaceBox.Text,
EnvDTE.vsFindTarget.vsFindTargetSolution,
searchPathBox.Text, filesOfTypeBox.Text,
findResultsLocation);}
```

The search and replace strings, search path, and "files of type" information are just a straight pass-through from the Text properties of the controls that set them.

The last thing to do is to make the Done button close our form:

```
private void DoneButton_Click(object sender, System.EventArgs e)
{
 this.Dispose();
}
```

That concludes the tour of the Find and Replace sample code.

Additional Resources for Add-Ins

See the previous and following chapters for more information on macros, wizards, and other examples of the DTE automation model. Remember, the DTE model is the same whether it is accessed from an add-in, a macro, or a wizard, so examples of DTE usage can be copied between any of these.

Information Resources Beyond This Book

The MSDN online help that comes with Visual Studio .NET is the most convenient resource for further information and reference. Check out the *Automation and Extensibility Reference* topic for information on the DTE automation model classes and methods. Online, the MSDN Automation Samples web page has additional samples beyond those included in the MSDN help, and is found at http://msdn.microsoft.com/vstudio/downloads/samples/automation.asp.

A complete book on the subject of add-ins is Les Smith's *Writing Add-Ins for Visual Studio .NET* from Apress. The book is based on Visual Basic.NET and Visual Studio 2002, but it is still valid for Visual Studio 2003, since little has changed in the DTE model. It is the only dedicated book on add-ins that I am aware of, and it has a wide variety of useful examples.

Summary

We have looked at what constitutes an add-in, to see how they differ from macros and wizards. We have investigated the COM-based architecture of add-ins, and how this affects use of the automation model and debugging.

Samples in this chapter have demonstrated how to add different commands for an add-in to the Visual Studio menus, and how to manipulate projects and code with the EnvDTE classes. As we've seen, the EnvDTE classes provide general-purpose editing support, which can be very useful in creating add-ins.

I hope the information in this chapter gives you a way to enhance your productivity by creating custom add-ins for your particular programming needs. In an upcoming chapter, we will look at Wizards, which are special-purpose add-ins that are a bit easier to create.

■ ■ ■

Macros

Developers usually create macros to help them simplify and automate repeated development tasks; tasks that involve executing a number of Visual Studio commands or changing the source code or visual elements in the designer. These tasks can be automated using macros. Visual Studio .NET allows you to create macros that will work in a similar way to Microsoft Office macros. As with Microsoft Office macros, the only programming language you can use is Visual Basic .NET.

From a programming point of view, a macro is a piece of code that is interpreted by Visual Studio for Applications. Macros have many things in common with add-ins, since they also use the DTE object exposed by Visual Studio .NET. There are two basic ways to create a macro. Either you can use the macro recorder or you can type the macro code into Macro IDE.

Let's jump right into the fray: we will take a closer look at how macros are recorded and managed, and finally, we will create a useful macro that will generate read and write properties for a private member under the caret (text cursor).

Recording Macros

Before we can start writing complex macros that manipulate the entire Visual Studio .NET environment, we need to familiarize ourselves with how simple macros work and how they are recorded.

You can record a macro using the macro recorder. The recorder operates just like a regular VCR; it also allows you to edit the recorded code. The macro is always recorded into a temporary macro, which is overwritten every time you finish recording another macro.

To prevent Visual Studio .NET from overwriting your macro, you must save it under a new name before recording a new macro. Even when you have started recording a new macro, you can prevent the existing temporary macro from being overwritten by canceling the recording. The recorded macro will contain macro code representing the actions you have performed while recording the macro.

To start recording a temporary macro, you can press Ctrl+Shift+R or select Tools ➤ Macros ➤ Record Temporary Macro (see Figure 12-1).

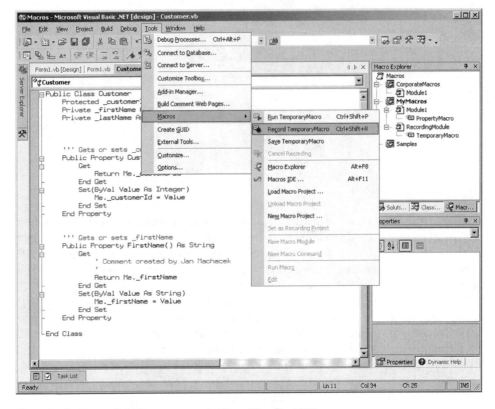

Figure 12-1. *Expanded Macros menu in Visual Studio .NET*

When you start recording, the Recorder toolbar will pop up. To stop recording click the Stop Recording button on the Recorder toolbar. This will stop the recording and create a new temporary macro or overwrite an existing one. You can pause the recording by clicking the Pause button or cancel the recording by clicking the Cancel button. See Figure 12-2.

Figure 12-2. *Macro Recorder toolbar*

When you stop the recording, Visual Studio .NET will create a new TemporaryMacro in a RecordingModule, which will also be shown in the Macro Explorer. The macro recorder will record all actions executed by the IDE. However, it will not record mouse moves. For example, if a user clicks on the File menu but does not select anything from it, and then clicks on Help and selects About, the Macro Recorder will record only one event: Help.About.

Managing Macros

A good way to manage macros is to use Macro Explorer (Figure 12-3). This feature works just like Solution Explorer; it lists macro projects, and allows you to create new macros, and delete and edit existing macro projects as well as individual macros within macro projects.

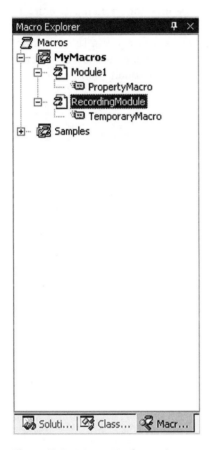

Figure 12-3. *Macro Explorer view*

To view the Macro Explorer, select View ➤ Other Windows ➤ Macro Explorer or press Alt+F8 (provided that you have not changed your keyboard mappings).

Macro Projects

A macro project is particularly useful in a corporate environment where the macro you create will be distributed to other developers in the company.

To start a new macro project, right-click on the Macros node in the Macro Explorer and select New Macro Project. Give the new macro project a name, and it will appear in the Macro Explorer. You can distribute the macro project by simply copying the macro project file; macro projects are by default created in your documents folder under Visual Studio Projects\ VSMacros71\Macro-Name.

Other developers in the team will then select the Load Macro Project option from the context menu that appears after right-clicking on the Macros node in the Macro Explorer.

Running and Editing Macros

When you are done recording a macro, you can run it, edit its source code, rename it, or delete it through the right-click context menu.

To view a macro's source code, right-click on the macro node and select Edit. This will bring up the Macro IDE, which is a development tool for macros. It looks and operates just like Visual Studio .NET, except that it is designed for macro development. You can modify, debug, and run your macros from the Macro IDE. See Figure 12-4.

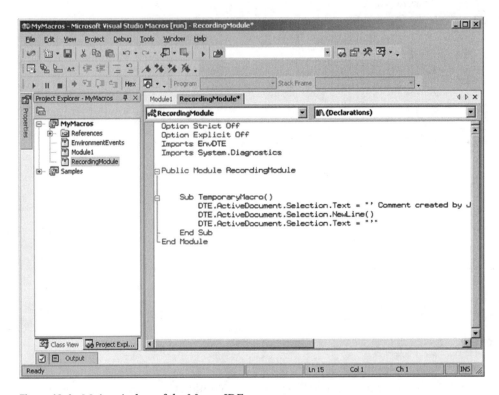

Figure 12-4. *Main window of the Macro IDE*

Hot Keys and IDE Integration

To further increase your productivity, you can assign a hot key to a macro. To do this, click Tools ➤ Options, select Keyboard under Environment, and select your macro from the list of available commands and then assign a hot key by pressing the required key combination. See Figure 12-5.

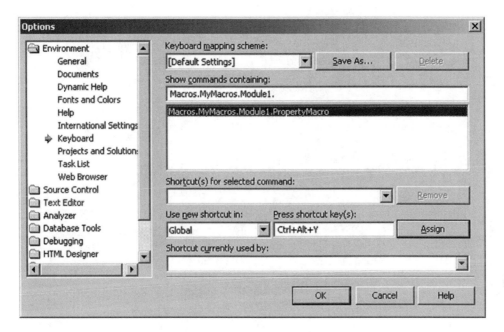

Figure 12-5. *Visual Studio .NET Options dialog*

Moreover, you can create a button that will appear in a toolbar in Visual Studio .NET. This is a good option if you have run out of shortcut keys. To add a button to a toolbar, click Tools ➤ Customize, select the Commands tab, make sure that Macros is selected in the categories listbox, and then select and drag your macro to the toolbar (Figure 12-6).

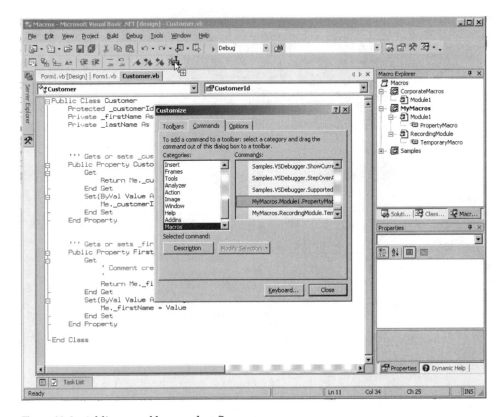

Figure 12-6. *Adding a tool button that fires a macro*

DTE

All commands available in Visual Studio .NET are a part of the Design Time Environment interfaces, or DTE. You can use methods and properties of the DTE in your macros to control the IDE just as you would using the menu or toolbar commands or the keyboard.

DTE interfaces are in the EnvDTE namespace. The MSDE page at http://msdn.microsoft.com/library/default.asp?url=/library/en-us/vsintro7/html/oricommonenvironmentobjectmodelcollections.asp lists Visual Studio .NET objects, and http://msdn.microsoft.com/library/default.asp?url=/library/en-us/vsintro7/html/vxgrfautomationobjectmodelchart.asp shows a complete diagram of DTE objects. It is an excellent resource for learning more about all DTE objects.

I'm going to give you a quick rundown of the most important objects and their properties, and provide simple sample code that explains how to use each interface where applicable.

DTE.ActiveDocument

The ActiveDocument property allows you to access the currently open document. There are several subclasses of the Document object.

When writing macros, you can assume that users want to run your macros from the current selection point; you can access the current selection using the Selection property.

You can also query a document's status using its properties. The properties are self-explanatory; you can refer to the MSDN online documentation for a more detailed description of the properties. For example, we can use a simple If statement in the macro code to determine whether the document is read-only:

```
If (ActiveDocument().ReadOnly) Then
     Macro code
End If
```

DTE.ActiveWindow

The ActiveWindow property represents the currently active window, or Nothing if there are no windows open. You can use ActiveWindow in a similar way to that of ActiveDocument, especially since a Window has the Document property that represents the document displayed in the current window. The Selection property of the ActiveWindow interface is a wrapper around the Document interface contained in the ActiveWindow:

```
Dim sel As TextSelection = DTE.ActiveWindow().Selection
```

When an ActiveWindow contains a window displaying a TextDocument, the following line is equivalent to the one just displayed:

```
Dim sel As TextSelection = DTE.ActiveWindow().Document.Selection
```

DTE.AddIns

Addins represent collections of individual addins registered in Visual Studio .NET. You can use this collection to verify that an addin that your macro needs to run is available:

```
Dim addins As AddIns = DTE.AddIns
Dim I As Integer
Dim addinFound As Boolean = False
Dim requiredGuid As String = "{5d1cb714-1c4b-11d4-bed5-005004b1f42f}"

If (addins.Count > 0) Then
    For I = 0 To addins.Count
        Dim addin As AddIn = addins.Item(I)
         If (addin.Guid() = requiredGuid) Then
            addinFound = True
            Exit For
        End If
    Next
End If

If (addinFound) Then
    ' process more macro code
End If
```

DTE.CommandBars

You may already be familiar with the CommandBars object if you have done some Microsoft Office add-in programming. This collection represents all command bars provided by the IDE; it also allows you to add new command bars and command buttons. However, CommandBars is not a property that you would normally use in a macro, because a macro that accesses a CommandBars object to register a new toolbar button must be executed at least once.

If you need to use the CommandBars object to create command buttons, your macro code will need to check whether a toolbar button is already registered with an event handler pointing to another macro. This object will typically be used by add-ins.

DTE.Commands

The Commands object is closely related to CommandBars. It allows you to associate a user interface object in a command bar with a command. You can implement the Execute event handler of a Command object to run your macro code. This object is not typically used in a macro for the same reasons as apply to the CommandBars object.

DTE.Documents

The Documents property represents a collection of all open documents in the IDE. Use the Item property of the Documents collection to access each individual Document.

DTE.Events

The Events collection allows your macro code to find an event available in the current Visual Studio .NET event list and implement an event handler for it:

```
Public Module Module1
    Dim WithEvents bldevents As BuildEvents
    Dim applicationObject As EnvDTE.DTE

    Sub EventsExample()
        Dim addInInstance As EnvDTE.AddIn

        applicationObject = CType(Application, EnvDTE.DTE)
        bldevents = CType(applicationObject.Events.BuildEvents, EnvDTE.BuildEvents)
    End Sub

    Private Sub bldevents_OnBuildDone(_
        ByVal Scope As EnvDTE.vsBuildScope, _
        ByVal Action As EnvDTE.vsBuildAction) _
        Handles bldevents.OnBuildDone
        ' commit to CVS
    End Sub
End Module
```

When you run the EventsExample macro, it will register an event handler for the OnBuildComplete event. However, this is not a typical example for a macro, since the bldevents_OnBuildDone will not run unless the macro is run at least once. If you want to make sure that an event handler is always executed, you should consider building an add-in.

DTE.Properties

The properties collection allows your macro code to change IDE properties. Manipulating the properties is very simple: the code follows the user interface of the Tools ➤ Options dialog:

```
DTE.Properties("TextEditor", "Basic").Item("ShowLineNumbers").Value = True
```

This simple macro asks the IDE to show the line numbers in all Visual Basic editor windows.

DTE.Solution

The Solution property allows you to access the current solution. Accessing the solution requires a bit more advanced processing, and this is why I recommend that you use the Solution property in add-ins rather than macros.

DTE.SourceControl

Unfortunately, Visual Studio .NET limits support for source control solutions to Visual SourceSafe. Visual SourceSafe works very well for smaller projects developed only in Visual Studio .NET. If you are dealing with bigger teams and projects that require tools other than Visual Studio .NET, you should consider using CVS or Subversion as your source control server. There are several implementations of Source Code Control Provider (SCC) that use CVS.

Whichever source control solution you decide to use in the end, you can use the SourceControl property in your macros. The problem with accessing source control from macro code is that it is very easy to introduce errors into your source code. It should always be up to the developer to manage versions of the source code files in a solution.

DTE.SupressUI

The SupressUI property can be used in your macros to instruct the macro processor not to display any user interface elements. This is usually used in wizard templates, because Visual Studio's templating engine will not allow the template code to access the user interface elements.

DTE.Windows

The Windows property provides access to all windows in Visual Studio .NET. You can access the source code windows, task list, etc. Because all items in the Windows collection are generic Window objects, you need to cast the item to the appropriate window type:

```
Dim win As Window = DTE.Windows.Item(EnvDTE.Constants.vsWindowKindTaskList)
Dim fileName As String = DTE.ActiveWindow.Document.FullName
Dim taskList As TaskList = win.Object
```

```
taskList.TaskItems.Add("Generated Code", "", _
    "Review the automatically generated code", _
    vsTaskPriority.vsTaskPriorityMedium, vbNull, True, _
    fileName, line - 8, True, True)
```

To gain access to an object displayed in the window, you need to use the `Window.Object` property and cast it to the expected type. The code sample just displayed shows this approach. We get an instance of a `TaskList` window and then use `win.Object` to gain access to the `TaskList` object displayed in the window.

Property Generator Macro

Now that we have covered the Visual Studio .NET extensibility model, we can implement a macro that will generate read and write properties for private members of a class. This is an ideal task for a macro, since it is relatively simple to program, very useful, and—most importantly—one of the most annoying points of writing code. We will start with a top-level implementation and then focus on implementation details of each function that goes into forming the macro.

Adding a Macro

We will start by adding a new macro to the project. To do this, open the Macro Explorer, select My Macros, right-click on Module 1, and select New Macro. See Figure 12-7.

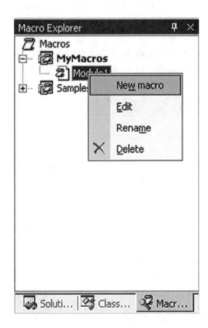

Figure 12-7. *New Macro popup menu*

This will open a Macro IDE window with Macro1 as the default macro name (Figure 12-8).

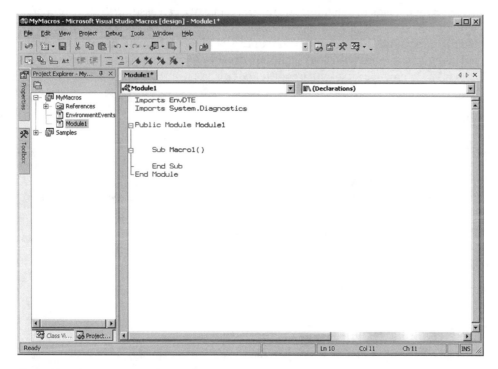

Figure 12-8. *Macro IDE with empty macro project*

To get started, we will rename the Macro1 `PropertyMacro` and then move ahead to start with the actual implementation.

Implementation

Let's look at the problem we will be dealing with. The simplest scenario is generating properties for a member in a class that does not contain any other code:

```
Public Class Customer
    Private _customerId As Integer

End Class
```

Even if the class we will be processing contains many other methods and properties, we just need to make sure that our macro does not change existing code.

The first thing we need to do in our macro is to determine whether the statement the cursor is positioned on is actually a `Private` or `Protected` member declaration. The code for checking whether the selected member is eligible for further processing by our macro should return the member name and type. We see from the code in the previous listing that this checking method should return `True`, since `Private _customerId As Integer` is indeed a valid declaration, and it should return "_customerId" as member name and "Integer" as member type.

The macro then needs to generate the property name. We can assume that the property name for `Private _customerId As Integer` should be `CustomerId`. However, there is no guarantee that developers will construct member names according to this pattern; in this case, the macro will insert "P" as the first character of the property name to make the property name unique.

This leads us to the following source code for our macro:

```
''' main macro code
Sub PropertyMacro()
    Dim memberName As String
    Dim type As String

    If (IsValidMember(memberName, type)) Then
        Debug.WriteLine("Got valid member name " & memberName & ", type " & type)
        ' get propertyName based on memberName
        Dim propertyName As String = GetPropertyName(memberName)
        ' finally, check that memberName and propertyName are not the same
        ' if they are, add P as the first character of propertyName

        If (memberName.ToUpper() = propertyName.ToUpper()) Then
            propertyName = "P" & propertyName
        End If

        ' propertyName variable now holds the correct property value
        Debug.WriteLine("Member name " & memberName & ", _
            Property name " & propertyName)

        InsertProperty(memberName, propertyName, type)
    End If
End Sub
```

We are still missing all supporting functions, but this code gives us a very good overview of what the macro is going to do. The first thing that `PropertyMacro` needs to do is to decide whether the text under the cursor is a valid property identifier. It calls the `IsValidMember(ByRef memberName As String, ByRef type As String)` method to determine whether this is the case. `IsValidMember` also sets `memberName` and `type` to the name and type of the selected member. If the caret is in `Private _customerId As Integer`, the function will return `True`, `memberName` will be set to "_customerId," and `type` will be set to "Integer."

The next thing our macro needs to do is to construct a valid, yet human-friendly, name for the generated property. It does so by calling `GetPropertyName`. This function checks the member name and returns a likely property name.

In the next step, the code needs to make sure that the generated property name and existing member name are not the same; if they are, it places a "P" in front of the property name.

Finally, we insert the property into the existing code by calling the function `InsertProperty`.

Dissecting PropertyMacro

We now have a very good overview of the steps the macro needs to perform, but since we are using some very interesting concepts in the supporting functions, it would be a shame not to discuss them further.

IsValidMember

The first thing we need to consider is how to place the entire range of a statement where the caret is. A simple solution would be to move to the start of the line and take the text on the entire line as our statement. This is all very well, but what if the member declaration is split into two lines, such as

```
Private _customerId As _
    Integer
```

We must also take into consideration that users may not position the cursor on the first line of the declaration. To make our macro really useful, we must not rely on our users to select the entire member declaration; we must write code to do all this. Luckily, with the help of the EditPoint class, the task is not overwhelmingly difficult. We need to get the selection from the current document and determine the current caret position:

```
''' Returns True if the current member under cursor
''' is a Private or Protected member
Function IsValidMember(ByRef name As String, ByRef type As String) As Boolean
    Dim sel As TextSelection = DTE.ActiveWindow().Selection

    Try
        Dim pt As EditPoint = sel.ActivePoint.CreateEditPoint
```

The EditPoint instance represents the position of the caret in the editor window. Once we have acquired the EditPoint, we need to move the current position to the beginning of the declaration. We do not need to implement all this ourselves; we can use the DTE interfaces to help us:

```
        '' find starting point of the statement
        pt.MoveToPoint(pt.CodeElement(_
            vsCMElement.vsCMElementDeclareDecl)._
            GetStartPoint(vsCMPart.vsCMPartWhole))
        '' move the selection to the start of the statement
        sel.MoveToPoint(pt, False)
        '' find ending point of the statement
        pt.MoveToPoint(pt.CodeElement(_
            vsCMElement.vsCMElementDeclareDecl)._
            GetEndPoint(vsCMPart.vsCMPartWhole))
```

The call to pt.CodeElement(vsCMElement.vsCMElementDeclareDecl).GetStartPoint (vsCMPart.vsCMPartWhole) does the job: it makes sure it sets the start property of the EditPoint object to the correct starting point.[1] On the next line we make sure that the selection start matches the start of the member declaration. Unfortunately, calling pt.CodeElement (vsCMElement.vsCMElementDeclareDecl).GetEndPoint(vsCMPart.vsCMPartWhole) does not set the end point of the EditPoint object to the end of the member declaration statement. An example will illustrate the situation:

```
Private _customerId As _
    Integer
```

The calls to GetStartPoint and GetEndPoint will return only the "Private _customerId" code fragment. We must then continue reading the selection until we reach the vbCrLf character. At the same time, we must still consider that a Visual Basic line of code may contain a continuation character, in which case we must ignore the vbCrLf character and continue reading:

```
        pt.EndOfLine()

        sel.MoveToPoint(pt, True)

        Dim line As String = sel.Text.Trim()
        While (line.EndsWith("_"))
            line = line.Replace("_", "")
            sel.LineDown()
            sel.SelectLine()
            line &= sel.Text.Trim()
        End While
```

After the macro interpreter has passed the End While statement, the variable line contains the entire member declaration, and we can pass control to another method whose task is to determine whether the line is actually a valid member:

```
        Return IsValidMemberString(line, name, type)
```

To finish off this function, we must add the catch block and return False if an exception is caught:

```
    Catch e As System.Exception
        Debug.WriteLine(e.Message)
        Return False
    End Try
End Function
```

---

1. The starting point is calculated based on the syntax rules of the current editor language. We could use the same code to process C# or J# code.

IsValidMemberString

The IsValidMemberString method examines the content of the member argument and decides whether the argument is a valid member declaration. If it is, the function sets name and type arguments to the member name and member type:

```
'' Returns true if the member identified by the member argument is
'' a valid member for creating a property
Function IsValidMemberString(ByVal member As String, _
    ByRef name As String, ByRef type As String) As Boolean
    Debug.WriteLine(member)
    Try
        Dim line() As String = member.Split()
```

We can safely assume that Visual Basic member declarations contain at least four words:[2]

```
        If (line.Length = 4) Then
            'members must be in form of <Access Modifier> <Name> As <Type>
            Dim accessModifier = line(0)
            name = line(1)
            Dim asKeyword = line(2)
            type = line(3)

            Debug.WriteLine(accessModifier & " " & name & " As " & type)

            'member is valid if
            ' * accessModifier = [Private, Protected] And
            ' * asKeyword = As
            Return _
                (accessModifier = "Private" Or accessModifier = "Protected") And _
                (asKeyword = "As")
        End If
```

This code simply extracts the expected words from the line() array and makes sure that they match the expected. We can check only the access modifier and As keyword. Name and type are user-defined, and we cannot make any assumptions about the content of those words:

```
    Catch e As System.Exception
        Debug.Write(e.Message)
    End Try

    Return False
End Function
```

Naturally, we need to finish the Try block and Function declaration.

---

2. Actually, Visual Basic members may contain five words if the member is a Shared member. I will leave implementation of this feature to the reader.

GetPropertyName

The next function to look at is quite a simple one: it will attempt to generate a human-friendly name for the property for the member. I have used only one rule: if a member starts with an underscore character, the property name will not contain the underscore character. The function also makes sure that the generated property name starts with a capital letter:

```
' this function tries to guess the property name
' from the memberName
Function GetPropertyName(ByVal memberName) As String
    Dim propertyName As String = memberName

    If (memberName.StartsWith("_")) Then
        propertyName = propertyName.Remove(0, 1)
    End If
    ' make sure the first character is in uppercase
    Dim pc As Char() = propertyName.ToCharArray()
    pc(0) = pc(0).ToUpper(pc(0))
    propertyName = New String(pc)

    Return propertyName
End Function
```

If you use a different naming convention in your code, you can modify this function to return the appropriate property name.

InsertProperty

We are getting closer to the final macro! InsertProperty is the function that will decide whether to insert the property declaration to the code file. The function must make sure that the property declaration is not already present in the file; it if is, the method will not do anything. If it is not, the function will call the GenerateProperty function to get the actual Visual Basic code for the property:

```
''' inserts the property into the active document
Function InsertProperty(ByVal memberName As String, _
    ByVal propertyName As String, ByVal type As String)
    Dim sel As TextSelection = DTE.ActiveWindow().Selection
    Dim pt As EditPoint = sel.ActivePoint.CreateEditPoint

    sel.SelectAll()
    If (sel.Text.IndexOf(String.Format("Property {0}()", propertyName)) = -1) Then
        pt.MoveToPoint(pt.CodeElement(_
            vsCMElement.vsCMElementClass)._
            GetEndPoint(vsCMPart.vsCMPartWhole))

        pt.LineUp()
        pt.EndOfLine()
        pt.Insert(vbNewLine)
```

```
        pt.Insert(GenerateProperty(memberName, propertyName, type))
    End If
End Function
```

GenerateProperty

The last function to look at is GenerateProperty, which simply writes out appropriate code:

```
''' This method generates the actual code that will be used
''' to process the property
Function GenerateProperty(ByVal memberName As String, _
    ByVal propertyName As String, ByVal type As String) As String
    Dim builder As StringBuilder = New StringBuilder()

    ' generate property declaration
    builder.AppendFormat(vbTab & "Public Property {0}() As {1}" & _
        vbNewLine, propertyName, type)
    ' generate getter code
    builder.AppendFormat(vbTab & vbTab & "Get" & vbNewLine)
    builder.AppendFormat(vbTab & vbTab & vbTab & "Return Me.{0}" & _
        vbNewLine, memberName)
    builder.AppendFormat(vbTab & vbTab & "End Get" & vbNewLine)
    ' generate setter code
    builder.AppendFormat(vbTab & vbTab & "Set(ByVal Value As {0})" & _
        vbNewLine, type)
    builder.AppendFormat(vbTab & vbTab & vbTab & "Me.{0} = Value" & _
        vbNewLine, memberName)
    builder.AppendFormat(vbTab & vbTab & "End Set" & vbNewLine)
    ' generate end property declaration
    builder.AppendFormat(vbTab & "End Property" & vbNewLine)

    ' return generated code
    Return builder.ToString()
End Function
```

Since this code is using a StringBuilder, you need to add an Imports System.Text statement at the beginning of the module.

Extending PropertyMacro

Now that our macro is finished, we can look at ways to extend its functionality. There are numerous ways to extend the macro; I have picked out two of the most interesting ones. The first one, adding comments, will not be very difficult. I am going to show it just to demonstrate how to extend the existing code in an elegant way. The second extension I am going to implement will add tasks to the Visual Studio .NET Task list.

The motivation behind this second extension is that in some cases you may need to perform custom code in the getter or setter code of the property. With generated code it is very easy to forget to add the validation code to your properties, which will make the Task list integration quite useful.

Comments Extension

Adding automatic comments may be one of desired extensions, and it will fit very well with the concept of macros: adding comments for properties that do not contain much custom code is a stereotypical task that usually involves repeating "Gets or sets member name." We can easily extend the macro to add these comments. To do this in a clean and extensible way, we will change the InsertProperty function:

```
''' inserts the property into the active document
Function InsertProperty(ByVal memberName As String, _
    ByVal propertyName As String, ByVal type As String)
    Dim sel As TextSelection = DTE.ActiveWindow().Selection
    Dim pt As EditPoint = sel.ActivePoint.CreateEditPoint

    sel.SelectAll()
    If (sel.Text.IndexOf(String.Format("Property {0}()", propertyName)) = -1) Then
        pt.MoveToPoint(pt.CodeElement(_
            vsCMElement.vsCMElementClass)._
            GetEndPoint(vsCMPart.vsCMPartWhole))

        pt.LineUp()
        pt.EndOfLine()
        pt.Insert(vbNewLine)

        Dim code As StringBuilder = New StringBuilder()
        code.Append(GeneratePreProperty(memberName, propertyName, type))
        code.Append(vbNewLine)
        code.Append(GenerateProperty(memberName, propertyName, type))
        pt.Insert(code.ToString())
    End If
End Function
```

We have introduced a new StringBuilder variable code, which is filled with text returned by the GeneratePreProperty and GenerateProperty functions. We also need to implement the GeneratePreProperty method. The actual implementation is not very difficult, for it simply adds the comments string:

```
''' This method generates the actual code that will be used
''' to process the property
Function GeneratePreProperty(ByVal memberName As String, _
    ByVal propertyName As String, ByVal type As String) As String
    Dim comments As StringBuilder = New StringBuilder()

    comments.AppendFormat(vbTab & "''' Gets or sets {0}", memberName)

    Return comments.ToString()
End Function
```

Task List Integration

We will use the same concept for the TaskList extension: we will create another function that will be executed once the property code is inserted into the code window:

```
''' function that is executed after inserting a property
Function GeneratePostProperty(ByVal memberName As String, _
    ByVal propertyName As String, ByVal type As String, _
    ByVal line As Integer)

    Dim win As Window = DTE.Windows.Item(EnvDTE.Constants.vsWindowKindTaskList)
    Dim fileName As String = DTE.ActiveWindow.Document.FullName
    Dim taskList As TaskList = win.Object

    taskList.TaskItems.Add("Generated Code", "", _
        "Review the automatically generated code", _
        vsTaskPriority.vsTaskPriorityMedium, vbNull, _
        True, fileName, line - 8, True, True)
End Function
```

This function shows how to access the DTE interfaces. It is just like using Visual Basic for Applications in Microsoft Office, including all the dangers of doing so. It is important to keep in mind that there is a lot of type casting performed in macro code and that the Macro IDE will not identify illegal type casts when writing the code. Errors will be reported when the macro is run.

Best Practices

The macro code we have just analyzed is a practical demonstration of a macro's capabilities; at the same time, it shows important considerations of macro programming. Macros may be quite long and complex; yet they do not perform difficult tasks. Looking at our PropertyGenerator macro, we see that the most complex task was analyzing the member at the caret position. The rest of the macro code was quite simple and straightforward. At the same time, the macro simplifies one of the dullest and boring tasks in programming.

Finally, I would like to add a quick note that will make it much easier for you to manage your macros in the future: include the string "DTE." in all statements that reference the DTE object model. This may sound like an inconvenience when you are writing macros, but it will become very useful if you decide to convert your macro into an add-in.

Running the Macro

Running your new macro is no different from running recorded macros as we have discussed earlier. The macro will process the code in the class file:

```
Public Class Customer
    Protected _customerId As Integer
    Private _firstName As _
```

```
        String
    Private _lastName As String

End Class
```

If we place the caret anywhere in `Private _customer As Integer`, it will modify the source code like this:

```
Public Class Customer
    Protected _customerId As Integer
    Private _firstName As _
        String
    Private _lastName As String

    ''' Gets or sets _customerId
    Public Property CustomerId() As Integer
        Get
            Return Me._customerId
        End Get
        Set(ByVal Value As Integer)
            Me._customerId = Value
        End Set
    End Property

End Class
```

As you can see, the generated property name is correctly named (no underscore character and capital C), and appropriate getter and setter code is also generated.

Assigning a hot key to run the macro can be the finishing touch that will speed up your Visual Basic .NET development.

Moving On

I am sure you are keen to learn how to extend the functionality of your macros even further. You can turn your macro into a full-blown add-in for Visual Studio .NET. Add-ins are covered in Chapter 11. I am only going to show you a simple way to convert an existing macro into an add-in.

New Add-In Project

In order to convert a macro into an add-in you must start a new add-in project using Visual Basic, since VB is the only language supported by the `MakeAddinFromMacroProj` macro. This project type is not shown under the usual folder for Visual Basic projects. Rather, you must select Other Projects ➤ Extensibility Projects. Give your add-in project a name and click OK. See Figure 12-9.

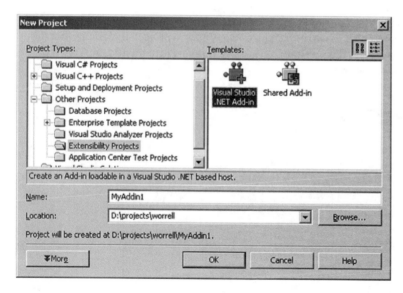

Figure 12-9. *New Project dialog with Visual Studio .NET Addin project type selected*

This will start an add-in wizard. Select Visual Basic as the programming language in the first step, because VB is the only language supported by the MakeAddinFromMacroProj macro. In the next step, select the host environments to which your add-in is going to be available. The add-in can be used in Visual Studio .NET or VS Macros IDE, or both. Next, give your add-in a friendly name and description.

Finally, make sure you have selected the "create tools" menu item. MakeAddinFromMacroProj will fail if this option is not selected. See Figure 12-10.

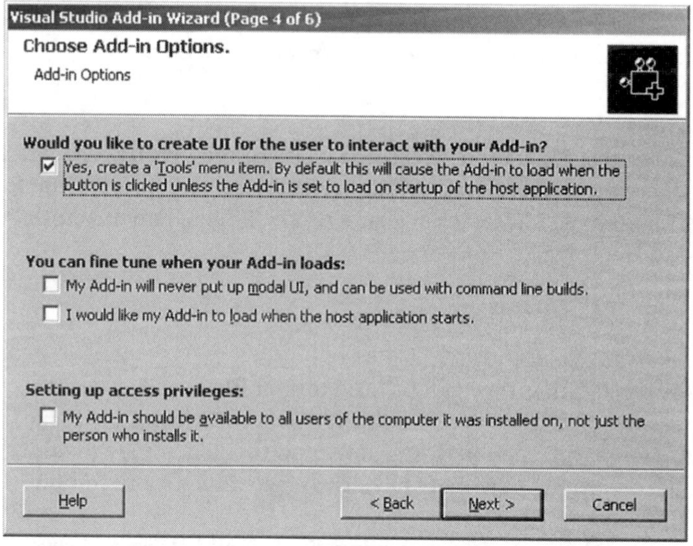

Figure 12-10. *Visual Studio .NET Addin wizard*

If you have added the add-in project to the existing solution, make sure you set the add-in project as a Start-up project. Once you have created a new add-in project, make sure that the macro project contains only a macro that you want to convert into an add-in. Then run `MakeAddinFromMacroProj`. See Figure 12-11.

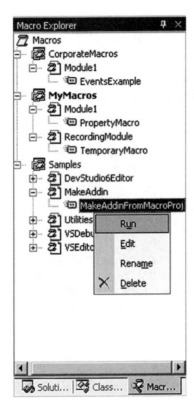

Figure 12-11. *Running the MakeAddinFromMacroProj macro from the Macro Explorer*

The macro will put up a warning that it is going to replace `Exec`, `QueryStatus`, and `OnConnection` methods; click Yes to continue running the macro. `MakeAddinFromMacroProj` will prompt you to enter the macro project name; for example **MyMacros** in Figure 12-11. The generator macro will modify the source code of the add-in.

Summary

You have learned what macros are and how they can be used to simplify your day-to-day development tasks. We have discussed basics of the DTE object model and created a real-life macro for generating properties for private members. You now know that macros are a simple way to extend your development environment without having to create much more complicated add-ins.

Even so, we have looked at a simple way to convert a macro into an add-in; we will cover add-ins in more detail in Chapter 11, but this is a good starting point for more coding adventures!

CHAPTER 13

■■■

Wizards

Wizards enable developers to extend the existing functionality of Visual Studio's built-in tools for creating new projects as well as adding new items to existing projects. At the same time, wizards are not particularly difficult to implement, even though—depending on the wizard type—there are some limitations; but these limitations are very minor, and I will show you a way to easily overcome them using a very simple Visual C++ project or a custom build script.

We will start the chapter by looking at how Visual Studio .NET organizes Wizards and how it executes the wizards. Then we will look at a simple wizard that can be implemented by supplying a custom script to Visual Studio's Wizard Engine. Finally, I will show you how to implement a full-blown wizard using Visual Basic .NET. Our wizard will put up a rich Windows Forms user interface, and it will represent a skeleton that you can use for building your own wizards.

Visual Studio .NET Wizards Overview

Visual Studio .NET uses a directory structure to locate the wizards that is very easy to understand (see Figure 13-1).

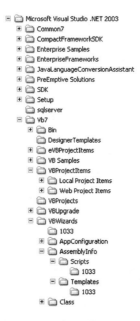

Figure 13-1. *Visual Studio .NET wizard directory structure*

I will explain the location of the files in more detail in the next section. In the meantime, however, I can tell you that you can drop a wizard definition file into almost any directory in this structure, and it will be picked up by Visual Studio .NET and presented in the correct category in the user interface.

Visual Studio uses this directory structure together with VSDIR and VZS files. The VZS file contains the textual definition for the wizard. You must start your VZS file with VSWizard 7.0, followed by the definition of the code that will be executed by Visual Studio .NET when the wizard is run. The MSDN page `http://msdn.microsoft.com/library/default.asp?url=/library/en-us/vsintro7/html/vxconvszfiles.asp` states that the version number must be set to 7.0, though setting it to 6.0 works just as well for Visual Studio .NET 2003. The code reference must be either CLSID or the class identifier of the COM library that implements the `IDTWizard` interface. We will return to the wizard COM libraries later, when we start implementing a COM-based wizard. Finally, you may include any number of custom parameters that will be passed to your wizard's execute method by specifying `Param=<parameter-value>` lines. The final result of the VSZ file may look like this:

```
VSWizard 7.0
Wizard={6B967689-DE9C-4fbc-9410-FC6A7C7C6F06}
Param="UpdateUri = http://localhost/wizard2/updates.asmx"
Param="Season = Spring"
```

We have set the wizard version to 7.0 and specified the wizard's CLSID and provided two custom parameters. Visual Studio will use only the first two lines to identify the add-in, and on execution it will pass the two `Param` values as parameters of the execute method.

The next file type Visual Studio .NET uses is a file with the `.vsdir` extension. This file contains further details about each VSZ file, specifically wizard name, description, icon, and wizard's capabilities. One VSDIR file usually contains definitions for more than one wizard; even so, you can have multiple VSDIR files in a wizard directory.

Let's now take a closer look at the values in the VSDIR file. You must specify these values correctly or Visual Studio .NET will not be able to load your wizard. Each line in the file contains the definition for one wizard, with values in the file separated by a vertical bar: |. Table 13-1 lists all columns, their names, and their meaning. Columns that must be set are marked with an asterisk. If you decide not to supply a value for an optional column, you must set it to 0:

```
Wizard2.vsz| |Wizard^2|110|Wizard for creating wizards|res.dll|1| |WizardProject
```

Table 13-1. *VSDIR file structure*

Column	Name	Description
1	RelPathName*	The name of the VSZ file, relative to the location of the VSDIR file.
2	{clsidPackage}	Optional. A GUID representing a product (such as Visual C++) that has a DLL containing localized resources. Normally, this field is blank for VSDIR files that correspond to third-party wizards.

Table 13-1. *VSDIR file structure (continued)*

Column	Name	Description
3	LocalizedName	Optional. This is the localizable name of the wizard or template and the name that appears in the Add Item dialog box. This can be a string or a resource identifier of the form #ResID. Since Wizards are COM libraries, you cannot use a .NET resource name.
4	SortPriority	Describes the order in which the add-in is going to be displayed. The add-ins will be sorted first by this column, then by add-in name. This means you can have more than one add-in with the same SortPriority value.
5	Description	Required. A localizable description of the template or wizard as it will appear in the Add Item dialog box when the item is selected. This can be a string or a resource identifier of the form #ResID. Applies only to template files, not folders. Again, you cannot use a .NET resource name.
6	DLLPath or {clsidPackage}	Required. Specifies a full path to a DLL or EXE file, or a GUID of a product that has a DLL file that contains an icon to load for the wizard. The icon is loaded as a resource out of a DLL/EXE file using the given IconResourceId. This setting overrides {clsidPackage}, if specified, for icon location. Applies only to template files, not folders.
7	IconResourceId	Optional. A resource identifier within the DLL file that determines the icon to display. If no icon is defined, the environment substitutes the default icon for a file with the same extension as the item. Applies only to template files, not folders.
8	Flags*	Flags for displaying the wizard. Visual Studio .NET uses this value to decide what elements of the New Project or New Item user interface to display or enable.
9	SuggestedBaseName	Required. Represents the name that will be suggested in the New Item window. It is either a string or a resource identifier defined as #ResId. If an item with the SuggestedBaseName already exists in the current scope, Visual Studio .NET will try to make the item name unique by appending an integer to the item's name.

As shown in Table 13-1, which explains the parameters, Visual Studio .NET will use the value in the Flags column to display or enable user interface elements in New Project or New Item dialog windows.

Table 13-2 lists all flags you can use in your VSDIR files.

Table 13-2. *VSDIR flag values*

Flag name	Value	Description
VSDIRFLAG_NonLocalTemplate	1	Use nonlocal user interface behavior and save mechanisms.
VSDIRFLAG_BlankSolution	2	Create a blank (empty) solution; do not create a project.
VSDIRFLAG_DisableBrowseButton	4	Disable the Browse button for this project or item.
VSDIRFLAG_DontAddDefExtension	8	Do not append a default extension to the name provided for the item. (This setting is not valid for projects.)
VSDIRFLAG_DisableLocationField	32	Disable the location field for this project or item.
VSDIRFLAG_DontInitNameField	4096	Do not initialize the name field for this project or item with a valid name.
VSDIRFLAG_DisableNameField	8192	Disable the name field for this project or item.

As you can tell, the flag values can be combined by simply adding the values. If you need to instruct Visual Studio .NET to disable the Browse button as well as to disable the location field for the item, set the flags to 4100. By adding the values you are actually setting the corresponding bits in the flags field.

Now that we know how Visual Studio .NET identifies and loads the wizards, we can jump into the action and implement a simple script-based wizard.

Script-Based Wizards

Let's start by creating a simple script-based wizard that will add an Exception to the Add New Item dialog under Local Project Items. It will simply create a new exception class with code for calling constructors from the inherited Exception. Overall, the wizard is not going to do anything spectacular. It will also be very easy to implement: all we are going to have to do is to modify VSZ and VSDIR files and provide a simple script that will perform the actions we need to create the new class file.

Scripting Engine

We do not have to implement our own scripting engine; we can use the existing Visual Studio .NET scripting engine that is defined in the COM library with program ID "VsWizard.VsWizardEngine.7.1."

Integrating into Visual Studio .NET

In this step, we will create the necessary VSZ file and modify the existing VSDIR file. This will allow Visual Studio .NET to recognize our wizard and to present it in the Add New Item dialog window.

Let's take a look at the final Exception.vsz file:

```
VSWIZARD 7.0
Wizard=VsWizard.VsWizardEngine.7.1
Param="WIZARD_NAME = Exception"
Param="WIZARD_UI = FALSE"
Param="PROJECT_TYPE = VBPROJ"
```

In it we are specifying the wizard version, the wizard's implementation, and several custom parameters. VsWizardEngine needs these custom parameters to correctly process the script.

In the next step, we need to modify the VSDIR file to allow Visual Studio .NET to identify our new VSZ file:

```
UI|{164B10B9-B200-11D0-8C61-00A0C91E29D5}|#3083|10
Code|{164B10B9-B200-11D0-8C61-00A0C91E29D5}|#3084|20
Data|{164B10B9-B200-11D0-8C61-00A0C91E29D5}|#3085|30
Web|{164B10B9-B200-11D0-8C61-00A0C91E29D5}|#3086|40
Utility|{164B10B9-B200-11D0-8C61-00A0C91E29D5}|#3087|50
Resources|{164B10B9-B200-11D0-8C61-00A0C91E29D5}|#3109|60
..\WinForm.vsz|{164B10B9-B200-11D0-8C61-00A0C91E29D5}|#3050|10|#3051|➥
{164B10B9-B200-11D0-8C61-00A0C91E29D5}|4527| |Form.vb
..\Class.vsz|{164B10B9-B200-11D0-8C61-00A0C91E29D5}|#3020|20|#3021|➥
{164B10B9-B200-11D0-8C61-00A0C91E29D5}|4510| |Class.vb
..\Exception.vsz| |Exception|20|Adds new Exception including inherited
constructors|➥
{164B10B9-B200-11D0-8C61-00A0C91E29D5}|4510| |Exception.vb
..\Module.vsz|{164B10B9-B200-11D0-8C61-00A0C91E29D5}|#3028|30|#3029|➥
{164B10B9-B200-11D0-8C61-00A0C91E29D5}|4514| |Module.vb
..\Component.vsz|{164B10B9-B200-11D0-8C61-00A0C91E29D5}|#3024|40|#3025|➥
{164B10B9-B200-11D0-8C61-00A0C91E29D5}|4512| |Component.vb
..\UserControl.vsz|{164B10B9-B200-11D0-8C61-00A0C91E29D5}|#3048|50|#3049|➥
{164B10B9-B200-11D0-8C61-00A0C91E29D5}|4526| |UserControl.vb
..\WinDataForm.vsz|{164B10B9-B200-11D0-8C61-00A0C91E29D5}|#3092|55|#3093|➥
 {164B10B9-B200-11D0-8C61-00A0C91E29D5}|4549| |DataForm.vb
```

We have added the line in boldface into the default VSDIR file located in C:\Program Files\ Microsoft Visual Studio .NET 2003\Vb7\VBProjectItems\Local Project Items\ LocalProjectItems.vsdir.

The location of this file may be different if you installed Visual Studio .NET onto another drive, but I'm sure you will be able to find the file on your system.

This is all we have to do to tell Visual Studio .NET that there is a new wizard; it will now offer an Exception as an option in the Add New Item dialog. See Figure 13-2.

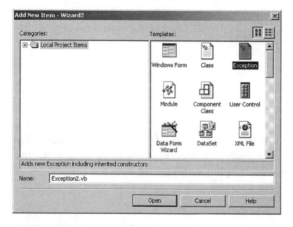

Figure 13-2. *Add New Item dialog*

Unfortunately, our wizard is not yet complete: it is missing the script that will be run when the wizard is activated.

Script Directories

The scripting language is JavaScript, and you have full access to the Visual Studio .NET DTE object. See Figure 13-3.

📁 Microsoft Visual Studio .NET 2003
⊞ 📁 Common7
⊞ 📁 CompactFrameworkSDK
⊞ 📁 Enterprise Samples
⊞ 📁 EnterpriseFrameworks
⊞ 📁 JavaLanguageConversionAssistant
⊞ 📁 PreEmptive Solutions
⊞ 📁 SDK
⊞ 📁 Setup
 📁 sqlserver
⊟ 📁 Vb7
  ⊞ 📁 Bin
   📁 DesignerTemplates
  ⊞ 📁 eVBProjectItems
  ⊞ 📁 VB Samples
  ⊞ 📁 VBProjectItems
   📁 VBProjects
  ⊞ 📁 VBUpgrade
  ⊟ 📁 VBWizards
    📁 1033
   ⊟ 📁 Exception
    ⊟ 📁 Scripts
      📁 1033
    ⊟ 📁 Templates

Figure 13-3. *Visual Studio .NET scripts directory structure*

We need to place our script into the Vb7\VBWizards\Exception directory under the Visual Studio .NET installation folder. Then we need to create two subdirectories within the Exception directory: Scripts and Templates. As you can guess, Scripts contains the code that will be executed by the scripting engine, and Templates contains code that will be preprocessed and copied into Visual Studio .NET as a result of the wizard execution.

Script Code

Now that we have created the necessary directories, we can create the actual script file. We will name the script file default.js and place it into the Scripts\1033 directory. Our script file will inherit all functions from the common.js file in Vb7\VBWizards\1033. All we need to do in our script file is to provide code for the OnFinish event handler. This event is fired when the scripting engine is done processing the user interface, and since our script wizard does not contain a user interface, it will be fired immediately:

```
function OnFinish(selProj, selObj)
{
    var oldSuppressUIValue = true;
    try
    {
        oldSuppressUIValue = dte.SuppressUI;
        var bSilent = wizard.FindSymbol("SILENT_WIZARD");
        dte.SuppressUI = bSilent;

        var strItemName = wizard.FindSymbol("ITEM_NAME");
        var strTemplatePath = wizard.FindSymbol("TEMPLATES_PATH");
        var strTemplateFile = strTemplatePath + "\\Exception.vb";

        var item = AddFileToVSProject(strItemName, selProj, selObj, _
            strTemplateFile, true);
        if( item )
        {
            item.Properties("SubType").Value = "Code";
            var editor = item.Open(vsViewKindPrimary);
            editor.Visible = true;
        }

        return 0;
    }
    catch(e)
    {
        switch(e.number)
        {
        case -2147221492 /* OLE_E_PROMPTSAVECANCELLED */ :
            return -2147221492;

        case -2147024816 /* FILE_ALREADY_EXISTS */ :
        case -2147213313 /* VS_E_WIZARDBACKBUTTONPRESS */ :
            return -2147213313;

        default:
            ReportError(e.description);
            return -2147213313;
        }
    }
    finally
    {
        dte.SuppressUI = oldSuppressUIValue;
    }
}
```

The code simply takes the `Exception.vb` file from `..\Templates\1033` and adds it to the current solution. A call to `AddFileToVSProject()` will take the template file, preprocess it, and add it to the current project. Preprocessing in this case consists of replacing [!output <name>] directives by the appropriate text.

Template

The template is a plain Visual Basic .NET file with specified preprocessor directives:

```
Public Class [!output SAFE_ITEM_NAME]
        Inherits Exception

        Public Sub New(ByVal message As String)
            MyBase.New(message)
        End Sub

        Public Sub New(ByVal message As String, ByVal cause As Exception)
            MyBase.New(message, cause)
        End Sub

        Public Sub New()
            MyBase.New()
        End Sub

End Class
```

Save this file under `Templates\1033\Exception.vb`. When the wizard executes the `OnFinish()` handler, this file will be included in the current project, and the first line will be replaced by the name you specified in the Add New Item dialog.

Summary

We have finished our first very simple wizard. It appears in the Add New Item dialog. We can execute custom code in the script file, and it is quite useful. Unfortunately, it does not allow us to do any advanced processing. To do that, we will need to create a COM-based wizard.

Wizards in Visual Basic .NET

The wizard we are going to write will be a skeleton that you can use to create your own wizards. We will implement the `IDTWizard` interface. This interface is actually very simple to implement, since it contains only one method: `Execute`. This method is called whenever Visual Studio .NET invokes the wizard. You must do all the processing in the method. Once the method returns, the wizard is unloaded.[1]

---

1. Technically speaking, the `IUknown.Release()` method is called on the interface, which should unload the wizard.

The general overview of the wizard's object model is on the UML model shown in Figure 13-4. The model shows only the most important classes and interfaces, not the actual implementation details.

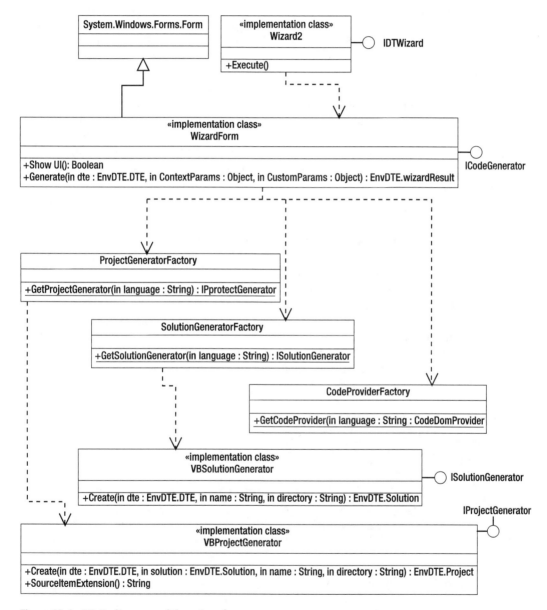

Figure 13-4. *UML diagram of the wizard*

As you can see, the Wizard2 class is a generalization of System.Windows.Forms.Form and depends on WizardForm, which implements the interface ICodeGenerator. The WizardForm, in turn, depends on ProjectGeneratorFactory, SolutionGeneratorFactory, and CodeProviderFactory, which depend on classes from the `Microsoft.*` and `System.CodeDOM.*` namespaces; Solution-GeneratorFactory depends on VBSolutionGenerator, and ProjectGeneratorFactory depends on VBProjectGenerator. The last two classes are implementation classes for the interfaces ISolutionGenerator and IProjectGenerator. I believe that this is the right level of modeling for any application: it describes the most important elements of the program, but does not go into unnecessary details.

Depending on the Visual Studio .NET languages you want to support, you will need to add references to the Code DOM assemblies. Depending on your installation of Visual Studio .NET, you will have at least `VBCodeProvider` in the `Microsoft.VisualBasic` assembly. If you have chosen to install C#, you will also have `CSharpCodeProvider` in `Microsoft.Csharp`, and if you have installed VC++, `MCppCodeProvider` defined in the assembly `Microsoft.MCpp` will also be available.

Because the wizard is going to have a Windows Forms user interface, we will also need a reference to `System.Windows.Forms`.

Getting Started

To get started, start a new Visual Basic class library project. Add references to `System.Windows.Forms`, `EnvDTE`, `System.CodeDOM`, and, depending on the Visual Studio .NET languages you wish to support, references to the code provider assemblies.

Once the assemblies have been added, add a new Windows Form to the project. We are now all set to dive in and implement the wizard details.

The wizard we are going to implement is going to be a standard COM in-process server. We can use any programming language that supports building COM servers. This means that we can also use Visual Basic .NET as long as we mark the implementation class with a GUID and we register the generated .NET library for the COM Interop server. To do this from Visual Studio .NET, make sure the Register for COM Interop is ticked. See Figure 13-5.

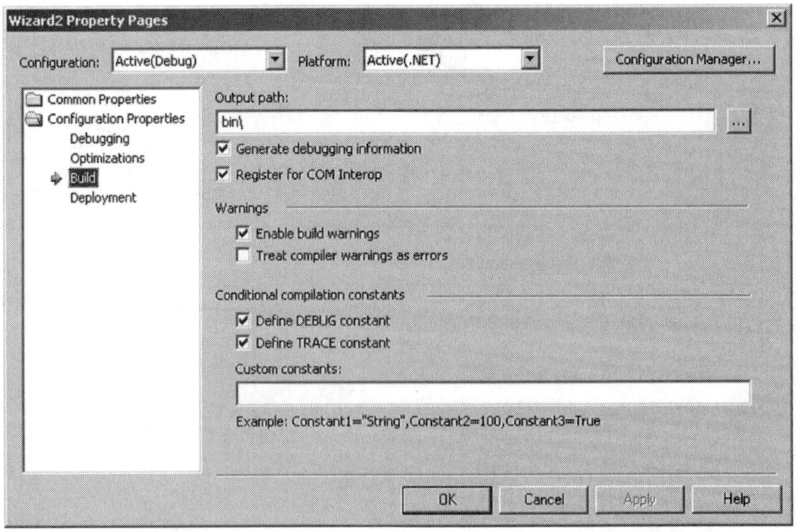

Figure 13-5. *Build properties dialog*

Setting this option instructs Visual Studio .NET to call regasm after a successful build. You must also mark the implementing class with a GUID attribute:

```vb
Imports EnvDTE
Imports System.Windows.Forms
Imports System.Runtime.InteropServices

Namespace Com.Apress.VSNET.Wizard2

    '''
    ''' Main implementing class. Implements Execute method where it
    ''' gathers input from the user interface
    ''' and finally builds the project
    '''
    <Guid("6B967689-DE9C-4fbc-9410-FC6A7C7C6F06")> _
    Public Class Wizard2
        Implements IDTWizard

        ''' IDTWizard.Execute implementation
        Public Sub Execute(ByVal Application As Object, _
            ByVal hwndOwner As Integer, _
            ByRef ContextParams() As Object, _
            ByRef CustomParams() As Object, _
            ByRef retval As EnvDTE.wizardResult) _
            Implements EnvDTE.IDTWizard.Execute

            ''' Wizard2 main code.

        End Sub
    End Class

End Namespace
```

The lines in bold represent import statements for EnvDTE, which exposes the Visual Studio .NET environment objects, and System.Runtime.InteropServices, which allows you to create a COM server from .NET managed code.

We must also mark the class that is going to be exposed as implementation of the IDTWizard interface with a GUID attribute. This will create a registry server entry, which identifies the created .NET library as a COM in-process server. See Figure 13-6.

Figure 13-6. *Registry entry for the COM server*

You will need either the CLSID or the program ID as a reference to the wizard's COM library. The program ID is generated from the namespace and class name: given the code from the previous listing, the program ID will be Wizard2.Com.Apress.VSNET.Wizard2.Wizard2.

IDTWizard

This is the core interface of the wizard object model; each wizard must implement this interface's Execute method. This method is incorrectly documented in the MSDN reference, but Visual Studio .NET will generate the correct method skeleton. The correct implementation is

```
Public Sub Execute(ByVal Application As Object, _
ByVal hwndOwner As Integer, ByRef ContextParams() As Object, _
        ByRef CustomParams() As Object, ByRef retval As EnvDTE.wizardResult)
```

Let's revisit the code we have created in the first listing and add code that will actually allow you to see what the wizard actually executes:

```
Imports EnvDTE
Imports System.Windows.Forms
Imports System.Runtime.InteropServices

Namespace Com.Apress.VSNET.Wizard2

    '''
    ''' Main implementing class. Implements Execute method where it
    ''' gathers input from the user interface
    ''' and finally builds the project
    '''
    <Guid("6B967689-DE9C-4fbc-9410-FC6A7C7C6F06")> _
    Public Class Wizard2
        Implements IDTWizard

        ''' IDTWizard.Execute implementation
        Public Sub Execute(ByVal Application As Object,
            ByVal hwndOwner As Integer, _
            ByRef ContextParams() As Object, _
            ByRef CustomParams() As Object, _
            ByRef retval As EnvDTE.wizardResult) _
            Implements EnvDTE.IDTWizard.Execute

            ''' Wizard2 main code.
            Dim generator As ICodeGenerator = New WizardGeneratorForm
```

```
    ' check whether we should generate the code
If (generator.ShowUI()) Then
    ' call generator's generate method to do the actual processing.
    retval = generator.Generate(CType(Application, _DTE),_
            ContextParams, CustomParams)
End If


    End Sub
End Class

End Namespace
```

I have decided to create the ICodeGenerator interface that must be implemented by a concrete class. This interface has two methods: ShowUI() and Generate(_DTE, Object(), Object()). The main code of the wizard calls ShowUI(), and if it returns True, it will proceed to call Generate. In our example, we are going to create a Windows Form that implements this interface.

The implementation I have chosen to show is a Form subclass that implements the ICodeGenerator interface. With this concept, the ShowUI() method simply calls the ShowDialog() method of the form. The Generate method will take care of the actual project creation and file generation.

Code Generation

We are now ready to move on to the actual implementation of the wizard. We will make good use of the introduction to DTE objects that we saw in chapter 12, on Macros, since we will use the _DTE object in the Generate method.

OK, now comes the fun part. We will write code that will create a new project, create source directories, and generate the source files. Before we can do this, we need to gather a few user settings, such as the wizard name and description.

I believe that I do not need to discuss Windows Forms settings in much detail, and so I will limit the description to simply stating that once the ShowDialog() method completes execution, our wizard will have gathered all user input and verified that the user input is in the correct format.

Even though the code generation can be done using simple StringBuilder objects, we are going to have a look at a more interesting, though a bit more complicated, way of using Code Document Object Model (DOM). Using Code DOM will allow us to generate code for any Visual Studio .NET programming language, not just Visual Basic.

Code DOM Support

We will start with creating a simple CodeProviderFactory class that will contain a single static method that will return an appropriate CodeDomProvider object for the specified programming language or throw an ArgumentException. The Generate method will use CodeProviderFactory to get an instance of CodeDomProvider that will be used to generate the actual source code. You must add a reference to the assemblies System.CodeDOM, System.CodeDOM.Compiler, and the CodeDOM assemblies for the Visual Studio.NET languages you wish to support. VBCodeProvider will be installed, and since you are using Visual Basic .NET, CsharpCodeProvider and MCppCodeProvider will be installed only if you have selected to install C# and VC++:

```
'''
''' Factory class that returns ICodeGenerator for the specific language
'''
Public Class CodeProviderFactory

'''
''' Returns ICodeGenerator for specified language
'''
Public Shared Function GetCodeProvider(ByVal language As String) As CodeDomProvider
    Dim provider As CodeDomProvider = Nothing
    If (language = "VB") Then
    provider = New VBCodeProvider
    ElseIf (language = "C#") Then
        provider = New CSharpCodeProvider
    ElseIf (language = "CPP") Then
        provider = New MCppCodeProvider
    Else
        Throw New ArgumentException(_
            String.Format("Language {0} is not supported", language))
    End If

    Return provider

End Function

End Class
```

Dissecting the Generate() Method

We are now ready to implement the heart of the wizard's functionality. Even though the final result is not going to be very complicated; the code is very dense:

```
' get settings from ContextParams
Dim projectName As String = ContextParams(1)
Dim projectDirectory As String = ContextParams(2)
```

Our Generate method gets called after the user has selected the project name and directory. We need to get the values entered by the user and use them to create the new solution. To do this, we can access the ContextParams array; the values in the array are different depending on the project type. As we are creating a project, the first value is the project name, and the second value is the project directory. More information on ContextParams can be found on the MSDN page http://msdn.microsoft.com/library/default.asp?url=/library/en-us/vsintro7/html/vxlrfcontextparamsenum.asp.

Now that we have the project's name and directory, we can create a new solution; we will use the project name and directory to do this. Once a solution is created, we will add a new project into it. We will use Visual Studio .NET standard templates; we need to get the path to these templates. The templates are usually located in C:\Program Files\Microsoft Visual Studio .NET 2003\Vb7. However, we do not want to hard-code the template paths directly. Instead, we will use dte.Solution.ProjectItemsTemplatePath() to get the templates path. The method accepts a single parameter, which identifies the template name whose path we want. We must add a reference to the VSLangProj assembly to get access to the VSLangProj namespace, which defines the constants for this method:

```
' get template paths
Dim templatesRoot As String = _
    dte.Solution.ProjectItemsTemplatePath(_
    VSLangProj.PrjKind.prjKindVBProject) & "..\VBWizards"
Dim projectTemplate = templatesRoot & _
    "\ConsoleApplication\Templates\1033\ClassLibrary.vbproj"
```

Once we have the paths to the files, we can use them to create a new project and add a new class file to it.

This is where we are going to use Code DOM to generate the contents of the new class file, save it to a temporary location, add a copy of the file into the project, and finally delete the temporary file:

```
' create wizard namespace, class, and main method.
Dim mainClass As CodeTypeDeclaration = New CodeTypeDeclaration("Demo")

Dim mainMethod As CodeEntryPointMethod = New CodeEntryPointMethod
mainMethod.Name = "Main"
mainMethod.ReturnType = Nothing
mainMethod.Attributes = MemberAttributes.Static Or MemberAttributes.Public

mainClass.Members.Add(mainMethod)

Dim rootNS As System.CodeDom.CodeNamespace = _
    New System.CodeDom.CodeNamespace("com.apress.vsnet.wizard")
rootNS.Types.Add(mainClass)

' generate the code and add it to the file
Dim tempClassFile As String = Path.GetTempFileName() & ".vb"
Dim stream As FileStream = New FileStream(tempClassFile, FileMode.Create)
Dim writer As StreamWriter = New StreamWriter(stream)
CodeProviderFactory.GetCodeProvider("VB").CreateGenerator().➥
GenerateCodeFromNamespace(rootNS, writer, Nothing)
writer.Close()
stream.Close()

' create a simple new class
Dim projectItem As ProjectItem
projectItem = project.ProjectItems.AddFromFileCopy(tempClassFile)
projectItem.Name = "Main.vb"

File.Delete(tempClassFile)
```

The first step is to create a `CodeTypeDeclaration` object, which represents the main class. The code then adds a `CodeEntryPointMethod` object to the model of the main class. This represents the application's Main method. Finally, we add the `CodeTypeDeclaration` instance to a `CodeNamespace`. All this code will result in the following code in Visual Basic .NET:

```
Namespace com.apress.vsnet.wizard
    Public Class Demo

        Public Shared Sub Main()
        End Sub
    End Class
End Namespace
```

Changing the language parameter to "C#" in a call to `CodeProviderFactory.GetCodeProvider` will generate the following code:

```
namespace com.apress.vsnet.wizard {

    public class Demo {

        public static void Main() {
        }
    }
}
```

Finally, changing the language parameter to "CPP" will generate the same code in managed C++:

```
namespace com {namespace apress {namespace vsnet {namespace wizard {

    using namespace System;
    public __gc class Demo;

    public __gc class Demo {

        public static void Main() {
        }
    };


    public static void Main() {
    }
}}}}
```

Unfortunately, we have a created Visual Basic project, so adding a C# or Managed C++ code file is not going to work, but you can see how easily we can generate valid source code for different Visual Studio .NET languages.

Debugging

Even if we are creating the simplest wizard, we will still need to debug it. Debugging usually involves starting a new instance of Visual Studio .NET and starting a testing project. I would not recommend debugging a wizard on an existing project because a small bug in the wizard's code could (and will) damage your existing source code. Before you start debugging your wizard, make sure that Visual Studio .NET will start a new instance and that it will attach a debugger to the new instance. To do this, change the project's Debugging settings under Configuration Properties. Make sure you have selected to start an external program as a start action and that the external program is Visual Studio .NET. See Figure 13-7.

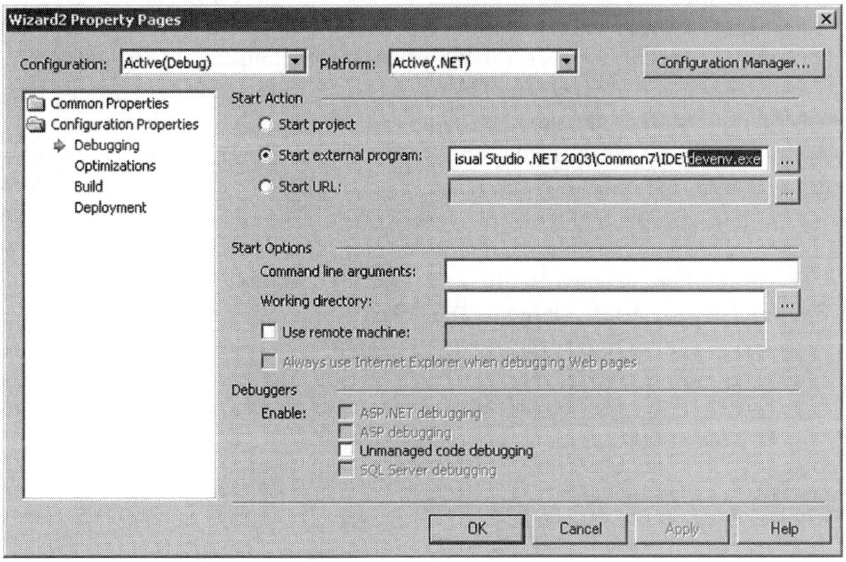

Figure 13-7. *Debug settings dialog*

Then start the wizard, and the debugger will stop on any breakpoints you have defined. See Figure 13-8.

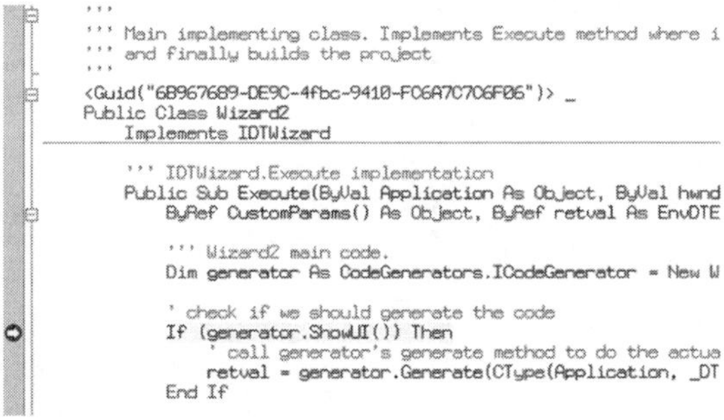

Figure 13-8. *Breakpoint hit in the debugger*

I am not going to discuss the debugger here, since it is covered elsewhere in the book. I am only going to add a warning that if you stop debugging, the new instance of Visual Studio .NET will be terminated, and any work in that new instance will not be saved.

Once you are happy that your wizard's code is working, you can take a look at ways to improve the wizard's user interface.

Resources

We need to have a look at Win32 resources that need to be included in the wizard's COM DLL to make the user interface more friendly. We should at least include an icon, and I would recommend including the resource identifiers to be used in the VSDIR file. We have two basic options: we can either use the vbc command line compiler to compile the whole wizard project manually, or we can create a resource-only DLL using Visual C++. Using a command-line compiler allows us to have only one project for the wizard, but we must maintain a build script that will use vbc to build the wizard. Every time you add or remove a file in the project or modify the directory structure, you must also update the build file. The advantage of this approach is that you have only one binary file that you must distribute. The second approach uses a Visual C++ resource-only library. A resource-only library is a DLL that contains only a DllMain entry point and Win32 resources. This approach allows you to maintain the entire solution using Visual Studio .NET. Moreover, you can change the language settings just by replacing the resource DLL without having to modify the wizard's binary. This is an approach that is used in large applications with many user interface elements. The disadvantage of using a resource-only DLL is that you have two pieces of binary files that you need to distribute. I am going to show you the Visual C++ resource-only DLL solution.

To start a resource-only project, add a new Visual C++ Win32 Project. See Figure 13-9.

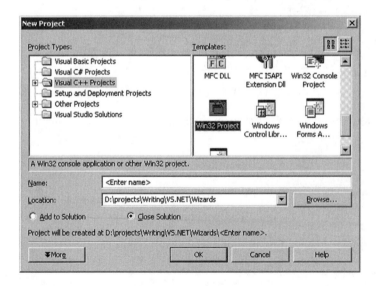

Figure 13-9. *New Visual C++ Project dialog*

To make sure that the newly created project compiles as resource-only DLL, remove all source code files except StdAfx.h. The resulting solution structure may look like that shown in Figure 13-10.

Figure 13-10. *Project structure with the resource DLL project*

This structure clearly shows that we have two projects in the wizard solution. The first project is the actual Visual Basic wizard COM library; the second project is the Visual C++ resource-only DLL project.

To make sure your newly created Visual C++ project compiles as a resource-only DLL, you must modify the project properties. See Figure 13-11.

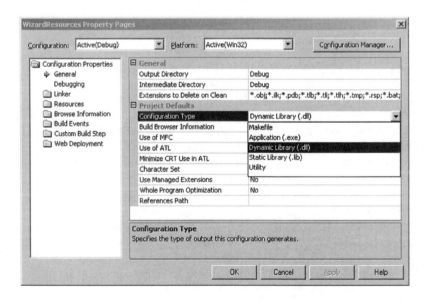

Figure 13-11. *Build properties dialog for the resource DLL project*

Make sure the project output is Dynamic Library (.dll). This is not enough, though. If we leave projects settings like this, the linker will include all standard libraries into the resulting binary file; the result of this will be a library that is far bigger than necessary. We must instruct the linker not to process any standard libraries and to include only the resources in the output DLL.

If you set Resource Only DLL to Yes and turn off AssemblyGeneration, the linker is going to produce just a standard PE DLL header followed by a Win32 resource block. The result will be a very compact resource-only Win32 unmanaged DLL.

All we need to do, then, is to edit the resources, such as strings, icons, and bitmaps. You can use Win32 resources from .NET code, and you can tell Visual Studio .NET to process your resource-only DLL in the VSDIR wizard definition file.

Refer to the installation paragraph to learn how to use the resource DLL instead of the main COM server library.

Installation

To install the wizard, you need to compile the resource project, create a VSZ file, and update the corresponding VSDIR file. We have already discussed the content of these files in detail, so I am going to summarize what we need to do in just a few lines.

We must create the file Wizard2.vsz with the following content:

```
VSWizard 7.0
Wizard={6B967689-DE9C-4fbc-9410-FC6A7C7C6F06}
```

The CLSID on the second line must match the CLSID in the Guid attribute of the IDTWizard implementation class.

The next step is to update the file Projects.vsdir; the line that was added to the file is shown in boldface:

```
ClassLibrary.vsz|{164B10B9-B200-11D0-8C61-00A0C91E29D5}|#3000|20|#3001|➡
{164B10B9-B200-11D0-8C61-00A0C91E29D5}|4500| |ClassLibrary
WindowsControl.vsz|{164B10B9-B200-11D0-8C61-00A0C91E29D5}|#3016|30|#3017|➡
{164B10B9-B200-11D0-8C61-00A0C91E29D5}|4508| |WindowsControlLibrary
WebControl.vsz|{164B10B9-B200-11D0-8C61-00A0C91E29D5}|#3010|60|#3011|➡
{164B10B9-B200-11D0-8C61-00A0C91E29D5}|4505| |WebControlLibrary
WindowsService.vsz|{164B10B9-B200-11D0-8C61-00A0C91E29D5}|#3018|80|#3019|➡
{164B10B9-B200-11D0-8C61-00A0C91E29D5}|4509| |WindowsService
EmptyProject.vbproj|{164B10B9-B200-11D0-8C61-00A0C91E29D5}|#3004|90|#3005|➡
{164B10B9-B200-11D0-8C61-00A0C91E29D5}|4502| |Project
EmptyWebProject.vbproj|{164B10B9-B200-11D0-8C61-00A0C91E29D5}|#3006|100|#3007|➡
{164B10B9-B200-11D0-8C61-00A0C91E29D5}|4503| 1|WebProject1|Web
ImportProjectFolderVB.vsz|{164B10B9-B200-11D0-8C61-00A0C91E29D5}|#3088|110|#3089|
➡ {164B10B9-B200-11D0-8C61-00A0C91E29D5}|4519|33|Project
Wizard2.vsz| |Wizard^2|110|Wizard for creating wizards|➡
D:\projects\Writing\VS.NET\Wizards\WizardResources\Debug\WizardResources.dll|1|➡
|WizardProject
```

The file WizardResources.dll must be specified only if you have decided to build a resource DLL. If you do not wish to use a resource DLL at all or if you have included Win32 resources in your Visual Basic wizard library, replace the DLL path with the wizard's CLSID.

When you are done modifying the files, start new instance of Visual Studio .NET or restart the existing one, and the Wizard^2 wizard will appear as an item in the New Project dialog, as shown in Figure 13-12.

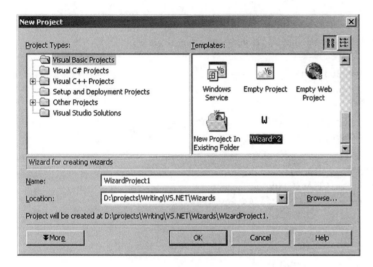

Figure 13-12. *Our wizard displayed in the New Project dialog*

When you click OK, Visual Studio .NET will run the wizard's Execute method, which will show the familiar user interface and generate a new wizard project.

Improving the Wizard

The final step in making the wizard completely language-independent is to create a class that implements ISolutionGenerator and IProjectGenerator interfaces that will take care of creating a solution and adding a project to the solution for the appropriate programming language.

ISolutionGenerator will have only one method, Create, which will create a solution; IProjectGenerator will have a method Create, which will create a new project, and a property SourceItemExtension(), which will return an extension for source files for the implementation.

The final source code for the wizard is going to be much more flexible and much easier to follow:

```
Imports EnvDTE
Imports System.Windows.Forms
Imports System.CodeDom
Imports System.CodeDom.Compiler
Imports System.Text
Imports System.IO
```

```vb
Imports Microsoft.CSharp
Imports Microsoft.VisualBasic
Imports Microsoft.MCpp

Namespace Com.Apress.VSNET.Wizard2.CodeSupport

    Public Interface IWizardCodeGenerator

        '''
        ''' Returns Form the wizard needs to generate the code
        '''
        Function ShowUI() As Boolean

        '''
        ''' Generates the code if GetForm() returns Nothing or
        ''' GetForm.ShowDialog() = DialogResult.OK
        '''
        Function Generate(ByVal dte As _DTE, _
            ByRef ContextParams() As Object, _
            ByRef CustomParams() As Object) As EnvDTE.wizardResult

    End Interface

    ''' Interface for generating new Solution
    Public Interface ISolutionGenerator
        ''' Creates new solution and returns the created Solution interface
        Function Create(ByVal dte As _DTE, ByVal name As String, _
            ByVal directory As String) As Solution
    End Interface

    ''' Interface for generating new Project
    Public Interface IProjectGenerator
        ''' Creates new project in a solution and returns the created
        ''' Project interface
        Function Create(ByVal dte As _DTE, _
            ByVal solution As Solution, ByVal name As String, _
            ByVal directory As String) As Project
        ''' Returns extension for the source code files
        ReadOnly Property SourceItemExtension() As String
    End Interface

    ''' Visual Basic .NET implementation for ISolutionGenerator
    Public Class VBSolutionGenerator
        Implements ISolutionGenerator
```

```vb
    Function Create(ByVal dte As _DTE, ByVal name As String, _
        ByVal directory As String) As Solution _
        Implements ISolutionGenerator.Create
        Dim sol As Solution = dte.Solution

        ' create new solution
        sol.Create(directory, name)

        Return sol
    End Function
End Class

''' Visual Basic .NET implementation for IProjectGenerator
Public Class VBProjectGenerator
    Implements IProjectGenerator

    Public Function Create(ByVal dte As _DTE, _
        ByVal solution As EnvDTE.Solution, _
        ByVal name As String, _
        ByVal directory As String) As EnvDTE.Project _
        Implements IProjectGenerator.Create
        Dim templatesRoot As String = _
            dte.Solution.ProjectItemsTemplatePath(_
                VSLangProj.PrjKind.prjKindVBProject) & _
                "\..\VBWizards"
        Dim projectTemplate = templatesRoot & _
            "\ConsoleApplication\Templates\1033\" & _
            "ConsoleApplication.vbproj"

        ' create project from existing
        Dim project As Project = _
            solution.AddFromTemplate(projectTemplate, _
                directory, name, True)

        Return project
    End Function

    Public ReadOnly Property SourceItemExtension() As String _
        Implements IProjectGenerator.SourceItemExtension
        Get
            Return ".vb"
        End Get
    End Property
End Class
```

```vb
'''
''' Factory class that returns ICodeGenerator for the specific language
'''
Public Class CodeProviderFactory

    '''
    ''' Returns ICodeGenerator for specified language
    '''
    Public Shared Function GetCodeProvider(_
        ByVal language As String) As CodeDomProvider
        Dim provider As CodeDomProvider = Nothing
        If (language = "VB") Then
            provider = New VBCodeProvider
        ElseIf (language = "C#") Then
            provider = New CSharpCodeProvider
        ElseIf (language = "CPP") Then
            provider = New MCppCodeProvider
        Else
            Throw New ArgumentException(_
                String.Format("Language {0} is not supported", _
                    language))
        End If

        Return provider

    End Function

End Class

''' Factory class for generating ISolutionGenerator
Public Class SolutionGeneratorFactory
    Public Shared Function GetSolutionGenerator(_
        ByVal language As String) As ISolutionGenerator
        If (language = "VB") Then
            Return New VBSolutionGenerator
        End If

        Throw New ArgumentException(_
            String.Format("language {0} is not supported", _
                language))
    End Function
End Class
```

```
''' Factory class for generating IProjectGenerator
Public Class ProjectGeneratorFactory
    Public Shared Function GetProjectGenerator(_
        ByVal language As String) As IProjectGenerator
        If (language = "VB") Then
            Return New VBProjectGenerator
        End If

        Throw New ArgumentException(_
            String.Format("language {0} is not supported", _
                language))
    End Function
End Class

End Namespace
```

This source file contains all improvements we have discussed and their Visual Basic .NET implementations (VBSolutionGenerator and VBProjectGenerator). The file also contains factories that return appropriate implementations for the generator interfaces. Currently, we support only Visual Basic .NET, but it would not be difficult to add support for another programming language by creating appropriate implementation classes for the generator interfaces and adding code to instantiate the implementation class to the factory methods:

```
Public Shared Function GetProjectGenerator(_
    ByVal language As String) As IProjectGenerator
    If (language = "VB") Then
        Return New VBProjectGenerator
    End If
    If (language = "C#") Then
        Return New CSharpProjectGenerator
    End If

    Throw New ArgumentException(_
        String.Format("language {0} is not supported", _
            language))
End Function
```

Finally, we will modify the Generate method of our add-in to use the newly created generators framework. There is one more thing to consider, though. We have flexible code generators, but our wizard appears only in Visual Basic projects. We are going to add the wizard definition (VSZ and VSDIR) to other language folders, and we will add a custom parameter to the VSZ file, which will specify the appropriate language:

```
VSWizard 7.0
Wizard={6B967689-DE9C-4fbc-9410-FC6A7C7C6F06}
param="language=VB"
```

The revised VSZ file includes the param field. The value will be passed to the Generate method in the CustomParams array. If you want to use the wizard as a C# project, modify the VSZ file's param value:

```
VSWizard 7.0
Wizard={6B967689-DE9C-4fbc-9410-FC6A7C7C6F06}
param="language=C#"
```

The wizard will then take C# templates for the project and will use the C# code DOM generator to create the project:

```
'''
''' Generate the code
'''
Public Function Generate(ByVal dte As EnvDTE._DTE, _
    ByRef ContextParams() As Object, _
    ByRef CustomParams() As Object) As EnvDTE.wizardResult _
    Implements IWizardCodeGenerator.Generate

    Dim language As String = "VB"

    For Each o As Object In CustomParams
        Dim params() As String = CType(o, String).Split("=")
            Dim param As String = params(0)
            Dim value As String = params(1)

            If (param = "language") Then
                language = value
            End If
    Next

    ' assign code names
    Dim className As String = wizardName.Text

    ' get settings from ContextParams
    Dim projectName As String = ContextParams(1)
    Dim projectDirectory As String = ContextParams(2)

    ' get the solution object
    Dim sol As Solution = _
        SolutionGeneratorFactory.GetSolutionGenerator(language).➥
        Create(dte, projectName, projectDirectory)

    ' create project from existing
    Dim project As Project =_
        ProjectGeneratorFactory.GetProjectGenerator(language). ➥
        Create(dte, sol, projectName, projectDirectory)
```

```
    ' create wizard namespace, class and main method.
    Dim mainClass As CodeTypeDeclaration = New CodeTypeDeclaration("Demo")

    Dim mainMethod As CodeEntryPointMethod = New CodeEntryPointMethod
    mainMethod.Name = "Main"
    mainMethod.ReturnType = Nothing
    mainMethod.Attributes = MemberAttributes.Static Or MemberAttributes.Public

    mainClass.Members.Add(mainMethod)

    Dim rootNS As System.CodeDom.CodeNamespace = _
        New System.CodeDom.CodeNamespace("com.apress.vsnet.wizard")
    rootNS.Types.Add(mainClass)

    ' generate the code and add it to the file
    Dim tempClassFile As String = Path.GetTempFileName()
    Dim stream As FileStream = New FileStream(tempClassFile, FileMode.Create)
    Dim writer As StreamWriter = New StreamWriter(stream)
    CodeProviderFactory.GetCodeProvider(language).CreateGenerator().➡
    GenerateCodeFromNamespace(rootNS, writer, Nothing)
    writer.Close()
    stream.Close()

    ' create a simple new class
    Dim projectItem As ProjectItem
    projectItem = project.ProjectItems.AddFromFileCopy(tempClassFile)
    projectItem.Name = String.Format("Main{0}",_
    ProjectGeneratorFactory.GetProjectGenerator(language). ➡
    SourceItemExtension)

    File.Delete(tempClassFile)
End Function
```

As you can see, the Generate method is now much cleaner, much easier to read, and most important, much more flexible. We now have a wizard skeleton that can create projects as well as source code files for any Visual Studio .NET programming language.

Summary

You have learned how Visual Studio .NET loads wizards, and you know how to write a simple script-based wizard as well as a more complicated COM wizard. You know how to use the Code DOM to create source code for any Visual Studio .NET programming language. You have also learned how to install the wizard, and with what you have learned from the chapter on macros, you possess the knowledge to extend the IDE in almost any way you like.

APPENDIX A

■ ■ ■

Project Files

This Appendix explains which files are created for each project type in Visual Studio .NET 2003 and their various descriptions. First, you'll see the project types and the files created by default with those project types. Then, in the second section, you'll see these various file types explained.

Project Types and Their Associated Files

Table A-1 presents the project types and their associated files. For an explanation of the file types themselves, please refer to the next section.

Table A-1. Project Types

Serial Number	Project Type	References Added by Default	Files Created by Wizard
1	**Windows Application** A project for creating an application with a Windows user interface.	`System.dll` `System.Data.dll` `System.Drawing.dll` `System.Windows.Forms.dll` `System.XML.dll`	**Assembly Information File:** `AssemblyInfo.cs` or `AssemblyInfo.vb` **Source Code File:** (vb or cs) **Resource File:** `resx` **Project file:** `csproj` or `vbproj` **Visual Studio Solution:** `Sln` **ICON File:** `Ico` (not created for VB) **Visual Studio Project User Options:** `Csproj.user` **Solution User Options:** `.suo`
2	**Class Library** A project for creating classes to use in other applications. By default, on creation of a Class Library, a class is also created for writing code.	`System.dll` `System.Data.dll` `System.XML.dll`	**Source Code File:** -(vb or cs) **Assembly Information File:** `AssemblyInfo.cs` or `AssemblyInfo.vb` **Project File:** `csproj` or `vbproj` **Visual Studio Solution:** `Sln` **Visual Studio Project User Options:** `csproj.user` or `vbproj.user` **Solution User Options:** `.suo`

Continued

Table A-1. Project Types (continued)

Serial Number	Project Type	References Added by Default	Files Created by Wizard
3	**Windows Control Library** A project for creating controls to use in Windows applications.	System.dl System.Data.dll System.Drawing.dll System.Windows.Forms.dll System.XML.dll	**Source Code File:** (vb or cs) **Assembly Information File:** AssemblyInfo.cs or AssemblyInfo.vb **Project File:** csproj or vbproj **Visual Studio Solution:** Sln **Visual Studio Project User Options:** csproj.user or vbproj.user **Resource File:** resx **Solution User Options:** .suo
4	**ASP.NET Web Application** A project for creating an application with a Web user interface. The source code file added has a class that inherits from System .Web.UI.Page. Note that the Solution file is created in the My Documents folder.	System.dll System.Data.dll System.Drawing.dll System.Web.dll System.XML.dll	**Assembly Information File:** AssemblyInfo.cs or AssemblyInfo.vb Global Application Class: Global.asax **Resource File:** Global.asax.resx **Source Code File:** Global.asax.cs or Global.asax.vb **Style Sheet:** Styles.css (not created for C# project) **Application Configuration File:** Web.config **Project File:** csproj or vbproj **WebInfo File:** .csproj.webinfo or .vbproj.webinfo **Web Form:** WebForm1.aspx **Resource File:** WebForm1.aspx.resx Source Code file (Code Behind): WebForm1.aspx.cs or WebForm1.aspx.vb **Visual Studio Solution:** Sln. **Solution User Options:** .suo

Table A-1. Project Types (continued)

Serial Number	Project Type	References Added by Default	Files Created by Wizard
5	**Web Service** A project for creating XML Web services to use from other applications. The source code file added has a class Inherits System. Web.Services.WebService. Note that the Solution file is created in the My Documents folder.	System.dll System.Data.dll System.Web.dll System.Web.WebServices.dll System.XML.dll	**Assembly Information File:** `AssemblyInfo.cs` or `AssemblyInfo.vb` **Global Application Class:** `Global.asax` **Resource File:** `Global.asax.resx` **Source Code File:** `Global.asax.vb` or `Global.asax.cs` **Application Configuration File:** `Web.config` **ProjectFile:** `Csproj` or `vbproj` **WebInfo File:** `.csproj.webinfo` or `.vbproj.webinfo` **Web Service:** `asmx` **Resource File:** `Service1.asmx.resx` **Source Code File (Code Behind):** `asmx.cs` or `asmx.vb` **Visual Studio Solution:** `Sln` **Solution User Options:** `.suo`
6	**ASP.NET Mobile Web Application** A project for creating an application viewable on PDAs, cellphones, and other mobile devices. The source code file added has a class that inherits from System.Web.UI.Mobile-Controls.MobilePage. The Solution file is created in the My Documents folder.	System.dll System.Data.dll System.Drawing.dll System.Web.dll System.Web.Mobile.dll System.XML.dll	**Assembly Information File:** `AssemblyInfo.cs` or `AssemblyInfo.vb` **Global Application Class:** `Global.asax` **Resource File:** `Global.asax.resx` **Source Code File:** `Global.asax.vb` or `Global.asax.cs` **Application Configuration File:** `Web.config` **Project File:** `csproj` or `vbproj` **WebInfo File:** `.csproj.webinfo` or `.vbproj.webinfo` **Web Form:** `WebForm1.aspx` **Resource File:** `WebForm1.aspx.resx` **Source Code File (Code Behind):** `WebForm1.aspx.cs` or `WebForm1.aspx.vb` **Visual Studio Solution:** `Sln` **Solution User Options:** `.suo`

Continued

Table A-1. Project Types (continued)

Serial Number	Project Type	References Added by Default	Files Created by Wizard
7	**Web Control Library** A project for creating controls to use in Web applications. The source code file added has a class that inherits from System.Web.UI.-WebControls.WebControl.	System.dll System.Drawing.dll System.Web.dll	**Assembly Information File:** AssemblyInfo.cs or AssemblyInfo.vb **Project File:** csproj or vbproj **Visual Studio Solution:** Sln **Visual Studio Project User Options:** csproj.user or vbproj.user **Source Code File:** vb or cs **Solution User Options:** .suo
8	**Console Application** A project for creating a command-line application. It is important to note in the source code file that a class is created for a C# project, while a module is created for a VB Project.	System.dll System.Drawing.dll System.Data.dll	**Assembly Information File:** AssemblyInfo.cs or AssemblyInfo.vb **Project File:** csproj or vbproj **Visual Studio Solution:** Sln **Visual Studio Project User Options:** csproj.user or vbproj.user **Source Code File:** vb or cs **ICON File:** Ico (not created for VB) **Solution User Options:** .suo
9	**Windows Service** A project for creating services for Windows. The source code file added has a class that inherits from System.ServiceProcess.-ServiceBase.	System.dll System.Data.dll System.ServiceProcess.dll System.XML.dll	**Assembly Information File:** AssemblyInfo.cs or AssemblyInfo.vb **Project File:** csproj or vbproj **Visual Studio Solution:** Sln **Visual Studio Project User Options:** csproj.user or vbproj.user **Source Code File:** vb or cs **Resource File:** resx **Solution User Options:** .suo

Project File Types Explained

Table A-2 explains a few file types that are associated with VS.NET 2003. The most important files are code files, Solution File, and the project files generated by the wizards.

Table A-2. File Types

Serial Number	File Type	File Extension	Description
1	Code File	`.vb` or `.cs`	Whenever a project is created in Visual Studio .NET, a code file is created in which the code is stored. Here are a few examples of what the code file could contain: Windows Form Class Module (Not in C#) Component Class User Control Custom Control Code File Inherited Form Web Custom Control Inherited User Control Windows Service COM Class Transactional Component Installer Class Web Form Web Service Web Custom Control
2	DataSet	`.xsd`	A file for creating an XML schema with DataSet classes.
3	XML File	`.xml`	XML files.
4	XML Schema	`.xsd`	Schema for XML documents.
5	HTML Page	`.html`	An HTML page that can include client-side code. Even Frameset can be saved as an HTML file.
6	Text File	`.txt`	Similar to creating a text file from Notepad.
7	XSLT File	`.xslt`	A file used to transform XML documents.
8	StyleSheet	`.css`	A cascading style sheet used for rich HTML style definitions.
9	Crystal Report	`.rpt`	Visual Studio .NET is integrated into Crystal Reports and provides a designer to help in the creation of a Crystal Report file that publishes data to a Windows or Web form.
10	Bitmap File	`.bmp`	Similar to creating a Bitmap file from MSPaint.
11	Cursor File	`.cur`	Win32 cursor file.
12	Icon File	`.ico`	Win32 icon file.
13	Assembly	`.resx`	These are Resource files that are used in the application.

Continued

Table A-2. File Types (continued)

Serial Number	File Type	File Extension	Description

14	Assembly Information File	.vb or .cs	This is the other file that is created with all types of projects under Visual Studio.NET. These files contain attributes that control general information about an assembly. Attributes added by default to the C# or VB Project differ. The important thing to note is that this file can contain the Key File attribute, which is used to add files to the GAC. A few examples or these attributes follow. Though the default Assembly Information files created for VB and C# differ, you always have the option of adding these attributes yourself. Here are few of these attributes to give you an idea of the possibilities:
			C#
			`[assembly: AssemblyTitle("")]`
			`[assembly: AssemblyVersion("1.0.*")]`
			`[assembly: AssemblyKeyFile("")]`
			`[assembly: AssemblyKeyName("")]`
			VB
			`<Assembly: Guid("6CBEBB65-5C1D-43B5-8A7F-02216B92BCDE")>`
			`<Assembly: CLSCompliant(True)>`

15	Application Configuration File	.config	Prior to configuration, we had INI files (or the registry) to change the settings of Applications. .NET now provides a standard way for changing these setting options. The file also contains other options and has standard tags to reduce the number of lines of code and promote ease of maintenance.
16	JScript File	.js	A script file containing JScript code.
17	VBScript File	.vbs	A script file containing VBScript code
18	Windows Script Host	.wsf	A file containing script that is run as a Windows program.
19	Web Forms	.aspx	ASPX files are ASP.NET files that are created for web applications. With previous versions, the ASP file extension was .asp. With ASP.NET the code and presentation are separated; the code is stored in the VB or CS file, while the ASPX file contains the presentation, i.e., HTML or server controls.
20	Web Service	.asmx	These files hold the web service code. But with the creation of a web service from VS.NET 2003, these files usually contain a single file, which points to the code behind the file, which contains the actual code.

Table A-2. File Types (continued)

Serial Number	File Type	File Extension	Description
21	User Controls for web applications	`.ascx`	File Names with an `.ascx` extension contain user controls that can be web applications, which could be one of the following: Web User Control Mobile Web User Control
22	Static Discovery File disco	`.disco`	Discovery Files are for locating and interrogating the web service. A Discovery file is an XML file with the `.disco` extension. The DISCO file is not automatically created for an XML web service. For creating a discovery file, refer to `http://msdn.Microsoft.com`.
23	Global Application Class	`.asax`	For a Global Application Class, also called an ASP.NET application file. In this file code is written to handle application-level events for ASP.NET applications. The class file inherits from System.Web.HttpApplication when you open the file in visual Studio.NET 2003, you will find a lot of events already added: Application_Start Session_Start Application_BeginRequest Application_EndRequest Application_AuthenticateRequest Application_Error Session_End Application_End
24	Solution File	`.sln`	A solution is a combination of one or more projects. It contains reference information about the projects that were added, and the path under which they can be located. It stores information about the project file `.vbproj` or `.csproj`. It also stores information about Debug and Release. Since all the files generated by VS.NET 2003 are simple text files, it's possible to open the solution file in Notepad.

Continued

Table A-2. File Types (continued)

Serial Number	File Type	File Extension	Description
25	Project file	`.vbproj` or `.csproj`	Similar to a Solution file, a Project file contains information about the particular project and can be opened in Notepad for access to more information. A Project file is an XML file, and for a C# project, the project file has a tag with CSHARP, and for a VB project, a tag with VisualBasic. A project is a combination or one or more files, and for each file added, an XML tag is added to the project file. You will also find a References tag, which has all the references that were added to your project the last time you saved your project file.
26	Visual Studio Project User Options	`.csproj.user` or `.vbproj.user`	As the name suggests, these files store information about the IDE settings that a user might have made. A User Options file is an XML file, and for a C# project the project file has a tag with CSHARP, and for a VB Project, a tag with VisualBasic. To explore more, open the Visual Studio Project User Options file in Notepad. When you right-click on the project in the Solution Explorer and select Properties from the context menu, a dialog box is shown. All the settings that you see here are stored in the User Options file. To see this in action, add a reference path and then save the solution; opening the user options file would not show you the reference path you added.
27	WebInfo File	`.csproj.webinfo` or `.vbproj.webinfo`	This is an XML file and URL Path of the Web tag that points to the virtual application root. These file are created only for ASP.NET applications.
28	Solution	`.suo`	Solution User Options file User Options is hidden by default; to view them in the Windows Explorer, select Folder Options from the Tools menu; select the View tab; then check the radio button labeled Show Hidden Files and Folders. These files store the options that you might have selected for your solutions; they also include the customizations made by you.
29	Program database	`.pdb`	Program Database files holds debugging and project state information.

APPENDIX B

■ ■ ■

Visual Studio .NET Directory Structure

Installation Directories

With the original release of Visual Studio .NET, Microsoft chose the rather inflexible directory name of `Microsoft Visual Studio .NET` to use as the default installation location, leading to a full default path of:

`C:\Program Files\Microsoft Visual Studio .NET`

With the release of Visual Studio .NET 2003, this has been amended slightly to include the version number, giving a default installation path of

`C:\Program Files\Microsoft Visual Studio .NET 2003`

Numerous other directories will be created as part of the installation to contain documentation, runtime resources, and so on. This directory contains the key Visual Studio-specific files, though: the IDE executable, further tools, the language compilers, settings, templates, sample graphics, and so on.

Language Directories

For each .NET language such as C#, VB.NET, and J#, a directory exists within the root installation path. If a full installation is performed, the following directories will exist:

- **Vb7:** Visual Basic .NET
- **Vc7:** Visual C++ (both .NET and unmanaged releases)
- **VC#:** C#
- **VJ#:** J#

As additional languages are installed, it's safe to assume that if they originate from Microsoft, they will continue to be installed in this location, as J# was when originally released as an addition to Visual Studio .NET. However, it is not a given that languages from third-party suppliers will be installed in this directory.

Within each of these directories there exist subdirectories that contain all of the templates available for that language: project templates, designer templates, file templates, and wizards. In the case of VB.NET, there are some coding samples, too.

Tools

There are numerous tools included with Visual Studio .NET, again all contained within subdirectories of the installation. Many of these, and reams of associated documentation, are found in the Framework SDK contained in the SDK directory. Any further SDKs that have been installed can be found in the Visual Studio SDKs subdirectory. The only two that come with Visual Studio are VS Analyzer, and DIA (to parse PDB debug-information files). It can be assumed that further SDKs will be installed in this directory as they become available. Additional utilities that were previously found in the platform SDK and Resource Kits, such as the `Generate Guid` tool found on the `Tools` menu in Visual Studio .NET, are located in the `Common7\Tools` directory.

MSDE

In the previous version of Visual Studio .NET, MSDE (the Microsoft Data Engine, a cut-down version of SQL Server) was included in certain versions of the distribution. It could be found in the `Setup\MSDE` subdirectory of the root installation directory. With this release, Microsoft has removed MSDE from the installation, and a ReadMe file now exists in that folder, redirecting the user to the following link for downloading MSDE:

`http://go.microsoft.com/fwlink/?linkid=13962`

Graphics

In the `Common7\Graphics` subfolder a selection of bitmap and metafile images, icons, cursors, and videos can be found. These are provided to be used in the applications created using Visual Studio, and can save a great deal of development time. While the icons may now appear outdated due to their being limited to 16 colors and small sizes, several useful standard Windows animations for file operations can be found here.

Templates

Whenever a new solution or new project is created in Visual Studio, or a new item is added to an existing project, these items are based on templates stored within the installation directory. These can be broken down into two categories:

- Template directories: Template directories contain entries for individual items that can be created, such as text files, XSD schemas, and ASPX pages. These are largely found in the directories `Common7\IDE\NewFileItems` and `Common7\IDE\NewScriptItems`. Additional items such as blank-solution templates can be found, too, in directories such as `SolutionTemplates` and `MacroProjects`.

- Enterprise templates: These templates are present in the two Enterprise editions of Visual Studio .NET 2003 (Enterprise Developer edition and Enterprise Architect edition), allowing software architects to base the design of applications on what is to be accomplished, freeing them from having to focus on the more detailed implementation aspects. Other than certain language-specific wizard files, all Enterprise Template files are located within an `EnterpriseFrameworks` subdirectory of the main installation location.

Interoperability

One final directory related to Visual Studio .NET, but existing out of the root Visual Studio folder, is as follows:

`C:\Program Files\Microsoft.NET\Primary Interop Assemblies`

This directory contains interoperability class libraries for some of the most common COM libraries that Microsoft has provided in the past, such as ADODB and MSHTML. These libraries have been developed with .NET developers in mind, to ensure that managed code can interoperate correctly with the functionality they provide. Further Primary Interop Assemblies are available for other applications, such as Microsoft Office XP, and are freely available for download from MSDN.

Project Directories

Further directories that are related to Visual Studio rather than the .NET Framework and runtime itself are those created by individual projects, and the compilers that act on them. For all code-related projects, irrespective of whether they produce a DLL or an executable as an output, the compiled binary files will be written within (a subdirectory of) a directory named "bin" (short for "binary") under the root of the project.

In the case of web projects (both Web Services and Web Forms projects), the DLL and debug files will reside directly in this "bin" directory. In the case of other project types, subdirectories named "Debug" and "Release" will contain the output files, depending on the Solution Configuration specified within Visual Studio .NET. As further Solution Configurations are added to these project types, further subdirectories will be created to contain their output. In addition to the output of the project itself, local copies of the output from all referenced projects will also be copied here by default. This can be changed by altering the value of the Copy Local property of each reference within Visual Studio.

Another difference between Web-based projects and class-library/executable projects is the creation of the "obj" (short for "object") directory. This acts as a working folder during compilation, containing all of the embedded resources, debug information, and so on that is to be compiled into the primary project output.

.NET Framework Directories

In addition to the directories that are created on a user's system for Visual Studio .NET, the underlying technology—the .NET Framework—has its own locations for storing files. There aren't as many of these as there are for Visual Studio, but they contain all that is needed to compile .NET solutions, albeit from a command-line environment, rather than a GUI. They also contain a multitude of applications, such as the ASP.NET worker process and ISAPI filter in addition to the DLLs that constitute the Framework classes. All these are vital for .NET applications to run.

Framework Versions

The main Framework files are all stored in the following location:

%SystemRoot%\Microsoft.NET\Framework

By default, %SystemRoot% will be C:\Winnt with server and professional editions of Windows up to Windows 2000, and C:\Windows with other versions such as Windows Server 2003 and Windows XP Professional.

This directory contains all of the versions of the .NET Framework that have been installed on the local machine, each stored in a separate directory. The name of this directory is the version number, such as v1.0.3705 or v1.1.4322 (as in the case of the Framework v1.1 release that comes with Visual Studio .NET 2003). Within each of these, a single version of the Framework is stored with all the necessary DLLs, tools, and configuration files, several of the most important files being the following:

- **csc.exe**: The C# compiler that can not only be used as a stand-alone compiler to compile projects. Other compilers such as vbc.exe and jsc.exe (for VB.NET and J#, respectively) are also located here, along with associated configuration files, csc.exe.config, for instance. The other tools that are required to compile .NET projects are installed in this directory, too: the assembly linker (al.exe), the Intermediate Language Assembler (ilasm.exe), and so on.

- **Installutil.exe**: This utility can be used to install .NET applications (such as Windows Services) from the command line, without the need for an MSI-based graphical installer.

- **aspnet_regiis.exe**: This is the tool that registers ASP.NET with IIS, a task that sometimes fails when Visual Studio .NET is installed on a system.

- **aspnet_state.exe**: This is the ASP.NET state service that allows Session information to be stored out-of-process and shared in a web-farm.

Other files found here include the SQL Scripts to install the SQL-Server ASP.NET Session State functionality. The subdirectories within each version of the framework are as follows:

- **CONFIG:** The most important file in this directory is the machine.config file, which stores the default settings that are overridden by individual applications. Another important file in this directory is DefaultWsdlHelpGenerator.aspx. It is this file that creates the WSDL help for web services. This can be amended in order to rebrand it or amend functionality, allowing restrictions to be made on the use of the features it provides. Further files in this directory define differing levels of security. These include `web_notrust.config`, and `web_hightrust.config`.

- **Temporary ASP.NET Files:** This directory contains the compiled versions of ASPX, ASCX, and other file types that are compiled at runtime, rather than as part of the build process within Visual Studio .NET. On rare occasions, the versions in this directory can get out of sync (such as when the files become locked), causing application errors. If this is the case, deleting the files in these directories will cause ASP.NET to recompile them, without raising any errors.

- **ASP.NETClientFiles:** This directory contains the `WebUIValidation.js` file, among others. It is this file that provides the mechanism for processing validation controls on the client side. It should be noted that the copies of the files found in these directories are not the ones executed. Those are detailed later in this appendix.

The Global Assembly Cache

The Global Assembly Cache (GAC) stores .NET assemblies that have been specifically designated to be shared across multiple applications on a single machine. This directory can be found in the `%SystemRoot%\assembly` location. The files it contains are not only those created by application developers, but also assemblies such as `System.Web.dll` that constitute the Framework classes themselves.

When Visual Studio .NET is installed, Explorer is updated via a Shell extension so that browsing to this directory will display a customized view, as can be seen in Figure B-1.

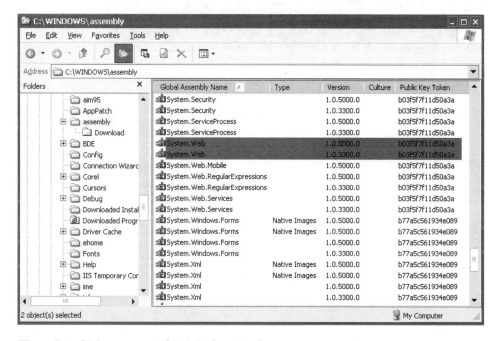

Figure B-1. GAC contents within Windows Explorer

The information displayed lets you see not only what assemblies are installed for use by your application, but also what versions are available. The two entries highlighted in the figure are different versions of the System.Web DLL, one of which was installed as part of v1.0 of the Framework, another as part of v1.1.

The directory structure of the assembly and its child entry Download shown in the tree-view to the left of the screenshot in the figure don't actually represent the directories that are present on the machine. The shell extension is hiding the true structure stored here. If we open a command prompt, we can see the true picture, as shown in Figure B-2.

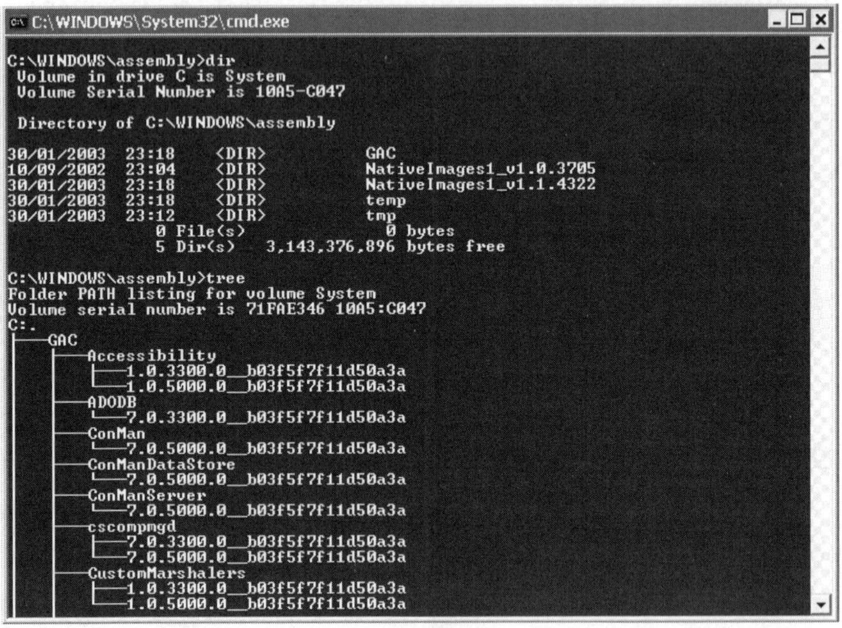

```
C:\WINDOWS\System32\cmd.exe

C:\WINDOWS\assembly>dir
 Volume in drive C is System
 Volume Serial Number is 10A5-C047

 Directory of C:\WINDOWS\assembly

30/01/2003  23:18    <DIR>          GAC
10/09/2002  23:04    <DIR>          NativeImages1_v1.0.3705
30/01/2003  23:18    <DIR>          NativeImages1_v1.1.4322
30/01/2003  23:18    <DIR>          temp
30/01/2003  23:12    <DIR>          tmp
               0 File(s)              0 bytes
               5 Dir(s)   3,143,376,896 bytes free

C:\WINDOWS\assembly>tree
Folder PATH listing for volume System
Volume serial number is 71FAE346 10A5:C047
C:.
├───GAC
│   ├───Accessibility
│   │   ├───1.0.3300.0__b03f5f7f11d50a3a
│   │   └───1.0.5000.0__b03f5f7f11d50a3a
│   ├───ADODB
│   │   └───7.0.3300.0__b03f5f7f11d50a3a
│   ├───ConMan
│   │   └───7.0.5000.0__b03f5f7f11d50a3a
│   ├───ConManDataStore
│   │   └───7.0.5000.0__b03f5f7f11d50a3a
│   ├───ConManServer
│   │   └───7.0.5000.0__b03f5f7f11d50a3a
│   ├───cscompmgd
│   │   ├───7.0.3300.0__b03f5f7f11d50a3a
│   │   └───7.0.5000.0__b03f5f7f11d50a3a
│   ├───CustomMarshalers
│   │   ├───1.0.3300.0__b03f5f7f11d50a3a
│   │   └───1.0.5000.0__b03f5f7f11d50a3a
```

Figure B-2. Command window listing of the GAC

The first command executed, dir, shows us that five directories are present:

- `Temp` and `tmp`: These directories contain temporary files when they are needed by the runtime, but for the most part remain empty.
- `GAC`: The GAC directory contains each assembly and assembly version registered with the global assembly cache in intermediate language (IL) format.
- **`NativeImages`**: Each of the `NativeImages` directories contains an assembly that, rather than being in IL, is compiled into native code for the processor of the machine. Once this has been done, the Native Image for an assembly is automatically used, improving performance, rather than all versions being probed. User-written assemblies can be converted into native images using the `Ngen.exe` utility provided with the framework.

The second command, tree, shows the structure within each of those directories. The pattern followed by the `NativeImages` directories is the same as that for the GAC directory, with each assembly name having its own subdirectory, each of which contains a further directory for each version of the assembly (this is suffixed by the Public Key Token for that assembly). It is in each of these bottom-level directories that the DLLs themselves are located, along with an INI file that gives details such as the DisplayName of the assembly (see Figure B-3).

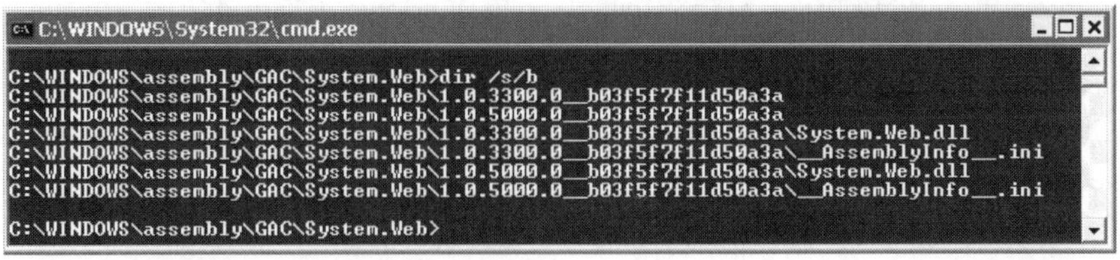

Figure B-3. Command window directory listing of a GAC entry

If you want to view the actual files from within Explorer, the shell extension can be disabled/deleted by renaming/deleting the file Desktop.ini, which resides in the Assembly directory. Since this file is hidden, it will not normally be listed, even with a Dir command.

ASP.NET Directories

In addition to the directories already discussed, there are several related to ASP.NET that are maintained both by the .NET runtime and by Visual Studio .NET. These can be split into two distinct types of directories, caches and support directories:

- **Caches:** These directories contain copies of applications being developed within Visual Studio .NET and compiled versions of ASP.NET pages and controls such as ASPX and ASCX files to be used by the runtime.

- **Support directories:** These contain extra information that is needed in order to provide the functionality of ASP.NET, such as the aspnet_client directory.

Temporary ASP.NET Files

When an initial request is made to a directory containing ASP.NET files such as those with ASPX and ASMX extensions, they are compiled to a library assembly by the ASP.NET ISAPI filter (aspnet_isapi.dll). These assemblies are then placed in the directory:

C:\Windows\Microsoft.NET\Framework\<Version>\Temporary ASP.NET Files

where they are executed each time a subsequent request for the page is made.

Within this directory, a separate directory is created for each virtual directory within IIS. Temporary names are used for subdirectories and DLL names, meaning that an application you create in a virtual directory named myApp would end up with an assembly in a location such as

...\Temporary ASP.NET Files\myApp\0cb50439\ae6e6bf9\hgpadoff.dll

The pseudorandom names for the files and directories are a hash of the original applica-tion/class names. Whenever the original source file is modified, the runtime recompiles it, maintaining this filename and replacing the existing assembly. If these DLLs are opened with ILDASM (the Intermediate Language disassembler), the original class names can be seen within them.

In addition to the Temporary ASP.NET Files directory, web services also make use of the system Temp directory, found by default at C:\Winnt\Temp in Windows 2000 and C:\Windows\ Temp in later versions, where temporary files and classes are written to.

If ASP.NET applications are being run on a machine that is a domain controller, then the worker process will run as a domain account as default, potentially requiring permissions to be changed. The Temporary ASP.NET Files and C:\Windows\Temp directories should both have write permissions enabled for the ASP.NET user defined in machine.config.

VSWebCache

The VSWebCache directory is, as its name suggests, used by Visual Studio .NET for caching web application data. By default, this directory is found at the following location:

```
C:\Documents and Settings\<Username>\VSWebCache
```

Within it, a directory is created for each web server (such as the local machine) on which web applications are being developed. These in turn each contain copies of the web projects being developed within Visual Studio, replicating the structure of IIS. These directories are maintained in order that work can be carried out on web applications even when the developer isn't connected to the web server. The contents of the directory are synchronized from within the Web Project submenu of the Project menu within Visual Studio (Figure B-4).

Figure B-4. The Project menu within Visual Studio

Whenever one of the bottom three options is selected, the version of the application cached locally is synchronized with that maintained on the web server. If the local machine is being used as a web server, this means that two copies of the site will exist on it.

aspnet_client

The `aspnet_client` directory exists within `C:\inetpub\wwwroot`. It contains the client-side JavaScript files used by ASP.NET to provide functionality for SmartNav and client-side form validation. SmartNav is used to improve the user experience on Internet Explorer v5.5 and above by performing the following operations:

- Eliminating the page-flash caused by navigation

- Persisting the scroll position when moving from page to page

- Persisting element focus between page navigations

- Retaining only the last page state in the browser's history

The individual script files are found within a subdirectory of the `aspnet_client` directory. In the case of the Framework version included with Visual Studio .NET 2003, the default location for these files is

`C:\inetpub\wwwroot\aspnet_client\system_web\1_1_4322`

In order to make use of these scripts, a virtual directory must be added to the root of each website (not virtual directory) in IIS that points to this directory; Visual Studio .NET does not create this entry for us.

FrontPage Extensions

Although the FrontPage Extensions directories aren't technically necessary for either ASP.NET or Visual Studio .NET to function, they are created as part of web projects as a means of publishing the files that constitute web applications to servers. The fact that they are named after Front-Page should not lead to their being associated with the web-design package that is part of Microsoft Office; they are a completely separate technology and are so named due to their original purpose of maintaining web servers and synchronizing files on them from within FrontPage.

These extensions now form one of the two main methods of accessing and updating files within Visual Studio .NET. The main benefit that they provide is that they work not only on the local machine, or even servers that are accessible through a LAN, but also on remote web servers over the Internet, making the location of the server transparent. Conversely, File Share mode (the other method of accessing files from within Visual Studio) works only with local machines: those that are contactable via UNC paths. The main advantage of File Share mode is that it allows for Visual Source Safe integration, which FrontPage Extensions do not.

The following directories are those created by the extensions. Not all of them are created at every level of the directory hierarchy within web applications, but all are created as hidden items:

- private

- vti_cnf

- vti_log

- vti_pvt

- vti_script

- vti_txt

If the File Share method is used for accessing a web project, the directories created to support FrontPage Extensions can be safely removed, making for a tidier directory structure within a project.

Special Directories

In addition to the directories that are used by Visual Studio .NET itself and system directories that are necessary for the runtime to function correctly, there are further Special Directories that can be referenced for I/O purposes during development and as part of Setup and Deployment Projects. Such directories represent predefined Windows directories, such as Program Files. The physical location of these directories can vary from one computer to another, possibly being located on a different drive, or having a different name; for example, the Windows directory itself could be located at `C:\Windows` on one computer, `D:\Windows` on another, or `C:\Winnt` on a third.

There are numerous special directories available to a developer in Visual Studio .NET:

- **Application Directory:** An application directory under the Program Files directory. Typically `C:\Program Files\Company Name\`*`App Name`*.

- **Common Files Directory:** A directory for components that are shared across applications. Typically `C:\Program Files\Common Files`.

- **Custom Directory:** A directory that you create on a target computer, or a predefined Windows directory that is not a special directory. Defaults to same location as the Application directory.

- **Fonts Directory:** A directory containing fonts. Typically `C:\Windows\Fonts`.

- **Module Retargetable Directory:** A custom directory that allows you to specify an alternative location for a merge module in a setup and deployment project.

- **Program Files Directory:** The root node for program files. Typically `C:\Program Files`.

- **System Directory:** The Windows System directory for shared system files. Typically `C:\Windows\System32`.

- **User's Application Data Directory:** A directory that serves as a repository for application-specific data on a per-user basis. Typically `C:\Documents and Settings\`*`username`*`\Application Data`.

- **User's Desktop:** A directory that contains files and directories that appear on the desktop on a per-user basis. Typically `C:\Documents and Settings\`*`username`*`\Desktop`.

- **User's Favorites Directory:** A directory that serves as a repository for the user's favorite items. Typically `C:\Documents and Settings\`*`username`*`\Favorites`.

- **User's Personal Data Directory:** A directory that serves as a per-user repository for documents. Typically `C:\Documents and Settings\`*`username`*`\My Documents`

- **User's Programs Menu:** A directory that contains a user's program groups. Typically `C:\Documents and Settings\`*username*`\Start Menu\Programs`.

- **User's Send To Menu:** A directory that contains a user's Send To menu items. Typically `C:\Documents and Settings\`*username*`\SendTo`.

- **User's Start Menu:** A directory that contains a user's Start menu items. Typically `C:\Documents and Settings\`*username*`\Start Menu`.

- **User's Template Directory:** A directory that contains document templates on a per-user basis. Typically `C:\Documents and Settings\`*username*`\Templates`.

- **Windows Directory:** Windows or system root directory. Typically `C:\Windows` or `C:\WinNT`.

- **Web Custom Directory:** A custom directory on a web server, identified by an HTTP address.

Unlike most I/O functions in .NET, access to these directories is available through the `System.Environment` class, rather than `System.IO`, since these values are platform-specific (and hence may not be available on mobile platforms and other ports of the .NET Framework). The individual directories are available through a call to the GetFolderPath method, passing in a value from the `SpecialDirectories` enumeration, as in the following example:

```
Dim specialDir As System.Environment.SpecialDirectory =
    Environment.SpecialDirectory.StartMenu
Dim path As String = System.Environment.GetFolderPath(specialDir)
```

This enumeration also includes extra values for locations such as My Computer, which, although not a physical directory, is a logical file-system location.

As previously mentioned, these locations can also be used in Setup and Deployment projects, being the target directories for the application data installed (see Figure B-5).

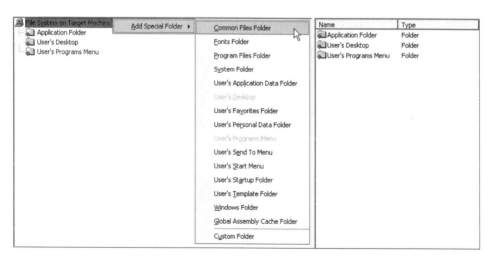

Figure B-5. Special folders in Setup and Deployment projects

APPENDIX C

■ ■ ■

Certification

Since you are reading this book, I will assume that you have more than a passing interest in Microsoft's .NET technology. If, like me, you have found that .NET offers you a powerful yet enjoyable environment in which to solve your programming problems, then you will no doubt want to start putting it to use in your day-to-day work. There may be others of you who are searching out new employment options and would relish the opportunity to work with the .NET technology. Regardless of whether you are trying to convince your existing employer to let you loose on .NET or demonstrate the breadth of your .NET knowledge to a prospective employer, having some kind of proof of your skills is going to come in useful.

That's where certification comes in. During this appendix we are going to take a look at the various options available that are related to the world of .NET programming. Specifically, we are going to start with a look at what certification levels Microsoft is offering, before focusing specifically on those that are related to development. While Microsoft would like to think they are the only vendor on the planet, our clients/employers don't often think that way. Since we can't develop our .NET applications in isolation from the rest of the computing community, I close this appendix with a look at some certification options available from other vendors that you might find useful for boosting your resume.

Overview of Microsoft Certification

Unless you have been living on the Moon for the past five years, you will no doubt be familiar with the wide range of certification options available from Microsoft. Covering almost all aspects of the desktop and server platforms as well as development tools, Microsoft Certification is a must for all developers wanting to improve their resumes. This appendix aims to provide you with a full overview of the certification options available and give you a roadmap for planning your certification campaign.

Certification Process

Currently, all Microsoft certifications are awarded based on the results of a set of examinations. Unlike Sun and Oracle, Microsoft certification does not require you to participate in any practical examinations or write any long essays. The only exception to this rule is the Microsoft Certified Trainer track, which requires you to demonstrate that you have good instructional and presentation skills.

Each certification level has a requirement on the number of exams you must pass, and the exams offered for each level are usually restricted to a subset of the full exam library. Once you have passed an exam, you can use it to count toward multiple certification levels, provided that the exam is included in that level's exam track. This means that if you pass exam 70-315, Developing and Implementing Web Applications with Microsoft Visual C#™ .NET and Microsoft Visual Studio .NET, to get your Microsoft Certified Professional (MCP) certificate, then you are already equipped with one of the exams needed to acquire the Microsoft Certified Application Developer (MCAD) certificate.

In this way, it is possible to progress gradually through the certification levels to your desired level, while minimizing the number of exams you will need to take.

Certification Tracks

There are currently ten different certification tracks on offer from Microsoft:

- **Microsoft Certified Professional (MCP):** This is the certification you will almost definitely obtain first. You can obtain this certification by demonstrating proficiency in a single Microsoft product. In practice, this means that if you pass any (or almost any!) of the available exams, you will be awarded the MCP certification.

- **Microsoft Certified Desktop Support Technician (MSDST):** This certification has just become available as I write this. This certification level is aimed at help-desk staff and requires the successful completion of two exams aimed at providing support on both the Windows operating system and applications running on it. As with most certification exams, either of these exams can be taken to obtain MCP status. I cannot speak with any experience on this certification, since it will be a cold day in hell before you find me on a help desk!

- **Microsoft Certified Systems Administrator (MCSA):** This certification is aimed at anyone whose job involves the running and maintenance of a Windows-based network environment. Currently there are two versions of this certification available, one for the Windows 2000 environment and one for Windows 2003. This certificate is looked at in more detail in the Non .NET Certification section.

- **Microsoft Certified Systems Engineer (MCSE):** The final step on the Microsoft track for all things infrastructure related. This certification is a natural progression from the MCSA certificate and also comes in Windows 2000 and Windows 2003 flavors. More coverage of this track can be found later in the appendix.

- **Microsoft Certified Database Administrator (MCDBA):** This track involves a mixture of exams; as well testing your skills on database administration, you will take exams focusing on network and server OS administration as well as database design and implementation.

- **Microsoft Certified Trainer (MCT):** This track requires that you have already obtained MCSE, MCSD, or MCDBA, and further requires that you have attended a specific course about Microsoft Learning and that you demonstrate practical presentation ability. Obtaining this certificate will enable you to teach any of the courses in the official Microsoft Curriculum.

- **Microsoft Certified Application Developer (MCAD)**: Most likely the next step after MCP for developers, the MCAD track requires that you pass three examinations to demonstrate your proficiency with a .NET language, Visual Studio, XML and Server Components, and at least one of the Microsoft server products such as SQL Server or BizTalk. This track is covered in more detail later in the appendix.

- **Microsoft Certified Solutions Developer (MCSD):** This is the final developer-oriented track available through Microsoft. Building on the foundations of the MCAD certification, MCSD requires that you take an extra two exams on top of the three required to obtain MCAD. One of these exams serves to further demonstrate your proficiency with your chosen .NET language, and the final exam is the Solutions Architecture exam, which tests your knowledge and ability in various areas related to application architecture, project management, and requirements analysis.

- **Microsoft Office Specialist:** The Office Specialist track is currently available in three versions covering the 2000, XP, and 2003 versions of the Office products. Each track is available in three levels, and exams are available for most of the Office products. The details of this certification are outside the scope of this appendix, but you can find more details at the Microsoft Certification site at http://www.microsoft.com/traincert.

- **Microsoft Office Specialist Master Instructor:** Currently available for the 2000 and XP versions of Microsoft Office, the Master Instructor certification requires that you gain the Office Specialist certification for every product in the suite. More details on this track can be found at the Microsoft Certification site.

Now that we have looked at all the available certification tracks, let's take a look at how the exams are structured, what kind of preparation is necessary, and what you can expect on the day of the exam.

Booking an Exam

Before you can take an exam, you must register for it and book a slot at an approved testing center in your area. Exams can be booked through either VUE at http://www.vue.com or Thomson Prometric at http://www.prometric.com. I have used both of these providers, and there really isn't much difference. Besides, you will find that your choice of test center is important, and both VUE and Prometric tend to offer the same selection of test centers.

I know it sounds stupid, but try to pick a test center that is as close to where you are as possible. When I took my first Microsoft test, I was booked at a test center about 15 miles from where I live. I had picked this test center because it was the only one I knew of, and I had attended a course there previously. I arrived just on time for my exam after a particularly stressful one-hour drive through early morning traffic. During the exam my concentration was abysmal; I still don't know how I managed to pass. Since then I have discovered that there is a test center about 3 minutes walking distance from where I live. I'm sure you can guess where I took the rest of my tests.

When booking your tests, be sure to give yourself enough time to prepare. I like to have at least three weeks before I have to take a test, giving me plenty of time to study and study some more.

Preparing for a Microsoft Exam

Preparation for the exam is split into two parts: what you do for the few weeks before the exam and what you do the night before the exam.

During the weeks prior to the exam, you will want to try to do as much studying as you can manage effectively, where the focus is on *effectively*. You don't want to try and cram in a mammoth 8-hour study session, since your brain will no doubt shut down early on and you will just be wasting your time. I have found it effective to limit myself to a maximum of an hour a night leading up the exam, giving my brain just enough exercise without risking long-term damage.

You should aim to plan your studying strategy in advance and then prepare all the materials that you need. You will find a full breakdown of all the areas on which you are going to be tested at the Microsoft Certification website, and these areas should be the focus of your study.

Everyone has different ways of studying. Some people like fancy flash cards or sticky notes all over the house. Others, like me, are content with just a good reference book (like this one!), a pen, and some paper. But one thing everyone needs is practice. If you are serious about passing your test, then you will want to obtain one or more practice tests that you can work through prior to taking the real thing. You can obtain practice tests from a variety of sources, each of which is discussed later in the appendix in the Exam Resources section.

■**Note** A note on practice tests: One problem I find with practice tests is that I tend to remember which answers are right and which answers are wrong. This doesn't mean that I understand that question or even know what the answer is. I simply know that the correct answer to question 16 is A. In this case, you may want to take a break from your practice tests to try to forget which answers match which questions. You should also strive to understand why a correct answer is correct, not just that it is so.

The night before your exam you will probably want to do a small amount of review to recap the topics on the exam. If you stay up all night and still feel like you need a cram session that would make a university student weep, then good luck on the exam. You will need it. You should aim to get a decent night's sleep so that you are fresh and attentive during the exam.

On the morning of the exam, the advice I can give you is make sure you are on time. You might want to consider getting to the test early, since you will probably be allowed to start early.

Taking the Exam

The exam is computer-based, and once you have completed the exam, you will be notified immediately whether you have passed or failed. You don't receive a grade. You are simply told whether you passed or failed, and there are no grades included on your actual certificate.

All the questions on the exam are multiple-choice, with some requiring just a single answer, while others require you to pick multiple correct answers. As you proceed through the exam, you can mark any questions you are unsure about, so that you can come back to them later on. There are no hard-and-fast rules on how to proceed during the exam, but I can offer the following advice:

- Go through the test once quickly, answering all the questions you are comfortable with and leaving those that you aren't.

- Go through the test again, this time spending more time on the unanswered questions. Don't linger too long on any one question. Instead, mark it and move on.

- As you near the end of your time, if you have any questions unanswered, then guess. You don't get penalized for wrong answers, so you might be lucky with your guesses and get a few extra questions correct. Just remember when you are making your guesses to choose the answers that lean more toward the "Microsoft way."

Once you have finished, print your results and relax. It's over. If you passed, congratulations! If not, don't worry; your results will highlight which particular topics you did badly in, so that you can concentrate your efforts for the next time you take the test.

Microsoft Certified Professional

Microsoft Certified Professional (MCP) is the first step along the certification path that many of you will take. The sheer number of exams available to gain this accreditation is overwhelming, with exams covering all facets of Microsoft-based computing. In this section we will look specifically at the exam aimed at .NET developers, focusing on what skills you will be tested on and what level of experience is required for the exam.

What You Are Being Tested For

With the MCP certificate, to say what exactly you are being tested for is at the same time a very easy and a very difficult question. It is very easy, because you are being tested for your knowledge in a single area of a single Microsoft product. It is very difficult to answer because of the massive number of options that are available. Gaining MCP is actually fairly simple for anyone who has more than two years of experience working with Microsoft Windows; choosing which exam to take, however, is a different matter!

Choosing Your Exam

As I mentioned previously, there is a wide array of exams available for the MCP certificate, some of which, like the Windows XP exam, you could no doubt pass without any extra work. However, if like me, you are planning to obtain the MCAD certification, then you will no doubt want to plan ahead and take an exam that not only gains you the MCP accreditation but that will also count toward the MCAD certification as well.

Fortunately, you don't have to be too clever with your planning at this stage, since any of the exams that count toward the MCAD accreditation will also give you MCP status. To this end, you should take whichever of the exams you feel more comfortable with, from those described in the Microsoft Certified Application Developer section.

Microsoft Certified Application Developer

The Microsoft Certified Application Developer (MCAD) certificate is a must for all .NET developers. From a career point of view, it provides a recognized way for you to prove that your skills in .NET are up to scratch. From a day-to-day programming point of view, you will almost certainly get some benefit out of working toward and gaining this certification. I found that during my preparations for the MCAD exams, my attention was more focused on topics that I used daily, and after a while, I found myself going to the MSDN library less and less to look up API references or class names. Finally, from a personal point of view, there is a great sense of achievement in gaining a certification in your chosen profession.

What You Are Being Tested For

The MCAD certification tests whether you are capable of putting together a full application using .NET technologies. Passing any of the tests required to gain MCAD certification will give you MCP status, so you may want to consider starting off with one of the MCAD exams in order to gain your MCP status. If you gain MCP using a non-MCAD exam, you will need to pass four exams to gain both MCP and MCAD, whereas gaining MCP via an MCAD exam means that you require only three passes to obtain both accreditations.

Some of the exams will expect you to select a language, either C# or VB.NET, in which to have the exam presented. For all exams you will be expected to have a good grasp of the syntax and nuances of that language. If you can't read C# code proficiently, then don't even consider taking a C# exam until you can.

For those who have used .NET in their day-to-day work, obtaining the MCAD certification should be a cinch. For those who haven't, you face a slightly more difficult, yet entirely achievable, task.

Core Exams

If you have looked at the MCAD exams on the Microsoft website (http://www.microsoft.com/learning/mcp/mcad/requirements.asp) already, you will have noticed that there appear to be six exams to choose from for your core tests. While this is true in a purely literal sense, there are actually only three tests, each of which comes in C# and Visual Basic .NET versions. The C# and Visual Basic .NET versions of each exam are almost identical, a fact that may interest you when you come to pick your elective exams.

■**Note** You do not have to take the exams in the order they are discussed here. You are free to take the exams in whatever order you like. The order in which they are presented here just seemed logical to me (and it just happens to coincide with the order in which I took my exams!).

Choosing Your Core Exams

You are required to select two exams from the core set, and you are restricted in which exams you may choose. For your first exam, you must select from one of the exams shown in Table C-1.

Table C-1. MCP Core Exams

Exam Number	Exam Title
70-305	Developing and Implementing Web Applications with Microsoft Visual Basic® .NET and Microsoft Visual Studio® .NET
70-306	Developing and Implementing Windows-Based Applications with Microsoft Visual Basic .NET and Microsoft Visual Studio .NET
70-315	Developing and Implementing Web Applications with Microsoft Visual C#™ .NET and Microsoft Visual Studio .NET
70-316	Developing and Implementing Windows-Based Applications with Microsoft Visual C# .NET and Microsoft Visual Studio .NET

As you can see, you basically have a choice of either Windows-based or Web-based applications in your language of choice. Which exam you choose is entirely up to you, and your choice will probably reflect your day-to-day work or what you would like to be working on. For instance, most of my .NET experience has been with ASP.NET applications, so I opted to take the C# ASP.NET exam, since I already had a thorough grounding in what was required.

I don't want to start regurgitating the content from the Microsoft Certification site, but I do want to address some of the core skills that each exam type will test you on.

Windows Exam Topics

Without further ado, let's take a look at the core skills covered in the Windows-based exams:

- **Creating User Services:** The biggest portion of the questions on the exam fall under this topic. You will be tested on your ability to build the user interface of an application using Windows Forms; this includes manipulating and instantiating controls, validating input, and handling errors. A few of the more advanced UI topics such as localization, accessibility, printing, and on-line help may also be tested, but the number of questions on these topics will be small. You should also be prepared to handle questions on working with a variety of business components, implemented using COM, .NET, Web Services, or native code.

- **Creating and Managing .NET Assemblies:** This topic covers the creation and manipulation of .NET assemblies. If you use Visual Studio .NET exclusively for your development, then you may be unfamiliar with some of the tools and concepts this topic tests. In order to be ready for this topic you should be comfortable using command-line tools to package up satellite and resource-only assemblies. You should also be comfortable creating Windows Controls and hosting them in Internet Explorer.

- **Consuming and Manipulating Data:** This is the part of the exam where you get tested on your ADO.NET knowledge. Specifically, you will be tested on your ability to interface with SQL Server using both ad hoc queries and stored procedures. You should be familiar with how ADO.NET is structured and with the major parts of the API. This topic also covers XML, so you should be familiar with the majority of classes in the System.Xml namespace and how XML is integrated with ADO.NET. Make sure you are comfortable with data-binding, since you are bound (get it?) to get a question or two on this. There will be quite a few questions on the exam pertaining to this topic, so you should make sure you are comfortable with it.

- **Testing and Debugging:** Fairly self-explanatory, this objective covers your ability to test and debug your applications. Specifically, you should be comfortable with the debugger in Visual Studio .NET, including setting and managing breakpoints, including some of the more unused settings. On my exam I was tested on how you break only when a certain condition evaluates to true. You will almost certainly get tested on tracing, so you should be familiar with how the tracing architecture is structured and how to configure the tracing settings for your applications. Also, and quite unexpectedly, I was tested on writing a unit test plan, so you should be familiar with this. I warn you now: your idea of a unit test plan may, and probably will, differ from Microsoft's, so you should consider getting one of the study guides mentioned later in the appendix to familiarize yourself with the "Microsoft Way."

- **Deploying a Windows-Based Application:** You should expect to see a couple questions on this topic on your exam. You are expected to know quite a bit about deploying Windows Forms applications using a variety of mechanisms, such as removable media, network, and the Web. You will almost certainly see a question about Windows Installer, so you should at least be familiar with it and the various setup projects associated with it. The requirements from Microsoft state that you should be familiar with the Windows Logo Program, so you should at least familiarize yourself with what this involves. If you are not familiar with the Global Assembly Cache (GAC), then you need to learn about it for this exam.

- **Maintaining and Supporting a Windows-Based Application:** This is probably the smallest topic on the exam. All you will need to know for this part of the exam is how to diagnose and resolve faults with your software, and how to analyze and optimize the performance of your application.

- **Configuring and Securing a Windows-Based Application:** For this topic you will be tested on your knowledge of the .NET application configuration file format. Some of the questions will present you with various options for configuration data that look alike and ask you to choose the correct one, so you should be able to recognize when the configuration is wrong as well as when it is right. You will be tested in more depth on your ability to configure the security of your application, including configuring the different types of authentication as well as managing the users and roles of the application. Some of the questions pay specific attention to the effect of the ordering of the user and role management elements on the behavior of the application.

Web Application Exam Topics

Now let's take a look at the topics covered by the Web Application exams. You will find that many of the skills overlap, especially in the areas that are not specific to your chosen environment, but that's the benefit of having a core class library like .NET.

- **Creating User Services:** Most of the topics from the Windows exam such as data validation, error handling, and localization are covered in the Web Application. Of course, the implementation of these features is specific to ASP.NET in this exam, so you should be comfortable using all these features in an ASP.NET environment. You should have a good grasp of ASP.NET Server Controls, User Controls, and the HTML controls, since these are covered extensively. Moreover, a wide range of the questions look at the intrinsic ASP.NET objects such as Request and Response, so you should be familiar with these as well.

- **Creating and Managing .NET Assemblies:** The only difference in this topic from the Windows exam is that instead of Windows Controls, you will be tested on Custom Controls and User Controls. You should be able to identify the differences between these two different types of control and also choose which type is appropriate for a given scenario.

- **Consuming and Manipulating Data:** Other than the differences in the data-binding mechanisms between ASP.NET and Windows Forms, the content for this topic will be the same as on the Windows exam.

- **Testing and Debugging:** This topic contains most of the content from the Windows exam, plus some extra content that is specific to ASP.NET. You should be familiar with the ASP.NET trace mechanism, including how to configure this for in-line and out-of-line viewing. You should make sure you know how to configure this at both the page and application levels.

- **Deploying a Web Application:** There isn't a great deal of difference between this topic on the Web Application exam and the corresponding topic on the Windows exam. Just make sure you are comfortable with the specific requirements of deploying to IIS such as virtual directory configuration and that you are familiar with the differing requirements of a Web garden, a Web farm, and a cluster.

- **Maintaining and Supporting a Web Application:** Almost identical to the Windows exam, the only difference is that you may be quizzed on performance analysis issues specific to the Web such as poor response time and timed-out requests.

- **Configuring and Securing a Web Application:** This topic differs greatly from the corresponding topic on the Windows exam. You will no doubt be tested on configuring your application within IIS as well as configuration options that are available in the machine.config and web.config files. You will need a full understanding of all the authentication mechanisms, especially forms authentication. Under this topic you will also find questions on configuring and implementing caching using both the Cache object and ASP.NET cache directives. As if this topic didn't have enough content already, you will also need to make sure you understand how to configure the different session management mechanisms and also how to configure various server services such as Frontpage Extensions. There will be quite a few questions relating to this topic on your exam, so you should be familiar with all the concepts mentioned.

You should now have more of an idea which exams best suit your situation and some kind of a starting point for your certification. With these exams you should find something that matches your day-to-day job, or at least the kind of job you are looking for. Then it can be quite easy to settle into getting ready for the exam, which is why I recommend that you take such an exam first. As I mentioned earlier, I started with the Web Application exam, and my familiarity really helped me settle into the certification process. Keep in mind also that passing one of these exams will give you MCP status if you don't already have it, so if you are looking for an MCP exam but thinking about moving onto MCAD later, you should really consider one of these exams as your starting point.

Second Core Exam

Once you have passed your first core exam, it's straight onto the second and final core exam. For your second core exam, you have two "choices." See Table C-2.

Table C-2. MCAD Additional Core Exam

Exam Number	Exam Title
70-310	Developing XML Web Services and Server Components with Microsoft Visual Basic .NET and the Microsoft .NET Framework
70-320	Developing XML Web Services and Server Components with Microsoft Visual C# and the Microsoft .NET Framework

I'm sure you can see why I chose to put the word "choices" in quotation marks. For your second core exam, the only choice you get is the language you want the exam presented in. The topic of XML Web Services and Server Components is fixed. Fortunately, this exam is quite interesting, and the topics covered are quite useful in day-to-day development, especially if your work involves server-based applications.

Okay, let's have a look at the requirements for these exams, and then we'll move on to look at the options for your elective exam:

- **Creating and Managing Microsoft Windows® Services, Serviced Components, .NET Remoting Objects, and XML Web Services:** This is a rather broad topic, as indicated by the excessively lengthy title, and most of the questions on the exam come under this category. You will tested on your ability to create and control Windows Services and XML Web Services. You should be extremely competent with .NET Remoting, understanding both the server and client sides of the Remoting architecture as well as how to configure your remote objects both declaratively and programmatically. The questions on Remoting can be quite advanced, and expect to see questions on the various formatter/channel combinations as well as asynchronous methods and object activation and lifetimes. Also covered under this topic is the concept of Serviced Components. You will need an understanding of what Serviced Components are and how they interact with COM+ services. You should be comfortable using the Component Services tool, as well as the various command-line tools needed for strong name creation and component registration. The exam will undoubtedly contain questions relating to security on some if not all of these different areas, and you should be aware of how security is implemented and managed in each context.

- **Consuming and Manipulating Data:** This topic builds on the foundation set by the corresponding topic in the Windows and Web Application exams. Specifically, you will need to be sure you fully understand how DataSet relationships work, and you undoubtedly will find a few questions on XPath and the XmlReader classes; so make sure you know how they work. I also found on my exam that a few questions on the XML capabilities of SQL Server had crept in. In particular, you will need to be comfortable querying

SQL Server for XML data and also with issuing an update command to SQL Server using XML input.

- **Testing and Debugging:** As with the previous topic, this topic builds on coverage of the Windows and Web Application tests. The additional areas covered under this exam are interactive debugging and testing, and debugging concepts specific to Web Services, Windows Services, and remote objects. You need to be familiar with how SOAP exceptions function and how to leverage SOAP exceptions to provide a mechanism for logging and debugging.

- **Deploying Windows Services, Serviced Components, .NET Remoting Objects, and XML Web Services:** For this topic, you will need to demonstrate a full understanding of deploying the four specialized components that are tested on this exam. You need to understand how an XML Web Service is deployed in IIS and how to publish your XML Web Service in a UDDI repository. You need to understand how versioning works, especially when Strong Names are used. You should be aware of how to redirect the .NET runtime assembly loader by specifying a binding policy. You will be tested on the various command line tools for installation and component registration, and some of the questions are intentionally misleading, so make sure you are awake when you take the test. If you thought the questions on security configuration on your previous exam were difficult, then brace yourself, for this exam tests your knowledge of identity impersonation and integration of custom authentication schemes.

As you can see, some of the topics on this exam are quite advanced, certainly not things that many readers will be using in their day-to-day development. You will find, though, that if you give yourself plenty of time to study and prepare for this exam, then you should pass it quite comfortably. I found that I got the most out of working toward this particular exam, since it forced me to look in detail at topics I tended to face only once every three months. If you are looking to impress a potential employer with your knowledge, then you could do a lot worse than to study some of the topics covered on this exam.

Elective Exams

When you get to this point you are almost there! All you have to do now is choose your elective exam. When choosing your elective exam you are faced with a small moral dilemma, due to Microsoft's somewhat lax certification requirements. For some reason, Microsoft permits you to take any of the core exams that you haven't already taken as your elective. At first glance, this doesn't seem like much of an issue, until you remember what I said about the similarity of the core exams. The Web Application exam in C# is almost identical to the Web Application exam in VB.NET, so identical, in fact, that you stand a good chance of getting almost all the same questions with just a difference in language.

■**Note** I was alerted to this "dirty little secret" by a Microsoft Certified Trainer who was running a course on which I won a place. During the break on the first day we were sitting around discussing our intentions regarding certification when the trainer let us all in on this secret. It turned out that he and most of his colleagues had obtained their MCSD certifications this way!

Under the current Microsoft rules it is perfectly acceptable for you to take the C# Web Application exam as your core exam and then take the almost identical Visual Basic .NET Web Application exam as your elective. I know what you are thinking; surely, Microsoft can't be that stupid; alas, these are the people that gave us Clippy, the awful and extremely annoying Office mascot. This is not only acceptable, but there is even a little note on the MCAD requirements page on the Microsoft Certification indicating as much! Any of the exams you choose here will count toward the MSCD certification, either as an additional core exam or as your elective exam for that certification as well.

The remaining elective exams available to you are shown in Table C-3.

Table C-3. MCAD Elective Exams

Exam Number	Exam Title
70-229	Designing and Implementing Databases with Microsoft SQL Server™ 2000 Enterprise Edition
70-230	Designing and Implementing Solutions with Microsoft BizTalk Server® 2000 Enterprise Edition
70-234	Designing and Implementing Solutions with Microsoft Commerce Server 2000

If you have a particular expertise in any of these products, you will undoubtedly want to take the exam in that product. I imagine that if you are reading this book, then you at least have a passing familiarity with SQL Server, so this may well be the choice for the majority of you. You should also note that if you plan to take the Microsoft Certified Database Administrator (MCDBA) certification at any point, then the 70-229 SQL Server exam will count toward that as well.

Now let's take a look at what skills are covered in each of the three elective exams.

SQL Server 2000 Exam Topics

As I mentioned earlier, the SQL Server 2000 exam may well be the one that the majority of you opt for. Out of all the .NET Enterprise Servers, SQL Server is the one you are most likely to have had a degree of real-world experience with. I actually took this exam as my elective due to my familiarity with SQL Server, and I found that familiarity helped me during my preparation and during the exam.

If you are currently looking for a job as a .NET programmer, then this exam is something of a safe bet. The chances are that your job will in some way involve using SQL Server, and showing your prospective employer that you have proven skills with the product may be the difference between getting the job or getting a letter in the post thanking you for your time.

Okay, let's look at the skills you will be tested on:

- **Developing a Logical Data Model:** This section of the exam is all about database design. You will be tested on your understanding of concepts such as normalization and entity modeling. You should be familiar with normalization up to at least third normal form, and you should be comfortable defining entities and their attributes. This section tests your ability to identify keys and specify constraints such as FOREIGN and PRIMARY keys. You should also be comfortable specifying data types, dealing with CHECK and UNIQUE constraints, and managing nullability of data. You will get a couple of questions on the more theoretical aspects of database design, so you may want to bone up on all the theory.

- **Implementing the Physical Database:** In this section of the exam you will be tested on your ability to get down and dirty and actually build your database. You will need quite extensive experience with Data Definition Language (DDL) commands as well as a good understanding of the various concepts associated with implementing a database. You should have some knowledge of capacity planning and how this translates into DDL commands for building tables with specific allocations for both data and log size. You need to understand how SQL Server file growth works and how you can affect this behavior for your databases. Your DDL knowledge will be tested with questions on the creation of a wide variety of schema objects such as triggers, stored procedures, functions, and views. On my exam I had a few questions on indexes that tested not only my knowledge of the syntax, but also my understanding of where each particular index type should or should not be employed. There is also no doubt that you will encounter a few questions on replication, so make sure you know the different types of replication available and when they are and aren't appropriate.

- **Retrieving and Modifying Data:** The core part of this section is coverage of Data Manipulation Language (DML). Most of you will use this as part of your regular programming experience, so it shouldn't pose too much of a problem. On top of run-of-the-mill DML, you will also be tested on SQL Server's XML support commands. I was tested on returning XML as the output from a query and also on executing an XPATH query as part of a larger SQL query. You should make sure you are familiar with some of the features that are less associated with .NET programming, such as linked servers, Bulk Insert, Data Transformation Services, and cursors.

- **Programming Business Logic:** This objective tests your ability to create and manage business logic using T-SQL. You will be tested on your knowledge of stored procedures, triggers, and user-defined functions. You should be comfortable within T-SQL constructs for error handling, flow control, and transaction management. You may see, as I did, a question or two on using Query Analyzer to debug your business logic.

- **Tuning and Optimizing Data Access:** I found this to be the hardest of the sections on the exam. This section tests your knowledge of various tools such as the SQL Profiler and the Index Tuning Wizard. You should be familiar with how to set up and run a profile and then how to use the results in the Index Tuning Wizard. You may also find some questions on the behavior of specific settings within the profiler or on what information the profiler must log in certain cases. You should also make sure you understand the different types of indexes, when they are appropriate, and how their use can affect database performance.

- **Designing a Database Security Plan:** For this part of the test you will be tested on your knowledge of Data Control Language (DCL) statements. You should fully understand how GRANT, REVOKE, and DENY apply in defining object security down to column level. You should be aware of the differences between managing security at user and role levels, and finally, there were two questions on my exam related to the use of application roles to secure your database. Specifically, you should be aware of how to create application roles as well as how to switch your current connection into an application role.

Now let's take a look at the BizTalk Server exam.

BizTalk Server Exam Topics

While many of you may not be too familiar with BizTalk Server, there are a lot of applications that use BizTalk for integration and information sharing with other, potentially legacy, applications. If you are looking for a job as a Systems Integrator or you are looking to work in some area of integration, then this exam would be ideally suited, since it covers skills directly related to your chosen line of work.

The skills covered in this exam are as follows:

- **Planning and Designing BizTalk Server Solutions:** This is a big topic. You will be tested on a wide variety of different concepts from planning your security architecture including SQL Server security to planning your installation for differing levels of security, reliability, and scalability. You need to have some level of experience installing and configuring a BizTalk solution.

- **Installing BizTalk Server:** For this section of the exam you will be expected to demonstrate your ability not only to successfully install BizTalk Server but also to troubleshoot failed installations. This section not only tests knowledge of BizTalk installation and configuration but also your ability to install SQL Server and configure the underlying operating system.

- **Building Document Interchanges:** In this part of the exam you are tested on your ability to create and configure document interchanges using BizTalk Server. This involves specifying the organizations and applications involved in the interchange as well as choosing and creating message envelopes in a variety of formats including EDI and XML. You should be able to create and configure inbound and outbound channels as well as a variety of receive scripts for receiving using FTP and Message Queuing.

- **Creating Auxiliary Components for BizTalk Server Solutions:** This section tests your ability to create custom transport logic, encapsulated as COM+ components.

- **Administering BizTalk Server Solutions:** This is quite a large part of the exam and involves many different facets of .NET Enterprise Server technology. You are expected to demonstrate an understanding of the various administration tools that make up a BizTalk installation, including Document Tracking and Activity, WMI, XLANG Event Monitor, and SQL Server Enterprise Manager. You should be able to diagnose any problems related to a BizTalk installation including security issues at the OS level and errors with external services such as SQL Server and WebDAV.

- **Creating Schemas and Transformations:** This section of the exam tests your knowledge of schema building and transformation definition. Specifically, you will be tested on your ability to import and modify schemas using the BizTalk Editor, as well on using the BizTalk Mapper to create schema mappings. You will also be tested on your ability to create schemas for flat files and to define XDR-based schemas for data in EDI format.

- **Implementing Business Processes Using BizTalk Orchestration Designer:** This section is quite involved. You are expected to demonstrate an understanding of how business processes are defined using BizTalk Flowchart shapes and how to bind your business process to concrete implementations using the Implementation shapes. You will be tested on your knowledge of building transactional business processes including both long- and short-lived processes.

Commerce Server Topics

- **Analyzing Business Requirements:** This section tests your ability to analyze a project and gather the appropriate requirements for use in defining a Commerce Server-based solution. You are tested on three main requirement types: architectural, integration, and functional. These types are further split into specific goals such as performance requirements for architectural and catalog requirements for functional.

- **Designing a Commerce Server Solution:** In this section you will be tested on all aspects of Commerce Server design. You must demonstrate an ability to design user profiles, shopping and checkout strategies, and a Data Warehouse and reporting model. In addition to this you will be tested on the design of an effective security framework along with deployment architectures for testing, staging, and production.

- **Installing and Configuring Commerce Server 2000:** This section is pretty much as the title implies: it tests your ability to install and configure an instance of Commerce Server. As part of this you are tested on your ability to install and configure both SQL Server and IIS, as well as your ability to diagnose any installation-related errors.

- **Developing a Commerce Server Solution:** This is a large part of the exam. It tests your ability to actually develop a site using Commerce Server. You are tested on your ability to create profile definitions and campaigns as well as catalogs using Business Desk, XML, and the BizTalk API. You are also tested on your ability to customize the Business Desk and to create an analytics solution using the Data Warehouse.

- **Deploying a Commerce Server Solution:** This section focuses on the packaging and deployment of Commerce Server sites. Much of this section relates to diagnosing errors that occur during deployment, but special note is given to the configuration of SSL within the deployment environment.

- **Maintaining and Supporting Your Commerce Server Solution:** This part of the exam tests your ability to manage a Commerce Server site on an ongoing basis. This involves managing catalogs, profiles, content, and campaigns as well as the management of any orders that are made using your site.

Microsoft Certified Solutions Developer

The Microsoft Certified Solutions Developer (MCSD) accreditation represents the pinnacle of Microsoft's certification track for developers. To obtain this certificate you need to pass a further two tests on top of those required to gain your MCAD certification. The intention of this certification is to show that the holder is capable of designing and building applications in both the Windows and Web environments as well as being proficient in defining and communicating a robust application architecture.

The actual requirements for this exam are four core exams and one elective, but two of your core exams and the elective are taken care of by your MCAD certification, so you are left with the remaining two core exams. For your first core exam you need to take the other platform exam that you didn't take for your MCAD. So if you took the Web Application exam, then you will need to take the Windows exam, and vice versa. For the remaining core exam you have one option, as shown in Table C-4.

Table C-4. MSCD Core Exam

Exam Number	Exam Title
70-300	Analyzing Requirements and Defining Microsoft .NET Solution Architectures

As the title implies, this exam is very much suited to architects and lead developers who have some level of experience working with clients to define and develop requirements and transforming these requirements into an effective architecture. I'd like to make a few comments at this point about this exam, since it is quite different from those we have discussed so far. First, this exam is a little more practical than the rest. It tests your decision-making abilities as well as your actual knowledge, so you will find that hands-on experience is very useful. Second, some of the topics on the exam are generally more suited to the role of a strategist or consultant. You should not be surprised to see a few questions on the exam talking about return on investment or total cost of ownership; it is expected that you will take these factors into consideration with your solution. My third and final point is that your idea of solutions architecture, and certainly mine, might differ quite substantially from Microsoft's. Unless you are a solid practitioner of the Microsoft Solutions Framework (MSF), you will need to get yourself into Microsoft mode before the exam. You might find that having a special hat can help in this case!

Solution Architectures Exam Topics

So, let's take a look at the skills that are covered in the Solution Architectures exam:

- **Envisioning the Solution:** This section of the exam is more oriented to analyzing feasibility and customer needs in specific areas than to any actual technical architecture. You should expect to see a few questions on risk management and also to be tested on your ability to match the concept and requirements of a project to the available resource/skill set.

- **Gathering and Analyzing Business Requirements:** This section covers what is generally the first appendix in any book on software architecture. You will expected to look at both functional and nonfunctional requirements during this section and demonstrate your ability to understand, document, and communicate a variety of business needs.

You should expect to see questions that are decidedly nontechnical in nature, such as those that address the requirements for training and staffing as well as those that expect you to assess a solutions position in the marketplace. You should be familiar with common concepts such as use cases, data modeling, and process management. This is probably the largest section on the exam.

- **Developing Specifications:** In this area you will be tested on your ability to transform a set of requirements into a working specification, paying particular attention to nonfunctional requirements such as security, operations, and infrastructure. This section includes questions on building a test plan that are more difficult and involved than those on the MCAD exams. Finally, for this section you might see a few questions on creating a training plan for the users of your solution.

- **Creating the Conceptual Design:** For this section of the exam you will be expected to demonstrate a good understanding of defining the conceptual model of your solution. You should understand Object Role Modeling (ORM) concepts and how to identify and describe facts, attributes, and constraints for the entities in your model. A variety of different constraint types are covered. If you don't have any experience in this topic, then you will certainly need to start reading up, since these questions are among the most difficult on the exam.

- **Creating the Logical Design:** This topic is something that most of you will already be quite familiar with. You will be tested on your ability to define logical architectures for your solution, including considerations of security, maintainability, and performance. You should be familiar with Entity Relationship modeling, since you will be tested on building a logical data model, including the process of data normalization. You will need some knowledge of XML schemas, since you are expected to be able to define the schema(s) for your data model. You will undoubtedly get tested on your ability to provide validation of your logical model, both against the initial set of requirements and via a proof of concept.

- **Creating the Physical Design:** This is where it gets technical! In this section you will be quizzed on topics relating to deployment, user interface design, and physical data design, including index creation and backup strategies. Most of the topics in this section relate to defining how the solution will actually be built, so you should expect questions on how to physically interconnect application components, managing validation and error-handling, implementing security in a distributed environment, and infrastructure issues related to building high-availability solutions. As with the previous topic, you are expected to be able to validate your design against the original requirements and via a proof of concept.

- **Creating Standards and Processes:** In this section you will need to show that you can establish a variety of standards within your solution. In this case, the term "standards" refers to those standards employed for coding, user interface, documentation, source code control, and testing. You should demonstrate your ability to create and enforce processes for the development of your solution, including code reviews, issue tracking, and change management. A few of the questions relate to Visual Studio .NET Enterprise Templates and their relation to enforcing certain constraints on developers.

The Solutions Architecture exam is quite difficult, but if it were otherwise, then everyone would be an MCSD. More so than the other exams, this one requires a degree of actual experience, but it's not completely impossible to pass this without any experience; you'll just need to study harder and longer.

So with that we have concluded our look at the MCSD exam. You should now have a better grasp of what is required for this exam as well as good idea of which path you want to take. Now let's a look at a few of the other Microsoft certification levels that you might want to consider after you have passed your MCSD.

After MCSD

So now that you are a fully fledged MCSD, what do you do next? Well, there are really three answers to that question:

- You can get some well-earned rest.

- You can work on some non-Microsoft certification (see the next section).

- You can work on some alternative Microsoft certification.

In this section we are going to look at the last option, specifically covering the MCDBA, MCSA, and MCSE certifications.

Microsoft Certified Database Administrator

This certificate is a good choice after taking MCSD or MCAD, since you can use one of the Web Application or Windows core exams from your MCAD as your elective for this certificate. To make things even better, if you took the SQL Server exam as your elective exam for MCAD or MCSD, it counts as one of the core exams for this certification. This leaves you needing the final two core exams, one of which will count toward the MCSA and MCSE certification. So as you can see, this certification is the perfect bridge between the development track and the administration track.

Okay, so what other exams do you need? Well, for your first core exam you need to take the SQL Server Administration exam. This exam is available in both 7.0 and 2000 editions, although the 7.0 version is scheduled to be discontinued, and considering that a new version of SQL Server is on the horizon, the 2000 exam seems the sensible choice. See Table C-5.

Table C-5. MCDBA Core Exam Options

Exam Number	Exam Title
70-228	Installing, Configuring, and Administering Microsoft SQL Server 2000 Enterprise Edition
70-028	Administering Microsoft SQL Server 7.0

I'm not going to go into as much detail here about the exams as I did for MCAD and MCSD, other than to state the obvious: the SQL Server exams here are much more oriented to the role of database administrator than the SQL Server exam for the MCAD/MCSD track. There are many developers familiar with how to develop applications using SQL Server, but not as many are familiar with how to correctly configure and maintain a running SQL Server installation. You may want to start being nice to your DBA so you can tap him for information. Interestingly enough, the SQL Server 2000 exam counts as the elective for MCSA, so once you have completed this certification you are left needing just one more pass to get MCSA.

■Note The full breakdown of the rest of the Microsoft exams described here can be found on the Microsoft Certification site at www.microsoft.com/traincert.

For the remaining core exam you have three choices, two of which (70-290 and 70-291) will count as a credit toward the MCSA and MCSE certifications. These exams are not really related to SQL Server, but rather they test your abilities to maintain the underlying operating system, in this case Windows Server, as part of the database's network environment. See Table C-6.

Table C-6. MCDBA Elective Exams

Exam Number	Exam Title
70-290	Managing and Maintaining a Microsoft Windows Server 2003 Environment
70-291	Implementing, Managing, and Maintaining a Microsoft Windows Server 2003 Network Infrastructure
70-215	Installing, Configuring, and Administering Microsoft Windows 2000 Server

For these exams, you will not find any questions relating to SQL Server itself. Instead, they are all related to the server operating system and the network environment. After all, what good is a perfectly configured database without a perfectly configured operating system?

When choosing your remaining core exam, you will want to consider what your plans are for MCSA and MCSE. Both the MCSA and MCSE are split into two separate subtracks: one for Windows 2000 Server and the other for Windows 2003 Server. If you are planning on getting the most up-to-date MCSA and MCSE certificates, then you will want to consider going for one of the 2003 exams at this stage, since they count toward the MCSA and MCSE 2003 tracks.

Microsoft Certified Systems Administrator

The Microsoft Certified Systems Administrator (MCSA) certificate is relatively new in comparison to the Microsoft Certified Systems Engineer (MCSE), which seems to have been available since computers were invented. The MCSA shares a similar relationship with the MCSE certificate that MCAD shares with MCSD, in that you cannot obtain MCSE without first obtaining the MCSA.

The MCSA certification is ideal if you are your development team's designated administrator, and it certainly won't do you any harm to have on your resume. If anything, having both development and operations-oriented certification on your resume will demonstrate a well-rounded knowledge of computer systems. You will also find that if you develop many Windows Server-based applications, especially those that integrate with Active Directory or Exchange, then the MCSA and MCSE certifications are a great way to consolidate your knowledge in those areas.

As I mentioned earlier, there are two subtracks for the MCSA and MCSE certifications: one for the Windows 2000 family and one for the Windows 2003 family. For the purposes of this book, I will look only at the 2003 track, but you can find more information about the 2000 track on the Microsoft Certification site.

To obtain MCSA certification, you need to pass two core exams and one elective. The first core exam covers server operating systems, and the second covers client operating systems. If you have already passed your MCDBA certification, then you will have already passed the server OS exam, so you just need to obtain the client OS exam. See Table C-7.

Table C-7. MCSA Core Client OS Exam Choices

Exam Number	Exam Title
70-270	Installing, Configuring, and Administering Microsoft Windows XP Professional
70-210	Installing, Configuring, and Administering Microsoft Windows 2000 Professional

In all honesty, the client OS exams should be a walk in the park for a developer, since you will already have more than a passing familiarity with most of the topics covered. There were certainly no topics, other than Remote Installation Services, on the exam that I was not already comfortable with.

For the elective exam you have five choices, one of which is the Installing, Configuring, and Administering Microsoft SQL Server 2000 Enterprise Edition exam covered by the MCDBA, so if you have already passed your MCDBA, you will not need to take an elective for MCSA. If you didn't go down the MCDBA route, then the remaining choices for your elective are as shown in Table C-8.

Table C-8. MCSA Elective Exams

Exam Number	Exam Title
70-286	Implementing and Supporting Microsoft Systems Management Server 2.0
70-227	Installing, Configuring, and Administering Microsoft Internet Security and Acceleration (ISA) Server 2000, Enterprise Edition
70-284	Implementing and Managing Microsoft Exchange Server 2003
70-299	Implementing and Administering Security in a Microsoft Windows Server 2003 Network

Any of the elective exams for MCSA, including the SQL Server exam, also count as an elective toward MCSE, so you can choose freely, knowing that you will not have to take more exams than absolutely necessary.

As an alternative to taking an elective exam for the MCSA certification, Microsoft will give you credit if you have passed any of the following combinations of CompTIA exams:

- CompTIA A+ and CompTIA Network+

- CompTIA A+ and CompTIA Server+

- CompTIA Security+

You can find out more details about CompTIA certification at `http://www.comptia.org`.

Microsoft Certified Systems Engineer

The MCSE certification is the top-level Microsoft certification for Systems Administrators and Engineers. It builds on the foundation of the MCSA and tests for more specific skills related to delivering secure, high-availability infrastructure based on the Microsoft platform. The MCSE exam requires the most passes to obtain: seven in all. Fortunately, the three passes gained toward your MCSA (by whichever means you got them) will count toward the MCSE certification, leaving you with just four remaining exams.

■Note Please note that only the CompTIA Security+ certification will count toward an elective for the MCSE certification.

The remaining four exams for the MCSE are all core exams, although there are a few extra options for the elective that I will discuss in a minute. The core set of exams is split into three categories, some of which will have been covered by the MCSA but are included here for completeness. The first category is Networking System, and all four exams are required; see Table C-9.

Table C-9. MCSA Core Networking System Exams

Exam Number	Exam Title
70-290	Managing and Maintaining a Microsoft Windows Server 2003 Environment
70-291	Implementing, Managing, and Maintaining a Microsoft Windows Server 2003 Network Infrastructure
70-293	Planning and Maintaining a Microsoft Windows Server 2003 Network Infrastructure
70-294	Planning, Implementing, and Maintaining a Microsoft Windows Server 2003 Active Directory Infrastructure

If you have already obtained MCSA status, then you will have no doubt passed either 70-290 or 70-291 already, so you will have just three of these exams to pass. The second category of core exams is the Client Operating Systems, the exams for which are exactly the same as the client exams for the MCSA exam, which you may have already passed. The third and final category of core exams is Design. In this category you are tested on your ability to develop some portion of the network infrastructure. You have two choices for this category, from which you must choose one exam, one aimed at security and the other at general network infrastructure and Active Directory. See Table C-10.

Table C-10. MCSE Core Design Exam Choices

Exam Number	Exam Title
70-297	Designing a Microsoft Windows Server 2003 Active Directory and Network Infrastructure
70-298	Designing Security for a Microsoft Windows Server 2003 Network

The last piece in the MCSE puzzle is the elective exam. If you have already passed your MCSA exam, then you will have already fulfilled this requirement. If not, you are free to choose from any of the electives from the MCSA exam, the other exam from the Design category (i.e., 70-298 if you took 70-297 for your core requirement), or either of the exams listed in Table C-11.

Table C-11. MCSE Elective Exam Choices

Exam Number	Exam Title
70-229	Designing and Implementing Databases with Microsoft SQL Server 2000 Enterprise Edition
70-232	Implementing and Maintaining Highly Available Web Solutions with Microsoft Windows 2000 Server Technologies and Microsoft Application Center 2000

Overall, the MCSE exam is a fairly difficult one to pass, but is certainly worth the effort, especially if your current or potential employer is interested in partnering with Microsoft. The standard Microsoft Certified Partner program requires a company to have two MCPs on full-time staff before it is considered eligible to participate. However, the Microsoft Certified Gold Partner Program requires five full-time MCSEs for eligibility, so if you pass this exam, your company may also be able to benefit as well.

Specialization

Recently introduced into the MCSA and MCSE tracks is the ability to extend your accreditation into a specific area. Currently, there are two specializations available for messaging and security. Obtaining a specialization usually involves taking one or two extra exams on top of the requirement for your certification. You can find out what extra exams are required for both the messaging and security specializations on the Microsoft Certification website.

Non-Microsoft Certification

It is becoming increasingly rare to see 100% Microsoft-based solutions, and in today's climate, placing all your eggs in a single basket is widely considered to be a bad move. Over the last month I have seen an increase in the number of clients who are looking to open-source solutions such as MySQL and PostgreSQL in place of SQL Server 2000. This is especially prevalent in cases in which SQL Server would be overkill but a Microsoft Access database would crumble under the pressure. Other cases can require more power than is available with SQL Server, which sees clients turning to alternative databases such as Oracle.

Databases are not the only area in which we see non-Microsoft technologies being integrated into a .NET environment. The advent of XML Web Services has unleashed a new wave of integration of previously isolated technologies. One area that looks set to boom is the use of Macromedia Flash as a client-side technology for rich applications. The newly released 2004 version of Macromedia Flash even offers a specific application authoring mode following the familiar forms/controls model.

With this wide variety of technologies outside the Microsoft camp you may need to look elsewhere to prove your worth to potential or current employers. Fortunately, Microsoft is not the only vendor with a certification offering. Many other vendors in the IT industry offer comprehensive certification paths for their own products. In this section we are going to take a brief look at the certification options available for the Oracle and MySQL database as well for Macromedia Flash.

Oracle 9i

Certification from Oracle Corporation comes in three flavors. The first level is Oracle Certified Associate (OCA), which demonstrates a level of knowledge in one area of Oracle's product range. The second level is Oracle Certified Professional (OCP), which builds on the foundations of OCA but tests your knowledge in some of the more practical aspects of Oracle technology as well as on a wider range of skills related to your chosen area. The third and final level of certification is Oracle Certified Master (OCM), the requirements for which are quite high. To obtain OCM you have to attend two compulsory Oracle University courses as well complete a practical test of your Oracle skills.

As with Microsoft certification, Oracle's certification for their database products is split into two main tracks, one for developers and one for administrators. Currently, the highest level you can obtain as a developer is OCP, since OCM is available only on the administration track.

The first step on the developer track is the OCA level certification Oracle9i PL/SQL Developer Certified Associate. To obtain this accreditation you are required to pass two exams that test your knowledge of common database concepts such as tables, indexes, and stored procedures, as well your grasp of Oracle's PL/SQL language. The skills tested at this level should be enough for any .NET developer who will be working with Oracle, since you will certainly build an appreciation and a thorough understanding of what can done with Oracle and how to achieve it.

The OCP level on the developer track requires that you pass an additional exam once you have obtained your OCA. This exam focuses on Oracle's Forms product used to build applications that run against an Oracle database. I had originally decided to stop after I obtained my OCA, since I couldn't foresee actually using Oracle Forms to build an application, and since this is a book on .NET development, I would imagine you too will be wondering where this particular skill might be put to use. However, recently, I have changed my mind on this, since I think that OCP will look better than OCA on my resume, so it seems worthwhile completing this one exam. For most of you, Oracle Forms will be an easy product to come to grips with, especially if you are already familiar with the Oracle database. The concept for building an application with Oracle Forms doesn't differ greatly from what you will already be used to.

More information on Oracle's certification offerings can be found at http://www.oracle.com.

MySQL

For those of you not familiar with MySQL, it is a freely available open-source database server that you can use to power your applications. Currently, MySQL can be accessed from .NET using either the OBDC or OLEDB .NET data providers. There are currently some open-source projects working on a full .NET data provider for MySQL that you can also play around with, but you may want to hold off using them in a production environment.

For many projects MySQL provides a great alternative to Microsoft Access, and in some cases SQL Server, since it is extremely quick and very stable. It is also a true database server, as opposed to the simple file-based database of Access, meaning that it can handle many more concurrent connections.

MySQL AB, the company behind MySQL, currently offers two levels of certification for their database product. The first level of accreditation is the MySQL Core certification, which has been available since March 2003. I am currently working with one of my developers on this certification, and we are finding it fairly easy going. The Core certification really serves as an introduction to the world of MySQL, and if you are familiar with other database products such as SQL Server or Oracle, then you will have no problem working through this certification.

The second level of certification available from MySQL AB is the Certified MySQL 4 Professional. This certification level requires that you have already obtained the MySQL Core certification and that you take a further exam. The Professional certification builds on Core level and tests your abilities in a much more advanced sense. At this level you are tested much more on your ability to secure, optimize, and maintain a MySQL database than at the Core level.

The MySQL website, `http://www.mysql.com`, contains much more information on these certification levels.

Macromedia Flash

Today's users expect a great deal from the user interface of a Web-based application. The advent of widely available broadband access means that users are looking for an ever richer experience from the applications that they use on the Web. While technologies such as DHTML and JavaScript can help to improve the usability of standard HTML applications, they are quite limited in their reach and difficult to implement across browsers. Macromedia Flash has been around on the Web for years and is almost always present on a user's machine. In recent years, Flash has expanded from being just an application for animations to a technology capable of supporting rich application user interfaces.

Proving your ability to build rich interfaces for your applications will almost certainly prove important in the coming years, if not months. Fortunately, Macromedia offers comprehensive certification for most of their products, and Flash is no exception. There are actually two certificates available for Flash: one aimed at designers and the other at developers. The developer exam covers all aspects of Flash relating to the development of rich applications, with particular focus on design and ActionScript coding. You will need some experience in Flash in order to be able to pass this exam, since some of the questions will quiz you on the actual use of Flash, as opposed to the theory.

You can find a full breakdown of the requirements for the Flash Certified Developer exam at `http://www.macromedia.com`.

Exam Resources

There is a wide range of resources available to help you pass your certification exams. Without taking advantage of some of these resources you may find it difficult to pass some of the exams unless you are particularly experienced in the area covered by the exam.

Exam Requirements

Your first step for any certification test should be to get a list of the topics that will be covered. You will almost definitely find these on the website of the vendor who is offering the certification test. Certainly, all the test sponsors discussed in this appendix offer comprehensive breakdowns of their exam requirements.

Looking at the exam requirements, you will be able to form an idea of how much work is necessary for you to pass the test. In some cases you may choose to work on other tests before attempting a particular test because there are just too many requirements that you are unfamiliar with. No matter what any other reference material says, you should always use the vendor's exam requirements as your master plan for exam preparation.

Study Guides

Study guides are an inexpensive, and usually quite effective, mechanism for preparing for a test. Certainly, if you work as freelancer or a contractor, then you may not be able to afford the cost of instructor-led training, in which case a study guide is invaluable.

I can honestly say that there is no particular provider of study guides that you should opt for. In the case of the Microsoft certification tracks, the study guides from Microsoft Press are an obvious choice, but you may want to back them up with some solid reference books. I can especially recommend the excellent Professional C#, second edition, by Simon Robinson, which I used during my C# exams.

Many of the study guides are offered as reduced-price packages for an entire certification track. This is most definitely the case for the MCSE study guides available from a wide variety of publishers, so you may want to consider investing in the whole set, as opposed to buying each book separately. You'll certainly save money in the long run.

Practice Tests

As the time nears for you to take your exam, you may want to try your hand at a practice test. These tests are built to mimic what you will see in the actual exam, so they can be useful for familiarizing yourself with the process.

Generally, you will get many more questions on your practice test than you will get on the actual exam. If you can successfully answer all the questions on the practice test, then you stand a good chance of passing the real thing.

Another point about practice tests is that it is not unusual for you to see the same (or almost the same) question on your practice test as on the real exam. In fact, the first test I took had at least five or six questions that were almost laughably similar to those on the practice test.

Most study guides come with a practice test or two on the accompanying CD. I have personally found these to be an absolute waste of time, and instead I opted to purchase my tests from an online provider. Depending on which vendor's tests you are taking, you can find good practice tests at both http://www.selftestsoftware.com and http://www.measureup.com. I have used tests from both providers, and I have never failed an exam yet.

Training

While some people are perfectly comfortable learning from a book, many prefer taking part in instructor-led training. You will find that most of the certification paths, the Microsoft ones included, offer official accompanying training courses operated throughout the world by vendor-approved training centers. Although you can purchase a decent holiday for the price of some of these training courses (see the following note), they are worthwhile, and you get a great deal of study material to take home.

Note As this book goes to print, one of my developers will be whisked off on an expensive training course that truly is a decent holiday! After spending two nights in Orlando, he will spend the next five days on a cruise ship sailing around the Caribbean learning about the wonders of PHP. More details can be found about this course at `http://www.phparchitect.com/cruise`.

I was fortunate enough to win a place on a Microsoft training course at a local provider, and I found it really useful, especially since such courses are specifically geared toward the exam you will be taking. You have the benefit of spending five days with an instructor who knows the exam inside and out, so you can gain some useful insights over a few pints at lunch.

For more information on instructor-led courses, either visit your chosen vendor's website or contact your local training provider.

Summary

In this appendix we have addressed a wide variety of certification options. We have looked in close detail at the Microsoft developer certifications, including:

- Microsoft Certified Professional

- Microsoft Certified Application Developer

- Microsoft Certified Solution Developer

We have also taken the time to look not only at the Microsoft certifications available for administrators and systems engineers, but also at the certification options available from other vendors such as Oracle, MySQL AB, and Macromedia.

Finally, we looked at the various resources available to help you pass your certification exams. After reading this appendix, you should have a much clearer idea of which accreditations you want to seek and how to go about achieving them in the most efficient way possible.

Index

forums.apress.com

FOR PROFESSIONALS BY PROFESSIONALS™

JOIN THE APRESS FORUMS AND BE PART OF OUR COMMUNITY. You'll find discussions that cover topics of interest to IT professionals, programmers, and enthusiasts just like you. If you post a query to one of our forums, you can expect that some of the best minds in the business—especially Apress authors, who all write with *The Expert's Voice*™—will chime in to help you. Why not aim to become one of our most valuable participants (MVPs) and win cool stuff? Here's a sampling of what you'll find:

DATABASES

Data drives everything.

Share information, exchange ideas, and discuss any database programming or administration issues.

INTERNET TECHNOLOGIES AND NETWORKING

Try living without plumbing (and eventually IPv6).

Talk about networking topics including protocols, design, administration, wireless, wired, storage, backup, certifications, trends, and new technologies.

JAVA

We've come a long way from the old Oak tree.

Hang out and discuss Java in whatever flavor you choose: J2SE, J2EE, J2ME, Jakarta, and so on.

MAC OS X

All about the Zen of OS X.

OS X is both the present and the future for Mac apps. Make suggestions, offer up ideas, or boast about your new hardware.

OPEN SOURCE

Source code is good; understanding (open) source is better.

Discuss open source technologies and related topics such as PHP, MySQL, Linux, Perl, Apache, Python, and more.

PROGRAMMING/BUSINESS

Unfortunately, it is.

Talk about the Apress line of books that cover software methodology, best practices, and how programmers interact with the "suits."

WEB DEVELOPMENT/DESIGN

Ugly doesn't cut it anymore, and CGI is absurd.

Help is in sight for your site. Find design solutions for your projects and get ideas for building an interactive Web site.

SECURITY

Lots of bad guys out there—the good guys need help.

Discuss computer and network security issues here. Just don't let anyone else know the answers!

TECHNOLOGY IN ACTION

Cool things. Fun things.

It's after hours. It's time to play. Whether you're into LEGO® MINDSTORMS™ or turning an old PC into a DVR, this is where technology turns into fun.

WINDOWS

No defenestration here.

Ask questions about all aspects of Windows programming, get help on Microsoft technologies covered in Apress books, or provide feedback on any Apress Windows book.

HOW TO PARTICIPATE:

Go to the Apress Forums site at **http://forums.apress.com/**.

Click the New User link.